KB140159

한영 · 영한

장기요양보험
용어사전

한영 · 영한

장기요양보험
용어사전

✚

스미이 히로시 · 사와다 유키
임춘식 · 선현규

Korean-English & English-Korean
LONG-TERM CARE DICTIONARY

머리말

2000년 한국의 65세 이상의 노인인구는 339만 명에 달해 전체 인구의 7%를 넘어 고령화 사회(Aging society)가 되었다. 2018년에는 고령화율이 14%를 넘어서 고령사회가 될 것으로 전망하고 있지만, 일본은 이미 2013년에 전체 인구 대비 65세 이상 노인인구가 무려 25%로 세계 최초로 초고령사회(Super aging society)로 진입하였다.

저출산·고령화 현상은 복지 선진 국가들에서 나타나는 일반적이고 공통적인 현상이지만, 한국의 인구 고령화 속도는 일본, 영국, 독일, 미국 등의 국가보다 빠르게 진행되고 있는 반면, 핵가족화와 여성의 취업 증가, 가족의 부양 가치관의 변화에 따른 가족의 간병기능 약화 등으로 인해 장기요양보호에 대한 사회적 수요가 더욱 증대되어 심각한 사회문제로 대두되었다.

이에 한국에서도 2000년부터 시작된 고령화 사회에서 심각하게 대두된 노인장기요양 보호 문제에 능동적으로 대처하고 노인의 인간다운 삶을 보장해 주기 위해 '노인장기요양보호정책기획단', '추진기획단', '실행위원회' 등 정부에서 자문위원회를 설치·운영하여 한국에 적합한 제도모형을 연구하였고, 정부에서는 본 실행모형을 기초로 입법과정을 거치게 되었다.

고령이나 치매·중풍 등으로 거동이 불편하여 혼자서 일상생활을 하기 어려운 노인 등에게 신체활동·가사지원 등의 장기요양급여를 사회보험방식에 따라 제공하여 노후의 건강증진과 생활안정을 도모하고 가족의 부담을 덜어 줌으로써 국민의 삶의 질을 향상시킬 수 있는 '노인장기요양보험제도'를 2008년 7월 1일부터 실행하였지만 선진국에서는 이미 이 제도를 실시해 왔다.

예를 들면, 네덜란드는 1968년 '장기요양보험' 전신인 '특별의료보험제도'를 오스트리아는 1993년에 '장기요양수당제도'를 도입했다. 또한 독일은 1994년 4월에 '요원호(要援護) 리스크의 사회적 보호에 관한 법률'을 제정하여, 1995년 4월부터 재가서비스, 1996년 7월부터는 시설서비스를 제공해 왔다. 또한 이웃 일본은 1997년 '개호보험법'을 제정하여 2000년 4월부터 '개호보험제도'를 성공적으로 실시하고 있다.

최근 중국에서도 2002년부터 '양로호리원(養老護理員)'이라는 제도를 제정하여 장기요양 서비스 인력을 양성하고 있으며, 대만에서도 장기요양보험 제도를 도입하기 위해 정책적 논의가 활발히 진행하고 있다. 특히 일본에서는 동남아 여러 나라와 경제협력협정(Economic Partnership Agreement: EPA)을 체결하여 2008년부터 인도네시아와 필리핀, 2012년부터는 베트남으로부터 간호사와 요양보호사 인력을 도입해 부족한 내국인의 요양인력난을 해결하고 있다.

이처럼 많은 국가들이 노인장기요양보험제도를 도입하게 된 것은 무엇보다도 고령이나 노인성 질병 등의 사유로 일상생활을 혼자서 수행하기 어려운 노인 등에게 신체활동 또는 가사지원활동 등의 장기요양급여에 관한 사항을 규정하여 노후의 건강증진 및 생활안정을 도모하고 그 가족의 부담을 덜어 줌으로써 국민의 삶의 질을 향상하도록 하는 데에 있다.

결과적으로 이 제도를 도입한 한국은 물론 일본 등에서도 첫째, 노인의 삶의 질이 크게 향상되었고, 가족의 부양부담이 경감되었다. 둘째, 여성 등 비공식적 요양인력의 사회경제적 활동의 활성화 셋째, 요양보호사, 간호사 등의 사회적 일자리 확대에 기여 넷째, 의료 및 요양전달체계 효율화로 인한 노인의료비 절감효과를 가져온 것으로 평가받고 있다.

그러나 향후 노인장기요양의 서비스 수준 향상을 통한 안정적 발전을 위해서는 장기요양 수급질서 확립, 장기요양 서비스 질적 제고, 노인성질환 예방사업의 활성화 등에 대한 과제를 안고 있으며, 나아가 장기요양보험제도를 제정한 국가 간의 공식적인 정책적 아젠다는 물론 장기요양 관련 학술연구 기반 조성을 위한 국제협력은 미진한 실정에 있다.

이러한 상황에서 최근 일본은 장기요양보험 관련 국제 학술교류를 진지하게 추진하고 있는 유일한 국가이다. 특히 일본에서는 장기요양보험 관련 전문 학술용어인 『개호복지 용어사전(1989)』이 이미 발간되었으며, 이어 2012년에는 『국제 개호보험 용어사전: 개호보험의 국제화』를 스미이 히로시(住居 廣士)와 사와다 유키(澤田 如) 교수에 의해 공동으로 발간되어 일본 학계뿐만 아니라 다른 나라에서도 화제가 되고 있다.

『국제 개호보험 용어사전』은 총 3부로, 1부에는 장기요양보험에 관련된 약 7,400개의 '영일용어'와 약 9,400개의 '일영용어'가 수록되어 있다. 2부에는 1부의 '일영용어'에 수록되어 있는 용어 중에서 다소 중요하다고 생각된 684개 용어가 일본어와 영어로 해설되어 있다. 3부에는 미국, 영국, 독일, 호주, 한국에서 보편적으로 인용되고 있는 약 2,300개의 장기요양보험 등의 관련 용어가 수록되어 있다.

또한, 부록으로서 2부에 게재된 684개 용어가 앞으로 국제 표준용어로 통용이 될 것으로 예상되고 있는 인도네시아어, 한국어, 스페인어, 타갈로그어,

중국어, 독일어, 힌디어, 프랑스어, 베트남어, 포르투갈 등 10개 국어로 수록된 세계 최초의 용어사전이다.

한국어판 『장기요양보험 용어사전』의 공동 집필 동기는 『국제 개호보험 용어사전』 저자가 장기요양 용어의 국제화 표준작업을 한일 공동으로 개발하자는 요청에 따라 임춘식, 선현규 교수가 공동으로 참여하여 약 2년 만에 4인의 공동 편저로 출판의 빛을 보게 되었다.

『장기요양보험 용어사전』은 "국제 개호보험 용어사전(일본, 2012)"을 근간으로 "Encyclopedia of Elder Care(미국, Facts on File, 1995)", "Encyclopedia of Social Work(영국, Blackwell Publishing Ltd. 1990)", 그리고 "노인복지학 사전(한국노인복지학회, 2005)" 등의 문헌을 참고로 노인복지, 의료, 간호, 장기요양, 재활, 교육, 보육 등의 영역으로부터 장기요양보험과 관련된 약 7,530개 용어를 추출한 후, 선현규 교수의 가교 역할로 4인이 공동으로 검증하여 3,030개 용어를 추가한 약 10,560개 용어로 집대성하였다.

이 용어사전은 총 4부로 구성되어 있다. 1부는 '한영용어', 2부는 '영한용어', 그리고 3, 4부에서는 1부의 '한영용어' 부분에 게재한 약 12,500개 용어 중에서, 영어에 의한 학술교류에 사용되는 빈도가 높다고 생각되는 사회복지, 노인복지, 장기요양보험 등 관련 700개 용어를 한국어와 영어로 해설했다.

본 용어사전에 수록된 용어는 세계 각국의 의료·보건, 장기요양기관, 행정기관 등에서 사용하고 관련 용어는 물론 사회복지이론과 실천에 근거, 재검증하여 수록했으나 번역의 정확성과 타당성에 대해서는 앞으로 개정판을 출판해 가면서 수정·보완해야 할 과제를 안고 있다.

앞으로 이 용어사전에 의해 장기요양 등에 관한 용어가 국제적으로 표준화되고 전문성이 구축되어 장기요양보험제도의 정착화, 그리고 제도 수립을 계획하고 있는 국가는 물론 시설 종사자와 관련 학술계에 보탬이 된다면 더할 수 없는 영광으로 생각한다. 또한 이 용어사전에 의해 장기요양보험의 국제화가 진전되기를 바라면서 독자 제현의 많은 지도편달을 바란다.

끝으로, 이 한국어판 용어사전이 출간될 수 있도록 동기를 부여했음은 물론 요양용어의 국제화 표준 작업을 세계 최초로 시도하고 있는 스미이 히로시, 사와다 유키 교수에게 특히 진심으로 감사의 말을 전한다. 그리고 흔쾌히 출판의 기회를 마련해 주신 한국학술정보(주) 채종준 대표님을 비롯한 편집담당 직원들에게도 감사를 표한다.

2014년 8월 15일

스미이 히로시住居 廣土 사와다 유키澤田 如

임춘식林春植 선현규宣賢奎

범례

* 영한 용어는 기본적으로 미국식 철자법을 알파벳 순서로 배열했다. 영국식 철자법 표기 용어는 다음과 같다.

  [예] 미국식   영국식

    behavioral   behavioural

    labor   labour

* 동일한 알파벳으로서 대문자와 소문자가 상이한 경우에는 대문자를 우선 배열했다.

* 한영 용어는 가나다 순서로 배열했다.

* 단체 및 조직명 등의 고유명사는 자칭의 일반 명칭으로 표기했다.

* 약칭이 일반적인 표기인 경우도 수록했다.

  [예] OECD

* 한 개의 용어에 두 개 이상의 번역 용어의 경우에는 세미콜론(;)으로 구분했다.

* 외국인 이름에는 ≪ ≫ 안에 성과 이름의 이니셜을 원어와 약어로 표기했다.

  [예] 알츠하이머 ≪Alzheimer, A.≫

* 학술적으로 사용 빈도가 높은 707개 용어는 한국어와 영어로 간략하게 해설했다.

PART 1

TERMS IN
KOREAN
ENGLISH

한영
용어

ㄱ

가격유지 price supports
가격차별 price discrimination
가격통제 price controls
가계 household budget ; family budget
가계대출 budgeting loans
가계도 genogram
가구 household
가구주민협의회 block organizations
가내노동 family labor
가동률 utilization rate
가동성 mobility ; workability
가동성 실내공기청정기 mobile room air cleaner
가동인구 utilization population
가두보도활동 street guidance
가든골절분류
  Garden classification system of fracture
가려움증 pruritus
가령 aging
가령성 질환 age-related disease
가령황반변성 age-related macular degeneration
가루약 powdered drug
가명령 interim order
가바펜틴 gabapentin
가변마찰 이음새 variable friction joint
가볍게 집기 pulp pinch
가부장제 patriarchalism
가브리엘바늘 Gabriel needle
가비트릴 Gabitril
가사 housekeeping ; household work
가사노동 housekeeping ; domestic labor
가사도움 domestic helper
가사분담 housekeeping assignment
가사서비스제공자 homemaker services provider

가사심판 household duties adjustment
가사원조 homemaker services
가사원조자 homemaker
가사활동도우미
  home helpers for household activities
가산 addition
가석방 parole
가석방심의위원회 parole board
가설 hypothesis
가성구마비 pseudobulbar paralysis
가성불량소년 pseudo delinquent
가성치매 pseudodementia
가스멸균 gas sterilization
가스트로그라핀관장 gastrografin enema
가슴통증 chest pain
가압류 impounding
가역성 plasticity
가옥수리사기 home repair scam
가옥평가 house evaluation
가옥화재 house fire
가와사키병
  mucocutaneous lymph node syndrome
가운착용법 gown technique
가운테크닉 gown technique
가의수
  temporary prosthesis of upper limb amputee
가이던스 guidance
가이드라인 guidelines
가이드헬퍼 guide helper
가입 enrollment ; participation
가입자 enrollee ; participant
가입제약
  enrollment restriction ; participation restriction

ㄱ

가정 home
가정 내 사고 accidents in the home
가정 내 폭력 domestic violence : DV
가정건강서비스 home health services
가정도구 utensil
가정도우미 home helpers
가정방문 home visits
가정법원 family court
가정보호 home care
가정복지 family welfare
가정복지과 Family Welfare Division
가정봉사 domestic help
가정봉사원 housekeeping service providers
가정봉사원서비스 homemaker service
가정봉사원파견사업
  delivery program of domestic helpers ;
  house keeping service providers dispatching ;
  dependent service business
가정봉사원파견사업소
  house keeping service providers dispatching
  office
가정봉사원파견시설
  house keeping service providers dispatching
  facilities
가정부 housekeeper
가정불화 family trouble
가정붕괴 family down
가정상담원 family adviser
가정양호 family child care
가정욕조 home bathtub
가정위탁 foster care
가정의 family doctor
가정의 기능 family doctor's function
가정일 housekeeping ; household work
가정재판소 family court
가정정책 family policy
가정조성서비스 homemaker services
가정조성자 homemaker
가정폭력 family violence
가정환경 family environment
가제 gauze
가족 family
가족 룰 family rule

가족갈등 family conflict
가족개호 family-provided care
가족개호자 family caregiver
가족계획 family planning
가족계획지도 family planning guidance
가족관계 family relationship
가족구성 family composition
가족구조 family structure
가족권 family right
가족규칙 family rules
가족급여 family benefit
가족기능 family function
가족긴장 family tension
가족도 family map
가족력 family history
가족면접 family interview
가족문제 family issue
가족법 family law
가족병리 family pathology
가족복지 family welfare
가족복지기관 family welfare service center
가족복지시설 institution of family welfare
가족봉사기관 family service organizations
가족부양 responsible for family ; family support
가족부양부담감척도
  Family Caregiver Burden Scale
가족부조계획 Family Assistance Plan : FAP
가족비밀 family secrets
가족사회학 sociology of the family
가족생활주기 family life cycle
가족성 대장포리포시스
  familial adenomatous polyposis : FAP
가족성 선종성용종증
  familial adenomatous polyposis : FAP
가족소시얼워커 family social worker
가족소시얼워크 family social work
가족수당 family allowance
가족시스템 family system
가족시스템이론 family system theory
가족시스템접근법 family systems approach
가족신화 family myths
가족역동성 family dynamics
가족역할 family role

가족요법 family therapy
가족요양비 dependent health care coverage
가족요양비지급신청서
　Dependent Care Service Coverage Payment
　Application Form
가족저항 family resistance
가족정책 family policy
가족조각 family sculpting
가족주기 family life cycle
가족주의 familism
가족중심케어 family-based care
가족중심케이스워크 family centered casework
가족지도 family education
가족지원 family support
가족지원센터 family support center
가족지향케어 family-oriented care
가족진단 family diagnosis
가족치료 family therapy
가족케이스워커 family case worker
가족케이스워크 family care work
가족투사 과정 family projection process
가족폭력 family violence
가족항상성 family homeostasis
가족해체 family disorganization
가족회 self-help group for families
가죽세공 leather work
가징수 provisional collection
가처분소득 disposable income
가출 run away from home
가출노인 runaway aged
가출노인찾기종합센터
　Center for Searching Runaway Aged
가출소 conditional release ; release on parole
가출옥 provisional release
가출자 runaway
가치 value
가치 명료화 values clarification
가치 있는 빈민 worthy poor
가치관 sense of value
가치법칙 law of value
가치지향 value orientation
가치판단 value judgment
가퇴원 conditional release

가프키도표 Gaffky table
가학성 성격장애 sadistic personality disorder
가학성애 sadistic
가학피학성애 sadomasochism
각막반사 corneal reflex
각본 scripts
각성 awake
각성제 awakening drug ; speed ; uppers
각인 imprinting
각장 leg length
각장부동 leg length inequality
각혈
　hemoptysis ; haemoptysis ; coughing up of
　blood
각화성 병변 keratotic lesions
각화증 keratosis
간 전문의 hepatologist
간경변 liver cirrhosis
간기능검사 liver function test : LFT
간단한 치료 brief therapy
간대성 근경련 myoclonus
간대성 근경련간질 myoclonus epilepsy
간동맥동주요법 hepatic arterial infusion
간반 liver spots
간병수당 attendance allowance
간병인 attendant
간상 rod
간성 intersex
간암 liver cancer
간염 hepatitis
간이구강위생검사
　Brief Oral Health Status Examination :
　BOHSE
간이동통조사표 Brief Pain Inventory : BPI
간이영양상태평가
　Mini Nutritional Assessment : MNA
간이욕조 simple bathtub
간이정신상태검사
　Mini Mental State Examination : MMSE
간이피로평가 Brief Fatigue Inventory : BFI
간장 liver
간장병학 hepatology
간장학 hepatology

간접비 indirect cost
간접세 indirect tax
간접언어 indirect language
간접원조기술 indirect social work
간접접촉감염 indirect contact infection
간접접촉전파 indirect contact spread
간접질문 indirect questions
간접처우 indirect treatment
간접처우직원 indirect treatment staff
간접치료 indirect treatment
간접활동 indirect practice
간주지정 deemed status
간주지정인정 deemed status accreditation
간질 epilepsy
간질발작 epileptic seizure
간체 rod
간헐견인 intermittent traction
간헐도뇨 intermittent urethral catheterization
간헐성 파행 intermittent claudication
간헐적 강화 intermittent reinforcement
간헐적 공기압박치료
    intermittent pneumatic compression
간헐적 양압호흡법
    intermittent positive-pressure breathing therapy
간호 nursing
간호계 대학 four-year nursing school
간호과 Nursing Division
간호관계자 nursing personnel
간호기초교육 basic nursing education
간호보조사 supporting nurse
간호보조원 nurse assistant
간호사 nurse
간호사부족 nursing shortage
간호사의 윤리강령 code of ethics for nurses
간호사장 director of nursing
간호의 기준
    standards of nursing ; standards of nursing
    practice
간호일지 nursing notes
간호전문 nursing profession
간호전문직 nursing professional
간호조무사
    nurse aide ; assistant service division of nursing

간호조수 nurse aide
간호종사자 nursing staff
간호직원 nursing staff
갈고리 소식자 hooked probe
갈고리 존데 hooked probe
갈등 conflict
갈등관리 conflict management
갈등유발 conflict induction
갈등이론 conflict theories
갈등해결 conflict resolution
갈란타민 galantamine
갈아입기 changing clothes
갈톤 Francis Galton
감가상각 depreciation
감각 sense
감각감퇴 hypesthesia
감각강화법 sensory enhancement
감각과민 hyperesthesia
감각기능 sensory function
감각대행 sensory substitution
감각둔마 hypesthesia
감각마비 sensory paralysis
감각성 실어 sensory aphasia
감각소실 anesthesia
감각신경 sensory nerve
감각신경전도속도
    sensory nerve conduction velocity
감각운동기 sensorimotor stage
감각장애 sensory disorder ; sensory disturbance
감각통합 sensory integration
감광색소 photopigment
감금증후군 locked-in syndrome
감기와 같은 증상 flu-like symptom
감독과 Inspection Division
감독과 보호 custody
감독과 보호권 child custody
감득욕구 felt needs
감리 surveillance
감마선멸균 gamma sterilization
감미 sweet
감별 assessment
감사 survey
감사관 surveyor

감세지진 tax quake
감수분열 meiosis
감수성 시험 sensitivity test
감수성 훈련집단 sensitivity group
감시 surveillance
감시안전과 Inspection and Safety Division
감시지도 · 마약대책과
  Compliance and Narcotics Division
감압 decompression
감압실 depressurized room
감액노령연금 low cost pension for the elderly
감염 infection ; incidence
감염경로 routes of infection
감염경로별 예방책 transmission-based precaution
감염관리 infection control
감염관리간호사 infection control nurse
감염관리예방 infection control and prevention
감염관리위원회 infection control committee
감염관리의사 infection control doctor
감염관리전문가 infection control practitioner
감염관리팀 infection control team
감염관리프로그램 infection control program
감염균 bacterium
감염대책 infection control
감염대책간호사 infection control nurse
감염대책예방 infection control and prevention
감염대책위원회 infection control committee
감염대책의사 infection control doctor
감염대책전문가 infection control practitioner
감염대책팀 infection control team
감염대책프로그램 infection control program
감염방어능저하환자 compromised patient
감염방어복 protective clothing
감염성 심내막염 infective endocarditis
감염성 의료폐기물 infectious medical waste
감염성 폐기물 infectious waste
감염식 low salt diet ; low sodium diet
감염예방
  prevention of infection ; infection prevention
감염원 source of infection
감염원격리 source isolation
감염율 incidence rate
감염율조사 incidence survey

감염전문간호사 infection clinical nurse specialist
감염제어 infection control
감염제어간호사 infection control nurse
감염제어예방 infection control and prevention
감염제어위원회 infection control committee
감염제어의사 infection control doctor
감염제어전문가 infection control practitioner
감염제어팀 infection control team
감염제어프로그램 infection control program
감염증 infectious disease
감염증감시 infection surveillance
감염후 기침 post-infection cough
감음난청 sensorineural deafness
감정기분질문표
  Feeling Tone Questionnaire : FTQ
감정반사 reflection of feeling
감정방산 emotional release
감정실금증 emotional incontinence
감정의 양면성 ambivalence
감정이입 empathy
감정전이 transference
감호 guardianship
감화교육 correctional education
감화사업 correctional relief activities
감화원 reformatory
갑상선기능저하증 hypothyroidism
갑상선기능항진증 hyperthyroidism
갑상선미분화암 anaplastic thyroid cancer
갑상선수양암 medullary thyroid cancer
갑상선암 thyroid cancer
갑상선여포암 follicular thyroid cancer
갑상선유두암 papillary thyroid cancer
갑상선자극호르몬
  thyroid-stimulating hormone : TSH
갑상선종 goiter
갑상선질환 thyroid disease
값싼 정부 cheap government
강간 rape
강도기간곡선 intensity-duration curve : I-D curve
강력한 약 multipotent drug
강박 compulsion
강박성 장애
  obsessive compulsive disorder : OCD

ㄱ

강박성 장애제
obsessive compulsive disorder medication
강박적 성격장애 compulsive personality disorder
강박증 obsession
강점 strength
강점관점 strengths perspective
강점모델 strength model ; strength-based model
강제 coercion
강제 버스통학 busing
강제가입 compulsory enrollment
강제보험 compulsory insurance
강제울음 forced crying
강제웃음 forced laughing
강제입소
compulsory admission ; involuntary admission
강제입원 involuntary hospitalization
강제적 성도착장애 paraphilic coercive disorder
강제조치 compulsory measure
강제징수
compulsory collection ; forcible collection
강제통고 enforcement notice
강제할당 levy
강직 rigidity
강찰법 stroking
강화 reinforcement
강화계획 schedule of reinforcement
강화물 reinforcer
강화운동 strength exercise
강화인자 reinforcer
개구색 모드 aperture color mode
개량주의 reformism
개발도상국 developing country
개발적 사회복지 developmental social welfare
개방등록기간 open enrollment period
개방명부제 open-panel
개방병원 attending system
개방성 permissiveness
개방성 골절 compound fracture ; open fracture
개방시설 open facility
개방식 드레나쥐법 open drainage system
개방입양 open adoption
개방집단 open-ended group
개방체계 open system

개방형 질문 open-ended questions
개별가족세션 individual family session
개별개호 individualized care
개별관리 individual management
개별교육계획 individualized educational plan
개별교육프로그램
individualized education program
개별사회사업 individualization service
개별사회사업 치료의 유형학
typology of casework treatment
개별원조기술 case work
개별이해 individual understanding
개별적 조정 individual manipulation
개별지도 individual guidance
개별처우 individual treatment
개별케어 individualized care
개별화 individualization
개별화의 원칙 principle of individualization
개선 scabies
개선명령 remedial order
개선활동 quality improvement : QI
개수대 sink
개업사회사업 private practice
개운동연쇄 open kinetic chain
개인내 변동 personal change
개인보호물품
personal protective equipment : PPE
개인실 private room
개인심리학 individual psychology
개인연금 personal pension
개인연금보험료 personal pension premium
개인연금플랜 personal pension scheme
개인위생 personal hygiene
개인적 구조기구 personal emergency device
개인적 커뮤니케이션 personal communication
개인정보 personal information
개인정보보호법
Personal Information Protection Act
개인정보절도 identity theft
개인주의 individualism
개인지원서비스 personal assistance services
개인케어 individualized care
개인퇴직연금계산

individual retirement account : IRA
개인할당 individual quota
개입 intervention
개입연구 intervention study
개입적 혈관조영 interventional angiography
개입적 화상진단 interventional radiology : IVR
개입초점 unit of attention
개정구빈법 The Reformed Poor Law
개정판 아동발현불안척도
　　Revised Children's Manifest Anxiety Scale :
　　RCMAS
개정판 웩슬러 기억검사
　　Revised Wechsler Memory Scale : WMS-R
개정판 웩슬러 성인지능척도
　　Revised Wechsler Adult Intelligence Scale :
　　WAIS-R
개치베드 gatch bed
개혁자 reformer
개호 care ; long-term care
개호강습 practical training for long-term care
개호계획 care plan
개호과정 care process
개호관계 care provider-recipient relationship
개호급여 long-term care insurance benefit
개호급여비납부금
　　government subsidy to care providers
개호기기 care equipment ; care device
개호기술 care skills
개호기술강습회
　　practical skills training for long-term care
개호노동 care work
개호노동안정센터 Care Work Foundation : CWF
개호노동자 care worker
개호노인보건시설 geriatric health care facilities
개호노인복지시설 geriatric welfare facilities
개호담당자 direct care staff
개호력 강화계획
　　empowerment plan for long-term care
개호로보트 care robot
개호모델 long-term care model
개호목표 care goal
개호보수 long-term care insurance payment
개호보험 long-term care insurance

개호보험과 Long-Term Care Insurance Division
개호보험료
　　long-term care insurance premium ; long-term
　　care premium
개호보험료가산
　　additional assistance for long-term care
　　insurance
개호보험료감면제도
　　deduction of long-term care insurance
　　premiums
개호보험료율
　　long-term care insurance premium rate ;
　　premium rate of long-term care insurance
개호보험법 Long-Term Care Insurance Law
개호보험법시행법
　　Act for Enforcement of the Long-Term Care
　　Insurance Act
개호보험사업계획 long-term care insurance plan
개호보험심사회
　　Review Committee on Long-Term Care
　　Insurance
개호보험인정조사
　　long-term care insurance eligibility assessment
개호보험제도 long-term care insurance system
개호보험지정사업자
　　long-term care insurance certified provider
개호보험피보험자
　　the insured of long-term care insurance
개호복지 care and welfare
개호복지사 certified care worker : CCW
개호복지사 국가시험
　　National Certification Examination for Care
　　Worker
개호복지사 국가시험 · 실기시험
　　National Certification Examination and
　　Practice Examination for Care Workers
개호복지사 등록 Certified Care Worker Registry
개호부담 burden of care
개호부문 direct care section
개호부조 long-term care assistance
개호비용지불 payments to care providers
개호비즈니스 long-term care business
개호사고 errors in long-term care

ㄱ

개호상담원
　long-term care advisor ; care advisor

개호서비스계획 　care services plan

개호서비스정보공개
　public reporting of long-term care services

개호서비스제공책임자 　care services manager

개호서비스제공표 　service provider report

개호서비스패키지
　long-term care services package

개호수당 　long-term care allowance

개호순서 　procedures of long-term care

개호시설 　long-term care facility

개호시설사업자 　institutional care provider

개호실습 · 보급센터
　practice and promotion center for long-term
　care

개호예방 　prevention of long-term care

개호예방단기입소생활개호
　preventive short-term care accommodation

개호예방방문입욕개호
　preventive home bathing care

개호예방복지용구대여
　preventive rental services of welfare equipments

개호예방사업 　preventive long-term care plan

개호예방서비스 　care-preventive services

개호예방일반고령자시책
　preventive aged-care approach for the
　independent

개호예방케어매니지먼트
　preventive care management

개호예방특정고령자시책
　preventive aged-care approach for the frail

개호예방특정시설입소자생활개호
　specific care home for the preventive long-term
　care

개호요양형의료시설 　long-term health care facility

개호욕구 　long-term care needs

개호용구 　care equipment ; care device

개호원조자
　care assistant ; long-term care assistant

개호의 사회화 　socialization of care

개호의 윤리 　ethics of long-term care

개호의 질 　quality of care

개호이념 　morality of long-term care

개호인정심사회
　Long-Term Care Certification Committee

개호자 　caregiver

개호자 불안 　anxiety for long-term caregivers

개호자 수당 　carer's allowance

개호전문
　direct care profession ; care profession

개호전문직
　direct care professional ; care professional

개호종사자 　direct care staff

개호지도 　care guidance

개호지원서비스 　care management services

개호지원서비스계획
　care management services plan

개호지원전문원 　care manager

개호직원 　direct care staff

개호판 매니지드케어 　managed long-term care

개호형 양로원 　custodial care facility

개호휴가 　family care leave

개호휴가제도 　family care leave system

개황조사 　general condition survey

객관성 　objectivity

객관적 욕구 　objective needs

객지벌이 　migrant work

객혈 　hemoptysis

갠트 도표 　GANT chart

갬블 　gambling

갱년기 　menopause

갱년기장애 　menopausal disorder

갱생 　regeneration

갱생보호 　offenders rehabilitation

갱생의료 　medical rehabilitation services

갱생협회 　Recovery, Inc.

갱신 　renewal

갱신신청 　renewal application

갱에이지 　gang age

갱의 　dressing

갱의동작 　dressing activity

각출제 　contributory scheme

거대세포동맥염 　giant cell arteritis : GCA

거르기 　straining

거부 　rejection ; denial

거상 팔 지지대 mobile arm support
거세 castration
거세불안 castration anxiety
거스트만 증후군 Gerstmann syndrome
거시적 실천 macro practice
거시적 지향 macro orientation
거식증 anorexia
거울문자 mirror writing
거적아구성 빈혈 megaloblastic anemia
거주케어 residential care
거주환경 residential environment
거출급여 contributory benefit
거출급여제 contributory benefit system
거택개호 home-based care
거택개호서비스 home-based care services
거택개호서비스계획
home-based care services plan
거택개호서비스사업소
home-based care services office
거택개호서비스사업자
home-based care services provider
거택개호지원 home-based care management
거택개호지원사업
home-based care management program
거택개호지원사업소
home-based care management office
거택개호지원사업자
home-based care management provider
거택부조 home-based assistance
거택부조계획
home-based assistance services plan
거택부조서비스 home-based assistance services
거택부조서비스계획
home-based assistance services plan
거택생활부조 home-based living assistance
거택생활부조사업
home-based living assistance program
거택생활부조서비스
home-based living assistance services
거택생활부조서비스사업소
home-based living assistance services office
거택생활부조서비스사업자
home-based living assistance services provider

거택생활원조 home-based living support
거택생활원조사업
home-based living support program ;
home-based living supportive program
거택생활원조서비스
home-based living support services ;
home-based living supportive services
거택생활원조서비스사업소
home-based living support services office ;
home-based living supportive services office
거택생활원조서비스사업자
home-based living support services provider ;
home-based living supportive services provider
거택서비스 home-based services
거택서비스계획 home-based care services plan
거택서비스사업 home-based services program
거택서비스사업소 home-based services office
거택서비스사업자 home-based services provider
거택원조 home-based support
거택원조서비스
home-based support services ; home-based
supportive services
거택의료 medical home-based care
거택의료서비스
medical home-based care services
거택의료서비스계획
medical home-based care services plan
거택의료서비스기관
medical home-based care services agency
거택의료서비스사업소
medical home-based care services office
거택의료서비스사업자
medical home-based care services provider
거품목욕 jacuzzi
거품목욕탕 whirlpool spa
건강 health
건강관련 QOL health-related quality of life
건강관리 health management
건강관찰 health observation
건강교육 health education
건강교육 가이드라인 health education guidelines
건강국 Health Service Bureau
건강대조자 healthy control

건강문화 health culture
건강보건재정운영국
 Health Insurance Finance Operations Agency
건강보균자 healthy carrier
건강보험 health insurance
건강보험급여 health insurance benefit
건강보험심사평가원
 Health Insurance Review Agency
건강보험재정안정종합대책
 Health Insurance Fiscal Stability Policy
건강보험제도 Medicare system
건강보험조합 health insurance society
건강보험증 health insurance card
건강보호 health care
건강보호재정국
 Health Care Financing Administration
건강복지의 질 quality of well-being : QWB
건강사정 health assessment
건강산업 health industry
건강상담 health counseling
건강상태 health condition
건강수첩 health handbook
건강식품 health food
건강신념모델 health belief model
건강염려증 hypochondria
건강위기관리 health risk management
건강유지 health maintenance
건강일본21 Health Japan 21
건강자원봉사 healthy volunteer
건강증진 health promotion
건강증진법 Health Promotion Act
건강지표 health indicator
건강진단 health examination
건강진단증명서 certificate of health examination
건강체크 medical check-up
건강프론티어전략 Health Frontier Strategic Plan
건강한 사람 healthy volunteer healthy subject
건강행동 health behavior
건강행동이론 health behavior theory
건고정 tenodesis
건고정 효과 tenodesis effect
건막류 bunion
건망증 amnesia ; forgetfulness

건식세탁 dry cleaning
건열 dry heat
건열멸균 dry heat sterilization
건열멸균기 hot air sterilizer
건조증 xerosis
건측 unaffected side of the body
건판손상 rotator cuff injury
걸쭉한 음식 thickened diet
걸쭉함 thickened
검사 편견 test bias
검시 autopsy
검안 optometry
검안사 optometrist
검안의 optometrist
검압법 manometry
검진 screening
검찰관 public prosecutor
검체수집 specimen collection
게르스트만 증후군 Gerstmann syndrome
게슈탈트요법 gestalt therapy
게스 후 테스트 guess-who test
게스탈트 심리학 gestalt psychology
게스탈트 치료 gestalt therapy
게실질환 diverticular disease
게인 프로그램 GAIN Program
게젤샤프트 Gesellschaft
겨드랑이 axilla
겨드랑이동맥 axillary artery
겨드랑이보조기 underarm brace
겨드랑이털 under arm hair
격리 isolation
격리병동 isolation unit
격리병원 pest house
격리실 isolation room
격리예방책 isolation precaution
격리장치 isolator
견갑상완리듬 scapulohumeral rhythm
견갑흉간절단술 forequarter amputation
견갑흉간절단용 의수
 forequarter amputation prosthesis
견건판손상 rotator cuff injury
견관절아탈구 shoulder subluxation
견관절주위염 adhesive capsulitis

견관절탈구 shoulder dislocation
견당식 orientation
견당식장애 disorientation
견수증후군 shoulder-hand syndrome
견습간호사 student nurse
견습기간
　apprenticeship period ; period of apprenticeship
견습생 apprentice
견의수 shoulder disarticulation prosthesis
견인 traction
견인요법 traction treatment
결과 consequence
결과의 평등 equality of result
결근 work absence
결막염 conjunctivitis
결사체 association
결속 bonding
결손가정 broken home
결연사업 sponsorship service program
결장내시경 colonoscope
결장내시경검사 colonoscopy
결장세정 colonic lavage
결장전처치 colon preparation
결장점막생검 colonic mucosal biopsy
결장통과검사 colonic transit study
결절성 동맥주위염 periarteritis nodosa
결정관절증 crystal arthropathy
결정론 determinism
결정성 능력 crystallized ability
결정성 지능 crystallized intelligence
결정유발성 관절염 crystal induced arthritis
결정적 critical
결함수분석 fault tree analysis
결핵 tuberculosis
결핵감염증과
　Tuberculosis and Infectious Diseases Control
　Division
결핵요양소 sanitarium
결핵종 tuberculoma
결핵환자 tuberculosis patient
결혼 marriage
결혼계약 marital contracts
결혼상담 marriage counseling

결혼상담소 marriage counseling center
결혼왜곡 marital skew
겸상 적혈구성 빈혈 sickle-cell anemia
겸자 forceps
겸자생검 forceps biopsy
겹쳐입음 layered clothing
경직형 spastic type
경계 boundary
경계구역 cold zone
경계선 borderline
경계선 성격장애 borderline personality disorder
경계선층 borderline class
경골고원 tibial plateau
경골근위부골절 proximal tibia fracture
경과관찰병동 observation unit
경과기록 progress record
경관영양 tube feeding
경구 by mouth : PO
경구감염 oral transmission
경구보액요법 oral rehydration therapy
경구섭취 oral intake
경도인지장애 mild cognitive impairment : MCI
경동맥협착 carotid artery stenosis
경두개자기자극
　transcranial magnetic stimulation : TMS
경량화 downsize
경련 convulsion ; spasm
경로 respect for the elderly
경로당 church for the senior citizen
경로당활성화사업
　project for activation of senior citizen churches
경로당활성화협의체
　Consultative Body Promoting Activation of
　Senior Citizen Churches
경로대학 university for the senior citizens for
　lifetime learning
경로분석 path analysis
경로사상 respect for the aged
경로식당 canteen for the senior citizen
경로연금 pension for the senior citizen
경로우대 special benefits for the senior citizens
경로우대서비스 special benefits service
경로우대제도

special benefit programs for the senior citizens

경로우대증
preferential certificate for the senior citizens

경로우대할인제도
special benefit and discounts programs for the senior citizens

경로의 날
Respect for the Elderly Day ; Respect for the Aged Day

경로헌장 Senior Citizen Charter

경로회 senior citizens club

경로효친사상 respecting filial obligation

경막외진통법 epidural analgesia

경막외혈종 epidural hematoma

경막하혈종 subdural hematoma

경면 somnolence ; drowsiness

경범죄 minor offence

경보 alarm

경보안전시스템 alert safety system

경부신경근증 cervical radiculopathy

경비 nasal

경비경관영양 nasal tube feeding

경비노인양로시설
low cost care service facilities for the aged

경비노인요양시설
low cost health care service facilities for the aged

경비노인전문요양시설
low cost specialized health care service facilities for the aged

경사로 ramp

경상비 recurrent expenditures

경성 spastic ; spasticity

경성S상 결장경검사 rigid sigmoidoscopy

경성경 rigid scope

경성대마비 spastic paraparesis

경성마비 spastic paralysis

경성사경 spastic torticollis

경수손상
cervical spinal cord injury ; cervical cord injury

경영문자 mirror writing

경영참가 management participation

경요도적 마이크로파 온열요법
transurethral microwave therapy : TUMT

경요도적 전립선절제술
transurethral incision of prostate

경요도적 절제 transurethral resection : TURP

경장영양법 transintestine nutrition method

경쟁가능한 시장 contestable market

경쟁원리 principle of competition

경쟁적 고용 competitive employment

경정맥신우조영 intravenous pyelogram : IVP

경제개발국
Office of Economic Development : OED

경제계획 economic planning

경제과 Economic Affairs Division

경제교육 economic education

경제기회국
Office of Economic Opportunity : OEO

경제기회법 Economic Opportunity Act

경제발전 economic development

경제불황 depression economic

경제사회이사회 Economic & Social Council

경제성장 economic growth

경제성장률 economic growth rate

경제연계협정
Economic Partnership Agreement : EPA

경제자문위원회
Council of Economic Advisers : CEA

경제재정자문회의
Council on Economic and Fiscal Policy

경제적 약탈 economic predation

경제적자유주의 economic liberalism

경제적학대 전문가팀
fiduciary abuse specialist team : FAST

경제정책 economic policy

경제체제 economic system

경제협력개발기구
Organization for Economic Co-operation and Development : OECD

경조병 hypomania

경직 ankylosis

경직성 ankylosing

경직성 보조기 plastic orthosis

경직성 척추염 ankylosing spondylitis

경직장적 초음파검사 transrectal ultrasonography

경직장적 초음파검사법

endorectal ultrasonography
경직형 사지마비 spastic quadriplegia
경직형 양마비 spastic diplegia
경찰법(輕擦法) eurage
경찰사회사업 police social work
경청 active listening
경추 cervical spine
경추견인 cervical traction
경추보조기 cervical orthosis ; halo-vest orthosis
경추보호대 cervical spine collar
경추성 두통 cervicogenic headache
경추염좌 neck distortion
경축 spasticity
경피 topical : TOP ; transdermal
경피감염 percutaneous infection
경피경간적 담관드레나지
　percutaneous transhepatic cholangiodrainage
경피경관적 관상동맥재개통술
　percutaneous transluminal coronary
　recanalization
경피경관적 관상동맥형성술
　percutaneous transluminal coronary angioplasty
경피내시경적 위루조설술
　percutaneous endoscopic gastrostomy : PEG
경피적 매입전극
　percutaneous implantable electrode
경피적 에탄올주입요법
　percutaneous ethanol injection
경피적 전기신경자극
　transcutaneous electrical nerve stimulation :
　TENS
경항문적 초음파검사 transanal ultrasonography
경험요율 experience rating
경험율 experience rating
경험의 empirical
경험자기 experiential self
경험적 치료 empiric therapy
경험주의적 치료 empiric therapy
경험치료 experiential therapy
경화증 cirrhosis
계급 class
계급사회 hierarchical society
계단 stairs

계단승강 scaling stairs
계단승강기 stair lift
계량경제학 econometrics
계면반사 interface reflection
계속이론 continuity theory
계속적 개선활동 continuous quality improvement
계속적 냉각요법 continuous cold therapy
계속적 케어 continuing care
계약 contract
계약서 contract document
계약수립 contracting
계약제도 contract system
계절노동 seasonal work
계절보육소 seasonal day nursery
계절성 정서장애
　seasonal affective disorder : SAD
계절적 실업 seasonal unemployment
계층 social stratum
계통적 논리재구성법
　systematic and rational reconstruction
계통추출법 systematic sampling
계획적 자상행위 deliberate self-harm
계획적 행동이론 theory of planned behavior
고객 customer
고객만족 customer satisfaction : CS
고관절골절 hip fracture
고관절의족 hip disarticulation prosthesis
고관절인공관절 전치환술
　total hip replacement : THR
고기능 인공발연구 energy storing prosthetic foot
고난 grief work
고도간호시설 skilled nursing home
고도경제성장 high economic growth
고도산업사회 high industrialized society
고도선진의료
　highly advanced medical technology : HAMT
고도전문간호사 advanced practice nurse
고도치료실 high dependency unit
고독 loneliness
고독사 solitary death
고등양성훈련제도 higher apprenticeships
고려장 Koryeo Funeral (leaving one's parents
　when they get older)

ㄱ

고령 · 장애인고용대책부
Employment Measures for the Elderly and
Persons with Disabilities Department

고령기 장애　old-age disorder

고령기 활동　later-life activity

고령동성애자　lesbian elder

고령발생 류마티스관절염
elderly-onset rheumatoid arthritis : EORA

고령사회　aged society

고령사회기본법　Basic Act for the Elderly

고령사회대책기본법　Aged Society Basic Act

고령성 질환　age-related disease

고령이민　immigrant elder

고령자　elderly

고령자 치과학분야　geriatric dentistry

고령자 케어매니지먼트　geriatric care management

고령자 케이스매니저　geriatric case manager

고령자 케이스매니지먼트
geriatric case management

고령자간호　geriatric nursing

고령자개호
elderly care ; caring for the elderly ;
geriatric care

고령자개호기관
long-term care agency for the elderly

고령자개호보험
long-term care insurance for the elderly

고령자개호사업자
long-term care provider for the elderly

고령자개호서비스
long-term care services for the elderly

고령자개호서비스기관
long-term care services agency for the elderly

고령자개호서비스사업소
long-term care services office for the elderly

고령자개호서비스사업자
long-term care services provider for the elderly

고령자개호시설
long-term care facility for the elderly

고령자개호지원　elderly care management

고령자개호지원서비스
elderly care management services

고령자개호지원서비스기관
elderly care management services agency

고령자개호지원서비스사업소
elderly care management services office

고령자개호지원서비스사업자
elderly care management services provider

고령자개호포기　elder neglect

고령자거주공동체
community living for the elderly ; senior
living community

고령자거택개호　home-based care for the elderly

고령자거택개호지원
home-based care management for the elderly

고령자거택부조
home-based assistance for the elderly

고령자거택생활부조
home-based living assistance for the elderly

고령자거택생활원조
home-based living support for the elderly

고령자거택원조
home-based support for the elderly

고령자고용
employment of older workers ; employment of
the elderly ; hiring older workers

고령자고용대책과
Employment Measures for the Elderly
Division

고령자고용장려금
incentives for employment of the elderly

고령자고용정보센터
Information Center for Employment of the
Elderly

고령자고용지원금
funding for employment of the elderly

고령자고용촉진
employment promotion for the elderly

고령자고용촉진대책
employment promotion policy for the elderly

고령자고용촉진법
Act for the Promotion of Employment of
Older Persons

고령자고용촉진장려금
incentives for promoting employment of the
elderly

고령자공동생활 group living for the elderly

고령자공동생활부조
group living assistance for the elderly

고령자공동생활원조
group living support for the elderly

고령자공동생활지원
group living management for the elderly

고령자급식 meal services for the elderly

고령자다목적복지센터 multipurpose senior center

고령자대상 공영주택
public housing for the elderly

고령자대상 민간서비스
private services for the elderly

고령자대상 우량임대주택
high-quality rental housing for the elderly

고령자대학 university for the elderly

고령자무시 elder neglect

고령자법률지원프로그램
elderly legal assistance program

고령자보건복지 geriatric health and welfare

고령자보건복지추진 10개년전략
Ten-Year Strategy to Promote Health and
Welfare for the Aged ; Gold Plan

고령자보건의료 health care for the elderly

고령자보건의료비
health care expenditures for the elderly ;
medical expenses for the aged

고령자보건의료서비스
health care services for the elderly

고령자보건의료제도
health care system for the elderly

고령자복지 welfare for the elderly

고령자복지서비스 welfare services for the elderly

고령자복지센터 senior center

고령자부조 assistance for the elderly

고령자부조서비스
assistance services for the elderly

고령자부조서비스기관
assistance services agency for the elderly

고령자부조서비스사업소
assistance services office for the elderly

고령자부조서비스사업자
assistance services provider for the elderly

고령자생활복지센터 welfare center for the elderly

고령자생활부조 living assistance for the elderly

고령자서비스조정팀
service management team for the elderly

고령자세대 elderly household

고령자스포츠 sports for the elderly

고령자약제처방기준 Beers criteria

고령자에 대한 약제부적절투여
inappropriate prescription for elderly

고령자에 대한 편견 prejudice against the elderly

고령자용주택 housing for the elderly

고령자원조 support for the elderly

고령자원조서비스
support services for the elderly ;
supportive services for the elderly

고령자원조서비스기관
support services agency for the elderly ;
supportive services agency for the elderly

고령자원조서비스사업소
support services office for the elderly ;
supportive services office for the elderly

고령자원조서비스사업자
support services provider for the elderly ;
supportive services provider for the elderly

고령자의 존엄 dignity of the elderly

고령자의료 medical care for the elderly

고령자의료 펠로우십프로그램
Geriatric Medicine Fellowship Program

고령자의료비
medical expenses for the elderly ; health care
expenditures for the elderly

고령자의료서비스
medical care services for the elderly

고령자의료서비스기관
medical care services agency for the elderly

고령자의료서비스사업소
medical care services office for the elderly

고령자의료서비스사업자
medical care services provider for the elderly

고령자의료제도
medical care system for the elderly

고령자인구 elderly population

고령자인재은행

ㄱ

Human Resource Agency of the Elderly
고령자재가개호지원

elderly home care management
고령자재가부조 home assistance for the elderly
고령자재가생활부조
home living assistance for the elderly
고령자재가생활원조
home living support for the elderly
고령자재가원조 home support for the elderly
고령자전문의 geriatrician
고령자전용임대주택 senior rental housing
고령자종합평가
Comprehensive Geriatric Assessment : CGA
고령자주택 elderly housing
고령자주택정책 housing policy for the elderly
고령자창업지원
support for business of the elderly
고령자취업 work for the elderly
고령자취업알선사업
agency program of the work of the elderly
고령자취업알선센터
Agency of the Work of the Elderly
고령자취업정보
information of the work for the elderly
고령자취업지원센터
Support Center for the Work of the Elderly
고령자케어 geriatric care
고령자케어 어드바이저 senior care advisor
고령자케어제공주택
elder care housing ; aged care home
고령자클럽
senior citizens club ; old people club
고령자평가 매니지먼트프로그램
geriatric evaluation and management program
고령자학교 school for the elderly
고령자학급 educational class for the elderly
고령자학대 elderly abuse ; elderly mistreatment
고령자학대 · 니글렉트 elder abuse and neglect
고령자학대방지 prevention of elder abuse
고령자학대방지법 Elder Abuse Prevention Act
고령자학대방지활동
elder abuse prevention activity
고령출산 advanced maternal age

고령친화산업 nursing care industry
고령친화산업지원센터
Support Center for the Nursing Care industry
고령친화산업진흥법
Law for Promotion of Nursing Care industry
고령화 population aging ; aging population
고령화사회 aging society
고령화위원회 Conference on Aging
고령화율 rate of population aging
고리 자물쇠 ring lock
고리대금 usury
고리대금업자 loan shark
고립 isolation
고막 tympanic membrane
고면책의료보험
high deductible health insurance plan
고밀도지단백 HDL < high-density Lipoprotein >
고발 whistle-blowing
고복지 · 고부담 high level of welfare
고부갈등
conflict between mothers-in-law and daughters-in-law ; conflict between mothers-in-law and brides
고비중리포단백질 high-density lipoprotein : HDL
고빈도접촉면 high touch surface
고살죄 manslaughter
고소뇌부종 high altitude cerebral edema
고소득층 upper income class
고소폐수종 high altitude pulmonary edema
고수준소독 high level disinfection
고실형성술 tympanoplasty
고아 orphans
고아원 orphanage
고압증기멸균 steam sterilization ; autoclaving
고압증기멸균기 autoclave
고액개호비용
catastrophic long-term care expenses
고액개호서비스
catastrophic long-term care services expenses
고액요양비 catastrophic health care expenses
고액의료비 catastrophic medical expenses
고액장기요양비용
catastrophic long-term care expenses

고액장기요양서비스
catastrophic long-term care services expenses
고연령노동자 older worker
고엽제 Agent Orange
고온생검 hot biopsy
고요산혈증 hyperuricemia
고용 employment
고용개발과 Employment Development Division
고용계약 employment agreements and contracts
고용계약서 indenture
고용계획 employment programs
고용균등·아동가정국 Equal Employment
고용균등정책과
Equal Employment Policy Division
고용기간
employment period ; period of employment
고용법 Employment Act
고용보험 employment insurance
고용보험과 Employment Insurance Division
고용보험법 Employment Insurance Law
고용보험제도 Employment Insurance System
고용율 employment rate
고용인원조계획
employee assistance programs : EAPs
고용정책 employment policy
고용정책과 Employment Policy Division
고용정책기본법 Employment Basic Law
고용조정 employment adjustment
고용종료 termination of employment
고용차별금지법
Employment Antidiscrimination Law
고용통계과 Employment Statistics Division
고용훈련 프로그램 (ET프로그램)
Employment training programs
고유감각 proprioception
고유수용성 결함 proprioception deficit
고유수용성 신경근촉통법
proprioceptive neuromuscular facilitation : PNF
고의적 자산축소 spending down
고의적 자상행위 deliberate self-harm
고인 deceased
고전적 조건형성 classical conditioning
고전적 조건화 classical conditioning

고정관계 fixator muscle
고정근육긴장이상 fixed dystonia
고정기 fixator
고정디스토니아 fixed dystonia
고정자산 fixed assets
고정자전거 stationary bicycle
고주파요법 diathermy
고주파투열요법 diathermy
고지혈증 hyperlipidemia
고질소혈증 azotemia
고차뇌기능 higher brain function
고차뇌기능장애 higher brain dysfunction
고착 fixation
고체온 hyperthermia
고칼로리수액 hyperalimentation
고콜레스테롤혈증 hypercholesterolemia
고탄산가스혈증 hypercapnia
고한산업 sweating industry
고혈당성 고삼투압증후군
hyperosmolar hyperglycemic syndrome : HHS
고혈당증 hyperglycemia
고혈압 hypertension
고형비누 bar soap
곤궁자 needy person
골감소성 osteopenia
골격 skeleton
골격근 skeletal muscle
골결핍증 osteopenia
골다공증 osteoporosis
골드플랜 Gold Plan
골드플랜21
Gold Plan 21 ; Gold Plan for 21st century
골밀도 bone density ; bone mineral density
골반골절 pelvic fracture
골반대 pelvic band
골반대부 하지보조기
hip-knee-ankle-foot orthosis : HKAFO
골반반절제술 hemipelvectomy
골반저이완 pelvic floor relaxation
골수이형성증후군 myelodysplastic syndrome
골연골염 costochondritis
골연화증 osteomalacia
골염량 bone mineral density

골위축증 bone atrophy
골절 fracture
골절관리 fracture management
골질환 bone disease
골화성 근염 myositis ossificans
공감 empathy
공감적 이해 empathic understanding
공감피로 compassion fatigue
공격 aggression
공격기제 aggressive mechanism
공격적 아동 aggressive child
공격적 행동 aggressive behavior
공공경제학 public economics
공공교통기관 public transportation
공공복지 public welfare
공공사업 public work
공공사업청 Public Works Administration : PWA
공공선택이론 public choice theory
공공정책 public policy
공공주택 public housing
공공직업안정소
　　public employment security office : PESO
공공직업훈련 public vocational training
공급보조금 supply subsidy
공급자 provider
공급주체 provider
공급체계 provision systems
공기감염
　　airborne infection ; airborne transmission
공기감염격리 airborne infection isolation : AII
공기기관지조영 air bronchogram
공기색전증 air embolism
공기시료채집 air sampling
공기시료채집기 air sampler
공기여과장치 air filter
공기예방책 airborne precaution
공기오염 air pollution
공기전파 airborne transmission
공기제거 및 증기침투시험 Bowie-Dick Test
공기조화 air conditioning
공기조화기
　　heating ventilation and air-conditioning :
　　HVAC

공동결정법 the law of codetermination
공동경제협력위원회 Joint Economic Committee
공동근 synergist
공동기금 joint funding
공동면접 joint interview
공동모금 community chest
공동모금활동 community chest campaign
공동모금회 Community Chest
공동보험 co-insurance
공동보호양육원 joint custody
공동부담 co-pay
공동사회 community
공동생활가정 group home
공동예산책정 joint budgeting
공동운동 synergy
공동치료 conjoint therapy
공리주의 utilitarianism
공립병원 public hospital
공립병원개혁 public hospital reform
공립시설 public institution
공무원 civil servants
공무원연금 pension of government servants
공민권 civil rights
공민권운동 civil rights movement
공복시 고혈당 impaired fasting glucose : IFG
공복시 혈당 fasting blood sugar
공사분리 public/private dichotomy
공사분리의 원칙
　　principle of private/public dichotomy
공산주의 communism
공상배회 fantasy wandering
공상적 사회개량가 do-gooder
공생 symbiosis
공생사회 symbiosis society
공설민영 privatization of public enterprise
공소증후군 empty nest syndrome
공식적조직 formal organization
공업화 industrialization
공영기업등 회계부문 public businesses account
공영기업직원 local public enterprise personnel
공영주택 public housing
공유성 편집장애 shared paranoid disorder
공유주택 shared housing

공의존 co-dependency
공익법인 public benefit corporation
공익사업 public utility
공익신탁 charitable trust
공익전당포 public pawnshop
공인 accreditation
공인사회사업가 certified social worker
공인사회사업가학회
　　Academy of Certified Social Workers : ACSW
공장법 Factory Act
공적개입 public intervention
공적개호보험 public long-term care insurance
공적개호보험제도
　　public long-term care insurance system
공적구제 public relief
공적기업 public enterprise
공적노인요양보장추진기획단
　　Public Planning Committee for Protection and
　　Promotion of Care Services for the Elderly
공적노인요양제도 long-term care system
공적부조 public assistance
공적부조기준 public assistance standards
공적부조비용 public assistance costs
공적부조수급자 public assistance recipient
공적서비스 public services
공적연금 public pension
공적연금일원화
　　integration of the public pension schemes
공적연금제도 public pension system
공적연금제도가입경과
　　public pension plan subscription process
공적의료보험 public health care insurance
공적의료보험제도
　　public health care insurance system
공적장기요양보험
　　public long-term care insurance
공적장기요양보험제도
　　public long-term care insurance system
공적책임 public responsibility
공적후견인 public guardian
공정원리 principle of justice
공정증서 notarial deed
공제 deduction

공제연금 mutual aid pension
공제제도 mutual aid system
공제조합 mutual aid association
공조 public support
공중먼지 airborne particle ; floating particle
공중보건 public health
공중보건서비스청 Public Health Service
공중보건의 public health doctor
공중부유균 airborne bacteria
공중부유균 측정기 airborne microbe sampler
공중부유미립자측정기 particle counter
공중부유분진 floating particle
공중세균 airborne bacteria
공중세균측정기 airborne microbe sampler
공중위생 public health
공중위생법 Public Health Service Act
공증인 notary public
공청회 public hearing
공평 equity
공포장애 phobic disorder
공포증 phobia
공해 pollution
공황 crisis
과각화증 hyperkeratosis
과도한 침흘림 excessive drooling
과민성 irritability
과민성 쇼크 anaphylactic shock
과밀인구 overpopulation
과보상 overcompensation
과보호 overprotectiveness of children
과부 [남성] widower
과부 [여성] widow
과부공제 reduction of taxes for widow
과부급여 widow benefit
과부복지자금대여 welfare fund loan for widows
과부세공제 tax deduction for widows
과부연금 widow's pension
과산화수소가스 플라스마멸균
　　hydrogen peroxide gas plasma sterilization
과소 depopulation
과시행위 demonstrative
과식 overeating
과식증 bulimia

과신장 hyperextension
과업중심치료 task-centered treatment
과오납액 overpayment of premium
과용 overuse
과용성 근력저하 over work weakness
과용증후군 overuse syndrome
과유연 sialorrhea
과잉미네랄 mineral excess
과잉병상 overbedding
과잉보상 overcompensation
과잉보호 overprotectiveness
과잉애 overloving
과잉인구 overpopulation
과정기록 process recording
과정모형 process model
과정으로서의 퇴직 retirement process
과정중심주의 process-centered social work
과제 assignment
과제분석 task analysis
과제수행능력 task performance ability
과제중심모델 task-centered model
과제중심접근방법 task-centered approach
과제중심접근법 task-centered approach
과중성장 overgrowth
과즙액체식 nectar liquid diet
과초산 peracetic acid
과태금 fines for default
과태료 non-penal fine
과학 science
과학연구비보조금
  grant-in-aid for scientific research
과학적 방법 scientific method
과호흡증 hyperventilation
관계 relationship
관계망 network
관계망 치료 network therapy
관계망 형성 networking
관계사고 ideas of reference
관계요법 relationship therapy
관념실행 ideational apraxia
관념운동실행 ideomotor apraxia
관념화 ideation
관동맥질환 coronary artery disease : CAD

관련전문가 팀 interprofessional team
관련통 referred pain
관료정치 bureaucracy
관료제 bureaucracy
관료화 bureaucratization
관리가능고정비 managed cost
관리경쟁 managed competition
관리과업 management tasks
관리영양사 registered dietitian
관리운영비 administrative cost
관리자훈련계획
  management training program : MTP
관리정보체계
  management information systems : MISs
관민경쟁 public-private competition
관민경쟁의 비용산정
  calculating public-private competition costs
관상동맥 coronary artery
관상동맥 연축성 협심증
  vasospastic angina pectoris
관상동맥성 심질환 coronary heart disease : CHD
관상동맥우회술
  coronary artery bypass graft surgery : CABG
관상동맥조영 coronary angiography
관상동맥질환 coronary artery disease : CAD
관상동맥질환집중치료실 coronary care unit : CCU
관선변호인 public defender
관음증 voyeurism
관장 enema ; bowel preparation
관절 joint
관절가동역 range of motion : ROM
관절가동역검사 range of motion testing :
  ROM-T
관절가동역운동 range of motion exercise
관절각도계 goniometer
관절구축 joint contracture ; joint stiffness
관절류머티즘 rheumatoid arthritis : RA
관절모멘트 joint moment
관절보철 joint prosthesis
관절염 arthritis
관절운동접근법 arthrokinematic approach : AKA
관절이단 disarticulation
관절치환술 joint replacement

관절통　arthralgia
관찰　observation
관찰에 기초한 실천　empirically-based practice
관해　remission
관호조치　detention and classification
광기　mania ; rage
광노화　photoaging
광니요법　fango therapy
광범성 발달장애
　pervasive developmental disorder : PDD
광선손상　actinic injury
광선역학요법　photodynamic therapy
광선요법　actinotherapy
광선혐기증　photophobia
광순응　light adaptation
광우병　mad-cow disease
광장공포증　agoraphobia
괴롭힘　bullying
괴사　necrosis
괴저　gangrene
교감신경　sympathetic nerve
교감신경피부반응　sympathetic skin response
교과과정정책설명서　curriculum policy statement
교구빈민구제　Parish Poor Rate
교대욕　contrast bath
교대제 근무　alternative work schedule
교도소　prison
교량직업　bridge job
교류　transactions
교류분석　transactional analysis
교부금　grant-in-aid
교섭　bargaining
교액성 신경장애　entrapment neuropathy
교우도식　sociogram
교원병　collagen disease
교육　education
교육 가능한　educable
교육급여　educational benefit
교육미팅　educational meeting
교육보조수당　educational maintenance allowance
교육부조　educational aid
교육분석　didactic analysis
교육비　educational expenses

교육심리학　educational psychology
교육에 있어서의 장애기준
　disability standards for education
교육유지수당　educational maintenance allowance
교육자역할　educator role
교육적 재활　educational rehabilitation
교정　corrections
교정시설　correctional facility
교정용보조기　corrective orthosis
교정장치　orthodontic appliance
교정정신의학　orthopsychiatry
교정화　corrective shoes
교차3점 보행　alternate three-point gait
교차감염　cross infection
교차계획　intersectoral planning
교차오염　cross contamination
교차표　cross-tabulation
교통사고 목손상　whiplash ; whiplash injury
교통수당　transportation allowance
교통장애물제거법
　Transportation Accessibility Improvement Law
교호보행보조기　reciprocating gait orthosis
교호식 보행기　reciprocal walking frame
교호원　home for training and education of juve-
　nile delinquent
구갈　dry mouth
구강　oral cavity
구강건조증　dry mouth ; xerostomia
구강기　oral stage
구강기능향상　improvement of oral functions
구강내장치　oral appliance
구강단계　oral propulsive phase
구강대 구강 인공호흡　mouth-to-mouth breathing
구강대 비강 인공호흡　mouth-to-nose breathing
구강보건평가　oral health assessment
구강상태　oral status
구강실행증　oral apraxia
구강악안면외과　oral and maxillofacial surgery
구강악안면외과의　oral and maxillofacial surgeon
구강암　oral cancer
구강온　oral temperature
구강위생　oral health
구강질환　oral disease

ㄱ

구강청소행동 oral hygiene
구강체온 oral thermometry
구강케어 oral health care
구급구명사 emergency medical technician : EMT
구급구명실 emergency room : ER
구급법 first aid
구급외래 emergency room : ER
구급의료 emergency medical services
구급지정병원 designated emergency hospital
구급차 ambulance
구동륜 wheel
구두실행증 oral apraxia
구두주걱 shoe horn
구두주걱보조기 shoe horn brace : SHB
구두형 장구 corrective shoes
구루병 rickets
구마비 bulbar palsy
구부린 자세 crouch posture
구빈법 poor law
구빈사업 poor relief
구빈원 almshouse ; poorhouse
구빈제도 poor relief system
구사 moxibustion therapist
구성실행 constructional apraxia
구성실행증 constructional apraxia
구성장애 constructive disability
구세군 salvation army
구속 restraint
구순기 oral phase
구순성격 oral character
구심성 수축 concentric contraction
구심성 시야협착
  concentric contraction of the visual field
구심적 가족구조 centripetal family structure
구아이악검사 guaiac test
구역질 nausea
구원 support ; assistance ; help
구원관계 therapeutic relationship
구음장애 articulation disorder ; dysarthria
구음훈련 articulation training ; dysarthria training
구제사업 relief work
구조 relive ; rescue ; save
구조적 가족치료 structural family therapy

구조적 사회변동 structural social change
구조적 사회사업 structural social work
구조적 증분주의 structural incrementalism
구조조정 restructuring
구조치입소 old placement system
구직자 job seeker
구직자급여 job seeker's benefit
구체적조작기 concrete operations stage
구축 contracture
구축예방
  contracture prevention ; prevention of
  contracture
구축현상 crowding-out theory
구충제 anthelmintic
구타 battery
구토 vomiting ; nausea
구호시설 relief institution
구화 verbal communication
구화법 oral method
구획계획 sectoral planning
구획증후군 compartment syndrome
국가독점자본주의 state monopolistic capitalism
국가보호 parents patriae
국가시험 · 실기시험
  National Certification Examination and Practice
  Examination
국가주의 nationalism
국가중심이론 state-centered theory
국가책임 national responsibility
국가최저기준 national minimum standards
국가최저임금 national minimum wage
국가최저임금감독관
  national minimum wage compliance officer
국경없는 의사회 Medecins Sans Frontieres : MSF
국고보조금 state subsidy
국균증 aspergillosis
국내총생산 gross domestic product : GDP
국립감염증연구소
  National Institute of Infectious Diseases
국립국제의료연구센터
  National Center for Global Health and
  Medicine
국립병원 national hospital

국립병원과　National Hospitals Division
국립보건원　National Institute of Health
국립보건의료과학원
　National Institute of Public Health
국립보건통계조사청
　National Center for Health Statistics Research :
　NCHSR
국립부흥청
　National Recovery Administration : NRA
국립사회보장·인구문제연구소
　National Institute of Population and Social
　Security Research
국립사회복지연수원
　National Academy of Practice : NAP
국립생육의료연구센터　National Center for Child
　Health and Development
국립순환기병연구센터
　National Cerebral and Cardiovascular Center
국립아동건강 및 인간발달연구원
　National Institute of Child Health and Human
　Development
국립아동학대 및 방임예방센터
　National Center on Child Abuse and Neglect
국립암연구센터　National Cancer Institute
국립의약품식품위생연구소
　National Institute of Health Sciences
국립장수의료연구센터
　National Center for Geriatrics and Gerontology
국립정신·신경의료연구센터
　National Center of Neurology and Psychiatry
국립정신보건연구원
　National Institute of Mental Health : NIMH
국민개호비용
　national long-term care expenditures ; national
　expenditures on long-term care services
국민건강만들기 대책
　national health promotion policy
국민건강만들기 운동
　national health promotion movement
국민건강보험　National Health Insurance
국민건강보험공단
　National Health Insurance Corporation
국민건강보험과

National Health Insurance Division
국민건강보험단체연합회불평처리위원회　Grievance
　Committee of the National Health Insurance
국민건강보험료
　National Health Insurance premiums
국민건강보험료감면
　deduction for National Health Insurance
　premiums
국민건강보험법　National Health Insurance Act
국민건강보험제도
　National Health Insurance System
국민건강보험조합
　National Health Insurance society
국민건강보험증　National Health Insurance card
국민기초생활보장제도
　National Basic Livelihood Security Act
국민기초생활수급자
　claimant of national basic human needs
　benefits
국민보건보험　national health insurance
국민보건서비스　national health service
국민복지지표　net national welfare
국민부담율　national burden rate
국민생활기초생활보장법
　National Basic Human Needs Security Law
국민생활센터
　National Consumer Affairs Center of Japan
국민소득　national income : NI
국민연금　National Pension
국민연금공단　National Pension Corporation
국민연금기금　National Pension Fund
국민연금법　National Pension Law
국민연금보험　National Pension Insurance
국민연금보험료　National Pension premiums
국민연금보험료감면
　deduction for National Pension premiums ; tax
　deduction for National Pension premiums
국민연금의 기호번호
　National Pension registration number
국민연금피보험자의 수급금액
　amount of National Pension Insurance benefit
국민의료비
　national medical expenditures ; national health

expenditures

국민주권 popular sovereignty

국민총복지 gross national welfare : GNW

국민총생산 gross national product : GNP

국민투표 referendum

국세조사 national census

국소 topical : TOP

국적 nationality

국제가족의 해 International Year of the Family

국제개발기구
Agency for International Development : AID

국제고령자의 해
International Year of Older Persons : IYOP

국제과 International Affairs Division

국제규격 International Standard : IS

국제년 international year

국제노년정신학회
International Psychogeriatric Association

국제노동기구
International Labour Organization : ILO

국제노인문화예술제
International Cultural and Art Festival for the Elderly

국제두통학회 두통분류위원회
Headache Classification Committee of the International Headache Society

국제보건 international health

국제보건복지 international health and welfare

국제복지 international welfare

국제부인의 해
International Women's Year : IWY

국제사회복지 international social welfare

국제사회복지협의회
International Council on Social Welfare : ICSW

국제사회복지협회
International Council on Social Welfare : ICSW

국제사회사업 international social work

국제사회사업가훈련프로그램협의회
Council on International Programs : CIP

국제사회사업대학협의회 International Association of Schools of Social Work : IASSW

국제생물다양성의 해
International Year of Biodiversity : IYB

국제생활기능분류 International Classification of Functioning, Disability and Health : ICF

국제아동복지연맹
International Union for Child Welfare : IUCW

국제아동복지연합
International Union for Child Welfare

국제아동의 해 International Year of the Child

국제여성의 날 International Women's Day

국제여성의 해 International Women's Year

국제연금과 International Pension Division

국제연맹 League of Nations : LON

국제연합 United Nations : UN

국제위생의 해
International Year of Sanitation : IYS

국제의료 international medicine

국제인권규약
International Covenant on Human Rights

국제인권단체 Human Rights Watch : HRW

국제인권헌장 International Bill of Human Rights

국제장수센터 International Longevity Center

국제장애분류
International Classification of Impairments Disabilities and Handicaps : ICIDH

국제장애인 10년
United Nations Decade of Disabled Persons

국제장애인의 해
International Year of Disabled Persons : IYDP

국제질병분류
International Classification of Diseases : ICD

국제질병분류 제10판 International Classification of Disease 10th revision : ICD-10

국제질병분류법
International Classification of Diseases : ICD

국제청년의 해 International Year of Youth

국제카리타스 Caritas Internationals

국제평화의해 International Year of Peace

국제표준화기구
International Organization for Standardization : ISO

국제화학의 해
International Year of Chemistry : IYC

국제후생사업단 Japan International Corporation of Welfare Services : JICWELS

국친사상 parent patriot
국한성 focal
국회예산국 Congressional Budget Office : CBO
군대사회사업 military social work
군립병원 county hospital
군발두통 cluster headache
군비축소 disarmament
군인연금 soldiers' pension
군인유족수당
  dependency and indemnity compensation
군중심리 mob psychology
군체형성 colonization
굴곡 flexion
굴곡구축 flexion contracture
굽 높은 구두 extension shoe
궁핍화이론 theory of deterioration
권고 recommendation
권력 authority ; power
권력집단 power group
권리 rights
권리 [자격) entitlement
권리능력 legal capacity
권리부여 empowerment
권리옹호 human rights advocacy
권리장전 Bill of Rights
권위 authority
권위적인 authoritarian
권위적인 관리 authoritarian management
권한부여 empowerment
권한부여모델 empowerment model
궐석재판 default judgment
궤양 ulcer
궤양형성 ulceration
귀 울림 tinnitus
귀가조치 homebound
귀납논리프로그래밍 inductive logic programming
귀납법 inductive method
귀납적 추론 inductive reasoning
귀납추리 inductive reasoning
귀머거리 deafness ; the deaf
귀머거리 노인 the deaf-mute elderly
귀먹음 deafness
귀속 attribution

귀화 naturalization
규모의 경제 economic of scale
규범 norms
규범적 normative
규제약물 controlled substances
규제완화 deregulation
균교대증 superinfection
균교대현상 microbial substitute
균등색공간 uniform color space
균등색도도 uniform chromaticity scale diagram
균일거출 flat rate contribution
균일급여 flat rate benefit
균일제 flat rate scheme
균혈증 bacteremia
그 밖의 위생재료 other sanitary supplies
그레셤의 법칙 Gresham's Law
그레이마켓 입양 gray market adoption
그레이브스병 Graves' disease
그레이팅 grating
그레이팬서 Gray Panthers
그룹다이내믹스 group dynamics
그룹레크리에이션 group recreation
그룹리빙 group living
그룹모델 group model
그룹슈퍼비전 group supervision
그룹운동 group exercise
그룹워커 group worker
그룹워크 group work
그룹워크기록 group work recording
그룹워크의 기술 skill of group work
그룹워크의 분야 field of group work
그룹진료 group practice
그룹카운셀링 group counseling
그룹홈 group home
그리스도교 여자청년회
  Young Women's Christian Association :
  YWCA
그리스도교 청년회
  Young Men's Christian Association : YMCA
그리스트교 사회사업 Christian social work
그린라이닝 greenlining
그물화 enmeshment
극도의 피로 burnout

극렬개인주의 rugged individualism
극복 coming out
극약 drastic medicine
극저출생체중아 very premature infant
극초단파요법 microwave therapy
극형 capital punishment
근 muscle
근 클램프 muscle cramp
근간대성 발작 myoclonic seizure
근경련 muscle cramp
근경련발작 myoclonic seizure
근경축 muscle cramp
근골격계 musculoskeletal system
근골격질환 musculoskeletal disease
근교감신경활동 sympathetic muscle nerve activity
근구축 muscle contracture
근구축증 muscle contracture
근근막성 동통증후군
　myofascial pain syndrome : MPS
근긴장 muscle tonus
근긴장성 이영양증 myotonic dystrophy
근긴장저하 hypotonia ; muscle hypotonia
근긴장증 myotonia
근긴장항진 muscle hypertonia ; hypertonia
근대화 modernization
근대화론 modernization theory
근력 muscle strength
근력강화 muscular strengthening
근력강화훈련 muscle strengthening exercise
근력유지 muscle maintenance
근력유지훈련 exercises for maintaining muscle
근력저하 muscular weakness
근력측정 muscle strength measurement
근로공제 deduction for employment
근로세공제 tax deduction for employment
근로소득세액공제
　earned income tax credit : EITC
근로여성복지 working women's welfare
근로자생활과 Workers' Life Division
근로자생활부 Workers' Life Department
근로청소년복지 working youth welfare
근린 neighborhood
근린정보센터 neighborhood information

근막릴리스 myofascial release
근막염 fasciitis
근막이완요법 myofascial release
근면성대열등감 industry versus inferiority
근비대 muscle hypertrophy
근생검 muscle biopsy
근섬유전도속도 muscle fiber conduction velocity
근섬유유형 muscle fiber type
근염 myositis
근위 proximal
근위단 proximal end
근위축 muscular atrophy
근위축성측색경화증
　amyotrophic lateral sclerosis : ALS
근육 muscle
근육간대경련 myoclonus
근육간대경련발작 myoclonic seizure
근육긴장이상 dystonia
근육긴장저하아 floppy infant
근육내 intramuscular
근육단면적 cross-sectional area of muscle
근육병 myopathy
근육위축증 muscular dystrophy
근육이완법 muscle relaxation technique
근이영양증 muscular dystrophy
근이완제 muscle relaxant
근재교육 muscle reeducation
근적외선 near-infrared
근전도 electromyogram : EMG
근전도검사 electromyography
근전의수 myoelectric upper limb prosthesis
근지구력 muscle endurance
근질근질 다리증후군 restless legs syndrome : RLS
근질환 myopathy
근친상간 incest
근친상간욕망 incestuous desire
근통성 뇌척수염 myalgic encephalomyelitis
근피로 muscle fatigue
글로벌리제이션 globalization
글로벌스탠다드 global standards
글로브쥬스법 glove juice method
글루코사민 glucosamine
글루코스 glucose

글루코스무수물 glucose anhydride
글루코코르티코이드 glucocorticoid
글루코파지 Glucophage
글루타르알데히드 glutaraldehyde
글씨쓰기훈련 writing exercise
긁음 scratching
금공세공 metal craft
금단 withdrawal
금단증상 withdrawal symptoms
금연 abstinence from smoking
금융자산 financial asset
금전가치 value-for-money : VFM
금전관리 money management
금전급여 cash benefit
금전보상기법 token economy
금주 abstinence from alcohol
금지명령 injunction
금티오말산나트륨 gold sodium thiomalate
급성 acute
급성간질성 폐렴 acute interstitial pneumonia
급성경막외혈종 acute epidural hematoma
급성골수성 백혈병
  acute myelocytic leukemia : AML ; acute
  myelogenous leukemia : AML ; acute myeloid
  leukemia
급성관증후군 acute coronary syndrome
급성기 acute phase
급성기 재활치료 acute phase of rehabilitation
급성림프구성 백혈병
  acute lymphoblastic leukemia ; acute
  lymphocytic leukemia ; acute lymphoid
  leukemia : ALL
급성백혈병 acute leukemia
급성세기관지염 acute bronchiolitis
급성소화관출혈 acute gastrointestinal bleed
급성신우신염 acute pyelonephritis
급성심근경색 acute myocardial infarction
급성요통증 strained back
급성요폐증 acute urinary retention
급성위염 acute gastritis
급성전각회백수염 acute anterior poliomyelitis
급성참조용량 acute reference dose
급성출혈후 빈혈 acute posthemorrhagic anemia

급성폐렴 acute pneumonia
급성폐부종 flash pulmonary edema
급성폐상해 acute lung injury
급성폐손상 acute lung injury
급성폐수종
  acute pulmonary edema ; flash pulmonary
  edema
급성호흡곤란증후군
  acute respiratory distress syndrome : ARDS
급성호흡부전
  acute respiratory failure ; acute respiratory
  insufficiency
급성환자치료 acute care
급성회백수염 acute anterior poliomyelitis
급성후두기관염 acute laryngotracheitis
급여 benefits
급여계산 salary calculator
급여공제 payroll deduction
급여관리업무 benefit management services
급여관리표 benefit management form
급여기간 benefit period
급여기준 benefits standards
급여비심사위원회 Benefit Review Committee
급여수준 benefit level
급여우선리스트 benefits priority list
급진적 사회사업 radical social work
긍정적 강화 positive reinforcement
긍정적 내포 positive connotation
긍정적 전이 positive transference
긍정적 차별 positive discrimination
기계세정 mechanical cleaning
기관 trachea
기관개발기금 sunk costs
기관내 마취 endotracheal anesthesia
기관내 이물 intratracheal foreign body
기관내 주입 intratracheal injection
기관위임사무 agency delegated function
기관장위원회 board of directors
기관절개 tracheostomy
기관지내시경 bronchoscopy
기관지드레나지 bronchial drainage
기관지배액 bronchial drainage
기관지염 bronchitis

ㄱ

기관지천식 bronchial asthma
기관지확장제 bronchodilator
기구관련감염 device-related infection
기금 endowment
기금소지 funding-holding
기금조성 funding
기기 equipment
기기관리서비스 equipment management services
기념병원 memorial hospital
기능 function
기능국소화 functional localization
기능분화 functional differentiation
기능사정 functional assessment
기능상실주부 displaced homemaker
기능상태질문표
　Functional Status Questionnaire : FSQ
기능성 체위 functional position
기능손상 functional impairment
기능심리학 functionalism
기능연령 functional age
기능유지 functional maintenance
기능장애 impairment ; dysfunction
기능재건 functional reconstruction
기능적 MRI
　functional magnetic resonance imaging : fMRI
기능적 국재화 functional localization
기능적 문맹 illiterate functional
기능적 예후 functional prognosis
기능적 자립 functional independence
기능적 자립도평가법
　Functional Independence Measure : FIM
기능적 작업요법 functional occupational therapy
기능적 잔기량 functional residual capacity
기능적 장비 functional brace
기능적 전기자극
　functional electrical stimulation : FES
기능적 접근법 functional approach
기능적 정신병 functional mental illness
기능적 지위 functional position
기능적 활동질문표
　Functional Activities Questionnaire : FAQ
기능주의 functionalism
기능주의 개별사회사업 functional casework

기능지역사회 functional community
기능집단 functional group
기능평가 functional assessment
기능평가표 Functional Assessment Inventory :
　FAI
기능회복 functional recovery
기능회복훈련 restorative training
기능훈련 functional training ; functional exercise
기능훈련사 function trainer
기도 airway
기도감염 sinopulmonary infection
기도감염격리 respiratory isolation
기도관리 airway management
기도내압 airway pressure
기도내압 시간곡선 airway pressure-time curve
기도마개 airway closure
기도세정 airway cleaning
기도스텐트 airway stent
기도저항 airway resistance
기도전도도 airway conductance
기도클리닝 airway cleaning
기도폐쇄
　airway closure ; airway obstruction ; airway
　occlusion
기도폐쇄법 supraglottic swallow
기도허탈 airway collapse
기도협착 airway stenosis
기도화상 airway burn
기도확보 airway maintenance
기독교세계봉사회 Church World Service
기독교여성청년회
　Young Women's Christian Association :
　YWCA
기독교청년회
　Young Men's Christian Association : YMCA
기로 abandoning elderly
기록 recording ; records
기록양식 recording style
기립 보행동작측정법 Timed Get-Up and Go Test
기립대 standing table
기립보행검사 Get-up and Go Test
기립성 저혈압 orthostatic hypotension
기립운동

sit-to-stand exercise ; standing exercise
기립침대 tilting table
기립훈련 standing exercise
기명력 memory retention
기명력장애 encoding disturbance
기명장애 memory disturbance
기미 liver spots
기본색채어 basic color term
기본수당 basic allowance
기본장기요양비 basic care fee
기본적 불안 basic anxiety
기본적 생활습관 fundamental habits
기본적 욕구 basic needs
기본적 인권
  fundamental human rights ; basic human rights
기본적 일상생활활동
  basic activities of daily living
기본적 지위 fundamental position
기본조사 basic survey
기부 donation
기부금세공제 tax deduction for charity donations
기부재산 donation
기부행위 donation practice
기분 mood
기분순환성장애 cyclothymic disorder
기분장애 mood disorder
기브스 cast
기소대상면제 decriminalization
기술철학 philosophy of technology
기술혁신 innovation
기아보호소 foundling hospitals
기억 memory
기억상실증 amnesia
기억장애 memory disorder
기억장애검사 Memory Impairment Screen : MIS
기업연금 corporate pension
기업연금국민연금기금과 Corporate Pension and
  National Pension Fund Division
기업자원봉사 corporate volunteer
기업조합 corporate union
기업화 corporatization
기여위험 attributable risk
기여위험비율 attributable risk percent : ARP

기왕경험연수 medical history ; anamnesis
기왕력 medical history
기왕조사 retrospective study
기원가족 family of origin
기이성 요실금 paradoxical incontinence
기저귀 diaper
기저귀 교환 diaper change
기저귀 떼기 diaper removal
기저귀 제거 diaper removal
기저귀 커버 diaper cover
기정양육 child rearing in the family
기제 mechanism
기종 emphysema
기종성 신우신염 emphysematous pyelonephritis
기좌위 sitting position
기좌호흡 orthopnea
기준 및 정도의 원칙
  principle of standards and extent
기준간호 standardized nursing
기준개호
  standardized care ; standardized long-term care
기준심사과 Standards and Evaluation Division
기준전극 reference electrode
기준체중비 ideal body weight : IBW
기증자 donor
기질금속단백질분해효소
  matrix metalloprotease enzyme
기질성 정신질환 organic mental disorder
기질적 장애 organic disturbance
기초공제 basic standard deduction
기초대사 basal metabolism
기초대사량 (기초대사율)
  basal metabolic rate : BMR
기초상환점수 basic reimbursement rate
기초식품 basic food group
기초연금 basic pension
기초연금거출금 contribution for basic pension
기초연금교부금 grant for basic pension
기초연금번호 basic pension number
기초연금제도 basic pension system
기초체온 basal body temperature
기침 cough
기침보조 assisted coughing

기침형천식 cough variant asthma : CVA
기타법과의 급여조정 adjustment with other laws
기탁식품 sustenance food
기포목욕 jacuzzi ; whirlpool spa
기포목욕탕 whirlpool spa
기포욕 bubble bath
기호 signage
기회감염 opportunistic infection
기회비용 opportunity costs
기회의 평등 equality of opportunity
기회이론 opportunity theory
기획 planning
기획프로그램 opportunity programs
긴급부조 emergency assistance : EA
긴급연락처 emergency contact information
긴급조치입원 urgent involuntary hospitalization
긴급통보 emergency call
긴급통보서비스 emergency call services
긴급통보시스템 emergency call system
긴급통보장치 emergency alarm system
긴급피폭의료관리

radiation emergency medical management
긴장 tension
긴장성 경반사 tonic neck reflex
긴장성 방광 bladder hypotonia
긴장저하 hypotonia
긴장항진 hypertonia
긴장형 두통 tension-type headache
길랑바레증후군 Guillain-Barre syndrome : GBS
길버트 법 Gilbert Act
길항근 antagonist
길항작용 antagonism
깃털알레르기 feather allergy
깔때기가슴 pectus excavatum
깔창 insole
깨끗이 닦기 sponge bath
깽 gang
꽃가루 알레르기 hay fever
꿈 분석 dream analysis
끓는 물 boiling water
끼움 filling-in

ㄴ

나 - 전달법 I-message
나딜 Nardil
나라별할당계획 national allocation plan
나르딜 Nardil
나르시시즘 narcissism
나멘다 Namenda
나무기법 tree analysis
나무분석 tree analysis
나병 leprosy
나선상 지주단하지보조기 spiral ankle-foot orthosis
나이아신 Niacin
나이트서비스 night services
나이트시터 night sitter
나이트케어 night care
나이트케어사업 night care project
나이트호스피털 night hospital
나이팅게일 Nightingale Florence
나트륨 sodium
나프로신 Naprosyn
나프록센 naproxen
낙상 fall
낙상사고 fall incident
낙상예방 falls prevention
낙상위험도 fall risk
낙오자 dropout
낙인 labeling
낙인화 stigmatization
낙태 abortion
낙하균측정법 setting plate sampling
난독 alexia
난민 refugee
난민구제 refugee relief program
난민서비스 refugee services

난병대책 policy for incurable diseases
난병인정
  incurable disease certification ; certification of
  incurable disease
난소암 ovarian cancer
난수표 table of random numbers
난시 astigmatism
난청 hearing loss : HL ; deafness
난청고령자 auditorially impaired elderly
난청아 auditorially impaired child
난청유아 auditorially impaired infant
난청유아통원시설
  day services facility for the auditory loss infants
난청자 auditorially impaired
난치병 incurable disease
날마다 every day : QD
날씨 weather
날트렉손 naltrexone
날품팔이 노동자 day laborer ; day labor employee
날품팔이 노동자건강보험
  Day Laborers Health Insurance
남근기 phallic stage
남녀고용기회균등법
  Equal Employment Opportunity Laws
남녀공동참가
  equal participation of women and men
남녀공동참가사회 gender-equal society
납골 · 기타 상제를 위해서 필요한 것
  cineration and any other things necessary for
  funerals
납세자의 반란 taxpayer's revolt ; tax revolt
납중독 lead poisoning
낭독봉사 reading volunteer services

낭독봉사원 reading volunteer
낭창 lupus
낮병원 day hospital
내각 cabinet
내과 internal medicine
내구성 endurance
내구의료기기 durable medical equipment : DME
내담자 client
내당능이상 impaired glucose tolerance : IGT
내독소시험 endotoxin test
내러티브적 접근 narrative approach
내러티브테라피 narrative therapy
내면화 internalization
내반 varus
내반첨족 equinovarus foot
내복약 oral medication
내부상호보조 cross-subsidization
내부장애 internal disorder
내부장애인갱생시설
　rehabilitative facility for people with internal
　disorders
내부환경 internal environment
내분비 endocrine
내분비의사 endocrinologist
내분비질환 endocrine disease
내분비학 endocrinology
내분비학자 endocrinologist
내성 tolerance
내셔널리즘 nationalism
내셔널미니멈 national minimum
내시경 endoscope
내시경검사 endoscopy
내시경수술 endoscopic
내시경적 역행성 담관체관조영
　endoscopic retrograde cholangiopancreatography
내시경적 초음파검사 endoscopic ultrasonography
내시경초음파검사 endosonography
내압대 pressure zone
내용성 tolerance
내용일일섭취량 tolerable daily intake
내원시 심장정지 dead on arrival : DOA
내의 underwear
내이염 labyrinthitis

내인성 endogenous
내인성 감염 endogenous infection
내인성 감염증 endogenous infection
내인성 괄약근부전
　intrinsic sphincter deficiency : SD
내인성 정신병 endogenous psychosis
내적 조합범위 internal frame of reference
내전 adduction
내출혈 bruise
내측단고이음새 시스템
　medial single hip joint system
내측휘프 medial whip
내향발굽 toe in
내향성 introversion
내회전 internal rotation
냉각살균제 cold sterilant
냉동요법 cryotherapy
냉멸균 cold sterilization
냉수공급장치 water cooler
냉습포 cold pack
냉찜질 cold compress
너클벤더 knuckle bender
널싱홈 nursing home
널싱홈 이용자 resident
널싱홈 이용자의 권리 rights of residents
네 개의 식품군
　four food groups ; four basic food groups
네발 기어가기 crawling
네발 기어가기 이동 creeping
네발 지팡이 quad cane ; four-legged cane
네블라이저 nebulizer
네이버후드길드 neighborhood guild
네이티브아메리칸 Native American
네트워크 network
네트워크모델 network model
네트워킹 networking
네프로제증후군 nephritic syndrome
노건국 Health and Welfare Bureau for the Elderly
노년개발 development of the aged
노년기 senium ; old-age
노년기 동성애자 gay elder
노년기 조우울증
　manic depressive psychosis in the elderly

노년병 geriatric disease
노년사회복지학 gerontological social work
노년성 난청 presbycusis
노년우울증스케일
　Geriatric Depression Scale : GDS
노년의학 geriatrics
노년인구 elderly population
노년인구비율 ratio of the elderly population
노년인구지수 old-age dependency ratio
노년인지증 senile dementia
노년자공제 deduction for the aged
노년자세공제 tax deduction for the seniors
노년증후군 geriatric syndrome
노년치매 senile dementia
노년학 gerontology
노년화지수 aging index
노노개호
　elder to elder care ; elderly care provided by
　elderly
노동3법 three act concerning with labor
노동가능인구 eligible population
노동경제학 labor economics
노동계약 employment contract
노동권 right of labor
노동기본권 fundamental rights at work
노동기준감독관 labor standards inspector
노동기준국 Labour Standards Bureau
노동력 labor force
노동력인구 labor force population
노동문제 labor problem
노동보험징수과
　Labour Insurance Contribution Levy Division
노동복지 labor welfare ; labour welfare
노동빈곤자 working poor
노동생산성 labor productivity
노동시간 work hours
노동시장 labor market
노동시장센터업무실
　Labour Market Center Operations Office
노동안전위생법 Industrial Safety and Health Act
노동안전위생청
　Occupational Safety and Health Administration :
　OSHA

노동위생과 Industrial Health Division
노동위원회 labor relation commission
노동유인정책 workfare
노동인구 work force
노동자생산협동조합 worker's collective
노동자재해보험관리과
　Workers' Compensation Administration
　Division
노동자재해보험보상부
　Worker's Compensation Department
노동자피해보상보험보상
　industrial accident compensation
노동장려계획 work incentive program : WIN
노동재해 occupational injury
노동재해보험 workers' compensation insurance
노동쟁의 strike
노동적응능력지표 work ability index
노동정책 labor policy
노동조건 working conditions
노동조정위원회 a labor relations board
노동조합 labor union
노동조합법 the Trade Union Law
노동조합주의 trade unionism
노동환경 work environment
노력협심증 effort angina
노력호흡 effort respiration
노령가산 supplemental payment to the aged
노령기초연금 basic old-age pension
노령보험 old-age insurance
노령복지연금 old-age welfare pension
노령부조 old-age assistance : OAA
노령선
　line of old age (age when a person is
　treated as old)
노령수당 allowances for the aged
노령연금 old-age pension
노령적립구좌 old-age reserve account
노령후생연금 old-age employees' pension
노로바이러스 norovirus
노르바스크 Norvasc
노르트립틸린 nortriptyline
노르프라민 Norpramin
노멀라이제이션 normalization

노무관리 labor management
노사관계 labor relation
노사협의회 labor management committee
노상생활자 homeless
노쇠 marasmus ; senility
노숙자 homeless
노스탤지어 nostalgia
노안 presbyopia
노이로제 neurosis
노인 the old aged
노인4고 four types of pain in elderly
노인가정도우미사업
　home helpers of elderly program
노인간호 geriatric nursing
노인간호센터 nursing center for the aged
노인간호학회 Nursing Academy for the Aged
노인개호
　elderly care ; caring for the elderly ; geriatric
　care
노인개호기관 long-term care agency for the aged
노인개호사업소
　long-term care office for the aged
노인개호서비스
　long-term care services for the aged
노인개호서비스기관
　long-term care services agency for the aged
노인개호서비스사업소
　long-term care services office for the aged
노인개호서비스사업자
　long-term care services provider for the aged
노인개호시설 long-term care facility for the aged
노인개호지원 elderly care management
노인개호지원센터
　care management center for the aged
노인거주복지시설
　residential welfare facilities for the aged
노인거택개호 home-based care for the aged
노인거택개호지원
　home-based care management the aged
노인거택개호지원센터
　home-based care management center for the
　aged
노인거택생활부조

home-based living assistance for the aged
노인건강&복지연구소
　Research Center for Health Check-ups & Welfare
　of the Aged
노인건강진단 health check-ups for the aged
노인건강체조경연대회
　Assembly of Health Gymnastics for the Aged
노인고용 employment of the aged
노인고용율
　employment rates of the aged ; employment
　rates for older people
노인고용촉진
　employment promotion for the aged
노인고용촉진대책
　employment promotion policy for the aged
노인공동생활 group living for the aged
노인공동생활지원
　group living support for the aged
노인공동작업장
　common work place for the aged
노인공포증 gerontophobia
노인교실 classroom for the aged
노인교육 education for the aged
노인권익보호당
　Party Protecting Interests of the Aged
노인능력은행 Talent Bank of the Aged
노인단기입소 short-stay for the aged
노인단기입소시설 short-stay facility for the aged
노인대상 공영주택 public housing for the aged
노인대상 민간서비스 private services for the aged
노인대학
　University of Lifelong Learning for the Aged
노인데이센터 adult day center
노인데이헬스케어 adult day health care
노인동료프로그램 Senior Companion Program
노인무료급식 free rationing to the aged
노인무직세대 aged retiree household
노인문제 the problem of the aged
노인문화제 Cultural Festival for the Aged
노인반점 senile plaque
노인방문개호케어 home health care for the aged
노인범죄 crime by the elderly
노인병 the diseases of the elderly

노인병원 geriatric hospital
노인보건 elderly health
노인보건계획 health plan for the aged
노인보건과
　　Division of the Heath for the Elderly
노인보건법
　　Health and Medical Services Law for the
　　Elderly
노인보건복지 health and welfare for the aged
노인보건복지계획
　　Health and Welfare Plan for the Aged
노인보건복지국
　　Health and Welfare Bureau for the Elderly
노인보건복지권영역
　　welfare administration district and health- welfare
　　of the aged
노인보건복지기관
　　health and welfare agency for the aged
노인보건복지대책위원회
　　Health and Welfare Committee for the Aged
노인보건복지사업
　　health and welfare program for the aged
노인보건복지사업소
　　health and welfare office for the aged
노인보건복지사업자
　　health and welfare provider for the aged
노인보건복지서비스계획
　　health and welfare services plan for the aged ;
　　health and welfare plan for the aged
노인보건복지시설
　　geriatric health and welfare facility
노인보건복지제도
　　health and welfare system for the aged
노인보건복지종합대책
　　health care and welfare services organization
　　for the aged
노인보건사업 health programs for the aged
노인보건서비스
　　health services for the aged ; elderly health
　　services
노인보건서비스계획
　　health services plan for the aged
노인보건시설 geriatric health care facilities

노인보건의료
　　medical and health care for the aged
노인보건의료계획
　　medical and health care plan for the aged
노인보건의료대책
　　policy of health and medical care of the
　　elderly
노인보건의료서비스
　　medical and health care services for the aged
노인보건의료시설
　　health care services facilities for the aged
노인보건의료제도
　　medical and health care system for the aged
노인보건제도 health care systems for the aged
노인보호전문기관
　　specialized institute for the protection of the
　　aged
노인복지 welfare for the aged
노인복지기관 welfare agency for the aged
노인복지법 Welfare Law for the Elderly
노인복지사 welfare worker for the aged
노인복지사업 welfare program for the aged
노인복지사업소 welfare office for the aged
노인복지사업자 welfare provider for the aged
노인복지상담 welfare counseling for the aged
노인복지상담원 welfare adviser for the aged
노인복지서비스 welfare services for the aged
노인복지센터
　　welfare center for the aged ; senior center
노인복지시설
　　geriatric welfare facilities ; welfare facility for
　　the elderly
노인복지시설연합회
　　Joint Association of Elderly Welfare Facilities
　　for the Aged
노인복지시책 welfare policy for the aged
노인복지제도
　　welfare system for the aged ; welfare system
　　for the elderly ; elderly welfare system
노인복지주택 welfare houses for the aged
노인복지지도주사
　　social worker for the elderly ; welfare supervisor
　　for the elderly

노인복지회관 welfare halls for the aged
노인부양 responsible for the age
노인부양공제 deduction for elderly dependents
노인부양기피현상
  support repellent phenomenon observed in elderly
노인부양비 old-age dependency ratio
노인부양세공제
  tax deduction for elderly dependents
노인부조 assistance for the aged
노인빈곤 poverty among the elderly
노인상담원 counselor for the aged
노인생활과학연구소
  Research Institute of Life Science of Elderly
노인성 난청 senile deafness
노인성 반점 senile plaque
노인성 우울증 senile depression
노인성 인지증 senile dementia
노인성 인지증질환센터 Senile Dementia Center
노인성 치매 senile dementia
노인성 폐렴 pneumonia in the elderly
노인수당 allowances for the aged
노인수발보험법안
  Bill for Care Services Insurance for the Elderly
노인수발제공주택
  elder care housing ; aged care home
노인승차권제도 Ticket System for the Elderly
노인아파트 apartments for the aged
노인양로시설 endowment facilities for the aged
노인에 대한 범죄 crimes against the elderly
노인여가 leisure time of the aged
노인여가복지시설
  leisure time welfare facilities for the aged
노인요양공동생활가정 group home for the aged
노인요양복지시설
  care service and welfare facilities for the aged
노인요양시설 care service facilities for the aged
노인요양원
  care service and health service facilities for the aged
노인우울증척도
  Geriatric Depression Scale : GDS
노인원조 support for the aged

노인유휴노동력 elderly idle work force
노인의 날 Aged Day
노인의 전화
  Information and Referral Service for the Aged
노인의 존엄 dignity of the elderly
노인의 종말간호 terminal care
노인의료
  geriatric medical care ; geriatric medicine
노인의료복지시설
  medical and welfare facilities for the aged
노인의료비
  medical care expenditures for the aged ; medical expenses for the aged
노인의료서비스
  medical care services for the aged
노인의료수급대상자
  target population of geriatric medicine
노인의료제도 medical care system for the aged
노인인력활용대책
  elderly personnel utilization policy
노인자살 suicide by the aged
노인자원봉사 elderly volunteers
노인자원봉사단
  group of elderly volunteer services
노인장기요양 long-term care for the aged
노인장기요양급여비용심사명세서
  Written Statement for Long-Term Care Benefit Cost
노인장기요양급여비용심사청구서
  Written Claim for Long-Term Care Benefit Cost
노인장기요양급여비용정산심사결정통지서
  Notice of Determination of Long-Term Care Benefit Cost Calculation
노인장기요양급여비용청구명세서접수증
  Receipt of Written Statement of Claim for Long-Term Care Benefit Cost
노인장기요양보장 long-Term care for the aged
노인장기요양보험
  long-term care insurance for the aged
노인장기요양보험법
  Long-Term Care Insurance Law for the Aged
노인장기요양보험법시행규칙

Enforcement of Long-Term Care and Insurance Act for the Aged

노인장기요양보험법시행령

Order of Enforcement of Long-Term Care and Insurance Act for the Aged

노인장기요양보험제도

Long-Term Care Insurance System for the Aged

노인장기요양보호종합대책

organization for long- term cares for the aged

노인재가개호지원 elderly home care management

노인재가개호지원센터

home care management center for the aged

노인재가복지사업소

in-home welfare office for the aged

노인재가복지시설

in-home welfare facilities for the aged

노인재가생활지원센터

living management center for the aged

노인재혼 elderly remarriage

노인전문병원 geniatric hospital ; elderly hospital

노인전문요양시설

specialized health care service facilities for the aged

노인전용주택 housing for the aged

노인정신보건 geriatric mental health care

노인정신보건대책

policy of geriatric mental health care

노인정신보건제도

geriatric mental health care system

노인종합복지관 general welfare center of elderly

노인종합상담센터

comprehensive counseling center for the aged

노인주간보호 adult day care

노인주간보호서비스센터 adult day services center

노인주간보호센터 adult day care center

노인주간보호시설 day care facilities for the aged

노인주거복지시설

dwelling welfare facilities for the elderly

노인주거연구소

Research Institute of Dwelling of the Elderly

노인주택 congregate housing for the aged

노인준비교육

preparatory education for the elderly

노인진료보수제도 geriatric medical fee system

노인집중치료실 geriatric intensive care unit

노인집합주택 congregate housing for the aged

노인촌 silver city

노인촌락 retirement community

노인케어제공주택

elder care housing ; aged care home

노인클럽 senior citizens club

노인학 gerontology

노인학교 school for the aged

노인학교지도사 school instructor for the aged

노인학급 educational class for the aged

노인학대 elderly abuse ; elder abuse

노인학대상담센터

Counseling Center for Elderly Abuse

노인헌장 charter for the Elderly

노인홈 care home for the aged

노인홈헬프 home help for the aged

노인홈헬프서비스

home help services for the aged

노인휴양소 rest areas for the aged

노인휴양시설 rest facilities for the aged

노인휴양홈

rest home for the aged ; recreational home for the aged

노재보험업무실 Compensation Operation Office

노친부양

responsible for an aging parent ; responsible for aging parents

노화 aging

노후생애설계전문가

experts designing post retirement life

녹내장 glaucoma

녹농균성 폐렴 pseudomonas pneumonia

녹색의료보호수첩 green medical care card

논렘수면

non-rapid eye movement < NREM > sleep

논리정동요법 rational-emotive therapy

논슬립 non-slip

논슬립매트 non-slip mat

논슬립테이프 non-slip tape

논크리티칼 non-critical

놀이치료 play therapy

농 deafness

농고령자 the aged deaf ; the deaf elderly

농노인 the aged deaf ; the deaf elderly

농뇨 pyuria

농아고령자 blind elderly ; the deaf-mute elderly

농아노인 blind elderly ; the deaf-mute elderly

농아아 the deaf-mute child

농아아동 blind child

농아아동시설 facility for the deaf-mute children

농아유아 blind infant ; the deaf-mute child

농아자 blind person ; deaf-mute

농아학교 school for the deaf mute

농자 the deaf

농촌 rural village

농촌과잉인구 rural over population

농촌문제 rural problem

농촌부의 고령자 rural elder

농촌사회 rural society

농축음료 thickened liquid

농학교 school for the deaf

농후 벌꿀상 액체식 ultra-honey-thick diet

농후음료 thickened liquid

뇌간 brain stem

뇌경색 cerebral infarction

뇌동맥경화증 cerebral arteriosclerosis

뇌부종 brain edema

뇌빈혈 cerebral anemia

뇌사 brain death

뇌사판정기준

　diagnostic criteria for clinical diagnosis of brain death

뇌색전 cerebral embolism

뇌성마비 cerebral palsy : CP

뇌신경 cerebral nerve

뇌신경외과집중치료실 neurosurgical care unit

뇌실복강단락술

　ventriculoperitoneal shunting : VP

뇌외상 traumatic brain injury : TBI

뇌장애 brain damage

뇌전도 electroencephalogram : EEG

뇌졸중 apoplexy ; stroke

뇌졸중 기능장애평가법

Stroke Impairment Assessment Set : SIAS

뇌졸중 집중치료실 stroke care unit

뇌종양 brain tumor

뇌좌상 cerebral contusion

뇌출혈 cerebral hemorrhage

뇌파 electroencephalogram : EEG

뇌혈관성 치매 cerebrovascular dementia

뇌혈관장애 cerebrovascular disorder : CVD ; cerebral vascular accident

뇌혈관조영 cerebral angiography

뇌혈전 cerebral thrombosis

뇌혈전증 cerebral thrombosis

누두흉 pectus excavatum

누수시험 water leakage test

누적이환율 cumulative incidence rate

누진세 progressive tax

눈내압 intraocular pressure

눈부신 빛 glare

눈부심 glare

뉴딜 New Deal

뉴딜정책 New Deal Policy

뉴로파치 neuropathy

뉴로피드백 neurofeedback

뉴론틴 Neurontin

뉴욕심장학회 분류

New York Heart Association functional Classification

느낀 욕구 felt needs

느린맥 bradycardia

느린호흡 bradypnea

늑간신경통 intercostal neuralgia

늑근 stirrup

늑목 stall bar

늑연골염 costochondritis

늙음 oldness

능동면역 active immunity

능동수송 active transport

능동투과 active permeation

능동핸드 utility hand

능동훅 작업용 수선구

　split hook and specialized tool

능력 ability ; competence ; power

능력개발과

Human Resources Development Division
능력저하 disability
능력주의 ability principle
능력평가과
Vocational Ability Evaluation Division
니글렉트 neglect
니드 need
니들스틱 needlestick
니들스틱사고 needlestick injury

니들스틱상처 needlestick injury
니즈 needs
니치 niche
니트로글리세린 nitroglycerin : NG
니트족
Not in Education, Employment or Training :
NEET
니패드 knee pad

ㄴ

ㄷ

다가불포화지방산
 polyunsaturated fatty acid : PUFA
다계통위축증 multiple system atrophy : MSA
다관절성 통풍 polyarticular gout
다나카 비네식 지능검사
 Tanaka-Binet Intelligence Test ; Tanaka-Binet
 Scale of Intelligence
다뇨 polyuria
다능 multipotent
다단계평가
 Multilevel Assessment Instrument : MAI
다동 hyperkinesia
다르본 Darvon
다른 의사의 의견 second opinion
다리길이 leg length
다면적 요법 multimodal therapy
다발경색성 치매 multi-infarct dementia : MID
다발뉴로파치 polyneuropathy
다발성 경화증 multiple sclerosis : MS
다발성 뇌경색 multiple cerebral infarction
다변량해석 multivariate analysis
다분화능 multipotent
다시냅스반사 polysynaptic reflex
다양성 diversity
다양성과 포괄성 diversity and inclusion
다운증후군 Down Syndrome
다원화된 사회 pluralistic society
다장기기능부전 multiple organ failure
다장기기능부전증후군
 multiple organ dysfunction syndrome : MODS
다제내성 multi-drug resistance : MDR
다제내성 결핵
 multi-drug resistant tuberculosis : MDR-TB

다제병용 polypharmacy
다제처방 polypharmacy
다중성격 multiple personality
다중인격성 장애 multiple personality disorder
다중채무 multiple debtor
다직종연계 interprofessional work
다직종연계교육 interprofessional education
다직종팀 interdisciplinary team : IDT
다진고기식 minced meal
다차원빈곤지수
 multidimensional poverty index : MPI
다차원적 기능평가
 multidimensional functional assessment
단가계약 unit price contract
단계이론 stage theories
단계적 보험료 step-up contribution
단골담당의사 primary care physician : PCP
단골의 primary care physician : PCP
단골의사
 primary doctor ; primary care physician : PCP ;
 family doctor
단기기억 short-term memory
단기목표 short-term goal
단기보호 short-stay
단기보호사업 short-stay project
단기보호사업소 short-stay office
단기보호서비스 short-stay services
단기보호시설 short-stay care facilities
단기입소요양개호 short-stay health care
단기입소케어 short-stay care
단기자원봉사 short-term volunteer
단기치료 brief therapy
단기케어시설 short-term care facility

단단 amputation stump
단단관리 stump care
단단단 short stump
단단대 stump sock
단단부하소켓 end-bearing socket
단단신경통 stump pain
단단통 stump pain
단당류 monosaccharide
단당무수물 monosaccharide anhydride
단대립보조기 short opponens hand orthosis
단독개업 solo practice
단독개업의사 solo practitioner
단독공포증 autophobia
단마비 monoplegia
단백뇨 albuminuria
단백질 protein
단백질에너지 protein energy
단백질에너지결핍증
　protein-energy malnutrition : PEM
단색광 monochromatic light
단속적 휴가 intermittent leave
단시간 · 재가노동과
　Part-Time Work and Home Work Division
단시냅스반사 monosynaptic reflex
단어찾기의 어려움
　word finding difficulty ; word finding disorder
단어찾기장애
　word finding difficulty ; word finding disorder
단일포톤방출단층촬영
　single photon emission computed tomography
　: SPECT
단좌위 sitting position
단차 threshold
단차해소 elimination of thresholds
단차해소기 lifting platform
단체교섭 collective bargaining
단체보험 group life insurance
단체협상 collective bargaining
단체협약 labor collective agreement
단추구멍변형 boutonniere deformity
단축이음새 single axis joint
단층촬영 tomography
단카이세대

baby boom generation ; baby boomer
단하지보조기
　ankle-foot orthosis : AFO ; short leg brace :
　SLB
달력나이 chronological age
담석 gallstone
담화치료 narrative therapy
당뇨병 diabetes mellitus : DM
당뇨병성 고혈당성 고삼투압성 혼수
　hyperglycemic hyperosmolar nonketotic coma :
　HHNKC
당뇨병성 망막증 diabetic retinopathy
당뇨병성 신경증 diabetic neuropathy
당뇨병성 신부전 diabetic nephropathy
당뇨병성 케톤산증 diabetic ketoacidosis : DKA
당뇨병성 혼수 diabetic coma
당뇨병식품교환표
　diabetes food exchange list ; food exchange
　list for diabetes
당뇨병약 diabetes medication
당분 sugar
당사자활동 self-help activity
당월부과 monthly charge
당일치기 개호
　ambulatory care ; outpatient care ; commuting
　for care
당일치기 재활
　ambulatory rehabilitation ; outpatient
　rehabilitation ; commuting for rehabilitation
당질 saccharide
당질코르티코이드 glucocorticoid
대광반사 light reflex
대기기간 waiting period
대기오염 air pollution
대기자 applicants on the waiting list
대기자 리스트 waiting list
대기적 심장카테터검사
　elective cardiac catheterization
대뇌동맥륜 circle of Willis
대도시권 metropolitan area
대독 reading assistance
대동맥변협착증 aortic stenosis
대동작기능 gross motor function

대둔근 gluteus maximus muscle
대리 substitution
대리결정 surrogate decision
대리보호 substitute care
대리수령 legal reception services
대리인 attorney-in-fact
대리전화 telephone assistance
대리출산 surrogacy ; surrogate delivery
대리판단 substituted judgment
대립 confrontation
대립바 opponens bar
대립보조기 opponens splint
대마 marijuana
대마비 paraplegia
대면집단 encounter group
대발생 outbreak
대변검사
  fecal examination ; feces examination ; stool
  specimen
대변자 advocate
대변잠혈검사 fecal occult blood test : FOBT
대부금제도 emplo1yee credit system
대부전마비 paraparesis
대비감도 contrast sensitivity
대사 metabolism
대사당량 metabolic equivalent of task : MET
대사성 질환 metabolic disease
대사이상 metabolic disorder
대사저해제 metabolic inhibitor
대사제 dormitory system
대상 compensation
대상관계이론 object relations theory
대상운동 compensatory movement
대상자 subject
대상포진 herpes zoster ; shingles
대상포진후 신경통 post-herpetic neuralgia : PHN
대상한정감시 targeted surveillance
대악 Five Giants
대역 substitute
대용 substitute
대우울증 major depression
대인관계 interpersonal relationship
대인관계스킬 interpersonal relationship skill

대인사회서비스 personal social services
대인원조기술 interpersonal helping skill
대인적 사회서비스 personal social services
대인케어서비스 personal care services
대장암 colon cancer
대장암검진 colorectal cancer screening
대장암집단검진
  group examination for the large bowel cancer
대장폴립
  colorectal polyps ; large intestine polyps
대적혈구성 빈혈증 macrocytic anemia
대전자 greater trochanter
대전자동통증후군
  greater trochanteric pain syndrome
대전자부 골절 greater trochanter fracture
대조군연구 case control study
대중매체 mass media
대중목욕탕 public bath house
대중사회 mass society
대중여가 mass leisure
대중탕 public bath house
대증요법 symptomatic therapy
대처 coping
대처전략 coping strategy
대처행동 coping behavior
대체기능 substitute function
대체요법 alternative medicine
대체의학
  alternative medicine ; complementary medicine
대체조제 substitute medication
대출혈 hemorrhaging
대퇴골 경부골절 femoral neck fracture
대퇴골 전자부골절 subtrochanteric fracture
대퇴사두근 quadriceps femoris
대퇴소켓 transfemoral socket
대퇴의족
  above-knee prosthesis ; transfemoral prosthesis
대퇴전자간골절 intertrochanteric fracture
대퇴절단 above-knee amputation
대퇴통 지각이상 meralgia paresthetica
대포냐 버터냐 guns or butter
대필 allograph
대한간학회

The Korean Association for the Study of the Liver
대한간호복지재단
Korean Nurses Welfare Foundation
대한간호협회 Korean Nurses Association
대한고관절학회 The Korean Hip Society
대한구강보건학회
Korean Academy of Oral Health
대한노인과학발명협회
Korean Institute of Science and Inventions for the Elderly
대한노인내과학회
Korean Society of Internal Medicines for the Elderly
대한노인물리치료학회
Korean Physical Therapy Academy for the Elderly
대한노인병원협의회
Korean Council of Hospitals for the Elderly
대한노인병학회 The Korean Geriatrics Society
대한노인복지신문
Korean Elderly Welfare Newspaper
대한노인요양병원협회
Korean Association of Geriatric Hospitals
대한노인의학회
The Korean Geriatric Medical Association
대한노인재활의학회
Korean Academy of Geriatric Rehabilitation Medicine
대한노인정신의학회
Korean Association for Geriatric Psychiatry
대한노인회
The Korea Senior Citizens Association
대한노화방지의학회
Korean Anti-Aging Medical Society
대한뇌졸중학회 Korean Stroke Society
대한당뇨병학회 Korean Diabetes Association
대한물리치료학회
The Korean Society of Physical Therapy
대한변호사협회 Korean Bar Association
대한실버산업협회
Korean Association of Senior Industry
대한요양보호사협회

Korean Institute for Medical Cares
대한은퇴자협회
An Independent NGO in the Public Service
대한임상노인의학회
The Korean Academy of Clinical Geriatrics
대한재활의학회
Korean Academy of Rehabilitation Medicine
대한전인케어복지협회
Korean Care and Welfare Association
대한정신약물학회
Korean College of Neuropsychopharmacology
대한치매학회 Korean Dementia Association
대한케어복지학회 Korean Care Welfare Academy
대행자 agent
댐퍼 damper
더글라스와천자 culdocentesis
더러운 상처 dirty wound
더메스틱 바이오런스 domestic violence : DV
더블바인드가설 double-bind theory
더블백 손기술 double bag technique
덤벨 dumbbell
덤핑증후군 dumping syndrome
데니슨 Edward Denison
데메롤 Demerol
데모그란트 demogrant
데시벨 decibel : dB
데시프라민 desipramine
데이 · 나이트서비스 day/night care
데이서비스 day services
데이서비스센터 day services center
데이케어 day care
데이케어센터 day care center
데이터베이스 database
데이호스피탈 day hospital
데이홈 day home
데프레닐 Deprenyl
덱스트로메토르판 dextromethorphan
덴버발달선별검사
Denver Developmental Screening Test : DDST
덴탈프로스 dental floss
도구 equipment
도구의 강박적 사용
compulsive manipulation of tools

도너 donor

도너츠현상 doughnut phenomenon

도네페질 donepezil

도덕적 해이 moral hazard

도랄 Doral

도박 gambling

도수근력검사 manual muscle testing : MMT

도수요법 manual therapy

도시계획 urban planning

도시문제 urban problem

도시생활 urbanism

도시화 urbanization

도시화 사회 urbanizing society

도어 door

도예 clay work

도제 apprenticing

도제제도
apprentice system ; apprenticeship system

도착즉시사망 dead on arrival : DOA

도착직후사망 dead on arrival : DOA

도치 inversion

도파민 dopamine

도파민 수용체 차단 dopamine receptor blockade

독거 solitary-living

독거고령자 solitary-living elderly

독거노인 solitary-living elderly

독거장애인 solitary-living disabled person

독립변수 independent variable

독립행정법인
independent administrative institution

독서안경 reading glasses

독서장애 print disabled

독서치료 bibliotherapy

독순술 lip-reading ; speech-reading

독신생활고령자 solitary-living elderly

독신생활노인 solitary-living elderly

독촉장 collection letter

독화 lip-reading ; speech-reading

돌보는 사람의 권리 rights of caregivers

돌봄 assistance ; assistant ; support

돌봄훈련 assistive exercise

돌아눕기 roll over

돌연사 sudden death

동거 cohabitation

동결어깨 frozen shoulder

동경노인종합연구소 활동능력지표
Tokyo Metropolitan Institute of Gerontology
index of competence : TMIG-IC

동계 palpitation

동공대광반사 pupillary light reflex

동기 motivation

동기부여 motivation

동기부여된 욕구 motivated needs

동기화 motivation

동료관계 peer relationship

동료집단 peer group

동맥 artery

동맥 재구축 arterial remodeling

동맥·호기종말 이산화탄소분압교차
arterial to end- tidal carbon dioxide tension
difference

동맥·혼합정맥 산소교차
arterial-mixed venous oxygen content difference

동맥경련 arteriospasm

동맥경직도 arterial compliance

동맥경화 arteriosclerosis

동맥경화성 심질환
arteriosclerotic heart disease : ASHD

동맥경화성 피질하백질뇌증
subcortical arteriosclerotic encephalopathy

동맥내 intraarterial

동맥내 디지털감산혈관조영술
intraarterial digital subtraction angiography

동맥내막염 endarteritis

동맥도관 arterial conduit

동맥류 aneurysm

동맥류 봉축술 aneurysmorrhaphy

동맥류 절제 aneurysmectomy

동맥박동 arterial pulse

동맥변 arterial valve

동맥색전 arterial embolism

동맥수 arterial tree

동맥수축기잡음 arterial systolic murmur

동맥신생 arteriogenesis

동맥신장성 arterial distensibility

동맥안압측정 arterial tonometry

동맥압 arterial blood pressure
동맥연속잡음 arterial continuous murmur
동맥연축 arteriospasm
동맥잡음 arterial bruit
동맥저항 arterial resistance
동맥조영 arteriography
동맥질환 arterial disease
동맥천자 arterial puncture
동맥폐쇄질환 arterial occlusive disease : AOD
동맥혈 arterial blood
동맥혈가스 arterial blood gas
동맥혈가스분석 arterial blood gas analysis
동맥혈산소분압 arterial oxygen tension
동맥혈산소포화도 arterial oxygen saturation
동맥혈이산화탄소분압
  arterial carbon dioxide tension
동맥혈채취 arterial blood sampling
동맥혈탄산가스분압
  arterial partial pressure of carbon dioxide :
  PaCO2
동맥혈포화도저하 arterial desaturation
동맥형성술 coronary angioplasty
동면 hibernation
동면심근 hibernating myocardium
동물개재요법 animal assisted therapy : AAT
동물개재활동 animal assisted activity : AAA
동물성 식품 animal food product
동물요법 animal therapy
동물원성 감염증 zoonose
동반자 companion
동성애 homosexuality
동시대비효과 simultaneous contrast effect
동시발생 synchronicity
동시성검토 concurrent review
동시입각기 double stance phase
동심형 침전극 concentric needle EMG
동양철학 eastern philosophies
동요 nursery rhymes
동요관절 frail joint
동요성 고혈압증 labile hypertension
동위색 metamer
동의 informed consent
동의능력평가도구

MacArthur Competence Assessment Tool for
  Treatment : MacCAT-T
동의서 agreement
동의입원 hospitalization with consent
동일성 위기 identity crisis
동일시 identification
동일화 identification
동작 movement
동작보행 point gait
동작분석 motion analysis
동작의 자유도 degree of freedom of motion
동적 안정성 dynamic stability
동적 컴퓨터단층촬영
  dynamic computed tomography
동정 sympathy
동조 conformity
동종요법 homeopathic remedies
동통 pain
동통 매니지먼트 pain management
동통관리 pain control ; pain management
동통성 장애 pain disorder
동통성 주관절증후군 tennis elbow
동통제 pain medication
동통회피성 보행 antalgic gait
동화 assimilation
동화교육 antidiscrimination education
동화작용 anabolism
두문불출 housebound ; social withdrawal
두문불출고령자 housebound elderly
두문불출노인 housebound elderly
두문불출병후군
  housebound syndrome ; withdrawal syndrome
두발지지 double support
두발지지기 double support period
두부외상
  traumatic brain injury : TBI ; head trauma
두타스테리드 dutasteride
두통 headache
둘러쌓기운동 enclosure movement
둘록세틴 duloxetine
뒷꿈치돋음 보행 vaulting
뒷방향연구 retrospective study
듀낭 Jean Henri Dunant

듀센느형 근이영양증
Duchenne muscular dystrophy
듀이 Dewey John
듀피트렌구축 Dupuytren's contracture
드라마테라피 drama therapy
드라이마우스 dry mouth
드라이브스루 출산 drive-through delivery
드라이샴푸 dry shampoo
드라이크리닝 dry cleaning
드레싱 dressing
드레싱스킬 dressing skill
드레이프 drape
드레인 drain
드롭아웃 dropout
들어올리기 elevation ; lifter
등간측정 interval measurement
등교거부 school absenteeism
등교거부아 pupil rejecting school attendance
등록 enrollment ; registration
등록간호사 registered nurse : RN
등록번호 registration number
등록자 enrollee
등록제약 enrollment restriction
등면적도 isoarea map
등받이 backrest
등색함수 color matching function
등속성 수축 isokinetic contraction
등속성 운동 isokinetic exercise
등용 isovolumetric ; isovolumic
등용성 수축
isovolumetric contraction ; isovolumic
contraction
등용성 수축시간
isovolumetric contraction time : ICT ;
isovolumic contraction time
등용수축

isovolumetric contraction ; isovolumic
contraction
등용수축시간
isovolumetric contraction time : ICT ;
isovolumic contraction time
등용이완
isovolumetric relaxation ; isovolumic
relaxation
등용이완시간
isovolumetric relaxation time : IRT ;
isovolumic relaxation time : IRT
등자 stirrup
등장성 수축 isotonic contraction
등장성 운동 isotonic exercise
등척성 수축 isometric contraction
등척성 운동 isometric exercise
디곡신 digoxin
디맨즈 demands
디바인 Edward T. Devine
디설피람 disulfiram
디스토니아 dystonia
디스포저블 disposable
디아제팜 diazepam
디아테르미 diathermy
디에틸스틸베스트롤 diethylstilbestrol : DES
디지털혈관조영 digital subtraction angiography
디프테리아 diphtheria
디플레이션〔통화수축〕 deflation
딜레마 dilemma
딜티아젬 diltiazem
딸꾹질 hiccups
땀띠 heat rash
또래집단 peer group
뛰기보행 swing-to gait
뜸사 moxibustion therapist
뜸요법 moxibustion

라멜테온 ramelteon
라모트리진 lamotrigine
라미부딘 lamivudine
라믹탈 Lamictal
라베타롤 labetalol
라벨 label
라벨링 labeling
라스파이레스 Étienne Laspeyres
라식스 Lasix
라우애하우스 rauhaus
라이브리엄 Librium
라이터증후군 Reiter's syndrome
라이트하우스 light house
라이프리뷰 life review ; reminiscence
라이프사이클 life cycle
라이프스타일 lifestyle
라이프스테이지 life stage
라이프이벤트 life event
라이프코스 life course
라자다인 Razadyne
라크나경색 lacunar stroke
라틴아메리카계고령자 Latino elder
라틴아메리카계인 Hispanics
라포 rapport
라포르 rapport
랄록시펜 raloxifene
래디니스 readiness
래디컬소시오워크 radical social work
러빙법 rubbing method
러셀세이지재단 Russell Sage Foundation
런닝코스트 running cost
레그레스트 leg rest
레그서포트 leg-support

레미닐 Reminyl
레미케이드 Remicade
레보도파 levodopa
레비아 Revia
레스리스버가 Frits Jules Roethlisberger
레스트홈 rest home
레스파이트케어 respite care
레스파이트케어서비스 respite care services
레이 복합도형검사 Rey figure copy
레이븐의 색채매트릭스검사
　Raven's colored progressive matrices
레이오프 lay-off
레이저도플러혈류측정기 laser doppler flowmetry
레이저수술 laser surgery
레이저치료 laser therapy
레저프로그램 leisure program
레즈비언 lesbian
레즈비언고령자 lesbian elder
레지덴셜소시얼워크 residential social work
레지덴셜케어워크 residential care work
레크리에이션 recreation
레크리에이션 프로그램 recreation program
레크리에이션활동 recreational activity
레플루노마이드 leflunomide
렉추어포럼 lecture forum
렐팍스 Relpax
렘수면 rapid eye movement < REM > sleep
로고테라피 logotherapy
로라제팜 lorazepam
로렌쯔곡선 Lorenz Curve
로르샤흐검사 Rorschach Test
로르샤흐잉크반점검사 Rorschach Inkblot Test
로박신 Robaxin

로살탄 losartan
로샤검사 Rorschach Test
로샤검사잉크반점검사 Rorschach Inkblot Test
로오샤크테스트 Rorschach Test
로저스 Carl Ransom Rogers
로제렘 Rozerem
로커모티브신드롬 locomotive syndrome
로크 John Locke
로페라미드 loperamide
로프레소 Lopressor
로프스트랜드 목발 Lofstrand crutch
로피니롤 ropinirole
론드 이그재큐티브 loaned executive
롤플레이 role play
롤플레잉 role playing
뢴트겐 roentgen
루게릭병 Lou Gehrig's disease
루복스 Luvox
루소 Jean-Jacques Rousseau
루이소체치매 Lewy body dementia
루즈벨트 F. D. Roosevelt
루테인 lutein
루프스 lupus
류마티스성 다발근통증 polymyalgia rheumatica
류머티즘 rheumatic disorder
류머티즘전문의 rheumatologist
류머티즘학 rheumatology
르프레이 Pierre Guillaume Frédéric Le Play
리더쉽 leadership
리도카인 lidocaine
리루텍 Rilutek
리리카 Lyrica
리멘뷰겔법 Riemenbugel method
리바미드 행동기억검사
  Rivermead Behavioural Memory Test : RBMT
리바스티그민 rivastigmine
리버스모기지 reverse mortgage
리버스모기지 프로그램 reverse mortgage program
리브락스 Librax
리브리엄 Librium
리비도 libido
리빙윌 living will

리빙케어 leaving care
리세드로네이트 risedronate
리소솜병 Lysosomal diseases
리소좀 Lysosomal storage disease
리소좀병 Lysosomal storage disease
리소좀축적병 Lysosomal storage diseases
리스크 risk
리스크 공유플랜 risk-sharing plan
리스크관리 risk control
리스크매니지먼트 risk management
리스키시프트 risky shift
리스페달 Risperdal
리스페리돈 risperidone
리스폰스코스트 response cost
리얼리티오리엔테이션 reality orientation
리오가나이제이션 reorganization
리자트립탄 rizatriptan
리쳐 reacher
리치먼드로 돌아가라 back to Richmond
리치아웃 reach out
리카도 David Ricardo
리캡 recap
리코펜 lycopene
리큅 Requip
리클라이닝형 휠체어 reclining wheelchair
리터러시 프로그램 literacy program
리튬 lithium
리팜핀 rifampin
리포단백질 lipoprotein
리포단백질수용체관련단백
  lipoprotein receptor-related protein : LRP
리프레이밍 reframing
리프트 lift
리프트버스 lift bus
리허빌리테이션 rehabilitation
린비트롤 Limbitrol
린스 rinse
릴랙세이션 relaxation
릴루졸 riluzole
링겔 Intravenous
링겔치료 intravenous therapy
링크널스 link nurse

ㅁ

마그네슘 magnesium
마데룽변형 Madelung deformity
마라스무스 marasmus
마르크스 Karl Marx
마르크스주의 Marxism
마른 걸레질 dry wiping
마모 abrasion
마법의 손 magic hand
마비 paralysis ; paresis ; palsy
마비측 paralytic side
마스타베이션 masturbation
마슬로우 A. H. Maslow
마약 narcotic ; narcotics
마약중독 narcotic addiction
마약중독유아 narcotic addicted infant
마약중독자 narcotic addicted
마음껏 먹기 뷔페 all-you-can-eat buffet
마음의 상처 trauma
마음의 케어 mental health care
마이너리티 minority
마이너리티그룹 minority group
마이오클로누스간질 myoclonus epilepsy
마이크로벌룬 micro balloon
마지막 기부 ultimate gift
마찰실업 frictional unemployment
마찰잠금 이음새 friction lock joint
마찰접종법 rubbing method
마취 anesthesia
마취제 anesthetic ; narcotics
마켓바스켓방식 market basket method
마켓테스팅 market testing
마크로레벨 macro level
마틴그류버접합 Martin-Gruber anastomosis

마플란 Marplan
막여과기 membrane filter
막연한 불안 free-floating anxiety
만능팔 지지기 mobile arm support
만모그라피 mammography
만성 chronic
만성골수성 백혈병 chronic myelocytic leukemia
만성관절류머티즘 rheumatoid arthritis : RA
만성기 chronic stage
만성기관지염 chronic bronchitis
만성긴장형 두통 chronic tension-type headache
만성동통 chronic pain
만성림프액성 백혈병
  chronic lymphoid leukemia : CLL
만성병 chronic illness
만성비소중독 chronic arsenic poisoning
만성신부전 chronic renal failure
만성신우신염 chronic pyelonephritis
만성신장병 chronic kidney disease
만성염증성 탈수성 다발뉴로파치
  chronic inflammatory demyelinating
  polyneuropathy
만성염증성 탈수성 다발신경염
  chronic inflammatory demyelinating
  polyneuropathy
만성염증성 탈수초성 다발신경병증
  chronic inflammatory demyelinating
  polyneuropathy
만성적 실업 chronic unemployment
만성질환 chronic disease
만성질환요법기능평가
  Functional Assessment of Chronic Illness
  Therapy : FACIT

만성폐쇄성 기도질환
　chronic obstructive airway disease

만성폐쇄성 폐질환
　chronic obstructive pulmonary disease : COPD

만성피로증후군　chronic fatigue syndrome

만족　satisfaction

만족도　satisfying

만족도측정　satisfaction measurement

만취　drunkenness

만혼화　late marriage

말 실행증　apraxia of speech

말걸기　verbal encouragement ; encouragement

말기신부전　end-stage renal disease : ESRD

말기치료　terminal care

말기환자보호치료　hospice care

말단부　distal end

말단비대증　acromegaly

말더듬이　stammer

말붙이기
　verbal encouragement ; encouragement

말초　distal

말초동맥질환　peripheral arterial disease : PAD

말초부종　peripheral edema

말초성 안면신경마비　peripheral facial nerve palsy

말초순환장애　peripheral vascular disease

말초신경　peripheral nerve

말초신경마비　peripheral nerve palsy

말초신경병증　polyneuropathy

말초신경장애　peripheral neuropathy

말초전정기능부전
　peripheral vestibular dysfunction

말초정맥영양법
　peripheral parenteral nutrition : PPN

맛사지　massage

맛사지요법　massage therapy

망막　retina

망막감도　retinal sensitivity

망상　delusion

망상성 장애　delusional disorder

망치수지　mallet finger

맞벌이가족　dual career family

맞벌이부부 아동　latchkey child

매 맞는 배우자　battered spouse

매 맞는 아동　battered child

매년관리지출액
　annually managed expenditure : AME

매니아　mania

매니지드케어　managed care

매니지드케어프랜　managed care plan

매니지드콘페티션　managed competition

매니지드헬스케어　managed health care

매니지먼트시스템　management system

매독　syphilis

매리어트 노인자원봉사조사
　Marriott Seniors Volunteerism Study

매스미디어　mass media

매스커뮤니케이션　mass communication

매스컴　mass communication

매슬로의 욕구5단계설
　Maslow's hierarchy of needs

매슬로의 욕구단계　Maslow's hierarchy of needs

매월　monthly : 1M

매음　prostitution

매일　every day : QD

매일아침　every morning : QAM

매일취침시간전　every night : QHS

매장　burial ; cremation

매직핸드　magic hand

매체　media

매춘　prostitution

매춘방지법　Prostitution Prevention Law

매칭기프트제도　matching gift

매트　mat

매트동작　mat activity

매트리스　mattress

매트리스패드　mattress pad

매트운동　mat exercise

매핑기법　mapping technique

매혈자　blood seller

맥길 통증질문지　McGill Pain Questionnaire : MPQ

맥박　pulse

맥살트　Maxalt

맥아더치료 동의능력평가도구
　MacArthur Competence Assessment Tool for Treatment : MacCAT-T

맨손요법 manual therapy
맬더스 Thomas Robert Malthus
맬더스주의 Malthusianism
맹 blindness
맹농아 deaf-blind child
맹농아아 deaf-blind and mute child
맹농아아시설 facility for deaf-blind children
맹농아유아 deaf-blind and mute infant
맹농아인 deaf-blind and mute
맹농유아 deaf-blind infant
맹농인 deaf-blind person
맹도견 guide dog ; seeing eye dog
맹아시설 blind child institution
맹인 blind person
맹인 가이드헬퍼 guide helper for the blind
맹인 가이드헬프 guidance for the blind
맹인교육 education for the blind
맹인시설 facility for the blind
맹인양로원
　long-term care home for the elderly blind
맹인학교 school for the blind
맹인홈 home for the blind
맹자시설 facility for the blind persons
맹증 blindness
맹학교 school for the blind
머더링 mothering
머리감기 shampooing
머리정돈 styling and setting hair
머리카락 hair
먹물법 India ink method
먼셀표색계 Munsell color system
메가트렌드 megatrend
메꿈 filling-in
메노포즈 menopause
메뉴 menu
메니에르병 Meniere's disease
메니에르신드롬 Meniere's disease
메디신볼 medicine ball
메디컬레터 medical letter
메디컬소시얼워크 medical social work
메디케어 Medicare
메디케이드 Medicaid
메로신결핍 선천성 근이영양증

merosin-deficient congenital muscular
　dystrophy
메리디아 Meridia
메리트재 merit goods
메만틴 memantine
메스메리즘 mesmerize
메인스트리밍 mainstreaming
메인트넌스 maintenance
메조레벨 mezzo level
메츠 metabolic equivalent of task : MET
메타메시지 metamessage
메타보릭크증후군 metabolic syndrome
메타인지 metacognition
메타포 metaphor
메탁살론 metaxalone
메토카르바몰 methocarbamol
메토트렉세이트 methotrexate
메토프롤롤 metoprolol
메톨라존 metolazone
메트레이 Mettray
메트포르민 metformin
메트포민 metformin
메티실린 내성 황색포도구균
　methicillin-resistant staphylococcus aureus :
　MRSA
메틸프레드니솔론 methylprednisolone
멜라닌세포 melanocyte
멜라토닌 melatonin
멜레나 melena
멤브레인 필터 membrane filter
면도생검 shave biopsy
면봉 cotton swab
면봉법 swab method
면봉채취 swab collection
면세조치 tax exemption
면역 immunity
면역결핍 immunosuppressed
면역결핍자 immunocompromised host
면역결핍증 immunodeficiency
면역결핍환자 immunocompromised patient
면역글로블린 immunoglobulin : Ig
면역글로블린 A immunoglobulin A : IgA
면역글로블린 E immunoglobulin E : IgE

면역글로블린 G immunoglobulin G : IgG
면역글로블린 M immunoglobulin M : IgM
면역부전 immunosuppressed
면역부전증 immunodeficiency
면역부전환자 compromised patient
면역시스템 immune system
면역신티그라피 immunoscintigraphy
면역억제 immunosuppressed
면역요법 immunotherapy
면역저하숙주 immunocompromised host
면역저하환자 immunocompromised patient
면역저항성 감약숙주 immunocompromised host
면역저항성 감약환자 immunocompromised patient
면역학적 변잠혈검사
   immunologic fecal occult blood test
면역화학적 변잠혈검사
   immunoassay fecal occult blood test
면접 interview
면접교섭권 visitation rights
면접조사 interview survey
면제 waiver
면책정률부담 co-payment
면책정액부담 deductible
멸균 sterilization
멸균공정 sterilization process
멸균기 sterilizer
멸균바리데이션 sterilization validation
멸균보증 sterility assurance
멸균보증수준 sterility assurance level : SAL
멸균수 sterilized water
멸균제 sterilant
멸종현상 extinction
명도 lightness
명목임금 nominal wage
명순응 light adaptation
명암순응 light/dark adaptation
명예 reputation
명예직 honorary position
명예훼손 defamation
명정 drunkenness
명확화 clarification
모노아민 산화효소저해약
   monoamine oxidase inhibitor

모니터 monitor
모니터링 monitoring
모니터측정 monitoring measurement
모답츠법 MODAPTS
모델링 modeling
모듈 module
모듈러 의지 modular prosthesis
모듈러 휠체어 modular wheelchair system
모듈식 좌위보지장치 modular seating system
모래놀이치료 sand play technique
모래주머니 sand bag
모럴 morale
모럴헤저드 moral hazard
모르피네 morphine
모르피네 의존 morphine dependence
모리타요법 Morita therapy
모방 imitation
모방약품 copycat medication
모비라이제이션 mobilization
모성 maternity ; motherhood
모성보호 maternity protection
모성적 양육 mothering
모스수술 Mohs surgery
모자가정 fatherless family ; single parent home
모자가족 mother-headed family
모자간염 mother-to-child transmission
모자건강수첩
   maternal and child health handbook
모자과부복지
   welfare for fatherless families and widows
모자과부복지대부금
   welfare loan for fatherless families and widows
모자과부복지센터
   welfare center for fatherless families and widows
모자과부복지시설 welfare facility for fatherless
   families and widows ; welfare facilities for
   fatherless families
모자문제 maternal and child problem
모자보건 maternal and child health care
모자보건과 Maternal and Child Health Division
모자복지 social services for fatherless families
모자복지연금 maternal and child pension
모자상담원 advisor for fatherless families

모자세대
single-mother household ; fatherless
household
모자수첩 maternal and child health handbook
모자연금 maternal and child pension
모자원 maternity homes
모자주택 housing for mothers and children
모자지도원 fatherless families advisor
모터포인트블록 motor point block
모험이행 risky shift
목공 woodworking
목발 crutch ; axillary crutch
목발보행 crutch gait
목욕 bathing
목욕동작 bathing activity
목욕보조 bathing assistance
목욕서비스 bathing services
목욕용 가운 bathrobe
목욕용구 bathing equipment
목욕탕 발판 draining board
목적세 earmarked taxes
목표 goal
목표설정 goal-setting
몬테소리 Maria Montessory
몰드형 좌위보지장치 molded seating system
몽고리즘 mongolism
묘지 cemetery
무감각증 anesthesia
무갹출제 noncontributory scheme
무거출급여 non-contributory benefit
무거출급여제 non-contributory benefit system
무거출연금 non-contributory pension
무거출퇴직연금
non-contributory retirement pension
무계급사회 classless society
무관심 apathy ; adiaphoria
무규범 (아노미) anomie
무균 asepsis
무균보증 sterility assurance
무균성 보증레벨 sterility assurance level : SAL
무균시험 sterility test
무균적 간헐도뇨법
aseptic intermittent catheterization : AIC

무균적 차폐 aseptic barrier
무균적 피복 aseptic barrier
무균조작 aseptic procedure
무기력 enervation
무기질 mineral
무기폐 pulmonary atelectasis
무뇨증 anuria
무능력 disability
무단결근 absenteeism
무단결석 truancy
무당파층 non-partisan voter
무료 free of charge
무료급식소 soup kitchen
무료노인양로시설
free endowment facilities for the aged
무료노인요양시설
free health care service facilities for the aged
무료노인전문요양시설 free specialized health care
service facilities for the aged
무료양로시설 free endowment facilities
무료접속 free access
무료진입 free access
무릎굽힘 knee giving way
무릎보조기 knee orthosis : KO
무릎보호대 knee pad
무릎불안정 knee giving way
무릎이음새 knee joint
무릎충격 terminal impact
무보험자 uninsured
무브먼트
red feather community chest movement
무산소성 역치 anaerobic threshold : AT
무산소성 훈련 anaerobic exercise
무산소증 anoxia
무산소혈증 anoxemia
무산소훈련 anaerobic exercise
무상노동 unpaid work ; unpaid labor
무상의료 free medical care ; free health care
무생물 표면 inanimate surface
무성증 aphonia
무수알코올 absolute alcohol
무시 neglect
무압이불 non-pressure bedding

무억제방광 uninhibited bladder
무연금자 unqualified person for public pension
무염 no added salt : NAS
무염식 no added salt diet
무의식 unconscious
무의지구 medically underserved area
무의촌 medically underserved area
무의탁노인 a senior citizen who does not have
무인가 unauthorized
무임승차 free rider
무자녀가족 childless family
무작위추출 random sampling
무작위할당 random assignment
무정부주의 anarchism
무정위운동증 athetosis
무조건반응 unconditioned response
무조건의 긍정적 배려 unconditional positive regard
무조건자극 unconditioned stimulus
무좀 tinea pedis
무증후성 보균자 asymptomatic carrier
무증후성 심근허혈 silent myocardial ischemia
무증후성 캐리어 asymptomatic carrier
무지 ignorance
무지외반증 bunion
무직 unemployment ; jobless
무차별 indiscrimination
무차별평등 non-discrimination and equality
무치증 edentulism
무코다당증 mucopolysaccharidosis
무톤 mouton
무한책임중간법인
  unlimited liability non-profit mutual benefit
  corporation
무해성 원리
  nonmaleficence principle ; principle of
  nonmaleficence
무해한 약제 innocuous drug
무호흡 apnea
무호흡발작 apneic spell
무호흡역치 apneic threshold
무호흡저호흡지수 apnea-hypopnea index : AHI
무호흡지수 apnea index
무홍채 – 소뇌성운동실조 – 정신박약증

Aniridia cerebellar ataxia mental deficiency
묵비 confidentiality
묵비의무 duty of confidentiality
문맹 illiteracy
문명 civilization
문제가족 problematic family
문제아 problem child
문제지향형 시스템 problem-oriented system :
  POS
문제해결 problem solving
문제해결과정 problem solving process
문제해결능력 workability
문제해결모형 problem solving model
문제해결접근법 problem solving approach
문제행동 problem behavior
문헌검토 philological study
문헌리뷰 literature review
문헌소개 literature review
문헌연구 philological research
문화변용 acculturation
문화양식 cultural pattern
문화인류학 cultural anthropology
문화적 동화 cultural assimilation
문화적 박탈 cultural deprivation
문화적 상대주의 cultural relativism
문화적 장벽 cultural barrier
문화지체 cultural lag
문화충격 culture shock
물가슬라이드제 price indexation
물가연동제 price indexation
물리의학 physical medicine
물리적 장벽 physical barrier ; symbolic barrier
물리치료 physical therapy
물리치료사 physical therapist=PT
물리치료사 실습가이드
  Guide to Physical Therapist Practice
물요법 hydrotherapy
물질남용 stimulant abuse
물질문화 material culture
물질유발정신병 substance-induced psychosis
물질적 학대 material abuse
물집 blister
미각 sense of taste ; gustation

미각저하 loss of taste
미국노인헌장 The Senior Citizen Charter
미국선주민 Native American
미국소시얼워커윤리강령
National Association of Social Workers Code
of Ethics
미국아동복지연맹 Children Welfare League
미끄럼방지 non-slip
미끄럼방지매트 non-slip mat
미끄럼방지테이프 non-slip tape
미네랄 mineral
미네랄결핍증 mineral deficiency
미네랄보급 mineral supplementation
미네소타 다면인격목록
Minnesota Multiphasic Personality Inventory :
MMPI
미니뇌졸중 mini stroke
미니멈 데이터세트 Minimum Data Set : MDS
미니프레스 Minipress
미드타운 맨하턴 연구조사
Midtown Manhattan Study
미라펙스 Mirapex
미란 erosion
미량영양소 trace nutrient
미만성 축색손상 diffuse axonal injury : DAI
미망인 widow
미분화 undifferentiated
미분화상태 undifferentiated status
미생물 비산자 disperser
미생물 살포자 disperser
미생물오염 microorganism contamination
미성년 minor ; under age
미성년보좌인
curator of minor ; court assistant for minors
미성년보좌인 선임
appointment of curator of minor
미성년보좌인의 지정
designation of curator of minor
미성년아이 minor child
미성년자 minor ; under age
미성년자 등기부 minor registry
미성년후견감독인
supervisor of guardian of minor

미성년후견인 guardian of minor
미성년후견인 선임
appointment of guardian of minor
미성년후견인의 지정
designation of guardian of minor
미세뇌기능장애 minimal brain damage : MBD
미세뇌손상 minor brain damage : MBD
미세먼지측정기 particle counter
미소혈관조영 microangiography
미숙련노동자 unskilled worker
미숙련장기요양노동자
unskilled long-term care worker
미숙아 premature infant
미술치료 art therapy
미신 superstition
미아 missing child
미야케식 기명력검사
Miyake Paired Verbal Association Learning Test
미열 slight fever
미오글로빈 myoglobin
미오크로누스 myoclonus
미오파치 myopathy
미크로레벨 micro level
미토콘드리아병 mitochondrial disease
미표정 micro-expressions
미혼모 unmarried mother
믹서식 blended diet
민간개호보험 private long-term care insurance
민간기관 private organization
민간기업 private enterprise
민간단체 private association
민간병원 private hospital
민간보험 private insurance
민간복지 private welfare
민간복지활동 private welfare activity
민간비영리조직 private non-profit organization
민간사업 private program
민간사업자 private program provider
민간사회복지 private social welfare
민간사회복지단체
private social welfare organization
민간사회복지사업 private social welfare program
민간산업복지 private industrial welfare

민간서비스 private services
민간섹터 private sector
민간시설 private facility
민간연금 private pension
민간영리조직 for-profit organization
민간요법 folk medicine
민간요법의사 curandero
민간의료보험 private medical insurance
민간장기요양보험
  private long-term care insurance
민간조성단체 private foundation
민간투자 private investment
민간홈 private home
민간화 privatization
민간활동 private activity
민법 Civil Law
민법전 Civic Code
민생위원 welfare commission volunteer

민생위원법 Welfare Commission Volunteers Act
민생위원의 협력
  cooperation of commission volunteers
민생행정 public welfare administration
민영화 privatization
민족 ethnic group
민족성 ethnicity
민족차별 ethnic discrimination
민주사회주의 democratic socialism
민주주의 democracy
민주주의사회 democratic society
민주화 democratization
민즈테스트 means test
민첩 dexterity
민화 folktale
밀 John Stuart Mill
밀입국자 undocumented alien
밀반찬배달서비스 meal delivery service

ㅂ

바닥 floor level
바닥청소 floor cleaning
바델척도 Barthel index
바라크루드 Baraclude
바륨 Valium
바륨조영 barium contrast radiography
바륨주장조영 barium enema
바륨죽 barium meal
바세르만반응 Wassermann reaction
바소텍 Vasotec
바스켓 겸자 basket forceps
바우처방식 voucher system
바이러스 virus
바이러스감염증 viral infection
바이러스감염후 피로증후군
  post-viral fatigue syndrome
바이러스성 간염 viral hepatitis
바이마르헌법 Weimarer Verfassung
바이브레이션 vibration
바이스테크의 7원칙 Biestek's principles
바이얼라지컬 인디케이터 biological indicator
바이오버든 Bioburden
바이오크린 시스템 bioclean system
바이오클린병실 biological clean room
바이오피드백 biofeedback
바이오피드백요법 biofeedback therapy
바이오필름 biofilm
바이오해저드마크 biohazard mark
바이킹식 all-you-can-eat buffet
바이탈사인 vital signs
바이패스수술 bypass surgery
바카 Roger Barker
바클레이 보고서 Barclay Report

바트레트 Harriet M. Bartlett
박리세포진 exfoliative cytology
박리세포학검사 exfoliative cytology
박사과정 doctoral programs
박사호
  Doctor of Philosophy degree ; doctorate degree
박애 philanthropy
박애사업 philanthropy
박탈 deprivation
반가부좌 half lotus sitting position
반감기 half-life
반대색 opponent color
반대색세포 color opponent cell
반동형성 reaction formation
반맹 hemianopia
반복 침삼키기검사
  repetitive saliva swallowing test : RSST
반복 타액연하검사
  repetitive saliva swallowing test : RSST
반복반사 reiterative reflection
반사 reflex
반사성 교감신경성 이영양증
  reflex sympathetic dystrophy : RSD
반사운동 reflex movement
반사작용 reflex
반사적 이익 reflection benefit
반사행동 respondent behavior
반사회성 anti-social group
반사회적 성격 antisocial personality
반사회적 집단 anti-social group
반상회 neighborhood association
반신불수 hemiplegia
반신욕 half-body bath

반월 cuff

반유동식 pureed diet

반응계층 response hierarchy

반응대가 response cost

반응비용 response cost

반응성 정신병 reactive psychosis

반응시간 reaction time

반응행동 respondent behavior

반장슬 back knee

반전 inversion

반조리 semi-prepared dish

반좌위
　semi-Fowler's position ; half-sitting position

반침습적 semicritical

반코마이신 내성 장구균
　vancomycin resistant enterococci : VRE ;
　vancomycin-resistant enterococcus : VRE

반항기 rebellious stage

반환청구 claims for refund

반흔구축 cicatricial contracture

발걸이 foot rest

발기 erection

발기부전 erectile dysfunction : ED

발끝떼기 toe off

발끝접지 toe contact

발달 development

발달검사 developmental test

발달과제 developmental tasks

발달단계 developmental stages

발달보장 development protection

발달연령 developmental age

발달이론 developmental theory

발달장애 developmental disorder

발달장애인지원법
　Developmental Disabilities Assistance Act

발달정신병리학 developmental psychopathology

발달지수 developmental quotient : DQ

발달지연 developmental delay

발달지체
　mental retardation : MR ; intellectual disorder

발돋움 보행 vaulting

발뒤꿈치 들림 heel off

발뒤꿈치 범퍼 heel bumper

발뒤꿈치 접지 heel contact

발때림 foot slap

발라시클로버 valacyclovir

발목상완지수 ankle-brachial index : ABI

발목욕 foot bath

발바닥굽힘 plantar flexion

발바닥접지 foot flat

발받침대 foot support ; leg rest

발병치료 podiatry

발병학 podiatry

발생 incidence

발생률 incidence rate

발암 carcinogenesis

발어실행 verbal apraxia

발열 fever

발열물질 pyrogen

발열물질검사 pyrogen test

발의 문제 foot problem

발작성 상실성 빈맥
　paroxysmal supraventricular tachycardia

발작성 장애 seizure disorders

발작이상 seizure disorder

발작제 seizure medication

발적 redness

발전도상국 developing country

발진 skin rash

발창 foot support

발톱 toenail

발톱이영양 onychodystrophy

발트렉스 Valtrex

발판 foot support ; foot board ; foot rest

발화지각지도 커리큘럼과 평가
　speech perception instructional curriculum and
　evaluation

밝기 brightness ; lightness ; luminance

밝기 항등성 lightness constancy

밤병원 night hospital

방계적자료원 collateral sources of data

방광경검사 cystoscopy

방광내압측정 cystometrography ; cystometry

방광류 cystocele

방광염 urocystitis

방광직장장애 bowel and bladder dysfunction

방광헤르니아 cystocele

방랑 vagrancy

방문간호 home health

방문간호경과기록부
progress note of the home visiting nurses

방문간호계획 home health plan of care

방문간호보조사교육
education of supporting nursing for the home
visiting nurses

방문간호사 home health nurse

방문간호스테이션
home health nurses station ; home care
nurses station

방문간호케어 home health care

방문간호케어기관 home health care agency

방문간호협회 Home Health Nurses Association

방문개호 home care

방문개호계획 care plan for home care

방문개호사업 home care project

방문개호사업소 home care office

방문개호사업자 home care provider

방문개호원 home care worker

방문개호원양성연수
home care worker training program

방문교사 서비스 visiting teacher service

방문교육 educational home visiting

방문구강위생 mobile oral health services

방문면접 on-site interview

방문세탁서비스 home laundry services

방문약제관리지도
home health medication management

방문영양식사지도
home nutrition education services ;
home-based nutrition education

방문요양 home care

방문요양보호사 home health aide

방문이미용서비스
home beauty services ; mobile beauty services

방문입욕 home bathing care ; home bathing

방문입욕서비스 home bathing services

방문재활 home care rehabilitation

방문조사
on-site assessment ; on-site evaluation ;

on-site survey ; site investigation

방문조사원 site investigator

방문지도 educational home visit

방문치과위생 mobile dental hygiene services

방문치과위생지도
mobile dental hygiene and educational services

방범교육 crime prevention education

방범대책 crime prevention policy

방법론통합화 integrating method

방부제 antiseptic

방사선 X-ray

방사선동영상촬영 cineradiography

방사선촬영 radiography

방사선치료 radiation therapy

방사선투시검사 fluoroscopy

방사성동위체 radioisotope

방사성알레르겐흡착시험 radioallergosorbent test

방사성옥소 radioactive iodine

방사성핵종혈관조영 radionuclide angiography

방수시트 waterproof sheet

방어 defense

방어기제 defense mechanism

방어행동 defensiveness

방염소재 flame-resistant material

방오소재 soil-resistant material

방위 defense

방위가족 family of orientation

방위의 분석 analysis of defenses

방임 neglect

방임형 지도 laissez-faire type leadership

방재 disaster prevention

방재대책 emergency planning

방충제 mothball

방향감각상실 disorientation

방향정위 orientation

방호의복 protective clothing

방호환경 protective environment : PE

방화대책 fire prevention

배경인자 contextual factor

배굴 dorsiflexion

배급할당 distribution quota

배뇨 urination

배뇨곤란 difficult urination

배뇨관리 urinary management

배뇨근괄약협동부전
　detrusor-sphincter dyssynergia : DSD

배뇨무력증 acraturesis

배뇨불능증 acraturesis

배뇨장애 urinary disorder ; micturition disorder

배뇨중추 micturition center

배뇨훈련 bladder training

배달 deliver

배담 bronchial drainage

배동주경첩 이음새 step-up elbow hinge

배리어 barrier

배리어 예방책 barrier precaution

배리어기재 barrier equipment

배리어널싱 barrier nursing

배리어프리 barrier free

배리어프리 디자인 barrier free design

배리어프리 문지방 barrier-free threshold

배리어프리 신법 New Barrier Free Law

배리어프리 주택 barrier free home

배리어프리 지도 barrier free map

배변 defecation

배변관리 bowel management

배변내압검사 defecometry

배변영화촬영술 cinedefecography

배변장애 dyschezia ; defecation disorder

배변조영검사 defecography

배변훈련 bowel training

배분 allocation

배분계획 allocation plan

배분금 allocated money

배상 indemnity

배설 excretion

배설개호 excretion care

배설관련용구 continence care product

배설물 fece

배설보조 toileting assistance

배설스케줄 toileting schedule

배설용구 excretion tool

배설장기요양 excretion care

배설장애 excretion disorder

배설케어 excretion care

배설훈련 excretion exercise

배수관 drain

배스로브 bathrobe

배식서비스 meal delivery services

배쓰보드 bath board

배우자 spouse

배우자공제 marital deduction

배우자세공제 tax deduction for a spouse

배우자학대 spouse abuse

배치 placement ; assign

배치결정 decision for the placement

배회 wandering

백내장 cataract

백레스트 backrest

백색인종 Caucasians

백서포트 back support

백선 tinea ; dermatophytosis

백신주사 vaccination

백조목변형 Swan neck deformity

백혈구 white blood cell : WBC

백혈병 leukemia

밸라-제롤드 증후군 Baller-Gerold syndrome

밸런스 balance

밸리데이션 validation

밸리데이션요법 validation therapy

밸프로산 valproic acid

밸프로인산 valproic acid

버그균형척도 Berg Balance Scale

버니언 bunion

버블배스 bubble bath

버즈세션 Buzz Session

버튼에이드 button aid

번아웃 burnout

번아웃신드롬 burnout syndrome

벌금 penalty

벌룬도뇨카테터 balloon catheter

벌룬배출시험 balloon expulsion test

벌룬보지시험 balloon retaining test

벌칙 penal regulation

범불안장애 generalized anxiety disorder

범이론적 모델 transtheoretical model

범죄 crime

범죄소년 juvenile offender

범죄심리학 criminal psychology

범죄피해 crime victimization
범죄피해자 구제 victim care
범죄회학 criminology
법 Law ; Act
법령위반 law violation
법령준수 compliance
법률 law
법률부조 legal aid
법률부조사업 legal aid service
법률상담 legal consultation
법률지원 legal assistance
법의사간호 forensic nurse
법의학간호학 forensic nursing
법의학병리학 forensic pathology
법의학병리학자 forensic pathologist
법의학복지 forensic social work
법의학심리학 forensic psychology
법의학심리학자 forensic psychologist
법의학인류학 forensic anthropology
법의학인류학자 forensic anthropologist
법의학정신간호 forensic psychiatric nursing
법인 corporation ; juridical person
법인세 corporation tax
법적 규제 legal regulation
법적 문제 legal issue
법적 별거 legal separation
법적 의무 legal obligation
법정고용율 statutory rates of employment
법정대리수령서비스 legal reception services
법정대리인 legal guardian
법정수탁사업 statutory functions entrusted
법정원조 court assistance
법정전염병
 legally designated communicable disease
베개 pillow
베니카 Benicar
베드 bed
베드사이드 테이블 bedside table
베라파밀 verapamil
베렐란 Verelan
베르너 증후군 Werner Syndrome : WS
베르니케 코르사코프 증후군
 Wernicke-Korsakoff syndrome

베르니케뇌증 Wernicke's encephalopathy
베르니케실어 Wernicke's aphasia
베르니케영역 Wernicke's area
베르테포르핀 verteporfin
베르토로티 증후군 Bertolotti's syndrome
베버리지 Beveridge M. William
베버리지 보고서 Beveridge Report
베이비부머 baby boomer
베이비붐 세대 baby boom generation
베이비시터 babysitter ; nanny
벡커형 근육퇴행위축 Becker muscular dystrophy
벤라팍신 venlafaxine
벤즈트로핀 Benztropine
벨 마비 Bell's palsy
벨패드법 bell and pad
벽지의료체제
 medical care system for remote areas
변 stool
변기 bedpan ; toilet
변기세정기 bedpan washer
변량 variance
변별자극 discriminative stimulus
변비 constipation
변색 discoloration
변생성 stool production
변성 degeneration
변성질환 degenerative disease
변수 variable
변실금 fecal incontinence ; bowel incontinence
변의 bowel movement
변잠혈검사 fecal occult blood test : FOBT
변통 bowel movement
변형 deformity
변형성 경추증 cervical spondylosis
변형성 고관절증 coxarthrosis
변형성 관절증 osteoarthritis : OA
변형성 슬관절증 gonarthrosis
변호사 attorney-at-law
변화매개인 change agent
변화매개체계 change agent system
변화분석 bivariate analysis
병 disease
병경험 illness experience

병관리 disease management : DM

병동 unit

병동청소 cleaning of the patient care unit

병리검사 pathology test

병상규제
control of hospital bed ; hospital bed- control

병소 focal ; nidus

병소감염 focal infection

병수당 sickness and injury allowance

병식 insight into disease

병실점유율 occupancy rate

병원 hospital

병원감염
hospital infection ; hospital-acquired infection ;
nosocomial infection

병원감염관리실천자문위원회
Hospital Infection Control Practices Advisory
Committee : HICPAC

병원감염폐렴 hospital-acquired pneumonia

병원기능평가 hospital accreditation

병원기반형 서비스 hospital-based services

병원사회사업 hospital social work

병원입원 hospitalization

병원자원봉사 hospital volunteer

병원정보시스템 hospital information system

병원체 pathogenic organism

병원퇴원 discharge from the hospital

병원환경 hospital environment

병의 징조 signs of disease

병의원간 진료연계 affiliation between outpatient
clinics and hospitals

병적 골절 pathological bone fracture

병적상태의 압축
compression of morbidity ; morbidity
compression

병적인 얽힘 enmeshment

병진전정동안반사
translational vestibulo-ocular reflex

병체험 illness experience

병행동 illness behavior

병행치료 concurrent treatment

병휴가 medical leave ; sick leave

보건 health

보건계획 health planning

보건복지 health and welfare

보건복지교육 health and welfare education

보건복지기관 health and welfare agency

보건복지기준 health and welfare standards

보건복지부 Ministry of Health and Welfare

보건복지사무소 health and welfare office

보건복지사업소 health and welfare office

보건복지서비스 health and welfare services

보건복지수준 level of health and welfare

보건복지시설 health and welfare facility

보건복지시책 policy of health and welfare

보건사 public health nurse : PHN

보건센터 health center

보건소 public health center

보건시설 health services

보건실 school infirmary

보건위생 health hygiene

보건지도 health guidance

보건행동 health behavior

보고 report

보관 safekeeping

보균자 carrier

보니바 Boniva

보더리스 borderless

보도 guidance

보드 앤드 케어홈 board and care home

보모 babysitter ; certified child care worker

보부 male nursery teacher

보산케트 Helen Bosanquet

보상 compensation

보상과 Compensation Division

보상교육 compensatory education

보석 bail

보속증 perseveration

보수비례거출
contribution in proportion to income

보수주의 conservatism

보수주의적 · 조합주의적 복지국가
conservative and corporatist welfare state

보스톤 이름대기검사 Boston Naming Test

보완대체의료
complementary and alternative medicine : CAM

보완의료 complementary medicine
보완적 의료보험
　Supplemental Social Security Insurance : SMI
보위딕 테스트 Bowie-Dick Test
보육 nursery child care
보육계획 nursery care programming
보육과 Day Care Division
보육니즈 nursery needs
보육단가 nursery unit cost
보육사 certified child care worker
보육소 child day care center
보육원 child day care center ; nursery school
보육정책 day nursery policy
보육제도 day nursery system
보이지 않는 손 invisible hand
보이콧 boycott
보장 security
보장구 orthosis ; prosthesis ; orthopedic appliance
보조 assistance
보조감염 community-acquired infection
보조견 assistance dog ; partner dog ; service dog
보조금 grants-in-aid
보조기 orthosis ; brace
보조기구 prosthetic equipment
보조기술 assistive technology
보조기요법 orthotic treatment
보조기학 orthotics
보조도구 technical aid
보조동근 assistant mover
보조모드 assist mode
보조사회사업가 case worker aide
보조양식 assist mode
보조원 assistant ; supporter
보조적 케어 custodial care
보조조절환기
　assist and/or controlled mechanical ventilation
보조호흡근 accessory respiratory muscle
보조훈련 assistive exercise
보존적 요법 conservative treatment
보존적 치료 conservative treatment
보좌감독인 supervisor of the curator
보좌인 curator ; court assistant
보증 guarantee

보증인 guarantor
보철 prosthetic
보청기 hearing aid
보충급부제도 Supplementary Benefit Scheme
보충급여 supplementary benefit
보충성 complementarity
보충성의 원리
　principle of supplementary nature of public
　assistance
보충적개념 residual conception
보충적용 supplemental coverage
보통보험료징수
　ordinary premium collection ; premium
　collection
보통비누 plain soap
보통세징수 ordinary tax collection
보통식 regular diet
보통징수 ordinary collection
보통출생율 crude birth rate
보통형 휠체어 standard wheelchair
보편적 예방책 universal precautions
보편적 욕구 universal needs
보편적 편리성 universal access
보편주의 universalism
보폭 step length ; stride length
보폭너비 stride width
보행 gait ; ambulation
보행곤란 gait difficulty
보행기 walker
보행기능평가 gait assessment
보행능력 gait ability ; walking ability
보행동작 ambulation activity
보행보조기기 mobility aid
보행보조도구 walking aid
보행분석 gait analysis
보행속도 gait velocity
보행실행 gait apraxia
보행연습 gait training
보행용 지팡이 walking cane
보행장애
　gait disability ; gait disturbance ; gait disorder
보행주기 gait cycle
보행패턴 gait pattern

보행훈련 gait training

보험 insurance

보험과 Employees' Health Insurance Division

보험국 Health Insurance Bureau

보험급여 insurance benefit

보험기간 insurance period ; period of insurance

보험기관 insurance agency

보험료 insurance premium

보험료감면 premium reduction

보험료기준액
standard rate of insurance premium

보험료납부필기간
period for the premium payment

보험료면제
immunity from premium contributions

보험료산정기준
insurance premium rate calculator standard

보험료소급부과 retroactive premium payment

보험료수준 insurance premium level

보험료율 insurance premium rate

보험료징수 collection of insurance premiums

보험료체납 non-payment of premium

보험사고 insured event

보험연구원 Korea Insurance Research Institute

보험의 insurance doctor

보험자 the insurer

보험증 insurance card

보험회사 insurance company

보호 protection care

보호감찰관 probation and parole officer

보호감찰제도 probation and parole system

보호감호 protective custody

보호격리 reversed isolation

보호견 service dog

보호고용 sheltered employment

보호과 Public Assistance Division

보호관찰 probation

보호관찰부가석방 parole

보호관찰부선고 probation

보호구치 protective custody

보호국 protective services

보호권 custody

보호사 parole officer ; probation officer

보호사법 Volunteer Probation Officers Act

보호서비스 protective service

보호수탁자 vocational guidance parent

보호시설 asylums

보호용 안경 eye goggle

보호율 public assistance ratio

보호의 보충성
supplementary nature of public assistance

보호의 종류 및 범위
types and scope of public assistance

보호의무자 person responsible for protection

보호자 guardian

보호자중심 parent-centered

보호주택 sheltered housing

보호처분 protective measure

보호형 개호시설 custodial care facility

보호형 케어 custodial care

보호율 walking rate

보훈연금 soldiers' pension

복강경수술 laparoscopic surgery

복강경하수술 laparoscopic surgery

복강세정 peritoneal lavage

복리후생 welfare program

복막조영 peritoneography

복막투석 peritoneal dialysis : PD

복부방사선사진 abdominal x-ray

복부천자 abdominocentesis

복부초음파검사 abdominal ultrasound

복서골절 boxer's fracture

복식호흡
abdominal respiration ; abdominal breathing

복압성 요실금 stress incontinence

복약관리 medication management

복약준수 medication compliance

복약치료지속성 medication adherence

복역수 prisoner

복와위 prone position

복지 welfare

복지경제학 welfare economics

복지공사 welfare public corporation

복지공장 welfare workshop for the disabled

복지관계자 welfare personnel

복지교육 welfare education

복지국가 welfare state
복지국가의 위기 welfare state in crisis
복지권 welfare rights
복지급여 welfare benefit
복지기금 welfare fund
복지기기
  care equipment ; welfare equipment ;
  technical aid for the disabled
복지기반과 Welfare Promotion Division
복지기준 welfare standards
복지노동 labor welfare ; labour welfare
복지레크리에이션 welfare and recreation
복지문화 welfare culture
복지반동 welfare backlash
복지비 welfare expenditure
복지사무소 welfare office
복지사무소소장
  superintendent of public welfare office
복지사회 welfare society
복지사회학 sociology of welfare
복지서비스 welfare services
복지서비스 제삼자평가제도
  third-party quality certification system for
  welfare services
복지수당 welfare allowance
복지수준 level of welfare
복지시설 welfare facility
복지시스템 welfare system
복지연금 welfare pension
복지욕구 welfare needs
복지용구
  technical aid for the disabled ; care equipment ;
  welfare equipment
복지용구구입
  purchase of welfare aids ; purchase of welfare
  equipments
복지용구대여
  welfare equipment rentals ; lending of welfare
  equipments
복지용구대여서비스 welfare equipment rental
  services
복지용구법 Welfare Equipment Law
복지용구분류코드

Classification Code of Technical Aids : CCTA
복지용구산업 welfare equipment industry
복지용구전문상담원 welfare equipments advisor
복지용구판매 welfare equipments trade
복지용구플래너 welfare equipments planner
복지용품 care equipment
복지원조 welfare assistance
복지원조자 welfare assistant
복지윤리 welfare ethics
복지인재 welfare manpower
복지인재정보센터
  Social Welfare National Center for Social
  Service Human Resources
복지자본주의 welfare capitalism
복지재원 welfare funds
복지전문 welfare profession
복지전문직 professional social work
복지전화
  telephone assistive device ; assistive listening
  and technology device
복지정보 welfare information
복지정책 welfare policy
복지제도 welfare system ; welfare regime
복지주거환경 코디네이터
  housing and environment coordinator
복지지표 welfare indicator
복지직원 welfare staff
복지차량 welfare vehicle
복지카드 welfare card
복지커뮤니티
  community organization for welfare
복지택시 welfare taxi ; welfare taxi services
복지행정 welfare administration
복지홈 welfare home
복지활동 welfare activity
복통 abdominal pain ; abdominalgia
복포 drape
복합가족 joint family
복합문제 가족 multiproblem family
복합시설 composite institute
본적 permanent domicile
본태성 고혈압 essential hypertension
볼런터리 voluntary

볼런터리즘 voluntarism
볼런티어 volunteer
볼런티어계획 volunteer plan
볼런티어뷰로 volunteer bureau
볼런티어센터 volunteer center
볼런티어스쿨 volunteer school
볼런티어활동 volunteer activity
볼비 John M. Bowlby
봉건사상 feudalistic thought
봉건사회 feudal society
봉사 voluntary work
봉사원 volunteer
봉와직염 cellulitis
부가 addition
부가가치세 value added tax : VAT
부가결실형 돌연변이 addition-deletion mutation
부가급부 fringe benefits
부가급여 fringe benefits
부가변이 addition mutation
부가연금 additional pension
부가중합 addition polymerization
부가중합체 addition polymer
부간호사장 assistant director of nursing
부검 autopsy
부과방식 imposition system
부교감신경 parasympathetic nerve
부녀보호 protective care for women
부녀복지 women's welfare
부녀복지상담원 counselor for women
부녀상담소 counseling center for women
부담 burden
부담금분담 share of cost
부담율 burden rate
부담질문표 burden interview
부당노동행위 unfair labor practice
부도덕가정 immoral family
부동 immobilization
부동성 immobility
부랑아 homeless child
부모교육훈련
    Parent Effectiveness Training : PET
부모모임 parent group
부목 splint

부부가족 conjugal family
부부간 공제 marital deduction
부부관계 marital relationship
부부상담 marriage counseling
부부역할 marital role
부부요법 marital therapy
부부재산계약 marital property agreement
부부치료 marital therapy
부분간절제 partial hepatectomy
부분목욕 partial bath
부분보조 limited assistance
부분세정 partial sponge bath
부분연금 partial pension
부분욕 partial bath
부분원조 limited assistance
부분입원 partial hospital
부분조사 partial enumeration
부분화 partialization
부비강기관지증후군 sinobronchial syndrome
부비동성 두통 sinus headache
부샤르결절 Bouchard's node
부성적 온정주의 paternalism
부시실장 assistant administrator
부신피질스테로이드 adrenocorticosteroid
부신피질호르몬관장 adrenocorticosteroid enema
부양 support ; sustenance
부양세공제 tax deduction for dependents
부양수당 dependency allowance
부양의무 responsibility to support dependents
부양의무자
    person responsible for dependent family ;
    person responsible for dependent family
    members
부양자세액공제 parenthood tax rebate
부업 side job
부엌도구 utensil
부유미립자 floating particle
부유입자 airborne particle
부의 강화 negative reinforcement
부의 벌 negative punishment
부의 소득세 negative income tax : NIT
부인 denial
부인과 gynecology

부인과의사 gynecologist
부인과의학 gynecology
부자가정
single parent home ; motherless family
부자세대
single-father household ; motherless household
부작용 side effect
부적격 inadequacy
부적응 maladjustment
부적응행동 maladjusted behavior
부전경수손상 incomplete cervical cord injury
부전대마비 paraparesis
부전마비 paresis
부전사지마비 incomplete quadriplegia
부정기형 indeterminate sentence
부정맥 arrhythmia
부정수급 public assistance fraud
부정약품 traffic drug
부정이득의 징수 collection of wrongful gain
부정적 강화 negative reinforcement
부정적 전이 negative transference
부정청구 unfair charge
부정행위 malpractice
부조 assistance
부조법 Public Assistance Law
부종 edema
부주치의 secondary physician
부착 cathexis
부처별 공공서비스협약
department public services agreement
부처별 세출한도액
Departmental Expenditure Limit : DEL
부하심전도 stress electrocardiogram
부호기 coder
부호화 coding
분광시감효율 spectral luminous efficiency
분권화 decentralization
분노 anger
분담금 allotted charge
분류 atheroma
분류수용 classified admission
분류처우 treatment based classification

분리 separation
분리가족 disengaged family
분리배양 differential culture
분리불안 separation anxiety
분리불안장애 separation anxiety disorder
분만마비 birth palsy
분만보조 assistance with delivery
분말약품 powdered drug
분무 fogging
분변검사 fecal examination
분변세균검사 stool microbiology
분변전 및 분변후 처치
treatment prior to and after delivery
분변키모트립신시험 fecal chymotrypsin test
분산분석 analysis of variance : ANOVA
분석 analysis
분석심리학 analytical psychology
분업 divisions of labor
분열 splitting
분열감정장애 schizoaffective disorder
분열장애 dissociative disorder
분열정서장애 schizoaffective disorder
분포 distribution
분포도 isoarea map
분포율 prevalence rate
분화 differentiation
분화복지국가 differentiated welfare state
불감증 frigidity
불결·감염수술 dirty/infected operation
불결구역 dirty area
불결창 dirty wound
불결행위 dirty behavior
불공평 inequity
불교사회사업 Buddhist social work
불균형 imbalance
불등교 school absenteeism
불량자세 malposture
불량주택지역 slum area
불량지위 malposition
불면 sleeplessness
불면증 insomnia
불명열 fever of unknown origin
불법입양 black market adoption

불법체류 illegal residence
불법취업 illegal employment
불복제기 appeal
불복제기제도 appeal system
불소 fluoride
불수의운동 involuntary movement
불안 anxiety
불안신경증 anxiety neurosis
불안장애 anxiety disorder
불안전고용 underemployment
불안정성 insecurity
불안증 anxiety
불완전고용 subemployment
불완전대마비 paraparesis
불응성 adiaphoria
불일치 incongruence
불치병대책 policy for incurable diseases
불치병인정
  incurable disease certification ; certification of
  incurable disease
불쾌지수 discomfort index
불평 complaint
불평등 inequality
불평처리 complaints handling
불평해결 grievances and complaints resolution
불포화지방산 unsaturated fatty acid
불현성 감염
  inapparent infection ; silent infection
불현성 오염 silent aspiration
불화 estrangement
불활성화계수 inactivation factor
붕대 bandage
붕대교환 dressing change
뷔페식 all-you-can-eat buffet
브라운씨쿼드증후군 Brown-Sequard syndrome
브라이유식 점자 Braille
브라이유식 점자블록 Braille block
브라이유식 점자용구 Braille writing equipment
브라이유식 점자타이프라이터 Braille typewriter
브라이유식 촉독 Braille reading
브러싱 brushing
브레스트지남력 기억집중검사
  Blessed Orientation-Memory-Concentration Test

브레인스토밍 brainstorming
브로카실어증 Broca's aphasia
브로카영역 Broca's area
브론스트롬 스테이지 Brunnstrom stage
브리프테라피 brief therapy
블록계약 block contract
블루칼라 blue collar
비결핵성 항산균증
  non-tuberculous mycobacterial infection
비경구영양 parenteral feeding
비공식보호 informal care
비공식부문 informal sector
비공식적 그룹 informal group
비공식조직 informal organization
비과세단체 tax-exempt organization
비과세세대 tax-exempt household
비과세수당 tax-exempt allowance
비관우울증 dysthymic disorder
비구골절 acetabular fracture
비구아니드 Biguanide
비네 지능검사 Binet Intelligence Test
비네시몬 지능검사법 Binet-Simon Test
비뇨기과 urology
비뇨기과의 urologist
비대 hypertrophy
비대칭 asymmetry
비대형 심근증 hypertrophic cardiomyopathy
비등수 boiling water
비디오 내시경검사 video endoscopy
비례분배 quota share
비만 obesity
비만저환기증후군
  obesity hypoventilation syndrome
비만증 adipositas
비만지수 obesity index
비말감염 droplet infection
비말예방책 droplet precaution
비말전파 droplet transmission
비말핵 droplet nuclei
비문증 myodesopsia
비밀보장 confidentiality
비밀보장의 원칙 principle of confidentiality
비밀보지 confidentiality

비밀보지의무 secrecy obligation
비배분의 원칙 non-distribution constraint
비사회성 unsocial behavior
비상근직원 part-time staff
비생물합성 abiotic synthesis
비소세포폐암 non-small cell lung cancer :
  NSCLC
비소중독 arsenic poisoning
비스마르크 Otto Eduard Leopold Bismarck
비스테로이드계 항염증약
  non-steroidal antiinflammatory drug : NSAID
비스포스포네이트 제재 bisphosphonate drug
비심판적 태도 non-judgmental attitude
비심판적 태도의 원칙
  principle of non-judgmental attitude
비암질환환자 non-cancer patient
비어스 C. W. Beers
비어스 기준 Beers criteria ; Beers list
비어테로머성 관상동맥질환
  non-atherosclerotic coronary artery disease
비언어적 의사소통 non-verbal communication
비언어적 커뮤니케이션
  non-verbal communication
비에스틱 7대 원칙 Biestek's 7 principles
비염 rhinitis
비영리 어드버커시 non-profit advocacy
비영리 nonprofit
비영리조직 non-profit organization : NPO
비오틴 biotin
비온스타드 증후군 Bjornstad syndrome
비용관리 managed cost
비용부담방식 cost-sharing formula
비용분담 cost sharing
비용산정 cost estimation
비용억제 cost containment
비용징수 collection of costs
비용편익 cost-benefit
비용편익분석 cost-benefit analysis
비용효율 cost-effective
비용효익 cost-benefit
비율 ratio
비자발적실업 involuntary unemployment
비자발적인 클라이언트 involuntary client

비전2030 Vision 2030
비정부조직 non-governmental organization : NGO
비정상 abnormal
비정상적 성관계 deviate sexual intercourse
비정형 정신병 atypical psychosis
비정형 항산균증 atypical mycobacteria
비정형 항정신병약 atypical antipsychotic
비죽상동맥경화증
  non-atherosclerotic coronary artery disease
비처방전약 non-prescription drug
비체중부하보조기
  non-weight bearing brace ; non- weight
  bearing orthosis
비침습성 검사 non-invasive diagnostic test
비침습적 non-critical
비타민 vitamin
비타민 A 결핍증 vitamin A deficiency
비타민 B1 결핍증 vitamin B1 deficiency
비타민 B2 결핍증 vitamin B2 deficiency
비타민 B6 결핍증 vitamin B6 deficiency
비타민 B12 결핍증 vitamin B12 deficiency
비타민 C 결핍증 vitamin C deficiency
비타민 D 결핍증 vitamin D deficiency
비타민 E 결핍증 vitamin E deficiency
비타민 K 결핍증 vitamin K deficiency
비합리적 신념 irrational belief
비해당 not applicable : N/A
비행 delinquency
비행소년 juvenile delinquent
비행원인론 etiology of criminal behavior
비행집단 delinquent gang
비행하위문화 delinquent subculture
비행행위 vice
비화폐적 욕구 non-monetary needs
빈 둥지증후군 empty nest syndrome
빈 의자기법 empty-chair technique
빈곤 poverty
빈곤가정 poor family
빈곤과의 전쟁 War on Poverty
빈곤문화 culture of poverty
빈곤선 poverty line
빈곤수준 poverty level
빈곤예방 prevention of poverty

빈곤의 악순환설 vicious circle of poverty
빈곤의 여성화 feminization of poverty
빈곤의 유형 type of poverty
빈곤의 재발견 rediscovery of poverty
빈곤자 poor
빈곤지수 poverty index
빈곤층 the poor strata
빈곤퇴치 프로그램 antipoverty programs
빈뇨 pollakiuria
빈맥 tachycardia
빈민 pauper
빈민가〔슬럼〕 slum
빈민감독관 overseers of the poor
빈민감독원 overseers of the poor
빈민구제위원 poor law guardians

빈민굴 shantytowns
빈민보호위원 poor law guardians
빈발두통 cluster headache
빈변 frequent bowel movements
빈스완거병 Binswanger's disease
빈터 Robert D. Vinter
빈혈 anemia
빈혈치료제 antianemia drug
빈호흡 tachypnea
빙낭 ice bag
빙침 ice pillow
빨간깃털모금
　red feather community chest movement
빨래판 rubbing board

사각코너 square corner
사건관련전위 event-related potential : ERP
사고발관 accidental extubation
사고장애 thought disorder
사고평가 accident evaluation
사기 fraud ; scam
사는보람이 있는 생활 life worth living
사닥다리이론 the extension ladder theory
사단법인 incorporated association
사라세미아 thalassemia
사람면역결핍바이러스
　human immunodeficiency virus : HIV
사람면역결핍바이러스감염 HIV infection
사람백혈구항원 human lymphocyte antigen
사람표피증식인자수용체 2형
　human epidermal growth factor receptor-2 :
　HER2
사례검토 case study
사례관리 case management
사례기록 case record
사례발견 case finding
사례사 case history
사례연구 case research
사례조사 case investigation
사례회의 case conference
사르코페니아 sarcopenia
사립병원 private hospital
사립학교교직원연금 Korea Teachers' Pension
사망 death
사망률 mortality rate
사망비율 proportional mortality indicator : PMI
사망율 death rate
사망자 deceased

사망진단서 death certificate
사면 amnesty
사무비 administrative cost
사무자동화 office automation
사무직노동자 white-collar worker
사무직원 clerical personnel
사법간호 forensic nurse
사법간호학 forensic nursing
사법병리학 forensic pathology
사법병리학자 forensic pathologist
사법복지 forensic social work
사법심리학 forensic psychology
사법심리학자 forensic psychologist
사법심사 judicial review
사법인류학 forensic anthropology
사법인류학자 forensic anthropologist
사법정신간호 forensic psychiatric nursing
사법해부 forensic autopsy
사변형 소켓 quadrilateral socket
사별 bereavement
사상관련전위 event-related potential : ERP
사생관 view of life and death
사생아 illegitimate
사생활 privacy
사스 severe acute respiratory syndrome : SARS
사업소 office ; agency
사업자 provider
사업주부담금 owner's payment
사영화 privatization
사용상 주의 patient's instructions for use
사용율 use rate
사유화 privatization
사이드레일 siderail

사이몬드 P. M. Symonds
사이코드라마 psycho drama
사이코세라피 psycho therapy
사이클로벤자프린 cyclobenzaprine
사이클로스포린 cyclosporine
사인별사망비율 proportional mortality rate
사일런트 킬러 silent killer
사임의족 Syme's prosthesis
사임절단 Syme's amputation
사자 deceased
사적개호 informal care
사적보험 personal insurance
사적부양 private support
사적부조 private assistance
사적사업채권 private activity bond
사적장기요양 informal care
사적활동 private activity
사전동의 informed consent : IC
사전조사 pre-test
사전평가 pre-evaluation ; pre-assessment
사정 assessment
사지 limbs
사지마비 quadriplegia
사찰 inspection
사찰지도원 inspector
사체안치소 morgue
사체해부 autopsy
사춘기 puberty
사춘기 거식증 adolescent nausea
사춘기 수척증 adolescent emaciation
사춘기 정신보건 adolescent mental health
사회 · 원호국
  Social Welfare and War Victims' Relief Bureau
사회개량 social reform
사회개발 social development
사회개혁 social reform
사회계급 social class
사회계약설 theory of social contract
사회계층 social stratification
사회계획 social planning
사회고용 social employment
사회공포증 social phobia
사회공학 social engineering

사회과학 social science
사회관계 social relation
사회교육 social education
사회구조 social structure
사회권 social rights
사회규범 social norm
사회기관 social agency
사회기능훈련 social skills training : SST
사회노년학 social gerontology
사회모델 social model
사회문제 social problems
사회민주주의 social democracy
사회민주주의적 복지국가
  social democratic welfare state
사회발전론 theories of social development
사회법 Social Law
사회변동 social change
사회병리 social pathology
사회병리학 social pathology
사회보장 Social Security
사회보장구조개혁
  structural reform of Social Security
사회보장급여 Social Security benefit
사회보장급여비 costs of Social Security benefit
사회보장법 Social Security Act
사회보장부담 Social Security burden
사회보장비용 Social Security costs
사회보장세 Social Security tax
사회보장심의회
  Advisory Council on Social Security
사회보장의 민영화 privatization of Social Security
사회보장제도 Social Security system
사회보장제도심의회
  National Advisory Council on the Social
  Security System
사회보장헌장 Social Security Charter
사회보험 social insurance
사회보험노무사
  certified social insurance and labor consultant
사회보험료 social insurance premium
사회보험료료공제
  tax deduction for social insurance premiums
사회보험방식 social insurance system

사회보험비 social insurance expenses
사회보험비용 social insurance costs
사회보험사무소 social insurance office
사회보험심사원 social insurance examiner
사회보험심사회
　Examination Committee of Social Insurance
사회보험업무센터
　social insurance operation center
사회보험진로보수지불기금
　Social Insurance Medical Fee Payments Fund
사회보험청 Social Insurance Agency
사회복지 social welfare
사회복지경영 social administration
사회복지계획 social welfare planning
사회복지계획법 social welfare planning method
사회복지관 social welfare center
사회복지관계 8법의 개정
　Revision of the Eight Acts related to Social
　Welfare
사회복지관리 social administration
사회복지관리사무소 Social Administration Office
사회복지교육 social work and welfare education
사회복지기관 social welfare agency
사회복지기준 social welfare standards
사회복지기초구조개혁
　Basic Structural Reform of Social Welfare
사회복지단체 social welfare organization
사회복지법 Social Welfare Service Law
사회복지법인 social welfare corporation
사회복지법제 social welfare registration
사회복지비용 cost of social welfare
사회복지사 certified social worker : CSW
사회복지사 및 개호복지사법
　Certified Social Worker and Care Worker Act
사회복지사무소 social welfare office
사회복지사무소직원 social welfare office staff
사회복지사양성시설 school of social work
사회복지사업 social welfare services
사회복지사업단 social welfare services agency
사회복지사업법 Social Welfare Service Law
사회복지서비스 social welfare services
사회복지수준 level of social welfare
사회복지시설 social welfare facility

사회복지운영관리 Social Welfare Administration
사회복지원조기술 social work and welfare practice
사회복지원조활동 social work and welfare activity
사회복지의 날 social welfare day
사회복지의 법제 social welfare legislation
사회복지전공과목
　degree requirements for social work
사회복지전문 social work profession
사회복지전문직 professional social work
사회복지전문직단체
　professional association of social workers
사회복지정보 social welfare information
사회복지정책 social welfare policy
사회복지정책분석 social policy analysis
사회복지제도 social welfare system
사회복지조사 social welfare research
사회복지주사 social welfare officer
사회복지진흥 · 시험센터
　Center of Social Welfare Promotion and
　National Examination
사회복지학사학위 bachelor of social work : BSW
사회복지학석사 master of social work : MSW
사회복지행정 social welfare administration
사회복지현장실습 social work practicum
사회복지협의회 Council of Social Welfare
사회봉사 volunteering
사회봉사교환소 social service exchange
사회부조 social assistance
사회불안 social unrest
사회비용 social cost
사회사업 social program
사회사업가 social worker : SW
사회사업교육 social work education
사회사업기술 social work skills
사회사업방법론 methods in social work
사회사업실천 social work practice
사회사업조사 social work research
사회생태학 social ecology
사회생활기능훈련 social skills training : SST
사회생활력 social functioning ability : SFA
사회서비스 social services
사회성숙도척도 social maturity scale
사회수당 social allowance

사회심리학 social psychology

사회악 social evil

사회안전망 social safety net

사회연대 social solidarity

사회욕구 social needs

사회운동 social movement

사회운동론 social movement theory

사회유대 social bond

사회의식 social consciousness

사회의학 social medicine

사회이동 social mobility

사회이론 social theory

사회인지이론 social cognitive theory

사회자본 social capital

사회자원 social resource

사회적 [아동] 보호 foster-child care

사회적 가치 social value

사회적 강자 socially advantaged person

사회적 개호 socialized long-term care

사회적 거리 social distance

사회적 격리 social isolation

사회적 기본권 social rights

사회적 긴장 social tension

사회적 네트워크 social network

사회적 무질서 anomie

사회적 문제해결법 social problem-solving

사회적 및 문화적 권리에 관한 국제규약
International Covenant on Economic, Social
and Cultural Rights

사회적 부담비 social charge

사회적 부양 social assistance

사회적 불리 handicap

사회적 상호작용 social interaction

사회적 손씻기 social hand washing

사회적 수용 social inclusion

사회적 약자 socially disadvantaged person

사회적 양호 social care

사회적 역할 social role

사회적 역할론 social role theory

사회적 요구 social needs

사회적 욕구 love belonging needs

사회적 위기관리 social risk management

사회적 위험 social risk

사회적 입원 social hospitalization

사회적 장벽 social barrier

사회적 장애 social handicapped

사회적 재활 social rehabilitation

사회적 적용 social adequacy

사회적 적응 social adjustment

사회적 지원 social support

사회적 지원네트워크 social support network

사회적 지위 social status

사회적 지지 social support

사회적 통합 social inclusion

사회적 포섭 social inclusion

사회적 행동 social action

사회적 행위 social action

사회적 행위이론 theory of social action

사회정책 social policy

사회제도 social institution

사회조사 social research

사회조직 social organization

사회주의 socialism

사회지리학 social geography

사회지원서비스 social support services

사회지표 social indicators

사회진단 social diagnosis

사회진화론 social evolutionism

사회질서 social order

사회집단 social group

사회참가 social participation

사회참가촉진 promotion of social participation

사회체제 social system

사회취로센터 Support of Employment

사회측정 sociometry

사회치료 social treatment

사회통계 social statistics

사회통계과 Social Statistics Division

사회통제 social control

사회통합 social integration

사회학 sociology

사회학습 이론 social learning theory

사회해체 social disorganization

사회행동 social action

사회행동가 social activist

사회행정 social administration

사회화 socialization
사회환경 social environment
사회활동 social activity
사후경직 rigor mortis
사후보호 after-care
사후처치 postmortem care
사후평가 post-evaluation ; post-assessment
산 acid
산도 acidity
산무수물 acid anhydride
산미 sour
산부인과 gynecology
산부인과의사 gynecologist
산부인과의학 gynecology
산성도 acidity
산소 oxygen
산소결핍증 anoxia
산소농축기 oxygen concentrator
산소섭취 oxygen intake
산소소비 oxygen consumption
산소요법 oxygen therapy
산아제한 birth control
산업민주주의 industrial democracy
산업사회사업 industrial social work
산업사회학 industrial sociology
산업심리학 industrial psychology
산업재해 workers accident
산업재해보상 workers' compensation
산업재해보상보험
 industrial accident compensation insurance
산업주의 industrialism
산업카운셀링 industrial counseling
산업케이스워크 industrial casework
산업혁명 industrial revolution
산업화 industrialization
산염기조절 acid-base regulation
산염기평형 acid-base balance
산욕감염증 puerperal fever ; childbed fever
산욕열
 puerperal fever ; puerperal sepsis ; childbed
 fever
산입불가능자산 non-countable asset
산테리아 santeria

산혈증 academia ; acidosis
산화에틸렌 가스멸균
 ethylene oxide gas sterilization
산후우울증 postpartum depression
살균작용 bactericidal action
살균제 germicide
살모네라균식중독 salmonella food poisoning
살모넬라균 salmonella
살인 murder
살포 spray
삼각건 sling
삼각지팡이 tripod cane
삼각코너 triangle corner
삼대 영양소 three major nutrients
삼자극치 tristimulus value
삼지마비 triplegia
삼차신경통 trigeminal neuralgia : TN
삼차원 CT three-dimension CT
삼차원 동작해석
 three-dimensional motion analysis
삼차원 보행분석 three-dimensional gait analysis
삼환계 항우울제 tricyclic antidepressant : TCA
상관계수 correlation coefficient
상관관계 correlation
상근환산 full-time equivalent : FTE
상기도기침증후군
 upper airway cough syndrome
상담 counseling
상담센터 advisory center
상담원 counselor
상담원조 counseling and support
상대위험 relative risk
상대적 과잉인구 relation over population
상대적인 위험 relative risk
상동증 stereotype
상동행동 stereotyped behavior
상동행위 stereotyped behavior
상드 Rene Sand
상병급여금 sickness benefit
상병수당금 sickness and injury allowance
상복 mourning
상부소화관 upper gastrointestinal
상부식도괄약근 upper esophageal sphincter : UES

상부식도괄약근장애
  upper esophageal sphincter dysfunction
상속 inheritance
상속세 death tax
상속재산설계 estate planning
상식적 아마추어 prudent lay person
상실 loss
상실체험 lost experience
상업적 활동 commercial activity
상염색체 autosome
상염색체 열성 autosomal recessive
상염색체 열성유전
  autosomal recessive inheritance
상염색체 열성유전병 autosomal recessive disorder
상염색체 우성 autosomal dominant
상염색체 우성유전
  autosomal dominant inheritance
상염색체 우성유전병
  autosomal dominant disorder
상완신경총마비 brachial plexus palsy
상완의수 transhumeral prosthesis
상완절단 above-elbow amputation
상용노동자 regular employee
상위인지 metacognition
상자형 이음새 box joint
상재균 resident bacteria
상재세균총 resident flora
상정요법 sand play technique
상제급여 burial and funeral benefit
상제부조 burial and funeral assistance
상제비용 burial and funeral costs
상제비지출 funeral expenses
상제수당 burial and funeral expenses allowance
상주세균총 indigenous bacterial flora
상지 upper extremity
상지보조기 upper extremity orthosis
상지절단 upper extremity amputation
상징적 장벽 symbolic barrier
상차리기 meal tray services
상처감염 wound infection
상처도포제 wound dressing
상처의 분류 wound classification
상하관계 vertical relationship

상해 injury
상호부조 mutual aid ; mutual assistance
상호원조집단 mutual aid groups
상호작용 reciprocal interactions
상호협력 mutual help
상환액결정방식
  Customary, Prevailing and Reasonable : CPR
상환지불 reimbursement
상황반사 situational reflection
새가슴 pectus excavatum
새니토리움 sanitarium
새디스트 sadist
새로마지플랜 2015 [저출산 · 고령사회 기본계획]
  Newly Introduced Plan 2015 (fundamental
  plan for low birth rate and aging society)
새틀라이트 방식 satellite system
색각항상 color constancy
색도 chromaticity
색맹 color blindness
색상 hue
색상해제 hue cancellation
색약 color weakness
색전 embolism
샌딩 sanding
생검 biopsy
생검겸자 biopsy forceps
생계보호 livelihood aid
생계비 cost of living
생계비 조정 Cost of Living Adjustment : COLA
생계비지수 cost-of-living index
생계수준 subsistence level
생년월일 date of birth
생리적 욕구 physiological needs
생리휴가 leave of absence by menstruation
생명 · 의료윤리 biomedical ethics
생명공학 bioengineering
생명보험 life insurance
생명보험료 life insurance premium
생명서포트서비스 advanced life support : ALS
생명윤리 bioethics
생명의 연장 extension of maximum life span
생명의 전화 life line
생명표 life table

생물연령 biological age
생물재해표시 biohazard mark
생물지표 biological indicator
생물학 패러다임 biological paradigm
생물학적 응답조절물질 biologic response modifier
생물학적 치료법 biological therapy
생물학적 클린룸 biological clean room
생사학 thanatology
생산력 productivity
생산연령인구 working-age population
생산적 복지 productive welfare
생산피로설 production fatigue
생식가족 family of procreation
생식기 genital stage
생식성 generatively
생애교육 lifelong education
생애발달 lifespan development
생애스포츠 lifelong sports
생애임금 lifelong wages
생애주택 lifelong housing
생업부조
    occupational aid ; occupational assistance
생전신탁 living trust
생존권 the right to a decent standard of living
생체간이식 living donor liver transplantation
생체검사 biopsy
생체공학 bioengineering
생체리듬 biological rhythm
생체물질격리 body substance isolation
생체소독 antisepsis
생체소독약 antiseptic agent
생체소독제 antiseptic agent
생체역학 biomechanics
생체전자기학 bioelectromagnetic
생체표면격리 body surface isolation
생태계 ecosystem
생태도 ecomap
생태학 ecology
생태학적 관점 ecological perspective
생태학적 심리학 ecological psychology
생태학적 접근법 ecological approach
생활공간 life space
생활공간위기개입 life space crisis intervention

생활관련활동
    activities parallel to daily living : APDL
생활구조 life structure
생활권 the right to live
생활기능 life functioning
생활기능훈련 life skills training
생활능력 ability to live
생활단계 life stage
생활력 life history
생활만족도 life satisfaction
생활모델 life model
생활모형 life model
생활문제 livelihood problem
생활보호 public assistance
생활보호기준
    public assistance standards ; standards of
    public assistance
생활보호법 Public Assistance Law
생활보호비용 public assistance costs
생활보호수급자 public assistance recipient
생활보호위원회 public assistance committee
생활보호제도 public assistance system
생활복지자금 welfare fund
생활복지자금대출제도 welfare fund loan system
생활부조 daily-needs assistance
생활비용 cost of living
생활비용조정 cost-of-living adjustment : COLA
생활상담원 life management advisor
생활설계 life design
생활수준 standard of living
생활습관 lifestyle
생활습관병 lifestyle-related disease
생활시설 living institution
생활양식 way of life style
생활욕구 life needs
생활원조
    home helping ; living assistance services
생활위생과 Environmental Health Division
생활의 질 quality of life : QOL
생활의 질 평가 quality of life assessment
생활자금 living expense
생활주기 life cycle
생활지도 guidance

생활지도원 daily life guidance counselor
생활지원서비스 living support services
생활협동조합 co-operative union : CO-OP
생활환경 living environment
샤르코관절 Charcot joint
샤워욕 shower bath
샤워용 휠체어 shower wheelchair
샤워의자 shower chair
샤워체어 shower chair
샤이드래거 증후군 Shy-Drager syndrome : SDS
샴푸 shampoo
섕크 shank
서맥 bradycardia
서베일런스 surveillance
서비스계약 service contract
서비스기술 service skill
서비스담당자회의 service staff meeting
서비스메뉴 service menu
서비스목표 goal of services
서비스수준 service level
서비스의 질 quality of service : QOS
서비스의 표준화 standardization of services
서비스이용자 service recipient
서비스접근성 accessibility of service
서비스제공권 service area
서비스제공책임자 service manager
서비스조정 service coordination
서비스체제 national service framework : NSF
서비스추진과
　Customer Service Promotion Division
서비스코드 service code
서비스패키지 services package
서비스평가 evaluation of services
서비스프레임워크
　national service framework : NSF
서스펜션프레임 suspension frame
서양의학 western medicine
서열측정 ordinal measurement
서지컬마스크 surgical mask
서커디안리듬 circadian rhythm
서포트 support
서포트그룹 support group
서포트시스템 support system

서호흡 bradypnea
석사호 master's degree
석세스풀 에이징 successful aging
석션 suction
선가정보호 · 후사회보장
　protection/social security of the elderly first by
　the family, then by the society
선고 truth telling
선골부 sacral region
선발약품 brand name medication
선별적 서비스 selective services
선별적 프로그램 selective programs
선별주의 selectivism
선불제 진료 prepaid medical practice
선불제 집단개원 prepaid group practice : PGP
선원보험 Seamen's Insurance
선원보험법 Seamen's Insurance Law
선종 adenoma
선진국 developed country
선천기형 congenital malformation
선천성 고관절탈구
　congenital hip dislocation ; luxatio coxae
　congenita
선천성 근긴장저하 congenital hypotonia
선천성 근이영양증 congenital muscular dystrophy
선천성 신증후군 congenital nephrotic syndrome
선천이상 congenital anomaly
선추적검사 Trail-Making Test
선취특권 preferential rights
선별고용 selective placement
선택적 세로토닌재흡수저해제
　selective serotonin reuptake inhibitor : SSRI
선택적 정보배포
　selective dissemination of information : SDI
선택적 제도곤궁대상자
　optional categorically needy
선택적 최적화론
　selective optimization with compensation
선택적 추출 selective abstraction
선택주의 selectivism
선행 beneficence
선행성 결장관장 antegrade colonic enema : ACE
선행원리 principle of beneficence

선회대 rotator strap
설근침하 tongue swallowing
설명책임 accountability
설문지 questionnaire
설사 diarrhea
설인신경통 glossopharyngeal neuralgia
설인호흡 glossopharyngeal breathing
설치기준 requirements for establishment
설트랄린 sertraline
설파살라진 sulfasalazine
설폰요소제 sulfonylurea
설하선 sublingual gland
설하정 sublingual tablet
섬광조영술 scintigraphy
섬망 delirium
섬망증 delirium tremens : DTS
섬망평가검사 Delirium Rating Scale
섬망평가척도 Delirium Rating Scale
섬유 fiber
섬유소 fibrin
섬유속자발수축 fasciculation potential
섬유속전위 fasciculation potential
섬유자발전위 fibrillation potential
섬유형 그룹화 fiber type grouping
섭식 food intake
섭식장애 eating disorder
섭식제한 feeding restriction
섭취열량 caloric intake
성 gender
성감염증 sexually transmitted disease : STD
성개발지수
  gender-related development index : GDI
성건강 sexual health
성격 personality ; character
성격검사 personality test
성격구조 personality structure
성격이상 character disorder
성격장애 character disorder
성격진단법 personality diagnosis methods
성격특성항목표 personality inventory
성공보수 contingent fee
성공적인 노화 successful aging
성교동통 dyspareunia

성교동통증 dyspareunia
성교육 sex education
성교통 dyspareunia
성기기 genital stage
성기능장애 sexual dysfunction
성기단계 genital stage
성년후견 adult guardianship
성년후견감독인 supervisor of adult guardian
성년후견인 adult guardian
성년후견제도 adult guardianship system
성동일성장애 gender identity disorder : GID
성문위삼킴 supraglottic swallow
성반응검사 introversion extroversion test
성범죄 sex crime
성별 gender
성별역할분업 sexual division of labor
성역할 gender role
성염색체 sex chromosome
성욕 libido
성인T세포백혈병 · 임파종
  adult T-cell leukemia : ATLL
성인교육 adult education
성인기 adulthood
성인데이센터 adult day center
성인데이헬스케어 adult day health care
성인발달 adult development
성인발병성 adult-onset
성인발병성 관절류머티즘
  adult-onset rheumatoid arthritis : AORA
성인병 adult disease ; diseases of adult people
성인보호서비스
  adult protective services ; adult
  protection services
성인아이 adult children
성인양호시설 adult foster care home
성인용 현재성 불안척도
  Adult Manifest Anxiety Scale
성인잠재성 자기면역성 당뇨병
  latent autoimmune diabetes in adults : LADA
성인주간보호 adult day care
성인주간보호서비스센터 adult day services center
성인주간보호센터 adult day care center
성인형 다능성 간세포

人

multipotent adult progenitor cell

성인호흡곤란증후군
adult respiratory distress syndrome

성장성장률제도
management system of growth rate

성장장애 failure to thrive : FTT

성장호르몬 growth hormone

성적 소수자 sexual minority

성적충동 libido

성적폭력 sexual violence

성적학대 sexual abuse

성적희롱 sexual harassment

성지향장애 sexual orientation disturbance

성차 gender difference

성차별 sex discrimination

성차별주의 sexism

성평등 sexual equality

성폭력 Sexual violence

성폭력피해자지원 간호직
sexual assault nurse examiner

성학대 sexual abuse

성행위 sexual activity

성행위감염증 sexually transmitted disease : STD

성희롱 sexual harassment

세간 E. O. Seguin

세계대공황 Great Depression

세계보건기구 World Health Organization : WHO

세계보건기구헌장
Constitution of the World Health Organization

세계인권선언 Universal Declaration of Human Rights : UDHR

세계인권의 날 World Human Rights Day

세계재활협회 Rehabilitation International : RI

세계적 노화 global aging

세균 bacterium ; bacteria

세균감염 fungal infection

세균뇨 bacteriuria

세균성 폐렴 bacterial pneumonia

세균정착카테터 colonization catheter

세균증식의 병소 focus of colonization

세금 tax

세금공제 tax deduction

세금체납 tax delinquency

세금체납정리기구
delinquent tax collection organization

세금환부 tax rebate

세대〔世帶〕 household

세대간 경계 generation boundary

세대간 관계 intergenerational relations

세대간 부양 intergenerational support

세대간 분쟁 intergenerational conflict

세대간 재분배 intergenerational redistribution

세대간 케어 intergenerational care

세대구조 family structure

세대단위의 원칙
principle of public assistance on a household basis

세돈분류 Seddon's classification

세동맥 arteriole

세동전위 fibrillation potential

세라피 therapy

세라피스트 therapist

세로발활 longitudinal arch

세로토닌 serotonin

세로토닌 노르에피네프린 재흡수억제제
serotonin norepinephrine reuptake inhibitor : SNRI

세면기 washbowl

세미크리티컬 semicritical

세비보 Sebivo

세손가락 집기 three-jaw chuck pinch

세수 face cleaning

세안 face cleaning

세액공제 tax rebate

세절채취법 punch biopsy

세정 washing

세정멸균기 washer sterilizer

세정법 wash method

세정세포진 lavage cytology

세정소독기 washer disinfector

세제 detergent

세제알레르기 detergent allergy

세컨드오피니언 second opinion

세탁 laundry

세탁기 washing machine

세탁실 laundry room

세탁용 비누 laundry soap

세탁용 합성세제 laundry synthetic detergent

세틀먼트 settlement

세틀먼트하우스 settlement house

세프티네트 safety net

섹슈얼 해러스먼트 sexual harassment

섹슈얼리티 sexuality

셀레길린 selegiline

셀레늄 selenium

셀레브렉스 Celebrex

셀리콕시브 celecoxib

셀프어드보카시 무브먼트 self-advocacy movement

셀프케어 self-care

셀프콘트롤 self-control

셀프헬프그룹 self-help group : SHG

소각로 incinerator

소개료 referral fee

소개서비스 referral services

소거현상 extinction

소규모다기능서비스
small-scale multi-functional services

소규모다기능형거택개호 small-scale multi-functional home-based care service

소규모다기능형거택장기요양
small-scale multi-functional home-based care service

소규모다기능형서비스
small-scale multi-functional services

소규모신체장애인요호시설
small-scale custodial facility for the physically disabled

소규모작업소 small-scale workshop

소규모특별양호양로원
small-scale geriatric welfare home for the aged

소급부과 retrospective charge

소급적용 retroactive indication

소나타 Sonata

소년 juvenile

소년감별소 juvenile classification office

소년검찰 juvenile prosecution

소년경찰 juvenile police

소년경찰제도 police work with juveniles

소년교도소 juvenile prison

소년범죄 juvenile delinquency

소년법 Juvenile Law

소년법원제도 juvenile court system

소년보호 juvenile probation

소년보호사 juvenile probation officer

소년비행 juvenile delinquency

소년심판 juvenile justice

소년원 reformatory

소년의 집 boy's house

소년전기 early adolescence

소년중기 middle adolescence

소년후기 late adolescence

소뇌 cerebellum

소독 disinfection ; antisepsis

소독위생처리 sanitization

소독제 disinfectant

소득검사 income test

소득보장 income security

소득분배 income distribution

소득분포 personal income distribution

소득세 income tax

소득월액보험료 monthly premium

소득유지 income maintenance

소득재분배 income redistribution

소득정책 income policy

소득제한 income limit

소득조사 earnings test ; income test

소멸시효 extinctive prescription

소멸현상 extinction

소미브레이스
SOMI brace ; sterno-occipital-mandibular-immobilizer brace

소방대원 Firefighter

소방서 Fire Department

소변 urine

소변기 urinary bottle holder ; urinal

소비생활협동조합
consumers' cooperative association

소비세 consumption tax

소비자 consumer

소비자가격 street value

소비자교육 consumer education

소비자권리그룹 consumer rights group

소비자물가지수 consumer price index : CPI

소비자보호 consumer protection

소비자보호사무소 consumer protection office

소비자운동 consumerism

소비자주의 consumerism

소비자중시의 케어 consumer-directed care

소비자청 Consumer Affairs Agency

소생조치거부 Do Not Resuscitate : DNR

소세포폐암 small cell lung cancer : SCLC

소수민족 ethnic minority

소수집단 minority group

소수파그룹 minority group

소숙사제도 cottage system

소시얼그룹워크 social group work

소시얼니드 social needs

소시얼서비스 social services

소시얼서포트 social support

소시얼서포트네트워크 social support network

소시얼스킬 social skill

소시얼스킬훈련 social skills training : SST

소시얼스터디 social study

소시얼워커 social worker : SW

소시얼워크 social work

소시얼워크박사호
Doctor of Philosophy (Ph. D.) in Social
Work

소시얼워크연구 social work research

소시얼위기관리 social risk management

소시얼인클루전 social inclusion

소시얼인터그룹워크 social intergroup work

소시얼지원 social support

소시얼케이스워크 social case work

소시얼트레이닝 social skills training : SST

소시오그램 sociogram

소시오메트리 sociometry

소아과 pediatric

소아과의사 pediatrician

소아기 붕괴성 장애
childhood disintegrative disorder

소아내시경검사 pediatric endoscopy

소아만성특정질환치료연구사업
medical aid for specific chronic diseases of
children

소아에 대한 2차 구명심폐소생법 및 처치
pediatric advanced life support

소아용 기능독립성평가 WeeFIM

소아자폐증 childhood autism

소아재가의료 pediatric home health

소아재가케어 pediatric home care

소아전문소생술 pediatric advanced life support

소양감 itching

소양증 pruritus

소외 alienation

소음 noise

소자녀화 depopulation

소자사회 society with the declined birth rate

소장 small intestine

소장기능장애
disorders of the small intestinal function

소장폴립 small intestinal polyps

소진 burnout

소집단토의 small group discussion

소켓 socket

소해면상뇌증
bovine spongiform encephalopathy : BSE

소화 digestion

소화관생리학 gastrointestinal physiology

소화기내과의 gastroenterologist

소화기병학 gastroenterology

소화기질환 digestive disease

소화성 궤양 peptic ulcer

소화흡수 digestion and absorption

속건성 손씻기용 제재
waterless handwashing product

속건성 찰식소독약 waterless antiseptic agent

속립결핵증 miliary tuberculosis

속박 constraint

속쓰림 heartburn

속임동작 trick motion

손 hand

손 소독마찰 antiseptic handrub

손가락 끝으로 집기 tip pinch

손가락도말평판법 finger streak plate method

손가락문자 fingerspelling

손가락사다리 finger ladder

손가락소독 hand antisepsis ; hand hygiene

손가락실인증 finger agnosia
손가락위생 hand hygiene
손가락의 오염제거 decontaminate hands
손가락평판도말배양법 finger streak plate method
손등관절보조기 knuckle bender
손발톱굽음증 onychogryphosis
손발톱염 onychia
손상 impairment
손씻기 hand wash
손씻기 소독 antiseptic handwash
손이음새 wrist joint
손자손녀양육 grandparenting
손자손녀키우기 grandparenting
손잡이 handrail
손잡이 설치 handrail installation
손재주 dexterity
손톱 nail ; fingernail
손톱이영양증 onychodystrophy
손해배상청구권
  the right to demand the compensation for
  damage
솜 cotton
송영 transportation
송영서비스 transportation services
송영차 transportation vehicle
쇄골하정맥도관삽입술
  subclavian vein catheterization
쇄골하정맥직접천자법
  subclavian vein catheterization
쇠약 marasmus
쇼그렌 증후군 Sjogren's syndrome
쇼크 shock
숄더서스펜션 shoulder suspension system
수계감염 waterborne infection
수관절배굴장구 cock-up wrist hand orthosis
수급권 the right to receive benefits
수급권 부여 vesting
수급요건 requirements to receive benefits
수급자 recipient
수급조정사업과
  Demand and Supply Adjustment Division
수뇨기 urine collector
수단적 ADL instrumental activities of daily

living : IADL
수단적 일상생활동작능력
  instrumental activities of daily living : IADL
수단적 일상생활활동
  instrumental activities of daily living : IADL
수당 allowance
수덱위축 Sudeck atrophy
수도과 Water Supply Division
수도물 tap water
수동브라이유식 점자타이프라이터
  manual Braille writer ; manual-type Braille
  writer
수동술 mobilization
수동점자타이프라이터 manual Braille writer
수동점자타자기 manual Braille writer
수동흡연 secondhand smoke
수두 chicken pox
수두감염 varicella infection
수두대상포진 varicella zoster
수두대상포진 바이러스 varicella zoster virus
수렴이론 convergence theory
수렴제 astringent
수료율
  percentage of patients receiving medical care
수리과 Actuarial Affairs Division
수리면접 intake interview
수마트립탄 sumatriptan
수막백혈병 meningeal leukemia
수막염 meningitis
수면 sleep
수면관련호흡장애 sleep-related breathing disorder
수면시 무호흡 sleep apnea
수면시 무호흡증후군 sleep apnea syndrome : SAS
수면장애
  sleep disorder ; sleep disturbance ; somnipathy
수면제
  hypnotic drug ; sleep medicine ; sleeping pill ;
  Ambien
수명 lifespan
수명연장 life extension
수반법 basin method
수반성 contingency
수발 assistance ; assistant ; support

수발자 assistant ; supporter
수분 fluid
수분밸런스 fluid balance
수분보급 rehydration
수분섭취 fluid intake
수분출납 fluid intake and output
수산사업 sheltered workshop services
수산시설 sheltered workshop facility
수송 transportation
수수파 minority
수술 surgery
수술부위감염 surgical site infection
수술시 손가락소독 surgical hand antisepsis
수술시 손씻기
　surgical scrub ; surgical hand washing
수술실 operating room : OR ; operating theater
수술실 간호사
　operation room registered nurse : ORRN
수술옷 operating suite
수술용 가운 operation gown
수술전불안 preoperative anxiety
수술전장관세정 preoperative bowel preparation
수술전장관준비 preoperative bowel preparation
수술전장관처리 preoperative bowel preparation
수술전장관처치 preoperative bowel cleaning
수술중 내시경검사 intraoperative endoscopy
수술중 초음파검사 intraoperative ultrasonography
수술창 surgical wound
수술창감염 surgical wound infection
수술창분류 surgical wound classification
수술후 감염 postoperative infection
수양부모 foster care
수양부모제도 foster care system
수양조부모 프로그램 foster grandparent program
수염깎기 shaving
수요 demands
수욕 hand bath
수용 acceptance
수용보호 indoor relief
수용성 가방 water-soluble bag
수용성 비타민 water-soluble vitamin
수용시설 asylum
수용의 원칙 principle of acceptance

수용자 inmate
수용적 태도 receptive attitude
수용치료 residential treatment
수은중독 mercury poisoning
수의수축 voluntary contraction
수의운동 voluntary movement
수익권 the right to receive benefits
수익사업 profit-making business
수익자 beneficiary
수익자부담 benefit principle
수익자부담의 원칙 beneficiary-to-pay principle
수익자청구금 charges to beneficiaries
수입조사 means test
수작업 세정 manual cleaning
수절지배분류 Zancolli classification
수정 물마시기검사 Modified Water Swallow Test
수정 바셀지수 modified Barthel index
수정 애쉬워스척도 Modified Ashworth Scale
수정체 crystal lens
수정체유화흡인술 phacoemulsification
수중운동 underwater exercise
수지검사 digital examination
수지균등의 원칙 principle of equivalence
수지상등의 원칙
　principle of equalization of income and
　expenditure
수지실인증 finger agnosia
수직감염 vertical disease transmission
수질오염 water pollution
수축기압 systolic pressure
수치료 hydrotherapy
수치심 sense of shame
수퍼바이져 supervisor
수퍼비전 supervision
수포 blister
수행기능장애 disorder of executive function
수행기능장애증후군 dysexecutive syndrome
수험수수료 examination fee
수혈 blood transfusion
수형도 tree diagram
수혜지역 catchment area
수화 sign language
수화법 sign language

수화봉사 sign language volunteer work
수화봉사원 sign language volunteer
수화원조 sign language support
수화원조자
　supporter of sign language ; sign language
　supporter
수화통역사 sign language interpreter : SLI
숙변 fecal impaction
숙주기생체관계 host-parasite relationship
순손익 net profit and loss
순어반사 word-for-word reflection
순응 habituation
순환기 cardiology
순환기외과집중치료실
　cardiac surgical intensive care unit
순환운동 circumduction
순환적 인과성 circular causality
순환혈액량감소성쇼크 hypovolemic shock
순회보육 mobile nursery service
순회진료 traveling clinic
술야감염 surgical site infection
숨가쁨 shortness of breath
숨은 문화적 장벽 hidden cultural barrier
숨을 헐떡임 wheeze
숫자등급척도 Numeric Rating Scale : NRS
숫자통증등급 Numeric Rating Scale : NRS
쉐도우워크 shadow work
쉐도윙 shadowing
쉐이핑 shaping
쉼터 shelters
슈트라스부르그시스템 Strassburger System
슈퍼바이저 supervisor
슈퍼바이지 supervisee
슈퍼비전 supervision
스네어 snare
스네어 전기응고 snare electrocoagulation
스노코 draining board (sunoko)
스몬병 subacute myeloopticoneuropathy : SMON
스미스 Adam Smith
스와브 채취 swab collection
스와브법 swab method
스완간즈 카테터 Swan-Ganz catheter
스완네크변형 Swan neck deformity

스웨덴식 무릎장구 Swedish knee cage
스위스형 무릎고정대 Swiss lock
스윙드루보행 swing-through gait
스케락신 Skelaxin
스쿨소시얼워커 school social worker
스쿨카운슬러 school counselor
스크래칭 scratching
스크러브법 scrub method
스크리닝 screening
스키너상자 Skinner box
스키너이론 Skinnerian theory
스키마 schema
스킨십 physical contact
스킬드 널싱홈 skilled nursing home
스태그플레이션 (불황) stagflation
스탬프한천법 stamp agar method
스탭모델 staff model
스터비 stubby
스테레오타이프 stereotype
스테로이드 steroid
스테빌라이저 stabilizer
스텐포드비네법 Stanford Binet test
스토마 stoma
스토마 용품 ostomy aid
스토마케어 stoma care
스트라이드 stride ; stride length
스트레서 stressor
스트레스 stress
스트레스 면역훈련 stress inoculation training
스트레처 stretcher
스트레칭 stretching
스트렝스 시점 strengths perspective
스티그마 stigma
스티그마티제이션 stigmatization
스포츠시설 sports facility
스폰지목욕 sponge bath
스프린트 splint
스프링클러 sprinkler
스피로놀락톤 spironolactone
스피리츄얼 케어 spiritual care
스피리츄얼 페인 spiritual pain
스핀햄랜드 Speenhamland
스핀햄랜드제도 Speenhamland system

슬관절 신장보조장치 knee extension assist
슬관절의족 knee disarticulation prosthesis
슬관절치환술 knee replacement
슬라이드제 sliding scale
슬라이딩 스케일 sliding scale
슬라이딩 튜브 sliding tube
슬럼 slum
슬로프 slope
슬링 sling
슬좌위 kneel sitting
습관성 약물 addictive drug
습성온열 moist heating
습식세탁 wet cleaning
습열멸균 moist heat sterilization
습진 eczema
습포 cataplasm
승낙 acceptance
승모판폐쇄부전 mitral regurgitation
승모판협착증 mitral stenosis
승수이론 theory of multiplier
승화 sublimation
시각 sense of sight
시각대행 vision substitution
시각상사척도 Visual Analog Scale : VAS
시각실인 visual agnosia
시각장애
  visual impairment ; visual deficit ; visual
  disability ; visual disorder ; visual disturbance
시각장애인
  the visually impaired ; visually disabled ;
  visually impaired
시각장애인 정보제공시설
  information services facility for the visually
  impaired
시각장애인갱생시설
  rehabilitation facility for the visually impaired
시각장애인용 신호기
  audible pedestrian traffic signal
시각장애인용 점자 Braille
시각장애인용 점자블록 Braille block
시각장애인용 점자용구 Braille writing equipment
시각장애인용 점자타이프라이터 Braille typewriter
시각장애인용 촉독 Braille reading

시각제한 visual limitation
시각통증척도 Visual Analog Scale : VAS
시계그리기 검사 Clock Drawing Test : CDT
시공간실인 visual spatial agnosia
시군구 city and wards
시능훈련사 orthoptist : ORT
시니어센터 senior center
시니어자원봉사 senior volunteer
시니어주택 senior housing
시니어컴퍼니언 프로그램
  Senior Companion Program
시력 visual acuity ; vision
시력장애
  visual impairment ; visual deficit ; visual
  disability ; visual disorder ; visual disturbance
시력저하 vision loss
시립병원 city hospital
시메티딘 cimetidine
시민 citizen
시민권 citizenship
시민권이론 citizenship theory
시민법 Civil Law
시민사회 civil society
시민생활상담소 citizen's advice bureau
시민운동 citizen movement
시민의식 civic consciousness
시민적 및 정치적 권리에 관한 국제규약
  International Covenant on Civil and Political
  Rights
시민참가 citizen participation
시봄보고서 Seebohm Report
시부트라민 Sibutramine
시빌미니멈 civil minimum
시사회복지협의회
  City Council of Social Welfare
시설 facility
시설개호 institutional care
시설개호서비스 institutional care services
시설관리 facility management
시설기반형 서비스 facility-based services
시설병 hospitalism
시설보호 institutional care
시설복지 institutional welfare

시설복지서비스 institutional welfare services
시설서비스 institutional services
시설서비스계획 institutional services plan
시설수용 admissions
시설실습 institutional training
시설운영 facility administration
시설자원봉사 facility volunteer
시설장 administrator
시설장기요양서비스 institutional care services
시설주의 institutionalism
시설케어 institutional care
시설케어서비스 institutional care services
시설케어플랜 care plan for institutional care
시설환경 institutional environment
시세포 photoreceptor
시스템적 시점 systems perspective
시안아미드 cyanamide
시야장애
    visual impairment ; visual deficit ; visual
    disability ; visual disorder ; visual disturbance
시야협착 visual field restriction
시용기간 probationary employment period
시장경제 market economy
시장바구니방식 market basket method
시장성 테스트 market testing
시장원리 market mechanism
시장의 성공 market success
시장의 실패 market failure
시정촌 municipality
시정촌 개호보험사업계획
    municipality's long-term care insurance
    program plan
시정촌 보건센터 municipal health center
시정촌 사회복지협의회
    municipal council of social welfare
시정촌 일반회계 municipality's general account
시정촌 특별급부 special municipal benefit
시정촌 합병
    consolidation of municipalities ; municipal
    consolidation
시지각 visual perception
시청각교육 audio visual education
시청각라이브러리 audio visual library

시청각장애인 정보제공시설
    information services facility for the visually
    and auditorially impaired
시체검안서
    medical certificate of the cause of death
시트교환 changing bed sheets
시판약 over-the-counter medication
식단 menu
식도 esophagus
식도내압검사 esophageal manometry
식도단계 esophageal phase
식도운동장애 esophageal motility disorder
식물군 flora
식물상 flora
식물상태 vegetative state
식물섬유 dietary fiber
식물성 식품 vegetable food
식사 meal
식사관리 meal management
식사동작 eating ; feeding activity
식사보조
    eating assistance ; assistance with eating
식사서비스 meal services
식사요법 nutrition therapy
식사용구 eating tool ; tools for eating
식사원조
    eating assistance ; assistance with eating
식사제한 dietary restriction
식사준비 meal preparation
식사케어
    eating assistance ; assistance with eating
식사택배서비스 delivered meals
식생활 dietary life
식습관 eating habit ; dietary habit
식염 salt
식욕 appetite
식욕부진 loss of appetite
식욕저하 loss of appetite
식욕중추 appetite center
식이장애 eating disorder
식중독 food poisoning
식품구입권 food stamps
식품안전부 Department of Food Safety

식품오염 food contamination
식품위생 food sanitation
식품위생감시원 food inspector
식품위생관리자
food safety and sanitation supervisor
식품위생법 Food Sanitation Law
식품조리 food preparation
식행동 이상 eating disorder
신결석 kidney stone
신경관계질환 neuromuscular disease
신경교액 nerve entrapment
신경근결출손상 root avulsion injury
신경근증 radiculopathy
신경근촉통법
neuromuscular facilitation technique
신경발달적 접근법 neurodevelopmental approach
신경변성 질환 neurodegenerative disease
신경블록 nerve block
신경생리학 neurophysiology
신경생리학자 neurophysiologist
신경생리학적 접근법 neurophysiological approach
신경성 관절 Charcot joint
신경성 대식증 bulimia nervosa
신경성 무식욕증 anorexia nervosa
신경성 방광 bladder hypotonia
신경성 식욕부진증 anorexia nervous
신경순환무력증 neurocirculatory asthenia
신경심리학 neuropsychology
신경심리학자 neuropsychologist
신경심리학적 검사 neuropsychological test
신경심리학적 평가 neuropsychological evaluation
신경안정제 barbiturates
신경안정제 남용 tranquilizer abuse
신경원성 근위축 neurogenic muscle atrophy
신경원성 동통 neuropathic pain
신경원성 쇼크 neurogenic shock
신경원성 폐수종 neurogenic pulmonary edema
신경인성 방광 neurogenic bladder
신경장애 neuropathy
신경전도속도 nerve conduction velocity : NCV
신경제거 denervation
신경조직 nervous tissue
신경종양의 neuro-oncologist

신경종양학 neuro-oncology
신경증 neurosis
신경증성 장애 neurotic disorder
신경통 neuralgia
신경학 neurology
신경학문적 검사 neurological examination
신경학문적 상태 neurological condition
신경학자 neurologist
신골드플랜 New Gold Plan for the Elderly
신구빈법 New Poor Law
신국국민생활지표 People's Life Indicators
신뢰 대 불신 trust versus mistrust
신뢰관계 rapport
신뢰관계의 구축 building rapport
신뢰도 reliability
신발 footwear
신변자립 physical independence
신보수주의 neoconservatism
신부전 kidney failure ; renal failure
신분증명서 identification
신산업도시 newly developed industrial city
신상감독과 보호 personal guardianship
신상감호 personal guardianship
신생아 neonate
신생아사망율 neonatal deaths rate
신생아집중치료실
neonatal intensive care unit : NICU
신생아행동평가
Neonatal Behavior Assessment Scale
신암 kidney cancer
신엔젤플랜 New Angel Plan for Children
신연방주의 new federalism
신용실추행위의 금지
prohibition of acts causing discredit ;
Prohibition of Acts to Damage Impartiality
신우신염 pyelonephritis
신우조영 pyelography
신의료임상연수제도
new clinical training system of primary care
신자유주의 neoliberal
신장 [伸長] extension
신장 [腎臟] kidney
신장구축 extension contracture

신장기능 renal function
신장기능장애 disorders of the kidney function
신장내과의 nephrologist
신장운동 stretching exercise
신장전문의 nephrologist
신장지속 prolonged stretching
신장질환 kidney disease
신장학 nephrology
신적제 nephrectomy
신종감염질병 emerging infectious disease
신중간층 new middle classes
신청보호의 원칙
  principle of public assistance based on
  application
신청자 applicant
신체개호 personal care
신체구속 physical restraint
신체기능 physical function
신체기능검사 physical performance test : PPT
신체둔감 physical deconditioning
신체메커닉스 body mechanism
신체반사 body reflection
신체보조 personal care
신체상 body image
신체원조 physical assistance
신체의존 physical dependence
신체장기요양 personal care
신체장애 physical disability
신체장애가 없는 빈곤자 able body poor
신체장애고령자 the physically disabled elderly
신체장애노인 physically disabled aged person
신체장애아 the physically disabled child
신체장애아개호지원
  care management for the physically disabled
  children
신체장애유아 physically disabled infant
신체장애인 (아) physical handicapped person
신체장애인간호
  nursing care for the physically disabled
신체장애인개호
  caring for the physically disabled ; care for the
  physically disabled
신체장애인개호지원

care management for the physically disabled ;
  disability care management
신체장애인갱생기금
  rehabilitation fund for the physically disabled
신체장애인갱생상담소
  rehabilitation counseling center for physically
  disabled
신체장애인갱생시설
  rehabilitation facility for the physically disabled ;
  rehabilitation facility for persons with
  disabilities
신체장애인갱생원호시설
  rehabilitation and assistance center for the
  physically disabled ; rehabilitation facility for
  persons with disabilities
신체장애인거택간호
  home-based care for the physically disabled
신체장애인거택개호지원
  home-based care management for the disabled
신체장애인고용
  employment of the physically disabled
신체장애인고용율
  employment rates of the physically disabled ;
  employment rates for persons with physically
  disabilities
신체장애인고용촉진
  employment promotion for the physically
  disabled
신체장애인고용촉진대책 employment promotion
  policy for the physically disabled
신체장애인단기입소
  short-stay for the physically disabled
신체장애인대상 민간서비스
  private services for the physically disabled
신체장애인복지
  welfare for the physically disabled
신체장애인복지법
  Act on Welfare of Physically Disabled Persons
신체장애인복지사
  welfare officer for the physically disabled
신체장애인복지센터
  welfare center for the physically disabled
신체장애인복지심의회

人

Advisory Council for the Welfare of Physically Disabled Persons

신체장애인복지작업소
welfare workshop for the physically disabled

신체장애인복지홈
welfare home for the physically disabled

신체장애인부조
assistance for the physically disabled

신체장애인사회참가촉진센터
promotion center of social participation for the physically disabled

신체장애인상담원
advisor for the physically disabled

신체장애인수산시설
sheltered workshop for the physically disabled

신체장애인수첩
physical disability certificate handbook

신체장애인요호시설
custodial care facility for the physically disabled

신체장애인운동
movement for the physically disabled

신체장애인원조
support for the physically disabled

신체장애인의료
medical care for the physically disabled

신체장애인작업소
workshop for the physically disabled

신체장애인장애정도등급표 list of disability grading

신체장애인재가개호지원
home care management for the disabled

신체장애인주간보호서비스
day care services for the physically disabled

신체장애인주간보호서비스센터
day services center for the physically disabled

신체장애인통소수산시설
sheltered workshop for the physically disabled

신체장애인홈헬프서비스
home help services for the physically disabled

신체적 공격 physical aggression

신체적 원인론 somatogenesis

신체적 일상생활동작능력
Physical Activities of Daily Living : PADL

신체적 학대 physical abuse

신체조정
physical conditioning ; body composition

신체지향심리요법 body-centered psychotherapy

신체형장애 somatoform disorders

신체활동량 physical activity

신체활동지원 personal hygiene assistance

신축법 sliding scale

신크로니시티 synchronicity

신티그래피 scintigraphy

신프로이트학파 neo-Freudian

신형특별양호케어 unit-based care

실금 incontinence

실금케어 incontinence care

실금평가 assessment of urinary incontinence

실기시험 professional practice examination

실내기후 room climate ; indoor climate

실내보행 walk in room

실레지아 밴드 Silesian bandage

실리콘제 소프트라이너 silicone soft liner

실리콘제내 소켓
Icelandic roll on silicone socket : ICEROSS

실명 blindness

실무경험증명서 proof of work experience

실무교육 field instruction

실무능력 competency-based practice

실무분야 fields of practice

실무이론 practice theory

실무지식 practice wisdom

실버라이프스타일 senior lifestyle

실버산업 elderly market

실버산업육성추진위원회
Elderly Market Development & Promotion Committee

실버서비스 silver service ; senior service

실버타운 silver town ; senior town

실버홈 senior home

실비노인복지주택
welfare housing at cost for the aged

실비양로시설 endowment facilities at cost

실비요양시설 private care home

실서증 agraphia ; dysgraphia

실성증 aphonia

실수입 actual income ; real income
실수입 이외의 수입
  income other than actual income
실습지도자 field instructor
실신 fainting
실어 aphasia
실어증 aphasia
실업 unemployment
실업급여 unemployment benefit
실업률 unemployment rate
실업문제 unemployment problem
실업보상 unemployment compensation
실업보험 Unemployment Insurance
실업수당 dole
실역연령 chronological age
실연령 chronological age
실용주의 pragmatism
실인 agnosia
실적주의 performance principle
실조 detrusor-sphincter dyssynergia : DSD
실조보행 ataxic gait
실조성 파행 ataxic gait
실존적 요법 existential therapy
실존주의 existentialism
실증주의 positivism
실지출 actual expenditure ; real expenditure
실질생계비 actual cost of living
실질수지 net balance of the settled account
실질임금 actual wage
실천연구 action research
실행증 apraxia
심계항진 palpitation
심근경색 myocardial infarction
심근허혈 myocardial ischemia
심기증 hypochondria
심령치료 mesmerize
심리 · 성적 단계 psychosexual stages
심리 · 성적 발달이론 psychosexual development
심리검사 psychological test
심리극 psychodrama
심리극요법 psychodrama therapy
심리사회발달이론
  psychological development theory

심리사회치료 psychosocial therapy
심리사회평가 psychosocial assessment
심리요법 psychotherapy
심리재활을 위한 작업치료
  diversional occupational therapy
심리적 외상 psychic trauma
심리적 재활 psychological rehabilitation
심리적 지지 psychological support
심리적 학대
  emotional abuse ; psychological abuse
심리치료 psychotherapy
심리치료자 psychotherapist
심리테스트 psychological test
심리판정원 psychological evaluator
심리평가 psychological assessment
심리학 psychology
심리학자 psychologist
심박수 heart rate
심박출량 cardiac output
심발타 Cymbalta
심방 atrium
심방기외 수축 premature atrial contraction : PAC
심방세포 atrial fibrillation
심방중격결손증 atrial septal defect
심부감각 deep sensation
심부뇌자극술 deep brain stimulation
심부전 heart failure
심부정맥혈전증 deep vein thrombosis
심사관리과 Evaluation and Licensing Division
심사청구 certification appeal
심상 image
심스위 Sims' position
심신모약 diminished capacity
심신상실 insanity
심신의학 mind-body medicine
심신장애 mental and physical disability
심신장애아
  the physically and mentally disabled child
심신장애아시설
  facility for the physically and mentally disabled
  children
심신장애아홈헬프서비스
  home help services for the physically and

mentally disabled children
심신장애인 the physically and mentally disabled
심신장애인시설
facility for the physically and mentally disabled
심신장애인홈헬프서비스
home help services for the physically and
mentally disabled
심신증 psychosomatic disease : PSD
심실기외 수축
premature ventricular contraction : PVC
심실세동 ventricular fibrillation
심실중격결손 ventricular septal defect : VSD
심에코 echocardiography ; cardiac ECHO
심원성 쇼크 cardiac shock
심원성 폐수종 cardiogenic pulmonary edema
심의회 council ; advisory committee
심인 psychogenesis
심인반응 psychogenic reaction
심장 heart
심장고동 palpitation
심장기능장애 disorders of the heart function
심장마사지 cardiac massage
심장병학 cardiology
심장부정맥 cardiac dysrhythmia
심장분로 cardiac shunt
심장외과관련감염
cardiac surgery-related infection
심장재활 cardiac rehabilitation
심장초음파검사 ultrasound cardiography
심장카테터법 heart catheterization

심장판막증 valvular heart disease
심장핵의학 cardiac nuclear medicine
심전도 electrocardiogram : ECG
심질환 heart disease
심첨박동 apex beat
심초음파 echocardiography
심초음파도 echocardiogram
심층케이스워크 intensive casework
심폐뇌소생법
cardiopulmonary cerebral resuscitation : CPCR
심폐소생법 cardiopulmonary resuscitation : CPR
심폐소생술거부 DNR< Do Not Resuscitate >
심포지움 symposium
심혈관·대사질환리스크 cardiometabolic risk
심혈관리스크 cardiovascular risk
심혈관질환 cardiovascular disease
심흉곽비 cardiothoracic ratio
심흉비 cardiothoracic ratio
십분위분배율 decimal distribution ratio
십쓰리A CYP-3A
싱크대 sink
쌍극 I형 장애 bipolar I disorder
쌍극 II형 장애 bipolar II disorder
쌍극성 장애 bipolar disorder
쌍무적 부양 bilateral support
쌕쌕거림 wheeze
쐐기 wedge
쐐기상 족저판 wedged insole
쓴 맛 bitter

아급성 케어시설 subacute care facility
아나킨라 anakinra
아나프라닐 Anafranil
아나프록스 Anaprox
아나필라틱 쇼크 anaphylactic shock
아네톨트리티온 anethole trithione
아노미 anomie
아놀드키아리증후군 Arnold-Chiari malformation
아니사키스 anisakis
아달리무맵 adalimumab
아데포비어 디피복실 adefovir dipivoxil
아동 children
아동 성적학대 child sexual abuse
아동 정신분석 child psychoanalysis
아동 정신치료 child psychotherapy
아동과 Children's Bureau
아동관
  child welfare residential facility ; children's
  house ; children's hall
아동구호연 Save the Children Federation
아동구호협회 Children's Aid Society
아동권리선언
  Declaration of the Rights of the Child
아동기 childhood
아동기 장애 childhood disorder
아동기 정신분열증 Childhood schizophrenia
아동긴급보호시설 children's shelter
아동문제 children's problems
아동문화 child culture
아동방임 child neglect
아동방치 child neglect
아동보호 child care
아동보호 사회사업가 child care worker

아동보호기금 Children's Defense Fund
아동보호서비스 child protective service
아동복지 child welfare
아동복지계획 child welfare plan
아동복지기관 child welfare agency
아동복지법 Child Welfare Law
아동복지사 child welfare officer
아동복지서비스 child welfare services
아동복지시설 child welfare facility
아동복지심의회
  Advisory Council on Child Welfare
아동상담소 child guidance center
아동상담원 advisor for children's issues
아동수당 children's allowances
아동수당법 Child Allowance Law
아동심리학 child psychology
아동양육보호권 custody of children
아동옹호 child advocacy
아동원 children's hall
아동원조협회 Children's Aid Society
아동위원 commissioned child welfare volunteer
아동유괴 child snatching
아동으로서의 의무 filial duty
아동자립지원 independence support for children
아동중심적교육 child centered education
아동지원국
  Office of Child Support Enforcement
아동학대 child abuse
아동학대방지법 Child Abuse Prevention Law
아동학대보호서비스 child protective services
아동행동과다증후군 hyperactive child syndrome
아동헌장 Children's Charter
아동후견 child custody

아동후생시설 children's recreational facility
아령 dumbbell
아리셉트 Aricept
아메리칸 인디언 American Indian
아미노산 amino acid
아미오다론 Amiodarone
아미트립틸린 Amitriptyline
아밀라아제 amylase
아베이론의 야생아 Wild Boy of Aveyron
아벨체위 Abel position
아보다트 Avodart
아브라함 Harold Maslow Abraham
아세트아미노펜 Acetaminophen
아스퍼거증후군 Asperger syndrome
아스페르질루스증 aspergillosis
아스피린 aspirin
아스피린요법 aspirin therapy
아시데미아 acidemia
아시드시스 acidosis
아시아계 미국인 Asian American
아시아계미국인사회사업가협회
　　Asian American Social Workers : AASW
아시클로버 acyclovir
아연 zinc
아웃리치 outreach
아웃브레이크 outbreak
아유르베다 의학 ayurvedic medicine
아이 child ; children
아이덴티티 identity
아이뱅크 eye bank
아이솔레이터 isolator
아이수당 child allowance
아이스팩 ice pack
아이싱 icing
아이큐 intelligence quotient : IQ
아이큐 테스트 IQ test
아자티오프린 Azathioprine
아치서포트 arch support
아카데미아 academia
아카티시아 akathisia
아캄프로세이트 acamprosate
아쿠아운동 aquatic exercise
아큐프릴 Accupril

아킬레스건 Achilles tendon
아킬레스건 연장술 Achilles tendon lengthening
아탈구 subluxation
아테롬 atheroma
아테토시스 athetosis
아테토제 athetosis
아토피 atopy
아토피기침 atopic cough
아토피성 피부염 atopic dermatitis
아티반 Ativan
아파르트헤이트 apartheid
아편류 관련장애 opioid-related disorder
아편의존 opiate dependence
아편중독 opiate addiction
아포 spore
아폴리포 단백질 apolipoprotein
아픈 쪽 affected part of the body
악력 grip strength
악마연구 demonology
악마추방 exorcism
악마학 demonology
악몽 nightmare
악성관절류머티즘 malignant rheumatoid arthritis
악성빈혈 pernicious anemia
악성종양 malignant tumor ; cancerous growth
악토넬 Actonel
안경 glasses
안경사 optometrist
안과의 ophthalmologist
안과학 ophthalmology
안구은행 eye bank
안내렌즈 intraocular lens : IOL
안내상담역 guidance counselor
안내서 hand-assisted escort
안내압 intraocular pressure
안드로겐 androgen
안드로겐 제거요법
　　androgen deprivation therapy : ADT
안락 comfort
안락뇨기 comfortable urinary aid
안락사 euthanasia
안락의자 rocking chair
안락의자형 rocking chair-type

안락한 체위 comfortable position
안마사[남성] masseur
안마사[여성] masseuse
안면 quiet sleep
안면견갑상완근이영양
  facioscapulohumeral muscular dystrophy
안면마비 facial paralysis
안면보호실드마스크 face shield mask
안면신경마비 facial paralysis ; Bell's palsy
안면실인증 prosopagnosia
안면원조 support of quiet sleep
안부확인 safety confirmation
안부확인시스템 safety confirmation system
안압계 tonometry
안전과 Safety Division
안전관리 safety control
안전관리체제 safety control system
안전대책과 Safety Division
안전망 safety net
안전문제 safety issue
안전벨트 harness
안전보건관리 safety and health control
안전욕구 safety needs
안전위생부
  Industrial Safety and Health Department
안전지도 safety education
안정성 stability
안정시 에너지소비량
  resting energy expenditure : REE
안정침상 lying position for rest ; bed rest
안정피로 asthenopia
안질 eye disease
안창 insole
알닥타자이드 Aldactazide
알닥톤 Aldactone
알람 alarm ; alert safety system
알래스카 원주민 Alaska Natives
알레르기 allergy
알레르기 반응 allergic reaction
알레르기성 기관지염 allergic bronchitis
알레르기성 비염 allergic rhinitis
알레르기성 소양증 allergic pruritus
알렌드로네이트 alendronate

알리 Alli
알마아타선언
  Alma-Ata Declaration ; Declaration of
  Alma-Ata
알모너 almoner
알아논 Al-Anon
알츠하이머병 Alzheimer's disease
알츠하이머형 치매
  senile dementia of the Alzheimer's type : SDAT
알츠하이머형인지증 불쾌평가척도
  Discomfort Scale for Dementia of the
  Alzheimer's Type : DS-DAT
알츠하이머형치매 불쾌평가척도
  Discomfort Scale for Dementia of the
  Alzheimer's Type : DS-DAT
알칼로혈증 alkalosis
알칼리혈증 alkalemia
알코올 alcohol
알코올 손세정제
  alcohol-based handrub ; alcohol- containing
  antiseptic handrub
알코올남용 alcohol abuse
알코올성 간염 alcoholic hepatitis
알코올성 뇌장애 alcoholic encephalopathy
알코올성 정신병 alcoholic psychosis
알코올소비 alcohol consumption
알코올의존증 alcoholism
알코올정신병 alcoholic psychosis
알코올중독 alcoholics ; alcoholism
알코올중독자갱생회 Alcoholics Anonymous : AA
알코올중독환자 alcoholics patient
알코올환각증
  alcoholic hallucinosis ; alcohol-related psychosis
암 cancer
암 레스트 armrest
암 서포트 arm support
암 슬링 arm sling
암내 axillary osmidrosis
암로디핀 Amlodipine
암명순응 dark/light adaptation
암모니아 ammonia
암모니아 해독 ammonia detoxification
암비엔 Ambien

암선고 truth telling
암성동통 carcinomatous pain
암소시휘도 scotopic luminance
암순응 dark adaptation
암스하우스 almshouse
암시된 동의 implied consent
암진료 연계거점병원 designated cancer hospital
암치료 cancer treatment
암치료기능평가
  Functional Assessment of Cancer Therapy :
  FACT
암페타민 amphetamine
암환자 cancer patient
압력단체 pressure group
압력파 pressure wave
압박 pressure
압박골절 compression fracture
압박궤양
  pressure ulcer ; decubitus ulcer ; pressure sore
압축기록 compressed recording
앙와위 supine position
앞치마 apron
애도 mourning
애도증 bereavement
애드버킷 advocate
애드보커시 advocacy
애드빌 Advil
애쉬워스척도 Ashworth Scale
애착 attachment
액모 under arm hair
액성조절 humoral regulation
액션 action
액션리서치 action research
액션시스템 action system
액와체온 axillary temperature
액체비누 liquid soap
액취 axillary osmidrosis ; osmidrosis axillae
액티버티 activity
액티버티 서비스 activity services
액틴 actin
앤지오텐신 angiotensin
앤지오텐신 변환효소 억제제
  angiotensin-converting- enzyme inhibitor : ACE

inhibitor
앤터뷰스 Antabuse
앨리지빌리티 eligibility
앰비밸런스 ambivalence
야간대응형 방문개호 night home care
야간병원 night hospital
야간보육 night care for children
야간보조기 night orthosis
야간보호 night care
야간섬망 night-time delirium
야간학교 night school
야경국가 night watchman state
야근 night shift
야뇨증 enuresis ; nocturia
야맹 night blindness
야비스클라이언트 YAVIS client
야콥병 Creutzfeldt-Jakob disease : CJD
야타베 기르포드 성격검사
  Yatabe-Guilford Personality Test
약 drug
약가기준 drug tariff standards
약값규제 drug price controls
약국 pharmacy
약리학적 변화 pharmacodynamic change
약물갱생시설 awakening recovery center
약물구속 chemical restraint
약물남용 drug abuse
약물남용 적발 drug abuse detection
약물내성 drug tolerance
약물동태적 변화 pharmacokinetic change
약물미사용 drug free
약물발진 drug rash
약물상호작용 medication interaction
약물알레르기 drug allergy
약물요법 pharmacotherapy
약물유발성 간염 drug-induced hepatitis
약물유발성 간질환 drug-induced liver disease
약물유발성 골다공증 drug-induced osteoporosis
약물유발성 급성췌장염
  drug-induced acute pancreatitis
약물유발성 루푸스 drug-induced lupus
약물유발성 만성췌장염
  drug-induced chronic pancreatitis

약물유발성 정신병 drug-induced psychosis
약물유발성 정신분열증
drug-induced Schizophrenia
약물유발성 췌장염 drug-induced pancreatitis
약물유발성 통합실조증
drug-induced Schizophrenia
약물유발성 파킨슨증 drug-induced Parkinsonism
약물유발성 혈소판감소성 자반병
drug-induced thrombocytopenic purpura
약물유발성 홍반성낭창
drug-induced lupus erythematosus
약물유해반응 adverse drug reaction : ADR
약물의존 drug dependence
약물중독 drug addiction
약물탐닉 drug habituation
약물항콜린제 Benztropine
약사감시 pharmaceutical inspection
약사감시원 pharmaceutical inspector
약사법 Pharmaceutical Affairs Law
약속 appointment
약시 weak eye sight
약식상해등급 Abbreviated Injury Scale : AIS
약어와 정의 acronym and definition
약제 medication
약제관리 medication management
약제기인성 정신병 drug-induced psychosis
약제기인성 혈소판감소증
drug-induced thrombocytopenia
약제비 pharmaceutical costs
약제사 pharmacist
약진 drug rash
약탈 predation
약품요법 pharmacotherapy
약해 drug-induced suffering
약화된 숙주 compromised host
약화예방 deconditioning prevention
약효과 소실현상 wearing-off phenomenon
양가감정 ambivalence
양극 anode
양극장애 bipolar disorder
양극화 polarization
양도소득과세 capital gains tax
양로시설 home for the aged

양로원
almshouse ; beadhouse ; care home for the aged
양면가치 ambivalence
양반다리 앉기 tailor sitting ; crossed leg sitting
양성 소유 androgyny
양성계면활성제 amphoteric surface active agent
양성모델 positive mold
양성소견 positive finding
양성애 bisexuality
양성예파 positive sharp wave
양성전해질 ampholyte ; amphoteric electrolyte
양성증상 positive symptom
양성훈련제도 apprenticeship
양수검사 amniocentesis
양수진단 amniocentesis
양심 conscience
양압실 pressurized room
양연보호 foster care
양육 bringing up ; care and education
양육방치 neglect
양육비용 costs for bringing up a child
양육비지출 expenses for bringing up a child
양육의료 medical aid for premature infants
양육자 person bringing up
양육지도
care and education for the disabled children
양자 adopted child
양자결연 adoption
양자발생 bimodal
양적연구 quantitative research
양적조사 quantitative investigation
양전자방출 단층촬영술
positron emission tomography : PET
양지위 proper functional position
양측마비 diplegia
양치질 gargling
양친자관계 foster parent
양키시티조사 Yankee City Study
양호교사 school nurse
양호노인홈 residential home for the elderly
양호시설
residential care home for children ; children's
home

양호실 school infirmary
양호아동 child in need of protection
양호학교 school for the physically and mentally disabled children ; school for the disabled children
어그레시브 케이스워크 aggressive casework
어깨 인핀지먼트 증후군 shoulder impingement syndrome
어깨걸이띠 shoulder suspension system
어깨뼈 외전보조기 airplane splint
어깨회전운동기 shoulder wheel
어덜트칠드런 adult children
어드미니스트레이션 administration
어메니티 amenity
어세스먼트 assessment
어세스먼트 시트 assessment sheet
어음청취역치 speech reception threshold : SRT
어음청취역치검사 speech reception threshold test
어치료 speech therapy
어카운터빌리티 accountability
억압 repression
억울 depression
억울형 depression type
억제 restraint
억제대 restraining tie
언더암 브레이스 underarm brace
언어 language
언어기능장애 speech disorders
언어능력 speech
언어성 기억 verbal memory
언어심리학 psycholinguistics
언어요법 speech therapy
언어요법사 speech therapist
언어의 명료성 speech clarity
언어장애 speech-language impediment ; verbal disorder
언어장애인 speech disorders
언어적 공격 verbal aggression
언어적 커뮤니케이션 verbal communication
언어청각사 speech-language-hearing therapist : ST
언어청각요법 speech-language therapy
언어청각재활 speech-language rehabilitation
언어청각훈련 speech-language training

언어치료 speech therapy
언어치료사 speech therapist : ST
언어훈련 speech and language training
얼라이먼트 alignment
얼룩빼기 stain removal
얼음베개 ice pillow
얼음주머니 ice bag
엄중격리 strict isolation
엄지손가락 버팀목 thumb post
엄지손가락 지문 thumbprint
업무독점 monopolization
업무메뉴얼 practice manual
업무상 폭로 occupational exposure
에고 ego
에나라프릴 enalapril
에나멜질 enamel
에너지 energy
에너지대사율 relative metabolic rate : RMR
에너지소비 energy expenditure
에너지필요량 energy requirement
에덴대안 Eden Alternative
에디슨병 Addison's disease
에로스 Eros
에르고노믹스 ergonomics
에르고미터 ergometer
에리스로포이에틴 erythropoietin
에비스타 Evista
에스니시티 ethnicity
에스타졸람 estazolam
에스테라제 esterase
에스테이트플래닝 estate planning
에스트로겐 estrogen
에스트로겐 보충요법 estrogen replacement therapy : ERT
에어레이션 aeration
에어리어 서비스 area services
에어리크 air leak
에어매트 air mattress
에어샤워 air shower
에어웨이 airway
에어커튼 air curtain
에어트래핑 air trapping
에어패드 air sleeping pad

에어필터 air filter

에이즈
acquired immune deficiency syndrome : AIDS

에이지즘 ageism

에이프런 apron

에이형 성격 Type A personality

에코맵 eco map

에코부머 echo boomer

에코주택 echo housing

에콜로지운동 ecology movement

에크린샘 eccrine gland

에타너셉트 etanercept

에토프로파진 ethopropazine

에티켓 etiquette

에틸렌옥시드 가스멸균
ethylene oxide gas sterilization

에피소드기억 episodic memory

엑셀론 Exelon

엑소시즘 exorcism

엑스 염색체 X chromosome

엔도톡신검사 endotoxin test

엔드 오브 라이프 케어 end-of-life care

엔브렐 Enbrel

엔젤플랜 Angel Plan

엔지오텐신 II 수용체 길항제
angiotensin II receptor antagonist

엔카운터집단 basic encounter group

엔클로우저운동 enclosure movement

엔타카폰 entacapone

엔테로바이러스 enterovirus

엔테카비어 entecavir

엔트로피 entropy

엘데프릴 Eldepryl

엘렉트라 콤플렉스 Electra complex

엘리자베스 1세 Queen Elizabrth I

엘리자베스 구빈법 Elizabethan Poor Laws

엘버펠드제도 Elberfeld System

엥겔 Christian Lorenz Ernst Engel

엥겔계수 Engel's coefficient

엥겔법칙 Engel's Law

엥겔스 Friedrich Engels

여가 leisure

여가관리 leisure time management

여가이용 use of leisure time

여가지도 leisure guidance

여가프로그램 leisure program

여과멸균 filtration sterilization

여권론 feminism

여권주위 사회사업 leisure time management

여권주의 치료 feminist therapy

여론 public opinion

여론조사 opinion survey

여론지도자 opinion leader

여섯가지 기초식품군 six basic food groups

여성경제활동 Women's economic activity

여성금주조직 Women for sobriety

여성노동 women's labor

여성노인사업 female elderly project

여성문제 women's problems

여성운동 women's movement

여성유권자연맹 League of Woman Voters

여성의 사회참가 social participation of women

여성자원봉사자 lady bountiful

여성참정권 women's franchise

여성해방운동 women's liberation movement

여행감염 레지오네라증
travel-associated legionellosis

역감염숙주 compromised host

역감염환자 compromised patient

역격리 reversed isolation

역과정 adversarial process

역기능 dysfunction

역동성 dynamic

역동적 진단 dynamic diagnosis

역량 competence

역방향성 전도 antidromic conduction

역선택 adverse selection

역설적 실금 paradoxical incontinence

역설적 지시 paradoxical directive

역설적 지향 paradoxical intention

역소득세 negative income tax : NIT

역연령 chronological age

역전관계 inverse relationship

역전도성 tendency to fall

역전이 countertransference

역진세 regressive tax

역차별 reverse discrimination
역치 threshold
역피로성 easy fatigability
역학 epidemiology
역학조사 epidemiological study
역할 role
역할갈등 role conflict
역할강도 role vigor
역할거리 role distance
역할기대 role expectation
역할긴장 role strain
역할모호성 role ambiguity
역할보충성 role complementaty
역할수행 role performance
역할연기 role play ; role playing
역할이론 role theory
역할인지 role perception
역할재평형 role re-equilibration
역할전환 role reversal
역할행동 role behavior
역행성 건망 retrograde amnesia
역행성 바륨소장조영 barium small bowel enema
역행성 신우조영 retrograde pyelography
역효과 치료환경 sociofugal arrangements
연간보증소득 guaranteed annual income
연계 cooperation
연계 · 협동고령자헬스케어
   geriatric interdisciplinary health care team
연고 ointment
연구개발진흥과
   Research and Development Division
연구보조금 획득수완 grantsmanship
연구소 research institution
연구윤리 ethics in research
연금 pension
연금과 Pension Division
연금국 Pension Bureau
연금급여 pension benefit
연금급여기준 pension benefits standards
연금급여기준법 Pension Benefits Standards Act
연금급여수준 level of pension benefits
연금기금 pension fund
연금보험 pension insurance

연금보험과 Pension Insurance Division
연금보험료 pension insurance premiums
연금보험료납부 payment of pension premiums
연금보험제도 pension insurance system
연금수급권 pensionable right
연금수급자 pensioner
연금수급자격 eligibility of employee pension
연금수급자격연령 pensionable age
연금수리 pension mathematics
연금수첩 pension handbook
연금슬라이드제 sliding scheme of pension
연금심의회 National Pension Council
연금적립기금 pension reserve fund
연금제도 pension system
연금지급개시연령 pensionable age
연기감지기 smoke alarm
연기성 성격장애 histrionic personality disorder
연대납부의무
   joint and several obligation for payments
연대채무 joint and several obligation
연대책임 joint and several liability
연동운동 peristalsis
연령차별 ageism
연명치료
   life-prolonging treatment ; life-sustaining
   treatment
연방범죄보험 프로그램
   Federal Crime Insurance Program
연방보험기여법
   Federal Insurance Contributions Act : FICA
연방정부 federal government
연방주택청
   Federal Housing Administration : FHA
연소근로자 juvenile labor
연소인구 young population
연속위기 crisis sequence
연속적 휴대식복막투석
   continuous ambulatory peritoneal dialysis : CAPD
연속절편 serial section
연속체 continuum
연쇄 chaining
연수 medulla oblongata
연식 mechanical diet ; mechanical soft diet

연식세탁 dry cleaning
연역법 deductive method
연역적 추론 deductive reasoning
연장보육 extended childcare
연장보호시설 extended care facilities : ECT
연장장기요양 extended care
연차유급휴가 yearly paid-holiday
연차조사 annual survey
연축 spasm
연하 swallowing
연하곤란 swallowing difficulty
연하기능 swallowing function
연하기능장애 dysphagia of swallowing function
연하문제 swallowing problem
연하반사 swallowing reflex
연하보조제 thickening agent
연하성 폐렴
  aspiration pneumonia ; deglutition pneumonia
연하운동 movement during swallowing
연하장애 dysphagia
연하조영검사 videofluorography : VF
연하통 odynophagia
연하훈련 swallowing training
연합 coalition
연합모금 united fund
연합운동 associated movement
연화제 emollient
연화좌 lotus position
연화증 malacia
열경련 muscle cramp
열공헤르니아 hiatus hernias
열등감 inferiority complex
열등처우의 원칙 less-eligibility principle
열사병 heat stroke
열상 burn
열성유전 recessive inheritance
열쇠구멍수술 keyhole surgery
열쇠아이 key child
열수소독 hot water disinfection
열악적 직장환경 hostile work environment
열중증 heat stroke
열피로 heat exhaustion
열피폐 heat exhaustion

염분섭취 sodium intake
염산필로칼핀 pilocarpine hydrochloride
염색체 chromosome
염색체이상 chromosomal abnormality
염좌 sprain
영 가설 null hypothesis
영구치 permanent tooth
영국청소년비행 프로그램 Borstal system
영리단체 for-profit organization
영성 spirituality
영속적 기획 permanency planning
영아사망 crib death
영아시설 infant institute
영아저긴장증후군 floppy infant
영양 nutrition
영양가 nutritive value of foods
영양개선 nutrition improvement
영양관리 nutritional management
영양권장량 recommended dietary allowance : RDA
영양문제 nutritional problem
영양보급 nutritional support
영양보조식품 dietary supplement
영양불량 malnutrition
영양사 dietitian
영양사법 Dietitian Law
영양상태 nutritional status
영양서비스 nutrition services
영양섭취 nutritional intake
영양섭취량 nutrient intake
영양소 nutrient
영양소요량 recommended dietary allowance : RDA
영양소요량위원회
  Committee on Dietary Allowances
영양스크리닝 nutritional screening
영양스크리닝추진재단
  nutrition screening initiative : NSI
영양실조 malnutrition
영양장애 nutritional disturbance
영양지도 nutritional education
영양지도원 nutrition consultant
영양처방 dietary prescription
영양케어계획 nutrition care plan
영양케어매니지먼트 nutrition care management

영양평가 nutritional assessment
영양필요량 nutritional requirement
영장 writ
영적만족감측정기구 (영적안녕척도)
　Spiritual Well-Being Scale
영점기준예산제 zero-base budgeting
영합지향 zero sum orientation
영향력 전술
　influence tactics ; tactics of influence
영향분석 impact analysis
옆으로 집기 side pinch
예견적 감사 prospective review
예견적 연구 prospective study
예금보험공사
　Korea Deposit Insurance Corporation
예리물질손상 sharps injury
예방 prevention
예방건강 프로그램 preventive health programs
예방격리 protective isolation
예방급여 preventive benefit
예방내복 prophylactic medication
예방노년학 preventive gerontology
예방서비스 preventive services
예방의학 preventive medicine
예방접종
　immunization ; preventive vaccination ;
　vaccination
예방접종증명서 proof of immunization
예방정신의학 preventive psychiatry
예방진료 primary care
예방진료의 primary care physician : PCP
예방처치 preventive treatment
예방케어 preventive care
예방투여 prophylactic medication
예비조사 preliminary survey
예산 budget
예산관리국
　Office of Management and Budget : OMB
예산직접관리일반개업의
　general practitioner fundholder
예산편성 budgeting
예술치료 art therapy
예약 appointment

예의 etiquette
예이츠보고서 Yates Report
예측변수 predictor variable
예행 behavioral rehearsal
예후 prognosis
예후예측 prognosis prediction
오그라듬 rigidity
오디오그램 audiogram
오디오미터 audiometer
오란자핀 olanzapine
오르가슴 장애 orgasmic impairment
오르기 push off
오르리스타트 orlistat
오르메사르탄 olmesartan
오리엔테이션 orientation
오목가슴 pectus excavatum
오목발바닥 받침 arch support
오물처리실 dirty utility room
오므린 입술 호흡법 pursed lip breathing
오버베드테이블 overbed table
오버킬 overkill
오브라이트 oblate
오스트메이트 ostomate
오십견 frozen shoulder
오아시스
　Outcome and Assessment Information Set :
　OASIS
오약 medication error
오연 pulmonary aspiration
오연성 폐렴 aspiration pneumonia
오염 contamination
오염관리 contamination control
오염구역 contaminated area ; hot zone
오염방지소재 soil-resistant material
오염상처 contaminated wound
오염수술 contaminated operation
오염제거처리 decontamination procedure
오염창 contaminated wound
오염통제 contamination control
오용 misuse
오용증후군 misuse syndrome
오웬 Robert Owen
오음 accidental ingestion

오이디푸스 콤플렉스 Oedipus complex
오이디푸스기 Oedipus phase
오존 ozone
오줌 urine
오진 misdiagnosis
오큐페이셔널테라피 occupational therapy : OT
오타와 헌장
    Ottawa Charter for Health Promotion
오토노미 autonomy
오토클레이브 autoclave
오피니언리더 opinion leader
오피오이드제 opioid medication
오한 chill
옥소 iodine
옥시코돈 oxycodone
옥시콘틴 OxyContin
온습포 hot pack
온실효과 greenhouse effect
온엄법 hot foment
온열요법 thermotherapy ; heat therapy
온정주의 paternalism
온찜질 hot compress
온천요법 balneotherapy
올터너티브메디슨 alternative medicine
옴 scabies
옴부즈맨 ombudsman
옴부즈퍼슨 ombudsperson
옵타콘 Optacon
옷갈아입기 dressing
옹호 advocacy
옹호활동 advocacy activity
와론 Henri Wallon
와류욕 whirlpool bath
와병도 판정기준 criteria for bedridden
와상 bedridden
와상고령자 [와상노인] bedridden elderly
와상고령자대책 policy for the bedridden elderly
와상고령자예방
    prevention of becoming bedridden elderly
와상노인제로작전
    bedridden eradication campaign
와상도 bedridden level
와상생활상태 bedridden status

와상예방 prevention of becoming bedridden
와위 lying position
와이 염색체 Y chromosome
와이스 검사 WAIS test
와파린 warfarin
완전 · 영속적 중증장애인부조
    Aid to the Permanently and Totally Disabled :
    APTD
완전고용 full employment
완전사회 perfect society
완전성 요실금 total incontinence
완전실업 unemployment
완전인공심장 total artificial heart
완전정맥영양 total parenteral nutrition : TPN
완전참가와 평등 full participation and equality
완하제 laxative
완화 palliative
완화케어 palliative care
완화케어병동 palliative care unit
완화케어병상 palliative care bed
왐네트 [의료복지기구]
    welfare and medical service network system :
    WAM NET
왕따 bullying
왕립위원회 royal commission
왕진 doctor's home visit
외과계 집중치료실 surgical intensive care unit
외과용 마스크 surgical mask
외국인 alien
외국인고용대책과
    Foreign Workers' Affairs Division
외국인노동관리소
    Alien Labor Certification Division
외국인입국허가증 green card
외국인장기요양노동자
    migrant care worker ; foreign care worker
외국인혐오증 xenophobia
외국태생고령자 foreign-born elderly
외동이정책 one-child policy
외래시 일부부담금
    lump sum payment for outpatient
외래재활
    outpatient rehabilitation ; ambulatory re

habilitation

외래진료 ambulatory medicine ; outpatient medicine

외래진료소 ambulatory clinic ; outpatient clinic

외래케어 ambulatory care ; outpatient care

외래환자 outpatient

외면화 externalization

외반 valgus ; eversion

외반모지 hallux valgus

외반족 talipes valgus

외부튜브 enteral tube

외분비샘 eccrine gland

외삽법 extrapolation

외상 trauma

외상성 뇌손상 traumatic brain injury : TBI

외상성 손상 traumatic injury

외상후 스트레스장애 post-traumatic stress disorder : PTSD

외인성 exogenous

외인성 감염 exogenous infection

외인성 홀몬 exogenous hormone

외적 조합범위 external frame of reference

외전 abduction ; eversion ; supination

외전방지 블록 abduction block

외전보행 abduction gait

외출지원 transportation and escort services

외측쐐기첨부 발바닥보조기 foot orthosis with lateral corrective wedge

외측휘프 lateral whip

외피 integumentary

외피계 integumentary system

외향발굽 toe out

외향성 extraversion

외향성의 사람 extrovert

외회전 external rotation

요가 yoga

요강 urinary bottle holder ; urinal

요개호 long-term care-required

요개호도 long-term care classification levels

요개호상태 long-term care status

요개호상태구분 category of long-term care status

요개호와상노인 bedridden long-term care recipient

요개호인정 certification of long-term care-required

요개호인정기준 certification standards for long-term care insurance benefits

요개호인정의 취소 cancellation of certification of long-term care-required

요개호자 long-term care recipient

요검사 urinalysis

요골동맥 radial artery

요골동맥류 radial artery aneurysm

요골동맥카뉴레삽입법 radial artery cannulation

요골동맥카테터 radial artery catheter

요골손상 lumbar spinal cord injury

요골신경근증 lumbar radiculopathy

요골원위단 골절 distal radius fracture

요구 demands

요구저지 frustration

요굴 radial deviation

요도 urethra

요도류 urethrocele

요도카테터 urethral catheter

요도카테터법 urethral catheterization

요독증 uremia

요로 urinary tract

요로감염 urinary tract infection : UTI

요로감염패혈증 urosepsis

요로관리 urinary management

요로스토미 urostomy

요리도구 cooking utensil

요모 dormitory matron

요보호가족 family in need of public assistance

요보호성 need for public assistance ; the need for public assistance

요보호세대 household in need of public assistance

요보호아동가족부조 Aid to Families with Dependent Children : AFDC

요보호자 person in need of public assistance

요산 uric acid

요선추보조기 lumbosacral orthosis
요실금 urinary incontinence
요약기록 summary records
요양 long-term health care
요양급여
long-term health care benefits ; medical care
benefit
요양급여비용
long-term health care benefit expenses
요양등급인정
certification of long-term care-required
요양등급지원인정
certification of long-term care
assistance-required
요양병상 long-term health care bed
요양병원요양비 long-term health care expenses
요양보호 long-term care
요양보호사 care worker
요양보호사 등록 Certified Care Worker Registry
요양보호사양성강좌
course for development of care worker
요양보호사양성시설
facilities for development of care worker
요양보호사양성커리큘럼
home care worker development curriculum
요양보호사양성표준교과서
standard text book for development of care
worker
요양비
long-term health care expenses ; medical care
expenses ; medical expenses
요양비용보상
compensation for long-term health care costs
요양비지출 geriatric care expenditures
요양원 nursing home
요양형병상군
long-term health care beds ; a group of beds
for long-term health care
요양형의료시설 long-term health care facilities
요역동학검사 urodynamic test
요양호노인 support-required elderly
요육의료
medical care and education for the disabled

children
요의 uresiesthesia
요인분석 factor analysis
요지원 long-term assistance-required
요지원인정
certification of long-term care assistance-
required
요지원인정의 취소
cancellation of certification of long-term
assistance-required
요지원자 long-term assistance-recipient
요추 lumbar vertebrae
요추견인 lumbar traction
요추천자 lumbar puncture
요측편위 radial deviation
요통 lumbago ; low back pain
요통예방
prevention of lumbago ; lumbago prevention
요통체조 lumbago exercise
요폐 urinary retention
요호 custodial care
욕구 needs
욕구5단계설 five-stage hierarchy of needs
욕구계층 hierarchy of needs
욕구불만 frustration
욕구불만내성 frustration tolerance
욕구사정 needs assessments
욕구서열 hierarchy of needs
욕구조사 needs survey
욕구집단 need group
욕구측정법 needs survey method
욕구평가 needs assessments
욕비 bath ratio
욕실 bathroom
욕조 bathtub
욕창
pressure ulcer ; decubitus ulcer ; pressure
sore ; decubitus ; bedsore
욕창발생예측척도
Braden Scale for Predicting Pressure Sore Risk ;
Braden Scale for Predicting Pressure Ulcer
Risk
욕창예방

prevention of pressure ulcer ; pressure ulcer prevention

욕창예방 및 치료
pressure ulcer prevention and treatment

욕창치료 pressure ulcer treatment

욕창치유과정스케일
Pressure Ulcer Scale for Healing : PUSH

용구 equipment

용수세정 manual cleaning

용해 fusion

용혈성 빈혈 hemolytic anemia

우대조치 preferential placement

우마미 umami

우발발관 accidental extubation

우생보호법
Eugenic and Maternal Protection Law

우생학 eugenics

우선석 priority seat

우선적 preferential

우선적 권리 preferential rights

우선좌석 priority seat

우성보호 eugenic protection

우성수술 eugenic operation

우성유전 dominant inheritance

우성학 eugenics

우송조사법 mail survey

우애 fraternity

우애방문 friendly visiting

우애방문원 friendly visitor

우애조합 friendly society

우연성 contingency

우울상태
depressive state ; state of depressed mood

우울신경증 depressive neurosis

우울자기평가척도
Center for Epidemiological Studies Depression Scale : CES-D

우울증 depression

우울한 반응 depressive reaction

우측와위 right lateral recumbent

우해면양뇌증
bovine spongiform encephalopathy : BSE

우호방문서비스 friendly visit services

운동 exercise ; movement

운동각 kinesthetic sense

운동감각 kinesthesia

운동강도 exercise strength

운동과다증 hyperkinesis

운동기 기능향상
improvement of body functions

운동기능 motor function ; motor skill

운동기능 · 프로세스기능평가
Assessment of Motor and Process Skills : AMPS

운동기증후군 locomotive syndrome

운동내용능 exercise capacity

운동뉴런 motor neuron

운동뉴런질환 motor neuron disease

운동단위 motor unit

운동단위활동전위
motor unit action potential : MUAP

운동마비 motor paralysis

운동발달 motor development

운동발달평가 motor developmental evaluation

운동부하 exercise load

운동부하검사 exercise tolerance test : ETT

운동분석 movement analysis

운동생리 exercise physiology

운동성 실어 motor aphasia

운동시험 exercise test

운동신경 motor nerve

운동신경기능 회복단계 Brunnstrom stage

운동신경전도속도
motor nerve conduction velocity

운동실어 motor aphasia

운동실조 ataxia ; motor ataxia

운동실행 motor apraxia

운동역학 kinetics

운동연령 motor age

운동연령검사 motor age test

운동요법 therapeutic exercise

운동유발전위 motor evoked potential

운동유지곤란 motor impersistence

운동장애
motor impairment ; dyskinesia ; movement disorder ; movement dysfunction

운동저하 hypokinesis ; hypokinesia
운동전문사 exercise instructor
운동점 motor point
운동점블록 motor point block
운동제어 motion control
운동제한
　restricted mobility ; movement-related
　functional limitation
운동처방 exercise prescription
운동평가 motor assessment
운동학 kinesiology
운동학문적 분석 kinematic analysis
운동학습 motor learning
운동항진 hyperkinesia
운드케어 wound care
운영 administration
운영적정화위원회
　Complaints Resolution Committee
울열 heat retention
울체성 피부염 stasis dermatitis
울혈 congestion
울혈성 심부전 congestive heart failure
움츠러진 걸음걸이 frozen gait
워너 증후군 Werner Syndrome : WS
워커-내담자관계 worker-client relationship
워커빌리티 workability
워커즈콜렉티브 worker's collective
워커홀릭 workaholic
워크샘플방법 work sample method
워크숍 workshop
워크쉐어링 work sharing
워크하우스 work house
워터필 water pill
원거리의료 long-distance medicine
원거리장기요양 long-distance care
원격교육 distance education
원격의료 remote medicine
원격의료시스템 remote medical system
원격조작용구 aid for extended reach
원격지의료 remote area medicine
원격케어 remote care
원격학습 distance learning
원규 folkways

원내감염
　hospital-acquired infection ; nosocomial
　infection
원내구조 indoor relief
원내폐렴 hospital-acquired pneumonia
원발개방우각녹내장
　primary open angle glaucoma : POAG
원발성 균혈증 primary bacteremia
원발성 담즙성 간경변 primary biliary cirrhosis
원발성 진행성 비유창성 실어
　primary progressive nonfluent aphasia
원발성 진행성 실어 primary progressive aphasia
원발성 혈류감염 primary blood stream infection
원상복구 restitution
원숙 mature
원시반사 primitive reflex
원심 공중부유물질채집기 centrifugal sampler
원심성 수축 eccentric contraction
원심적 가족구조 centrifugal family structure
원예요법 horticultural therapy
원외구조 outdoor relief
원위 distal
원위단 distal end
원위잠복기 distal latency
원인 대 기능 논쟁 cause-versus-function issue
원인적 진단 etiological diagnosis
원인지향적 조직 cause-oriented organization
원자 atom
원자극 primary stimulus
원자폭탄 atomic bomb
원조 assistance ; assistant ; support
원조관계 therapeutic relationship
원조자 assistant ; supporter
원조첨부고용 supported employment
원좌 circle mat
원천과세 withholding tax
원천징수 tax deduction at source
원초적집단 primary group
원추 cone
원호 protection
원호과 Relief Division
원호기획과
　Planning Division of War Victims' Relief

원회전 circumduction
원회전 보행 circumduction gait
월 2회 twice every month : 2M
월보험료 monthly premium
월부과 monthly charge
웩슬러 David Wechsler
웩슬러 성인용 지능검사
　Wechsler Adult Intelligence Scale : WAIS
웩슬러 아동용 개정판
　Wechsler Intelligence Scale for
　Children-Revised : WISC-R
웩슬러 아동용 지능검사
　Wechsler Intelligence Scale for Children : WISC
웩슬러 지능검사 Wechsler Intelligence Scale
웰부트린 Wellbutrin
웰빙 well-being
웹부처 Sydney Webb and Beatrice Potter Webb
위궤양 gastric ulcer
위기 crisis
위기개입 crisis intervention
위기개입접근법 crisis intervention approach
위기경로 critical pathway : CP
위기관리 risk management ; crisis management
위기교섭 crisis bargaining
위기긴급전화 crisis hot line
위기보호센터 crisis care centers
위기분석중점관리제도
　Hazard Analysis Critical Control Point system :
　HACCP
위기이론 crisis theory
위기중재 crisis intervention
위대한 사회 Great Society
위루 gastrostomy
위루튜브 gastrostomy tube
위루형성술 gastrostomy
위생 hygiene
위생검사기사 hygiene laboratory technician
위생적 손씻기 hygienic hand washing
위생학 hygienics
위세정 gastric lavage
위식도역류증
　gastroesophageal reflex disease : GERD
위암 gastric cancer ; stomach cancer

위약 placebo
위염 gastritis
위운동촉진제 prokinetic medication
위원회 council
위임권 power of attorney
위자료 alimony
위장실업 disguised unemployment
위절제술 gastrectomy
위축 atrophy
위축성 위염 atrophic gastritis
위축성 질염 atrophic vaginitis
위탁 referral
위탁사업 assignment program
위탁행위 commitment
위험구역 hot zone
위험물 hazardous material
위험방지 risk prevention
위험분담의 원칙 risk-sharing plan
위험유해물질 hazardous material
위험율평가 risk assessment
위험인자 risk factor
윅 프로그램 WIC program
윌리스 써클 circle of Willis
윌슨병 Wilson's disease
유각단계 swing phase
유각중기 mid swing
유교 Confucianism
유교사상 the ideas of Confucianism
유급휴가 paid time off : PTO
유기 desertion
유기아 neglected child
유기체적 윤리 bioethics
유나이티드웨이 united way
유네스코
　United Nations Educational, Scientific and
　Cultural Organization : UNESCO
유뇨증 enuresis
유니버설디자인 universal design
유니버설패션 universal fashion
유니세프
　United Nations Children's Fund : UNICEF
유니크 색상 unique hue
유니트케어 unit-based care

유대인 사회기관 Jewish social agency
유도접골사 judo orthopedist
유독소 toxoids
유동성 능력 fluid ability
유동성 지능 fluid intelligence
유동식 liquid diet
유랑생활 nomadism
유량여성 bag lady
유로복지사업 entrepreneurial practice
유로사회봉사 proprietary social services
유료노인복지주택
　　paid welfare houses for the aged
유료노인양로시설
　　paid endowment facilities for the aged
유료노인요양시설
　　paid health care facilities for the aged
유료노인전문요양시설
　　paid specialized health care facilities for the
　　aged
유료노인홈
　　private residential home for the elderly
유료사회단체 proprietary
유료양로시설 paid endowment facilities
유료행위 proprietary practice
유리 disengagement
유리지방산 non-esterified fatty acid
유발근전도 evoked electromyogram
유발전위 evoked potential
유방보철물 breast prosthesis
유방암 breast cancer
유방온존수술 breast-sparing surgery
유방재건술 breast reconstruction
유방절단술 mastectomy
유방촬영술 mammogram
유병 prevalence
유병율 prevalence rate
유사관절염 crystal arthropathy
유사빈곤층 'near poor' population
유산세 estate tax
유상볼룬터리 paid voluntary
유상자원봉사 paid volunteer
유색소수인종 minorities of color
유색인 nonwhite

유선종양적출방법 lumpectomy
유수증 ptyalism
유스호스텔 youth hostel : YH
유아 infant
유아교육 preschool education
유아급사증후군
　　sudden infant death syndrome : SIDS
유아기 newborn infant period
유아기 반추장애 rumination disorder of infancy
유아돌연사증후군 sudden infant death syndrome
유아반 toddler class
유아사망률 infant mortality rate
유아살해 infanticide
유아자폐증 infantile autism
유언서 testament ; will
유언자 testator
유언장 last will
유엔난민고등판무관사무소
　　United Nations High Commissioner for
　　Refugees : UNHCR
유엔인권선언
　　United Nations Declaration of Human Rights
유연 drooling
유연성 flexibility
유연증 ptyalism ; sialorrhea
유연처리제 softener agent
유연체조 flexibility exercise
유예기간 grace period
유의도 significance level
유의차 significant difference
유인 incentive
유인적 계약 incentive contracting
유자격 간호사 licensed nurse
유자격 소시얼워커 licensed social worker
유자격 의료복지직
　　licensed heath care practitioner : LHCP
유자격 임상소시얼워커
　　licensed clinical social worker : LCSW
유전 heredity
유전병 genetic diseases
유전상담 genetic counseling
유전성 비용종성 대장암
　　hereditary nonpolyposis colorectal cancer :

HNCC

유전자 gene

유전자검사 genetic testing

유전자의 돌연변이 mutations of genes

유전자진단 genetic diagnosis

유전체각인 genomic imprinting

유전학 genetics

유족급여 survivors allowance

유족기초연금 basic survivors pension

유족보상금

Dependency and Indemnity Compensation : DIC

유족연금 survivors pension

유죄답변 거래 genetic counseling

유지기 재활 late phase rehabilitation

유착물질 cadherin

유치도뇨관 indwelling catheter

유치도뇨관 감염 indwelling catheter infection

유치원 kindergarten

유치조사 placement questionnaire

유치카테터 indwelling catheter

유치카테터감염 line sepsis

유치카테터패혈증 line sepsis

유치함 infantilization

유토피아 Utopia

유한책임중간법인

limited liability non-profit mutual benefit corporation

유해환경 noxious environment

유행병 pandemic

유행성 epidemic

유행성 각결막염

epidemic keratoconjunctivitis : EKC

유행성 이하선염 mumps

유행점 point prevalence

유행조사 prevalence survey

유형학 typologies

유효수요 effective demand

유효시야 useful field of view

유희요법 play therapy

육성 nurturance

육성의료

medical aid for children with potential

disability

육성지원과

Vocational Training Promotion Division

육성환경과 Child-Rearing Promotion Division

육아 parenting

육아·개호휴업급여

child and family care leave benefit

육아·개호휴업제도

child and family care leave system

육아급여 child care benefit

육아노이로제 maternity neurosis

육아방기 child neglect

육아수당 child care allowance

육아지원 parenting support

육아태만 child neglect

육아휴업 parental leave ; child care leave

육아휴업수당금 parental leave allowance

육안적으로 오염된 손가락 visibly soiled hands

육영사업 scholarship program

육체노동자 blue-collar worker

윤락행위 prostitution

윤리 ethics

윤리강령 code of ethics

윤리규정 ethical code

융 심리학 Jungian psychology

융모막하혈종 subchorionic hematoma

은급 soldiers' pension

은유 metaphor

은퇴 retirement

은퇴농장 post retirement farming

은퇴이민 retired immigrants

은퇴촌 retirement community

은행 ginkgo biloba

음료수 potable water

음모이론 conspiracy theory

음부닦기 genital hygiene

음부세정

genital hygiene ; peri < perineal > care ; perineal < peri > care

음성기능장애 speech disorder

음성모델 negative mold

음성안내 voice guidance

음성언어기능장애 voice-speech disorder

음성증폭기 sound amplifier
음식 food
음식관련장애 food-related disorder
음식매개감염 food-borne infection
음식물쓰레기 garbage
음식물쓰레기처리 disposal of garbage and swill
음악요법 music therapy
음압성 폐수종
  negative pressure pulmonary edema
음위 impingement
음이온 계면활성제 anionic surface active agent
응급수단 emergency first aid
응급정신질활 psychiatric emergency
응급처치 emergency first aid
응능부담 ability-to-pay principle
응능원칙 ability-to-pay principle
응능주의 ability principle
응보 retribution
응용심리학 applied psychology
응용조사 applied research
응익부담 benefit-received principle
응익원칙 benefit principle
응익자부담 benefit principle
의도적 배회 purposeful wandering
의도적 자기방임 active self-neglect
의도적인 감정표현
  purposeful expression of feelings
의도적인 감정표현의 원칙
  principle of purposeful expression of feelings
의례 ritual
의뢰인 client
의뢰인중심요법 client-centered therapy
의료 medicine
의료감시원 medical inspector
의료개별사회사업 medical casework
의료경보 Medic Alert
의료경제 medical economic
의료경제지수 medical economic index
의료계획 health planning
의료곤궁대상자 medically needy
의료공제 deduction for medical care
의료과 Medical Economics Division
의료과소지역 medically underserved area

의료과실 medical malpractice
의료과오 medical malpractice
의료과오보상보험
  medical malpractice liability insurance
의료과오보험 malpractice insurance
의료과오소송 medical malpractice suit
의료관계자 medical personnel
의료관련서비스 health-related services
의료교육제도 medical education system
의료급부 medical benefit
의료급여 medical care benefit
의료급여법 Law for Medical Benefits/Care
의료급여수급자 claimant of medical benefits
의료기기 medical device ; medical equipment
의료기기분류 classification of medical devices
의료기록 medical records
의료기사등에 관한 법률
  Law for Medical Surgeons
의료기재 medical device ; medical equipment
의료대마 medical marijuana
의료도구 medical device ; medical equipment
의료면접 medical interview
의료모델 medical model
의료문제 medical problem
의료미스 medical error
의료법 Medical Services Law
의료법인 medical corporation
의료보장 medical security
의료보장제도 medical social security
의료보장프로그램 medical security program
의료보험 medical insurance
의료보험과 Health Insurance Division
의료보험제도
  health insurance system ; medical insurance
  system
의료보험제도의 일원화
  unification of health care insurance programs
의료보호 medical aid
의료보호대상자 medically needy
의료보호법 Medical Benefits Law
의료보호사업 medical care service
의료보호시설
  medical facility for public assistance recipients

의료보호입원
admission for medical care and custody
의료복지 medicine and welfare
의료복지연계
affiliation of medical care and social welfare
의료복합체 integrated health care delivery system
의료부담 burden of health care
의료부조 medical assistance
의료비
medical care expenses ; medical expenses
의료비공제 deduction for medical expenses
의료비급여 benefit for medical care expenses
의료비부담금분담 share of cost of medical care
의료비세공제
tax deduction for medical care expenses
의료비억제책 health care cost containment
의료비적정화 moderation in medical care costs
의료비적정화계획
health expenditure rationalization plan
의료사고 medical error
의료사회복지 medical social work
의료사회복지사 medical social worker
의료사회복지사업 medical social services
의료사회사업 medical social work : MSW
의료사회사업가 medical social worker
의료산업복합체 medical industrial complex
의료서비스계획 medical service plan
의료서비스부족지역 medically underserved area
의료서비스위원회 Health Services Commission
의료서비스패키지 health services package
의료세공제 tax deduction for medical care
의료수급자증 medical insurance card recipient
의료신용제 Medicredit
의료용 분무기 nebulizer
의료용구 medical device ; medical equipment
의료원조자 medical support assistant
의료위임장 health care proxy
의료윤리 medical ethics
의료의 기준 standards of medical practice
의료의 사회화
socialization of medical care ; socialization of medicine
의료의 질 quality of medical care

의료인류학 medical anthropology
의료인류학자 medical anthropologist
의료자원 medical resources
의료적 재활 medical rehabilitation
의료전달체계 medical delivery system
의료전문 health profession ; medical profession
의료전문직
health professional ; medical professional
의료전문직 부족지역
health professional shortage area
의료정책 health policy
의료제도개혁 health care reform
의료종사자 medical staff
의료케이스워커 medical caseworker
의료팀 medical team
의료폐기물 medical waste
의료품 medical supply
의료행위 medical practice
의류장애 clothing irritation
의무교육 compulsory education
의무실 dispensary
의미기억 semantic memory
의미성 치매 semantic dementia : SD
의미치료 logotherapy
의복 clothes
의복 갈아입기 changing clothes
의복기후 clothing climate
의복생활 clothing life
의복압 clothing pressure
의붓가정 stepfamily
의사 doctor ; physician
의사결정 decision-making
의사결정대리자 proxy decision maker
의사결정이론 decision theory
의사공개법 sunshine laws
의사과 Medical Professions Division
의사능력평가 mental capacity assessment
의사등록법
Medical Practitioners' Registration Act
의사법 Medical Practitioners Law
의사성숙 pseudomutuality
의사소개서비스
doctor referral services ; physician referral

services

의사소통 communication

의사소통이론 communication theory

의사시장 quasi-market

의사양성제도 medical education system

의사와의 연계 cooperation with physicians

의사장 medical director

의사전달 expressions of desires

의사전달장치 communication aid

의사조력자살 physician-assisted suicide

의수 upper limb prosthesis

의술업 medical practice

의식 consciousness

의식고양 consciousness-raising

의식상실 syncope

의식소실발작 presyncope

의식수준 level of consciousness

의식의 conscious

의식장애 disturbance of consciousness

의식적 조정 conscious manipulation

의식조사 opinion survey

의식혼탁 clouding of consciousness

의식화 conscientization

의안 false eye

의약분업

  separation of dispensary from medical practice

의약식품국

  Pharmaceutical and Food Safety Bureau

의업 medical practice

의업유사행위 quasi-medical practice

의역 paraphrasing

의욕 conation

의욕장애 volitional disorder

의원 재할당 reapportionment

의원간 진료연계

  affiliation between outpatient clinics

의원병 iatrogenesis

의원성 iatrogenic

의정국 Health Policy Bureau

의제가정 cohabiting dyad

의족

  solid ankle cushion heel foot : SACH ; lower
  limb prosthesis

의존성 anaclitic

의존성 성격장애 dependent personality disorder

의존증 addiction

의지 (義肢) prosthesis ; artificial limb

의지 (意志) will

의지보조기 orthosis and prosthesis

의지장비사 prosthetist and orthotist : PO

의지장착 prosthesis fitting

의지학 prosthetic

의지훈련 prosthetic training

의치 denture ; artificial teeth

의학모델 medical model

의학분야문제 medical issue

의학적 재활 medical rehabilitation

의학지시거부 against medical advice : AMA

의행위 medical practice

이 teeth

이개혈종 aural hematoma

이너시티현상 inner-city phenomenon

이뇨제 diuretic ; water pill ; Aldactone

이닦기 tooth brushing

이데올로기 ideology

이동 locomotion ; transfer and locomotion

이동개호 transfer assistance

이동관련복지용구 mobility aid

이동기능 mobility skill

이동대 grab bar ; transfer bar

이동동작 locomotion activity

이동바 grab bar ; transfer bar

이동보조도구 mobility aid

이동보호 ambulatory care

이동성 mobility

이동욕조 portable bathtub

이동의자 commode chair

이동척도법 movement scale

이동학대부모모임 Parents Anonymous : PA

이동화장실 commode ; bedside commode

이드 id

이든 Frederic Morton Eden

이레우스 ileus

이론 theory

이론생계비방식 market basket method

이론적 최대일일섭취량

theoretical maximum daily intake
이명 tinnitus
이미트렉스 Imitrex
이미프라민 imipramine
이민 immigration
이민노동자 migrant laborer
이민자 immigrant
이반드로네이트 ibandronate
이발 haircut
이방인 불안 (낯가림) stranger anxiety
이부프로펜 ibuprofen
이분척추 spina bifida
이분할 신뢰도검사 split-half reliability
이불건조서비스 futon mattress drying service
이브닝케어 evening care
이비인후검사 ear, nose and throat evaluation
이비인후과의 otolaryngologist
이비인후전문의 ear, nose and throat specialist
이비인후학 otolaryngology
이빨 teeth
이사 change of residence
이사스트레스 relocation stress
이산화질소 nitrogen dioxide
이산화탄소 carbon dioxide
이상 out of bed
이상발견 finding abnormality
이상보행 abnormal gait
이상불수의 운동평가척도
 Abnormal Involuntary Movement Scale : AIMS
이상심리학 abnormal psychology
이상운동증 dyskinesia
이상자세 abnormal posture
이상적 자아 ego ideal
이상적응기제 abnormal adjustment mechanism
이상지각 dysesthesia
이상지질혈증 dyslipidemia
이상출산 difficult delivery
이상행동 abnormal behavior
이상화 idealization
이성애 heterosexuality
이성성 골화 heterotopic bone formation
이소성 리듬 ectopic rhythm
이소성 요관 ectopic ureter

이소성 요관류 ectopic ureterocele
이소성 피지선 ectopic sebaceous gland
이소신 ectopic kidney
이소카복사지드 Isocarboxazid
이솝틴 Isoptin
이송비 transportation fee
이송서비스 transportation services
이수시간 curriculum hours
이스터 실 협회 Easter Seal Society
이승 transfer ; transfer and locomotion
이승관련용구 transfer aid
이승동작 transfer motion
이승동작훈련 transfer motion training
이승보조도구 transfer aid
이승훈련 transfer exercise
이식증 malacia
이식행위 abnormal eating habit
이식형 제세동기 implantable defibrillator
이야기접근법 narrative approach
이야기치료 narrative therapy
이엠지 electromyography : EMG
이온도입법 iontophoresis
이완 flaccid ; relaxation
이완성 마비 flaccid paralysis
이용감사 utilization review : UR
이용관리 utilization management : UN
이용료 usage cost ; fee
이용자 recipient ; client ; resident
이용자본위 client-oriented ; person-oriented
이용자부담 user fee
이용자부담금 charges for recipients
이용자지불 client payment
이용자평가
 client evaluation ; recipient evaluation
이음새 joint
이의신청 appeal
이의신청제도 appeal system
이익단체 interest group
이익집단 interest group
이익집단이론 interest group theory
이인장애 depersonalization disorder
이인정신병 Folie à Deux
이인증 depersonalization disorder

이전소득 transfer income
이전지급 transfer payments
이중경제 dual economy
이중구속 (이중맹검) double bind
이중구속이론 double bind theory
이중방사선조영법
　double contrast roentgenography
이중양동이법 double bucket system
이중에너지 방사선 dual-energy X-ray
이중에너지 방사선흡수법
　dual-energy X-ray absorptiometry : DEXA
이지 toe off
이직율 turnover rate
이질의 heterogeneous
이케이지 EKG < electrocardiogram >
이코맵 eco map
이타드 Jean Marc Gaspard Itard
이타이이타이병 Itai-itai disease
이타주의 altruism
이탈 disengagement
이탈이론 disengagement theory
이튼람베르트 증후군 Eaton-Lambert syndrome
이틀에 한번 every other day
이펙사 Effexor
이피가 cradle
이하선염 mumps
이학요법 physical therapy
이학요법사 physical therapist : PT
이학요법사 실습가이드
　Guide to Physical Therapist Practice
이행기 케어 transitional care
이행역 transition zone
이혈종 aural hematoma
이형성증 dysplasia
이혼 divorce
이혼자 divorced person
이혼중재 divorce mediation
이혼증명서 divorce certificate
이혼치료 divorce therapy
이환 incidence
이환율 incidence rate
인가 accreditation ; approval
인가기준 accreditation standards

인간개발 human development
인간게놈프로젝트 Human Genome Project
인간공학 ergonomics ; human engineering
인간과학 human science
인간관계 human relations
인간관계관리 human relation management
인간발달단계 life stage
인간빈곤지수 human poverty index
인간소외 alienation
인간의 존엄 human dignity
인간적 실존치료
　humanistic and existential therapy
인간행동과학 human behavioral science
인건비용 personnel costs
인건비지출 personnel expenditures
인격 personality
인격검사 personality test
인격검사질문지 personality inventory
인격장애 personality disorder
인공고관절형성술 total hip arthroplasty
인공골두치환술 hemiarthroplasty
인공내이
　artificial cochlea ; cochlear implant ; hearing
　aid used in connection with implant
인공두뇌학 cybernetics
인공렌즈 artificial lens
인공방광 artificial bladder
인공수정 artificial insemination
인공심장 artificial heart
인공심장변 artificial heart valve
인공영양 artificial feeding
인공임신중절 elective abortion
인공장기 artificial organ
인공투석 hemodialysis
인공폐 artificial lung
인공항문 artificial anus
인공혈관 artificial blood vessel
인공호흡
　artificial respiration ; artificial ventilation ;
　rescue breathing
인공호흡기 artificial respirator ; respirator
인공호흡기의존 사지마비
　respirator dependent quadriplegia

인공환기 artificial ventilation
인공후두 voice generator
인구구조 population structure
인구동태 population dynamics
인구동태·보건통계과
  Vital and Health Statistics Division
인구동태통계 vital statistics
인구문제 population problem
인구의 제로성장 zero population growth
인구이동 population movement
인구전환론 demographic transition theory
인구정책 population policy
인구조사 population census
인구통계 demographic statistics
인구통계학 demography
인구폭발 population explosion
인구학 demography
인구학문적 종속인구비율
  demographic dependency ratio
인권 human rights
인권보장 safeguard for human rights
인권옹호위원회 civil liberties commission
인권존중 protection of human rights
인내력 frustration tolerance
인데랄 Inderal
인도신 Indocin
인도주의 humanism
인두 pharynx
인두단계 pharyngeal phase
인두배양 throat swab culture
인두세 payroll tax
인두제 선불정액제 capitated plan
인두지불제 capitated payment
인두통과시간 pharyngeal passage time
인드메타신 indomethacin
인디언 업무국 Bureau of Indian Affairs
인디케이터 indicator
인력개발 및 훈련법
  Manpower Development and Training Act
인력기획 manpower planning
인민자본주의 people's capitalism
인보관 settlement house
인보사업 settlement house work

인보운동 neighborhood movement
인본주의적 지향 humanistic orientation
인비져블 핸드 invisible hand
인사관리 staffing
인성검사 personality test
인성학 Ethology
인솔 insole
인수공통전염병 zoonosis
인슐린 insulin
인슐린비의존성 당뇨병
  non-insulin-dependent diabetes mellitus :
  NIDDM
인슐린의존성 당뇨병
  insulin-dependent diabetes mellitus : IDDM
인슐린자기주사 insulin self-injection
인스턴트식품 tertiary processed food
인스티튜셔널리즘 institutionalism
인습적 의료 conventional medicine
인습적 장기요양 conventional care
인식 recognition
인식론 epistemology
인식장애 cognitive impairment
인신공격방지위원회
  Anti-Defamation League of B'nai B'rith
인신보호영장 habeas corpus
인에이블러 enabler
인위적인 장애 factitious disorder
인자분석 factor analysis
인적서비스 personal social services
인적자본 human capital
인적자원 human resources
인정 accreditation ; certification
인정NPO법인 approved non-profit corporation
인정간호사 certified nurse : CN
인정간호조산사 certified nurse midwife
인정건강교육사
  certified health education specialist
인정조사 accreditation survey
인젝션 플러그 injection plug
인조섬유 artificial fiber
인종적 민족적 차이 racial and ethnic difference
인종차별 racism
인종차별주의 racism

인종할당 racial quotas
인증기준 certification standards
인지 cognition
인지 불일치 cognitive dissonance
인지도 cognitive map
인지모델 cognitive models
인지발달 cognitive development
인지상태 cognitive status
인지요법
  cognitive remediation ; cognitive therapy
인지유형 cognitive style
인지이론 cognitive theory
인지장애 cognitive disorder
인지재활 cognitive rehabilitation
인지적 재구성 cognitive restructuring
인지적 · 경험적 자기이론
  cognitive experiential self theory
인지증 dementia
인지증개호연구 · 연수센터
  Dementia Care Research and Training Center
인지증개호정보네트워크
  Dementia Care Information Network
인지증고령자 people with dementia
인지증고령자대책
  policy for the elderly with dementia ; policy
  for dementia
인지증고령자의 일상생활자립도
  independence level of elderly with dementia
인지증그룹홈
  group home for people with dementia ; group
  home for the elderly with dementia
인지증노인 the elderly with dementia
인지증노인대책 policy for elderly with dementia
인지증대응형공동생활개호
  group home for the demented
인지증대응형통소개호
  day care services for the demented
인지증도 level of dementia ; stage of dementia
인지증전문병동 special care unit
인지증케어전문병동 dementia special care unit
인지치료 cognitive therapy
인지패러다임 cognitive paradigm
인지행동요법 cognitive behavioral therapy

인지훈련 cognitive remediation
인체공학 ergonomics
인칭술 inching technique
인카운터그룹 encounter group
인클루전 inclusion
인터그룹워크 intergroup work
인터벤션 intervention
인터뷰 interview
인터섹스 intersex
인터페론 interferon
인터페론α interferon alfa
인터페론β interferon beta
인터페론γ interferon gamma
인터페이스 interface
인테그레이션 integration
인테이크 intake
인테이크 컨퍼런스 intake conference
인테이크면접 intake interview
인텐시브 케이스워커 intensive caseworker
인텔리전트 의족 intelligent prosthesis
인트론 A Intron A
인포멀 informal
인포멀네트워크 informal network
인포멀서비스 informal services
인포멀시스템 informal system
인포멀자원 informal resources
인포멀케어 informal care
인폼드초이스 informed choice
인폼드콘센트 informed consent : IC
인플레이션 inflation
인플루엔자 influenza
인플루엔자 바이러스 influenza virus
인플루엔자 백신 Influenza vaccine
인플릭시맙 infliximab
인핀지먼트 impingement
일 work
일고 day labor
일과성 균총 transient flora
일과성 뇌허혈발작 transient ischemic attack : TIA
일과성 세균총 transient flora
일광소독
  sunlight disinfection ; solar disinfection
일광욕 sunbathing

일군연계분석 cohort sequential analysis

일내변동 circadian variation

일레트립탄 eletriptan

일류성 요실금 overflow incontinence

일몰증후군 sundown syndrome

일몰행동 sundowning

일반개업자 generalist

일반건강교육 general health education

일반고용 competitive employment

일반공무원제도 서열화 GS civil service ranks

일반급부 demogrants

일반병상 general bed

일반병원 general hospital

일반부조 general assistance

일반사회사업 generic social work

일반사회사업가 generic social worker

일반세대조사 general household survey : GHS

일반소시얼워크 generic social work

일반시스템이론 general system theory

일반욕조 general bathtub

일반의 general practitioner : GP

일반적-특수적 논쟁 generic-specific controversy

일반주가지수

common stock price ; price of common stock

일반진료소 general medical clinic

일반체계이론 general system theory

일반행정부문 general administrative field

일반화 generalization

일반회계 general account

일본 생명의 전화연맹

Federation of Inochi No Denwa Inc.

일본WHO협회 WHO Association of Japan

일본개호복지사회

Japan Association of Certified Care Workers

일본고령자학대방지센터

Japanese Center for the Prevention of Elder Abuse

일본공업규격 Japanese Industrial Standards : JIS

일본구강외과학회

Japanese Society of Oral and Maxillofacial Surgeons

일본구급구명사협회

Japanese Paramedics Association

일본미량영양소학회

Japan Trace Nutrients Research Society

일본방사선기사회

Japan Association of Radiological Technologists : JART

일본사회복지사회

Japan Association of Certified Social Workers

일본소시얼워크협회

Japanese Association of Social Workers

일본식 변기 squat toilet

일본식 혼수척도 Japan Coma Scale : JCS

일본아이뱅크협회 Japan Eye Bank Association

일본약제사회 Japan Pharmaceutical Association

일본의사회 Japan Medical Association

일본임상공학기사회

Japan Association for Clinical Engineering Technologists

일본임상위생검사기사회

Japanese Association of Medical Technologists : JAMT

일본존엄사협회

Japan Society for Dying with Dignity

일본집중치료의학회

Japanese Society of Intensive Care Medicine

일본치과의사회 Japan Dental Association

일본치매노인가족회

Alzheimer's Association Japan

일본판 덴버식 발달스크리닝검사

Japanese Version of Denver Developmental Screening Test : JDDST-R

일부다처제 (일처다부제) polygamy

일부보조 limited assistance

일부부담금 co-payment

일부사무조합 partial affairs association

일부일처제 monogamy

일부치매 lacunar dementia

일산화탄소 carbon monoxide

일산화탄소 중독 carbon monoxide poisoning

일상생활동작 activities of daily living : ADL

일상생활용구

equipments for daily living activities

일상생활자립도 판정기준

index of independence in activities of daily

living
일상생활지도 routine daily-life guidance
일상생활활동 activities of daily living : ADL
일상적 금전관리
　daily money management : DMM
일상적 손씻기 social hand washing
일상적 처우 daily treatment
일상지속적 두통
　new daily persistent headache : NDPH
일상청소 usual cleaning
일시고용 temporary employment
일시급여금 temporary allowance
일시보호 temporary protection
일시부조 temporary aid ; temporary assistance
일시적 temporary
일시적 경기침체 recession
일시적 서비스 temporary services
일시적 신체장애휴업제도
　temporary disability leave
일안 daily program
일어나기 getting up
일어서기 sit to stand
일어서기운동 sit-to-stand exercise
일용근로자 day laborer
일일 이용료 basic daily fee
일중독자 workaholic
일지 diary
일차과정 primary process
일차구심성 섬유 primary afferent fiber
일차예방 primary prevention
일차예방 primary prevention
일차이득 primary gain
일차적 사고과정 primary process thinking
일차적 치료 primal therapy
일차집단 primary group
일차판정
　initial assessment ; preliminary assessment
일탈 deviance
일탈행동 deviant behavior
일화기억 episodic memory
일회성 집단 single-session group
일회용 disposable
임금 wage

임금격차 wage disparity
임금복지통계과
　Wages and Labour Welfare Statistics Division
임금슬라이드 wage indexation
임금체계 wage system
임금통제 wage controls
임금피크제 salary peak
임대료쟁의 rent strike
임대료통제 rent control
임대주택 rental housing
임무 assignment
임산부 maternal
임산부사망율 Maternal death rate
임상가 clinician
임상검사 clinical examination
임상검사기사
　clinical laboratory technologist and technician
임상경로 clinical pathway
임상공학기사 clinical engineering technologist
임상사회복지사
　Licensed Clinical Social Worker : LCSW
임상사회사업 clinical social work
임상세균검사기사
　clinical microbiological technician
임상시험 clinical trial
임상시험결과 clinical trial result
임상심리사 clinical psychologist
임상심리학 clinical psychology
임상약제사 clinical pharmacist
임상영양평가 clinical nutritional assessment
임상의 clinician
임상적 개입 clinical intervention
임상적 면접 clinical interview
임상적 진단 clinical diagnosis
임상적 치매평가척도
　Clinical Dementia Rating Scale : CDR
임상호흡치료서비스
　clinical respiratory care and services
임시적 임용 temporary appointment
임시휴직 lay-off
임신 gestation
임신당뇨병 gestational diabetes
임원 director

임의가입 optional enrollment
임의단체 unincorporated association
임의보험 voluntary insurance
임의성 자금 discretionary funds
임의입원 conditional voluntary admission
임의후견제도 voluntary guardianship system
임종 dying
임종간호 caring for the dying
임질 gonorrhea
임파워먼트 empowerment
임파워먼트 접근법 empowerment approach
임펄스 impulse
임페어먼트 impairment
임포텐츠 impotence
입각기 stance phase
입각중기 mid-stance phase
입면 falling asleep
입법자 lawmaker
입소 admission
입소결정 admission ; admission decision
입소기간 length of stay : LOS
입소시설 residential facility

입소자 resident
입소형 시설이용자의 권리 rights of residents
입술 오므리고 숨쉬기 pursed lip breathing
입양 adoption
입양보조금 subsidized adoption
입원 hospitalization
입원결정 admission decision
입원기간 length of stay : LOS
입원료 admission charge
입원보험 hospital insurance : HI
입원조치 involuntary hospital admission
입원치료단계 hospital level of care
입원형 완화케어 inpatient hospice
입원환자 inpatient
입위 standing position
입위보지장치 stabilizer
입위운동 standing exercise
입회 enrollment
입회자 enrollee
입회제약 enrollment restriction
잇몸 gingival
잉크블롯 테스트 inkblot test

자가분해 autolysis
자가수용기 autoreceptor
자가중독 self-poisoning
자격 제거 decertification
자격임용제도
system for appointing a qualified person ;
system for appointing qualified persons
자격증 certification
자궁경부형성장애증 cervical dysplasia
자궁경암 cervical cancer
자궁난관조영 hysterosalpingography
자궁외임신 ectopic pregnancy
자궁탈 uterine prolapse
자극 impulse
자극감수성 irritability
자극반응이론 irritation response theory
자극법 stimulation method
자극일반화 stimulus generalization
자기각지 self-awareness
자기감염 self-infection
자기개념 self-concept
자기개선 self-improvement
자기건강관리 self-care
자기건강관리 매니지먼트 self-care management
자기건강관리 플랜 self-care plan
자기결정 self-determination
자기결정의 원칙
principle of client self-determination
자기공명장치 magnetic resonance imaging : MRI
자기공명혈관촬영
magnetic resonance angiography : MRA
자기교시훈련 self-instructional training
자기권리주장운동 self-advocacy movement

자기도뇨 self-catheterization
자기동일성 self-identity
자기면역 autoimmunity
자기면역성 간염 autoimmune hepatitis
자기민족중심주의 ethnocentrism
자기방어 ego defense
자기방위형 self-protection type
자기방임 self-neglect
자기부담금 co-payment
자기분해 autolysis
자기수용체 autoreceptor
자기실현 self-actualization ; self-realization
자기애성 인격장애
narcissistic personality disorder
자기애성 장기요양자 narcissistic caregiver
자기옹호운동 self-advocacy movement
자기용균 autolysis
자기이해 self-understanding
자기인식 self-awareness
자기자극 magnetic stimulation
자기조절 autoregulation
자기조절진통법 patient-controlled analgesia : PCA
자기조정 self-maintenance
자기주장 assertiveness
자기주장훈련 assertiveness training
자기중심주의 egocentrism
자기지불 out-of-pocket
자기집 own house
자기책임 self-responsibility
자기치료 self-medication
자기컨트롤이론 self-control theory
자기타동운동 self-assisted exercise
자기통제 self-control

자기투자형 개인연금
self-invested personal pension
자기파괴적 성격장애
self-defeating personality disorder
자기파산 voluntary bankruptcy
자기평가 self-evaluation
자기폭로 self-disclosure
자기표현 self-expression
자기혐오 self-hatred
자기효력감 self-efficacy
자녀보호권이 박탈된 어머니회
Mother without Custody
자녀양육권 child custody
자동가동역 active range of motion : AROM
자동기술법 automatism
자동내시경세정장치
automated endoscope reprocessor : AER
자동보조운동 active assisted exercise
자동복막투석 automatic peritoneal dialysis
자동사고 autonomic thought
자동수축 voluntary contraction
자동안전장치 self-hate
자동열림식 훅 voluntary opening hook
자동운동 active movement
자동잠김식 훅 voluntary closing hook
자동제세동기 automated external defibrillator
자동조절 autoregulation
자동차사고 motor vehicle accident
자동차수당 automobile allowance
자동청성 뇌간반응
automated auditory brainstem response
자동청성 뇌간반응평가
automated auditory brainstem response
evaluation
자동훈련 active exercise
자록솔림 Zaroxolyn
자립 independence
자립도 level of independent
자립생활 independent living : IL
자립생활기구 independent living aid
자립생활센터
Center for Independent Living : CIL
자립생활스킬 independent living skill

자립생활운동 independent living movement
자립생활원조 self-reliant living assistance services
자립성 존중원리
principle of respect for autonomy
자립센터 independence center
자립의 개념 concepts of independence
자립조장 help the clients help themselves
자립지원 independence support
자문 consultation
자문기관 advisory council
자문제공 advice giving
자문조정정신의학 consultation-liaison psychiatry
자발성 대 죄악감 initiative versus guilt
자발적 voluntary
자발적 반응기법 operant technique
자발적 반응조건부여 operant conditioning
자발적 실업 voluntary unemployment
자발활동 spontaneous activity
자본의 전형운동 metamorphosis of capital
자본조사 means test
자본주의 capitalism
자비소독 boiling sterilization
자비지불 out of pocket
자산 assets
자산세 property tax
자산조사 means test
자살 suicide
자살방조 assisted suicide
자살성 사고 suicidal ideation
자살예방 suicide prevention
자상타해 danger to self or others
자상행위 self-harm : SH ; self-injury
자선 charity
자선남비 charity pot
자선병원 charity hospital
자선사업 charity work
자선조직협회
Charity Organization Societies : COS
자선조직화운동
The Charity Organization Movement
자선활동 philanthropy
자세 posture
자세반사 postural reflex

자세반응 postural reaction
자세훈련 postural exercise
자식의 책임 filial responsibility
자신의 사망처리에 관한 유서 living will
자아 ego
자아기능 ego functioning
자아도취 narcissism
자아동일성 ego identity
자아력 ego strengths
자아분석 ego analysis
자아성취 기대 self-fulfilling prophecy
자아실현 self-actualization
자아심리학 ego psychology
자아욕구 esteem needs
자아지향적 사회사업 ego-oriented social work
자아통합 ego integration
자연발생적 동기부여 intrinsic motivation
자연발생적 퇴직자커뮤니티
    naturally occurring retirement community
자연발생적집단 spontaneous group
자연법사상 the principle of natural law
자연연상 free association
자연원조망 natural helping network
자연재해 natural disaster
자연집단 natural group ; informal group
자영 사회복지기관 private social agencies
자영업 self-employment
자영업자 self-employed
자영업자 건강보험공제
    self-employed health insurance deduction
자외선 ultraviolet
자외선살균 ultraviolet disinfection
자외선요법 ultraviolet therapy
자외선조사 ultra violet radiation
자외선차폐소재
    ultraviolet rays protection material
자원 resources
자원기준 상대가치측정법
    Resource-Based Relative Value Scale : RBRVS
자원봉사 volunteer
자원봉사 어드바이저 volunteer adviser
자원봉사 코디네이터 volunteer coordinator
자원봉사계획 volunteer plan

자원봉사국 volunteer bureau
자원봉사그룹 volunteer group
자원봉사기금 volunteer fund
자원봉사센터 volunteer center
자원봉사자 volunteer
자원봉사자육성사업
    volunteer service providers development
    association
자원봉사자카드 volunteer card
자원봉사주의 volunteerism
자원봉사활동 volunteer activity
자원봉사활동국
    Office of Voluntary Action : VAC
자원정신 voluntarism
자원주의 voluntarism
자원체계 resource systems
자원할당 resource allocation
자유권 the right of freedom
자유기업제도 free enterprise system
자유무역협정 Free Trade Agreement : FTA
자유방임 laissez-faire
자유연상 free association
자유재량고정원가 managed cost
자유주의자 liberal
자유주의적 복지국가 liberal welfare state
자유진료 point-of-service
자율사회사업 autonomous practice
자율성 autonomy
자율성 대 수치심과 의심
    autonomy versus shame and doubt
자율신경 autonomic nerve
자율신경계 autonomic nervous system
자율신경과반사
    autonomic dysreflexia ; autonomic
    hyperreflexia
자율신경기능장애 autonomic dysfunction
자율신경실조 dysautonomia
자율신경장애
    dysautonomia ; autonomic nerve disorder
자율훈련법 autogenic training
자이프렉사 Zyprexa
자재고리 caster
자제 continence ; self-restraint

자조 self-help
자조도구 self-help device
자조원칙 principle of self-help
자조조직 self-help organization
자조집단 self-help groups
자존심 self-esteem
자주선택성 autonomous choice
자주성 autonomy
자주재원 independent source of revenue
자주퇴원 against medical advice : AMA
자치사무 autonomous affairs
자치체 재판소 municipal court
자치회 self-government association
자택화재 home fire
자폐아 autistic child
자폐증 autism
자폐증 스펙트럼장애
  autism spectrum disorder : ASD
자활보호 occupational aid
작업기억 working memory
작업내성 work tolerance
작업능력 work capacity
작업동기 work incentives
작업요법 occupational therapy
작업요법사 occupational therapist : OT
작업용 의수 work arm
작업장 workhouse
작업장법 The Workhouse Act
작업장테스트법 Workhouse Test Act
작업조정 work adjustment
작업치료 occupational therapy
작업치료사 occupational therapist : OT
작업테이블 work-table
작열통 causalgia
작용 action
작은 정부 small government
작화증 confabulation
잔뇨 residual urine
잔뇨감 residual sensation
잔여적 모델 대 제도적 모델
  residual versus institutional model
잔여적 복지시책 residual welfare provision
잔존감각 remaining sense

잔존능력 [잔존기능]
  remaining function ; residual functional
  capacity
잔존능력평가
  residual functional capacity assessment
잘 쓰는 손 handedness
잘레플론 zaleplon
잠들기 falling asleep
잠복감염 latent infection
잠복기 latency period
잠복기 보균자 incubation carrier
잠시 latency
잠재기 latency stage
잠재내용 latent content
잠재니즈 potential needs
잠재실업 latent unemployment
잠재연령기 latency-age child
잠재욕구 potential need
잠재의식 subconscious mind
잠재적 과잉인구 latent overpopulation
잠재적 동성애 homosexuality latent
잠재적 동성애자 latent homosexual
잠재적 욕구 latent needs
잠재적 정신분열증 환자 latent schizophrenic
잠재적 충성 invisible loyalties
잠정거택서비스계획
  tentative plan for home-based care services
잠정적 분석 wild analysis
잠혈검사 guaiac test
잠혈시험 occult blood test
장 전처치 bowel preparation
장 탈장 Enterocele
장관 이송능검사 transit study
장구
  orthosis ; brace ; prosthesis ; orthopedic
  appliance
장굴 palmar flexion
장기개호 long-term care
장기기억 long-term memory
장기기획 long-range planning
장기능 bowel function
장기능장애 encopresis
장기목표 long-term goal

장기보호시설 long-term care facilities
장기시설케어 long-term institutional care
장기요양 care ; long-term care
장기요양계획 care plan
장기요양과정 care process
장기요양관계 care provider-recipient relationship
장기요양급여 long-term care insurance benefit
장기요양급여비용
  long-term care insurance payment
장기요양기관 long-term care institute
장기요양기기 care equipment ; care device
장기요양기록 nursing records
장기요양기술 care skills
장기요양노동 care work
장기요양노동자 care worker
장기요양노인보건시설 geriatric health care facilities
장기요양노인복지시설 geriatric welfare facilities
장기요양담당자 direct care staff
장기요양대상 long-term care-required
장기요양등급 long-term care classification levels
장기요양등급인정
  long-term care classification levels
  authorization
장기요양등급자 long-term care recipient
장기요양등급판정위원회
  Long-Term Care Classification Committee ;
  Long-Term Care Certification Committee
장기요양로보트 care robot
장기요양만족감 satisfaction in caregiving
장기요양목표 care goal
장기요양보험료
  long-term care insurance premium
장기요양보험료감면제도
  deduction of long-term care insurance
  premiums
장기요양보험료율 Long-Term care insurance
  premium rate
장기요양보험법 Long-Term Care Insurance Law
장기요양보험사업계획
  long-term care insurance plan
장기요양보험제도
  long-term care insurance system
장기요양보호 long-term care

장기요양복지 care and welfare
장기요양부담 burden of care
장기요양비용 long-term care costs
장기요양서비스 long-term care services
장기요양서비스계획 care services plan
장기요양수가 long-term care pricing
장기요양시설 long-term care facility
장기요양심사위원회
  Long-Term Care Review Committee
장기요양심판위원회
  Long-Term Care Referee's Committee
장기요양예방 prevention of long-term care
장기요양예방사업 preventive long-term care plan
장기요양예방서비스 care-preventive services
장기요양옴부즈맨 long-term care ombudsman
장기요양욕구 long-term care needs
장기요양원조자
  care assistant ; long-term care assistant
장기요양으로의 접근 access to care
장기요양의 기준 standards of care
장기요양의 질 quality of care
장기요양인정서 long-term care certification
장기요양인정심사회
  Long-Term Care Certification Committee
장기요양인정점수 long-term care approval score
장기요양인정조사
  long-term care insurance eligibility assessment
장기요양인정조사표
  long-term care approval survey
장기요양일지 nursing notes
장기요양자 caregiver
장기요양자 부담 caregiver burden
장기요양자 부담지표 caregiver strain index : CSI
장기요양자 부담질문표 caregiver burden interview
장기요양자 부담척도 Caregiver Burden Scale
장기요양자 수당 carer's allowance
장기요양자 스트레스 caregiver stress
장기요양자세 attitudes toward care
장기요양자의 2차적 스트레스
  secondary stress on caregivers
장기요양자의 감정적 탈진증후군 caregiver burnout
장기요양자의 권리 rights of caregivers
장기요양종사자 direct care staff

장기요양지도 care guidance
장기요양지원전문원 care manager
장기요양직원 direct care staff
장기요양판정위원회
　Long-Term Care Certification Committee
장기요양행위 care practice
장기요양휴가 family care leave
장기요양휴가수당금 family care allowance
장기이식 organ transplantation
장기입소 long-term stay
장기자원봉사 long-term volunteer
장기제공 organ donation
장기치료 long-term care
장기침상요양 bed rest
장기케어 long-term care
장기케어시장 long-term care industry
장끈 intestinal string
장년봉사단 Group of Elderly Volunteers
장님아시설 facility for the blind children
장대립보조기 long opponens wrist hand orthosis
장래추계인구 population projection
장루설치환자 ostomate
장물아비 fence
장바이러스 enterovirus
장세정 bowel irrigation
장수 longevity
장수과학 longevity science
장수사회 longevity society
장수사회복지기금
　Social Welfare Funds for Longevity Society
장수의료제도
　Health Insurance System for Elderly Aged 75
　and Above
장식용 의수
　cosmetic < non-functional > upper limb
　prosthesis
장식핸드 cosmetic hand
장신의료사회사업 psychiatric social work
장애 disability
장애고령자 disabled elderly
장애고령자의 일상생활자립도
　independence level of the disabled elderly
장애군인 프로그램 Veterans Disability Program

장애군인연금 프로그램
　Veterans Disability Pension Program
장애급여 disability benefit
장애기초연금 basic disability pension
장애노인 the disabled elderly
장애동결 disability freeze
장애등급 disability levels
장애등급구분 degree of disability
장애모델 model of disability
장애보건복지부
　Department of Health and Welfare for
　Persons with Disabilities
장애보상급부 disability compensation
장애보험 disability insurance : DI
장애복지과
　Welfare Division for Persons with Disabilities
장애복지수당 disability welfare allowance
장애복지연금 disability welfare pension
장애아 disabled child
장애아간호
　nursing care for the disabled children
장애아개호
　caring for the disabled children ; care for the
　disabled children disabled children's care
장애아개호지원
　care management for the disabled children
장애아교육 education for the disabled children
장애아동교육법
　Education for All Handicapped Children Act
장애아동법 Handicapped Children Act
장애아보육 nursery for the disabled children
장애아복지수당 child disability allowance
장애아부조 assistance for the disabled children
장애아양육
　care with education for the disabled children
장애아의료
　medical care for the disabled children
장애아일시급여금
　temporary disability child allowance
장애연금 disability pension
장애유아 the disabled infant
장애의 개념
　concept of the disablement ; concept of

disability

장애의 사회모델 social model of disability

장애의 수용 acceptance of disability

장애의 의학모델 medical model of disability

장애인 disabled

장애인 올림픽 Olympic for the disabled

장애인 일시급여금 temporary disability allowance

장애인 정보네트워크

information network for the disabled

장애인간호 nursing care for the disabled

장애인개호

caring for the disabled ; care for the disabled

장애인개호지원 disability care management

장애인갱생상담소

rehabilitation counseling center for the disabled

장애인갱생센터

rehabilitation center for the disabled

장애인고용 employment of the disabled

장애인고용대책과

Employment Measures for Persons with

Disabilities Division

장애인고용율 employment rates of the disabled

장애인고용촉진

employment promotion for the disabled

장애인고용촉진대책

employment promotion policy for the disabled

장애인고용촉진법

Law for Employment Promotion of Persons

with Disabilities

장애인교육 education for the disabled

장애인권리운동 disability rights movement

장애인기본계획

basic pension for persons with disabilities

장애인기본법

Basic Act for Persons with Disabilities

장애인단체 organization for the disabled

장애인대상 민간서비스

private services for the disabled

장애인복지 welfare for the disabled

장애인복지상담원 welfare adviser for the disabled

장애인복지수당 disability welfare allowance

장애인복지연금 disability welfare pension

장애인부조 assistance for the disabled

장애인생활수당 disability living allowance

장애인생활지원수당 disability living allowance

장애인세공제 tax deduction for the disabled

장애인수당 disability allowance

장애인스포츠 disabled sports

장애인운동 disability movement

장애인원조 support for the disabled

장애인의 권리선언

Declaration on the Rights of Disabled Persons

장애인의 존엄 dignity of the disabled

장애인의 참이웃 모임

People-to-People Committee for the

Handicapped

장애인의료 medical care for the disabled

장애인자립생활

independent living for the disabled

장애인자립생활센터

independent living center for the disabled

장애인자립생활운동

independent living movement of the disabled

장애인자립센터

independence center for the disabled

장애인작업소 workshop for the disabled

장애인장기요양보험제도

Long-Term Care Insurance System for the

Disabled People

장애인정

disability certification ; certification of

disability

장애인주차허가증 disabled parking permit

장애인직업훈련

vocational training for the disabled

장애인직업훈련시설

vocational training facility for the disabled

장애인케어매니지먼트

care management for the disabled ; disability

care management

장애인플랜 federal plan for the disabled

장애인학대 disabled abuse

장애일시급여금

temporary disability allowance ; temporary

allowance for the disabled

장애정도구분 disability levels

장애정도구분의 인정
 certification of disability level

장애체험 experienced illness

장애학 disability study

장애후생연금 employee pension for disability

장염 비비리오 vibrio parahaemolyticus

장용성 제피 enteric-coating

장용코팅 enteric-coating

장용피 enteric-coating

장제보호 funeral care

장좌위 long-sitting position

장줄 intestinal string

장티푸스 typhoid fever

장폐쇄 ileus

재가간호 home health

재가간호사 home health aide

재가간호케어 home health care

재가간호케어기관 home health care agency

재가개호 home care

재가개호복지사 certified home care worker

재가개호사 home care aide

재가개호상담원 home care advisor

재가개호서비스기관 home care services agency

재가개호서비스사업소 home care services office

재가개호서비스사업자
 home care services provider

재가개호지원 home care management

재가개호지원센터 home care management center

재가고령자개호서비스
 home care services for the elderly

재가고령자복지서비스
 in-home welfare services for the elderly

재가노인개호서비스
 home care services for the aged

재가노인복지사업
 in-home welfare program for the aged

재가노인복지서비스
 in-home welfare services for the aged

재가보호서비스 home care service

재가복지 domiciliary care

재가복지대책 in-home welfare policy

재가복지봉사센터 in-home welfare service center

재가복지사업 in-home welfare service project

재가복지서비스 in-home welfare services

재가복지서비스기관
 in-home welfare services agency

재가복지서비스사업소
 in-home welfare services office

재가복지서비스사업자
 in-home welfare services provider

재가부조 home assistance

재가산소요법 home oxygen therapy : HOT

재가서비스 home care services

재가서비스기관 home care services agency

재가서비스사업소 home care services office

재가서비스사업자 home care services provider

재가서비스제공자 home care services provider

재가요양 home health care

재가요양지원진료소
 home health care support clinic

재가원조 home support

재가의료 medical home care

재가의료대책 medical home care plan

재가의료서비스 medical home care services

재가의료추진회의
 Commission for Promotion of Home Care

재가의사 home care physician

재가의학 home care medicine

재가장애인개호서비스
 home care services for the disabled

재가장애인복지서비스
 in-home welfare services for the disabled

재가장애인복지서비스기관
 in-home welfare services agency for the disabled

재가장애인복지서비스사업소
 in-home welfare services agency for the disabled

재가장애인복지서비스사업자
 in-home welfare services provider for the disabled

재가재활 home rehabilitation

재가중심정맥영양
 home parenteral nutrition : HPN

재가치료 home treatment

재가케어 home care

재가케어서비스 home care services
재가케어서비스기관 home care services agency
재가케어서비스사업소 home care services office
재가케어서비스사업자
  home care services provider
재가케어평가
  Outcome and Assessment Information Set :
  OASIS ; home care assessment
재가케어플랜 care plan for home care
재가투석요법 home dialysis therapy
재결합가정 reconstituted family
재고용 reemployment arrangements
재과제분석 reanalysis of problems
재교육증명 re-certification
재구성 reframing
재난 disaster
재단 (기금) foundations
재단법인 incorporated foundation
재래형 conventional
재명명 relabeling
재무관리 financial management
재무위원회 Committee of Ways and Means
재무제표 financial statement
재범 (재발) 률 (상습적 범행률) recidivism rate
재범자 (상습자) recidivist
재보증 reassurance
재분류 reclassification
재분배 redistribution
재분배효과 redistributive effect
재사용 reuse
재사회화 집단 resocialization group
재산분여 property division
재산조사 means test
재생불량성 빈혈 aplastic anemia
재생의료 regeneration medicine
재원 hospital stay
재인정 re-certification
재정력지수 financial capability index
재정복지 financial welfare
재정안정화기금 financial stability fund
재정중재기구 fiscal intermediaries
재정착 resettlement
재정투융자 treasury investment and loan

재정파탄 budget buster
재조직화 reorganization
재지정 re-certification
재직증명서 proof of employment letter
재평가 reassessment ; reevaluation
재해 accident
재해과학 disaster science
재해급여 disaster benefit
재해보상 accident compensation
재해보험 accident insurance
재해복구 charette
재해예방 disaster prevention
재해증후군 disaster syndrome
재허가 recognition
재혼 remarriage
재혼가정 remarried family
재활 rehabilitation
재활간호 rehabilitation nursing
재활간호사 rehabilitation nurse
재활개호 rehabilitative care
재활공학 rehabilitation engineering
재활기기 rehabilitation equipment
재활사회사업가 rehabilitation worker
재활서비스 rehabilitation
재활소시얼워커 social worker for rehabilitation
재활소시얼워크 social work in rehabilitation
재활시설 rehabilitation institute
재활의 physiatrist
재활의학 rehabilitation medicine
재활전문 안내서
  Rehabilitation Specialty's Handbook
재활접근법 rehabilitation approach
재활중지기준 inhibitor for rehabilitation
재활처방 rehabilitation prescription
재활프로그램 rehabilitation program
재흥감염증 re-emerging infectious diseases
쟁의권 right to strike
저긴장성 방광 bladder hypotonia
저나트륨혈증 hyponatremia
저능 imbecile
저능자 moron
저밀도지단백 low-density lipoprotein : LDL
저밀도콜레스테롤 low-density lipoprotein : LDL

저산소증 anoxia

저산소혈증 anoxemia ; hypoxemia

저상버스 low floor bus

저소득 low income

저소득가정 low income family

저소득가정 에너지원조 프로그램
Low Income Home Energy Assistance
program

저소득고령자대상 임대주택
low-income rental housing for the elderly ;
rental housing for low-income elderly

저소득국 low income country

저소득세대 low income household

저소득자세대 borderline family

저소득층 low income class

저속진행성 인슐린의존 당뇨병
slowly progressive insulin dependent diabetes

저수준소독 low level disinfection

저시력 low vision

저영양상태 undernutrition

저온살균 pasteurization ; cold sterilization

저온살균기 pasteurizer

저온화상 low temperature burn

저임금노동 low-wage labor

저임금노동시장 low-wage labor market

저작 mastication

저작권 copyright

저작근염 masticatory myositis

저작기능장애 masticatory disorder

저작문제 chewing problem

저작장애
mastication disorder ; masticatory disturbance

저장성 탈수 hypotonic dehydration

저주파요법 low frequency current therapy

저지방식 low-fat diet

저체온 hypothermia

저출산 · 고령사회기본법
Basic Act for the Low Birth Rate and the
Aging Society

저출산 · 고령사회위원회
Low Birth Rate and Aging Society
Commission

저출산고령화 depopulation and aging

저출산화 depopulation

저출생체중아 low birth weight infant

저항 resistance

저항운동 resistance exercise

저항훈련 resistance training

저해인자 inhibitor

저혈당 hypoglycemia

저혈당증 hypoglycemia

저혈압 hypotension

적격성 eligibility

적극적개별사회사업 reaching out casework

적당하고 질 좋은 케어
quality affordable health care

적립금 accumulation

적립방식 accumulative method

적법 증거 competent evidence

적변 stool extraction

적색지대 redlining

적십자 Red Cross

적십자사 Red Cross

적외선요법 infrared therapy

적용 adequacy

적응 adaptation

적응과 부적응 adjustment and maladjustment

적응기제 adjustment mechanism

적응성 adaptedness

적응성진단테스트 adjustment diagnosis test

적응장애 maladjustment disorder

적자 deficit

적자생존 the survival of the fittest

적정검사 aptitude test

적합 fitting

적합판정 fitting evaluation

적혈구 red blood cell : RBC

적혈구용적률 hematocrit

적혈구침강속도
erythrocyte sedimentation rate : ESR

전개호보험 universal long-term care insurance

전개호보험제도
universal long-term care insurance system

전공학습 concentrations

전국건강복지축제
National Health and Welfare Festival

전국노인건강축제
National Health Festival for the Elderly

전국노인데이케어연락협의회
Adult Day-care Liaison Council Japan

전국노인병원협의회
National Council of Hospitals for Elderly

전국노인보호전문기관
National Specialized Agency for Protection of Elderly

전국노인복지관대회
National Welfare Center for the Elderly

전국노인복지단체연합회
National Union of Welfare Association for the Elderly

전국노인복지단체협의회
National Institute of Welfare Association for the Elderly

전국노인클럽연합회
Japan Federation of Senior Citizens' Club

전국도시연맹 National Urban League

전국민연금 universal pension

전국민의료보험
national universal medical insurance

전국사회복지협의회
Japan National Council of Social Welfare

전국사회사업가협회 윤리강령
NASW Code of Ethics

전국소비자연맹 Consumer's League National

전국요양보호사협회
Korean Care Workers' Association

전국유료양로원협회
Japanese Association of Retirement Housing

전국카톨릭자선단체대회
National Conference on Catholic Charities

전국푸드뱅크 National Food Bank

전극 electrode

전근비용 moving expenses

전기경련요법 electroconvulsive therapy : ECT

전기고령자
elderly aged between 65 and 74 ; young-old

전기관절각도계 electrogoniometer

전기생리학 electrophysiology

전기쇼크요법 electroshock therapy : EST

전기요법 electrotherapy

전기자극 electrostimulation

전기자극장치 electrostimulator

전기진단법 electrodiagnosis : EDX

전기충격치료 electroshock therapy : EST

전기치료 electrotherapy ; elektrotherapie

전도성 distractibility ; conductive deafness

전도성 난청 conductive deafness

전도성 실어증 conduction aphasia

전도후 증후군 post-fall syndrome

전동브라이유식 점자타이프라이터
electric Braille writer

전동의수 electric upper limb prosthesis

전동점자타이프라이터 electric Braille writer

전동점자타자기 electric Braille writer

전동침대 electric bed

전동칫솔 electric toothbrush

전동휠체어 electric wheelchair

전동흡인기 electric aspirator

전두엽 frontal lobe

전두엽장애 frontal lobe dysfunction

전두엽증상 frontal lobe syndrome

전두측두엽치매 front-temporal dementia

전략적 가족치료 strategic family therapy

전략적 계획 strategic marketing

전략적 마케팅 strategic marketing

전략적 파괴행동 disruptive tactics

전륜보행기 front-wheel walker

전륜절첩보행기 front wheel folding walker

전립선비대증 benign prostatic hyperplasia

전립선암 prostate cancer

전립선염 prostatitis

전립선질환 prostate disease

전립선특이항원 prostate specific antigen

전만 lordosis

전망적 리뷰 prospective review

전망적 연구 prospective study

전맹 total blindness

전면개호 total care

전면발달 holistic-faceted development

전면보조 total assistance

전면원조 total assistance

전면의존 total dependence

전면장기요양 total care
전면접촉 소켓 total contact socket
전문 profession
전문가 specialist
전문기증언 expert witness
전문간호사 nurse practitioner
전문개별사회사업 specific casework
전문기준심의기구
　Professional Standards Review Organizations
전문사회사업 specific social work
전문성 professionalism
전문요양시설 skilled nursing facility
전문의 medical specialist
전문적 태도 professional attitude
전문직 profession
전문직단체 professional association
전문화 professionalization
전반적 기능평가
　Global Assessment of Functioning : GAF
전반적 평가척도 Global Assessment Scale : GAS
전보험 universal insurance
전보험제도 universal health insurance system
전분 amylum ; starch
전사반부절단 forequarter amputation
전색맹 total color blindness
전성기기 pregenital
전수조사 complete survey
전신닦기 full-body sponge bath
전신목욕 full-body bath
전신샤워욕 whole-body bathing
전신성 진행성 경화증
　progressive systemic sclerosis
전신성 홍반성 낭창
　systemic lupus erythematosus : SLE
전신성 홍반성 루프스
　systemic lupus erythematosus : SLE
전신세정 full-body sponge bath
전신욕 full-body bath
전실 anteroom
전실어 total aphasia
전연금 universal pension
전연금보험 universal pension insurance
전연금보험제도

universal pension insurance system
전염병 communicable disease
전염병예방법
　Communicable Diseases Prevention Law
전염성 질환 transmissible disease
전완의수 transradial prosthesis
전완절단 below-elbow amputation
전원 hospital transfer
전의료보험 universal medical care insurance
전의료보험제도
　universal medical care insurance system
전의식 preconscious
전이 transference
전이신경증 transference neurosis
전이초점화 정신요법
　transference focused psychotherapy
전인격적 케어 total personal care
전인적의료 holistic medicine
전자건강기록 electronic health records
전자기록 electric records
전자내시경검사 electronic endoscopy
전자부 골절 trochanteric fracture
전자빔 전산화단층촬영
　electron beam computed tomography
전자빔CT electron-beam computed tomography
전자선멸균 electron beam sterilization
전자정부 cyber government
전자진료기록카드 electronic health records
전자처방 e-prescription
전자활액포염 trochanteric bursitis
전정동안반사 vestibulo-ocular reflex
전정안반사 vestibulo-ocular reflex
전정장애 vestibular dysfunction
전조작기 preoperational stage
전족부 접촉 foot slap
전직 occupational change
전척수동맥증후군 anterior spinal artery syndrome
전체론 holism
전체론적 연구 holistic
전치 displacement
전향성 건망 anterograde amnesia
전화 inversion
전환 conversion

전환성 장애 conversion disorder
전환성 히스테리 신경증
 hysterical neurosis, conversion type
전환자 역할 distracter role
전환장애 conversion disorder
전환증상 conversion symptoms
절단 amputation
절단단 amputation stump
절대근력 absolute muscle strength
절대부조 categorical assistance
절대불응기 absolute refractory period
절대습도 absolute humidity
절대역 absolute threshold
절대적 빈곤 absolute poverty
절도죄 larceny
절뚝걸음 antalgic gait
절박성 요실금 urge incontinence
절식 nothing by mouth< nulla per os > : NPO
절제 abstinence
절주회
 drinking giving-up organization ; Stop
 Drinking Alcohol Support Group
절충 mediation
절충적 eclectic
점묵법 tattooing
점안액 eye drop
점역 translation into Braille
점역봉사자 volunteer Braille Services
점자 Braille
점자도서관 Braille library
점자블록 Braille block ; tactile floor tile
점자용구 Braille writing equipment
점자타이프라이터 Braille typewriter
점적주입담도조영술
 drip infusion cholecystography
점증저항훈련 progressive resistance exercise
점진적 사회변화 incremental social change
점진주의 incrementalism
접골치료용 부목 splint
접근하기 어려운 클라이언트 hard-to-reach clients
접수단계 intake
접수면접 intake interview
접수면접원 intake worker

접수절차 admissions procedures
접수처 admissions
접촉감염 contact infection
접촉감저하 loss of touch sensation
접촉반사 contact reflection
접촉배양지 contact plate
접촉배양지법 stamp agar method
접촉법 contact method
접촉예방책 contact precaution
접촉전파 contact transmission
접촉한천배지 contact plate
정관 articles of incorporation
정구성 빈혈 normocytic anemia
정규간호사 registered nurse: RN
정규고용 full-time employment
정규곡선 normal curve
정균작용 bacteriostatic action
정기건강진단 routine health examination
정기적 건강진단 periodic health evaluation : PHE
정년 retirement
정년제 mandatory retirement system
정년퇴직 mandatory retirement
정년퇴직자계속고용장려금
 incentives for the continued employment of
 the retired people
정당화 legitimation
정동 emotion
정량분무식 흡입기 metered-dose inhaler
정령지정도시
 government ordinance city ; city designated by
 government ordinance
정률부담 fixed charge rate
정리의향서 living will
정마찰 이음새 constant friction joint
정맥 eurhythmia ; vein
정맥류 varix
정맥영양법 parenteral nutrition
정맥혈 venous blood
정보 및 의뢰서비스
 information and referral service
정보개시 information disclosure
정보공개 information disclosure
정보기술 information technology : IT

ㅈ

정보네트워크 information network
정보시스템 information system
정보이론 information theory
정보자유법 Freedom of Information Act
정보제공 dissemination of information
정보화 사회 informationalized society
정부개발원조
official development assistance : ODA
정부고유활동 inherently governmental activity
정부관계법인노동조합연합
Labor Federation of Government Related
Organizations
정부관장 government administered
정부관장건강보험
government administered health insurance ;
government sponsored health insurance
정부지출금 appropriation
정상 normal
정상둔자 dull-normal
정상분포 normal distribution
정상세균총 normal flora
정상압수두증 normal pressure hydrocephalus
정상온도 normal temperature
정상인 healthy person ; healthy volunteer
정상적응기제 normal adjustment mechanism
정상치 normal value
정상혈압 normal blood pressure
정상화 normalization
정서 emotion
정서발달 emotional development
정서불안정 emotional insecurity
정서일치 affective congruency
정서장애 affective disorders
정서장애아 children with emotional disturbances
정서장애아단기치료시설
short-term treatment facility for children with
disabilities and emotional disturbances
정서적 단절 emotional divorce
정서적 불안정 emotional lability
정서테스트 emotional test
정신 내면의 intrapsychic
정신 및 행동장애 mental and behavioral disorder
정신 · 장애보건과

Mental Health and Disability Health Division
정신간호학회
The Korean Academy of Psychiatric and
Mental Health Nursing
정신건강 mental health
정신건강 사회사업가 mental health workers
정신건강 전문가 mental health professional
정신건강 팀 mental health team
정신건강협회 mental Health Association
정신과데이케어 psychiatric day care
정신과데이케어센터 psychiatric day care center
정신과방문간호케어 psychiatric home health care
정신과소시얼워커 psychiatric social worker : PSW
정신과의사 psychiatrist
정신과재활 psychiatric rehabilitation
정신박약 mental retardation
정신발달지체아
children with delayed mental development
정신병 psychosis
정신병 및 건강공동위원회
Joint Commission on Mental Illness and
Health
정신병리학 psychopathology
정신병리학자 psychopathologist
정신병약 psychoactive drugs
정신병원 mental hospitals
정신병적 psychotic
정신병적 행동 psychotic behavior
정신병질적 psychopath
정신병질적 인격 psychopathic personality
정신병학적 psychogenic
정신병환자 psychiatric patient
정신보건 mental health
정신보건 및 정신장애인복지에 관한 법률
Health and Welfare Law for People with
Mental Disabilities
정신보건복지 mental health and welfare
정신보건복지법
Health and Welfare Law for People with
Mental Disabilities
정신보건복지사
certified psychiatric social worker : CPSW ;
psychiatric social worker : PSW

정신보건복지사법
Certified Psychiatric Social Workers Act

정신보건복지상담원
advisor for the health and welfare of people
with mental disabilities ; mental health and
welfare counselor

정신보건복지센터
mental health and welfare center

정신보건사회복지사
psychiatric social worker : PSW

정신보건서비스 mental health services

정신보건센터 mental health center

정신보건지정의 designated psychiatrist

정신보건카운셀러 mental health counselor

정신보건행정 mental health administration

정신분석 psychoanalysis

정신분석가 psychoanalyst

정신분석요법 psychoanalytic therapy

정신분석을 받는 환자 analysand

정신분석의 패러다임 psychoanalytic paradigm

정신분석이론 psychoanalytic theory

정신분석적 심리요법
psychoanalytical psychotherapy

정신분석학 psychoanalysis

정신분열성 schizoid

정신분열성 성격장애
schizoid personality disorders

정신분열증 schizophrenia

정신분열증 유발형 부모 schizophrenogenic parent

정신분열증 장애 schizophreniform disorder

정신상태검사 mental status exam

정신성 spirituality

정신성적 발달이론
psychosexual development theory

정신성적 역기능 psychosexual dysfunction

정신성적 장애 psychosexual disorder

정신신체의학 psychosomatic medicine

정신신체증 psychosomatic

정신약 psychiatric medication

정신약리학 psychopharmacology

정신역동론 psychodynamics

정신역학 psychodynamics

정신연령 mental age : MA

정신요법 psychotherapy ; psychological therapy

정신위생 mental health

정신위생운동 mental hygiene movement

정신위생케어 mental health care

정신위생클리닉 mental health clinic

정신의료심사회
Committee on Mental Health ; Mental Health
Committees

정신의존 psychological dependence

정신의학 psychiatry

정신의학자 psychiatrist

정신작용제 psychoactive drug

정신장애 psychiatric disorder ; mental disability

정신장애 진단 통계편람
Diagnostic and Statistical Manual of Mental
Disorders

정신장애고령자 elderly with mental disabilities

정신장애노인 elderly with mental disabilities

정신장애아 children with mental disabilities

정신장애유아 infants with mental disabilities

정신장애인
people with mental disorders

정신장애인 생활훈련시설
daily living training facility for people with
mental disabilities

정신장애인간호
nursing care for people with mental disabilities

정신장애인개호
caring for people with mental disabilities

정신장애인개호지원
care management for people with mental
disabilities

정신장애인갱생상담소
rehabilitation counseling center for people with
mental disabilities

정신장애인거택간호
home-based care for people with mental
disabilities

정신장애인거택개호지원
home-based care management for people with
mental disabilities

정신장애인고용
employment of people with mental disabilities

정신장애인고용율
employment rates for persons with mental disabilities

정신장애인고용촉진
employment promotion for people with mental disabilities

정신장애인고용촉진대책
employment promotion policy for people with mental disabilities

정신장애인대상 민간서비스
private services for the psychiatric patient

정신장애인복지작업소
welfare workshop for people with mental disabilities

정신장애인복지홈
welfare home for people with mental disabilities ; welfare home for people with mental disorders

정신장애인부조
assistance for people with mental disabilities

정신장애인사회복귀시설
social rehabilitation and training facility for people with mental disabilities ; rehabilitation center for people with mental disabilities

정신장애인사회적응훈련
social skills training for people with mental disabilities ; social rehabilitation and training for people with mental disorders

정신장애인소규모작업소
small-scale workshop for people with mental disabilities

정신장애인수산시설
sheltered workshop for people with mental disabilities ; sheltered workshop for people with mental disorders

정신장애인요호시설
custodial care facility for people with mental disabilities

정신장애인운동
movement for people with mental disabilities

정신장애인원조
support for people with mental disabilities

정신장애인의료
medical care for people with mental disabilities

정신장애인작업소
workshop for people with mental disabilities

정신장애인재가개호지원
home care management for people with mental disabilities

정신장애인지역생활원호
community living support for people with mental disabilities

정신장애인지역생활지원사업
community living support program for people with mental disabilities

정신장애인지역생활지원센터
community living support center for people with mental disabilities

정신장애인통소수산시설
sheltered workshop for people with mental disabilities

정신장애진단 및 통계편람
Diagnostic and Statistical Manual of Mental Disorders : DSM

정신적 의존 emotional dependency

정신적 적응력 mental competency

정신적 학대 mental cruelty

정신제 psychiatric drug

정신지체 mental retardation

정신질환 mental illness

정신치료 psychotherapy

정신후유증 (외상후유증)
posttraumatic stress disorder

정액교부금 block grant

정액부담 fixed charge

정액요금 flat-rate fee

정액자기부담 deductible

정액제 fixed amount system

정액청부 fixed charge ; fixed price

정용 personal hygiene

정용개호 personal hygiene care

정용동작 personal hygiene activity

정용보조 personal hygiene assistance

정위반응 righting reaction

정적 강화 positive reinforcement

정적 안정성 static stability

정적 처벌 positive punishment

정제 tablet

정족수 quorum

정좌불능 akathisia

정좌위 kneel sitting

정주법 The Settlement Act

정주법 및 이주법

  Law of Settlement and Removal

정착 social settlement

정책 policy

정책결정론 policy decision-making theories

정책분석 policy analysis

정책성명서 policy statement

정책실시 policy implementation

정책입안자 policymaker

정책커뮤니티 policy community

정체성 identity

정체성 대 역할 혼란

  identity versus role confusion

정체성 위기 identity crisis

정체이형 heterostasis

정치적 행위 political action

정치적 활동 political activism

정형구두 corrective shoes ; orthopedic shoes

정형외과 orthopedics

정화 catharsis

젖산역치 anaerobic threshold : AT

제1단계 변화 first-order change

제1차 빈곤 primary poverty

제1형 당뇨병

  type 1 diabetes ; type 1 diabetes mellitus

제1호 피보험자 the first insured

제2단계 변화 second-order change

제2차 빈곤 secondary poverty

제2축 장애 Axis II disorder

제2형 당뇨병

  type 2 diabetes ; type 2 diabetes mellitus

제2호 피보험자 the secondary insured

제3부문 the third sector

제3부문 지불 third-party payment

제3세계 the third world

제3섹터 third sector

제3의 인생 the third age

제3차 교육 tertiary education

제공자 provider

제노믹각인 genomic imprinting

제노믹임프린팅 genomic imprinting

제니칼 Xenical

제대군인원호법 GI Bill

제도 institution

제도망 institutional network

제도적 개념 institutional concept

제도적 복지급여 institutional welfare provision

제로베이스 예산편성 zero-based budgeting

제로자세 zero position

제로지위 zero position

제모 hair removal ; shaving

제산제 acid-suppressive medication ; antacid

제삼세계 Third World

제삼의 길 Third Way

제삼자위원 third-party panel

제삼자평가 third-party quality endorsement

제삼자평가제도

  third-party quality endorsement system

제스트릴 Zestril

제압 decompression

제어 control and prevention

제지방체중 lean body mass : LBM

제출대행자

  person submitting application on behalf of the

  applicant ; person authorized to submit

  applications on behalf of the applicant

제한적 서비스 restrictive services

제한진료 limited medical care

제휴 collaboration

제휴간호사 link nurse

젠더 gender

젠더트랙 gender track

조각기법 sculpting

조갑구만증 onychogryphosis

조건등색 metamerism

조건등색지수 metamer

조건반사 conditioned reflex

조건반응 conditioned response

조건부 계약 contingency contracting

조건부 금지 conditioned inhibition

ㅈ

조건자극 conditioned stimulus

조건화 conditioning

조기개입 early intervention

조기교육 Head Start

조기발견 early detection

조기발생 알츠하이머병
early-onset Alzheimer's disease

조기이상 early ambulation

조닝 zoning

조례 ordinance

조로증 progeria

조리 cooking

조리공간 cooking space

조리기구 cooking tool

조리방법 cooking recipe

조리필 ready-to-serve dish

조립주택 prefabricated home

조명 lighting

조믹 Zomig

조백선 onychomycosis

조부 조항 grandfather clause

조부모 양연 foster grandparents

조비락스 Zovirax

조사 research ; study ; survey

조사대상 research subjects

조사망률 crude mortality rate

조사-재조사 신뢰도 test-retest reliability

조사표 questionnaire

조산 premature birth

조산사 midwife

조산시설 maternity home

조산원 midwife

조성금 grant-in-aid

조세 tax

조세부담 tax burden

조세부담률 tax burden ratio

조세비용 tax cost

조세우대 tax-privileged

조세지출 tax expenditure

조세징수 tax collection

조수 assistant ; supporter

조스타박스 Zostavax

조염 onychia

조우울증
manic depressive psychosis ; bipolar disorder

조울병 manic-depressive illness

조울증 manic depressive psychosis

조이영양증 onychodystrophy

조작적 개념 operational definition

조작적 조건화 operant conditioning

조작적 치료 operant therapy

조장자 enabler

조장자 역할 enable role

조절 accommodation

조정 mediation ; adjustment

조정간격 계획표 fixed-interval schedule

조정교부금
adjustment subsidy ; subsidy adjustment

조정자 coordinator

조정적 기능 coordinative function

조제서비스 pharmaceutical services

조준 focus

조증 mania

조증 에피소드 manic episode

조직 organization

조직관류 tissue perfusion

조직사회화 organizational socialization

조직인 organization man

조직적 성공 systemic success

조직적 실패 systemic failure

조진균증 onychomycosis

조출생률 crude birth rate

조치권자 administering authority

조치기간 placement period

조치비용 client allocation cost

조치제도 client allocation system

조하혈종 subungual hematoma

조합 union

조합관장건강보험
society-managed health insurance

조합복지 corporate welfare

조합주의 corporatism

조합주의적 (보수주의적) 복지국가
corporatist welfare state

조형 shaping

족관절 ankle joint

족백선 tinea pedis
족병 podiatric medicine
족병의 podiatrist
족욕 foot bath
족저굴곡 plantar flexion
족판 foot plate
존엄 dignity
존엄사 death with dignity
존엄사법 Death with Dignity Act
존엄사선언서 living will
존엄의 보지 maintenance of the dignity
존엄있는 생활 life with dignity
졸로프트 Zoloft
졸림 somnolence
졸미트립탄 zolmitriptan
졸음운전 sleep-driving
졸피뎀 zolpidem
종결단계 termination phase
종교 religion
종교법인 religious corporation
종교사회사업 religious social work
종교적 사회복지 sectarian services
종단적 연구 longitudinal study
종단적 조사 longitudinal study
종말기 terminal stage
종말기간호 terminal nursing care
종말기의료 terminal medical care
종말기장기요양 terminal care
종말기치료 terminal treatment
종말기케어 terminal care ; end-of-life care
종속변수 dependent variable
종속인구 dependent population
종속인구지수 dependency ratio
종신고용 lifelong employment
종신고용제도 lifelong employment system
종신연금 lifelong pension
종양괴사인자 tumor necrosis factor : TNF
종양괴사인자α저해제
  tumor necrosis factor-alpha inhibitor
종양의 oncologist
종양학 oncology
종업원 employee
종업원대표제도 employee representation

종업원만족도 employee satisfaction : ES
종업원퇴직소득보증법 ERISA
종이기저귀 paper diaper
종족궁 longitudinal arch
종족변형 talipes calcaneus
종창 swelling
종파〔예식〕 cult
종합건강증진운동 total health promotion : THP
종합고용 및 직업훈련법
  Comprehensive Employment and Training Act
종합구입 total purchasing
종합기획 comprehensive planning
종합병원 comprehensive hospital
종합상담 comprehensive consultation
종합세대조사 general household survey
종합적 품질경영활동
  total quality management : TQM
종합적 품질관리활동
  total quality management : TQM
좋은 이웃들 Good Finders
좌골지지 ischial weight-bearing
좌불안석증 akathisia
좌심실비대 left ventricular hypertrophy
좌약 suppository
좌우실인 left-right disorientation
좌위 sitting position
좌위보조구 seating aid
좌위보지 maintain a sitting position
좌위보지장치 seating system
좌위유지 balance in a sitting position
좌위자세 sitting posture
좌위훈련 sitting exercise
좌절 frustration
좌절감 frustration
좌절감내성 frustration tolerance
좌측와위 left lateral recumbent
좌파 leftist
죄의식 guilt
주 2회 two times weekly : 2W
주 3회 three times weekly : 3W
주 4회 four times weekly : 4W
주 5회 five times weekly : 5W
주 6회 six times weekly : 6W

ㅈ

주·야간보호 day/night care
주간과다졸림증 excessive daytime sleepiness
주간병동 day hospital
주간보호[보육] day care
주간보호사업 day care project
주간보호사업소 day care office
주간보호센터 day care center
주간보호소 adult day care
주간보호시설 day care center
주간재활
　outpatient rehabilitation ; ambulatory
　rehabilitation ; commuting for rehabilitation
주간재활센터 rehabilitation center
주간케어계획
　weekly service plan ; weekly care plan
주개호자 primary caregiver
주거제한법 residency laws
주거환경 living environment
주관적 욕구 subjective needs
주관적 행복감 subjective happiness
주관적 행복감척도 Subjective Happiness Scale
주관적 행복도 subjective well-being
주관절골절 elbow fracture
주관절욕 elbow bathing
주관절의지 elbow disarticulation prosthesis
주기성 사지운동 periodic leg movement
주기성 사지운동이상증
　periodic leg movement disorder : PLMD
주기성 사지운동장애
　periodic limb movement disorder
주기적 실업 cyclical unemployment
주동근 agonist ; prime mover
주류화 mainstreaming
주민 resident
주민기본대장 basic resident registration
주민기본대장 카드 basic resident registration card
주민리더 citizen leader
주민세 resident tax
주민운동 resident movement
주민자치 citizen autonomy
주민참가 resident participation
주변시야 peripheral vision
주변언어학 paralinguistics

주보충프로그램 State Supplemental Program
주사 injection
주사침 등의 손상 sharps injury
주산기 사망율 perinatal mortality rate
주소 chief complaint
주술치료사 curandero
주식 regular diet
주안 weekly schedule
주요성공요인 critical success factor : CSF
주요실패요인 critical failure factor
주요정서장애 major affective disorder
주요호소증상 chief complaint
주우울증 major depression
주의결함·다동성장애
　attention deficit hyperactivity disorder : ADHD
주의력 결핍장애 attention deficit disorder
주의장애 inattention
주임 chief
주임 홈헬퍼 chief home helper
주입기재관련 혈류감염
　infusate-related bloodstream infection
주입제관련 혈류감염
　infusate-related bloodstream infection
주장기요양자 primary caregiver
주제집단 theme group
주제통각검사 thematic apperception test : TAT
주치의 primary doctor ; attending doctor
주치의 의견서
　doctor's note ; report from the primary
　doctor
주택개량
　home improvement ; home modification
주택개량급여 home modification benefit
주택개량수당 home modification allowance
주택개선
　home improvement ; home modification
주택개조
　home improvement ; home modification
주택관리 housing management
주택보수자금 house repair allowance
주택부조 housing assistance
주택안전 home safety
주택융자 housing loan

주택자금　housing allowance
주택정책　housing policy
주택지구 상류화　gentrification
주택프로그램　housing programs
주프텐 고령자연구　Zutphen Elderly Study
주휴 2일제　two-daysoff a week system
죽음　death
죽음에 대한 관심　concern for the dying
죽종　atheroma
준개인실　semi-private room
준거집단　reference group
준거집단론　reference group theory
준비성　readiness
준수율　compliance rate
준시장　quasi-market
준실업　semi-unemployment
준의료직원　paramedical staff
준전문가　paraprofessional
준청결수술　clean-contaminated operation
준청결창　clean-contaminated wound
줄기세포　stem cell
중간값　median
중간법인법
　Non-Profit Mutual Benefit Corporation Law
중간시설　halfway houses ; intermediate facility
중간위　neutral position
중간지불기관　intermediary
중간평가항목　items of intermediate assessment
중개자 역할　broker role
중국잔류고아　Japanese orphans in China
중년　middle age
중년위기　midlife crisis
중도시각장애　acquired visual impairment
중도시각장애자
　person with acquired visual impairment ;
　newly blind
중도신체장애아
　children with acquired severe physical
　disabilities
중도신체장애인
　people with acquired severe physical disabilities
중도신체장애인갱생시설
　rehabilitation facility for people with acquired

severe physical disabilities
중도신체장애인갱생원호시설
　rehabilitation and assistance center for people
　with acquired severe physical disabilities
중도신체장애인수산시설
　sheltered workshop for people with acquired
　severe physical disabilities
중도실명　acquired blindness
중도실천　mezzo practice
중도장애　acquired disability
중도장애아
　children with acquired severe disabilities
중도장애인
　people with acquired severe disabilities
중도정신장애아
　children with acquired severe mental disabilities
중도정신장애인
　people with acquired severe mental disabilities
중도지각장애　acquired sensory impairment
중도지적장애아
　children with acquired severe mental
　retardation
중도지적장애인
　people with acquired severe mental retardation
중도청각장애　acquired hearing impairment
중도청각장애자
　person with acquired hearing impairment
중독　addiction ; intoxication
중독정신병　toxic psychosis
중류의식　middle-class consciousness
중립위　neutral position
중범위이론　middle range theory
중복면접　multiple interviews
중복장애
　multiple disabilities ; multiple handicaps
중복장애아　multiple handicapped child
중복장애인　multiple handicapped
중상주의　mercantilism
중성세제　neutral detergent
중성지방　triglyceride
중수준소독제　intermediate disinfection
중심　center of gravity : CG
중심경향측정　measure of central tendency

중심도 locus of center of gravity

중심성 경골수손상 central cord syndrome : CCS

중심암점 central scotoma

중심정맥고칼로리수액법
intravenous hyperalimentation : IVH

중심정맥압 central venous pressure

중심정맥영양법
intravenous hyperalimentation : IVH ; central
parenteral nutrition

중심정맥카테터 central catheter

중심카테터 central catheter

중앙공급 central supply

중앙노동위원회
Central Labour Relations Commission

중앙노인보호전문기관
Specialized Central Organization for Care of
Elderly

중앙멸균공급부
central sterile and supply department

중앙멸균재료부
central sterile and supply department

중앙집중화 centralization

중요성공요인 critical success factor : CSF

중요실패요인 critical failure factor

중요인물 key person

중요한 타자 significant others

중위수 mode

중이염 otitis media

중재 mediation

중재역할 go-between role

중재이혼 mediation divorce

중재자 역할 mediator role

중족골지지대 metatarsal bar

중죄 felonies

중증근무력증 myasthenia gravis : MG

중증급성 호흡증후군
severe acute respiratory syndrome : SARS

중증심신장애
severe physical and mental disabilities

중증심신장애아
children with severe physical and mental
disabilities

중증심신장애아시설
facility for children with severe physical and
mental disabilities

중증심신장애아통원사업
day care services program for children with
severe physical and mental disabilities

중증심신장애인
people with severe physical and mental
disabilities

중증심신장애인시설
facility for people with severe physical and
mental disabilities

중증심신장애인통원사업
day care services program for people with
severe physical and mental disabilities

중증외상환자에 대한 접근법
approach to the critically injured patient

중창 insole

중추성 청각처리장애
central auditory processing disorder

중추신경계 central nervous system

중풍 apoplexy

중혼 bigamy

쥐 spasm

쥐어짜는 듯한 아픔 squeezing pain

증거에 기초한 간호 evidence-based nursing

증거에 기초한 개호 evidence-based care : EBC

증거에 기초한 의료
evidence-based medicine : EBM

증거에 기초한 장기요양
evidence-based care : EBC

증거에 기초한 지역계획
evidence-based community planning

증거에 기초한 케어 evidence-based care : EBC

증기멸균 steam sterilization ; autoclaving

증명서 certificate

증명서의 사본 copy of certificate ; copy of proof

증명카드 donor card

증분역 incremental threshold

증상 symptom

증상설명 prescribing the symptom

증서제도 voucher system

증후군 syndrome

증후성 빈혈 symptomatic anemia

증후학　semiotics
지각　perception
지각능력변이　sensory change
지각마비　sensory paralysis
지각왜곡　perceptual distortion
지각장애　sensory impairment
지각재교육　re-education of sensation
지각충추〔감각〕　sensorium
지구력운동　endurance exercise
지구성　endurance
지구진단　community diagnosis
지급불능　insolvency
지급요건　requirements for benefits
지남력　orientation
지남력장애　disorientation
지노트　Haim G. Ginott
지능　intelligence
지능검사　intelligence test
지능연령　intellectual age
지능장애　intelligence disorder
지능지수　intelligence quotient : IQ
지능진단　intelligence diagnosis
지능편차치　intelligence standard score
지니 매　Ginnie Mae
지니계수　Gini coefficient
지대설정　zoning
지대형 근이영양증　limb-girdle muscular dystrophy
지도감독　supervision
지도과　Guidance of Medical Service Division
지면반력　ground reaction force
지문법　finger print plate method
지발성 디스키네지아　tardive dyskinesia
지발성 알츠하이머병　late-onset Alzheimer's disease
지방　fat
지방공공단체　local public entity
지방교부세　local allocation tax
지방분권　decentralization
지방분권화　decentralization
지방산　fatty acid
지방자치　local autonomy
지방자치법　Local Autonomy Law
지방자치체　local government
지방자치체연합　local authority association

지방재판소　district court
지방조직　adipose tissue
지방질　lipid
지방질이상증　dyslipidemia
지방질축적증　lipid storage disease
지방행정　local administration
지방행정부　local governing authority
지방흡수억제제　Alli
지불기금　payment fund
지불능력　solvency
지불보류　withhold
지불유예　moratorium
지성화　Intellectualization
지속견인　continuous traction
지속성　substantivity
지속성 흡식　apneusis
지속적 강화　continuous reinforcement
지속적 양압호흡
　continuous positive air pressure : CPAP
지속적 지지수속　sustaining procedures
지속타동운동　continuative passive motion : CPM
지시적 치료　directive therapy
지식기초　knowledge base
지실인증　finger agnosia
지압　acupressure
지압사　acupressurist
지어낸 이야기　confabulation
지역　community
지역가산　additional payment to community
지역간호　community nursing
지역개발　community development
지역거주시설서비스　community residential care
지역거주시설케어서비스
　community residential care services
지역격차　regional gap ; community difference
지역계획
　community planning ; regional planning ;
　community plan
지역고령자복지　community welfare for the elderly
지역고령자복지활동
　community welfare activities for the elderly
지역공동사회개발　community social development
지역노인복지　community welfare for the aged

지역노인복지활동
community welfare activities for the aged
지역밀착서비스 community-based service
지역밀착형방문간호케어
home and community-based health care
지역밀착형방문개호
home and community-based care
지역밀착형재활 community-based rehabilitation
지역밀착형통소개호
community-based day care services
지역밀착형통소재활
ambulatory community-based rehabilitation ;
community-based and outpatient rehabilitation
지역병원 community hospital
지역보건 community health
지역보건법 Community Health Act
지역보건의료 community health and medical care
지역보건의료계획
community health and medical care plan
지역보호 community care
지역복지 community welfare
지역복지 코디네이터
community welfare services coordinator
지역복지계획 community welfare planning
지역복지과
Community Welfare and Services Division
지역복지권리옹호사업
community advocacy services
지역복지기관 community welfare facility
지역복지기금 community welfare fund
지역복지사업 community welfare program
지역복지사업소 community welfare office
지역복지사업자 community welfare provider
지역복지서비스 community welfare services
지역복지센터 community welfare center
지역복지시설 community welfare facility
지역복지원조기술 community welfare work
지역복지협력사업
Association of Area Welfare Institutes
지역복지활동 community welfare activity
지역사회 community
지역사회 의사결정 조직망
community decision network

지역사회개발 community development
지역사회계획 community planning
지역사회관계 community relations
지역사회보호 community care
지역사회복지관 Area wise Social Welfare Center
지역사회사업 community work
지역사회사업가 community worker
지역사회서비스 정액교부금 프로그램
Community Service Block Gran program
지역사회센터 community center
지역사회자조 community self-help
지역사회접근방법 community approach
지역사회정신건강센터
community mental health center
지역사회정신의학 community psychiatry
지역사회조직 community organization : CO
지역사회조직 및 개발사무소
Community Planning and Development Office
지역사회조직가 community organizer
지역사회조직의 실천모델
community organization model
지역사회진단 community diagnosis
지역사회포럼 community forum
지역사회해체 community disorganization
지역설정계획 zoning
지역실습배치 block placement
지역연계패스 liaison critical pathway
지역의료 community medical care
지역의료계획 community medical care plan
지역일반병원 community general hospital
지역장애인복지 community welfare for the disabled
지역장애인복지활동
community welfare activities for the disabled
지역재활 community rehabilitation
지역정보보건활동 community mental health service
지역제 zoning
지역조사 community study
지역조직활동 community organization activity
지역지원 community support
지역지원사업 community support project
지역차조정계수
geographic adjustment factor : GAF
지역청소년단 Neighborhood Youth Corps

지역케어 community care
지역케어네트워크 community care network
지역케어시스템 community care system
지역케어회의 community care meeting
지역포괄지원센터 community-based care center
지역포괄케어 comprehensive community care
지역활동조직 community organization : CO
지연성 community bond
지용성 비타민 fat-soluble vitamin
지원그룹 support group
지원기기 assistive device
지원대상 long-term care assistance-required
지원대상자 long-term care assistance recipient
지원비제도 support payment system
지원집단 support group
지원체계 support system
지위 status
지위위반자 status offender
지유각보행 swing-to gait
지인 acquaintance ; a friend
지적소유권 intellectual property right
지적수준 intellectual level
지적장애 mental retardation : MR
지적장애고령자
 elderly person with mental retardation
지적장애노인
 elderly person with mental retardation
지적장애아 child with mental retardation
지적장애아시설
 facility for children with mental retardation
지적장애유아
 the mentally retarded infant ; infant with
 mental retardation ; baby with mental
 retardation
지적장애인 people with mental retardation
지적장애인개호
 caring for people with mental retardation ;
 care for people with mental retardation
지적장애인개호지원
 care management for people with mental
 retardation
지적장애인갱생상담소
 rehabilitation counseling center for people with

mental retardation
지적장애인갱생시설
 rehabilitation facility for people with mental
 retardation
지적장애인거택간호
 home-based care for people with mental
 retardation
지적장애인거택개호지원
 home-based care management for people with
 mental retardation
지적장애인거택개호지원사업
 home-based care management program for
 people with mental retardation
지적장애인그룹홈
 group home for people with mental
 retardation
지적장애인단기입소
 short-stay for people with mental retardation
지적장애인단기입소사업
 short-stay program for people with mental
 retardation
지적장애인대상 민간서비스
 private services for people with mental
 retardation
지적장애인복지
 welfare for people with mental retardation
지적장애인복지기관
 welfare agency for people with mental
 retardation
지적장애인복지사
 welfare officer for people with mental
 retardation
지적장애인복지사업소
 welfare office for people with mental
 retardation
지적장애인복지시설
 welfare facility for people with mental
 retardation
지적장애인복지작업소
 welfare workshop for people with mental
 retardation
지적장애인복지홈
 welfare home for people with mental

retardation

지적장애인부조
assistance for people with mental retardation

지적장애인상담원
counselor for people with mental retardation

지적장애인수산시설
sheltered workshop for people with mental
retardation

지적장애인운동
movement for people with mental retardation

지적장애인원조
support for people with mental retardation

지적장애인의 권리선언
Declaration on the Rights of Mentally
Retarded Persons

지적장애인의료
medical care for people with mental
retardation

지적장애인작업소
workshop for people with mental retardation

지적장애인재가개호지원
home care management for people with mental
retardation

지적장애인주간보호서비스
day care services for people with mental
retardation

지적장애인주간보호서비스사업
day care services program for people with
mental retardation

지적장애인주간보호서비스센터
day services center for people with mental
retardation

지적장애인홈헬프서비스
home help services for people with mental
retardation

지적재산 intellectual property

지절운동실행 limb kinetic apraxia

지정 designation ; certification

지정기부금 designated donation

지정병 designated hospital

지정의료기관 designated medical care agency

지정의제도
designation system for medical providers

지정정보공표센터
designated public information center

지정주택개호지원사업자
designated home-based care management
provider

지정주택서비스
designated home-based care services

지정취소
cancellation of designation ; cancellation of
certification

지주막하출혈 subarachnoid hemorrhage : SAH

지지 support

지지대 tipping lever

지지봉 support bar

지지적 과정 sustaining procedures

지지적 실인 topographical agnosia

지지적 작업요법 supportive occupational therapy

지지적 치료 supportive treatment

지지적 케이스워크 supportive casework

지지패드 applying pad

지체 retardation

지체부자유 crippled

지체부자유아 crippled child

지체부자유아갱생시설
rehabilitation facility for crippled children

지체부자유아시설 facility for crippled children

지체부자유아양호학교
special school for crippled children

지체부자유아요호시설
custodial care facility for crippled children

지체부자유아통원시설
day care services facility for crippled children

지체부자유자 crippled person

지체성 의식장애
persistent disturbance of consciousness

지체장애인 crippled people

지출 expenditure

지팡이 cane

지팡이 보행 cane-assisted gait

지표 indicator

지향가족 family of orientation

지혈 hemostasis

직계가족 stem family

직능판정원 vocational aptitude assessor
직무분석 job analysis
직선적 인과율 linear causality
직시하 생검 open biopsy
직업가정양립과
　Work and Family Harmonization Division
직업감염 occupational infection
직업교육 on the job training
직업능력개발국
　Human Resource Development Bureau
직업단 Job Corps
직업병 occupational disease
직업복귀 return to work
직업상담 career counseling
직업설명〔회〕 job description
직업성 폭로 occupational exposure
직업안정국 Employment Security Bureau
직업안정법 Employment Security Law
직업안정프로그램 job placement program
직업의식 professionalism
직업재활 vocational rehabilitation
직업적 vocational
직업적 아이덴티티 occupational identity
직업적 재활 vocational rehabilitation
직업전 prevocational
직업지도〔직업안내〕 vocational guidance
직업지도원 vocational counselor
직업카운셀링 vocational counseling
직업평가 vocational evaluation
직업프로그램 JOBS program
직업학교 trade school
직업훈련 job training ; vocational training
직업훈련수당 vocational training allowance
직업훈련시설 vocational training facility
직업훈련협력법 Job Training Partnership Act
직역보험 occupational group insurance
직원개발 staff development
직원배치 staffing
직원연수 staff development
직원회의 staff conference
직장S장결장경 proctosigmoidoscope
직장S장결장경검사 proctosigmoidoscopy
직장경 proctoscope

직장경검사 proctoscopy
직장내 rectal
직장내 초음파검사법 endorectal ultrasonography
직장내 코일 endorectal coil
직장보건 occupational health
직장사회사업 occupational social work
직장생검 rectal biopsy
직장세정 rectal irrigation
직장수지검사 digital rectal examination
직장실습형 훈련제도 apprenticeship
직장외 훈련 off-the-job-training : OFF-JT
직장조영 proctography
직장진찰 rectal examination
직장탈 rectal prolapse
직장항문탈출 anorectal prolapse
직장혹 rectocele
직장환경 악화형 성희롱
　hostile work environment harassment
직장훈련 on-the-job-training : OJT
직접계약모델 direct contract model
직접대광반사 direct light reflex
직접비용 direct cost
직접빛반사 direct light reflex
직접세 direct tax
직접실천 direct practice
직접언어 direct language
직접영향 direct influence
직접원조기술 direct social work practice
직접접촉감염
　direct contact infection ; direct contact
　transmission
직접질문 direct questions
직접처우 direct treatment
직접처우직원 direct treatment staff
직접치료 direct treatment
직종지정 designated employment
직책에 의한 성원 ex office member
진균감염 fungal infection
진균성 안내염 fungal endophthalmitis
진균증 mycosis
진균혈증 fungemia
진단 diagnosis
진단관련집단 diagnostic related groups

진단군별정액지불방식
diagnosis-related groups prospective payment
system : DRG-PPS

진단군별포괄지불제
diagnosis-related groups prospective payment
system : DRG-PPS

진단군분류 diagnosis procedure combination : DPC

진단군분류별 계수
coefficients for diagnosis procedure
combination : DPC

진단범주 diagnostic category

진단주의 사회사업학파
diagnostic school in social work

진단주의 케이스워크 diagnosis casework

진동법 vibration

진로지도 guidance for career direction

진로지도교관
school counselor ; guidance counselor

진료기록카드 patient records

진료방사선기사 clinical radiologic technologist

진료보수 medical fee

진료보수제도 medical treatment fee system

진료소 clinic

진료예약 doctor appointment

진료의 기준 standards of medical practice

진료정보관리사계 medical coder

진료환자수
number of patients receiving medical care

진보주의적 시대 Progressive Era

진성구급 true emergency

진성요실금 true incontinence

진실성 genuineness

진양제
antipruritic ; antipruritic drug ; antipruritic
medication

진요통과보행 swing-through gait

진자시험 pendulum test

진전 tremor

진전섬망 delirium tremens

진정 petition ; appeal

진정제 downers ; sedatives

진정최면제 sedative-hypnotic drug

진지 genuineness

진찰선택 point-of-service

진통보행 antalgic gait

진통약 analgesic drug

진통제 analgesic

진폐증 보상프로그램 Black Lung program

진해약 antitussive drug

진해제 antitussive drug

진행성 구마비 progressive bulbar palsy

진행성 근이영양증
progressive muscular dystrophy : PMD

진행성 마이오클로누스간질
progressive myoclonus epilepsy

진흥과 Promotion Division

질 좋은 널싱케어 quality nursing home care

질 좋은 재가간호케어 quality home health care

질 좋은 재가장기요양 quality home care

질문 questioning

질문지 questionnaire

질문지법 questionnaire method

질문지조사 investigation questionnaire

질병 morbid

질병관리 disease management : DM

질병관리예방센터
Center for Disease Control and Prevention : CDC

질병군별포괄수가제
diagnosis-related groups prospective payment
system : DRG-PPS

질병급여 sickness benefit

질병대책과 Specific Diseases Control Division

질병률 morbidity rate

질병보험 sickness insurance

질병부인 denial of illness

질병분류학 nosology

질병연금 sickness pension

질병영향 프로파일 sickness impact profile : SIP

질병의 압축 morbidity compression

질병인식불능증 anosognosia

질병통제센터 Centers for Disease Control

질병편력 flight into illness

질병휴가 sick leave

질산염 nitrate

질식 asphyxia

질식할 것 같은 아픔 strangling pain

질염 vaginitis
질적연구 qualitative research
질적조사 qualitative investigation
질케어 vaginal care
질환 disease
질환관리 disease management : DM
질환수식성 항류마티스약제
　disease-modifying antirheumatic drug : DMARD
집 없음 homelessness
집계분석 tabulation
집기 pinch
집단 group
집단간의 집단지도 intergroup work
집단검진
　group physical examination ; group medical
　examination
집단격리 cohort isolation
집단경험 group experiences ; encounter group
집단과정 group process
집단관계 intergroup relations
집단괴롭힘 bullying
집단구조 group structure
집단급식서비스 congregate meal program
집단기능 group function
집단따돌림 bullying
집단민원 class action suit
집단발달 group development
집단발생 outbreak
집단보육 collective child care
집단비행 group delinquency
집단사회사업 social group work ; group work
집단사회사업가 group worker
집단사회사업발전위원회
　Committee for the Advancement of Social
　Work with Group
집단상담 group counseling

집단상호작용 group interaction
집단생활지도집단 T-group
집단시설보호 group institutional care
집단심리치료 group psychotherapy
집단압력 group pressure
집단역학 group dynamics
집단요법 group therapy
집단원조기술 group work
집단응집성 group cohesiveness
집단적격성 group eligibility
집단정신치료법 group psychotherapy
집단정체성 group identity
집단주택 congregate home
집단주택센터 congregate housing center
집단지도 group work
집단지도자 group leader
집단책임 collective responsibility
집단처우 group treatment
집단치료 group therapy
집단학살 genocide
집중개혁플랜 intensive reform plan
집중적 케어매니지먼트
　intensive care management
집중치료실 intensive care unit : ICU
집중치료실감염 ICU-acquired infection
집합적 무의식 collective unconscious
집행기능장애증후군 dysexecutive syndrome
집행유예자 보호관찰 probationer system
집행통고 enforcement notice
짓무름 erosion
징계 disciplinary punishment
징수 collection
짠맛 salty
찍어냄생검 punch biopsy
찜질 foment

ᄌ

차 승강 getting in and out of the car
차별 discrimination
차별대우폐지 desegregation
차별수정계획 affirmative action
차별적 반응 differential response
차세대육성능력 generatively
차아염소산나트륨 sodium hypochlorite
차압 foreclosure
차액징수 collection to make up a difference
차액청구 balance billing
차액침상 beds with an extra charge
차티스트운동 the Chartist Movement
착각 illusion
착상전진단 preimplantation genetic diagnosis
착어 paraphasia
착용신분증명서 wearable identification
착의스킬 dressing skill
착탈의 changing clothes
착행증 parapraxis
찰과상 abrasion
찰과상저항 abrasion resistance
찰과세포진 brushing cytology
찰머즈 Thomas Chalmers
참가 participation ; enrollment
참가자 participant ; enrollee
참가제약
  participation restriction ; enrollment
  restriction
참만남 집단 encounter group
참여관리 participative management
참여관찰 participant observation
참여모델 participant modeling
창감염 wound infection

창상케어 wound care
창상피복제 wound dressing
창설가족 family of procreation
채광 daylighting
채권압류 통고 garnishment
채권회수회사 collection agency ; debt collector
채뇨 urine sampling
채도 saturation
채변 feces sampling
책임 responsibility
책임성 accountability
챔버린 Joseph Chamberlain
처리 disposal
처방 prescription
처방약제프로그램
  prescription medication program
처방전 prescription
처방집 formulary
처벌 punishment
처우개선명령 order for improvement of services
처우계획 treatment plan
처우기록 case record
처우방침 treatment policy
처우제한의 원칙 principle of less eligibility
척굴 ulnar deviation ; ulnar flexion
척수반사 spinal reflex
척수소뇌변성증 spinocerebellar degeneration
척수손상 spinal cord injury : SCI
척수증 myelopathy
척주관협착증 spinal canal stenosis
척주기립근 erector spinae
척주지압요법 chiropractic
척추 X선 spinal X-ray

척추간반헤르니아
 hernia of the intervertebral disc
척추방사선 spinal X-ray
척추뼈 갈림증 spina bifida
척추압박골절 vertebral compression fracture
척추전만증 lordosis
척추천자 spinal tap
척추측만증보조기 Milwaukee brace
척추파열 spina bifida
척추후만증 kyphosis ; roundback
척측편위 ulnar deviation ; ulnar flexion
천명 wheeze
천식 asthma
천식발작 asthmatic attack
천연섬유 natural fiber
천자생검 needle biopsy
천자세포진 needle cytology
천자술 culdocentesis
천자흡인세포진 aspiration cytology
천장골하지절단의지 hemipelvectomy prosthesis
천장주행형 리프트 slide-on-ceiling type of lift
천재지변 natural disaster
철분 iron
철분결핍빈혈증 iron deficiency anemia
철분결핍증 iron deficiency
첨단거대증 acromegaly
첨도 kurtosis
첨족 foot drop
청각 auditory sense ; sense of hearing
청각과민 hyperacusis
청각기독성물질 ototoxic substance
청각실인 auditory agnosia
청각음성센터 auditory-verbal center
청각음성테라피스트 auditory-verbal therapist
청각장애
 auditory impairment ; auditory disability ;
 auditory disorder ; auditory deficit
청각장애인 정보제공시설
 information services facility for people with
 auditory impairments
청각장애자
 the auditorially disabled ; people with auditory
 impairments

청각장애자갱생시설
 rehabilitation facility for people with auditory
 impairments
청각적 평가 audiology assessment
청결 cleanness
청결간헐도뇨법
 clean intermittent catheterization : CIC
청결구역 clean area
청결수술 clean surgery
청결창 clean wound
청교도 윤리 Protestant ethic
청구대상기간 billing period
청구서 billing statement
청년기 youth adolescent
청년기 심리학 adolescent psychology
청년문화 youth culture
청년성 juvenile
청능훈련사 audiologist
청력 hearing ; hearing ability
청력검사 audiometry ; hearing test
청력도 audiogram
청력레벨 hearing level
청색증 cyanosis
청소 cleaning ; cleanup
청소기 vacuum cleaner
청소년 juvenile ; adolescence youth
청소년관절류머티즘 juvenile rheumatoid arthritis
청소년근육간대경련간질
 juvenile myoclonic epilepsy ; Janz syndrome
청소년기 adolescence
청소년단체 youth organization
청소년당뇨병 juvenile diabetes
청소년대책사업 youth programs
청소년범죄 juvenile crime offence
청소년범죄자 juvenile offenders
청소년보호 juvenile protection
청소년봉사기구 youth service organization
청소년비행 juvenile delinquency
청소년사법과 비행방지법
 juvenile Justice and Delinquency Prevention Act
청소년사법정책 juvenile justice policy
청소년사법제도 juvenile justice system
청소년상담사 youth counselor

ㅊ

청소년을 위한 이동사업 Mobilization for Youth
청소년특발성 류머티즘 juvenile idiopathic arthritis
청소년파킨슨병 juvenile Parkinsonism
청소년폴립 juvenile polyps
청소용구 cleaning equipment
청십자사 Blue Cross Association
청원 petition
청정도 클래스 cleanliness class
청정실 clean room
체간 truncus
체간보조기 spinal orthosis
체계 system
체계모델 four system
체계이론 system theory
체계적 추출법 systematic sampling
체계적 탈감각화 systematic desensitization
체계적 필수조건 systemic requisites
체납 non-payment
체드위크 Edwin Chadwick
체력 physical fitness
체성감각유발전위
  somatosensory evoked potential : SEP
체액 body fluid
체액조절 humoral regulation
체온 body temperature
체온계 thermometer
체온조절 thermoregulation
체온조절장애 disturbance of thermoregulation
체온측정 measurement of body temperature
체온측정계 medical thermometer
체외진단검사 in vitro diagnostic test
체외진단제 in vitro diagnostic reagent
체위 position
체위드레나지 postural drainage
체위배액 postural drainage
체위변환 change of position
체위설정 positioning
체육 gymnastics
체인스토크스 정신병 Cheyne-stokes psychosis
체인스토크스 호흡 Cheyne-stokes respiration
체조 exercise
체중부하 weight-bearing
체질감각 somatic sensation

체질량지수 body mass index : BMI
체험으로서의 장애 experienced illness
초경 menarche
초고령사회 super-aged society
초고성능여과공기기
  high efficiency particulate air filter
초고성능필터 high efficiency particulate air filter
초기 단음절 말지각검사
  Early Speech Perception Test
초기면접 initial intake
초기비용 initial cost
초단파요법 short wave diathermy
초로기 우울증 presenile depression
초로기 치매 presenile dementia
초산 acetic acid
초산염 acetate
초상 mourning
초음파 ultrasound
초음파검사 ultrasonography : US
초음파심장진단 echocardiography
초음파심장진단도 echocardiogram
초음파요법 ultrasound therapy
초음파유도천자 ultrasonically guided puncture
초음파응고절개장치
  ultrasonically activated device : USAD
초인지 metacognition
초자아 superego
초저출산고령사회
  hyper-aged and depopulating society
초점맞추기 focusing
초점조정 focusing
초청정공기 ultraclean air
촉각 sense of touch
촉각과민 hyperesthesia
촉각둔마 hypesthesia
촉각소실 anesthesia
촉독 Braille reading
촉매자 역할 catalyst role
촉지각저하 loss of touch sensation
촉진 facilitation
촉진기법 facilitation technique
촉진원인 precipitating cause
촉진자 역할 facilitator role

ㅊ

촌놈 redneck
총괄기능평가
  Global Assessment of Functioning : GAF
총무과 General Affairs Division
총의료비용 total medical costs
총의료비지출 total medical expenditures
총의치 full denture
총출산율
  total fertility rate : TFR ; total period fertility
  rate : TPFR
총콜레스테롤 total cholesterol
총혈구수 complete blood count : CBC
최강점 point of maximum intensity
최고범죄연령 the age of maximum criminality
최대근력 maximum muscle strength
최대내용량 maximum tolerable volume
최대다수의 최대행복
  greatest happiness for the greatest number
최대보행속도 maximal gait velocity
최대산소소비량 maximum oxygen consumption
최대수의수축압 maximum squeeze pressure : MSP
최대전도속도 maximum conduction velocity : MCV
최대정지압 maximum resting pressure : MRP
최면 hypnosis
최면상태 hypnosis
최면술 mesmerize
최면요법 hypnotherapy
최면치료 hypnotherapy
최빈국 least developed country : LDC
최선의 치료 best practice
최소가청치 absolute threshold of hearing
최소두뇌장애 minimal brain dysfunction
최소침습수술 minimally invasive surgery
최소홍반량 minimal erythema dose : MED
최저국민수준 national minimum
최저생계비 minimum cost of living
최저생존수준 minimum subsistence level
최저생활 minimum standard of living
최저생활가계부 minimum market basket
최저생활보장
  guaranteed minimum standard of living
최저생활비 minimum cost of living
최저수준 minimum standard

최저요구 측정 minimum needs estimation
최저임금 minimum wage
최저임금제도 minimum wage system
최종멸균 terminal sterilization
최종장기침상요양기간
  bedridden period before death : BPbd
추가급여 additional benefit
추가서비스 additional service
추가질문 probing
추골뇌저동맥조영 vertebral angiography
추골동맥 vertebral artery
추상지 mallet finger
추수과정 follow-up process
추수지도 follow-up
추장량 recommended dietary allowance : RDA
추적조사 follow-up study
추정일일섭취량 estimated daily intake
추지 mallet finger
추체 cone
추체로 pyramidal tract
추출법 sampling method
추출오차 sampling error
추출조사 sample survey
축 axis
축뇨이상 disturbance of urinary storage
축뇨장애 urinary storage disorder
축동 miosis
축동제 pilocarpine hydrochloride
축색변성 axonal degeneration
축소주의 reductionism
축어적 반사 word-for-word reflection
축일 holiday
축일보조 holiday sharing
축적효과 cumulative effect
출구부감염 exit-site infection
출산 childbearing
출산가족 family of procreation
출산력 fertility
출산부조 maternity assistance
출산수당 maternity allowance
출산수당금 maternity allowance
출산율 birthrate
출산적령기 childbearing age

출산휴가 maternity leave

출생률 감소사회
  society with the declining birth rate

출생서열이론 birth-order theories

출생율 fertility rate

출생전진단 prenatal diagnosis

출생증명서 birth certificate

출세이야기 Horatio Alger story

출이민 emigrant

출입구유효폭 effective width of doorway

출향 (적극적) 원조 reaching out

출혈 bleeding

출혈성 뇌졸중 hemorrhagic stroke

출혈성 수포 hemorrhagic bullae

충격 shock

충격치료 shock therapy

충동 drive

충동성 impulsiveness

충양근대 lumbrical bar

충혈 hyperemia

충혈제거제 decongestant

췌장 pancreas

췌장암 pancreatic cancer

췌장염 pancreatitis

취득시효 acquisitive prescription

취소 revocation

취업구조 employment structure

취업규칙
  employee rules and regulations ; working rule

취업인구 working population

취업지도 job placement guidance

취업지원 employment assistance

취침시 at bedtime

취학전교육 preschool education

취한 상태 drunkenness

측만 scoliosis

측면잡기 lateral pinch

측색 colorimetry

측와위 side-lying position

측정 measurement

층류 laminar air flow : LAF

층화추출법 stratified sampling

치간치솔 flossing teeth

치과 dentistry

치과검진수료율
  percentage of patients receiving annual dental
  exams

치과보건과 Dental Health Division

치과위생사 dental hygienist

치과위생사법 Dental Hygienists Law

치과의사 dentist

치과의사법 Dental Practitioners Law

치과질환 dental disease

치료 cure ; therapy ; treatment

치료 대 케어 care versus cure

치료거부권 right to refuse treatment

치료경험연수 medical history

치료공동체 therapeutic community

치료교육 therapeutic education

치료권 right to treatment

치료기법 therapeutic technique

치료력 medical history

치료모델 remedial model

치료보수 physician fee

치료식 therapeutic diet

치료자 therapist

치료적 내시경검사 therapeutic endoscopy

치료적 전기자극
  therapeutic electrical stimulation : TES

치료적 지역사회 therapeutic community

치매 dementia

치매 · 뇌졸증가족교실
  Family Classroom for the Dementia/
  Cerebrovascular Disease

치매고령자대책
  policy for the elderly with dementia ; policy
  for dementia

치매노인 people with dementia

치매노인대책 policy for people with dementia

치매노인일상생활자립도
  independence level of elderly with dementia

치매대응공동생활개호
  group home for people with dementia

치매대응형공동생활장기요양
  group home for people with dementia

치매대응형주간보호

day care services for people with dementia

치매도 level of dementia

치매성 고령자 elderly with dementia

치매성 고령자의 일상생활자립도
independence level of elderly with dementia

치매성 노인 elderly with dementia

치매성 노인그룹홈
group home for elderly with dementia

치매예방 prevention of dementia

치매의 행동정신증상 behavioral and psychological
symptoms of dementia : BPSD

치매전문병동 special care unit

치매전문병원
specialized hospital for people with dementia

치매진단 diagnosis of dementia

치매케어전문병동 special care unit

치매평가검사 Dementia Rating Scale

치매평가척도 Dementia Rating Scale

치명적 가족성 불면증 fatal familial insomnia

치사율 case-fatality rate

치실 dental floss

치아 teeth

치아 및 구강부위 호흡시스템
designation system for teeth and areas of the
oral cavity

치아노제 cyanosis

치아상실 tooth loss

치아졸리딘다이온계 약제 thiazolidinedione

치은염 inflamed gum

치조농루
blennorrhoea alveolaris ; alveolar ; pyorrhea

치주병
periodontitis ; periodontal disease ;
gum disease

치주조직 periodontium

치카노 Chicano

치프 chief

치환 substitution

친권 parental authority

친밀감 대 고립감 intimacy versus isolation

친사회행동 prosocial behavior

친자관계 parent-child relationship

친족 kinship

친족법 law of domestic relations

친족의무 relative's responsibility

친족케어 kinship care

침과다증 sialorrhea

침구 bedclothes ; acupuncture and moxibustion

침구사 acupuncture and moxibustion therapist

침구정리 bed making

침근전도 needle electromyogram

침대 bed

침대 리프트 bed lift

침대 옆 탁자 bedside table

침대난간 bedside rail

침대에서 휠체어로
transfer from bed to wheelchair

침대용 접이식 탁자 overbed table

침상 bedding

침상 상지위 bed positioning

침상기후 microclimate of sleeping floor

침상동작 bed mobility

침생검 needle biopsy

침술사 acupuncturist

침습적 critical

침식 erosion

침실용변기 chamber pot

침천자 needle puncture

침투지법 basin method

침흘리기 drooling

ㅊ

카롤리병 Caroli disease
카르바마제핀 carbamazepine
카리타스 caritas
카운셀러 counselor
카운셀링 counseling
카이로프랙틱 chiropractic
카츠 ALD 도구 Katz ADL index
카타르시스 katharsis
카타르시스법 cathartic method
카테콜-오-메틸트랜스라제
  catechol-O-methyltransferase : COMT
카테터 catheter
카테터관련감염 catheter-associated infection
카테터관련피유행성 감기염
  catheter-associated bloodstream infection :
  CABSI
카테터유래감염 catheter-related infection
카테터유래균혈증 catheter-related bacteremia
카테터유래피유행성 감기염
  catheter-related bloodstream infection : CRBSI
카테터유치법 catheterization
카톨리시즘 Catholicism
카페인 caffeine
칸나비스 cannabis
칸데사르탄 candesartan
칸디다 알비칸스 candida albicans
칼디젬 Cardizem
칼란 Calan
칼러니제이션 colonization
칼러니형성단위 colony forming unit : CFU
칼로리 제한 caloric restriction
칼비니즘 Calvinism
칼슘 calcium

칼슘 파이로인산염 축적질환
  calcium pyrophosphate deposition disease
칼슘결핍증 calcium deficiency
칼슘길항제 calcium channel blocker
칼슘통로차단제 calcium channel blocker
칼시토닌 calcitonin
캐나다식 고의족
  Canadian-type hip disarticulation prosthesis
캐넌 Ida M. Cannon
캐뉼라 cannula
캐릭터 character
캐보트 R. C. Cabot
캐스터 caster
캘리퍼 caliper
캠페인 campaign ; press campaign
캡사이신 capsaicin
캣 스캔 CAT scan
커너 위원회 Kerner Commission
커러퀴 colloquy
커뮤니케이션 communication
커뮤니케이션 노트 communication notes
커뮤니케이션 능력 communicative ability
커뮤니케이션 보드 communication board
커뮤니케이션 에이드 communication aid
커뮤니케이션 장애 communication disorder
커뮤니케이션이론 communication theory
커뮤니티 community
커뮤니티병원 community hospital
커뮤니티센타 community center
커뮤니티소시얼워크 community social work
커뮤니티오거니제이션
  community organization : CO
커뮤니티워커 community worker

커뮤니티워크 community work
커뮤니티재생 community revitalization
커뮤니티조직 community organization : CO
커뮤니티체스트 community chest
커뮤니티케어 community care
커뮤니티케어네트워크 community care network
커뮤니티케어시스템 community care system
커뮤니티활동기관 community action agency
커플요법 couple therapy
컨디셔너 conditioner
컨퍼런스 conference
컴파트먼트증후군 compartment syndrome
컴패니언 companion
컴퓨터단층촬영
  computed tomography : CT ; electron beam
  computed tomography
컴퓨터체축단층촬영
  computerized axial tomography : CAT
컴플라이언스 compliance
컴플렉스 complex
케겔운동 Kegel exercise
케니식 자기건강관리평가
  Kenny Self-Care Evaluation
케드헤린 cadherin
케어 care
케어가이드라인 care guideline
케어기버 caregiver
케어매니저 care manager
케어매니지먼트 care management
케어매니지먼트기관 care management provider
케어매니지먼트모델 care management model
케어목표 care goal ; goal of care
케어믹스 care mix
케어복지사 care worker
케어서비스 care services
케어워커 care worker
케어워크 care work
케어의 미래 future of care
케어의 질 quality of care
케어제공고령자주택
  elder care housing ; aged care home
케어제공주택
  adult care housing ; aged care home

케어주택 care home
케어카드 care card
케어컨퍼런스 care conference
케어코디네이션 care coordination
케어팀 care team
케어패스 care pathway
케어플랜 care plan
케어하우스 care home
케어환경 environment of care
케이블보관집 cable housing
케이블하우징 cable housing
케이스 case
케이스기록 case record
케이스담당량 case load
케이스로드 case load
케이스매니지먼트 case management
케이스믹스 case mix
케이스믹스지수 case mix index : CMI
케이스슈퍼바이저 case supervisor
케이스슈퍼비전 case supervision
케이스스터디 case study
케이스에이드 case aid
케이스에이드워커 case aid worker
케이스워커 case worker
케이스워크 case work
케이스워크 과정 casework process
케이스워크 관계 casework relationship
케이스워크 진단 casework diagnosis
케이스컨트롤연구 case control study
케이스컨퍼런스 case conference
케이스파일 case file
케이스할당문제 turf issues
케이스회의 case meeting
케이스히스토리 case history
케인즈 John Maynard Keynes
케인즈경제학 Keynesian economics
케인즈주의 Keynesianism
케인즈주의적 복지국가 Keynesian Welfare State
켈리패드 Kelly pad
코골이 snoring
코그넥스 Cognex
코넬건강지수 Cornell medical index : CMI
코넬메디컬인덱스 Cornell medical index : CMI

ㄱ

코넬의학조사표 Cornell medical index : CMI
코넬치매우울척도
　Cornell Scale for Depression in Dementia :
　CSDD
코데인 codeine
코디네이터 coordinator
코르사코프 정신병 Korsakoff's psychosis
코르셋 corset
코르티코스테로이드 corticosteroids
코스정신발달검사 Kohs Block Design Test
코스트계약 cost-volume contract
코어타임 core time
코자 Cozaar
코카인 cocaine
코크런리뷰 Cochrane review
코포라티스트 복지국가 corporatist welfare state
코핑 coping
코핑행동 coping behavior
코호트 cohort
코호트분석 cohort analysis
코호트연구 cohort study
코호팅 cohorting
콘드로이친황산 chondroitin sulfate
콘트라스트감도 contrast sensitivity
콜라겐 collagen
콜레스테롤 cholesterol
콜로니 colony
콜린성 요법 cholinergic therapy
콜린에스터레이즈억제제 cholinesterase inhibitor
콜버그의 도덕발달 이론
　Kohlberg moral development theory
콤플렉스 complex
쾌락원칙 pleasure principle
쿠마딘 Coumadin
쿠션 cushion
쿠싱증후군 Cushing's syndrome
쿠아제팜 quazepam
쿨링오프 cooling off
퀴나프릴 quinapril
퀴블러로스 사망단계
　Kubler-Ross's five stages of grief ;
　Kubler-Ross model ; the five stages of grief
큐분류법 q-sort technique

큐어 cure
크라우딩아웃이론 crowding-out theory
크래들 cradle
크랙 crack
크러치 crutch
크레졸비누액 saponated cresol solution
크로스집계 cross tab ; cross tabulation
크론카이트 - 카나다 증후군
　Cronkhite-Canada syndrome
크리밍 creaming
크리티니즘 cretinism
크리티컬 critical
크리프트 후크 crypt hook
크린벤치 clean bench
크림스키밍 cream-skimming
크산틴 xanthines
큰 정부 big government
클라이언트 client
클라이언트 본위 client-oriented
클라이언트 중심기록방법 person-oriented record
클라이언트 중심요법 client-centered therapy
클라이언트 중심치료 client-centered therapy
클라이언트 참가 client participation
클라이언트 체계 client system
클락포지션 clock position
클럽활동 club activity
클렌자크식 발목관절 이음새 Klenzak ankle joint
클렙시엘라폐렴 Klebsiella pneumonia
클로나제팜 clonazepam
클로노핀 Klonopin
클로디아 제폭시드 클리디니움
　clidinium-chlordiazepoxide
클로르디아 제폭사이드 Chlordiazepoxide
클로르디아 제폭사이드 아미트리프틸린
　chlordiazepoxide-amitriptyline
클로르제페이트 clorazepate
클로르제프산 clorazepate
클로르족사존 chlorzoxazone
클로르프로마진 chlorpromazine
클로미프라민 clomipramine
클로스트리듐 디피실리균 clostridium difficile
클로자핀 clozapine
클로피도그렐 clopidogrel

클뤼버부시증후군 Kluver-Bucy syndrome
클리니컬 스킬 clinical skill
클리니컬 패스웨이 clinical pathway
클리어링법 clearing technique
클린룸 clean room

클린존 clean zone
키너렛 Kineret
키브츠 Kibbutz
키홀수술 keyhole surgery
킹슬리 홀 Kingsley Hall

ㅋ

타당성 validity
타당성 구축 construct validity
타당성 연구 feasibility study
타동가동역 passive range of motion
타동운동 passive exercise
타라소프 Tarasoff
타박상 bruise
타액 saliva
타액과다분비 hypersalivation
타액기능 saliva functioning
타액분비과다 ptyalism ; sialorrhea
타운센드 계획 Townsend Plan
타워법 TOWER system
타의적 운동 passive exercise
타이레놀 Tylenol
타이아자이드계 이뇨제 thiazide diuretic
타이제카 Tyzeka
타이틀 20 Title XX
타인종 입양 transracial adoption
타일모자이크 tile mosaic
타임아웃 time-out
타진 percussion
타크린 tacrine
타해행위 danger to others : DTO
타협 compromise
타협숙주 compromised host
탁노소 adult day care center
탁아보호 day care
탄닌 tannin
탄력성 elasticity
탄수화물 carbohydrate
탄원 petition
탈감각화 desensitization

탈건착환 put clothing on the affected side and take the clothing off the unaffected side
탈구 luxation ; disarticulation
탈락세포검사 exfoliative cytology
탈륨스캔검사 thallium scanning
탈리도마이드 thalidomide
탈모치료제 Avodart
탈수 demyelination
탈수증 dehydration
탈수초 demyelination
탈수초성 질환 demyelinating disease
탈시설 deinstitutionalization
탈시설화 deinstitutionalization
탈신경 denervation
탈억제 disinhibition
탈의실 dressing room
탈의장 dressing room
탈지면, 거즈, 그 밖의 위생재료 absorbent cotton gauze and other sanitary supplies
탈지행위 cream-skimming
탈진증후군 burnout syndrome
탈퇴일시금 lump-sum withdrawal payments
탈퇴일시금재정청구서 claim form for the lump-sum withdrawal payments
탐색과정 working through
탐색전극 exploring electrode
탐스로신 tamsulosin
탑승자제어 휠체어 manual attendant controlled wheelchair
태극권 tai chi
태만 negligence

태아 fetus
태아기 prenatal
태아기 알코올증후군 fetal alcohol syndrome
태아기 장애 fetal disorder
태아알코올스펙트럼장애
  fetal alcohol spectrum disorder
태아알코올증후군 fetal alcohol syndrome
태아학 fetology
태양광 식수살균법 solar water disinfection : SODIS
태평양 섬주민 Pacific Islanders
태평양제도〔諸島〕출신자 Pacific Islander
택스코드 tax code
터미널케어 terminal care
털 제거 hair removal
테그레톨 Tegretol
테니스엘보 tennis elbow
테라토마 teratoma
테스토스테론 testosterone
테오피린 theophylline
테이색스병 Tay-Sachs disease
테일러 Frederic Winslow Taylor
테일러의 표출불안척도
  Taylor's Manifest Anxiety Scale : TMAS
테크노에이드협회 Association for Technical Aids
테타니 tetany
텔레톤 telethon
텔비부딘 telbivudine
템플대학 세대간 학습센터 Center for Intergenerational Learning of Temple University
팁핑레버 tipping lever
토글 브레이크 toggle brake
토레트병 Tourette's disorder
토론 debate
토론회 debate forum
토양감염 soil-borne infection
토우 브레이크 toe-break
토우 인 toe in
토인비 Arnold Toynbee
토인비 홀 Toynbee Hall
토착인 사회복지사 indigenous social worker
토착인 사회사업가 indigenous social worker
토털헬스프로모션 total health promotion : THP

토프라닐 Tofranil
토피라메이트 topiramate
토혈 hematemesis
톨카폰 tolcapone
통각 algesia
통각과민 hyperalgesia
통각과민증 algesia
통각잔류 remaining sense of pain
통계 statistics
통계적 가설검정 statistical hypothesis test
통계적 검정 statistical test
통계적 유의도 statistical significance
통계정보부
  Statistics and Information Department
통계조사 statistical research
통계청 Statistic Korea
통과균 transient bacteria
통과세균 transient flora
통과의식 rite of passage
통과증후군 transitional syndrome
통기 aeration
통산노령연금 aggregate old age pension
통소개호 day care services
통소개호시설 day care services center
통소재활 ambulatory rehabilitation
통신교육 online education
통원 doctor's office visit
통원의료 ambulatory health care services
통원자율 outpatient rate
통원환자 outpatient
통음 binge drinking
통정 integration
통제 control
통제된 정서적 관여
  controlled emotional involvement
통제된 정서적 관여의 원칙
  principle of controlled emotional involvement
통제범위 span of control
통제변수 control variable
통제집단 control group
통증생활장애평가척도
  Pain Disability Assessment Scale : PDAS
통증클리닉 pain clinic

E

통찰 insight
통찰요법 insight therapy
통풍 gout
통풍성 관절염 gouty arthritis
통합 integration
통합공급시스템 integrated delivery system : IDS
통합교육 integrated education
통합된 복지국가 integrated welfare state
통합된 환경 integrated setting
통합방법론 integrated method
통합실조증 schizophrenia
통합의료공급시스템
　integrated health care delivery system
통합적 방법 integrated method
통합지불 single-payer
통화침투이론 trickle-down theory
퇴거 eviction
퇴보형 아동 withdrawn child
퇴소 discharge from the facility
퇴소시 정보 discharge information
퇴소후 방문지도 follow-up visit after discharge
퇴역군인 veteran
퇴원 discharge
퇴원계획 discharge planning
퇴원시 청소 discharge cleaning
퇴원조정 discharge management
퇴직 retirement
퇴직검사 retirement test
퇴직소득조사 retirement earnings test
퇴직수당
　retirement allowance ; severance package
퇴직연금 retirement pension
퇴직일시금 retirement lump sum grant
퇴직자 의료보험제도
　retiree health care insurance system
퇴직자 의료제도 retiree health care system
퇴직조사 retirement test
퇴행 regression
퇴행행동 regression behavior
퇴화 atrophy
퇴화성 기억상실증 retrograde amnesia
투사 projection
투사 동일시 projective identification

투석 dialysis
투석요법 dialysis therapy
투시검사법 projective test
투약 assistance with the self-administration of
　medication
투약과오 medication error
투약량 조정 dosage modification
투약제한 medication restriction
투여 administration
투영 projection
투영검사 projective test
투영법 projective method
투옥 incarceration
투입 introjection
투입-산출분석 input-output analysis
투자 대 소비 개념
　investment-versus-consumption concept
튜브영양 tube feeding
트라닐시프로민 tranylcypromine
트라스투주맙 trastuzumab
트라우마 trauma
트란데이트 Trandate
트랑센 Tranxene
트래이너 trainer
트랜델렌버그 징후 Trendelenburg sign
트랜델렌버그 체위 Trendelenburg position
트랜스퍼 transfer
트랜스퍼보드 transfer board
트레드밀 treadmill
트레드밀 부하시험 treadmill testing
트리거 trigger
트리거 포인트 trigger point
트리법 tree analysis
트리트먼트 treatment
트리프탄 제재 triptan drug
트릭모션 trick motion
특기사항 special notes
특례요양비 special home care benefits
특발성 혈소판감소성 자반병
　idiopathic thrombocytopenic purpura : ITP
특별공제 special exemption
특별구 special ward
특별기준 special standard

특별니즈플랜 special needs plan
특별보험료징수 special premium collection
특별세액공제 special tax rebate
특별수당 special benefit allowance
특별식 special meal
특별양호노인홈 geriatric welfare home
특별임시위원회 adhocracy
특별자원봉사기금 special volunteer fund
특별장애인공제
  special deduction for people with disabilities
특별장애인세공제
  special tax deduction for people with
  disabilities
특별장애인수당 special disability allowance
특별지역가산
  additional payment to special region
특별지원교육 special needs education
특별지원학교 special school
특별지원학급
  special class for children with disabilities
특별징수 special collection
특별치료식 special therapeutic diet
특별현금급여 special cash benefits
특별회계 special account
특수교육 special education
특수교육제학교 special education school
특수법인 special juridical person
특수아동 exceptional children
특수연합 ad hoc coalition
특수욕조 specialized bathtub
특수이익집단 special interest group
특수자격 exceptional eligibility
특수직역연금
  special occupation retirement pension
특수침대 specialized bed
특이적 독서장애 specific reading disorder

특이한 idiosyncratic
특정독서장애 specific reading disorder
특정발달장애
  specific developmental disorder : SDD
특정복지용구 special welfare equipment
특정복지용구판매
  certified welfare equipment trade
특정비영리활동촉진법
  Law to Promote Specified Non-Profit
  Activities : NPO Law
특정산수능력장애
  specific disorder of arithmetical skills
특정승인 보험의료기관
  certified medical facility for health insurance
특정요양비 specific geriatric care costs
특정재원 earmarked revenue
특정질병 intractable disease
특정질환 intractable disease
특정철자장애 specific spelling disorder
특정활동 designated activity
특허매약 proprietary medicine
틀니 denture
티넬징후 Tinel sign
티아가빈 tiagabine
티아민결핍증 thiamine deficiency
티에체 증후군 Tietze's syndrome
티오레독신 Thioredoxin
티켓제도 ticket system
티트머스 Richard Morris Titmuss
티핑레버 tipping lever
틸팅테이블 tilting table
팀워크 teamwork
팀의료 team medicine
팀접근법 team approach
팀케어 team care
팀케어의 확립 establishment of the team care

E

ㅍ

파견노동자 dispatch worker
파괴성 정신분열증 hebephrenic schizophrenia
파괴행위 vandalism
파네이트 Parnate
파라메디컬 스태프 paramedical staff
파라프레니아 paraphrenia
파라핀욕 paraffin bath
파레토 최적 Pareto optimum
파메라 Pamelor
파블로프 Ivan Petrovich Pavlov
파상풍 tetanus
파스퇴르제이션 pasteurization
파슨즈 Talcott Parsons
파악 lateral pinch
파우치 pouch
파울러씨 체위 Fowler's position
파워재활 power rehabilitation
파이로인산염침착증
　pyrophosphate deposition disease
파이로젠 pyrogen
파이로젠검사 pyrogen test
파이로트 켐페인 pilot campaign
파이의 논리 logic of pie
파일로트 스터디 pilot study
파자마 pajamas
파종성 혈관내응고증
　disseminated intravascular coagulation
파지 prehension
파지보조기 prehension orthosis
파지부목 tenodesis splint
파지용구 aid for grasping
파킨소니즘 Parkinsonism
파킨슨병 Parkinson's disease

파킨슨병 체조
　physical exercise for Parkinson's disease
파킨슨증후군 Parkinson's syndrome
파킨슨체조
　physical exercise for Parkinson's disease
파트타임 part time
파트타임노동 part-time work
파트타임노동자 part-time worker
파티클 카운터 particle counter
파페츠회로 Papez circuit
파행 claudication
팍시팜 Paxipam
팍실 Paxil
판결 adjudication
판결감시프로젝트 Sentencing Project
판막증 valvular disease
판매자 provider
판정 judgment
판정회의 decision-making meeting
판타지배회 fantasy wandering
판토텐산 pantothenic acid
팔걸이 armrest ; arm sling
팔굽혀펴기운동 push up workout
팔꿈치 기어가기 creeping
팔꿈치 욕 elbow bathing
팔로우업 follow-up
팜비어 Famvir
팜시클로버 famciclovir
팡고테라피 fango therapy
패거리 gang
패널토의 panel discussion
패널히터 panel heater
패닉장애 panic disorder

ㅍ

패드 pad
패러다임 paradigm
패러사이트싱글 parasite single
패럴림픽 Paralympics
패밀리 그룹홈 family group home
패밀리서포트 family support
패밀리서포트센터 family support center
패밀리소시얼워크 family social work
패밀리케이스워크 family case work
패터널리즘 paternalism
패혈 sepsis
패혈증 septicemia ; blood poisoning
패혈증성 쇼크 septic shock
퍼거슨리포트 Ferguson Report
퍼블리시티 publicity
퍼스낼리티 personality
펀치생검법 punch biopsy
펄만 Harris R. Perlman
펄스옥시미터 pulse oximeter
페가시스 Pegasys
페그보드 pegboard
페그인터페론 pegylated interferon
페넬진 phenelzine
페놀블록 phenol block
페미니즘 feminism
페니실린 penicillin
페린도프릴 perindopril
페미니스트소시얼워크 feminist social work
페미니즘이론 feminist theory
페비안 사회주의 Fabian socialism
페서리 pessary
페스탈로찌 Johann Heinrich Pestalozzi
페어쉐어플랜 fair share plan
페이비안주의 (페이비어니즘) Fabianism
페이스마스크 face mask
페이스메이커 pacemaker
페이스시트 face sheet
페이스트식 paste meal ; chopped diet
페인클리닉 pain clinic
펜듈럼테스트 pendulum test
펠라그라 pellagra
펫 PET < positron emission tomography >
편견 prejudice ; bias

편도선 tonsil
편두통 migraine headache
편리 access
편리성 accessibility
편마비 hemiplegia
편무적 부양 unilateral support
편부모가정 single-parent family
편의적 선취 cream-skimming
편집 editing
편집성 치매 paraphrenia
편집장애 paranoid disorders
편집증 paranoid
편집형 사고 paranoid ideation
편집형 성격장애 paranoid personality disorder
편집형 정신분열증 paranoid schizophrenia
편측골반용의족 hemipelvectomy prosthesis
편측골반절단 hemipelvectomy
편측공간무시 unilateral spatial neglect : USN
편측공간실인 unilateral spatial agnosia
편측무시 unilateral neglect
편타손 손상 whiplash ; whiplash injury
편파적 중재 side-taking
편평족 pes planus
편평표피암 squamous cell carcinoma
평가 assessment ; evaluation
평가액 assessed value
평가자 간의 신뢰도 inter-rater reliability
평가조사 evaluation research
평가툴 assessment tool
평가항목 evaluation criteria ; assessment item
평균 mean
평균세대인원
　　average size of households ; average
　　household size
평균수명 average life span
평균약가 average price of drugs
평균양육비용 average cost of bringing up a child
평균여명 life expectancy
평균입원일수 average length of stay : ALOS
평등 equality
평등권 equal rights
평생교육
　　continuing education ; lifelong education

평생학습 lifelong learning
평판 reputation
평행봉 parallel bar
평행봉이론 the parallel bars theory
평형 equilibrium
평형기능장애 disturbance of balance
평형상태 equilibrium
평형장애 impairment of balance function
평화 peace
평화봉사단 Peace Corps
평화운동 peace movement
평화학 peace study
폐결핵 pulmonary tuberculosis
폐경 menopause
폐기 disposal
폐기관장애 pulmonary disorders
폐기능검사 pulmonary function test
폐기량측정법 spirometry
폐기물처리 refuse disposal
폐기물처리법
　Waste Disposal and Public Cleaning Law
폐기종 pulmonary emphysema ; emphysema
폐노카르디아증 pulmonary nocardiosis
폐동맥폐쇄증 pulmonary atresia
폐렴 pneumonia
폐렴구균성 수막염 pneumococcal meningitis
폐렴구균성 폐렴 pneumococcal pneumonia
폐렴구균예방접종 pneumococcal vaccination
폐렴연쇄구균 streptococcus pneumoniae
폐렴연쇄상구균 streptococcus pneumoniae
폐쇄 closed system
폐쇄가족 closed family
폐쇄병동 locked unit
폐쇄성 동맥경화증 arteriosclerosis obliterans
폐쇄시설 locked facility
폐쇄식 기관내흡인튜브
　closed endotracheal suction tube
폐쇄식 드레이니지 closed drainage
폐쇄식 지속도뇨시스템
　closed system of urinary drainage system
폐쇄운동사슬 closed kinetic chain
폐쇄전 pulmonary embolus
폐쇄체계 closed system

폐쇄형 수면무호흡 obstructive sleep apnea
폐쇄형 수면무호흡증후군
　obstructive sleep apnea syndrome : OSAS
폐쇄형 질문 closed-ended question
폐수종 pulmonary edema
폐암 lung cancer
폐용 disuse
폐용량감소술 lung volume reduction surgery
폐용성 골위축 disuse bone atrophy
폐용성 근위축 disuse muscle atrophy
폐용위축 disuse atrophy
폐용증후군 disuse syndrome
페이식 lung transplant
폐질 total disability
폐질환 pulmonary disease
폐포 alveolus
폐포 · 모세혈관관문 alveolar-capillary barrier
폐포 · 모세혈관장벽 alveolar-capillary barrier
폐포가스교환 alveolar gas exchange
폐포강 alveolar space
폐포구축 alveolar structure
폐포기 alveolar air
폐포기 · 동맥혈 산소분압교차
　alveolar-arterial oxygen tension difference
폐포기식 alveolar air equation
폐포내압 alveolar pressure
폐포대식세포 alveolar macrophage
폐포리크루트먼트 alveolar recruitment
폐포막 alveolar membrane
폐포매크로파지 alveolar macrophage
폐포부종 alveolar edema
폐포사강 alveolar dead space
폐포상피 alveolar epithelium
폐포상피세포 alveolar epithelial cell ; alveolar cell
폐포상해 alveolar damage
폐포서팩턴트 alveolar surfactant
폐포성 저산소 alveolar hypoxia
폐포세정 alveolar lavage
폐포수종 alveolar edema
폐포저환기 alveolar hypoventilation
폐포표면장력 alveolar surface tension
폐포표면활성물질 alveolar surfactant
폐포허탈 alveolar collapse

폐포환기 alveolar ventilation
폐합유역 closed drainage
폐활량 lung capacity
포괄의료 comprehensive medicine
포괄적 감시 comprehensive surveillance
포괄적 의료 comprehensive health care
포괄적 재활접근법
  holistic rehabilitative intervention
포괄적 지시 comprehensive order
포괄적 지역케어시스템
  comprehensive community care system
포괄적 지출리뷰 comprehensive spending review
포괄적 환경요인조사표
  Multiphasic Environmental Assessment
  Procedure : MEAP
포괄지불제도 prospective payment system
포괄평가 inclusive evaluation
포괄형지역생활지원
  assertive community treatment
포도당 glucose
포도당 부하시험 glucose tolerance test
포도당 비발효균
  glucose-non-fermentative bacteria
포드주의 fordism
포럼 forum
포멀네트워크 formal network
포멀서비스 formal service
포멀섹터 formal sector
포멀케어 formal care
포사맥스 Fosamax
포섭 cooptation
포스트모던 post-modern
포오쿼터절단 forequarter amputation
포자 spore
포지셔닝 positioning
포지트론CT positron emission tomography : PET
포지트론단층법
  positron emission tomography : PET
포지트론에미션 토모그래피
  positron emission tomography : PET
포진 herpes
포커싱 focusing
포켓감염 pocket infection

포켓러스감염 pocket infection
포터블욕조 portable bathtub
포터블화장실 commode ; bedside commode
포함 inclusion
포화증기 saturated vapor
폭 width
폭력 violence
폭로 exposure
폭로자 muckrakers
폭로허용농도 permissible exposure limit : PEL
폭식 adephagia
폭식증 bulimia nervosa
폭음 binge drinking
폰베 Pompe van Meerdervoort
폴로우업 follow-up
폴리에스테르 알레르기 polyester allergy
폴리오 poliomyelitis
폴리오후증후군 post-polio syndrome : PPS
폴립 polyps
폴크만연축 Volkmann's contracture
표면근전도 surface electromyogram
표면색모드 surface color mode
표면적 타당성 face validity
표면전극 surface electrode
표백 bleaching
표백액 bleach solution
표백제 bleaching agent
표본 sample
표본오차 sampling error
표본조사 sample survey
표본추출 sampling
표본추출법 sampling design
표재감각 superficial sensation
표적상 소견 bull's eye appearance
표적체계 target system
표적행동 target behavior
표정반사 facial reflection
표준가구 standard household
표준검사 standardized tests
표준공제 standard deduction
표준근로계약서 standard labor agreement
표준급여비용액 cost of standard benefits
표준급여패키지 standard benefits package

표준보수 standard for remuneration

표준보수제 standard pay system

표준부담액 cost of standard payment

표준생계비 standard cost of living

표준실어증검사
standard language test of aphasia : SLTA

표준연금 standard pension

표준예방책 standard precaution

표준온도 normal temperature

표준장기요양이용계획서
standard long-term care usability document

표준편차 standard deviation

표준화 standardization

표준화 사망비 standardized mortality ratio : SMR

표지 face sheet

표출된 문제 presenting problem

푸드박스 food box

푸드뱅크 Food Bank

푸드뱅크식품 food bank food items

푸딩대사저해제 purine metabolism inhibitor

푸로세마이드 furosemide

푸로세미드 furosemide

푸시업 push up

푸시오프 push off

풀뿌리민주주의 grass roots democracy

품질관리 quality control

품질관리활동 quality control : QC

품질보증 quality assurance

풋레스트 foot rest

풋보드 footboard

풍미 flavor

풍요사회 affluent society

풍진 rubella

풍토병 endemic

퓌레상태 pureed solids

퓌레식 pureed diet

퓨리터니즘 (청교도주의) Puritanism

프라미펙솔 pramipexole

프라스테론 dehydroepiandrosterone : DHEA

프라이 Elizabeth Fry

프라이머리케어 primary care

프라이머리헬스케어 primary health care : PHC

프라이버시 privacy

프라이버시보호 privacy protection

프라이버타이제이션 privatization

프라조신 prazosin

프란켈분류 Frankel classification

프래그머티즘 pragmatism

프레드니손 prednisone

프레임 frame

프로게스테론요법 progesterone therapy

프로그램 기획 및 예산제도
Program Planning and Budgeting system

프로그램 평가 및 검토기법
Program Evaluation and Review Technique

프로덕티브에이징 productive aging

프로드로말 현상 prodromal phase

프로막스 Flomax

프로바트립탄 frovatriptan

프로브 probe

프로섬 ProSom

프로세스 골 process-goal

프로스카 Proscar

프로이드 Sigmund Freud

프로이트과실 Freudian slip

프로이트이론 Freudian theory

프로작 Prozac

프로젝트 project

프로테스탄티즘 Protestantism

프로텍티브 서비스 protective service

프로폭시펜 propoxyphene

프로프라놀롤 propranolol

프로필 profile

프롬 Erich Fromm

프리가발린 pregabalin

프리드먼 사무소 Freedmen's Bureau

프리라이더 free rider

프리엑세스 free access

프리터 freeter

프리테스트 pre-test

플라빅스 Plavix

플라스틱보조기 plastic orthosis

플라시보효과 placebo effect

플래닝 planning

플래시백현상 flashback

플래토 plateau

플랫폼크러치　platform crutch
플랫폼형 지팡이　platform crutch
플러그피트소켓　plug-fit socket
플렉세릴　Flexeril
플렉스 타임제　flexible working hours system
플렉스너 보고서　Flexner Report
플렉스타임　flextime
플로어링　flooring
플로옥세틴　fluoxetine
플로톤펌프 저해약　proton pump inhibitor
플록세틴　fluoxetine
플루복사민　fluvoxamine
피고용자　employee
피고용자건강보험　employees health insurance
피고용자보험　employee insurance
피고용자연금　employee pension
피구　Alfred C. Pigou
피나스테라이드 (피네스테리드)　finasteride
피난민 (망명자, 도피자)　refugee
피난장소　evacuation site
피난처　sanctuary
피라지나마이드　pyrazinamide
피로　fatigue
피로연구　fatigue study
피버퓨　feverfew
피보험자　the insured
피보험자균등할　premiums on a per capita basis
피보험자기간　insured period
피보호자　public assistance recipient
피보호자세대　households on public assistance
피복　clothes
피복수당　clothing allowance
피복재　coating flux
피복제　coating drug
피부　skin
피부감각　superficial sensation
피부과 전문의　dermatologist
피부과의사　dermatologist
피부과학　dermatology
피부근육염증　dermatomyositis
피부보호제　skin barrier
피부사상균　dermatophyte
피부사상균증　dermatophytosis

피부소독　skin antiseptic
피부소양감　cutaneous pruritus
피부소양증　skin pruritus
피부손상　skin tear
피부암　skin cancer
피부양자　dependent
피부장애　skin disorder
피부전위반응　electrodermal responding
피부진균　dermatophyte
피부질환　skin disease
피부표면세균배양법　skin surface culture method
피브린　fibrin
피아제　Jean Piaget
피아제이론　Piaget's theory
피알　public relations : PR
피어그룹　peer group
피어그룹 슈퍼비전　peer group supervision
피어서포트　peer support
피어슈퍼비전　peer supervision
피어슨의 알 상관　Pearson's r correlation
피어카운셀링　peer counseling
피용자　employee
피용자보험
　employee insurance ; employees' insurance
피용자연금
　employee pension ; employees' pension
피이드백　feedback
피임법　contraception
피질하 혈관성 치매　subcortical vascular dementia
피트　feet
피트니스　fitness
피티에스디
　PTSD< post-traumatic stress disorder >
피폭자　atomic bomb survivor
피하　subcutaneous : Sub-Q
피하출혈　subcutaneous bleeding
피하터널감염　tunnel infection
피학대 고령자　abused elderly
피학대 노인　abused elderly
피학대 아동　abused child
피학성　masochism
피해망상　delusion of persecution
피해망상증　paranoia

피해자 보상 victim compensation
피해자 연구〔학〕 victimology
피해자 책임전가 victim blaming
픽병 Pick's disease
필기불능증 agraphia
필기시험 written examination
필담 written communication
필림포럼 film forum

필링인 filling-in
필수아미노산 essential amino acid
필요시 as needed : PRN
필요영양량 essential nutrition
필요전제기준 prerequisite criteria
필요즉응의 원칙 needs-response principle
핍뇨 oliguria
핑크노이즈 프로토콜 pink noise protocol

ㅍ

하니스 harness
하드웨어 hardware
하라제팜 halazepam
하루 2회 two times daily : BID
하루 3회 three times daily : TID
하루 4회 four times daily : QID
하루 5회 five times daily : 5D
하루 걸러 every other day : QOD
하루섭취권장량 reference daily intake : RDI
하류계층 lower class
하리스베네딕트 기초에너지방정식
　　Harris-Benedict caloric intake equation
하리스베네딕트 방정식 Harris-Benedict equation
하리스베네딕트 열량섭취방정식
　　Harris-Benedict caloric intake equation
하반신마비 paraplegic
하버드 의료과오연구
　　Harvard Medical Malpractice Study
하부구조 infrastructure
하부소화관 lower gastrointestinal
하부식도괄약근 lower esophageal sphincter : LES
하부식도괄약근 기능장애
　　lower esophageal sphincter dysfunction
하부체계 subsystem
하세가와 치매척도 Hasegawa Dementia Scale : HDS
하세가와 치매척도개정판
　　Hasegawa Dementia Scale-Revised : HDS-R
하세가와식 간이지능평가스케일 개정판
　　Revised Hasegawa's Dementia Scale : HDS-R
하시모토 갑상선염 Hashimoto's thyroiditis
하시모토병
　　Hashimoto disease ; Hashimoto's thyroiditis
하아트누프병 Hartnup disease

하아트누프증 Hartnup disorder
하열제 antipyretic drug ; antipyretic ; antipyretic
　　medication
하워드 John Howard
하위운동뉴런 lower motor neuron
하위운동신경원 lower motor neuron
하위집단 sub-group
하의식 subconscious
하이드랄라진 hydralazine
하이드로컬레이터 hydrocollator
하이드로코돈 hydrocodone
하이드로테라피 hydrotherapy
하이드록시클로로퀸 hydroxychloroquine
하이리스크 high risk
하이브리드 인공장기 artificial hybrid organ
하인리히 법칙 Heinrich's law
하임리히법 Heimlich Maneuver
하지 lower extremity
하지보조기
　　knee-ankle-foot orthosis : KAFO ; lower
　　extremity orthosis
하지불안증후군 restless legs syndrome : RLS
하지장 leg length
하지절단 lower limb amputation
하층계급 underclass
하층사회 lower social stratum
하코미테라피 body-centered psychotherapy
하퇴소켓 transtibial socket
하퇴의족 transtibial prosthesis
하퇴절단 below-knee amputation
하트넙병 Hartnup disease
하트넙증 Hartnup disorder
하프웨이하우스 halfway house

ㅎ

하혈 melena
학교공포증 school phobia
학교급식 프로그램 School Lunch program
학교법인 private school corporation
학교사회사업 school social work
학교상담 school counseling
학대 abuse ; maltreatment
학대아 abused child
학동 elementary school children
학사호 bachelor's degree
학생보조 프로그램 student aid programs
학습경험 learning experience
학습능력 learning ability
학습된 무기력 learned haplessness
학습불능자 learning disabled
학습사회 learning society
학습성 무력감 learned helplessness
학습성 무력감이론 learned helplessness theory
학습이론 learning theory
학습장애 learning disability : LD
학습패러다임 learning paradigm
학제간 활동 interdisciplinary activity
학제적 interdisciplinary
학제적 연구 interdisciplinary approach
한 쌍[한 단위로서] dyad
한 아이정책 one-child policy
한계취락 marginal village
한국가족관계학회
　Korea Association of Family Relations
한국가족법학회
　The Korean Society of Family Law
한국가족치료학회
　Korean Association of Family Therapy
한국가족학회 Korean Family Studies Association
한국가톨릭노인복지협의회
　Korea Catholic Old People's Welfare
　Organization
한국갤럽 Gallup Korea
한국교정학회
　Korean Society for Correction Service
한국교회노인학교연합회
　The Korean church aged school
한국노년유권자연맹

Korean Federation of Elderly Voters
한국노년자원봉사회
　Korea Geriatrics Society of Volunteer Service
한국노년학연구회
　Korea Research Institute of Gerontology
한국노년학회 The Korean Gerontological Society
한국노동연구원 Korea Labor Institute
한국노사관계학회
　Korea Industrial Relations Association
한국노인과학학술단체엽합회
　Korean Joint Association of Scientific
　Institutions for the Aged
한국노인대학복지협의회
　Korean Universities and Welfare Council for
　the Aged
한국노인대학연구회
　Korean Research Institute of the Universities
　for the Aged
한국노인문제연구소
　Korean Research Institute for the Problems of
　the Aged
한국노인문화센터
　Korean Cultural Center for the Aged
한국노인방송 Korea Noin Broadcast
한국노인병연구소 Korean Institute of Geriatrics
한국노인보호전문기관
　Korean Specialized Agencies for Protection of
　the Aged
한국노인복지개인시설협회
　Korean Association of Personal Welfare
　Facilities for the Aged
한국노인복지상담협회
　Korean Welfare Counseling Association for the
　Aged
한국노인복지선교협의회
　Korean Welfare Missionary Council for the
　Aged
한국노인복지센터 Korea day care center
한국노인복지시설협회
　Korean Welfare Facilities Association for the
　Aged
한국노인복지운동
　Korean Welfare Movement for the Aged

ㅎ

한국노인복지장기요양기관협회
Korean Long-Term Care Institutes Association for the Aged
한국노인복지중앙회
Korea Federation of Senior Welfare
한국노인복지학회
Korean Social of Welfare for the Aged
한국노인복지회 Help Age International
한국노인상조회
Korean Mutual Aid Society for the Elderly
한국노인생활지원재단
Korean Foundation for Supporting Life of the Aged
한국노인성교육연구소
Korean Research Institute of Sexual Education for the Aged
한국노인시설물리치료사협의회
Korean Council of Geriatric Physical Therapy
한국노인여가전문지도자협회
Korean Association of Leisure Time Specialized Coach for the Aged
한국노인연합회
Korean Joint Association of the Aged
한국노인요양센터
Korean Care Serves Center for the Aged
한국노인요양시설경영연구회
Korean Management Institute of Care Serves Facilities for the Aged
한국노인의 전화 Phones for the Aged, Korea
한국노인인권센터
Korean Center for Human Rights for the Aged
한국노인인력개발원
Korea Labor Force Development Institute for the aged
한국노인종합복지관협회
Korea Association of Senior Welfare Centers
한국노인체육협회
Korean Athletic Association for the Aged
한국노인치매건강협회
Korea Elderly Healthcare Association
한국노인학대방지정보망
Korean Information Network for Preventing Mistreatment to the Aged
한국노인학대연구소
Korean Research Center for the Mistreated Aged
한국노인학대피해상담센터
Korean Counseling Center for the Suffered Mistreated Aged
한국노화학회 Korean Aging Society Academy
한국민간자격협회 Korea Qualification Association
한국방송공사 KBS
한국보건경제정책학회
The Korean Association of Health Economics and Policy
한국보건사회연구원
Korea Institute for Health and Social Affairs
한국보건산업진흥원
Korea Health Industry Development Institute
한국보건의료인국가시험원
National Health Personnel Licensing Examination Board
한국보험학회
Korean Insurance Academic Society
한국사회복지사협회
Korea Association of social workers
한국사회복지학회
Korean Academy of Social Welfare
한국사회복지행정학회
Academy of Korean Social Welfare Administration
한국사회복지협의회
Korea National Council on Social Welfare
한국사회사업[복지] 대학협의회
Korean Association of Schools of Social Work
한국사회사업정책 및 실무센터
National Center on Social Work Policy and Practice
한국상담개발원
Korea Counseling Development Institute
한국상담학회
Korean Counseling Association
한국선명회 Korea World Vision
한국소비자보호원 Korea Consumer Agency
한국소비자원 Korea Consumer Agency

한국시니어클럽협회
Korea Association of Community Senior Club

한국여가레크리에이션협회
Korean Leisure Recreation Association

한국요양보호사협회
Korea Long-Term Care Worker Association

한국요양보호협회 Korea Care Association

한국인구학회 The Population Association of Korea

한국장애인연맹
Disabled Peoples' International KOREA : DPI

한국재가노인복지협회
Korea Association in Community Care for the Elderly

한국전쟁퇴역군인 Korean War veteran

한국정년퇴직인협회
Korean Retired Worker's Association

한국정보화진흥원
National Information Society Agency

한국정신보건사회복지학회
Korea Academy of Mental Health Social Work

한국주택협회 Korea Housing Association

한국지방자치학회
the Korean Association for Local Government studies

한국치매가족정보망
Korean Dementia Family Information Network

한국치매가족협회 Alzheimer's Association Korea

한국치매미술치료협회
Korean Dementia Art Therapy Association

한국치매미아방지협회
Korean Society for the Prevention of Lost Dementia Patients

한국치매협회
The Korean Association for Dementia

한국케어사회복지대학협의회
Korean Association of Care Work

한국평생교육노인대학협의회
Korean Lifetime Education University Council for the Aged

한국표준질병 · 사인분류
The Korean Standard Classification of Disease-Cause of Death

한국헬프에이지 HelpAge International

한냉지가산 additional cold district allowance

한랭스트레스 cold stress

한랭요법 cold therapy

한방약 herbal medicine

한방의 a herb doctor

한방의학 Korean medicine

한센병 Hansen's disease ; leprosy

한센병대책
Hansen's disease control policy ; leprosy control policy

한센씨병 Hansen's disease

한손동작 one-handed activity

한정명부제 closed panel

한정책임능력 diminished responsibility

할당 [고용] 제도 quota system

할당계획 allocation plan

할당고용 employment quota

할당고용제도 quota employment system

할당제 quota system

할당제한 quota restriction

할로베스트 halo-vest orthosis

할로보조기 halo orthosis

할로페리돌데카노에이트 haloperidol decanoate

할인요금 discount price

함구증 mutism

함부루크제도 Hamburg System

함입조 ingrown toenail

함축소리 muted voice

합계출산율
total fertility rate : TFR ; total period fertility rate : TPFR

합계특수출생률
total fertility rate : TFR ; total period fertility rate : TPFR

합동 collaboration

합동가족치료 conjoint family therapy

합동모금 United Fund

합동치료 collaborative therapy

합류 joining

합리적 개별사회사업 rational casework

합리적 정서적 치료 rational-emotive therapy

합리화 rationalization

합법성 de jure

합법취업 legal employment
합병증 complication
합성섬유 synthetic fiber
합성세제 synthetic detergent
합의 consensus
합의적 입증 consensual validation
합의형성 consensus building
핫라인 hot line
핫팩 hot pack
항간질제 antiepileptic drug ; carbamazepine
항갑상선약
  antithyroid drug ; antithyroid ; antitussive
  medication
항갑상선제
  antithyroid ; antithyroid drug ; antithyroid
  medication
항건선제 antipsoriatic drug
항고혈압제 candesartan ; Benicar
항구토제 antiemetic
항균 antimicrobial
항균·방취소재
  antibacterial and deodorization material
항균물질
  antibacterial agent ; antimicrobial agent
항균성 비누 antimicrobial soap
항균스펙트럼
  antibacterial spectrum ; antimicrobial spectrum
항균제
  antibacterial drug ; antibacterial agent ; anti
  microbial agent
항균제저항성 antimicrobial resistance
항균제함유비누
  antimicrobial soap ; antibacterial soap
항당뇨병제 antidiabetic
항목기록 item record
항문 anus
항문경 anoscope ; anal speculum
항문경검사 anoscopy
항문관초음파검사 anal endosonography
항문괄약근 anal sphincter muscle
항문괄약근 근전도검사
  electromyography of anal sphincter
항문기 anal phase

항문기 성격 anal personality
항문내압측정 anal manometry
항문벌리개 anal speculum
항문자극장치 anal stimulator
항문점막전류감각역치
  anal mucosal electrosensitivity
항문직장수지검사 digital anorectal examination
항문확장기 anal dilator
항바이러스 antiviral
항바이러스제 antiviral drug
항부종성 antiedemic
항불안제
  antianxiety medication ; anxiolytic medication ;
  anxiolytic
항산화물 antioxidant
항산화비타민 antioxidant vitamin
항산화요법 antioxidant therapy
항산화제 antioxidant agent
항상성 homeostasis
항상성유지기능 homeostasis
항생물질 antibiotic
항생물질내성균감염 antibiotic resistant infection
항생제 antibiotic
항암제 anticancer drug
항염증제
  antiinflammatory drug ; antiinflammatory
  medication
항우울제 antidepressant medication
항원 antigen
항원성 antigenicity
항응고제 anticoagulant
항이뇨 antidiuresis
항정신병 치료제 antipsychotic medication
항정신병약
  antipsychotic ; antipsychotic medication
항정신병제 antipsychotic drug ; antipsychotic
항중력근 antigravity muscle
항진균성 항생물질 antifungal antibiotic
항진균제 antifungal
항체 antibody
항체가 antibody titer
항체결합가 antibody valence
항통풍제 antipodagric

ㅎ

항파킨슨병약 anti-Parkinsonian medication
항파킨슨병제 anti-Parkinsonian drug
항혈소판제 antiplatelet agent
항혈전제
　antithrombotic drug ; antithrombotic
　medication
항혈청 antiserum
항히스타민제 antihistamine
해결지향적 접근법 solution-focused approach
해고 termination of employment
해독 detoxification
해독력 literacy
해독제 antidote
해리동일성 장애 dissociative identity disorder
해리성 감각장애 dissociated sensory disturbance
해리성 장애 dissociative disorder
해리성 지각장애 dissociated sensory disturbance
해머지 mallet finger
해밀턴 Hamilton Gordon
해밀턴우울평가척도
　Hamilton Rating Scale for Depression : HamD
해방 emancipation
해부학적 자세 anatomical position
해빌리테이션 habilitation
해석 interpretation
해시시 hashish
해썹 Hazard Analysis Critical Control Point
　system : HACCP
해열제 antipyretic ; antipyretic drug ; antipyretic
　medication
해외협력과 Overseas Cooperation Division
핵가족 nuclear family
핵스캔 nuclear scanning
핵심성공요소 critical success factor : CSF
핵심실패요인 critical failure factor
핵심장스캔 nuclear heart scan
핵심장학 nuclear cardiology
핵황달 kernicterus
핸드 hand
핸드레일 handrail
핸드림 handrim
핸드워시 hand wash
핸디캡 handicap

행동 behavior
행동과다증 hyperactivity
행동과학 behavior science ; behavioral science
행동관찰 behavioral observation
행동대가 response cost
행동리허설 behavior rehearsal
행동사정 behavioral assessment
행동수정 behavior modification
행동수정법 behavior modification
행동수정접근법 behavior modification approach
행동양식 behavior pattern
행동언어 behavioral language
행동연구 action research
행동요법 behavior therapy
행동의 일반화 generalization behavioral
행동이론 action theory
행동장애 conduct disorder
행동조사 action research
행동주의 behaviorism ; activism
행동주의자 역할 activist role
행동체계 action system
행동치료 action therapy ; behavior therapy
행동패턴 behavior pattern
행동평가 behavior assessment
행동화 acting out
행복추구권 the right to the pursuit of happiness
행복한 늙음 successful aging
행불자 missing person
행위 act ; action ; practice
행위별수가제 fee-for-service : FFS
행위장애 conduct disorder
행정 administration
행정감사 administrative inspection
행정개혁 administrative reform
행정계획 administrative plan
행정사무 Administrative Affairs
행정입법 statutory instrument
행정지도 administrative guidance
향기치료 aromatherapy
향상 improvement
향성검사 introversion extroversion test
향정신약 psychotropic drug
향정신제 psychotropic

허리둘레 waist circumference
허바드탱크 hubbard tank
허브 hub
허세 grandiosity
허셉틴 Herceptin
허약 frailty ; physically weak ; weakness
허약고령자 frail elderly ; the frail elderly ;
  the physically frail elderly
허약노인 frail elderly ; the frail elderly ;
  the physically frail elderly
허약아 frail child
허용일일섭취량 acceptable daily intake
허트빌딩법 Heart Building Law
허혈성 발작 ischemic stroke
허혈성 심질환 ischemic heart disease : IHD
허혈성 장염 ischemic colitis
헌법 constitution
헌팅턴무도병 Huntington's chorea
헌팅턴병 Huntington's disease
헌혈 blood donation
헐하우스 Hull House
헤게모니 hegemony
헤로인 heroin
헤로인 의존 heroin dependence
헤르셉틴 Herceptin
헤르쯔 hertz
헤마토크릿 hematocrit
헤모글로빈 hemoglobin : Hb
헤버덴결절 Heberden's nodes
헤베르덴결절 Heberden's nodes
헤이글런드 기형 Haglund's deformity
헤파린 heparin
헨드릭 낙상위험사정도구
  Hendrich's Fall Risk Assessment Tool
헨리 구빈법 Henrician Poor Law
헬러 증후군 Heller's syndrome
헬리코박터 파일로리 Helicobacter pylori
헬스케어 health care
헬스프로모션 health promotion
헬싱키선언 Declaration of Helsinki
헵세라 Hepsera
현금급부 cash grant
현금급여 cash benefit

현기증 dizziness ; vertigo
현대자본주의 contemporary capitalism
현대화 modernization
현물급부 price grant
현물급여 benefit in kind
현미경시야 field of microscope
현상학 phenomenology
현성행동 over behaviors
현수장치 suspension system
현수프레임 suspension frame
현실검증 reality testing
현실견당식 reality orientation
현실견당식훈련 reality orientation training : ROT
현실도피경향 tendency to escape from reality
현실원칙 reality principle
현실지남력 reality orientation
현실지남력훈련 reality orientation training : ROT
현실치료 reality therapy
현임훈련 in-service training
현장실습 field placement
현장연구 field study
현재내용 manifest content
현재성 불안척도 Manifest Anxiety Scale
현재적 욕구 the manifested needs
현저한 변화 significant change
현지조사 field research
현직훈련 in-service training
혈관내 유치카테터 intravascular catheter
혈관내 유치카테터관련감염증
  intravascular catheter- elated infection
혈관내 초음파법 intravascular ultrasound
혈관성 치매 vascular dementia
혈관우회로술 bypass surgery
혈관원성 쇼크 vasogenic shock
혈관원성 절단
  amputation for peripheral vascular disease
혈관조영 angiogram ; vascular imaging
혈관형성술 angioplasty
혈관확장제 vasodilator
혈뇨 hematuria
혈당 blood sugar
혈당량 glucose level
혈당치 blood sugar level ; glucose level

ㅎ

혈류감염 bloodstream infection

혈변 hematochezia

혈압 blood pressure

혈압계 blood pressure manometer

혈액검사 blood test

혈액대책과 Blood and Blood Products Division

혈액매개감염 bloodborne infection

혈액매개바이러스감염증
  bloodborne virus infection

혈액요소질소 blood urea nitrogen : BUN

혈액유래병원체 bloodborne pathogen

혈액은행 blood bank

혈액투석 hemodialysis

혈액학 hematology

혈연가족 consanguinity family

혈우병 hemophilia

혈우병성 관절증 hemophilic arthropathy

혈장 blood plasma

혈장글루코스 plasma glucose

혈전 thrombosis

혈전용해요법 thrombolytic therapy

혈전용해제 thrombolytic

혈전증 thrombosis

혈종 hematoma

혈중바이러스 감염증 bloodborne virus infection

혈청 blood serum

혈청학적 매독검사 serologic test for syphilis

혈침치 erythrocyte sedimentation rate : ESR

혈행재건술 revascularization

혐기성 균 anaerobe

혐오요법 aversion therapy

혐오자극 aversive stimulus

혐오치료 aversion therapy

협동조합 cooperative association

협동치료 collaborative therapy

협상 negotiation

협심증 angina pectoris

협심증 발작 angina attack

협의회 council

협조 coordination

협조운동장애 coordination disorder

협회 association

형광내시경검사 fluorescein endoscopy

형무소 prison

형벌학 penology

형법 criminal law

형법전 criminal code ; penal code

형사 사법정책 criminal justice policy

형사 사법제도 criminal justice system

형선고문제연구 Sentencing Project

형성집단 formed group

형식적 조작기 formal operations stage

형제〈자매〉간 갈등 sibling conflict

형제〈자매〉간 경쟁 sibling rivalry

형태발생 morphogenesis

형태소 morpheme

형태안정 morphostasis

형평 equity

호너증후군 Horner syndrome

호르몬 hormone

호르몬보충요법 hormone replacement therapy

호르몬수용체검사 hormone receptor test

호손효과 Hawthorne effect

호스피스 hospice

호스피스 보호 hospice care

호스피털리즘 hospitalism

호손 실험 Hawthorne experiment

호적상태 goodness of fit

호텔비용 hotel costs

호흡 respiration ; breathing

호흡곤란 dyspnea

호흡기 respiratory organ

호흡기감염 respiratory infection

호흡기능장애 respiratory functional disorder

호흡기질환 respiratory disease

호흡마비 respiratory paralysis

호흡부전 respiratory failure

호흡연습 respiratory exercise

호흡요법 respiratory therapy

호흡장애 respiratory disorder

호흡재활 pulmonary rehabilitation

호흡정지 apnea

호흡훈련 breathing exercise ; respiratory training

혼과 야의 스케일 Hoehn-Yahr stage

혼미 disorientation

혼수 coma

혼수상태 comatose
혼-야 단계 Hoehn-Yahr stage
혼인 marriage
혼인증명서 marriage certificate
혼전합의 prenuptial agreement
혼합가족 blended family
혼합경제 mixed economy
혼합사례 상환 case-mix reimbursement
혼합성 난청 mixed hearing loss
혼합형 치매 mixed dementia
홀론 holon
홀리스-테일러 보고서 Hollis-Taylor Report
홀리스틱의학 holistic medicine
홀씨 spore
홀터심전도 holter electrocardiogram
홈 엘리베이터 home elevator
홈리스 homeless
홈스테드 법 Homestead Act
홈케어서비스 home care service
홈케어촉진사업 home care promotion plan
홈프로그램 home program
홈헬스서비스 home health services
홈헬퍼 home helper
홈헬프 home help
홈헬프 코디네이터 home help coordinator
홈헬프서비스 home help services
홉킨즈 Harry Hopkins
홍등가 red-light district
홍보 public relations
홍보교육 public relations education
홍수[법) flooding
홍역 measles ; rubeola ; morbilli
화를 잘 냄 irritability
화상 burn
화상진단 diagnostic imaging
화상진단적 개입치료 interventional radiology : IVR
화염멸균 flame sterilization
화이트칼라 white collar
화이트칼라 범죄 white-collar crime
화장 cremation
화장실 restroom
화장실 스크린 toilet screen
화재위험도 fire risk

화폐적 욕구 monetary needs
화학물질관련장애 substance-related disorder
화학물질대책과 Chemical Hazards Control Division
화학색전 chemoembolization
화학섬유 chemical fiber
화학요법 chemotherapy
화학적 지시약 chemical indicator
화학치료 chemotherapy
화해 conciliation
화해자 역할 placater role
확대가족 extended family
확대내시경검사 magnifying endoscopy
확대독서기 enlarging reading device
확률표본 추출 probability sampling
확산이론 diffusion theory
확인된 환자 (또는 클라이언트)
　identified patient (or client)
확장기혈압 diastolic pressure
확정거출연금 defined contribution
환각 hallucination
환각제 hallucinogen
환경 environment
환경 속의 인간관점
　person-in-environment perspective
환경감시 environmental surveillance
환경개선 environmental reform
환경결정론 environmental determinism
환경권 environmental rights
환경문제 environmental problem
환경미생물조사 microbial sampling
환경보전 environmental protection
환경보호기관 environmental protection agency
환경수정 environmental modification
환경오염 environmental pollution
환경요법 environmental treatment
환경운동 ecology movement
환경위험물질 environmental hazards
환경유래질환 disorder of environmental origin
환경음악 back ground music : BGM
환경인자 environmental factor
환경정비 environmental maintenance
환경제어장치 environmental control system : ECS
환경조사 environmental sampling

ㅎ

환경조정 environmental coordination

환경치료 environmental treatment ; milieu therapy

환경평가 environmental assessment

환과고독 lonely people

환기 ventilation ; air insufflation

환기법 ventilation

환류 feedback

환상배회 fantasy wandering

환상사지감각 phantom limb sensation

환시 visual hallucination

환어곤란
word finding difficulty ; word finding disorder

환어장애
word finding difficulty ; word finding disorder

환자 patients

환자 제공자간 관계 patient-provider relationship

환자기록 patient records

환자만족도조사 patient satisfaction survey

환자옹호 patient advocacy

환자의 권리 patients' rights ; rights of patients

환자의 안전 patient safety

환자조사 patient survey

환자조절진통법
personal-controlled analgesia : PCA

환자중심요법
patient-centered therapy ; client-centered therapy

환자중심의료 patient-centered medicine

환지 phantom limb sensation

환지통 phantom limb pain

환청 auditory hallucination

환측 affected part of the body

활동 activity

활동이론 activity theory

활동일주기 circadian rhythm

활동적 평균여명 active life expectancy

활동전위 action potential : AP

활동제한 activity limitation

활동집단 activity group

활막절제술 synovectomy

활성산소 active oxygen

활성수송 active transport

활성지속 persistent activity

활성탄 active charcoal

활성탄소 active carbon

활약근장애 sphincter disturbance

활약근형성술 sphincteroplasty

활용부족 underutilization

활차 pulley

황달 jaundice

황반변성 macular degeneration

황산 키니네 quinine sulfate

황산염 quinine sulfate

황색육아종성 신우신염
Xanthogranulomatous pyelonephritis

황색의료보호수첩 yellow medical care card

황색포도상구균 staphylococcus aureus

황색포도상구균성 폐렴 staphylococcal pneumonia

황혼이혼 December divorce

황혼재혼 remarriage in matured age

회계감사 audit of financial accounts

회계년도 fiscal year

회고적 감사 retrospective review

회고적 연구법 retrospective study

회귀분석 regression analysis

회내 pronation

회백수염 poliomyelitis

회복 remission

회복기 보균자 convalescent carrier

회복기 시설 convalescent home

회복기 재활
recovery phase rehabilitation ; convalescent rehabilitation

회복반응 righting reaction

회상 life review ; reminiscence

회상법 reminiscence therapy

회상치료 reminiscence therapy

회선 수정체유화흡인방법
torsional phacoemulsification

회수대행업자 collection agency : debt collector

회음 perineum

회의록 minutes

회저 gangrene

회전전정동안반사
rotational vestibulo-ocular reflex

회절격자 grating

ㅎ

회진 physician rounds
회피 avoidance
회피성 성격장애 avoidant personality disorder
회피조건형성 avoidance conditioning
회피학습 avoidance learning
회화음성양해도검사
  Picture Speech Intelligibility Evaluation : PSINE
횡격막 diaphragm
횡단면조사 cross-sectional survey
횡단아치 transverse arch
횡단적 조사 cross-sectional research
횡령 embezzlement ; graft
횡족궁 transverse arch
횡축족궁 transverse arch
효과 efficacy
효과의 법칙 law of effect
효과적 치료환경 sociopetal arrangements
효도 filial piety to parents
효용이론 utility theory
효용재고 utilization review
효행 piety
후각 sense of smell
후각소실증 anosmia
후각저하 loss of smell
후견인 guardian
후견인선임 appointment of guardian
후견인의 지정 designation of guardian
후광효과 halo effect
후기고령자 elderly aged 75 and above
후기고령자의료제도
  Health Insurance System for the Elderly Aged
  75 and Above
후두신경통
  occipital neuralgia ; C2 neuralgia ; Arnold's
  neuralgia
후만 kyphosis ; roundback
후발의약품 generic drug
후복막혈종 retroperitoneal hematoma
후비루증후군 post-nasal drip syndrome : PNDS
후사반부절단 hindquarter amputation
후생경제학 welfare economics
후생과학과 Health Science Division
후생노동백서 Annual Health

후생노동부 Ministry of Health
후생보험
  employee insurance ; employees' insurance
후생연금 employee pension
후생연금기금 employees pension fund : EPF
후생연금보험 employees' pension insurance
후생연금보험법
  Employees' Pension Insurance Law
후성설 epigenesis
후유증 sequela
후임자 우선해고원칙 last hired-first fired
후족부 내반변형 rearfoot varus deformity
후종인대골화증
  ossification of the posterior longitudinal
  ligament : OPLL
후천성면역부전증후군
  acquired immune deficiency syndrome : AIDS
후쿠야마형 선천성 근이영양증
  Fukuyama type congenital muscular dystrophy
후향성 연구 retrospective study
훈련 exercise ; training ; habilitation
훈련급여 training benefit
훈련용 가의족 temporary lower limb prosthesis
훈련용 가의지 temporary prosthesis
훈련용 고정자전거 stationary bicycle
휘도 luminance
휠체어 wheelchair
휠체어동작 wheelchair activity
휠체어보조 wheelchair assistance
휠체어스포츠 wheelchair sports
휠체어에서 침대로 transfer from wheelchair to bed
휠체어에서 평행봉
  transfer from wheelchair to parallel bar ;
  wheelchair to parallel bar
휠체어이동 moving around by wheelchair
휠체어이승 wheelchair transfer
휠체어이승원조 wheelchair transfer assistance
휴가 leave of absence : LOA
휴대용 화장실 commode ; bedside commode
휴머니즘 humanism
휴먼라이츠워치 Human Rights Watch : HRW
휴먼서비스 human services
휴미라 Humira

ㅎ

휴식서비스 respite service
휴양설비 rest equipment
휴업보상 compensation for leave
휴직 leave
휴직급여 leave benefit
흉강천자 thoracocentesis
흉곽물리요법 chest physical therapy
흉곽밴드 chest strap
흉부 X선 chest X-ray : CXR
흉부압박 chest compression
흉수손상 thoracic spinal cord injury
흉식호흡 chest respiration
흉통 chest pain
흑백도항등성 lightness constancy
흑색변 melena
흑인 민권운동 black power
흑인 소수민족 blacks
흔들의자 rocking chair
흡수 absorption
흡수계수 absorption factor
흡수성 무기폐 absorption atelectasis
흡수성 섬유 water-absorbing fiber
흡수속도 absorption rate
흡수속도정수 absorption rate constant
흡수율 absorption ratio

흡수장치 absorption train
흡습성 섬유 hygroscopic fiber
흡식 inhalation
흡연 smoking
흡인 suction ; suctioning
흡인생검 suction biopsy
흡입 aspiration ; inhalation
흡착 absorption
흡착식 소켓 suction socket
희망 hope
희생양 scapegoat
흰 지팡이 white cane
히스타민 H1 수용체차단제
    histamine H1 receptor blocker
히스타민 H2 수용체차단제
    histamine H2 receptor blocker
히스타민 수용체차단제 histamine receptor blocker
히스테리 hysteria
히스테리적인 hysteric
히포크라테스의 맹세 Hippocratic Oath
히프노테라피 hypnotherapy
힘 power
힘줄고정작용 tenodesis effect
힘측정판 force plate

영 어

ABCDE모델 ABCDE model

ADL activities of daily living

ADL테스트 ADL test

ADP adenosine diphosphate

ALS amyotrophic lateral sclerosis

APDL activities parallel to daily living

ATP adenosine triphosphate

α 글루코시다아제 억제제
alpha-glucosidase inhibitor

α 차단제 alpha-blocker

A형 간염 hepatitis A

A형 간염바이러스 hepatitis A virus

BADL basic activities of daily living

BBS운동 Big Brothers and Sisters Movement

BECK 우울증 진단
Beck Depression Inventory : BDI

BMI body mass index

β 수용체 차단제 beta receptor blockage

β 아밀로이드 펩티드 beta-amyloid peptide

β 차단제 beta-blocker

β 카로틴 beta-carotene

B형 간염 hepatitis B : HBV

B형 간염바이러스 hepatitis B virus

CT검사 computed tomography : CT

CYP-3A CYP-3A

C바 C bar

C반응성 단백 C-reactive protein

C형 간염 hepatitis C

C형 간염바이러스 hepatitis C virus

D2 도파민수용체길항제
dopamine receptor D2 blockade

DOA dead on arrival

DV domestic violence

D치

D-value ; decimal reduction value ; decimal
reduction time

D형 간염 hepatitis D

D형 간염바이러스 hepatitis D virus

ECG electrocardiogram

EMG electromyography

EMG 바이오피드백 EMG biofeedback

E형 간염 hepatitis E

E형 간염바이러스 hepatitis E virus

F파 F wave

HDL high-density lipoprotein

HDL 콜레스테롤
high-density lipoprotein cholesterol ; HDL
cholesterol ; good cholesterol

H반사 H reflex

H파 H wave

IADL instrumental activities of daily living

ICD International Classification of Diseases

ICF International Classification of Functioning,
Disability and health

ICIDH International Classification of Impairments
Disabilities and Handicaps

ICU intensive care unit

ICU감염 ICU-acquired infection

IL운동 independent living movement

IPPB요법
intermittent positive-pressure breathing therapy

IQ intelligence quotient

IQ검사 IQ test

ISO국제규격분류 ISO International Classification
for Standards : ICS

ISO국제표준화기구 International Organization for
Standardization : ISO

JCS [일본식혼수척도] Japan Coma Scale

영어

KBM식 하퇴의족
  Kondylen Bettung Munster transtibial

LA 상호억제 reciprocal Ia inhibition

LD learning disability

LD 스크리닝검사 learning disability screening

LDL low-density lipoprotein

LDL 콜레스테롤 low-density lipoprotein : LDL

LOL length of life

MID multi-infarct dementia

MMSE Mini Mental State Examination

MMT Manual Muscle Testing

MP굴곡보조기 knuckle bender

MRA magnetic resonance angiography

MRI magnetic resonance imaging

MRSA methicillin-resistant staphylococcus aureus

M파 M wave

NGO non-governmental organization

NM스케일 Nishimura Dementia Scale : NMS

NPO non-profit organization

NPO지원세제 NPO tax support system

N식 정신기능검사
  Nishimura Dementia Scale : NMS

OA화 office automation

ODA official development assistance

OECD Organization for Economic Co-operation and Development

OSHA
  Occupational Safety and Health Administration

OT occupational therapist

PET positron emission tomography

PET법 positron emission tomography

PHN post-herpetic neuralgia

PT physical therapist

PTB식 단하지보조기 patellar tendon bearing ankle-foot orthosis

PTB식 체중부하식 하지보조기 patellar tendon bearing ankle-foot orthosis

PTB식 하퇴의족 patellar tendon bearing transtibial prosthesis

PTSD post-traumatic stress disorder

QOL quality of life

RCS 공중부유물질채집기 Reuter centrifugal sampler

SARS severe acute respiratory syndrome

SEK마크 SEK mark

SNRI serotonin-norepinephrine reuptake inhibitor

ST speech-language-hearing therapist

S장결장 sigmoid colon

S장결장경검사 sigmoidoscopy

TIA transient ischemic attack

TSB 소켓
  total surface bearing below-knee prosthesis

TSB 하퇴의족
  total surface bearing below-knee prosthesis

t검정 t-test

T스트랩 T-strap

T자 지팡이 T-cane

ULPA 필터 ultra low penetration air filter

VP션트 ventriculoperitoneal shunting

WAB 실어증검사 western aphasia battery : WAB

WAC법 Well Aging Community Law : WAC Law

WHO World Health Organization

WHO 3단계 진통제사다리
  WHO's three-step pain ladder

xy색도도 xy chromaticity diagram

X레이 roentgen

X선 X-ray

X선촬영 radiography

X선투시검사 fluoroscopy

X연쇄우성유전 X-linked dominant inheritance

X염색체 연관우성유전
  X-linked dominant inheritance

YMCA Young Men's Christian Association

YWCA Young Women's Christian Association

Zung 자가평가우울척도
  Zung Self-Rating Depression Scale : SDS

Z치 z value

숫 자

10대 denarian

100대 centenarian

110세 이상 supercentenarian

1분간 타임스터디 one-minute time study

1시간 마다 every hour : QH

1차 진료 primary medical care

1차 집단 primary group

1차적 욕구 primary needs

1회사용기재 single-use device

20대 vicenarian

21세기 복지비전
Welfare Vision for the 21st Century

21세기에 있어서의 국민건강만들기 운동
National Health Promotion Movement in the21st Century ; Healthy Japan 21

21트리소미 trisomy 21

24시간 연락체제
twenty-four-hour on call

24시간 주시 twenty-four-hour protective oversight

24시간 케어 twenty-four-hour care

2색형 반사모델 dichromatic reflection model

2시간 마다 every 2 hours : Q2H

2인실 semi-private room

2족 보행 two-point gait

2차 감염 secondary infection

2차 과정 secondary process

2차 구명심폐소생법·처치
advanced cardiac life support

2차 구명처치 advanced life support : ALS

2차 심폐소생법
advanced cardiovascular life support : ACLS

2차 예방 secondary prevention

2차 의료권 secondary medical service area

2차 장애 secondary disorder

2차 진료 secondary medical care

2차 집단 secondary group

2차 판정 secondary assessment

2차적 이득 secondary gain

30대 tricenarian

36항목 건강설문지
Medical Outcomes Study 36-Item Short-Form Health Survey : MOS SF-36

3대사인 three biggest causes of death

3동작 보행 three-point gait

3세대가족 three-generation family

3시간 마다 every 3 hours : Q3H

3인 이승법 three-person transfer

3점 보행 three-point gait

3차 진료 tertiary health care

401K 플랜 401K plan

40대 quadragenarian

4P Person, Problem, Place, Process

4시간 마다 every 4 hours : Q4H

4점 보행 four-point gait

4체계 모델 four system

50대 quinquagenarian

5대 사회악 Five Giants

5대 영양소 five major nutrients

60대 sexagenarian

6시간 마다 every 6 hours : Q6H

70대 septuagenarian

80대 octogenarian

8시간 마다 every 8 hours : Q8H

90대 nonagenarian

숫자

PART 2

영한
용어

A

A. H. Maslow 마슬로우
abandoning elderly 기로
Abbreviated Injury Scale : AIS 약식상해등급
ABCDE model ABCDE모델
abdominal breathing 복식호흡
abdominal pain 복통
abdominal respiration 복식호흡
abdominal ultrasound 복부초음파검사
abdominal x-ray 복부방사선사진
abdominalgia 복통
abdominocentesis 복부천자
abduction 외전
abduction block 외전방지. 블록
abduction gait 외전보행
Abel position 아벨체위
ability 능력
ability principle 능력주의 ; 응능주의
ability to live 생활능력
ability-to-pay principle 응능부담 ; 응능원칙
abiotic synthesis 비생물합성
able body poor 신체장애가 없는 빈곤자
abnormal 비정상
abnormal adjustment mechanism
  이상적응기제
abnormal behavior 이상행동
abnormal eating habit 이식행위
abnormal gait 이상보행
Abnormal Involuntary Movement Scale :
  AIMS 이상불수의 운동평가척도
abnormal posture 이상자세
abnormal psychology 이상심리학
abortion 낙태
above-elbow amputation 상완절단

above-knee amputation 대퇴절단
above-knee prosthesis 대퇴의족
abrasion 찰과상 ; 마모
abrasion resistance 찰과상저항
absenteeism 무단결근
absolute alcohol 무수알코올
absolute humidity 절대습도
absolute muscle strength 절대근력
absolute poverty 절대적 빈곤
absolute refractory period 절대불응기
absolute threshold 절대역
absolute threshold of hearing 최소가청치
absorbent cotton gauze and other
  sanitary supplies 탈지면, 거즈, 그 밖의 위생
  재료
absorption 흡수 ; 흡착
absorption atelectasis 흡수성 무기폐
absorption factor 흡수계수
absorption rate 흡수속도
absorption rate constant 흡수속도정수
absorption ratio 흡수율
absorption train 흡수장치
abstinence 절제
abstinence from alcohol 금주
abstinence from smoking 금연
abuse 학대
abused child 피학대 아동 ; 학대아
abused elderly 피학대 고령자 ; 피학대 노인
academia 산혈증 ; 아카데미아
Academy of Certified Social Workers :
  ACSW 공인사회사업가학회
Academy of Korean Social Welfare
  Administration 한국사회복지행정학회

A

acamprosate 아캄프로세이트
acceptable daily intake 허용일일섭취량
acceptance 수용 ; 승낙
acceptance of disability 장애의 수용
access 편리
access to care 장기요양으로의 접근
accessibility 편리성
accessibility of service 서비스접근성
accessory respiratory muscle 보조호흡근
accident 재해
accident compensation 재해보상
accident evaluation 사고평가
accident insurance 재해보험
accidental extubation 우발발관 ; 사고발관
accidental ingestion 오음
accidents in the home 가정내 사고
accommodation 조절
accountability 책임성 ; 설명책임 ;
  어카운터빌리티
accreditation 인가 ; 인정 ; 공인
accreditation standards 인가기준
accreditation survey 인정조사
acculturation 문화변용
accumulation 적립금
accumulative method 적립방식
Accupril 아큐프릴
acetabular fracture 비구골절
Acetaminophen 아세트아미노펜
acetate 초산염
acetic acid 초산
Achilles tendon 아킬레스건
Achilles tendon lengthening
  아킬레스건 연장술
acid 산
acid anhydride 산무수물
acid-base balance 산염기평형
acid-base regulation 산염기조절
acidemia 아시데미아
acidity 산성도 ; 산도
acidosis 산혈증 ; 아시드시스
acid-suppressive medication 제산제
acquaintance 지인
acquired blindness 중도실명

acquired disability 중도장애
acquired hearing impairment 중도청각장애
acquired immune deficiency syndrome :
  AIDS 후천성면역부전증후군 ; 에이즈
acquired sensory impairment 중도지각장애
acquired visual impairment 중도시각장애
acquisitive prescription 취득시효
acraturesis 배뇨무력증 ; 배뇨불능증
acromegaly 말단비대증 ; 첨단거대증
acronym and definition 약어와 정의
Act 법 ; 행위
Act for Enforcement of the Long-Term
  Care Insurance Act 개호보험법시행법
Act for the Promotion of Employment of
  Older Persons 고령자고용촉진법
Act on Welfare of Physically Disabled
  Persons 신체장애인복지법
actin 액틴
acting out 행동화
actinic injury 광선손상
actinotherapy 광선요법
action 액션 ; 작용 ; 행위
action potential : AP 활동전위
action research
  행동연구 ; 행동조사 ; 실천연구 ; 액션리서치
action system 액션시스템 ; 행동체계
action theory 행동이론
action therapy 행동치료
active assisted exercise 자동보조운동
active carbon 활성탄소
active charcoal 활성탄
active exercise 자동훈련
active immunity 능동면역
active life expectancy 활동적 평균여명
active listening 경청
active movement 자동운동
active oxygen 활성산소
active permeation 능동투과
active range of motion : AROM 자동가동역
active self-neglect 의도적 자기방임
active transport 능동수송 ; 활성수송
activism 행동주의
activist role 행동주의자 역할

activities of daily living : ADL
일상생활동작 ; 일상생활활동

activities parallel to daily living : APDL
생활관련활동

activity 액티버티 ; 활동

activity group 활동집단

activity limitation 활동제한

activity services 액티버티 서비스

activity theory 활동이론

Actonel 악토넬

actual cost of living 실질생계비

actual expenditure 실지출

actual income 실수입

actual wage 실질임금

Actuarial Affairs Division 수리과

acupressure 지압

acupressurist 지압사

acupuncture and moxibustion 침구

acupuncture and moxibustion therapist
침구사

acupuncturist 침술사

acute 급성

acute anterior poliomyelitis
급성회백수염 ; 급성전각회백수염

acute bronchiolitis 급성세기관지염

acute care 급성환자치료

acute coronary syndrome 급성관증후군

acute epidural hematoma 급성경막외혈종

acute gastritis 급성위염

acute gastrointestinal bleed 급성소화관출혈

acute interstitial pneumonia 급성간질성 폐렴

acute laryngotracheitis 급성후두기관염

acute leukemia 급성백혈병

acute lung injury 급성폐상해 ; 급성폐손상

acute lymphoblastic leukemia
급성림프구성 백혈병

acute lymphocytic leukemia
급성림프구성 백혈병

acute lymphoid leukemia : ALL
급성림프구성 백혈병

acute myelocytic leukemia : AML
급성골수성 백혈병

acute myelogenous leukemia : AML
급성골수성 백혈병

acute myeloid leukemia 급성골수성 백혈병

acute myocardial infarction 급성심근경색

acute phase 급성기

acute phase of rehabilitation
급성기 재활치료

acute pneumonia 급성폐렴

acute posthemorrhagic anemia
급성출혈후 빈혈

acute pulmonary edema 급성폐수종

acute pyelonephritis 급성신우신염

acute reference dose 급성참조용량

acute respiratory distress syndrome :
ARDS 급성호흡곤란증후군

acute respiratory failure 급성호흡부전

acute respiratory insufficiency 급성호흡부전

acute urinary retention 급성요폐증

acyclovir 아시클로버

ad hoc coalition 특수연합

adalimumab 아달리무맵

Adam Smith 스미스

adaptation 적응

adaptedness 적응성

addiction 중독 ; 의존증

addictive drug 습관성 약물

Addison's disease 에디슨병

addition 가산 ; 부가

addition mutation 부가변이

addition polymer 부가중합체

addition polymerization 부가중합

additional assistance for long-term care
insurance 개호보험료가산

additional benefit 추가급여

additional cold district allowance
한냉지가산

additional payment to community 지역가산

additional payment to special region
특별지역가산

additional pension 부가연금

additional service 추가서비스

addition-deletion mutation
부가결실형 돌연변이

adduction 내전

A

adefovir dipivoxil 아데포비어 디피복실
adenoma 선종
adenosine diphosphate ADP
adenosine triphosphate ATP
adephagia 폭식
adequacy 적용
adhesive capsulitis 견관절주위염
adhocracy 특별임시위원회
adiaphoria 불응성 ; 무관심
adipose tissue 지방조직
adipositas 비만증
adjudication 판결
adjustment 조정
adjustment and maladjustment 적응과 부적응
adjustment diagnosis test 적응성진단테스트
adjustment mechanism 적응기제
adjustment subsidy 조정교부금
adjustment with other laws
　기타법과의 급여조정
ADL test ADL테스트
administering authority 조치권자
administration
　행정 ; 어드미니스트레이션 ; 운영 ; 투여
Administrative Affairs 행정사무
administrative cost 관리운영비 ; 사무비
administrative guidance 행정지도
administrative inspection 행정감사
administrative plan 행정계획
administrative reform 행정개혁
administrator 시설장
admission 입소
admission charge 입원료
admission decision 입소결정 ; 입원결정
admission for medical care and custody
　의료보호입원
admissions 시설수용 ; 접수처
admissions procedures 접수절차
adolescence 청소년기
adolescence youth 청소년
adolescent emaciation 사춘기 수척증
adolescent mental health 사춘기 정신보건
adolescent nausea 사춘기 거식증
adolescent psychology 청년기 심리학

adopted child 양자
adoption 양자결연 ; 입양
adrenocorticosteroid 부신피질스테로이드
adrenocorticosteroid enema
　부신피질호르몬 관장
adult care housing 케어제공주택
adult children 어덜트칠드런 ; 성인아이
adult day care
　주간보호소 ; 노인주간보호 ; 성인주간보호
adult day care center
　성인주간보호센터 ; 노인주간보호센터 ; 탁노소
adult day center 성인데이센터 ; 노인데이센터
adult day health care
　노인데이헬스케어 ; 성인데이헬스케어
adult day services center
　성인주간보호서비스센터 ; 노인주간보호서비스센터
Adult Day-care Liaison Council Japan
　전국노인데이케어연락협의회
adult development 성인발달
adult disease 성인병
adult education 성인교육
adult foster care home 성인양호시설
adult guardian 성년후견인
adult guardianship 성년후견
adult guardianship system 성년후견제도
Adult Manifest Anxiety Scale
　성인용 현재성 불안척도
adult protective services 성인보호서비스
adult respiratory distress syndrome
　성인호흡곤란증후군
adult T-cell leukemia : ATLL
　성인T세포백혈병·임파종
adulthood 성인기
adult-onset 성인발병성
adult-onset rheumatoid arthritis : AORA
　성인발병성 관절류머티즘
advanced cardiac life support
　2차 구명심폐소생법·처치
advanced cardiovascular life support :
　ACLS 2차 심폐소생법
advanced life support : ALS
　2차 구명처치 ; 생명서포트서비스
advanced maternal age 고령출산

advanced practice nurse 고도전문간호사
adversarial process 역과정
adverse drug reaction : ADR 약물유해반응
adverse selection 역선택
advice giving 자문제공
Advil 애드빌
advisor for children's issues 아동상담원
advisor for fatherless families 모자상담원
advisor for the health and welfare of
people with mental disabilities
정신보건복지상담원
advisor for the physically disabled
신체장애인상담원
advisory center 상담센터
advisory committee 심의회
advisory council 자문기관
Advisory Council for the Welfare of
Physically Disabled Persons 신체장애인복
지심의회
Advisory Council on Child Welfare
아동복지심의회
Advisory Council on Social Security
사회보장심의회
advocacy 애드보커시 ; 옹호
advocacy activity 옹호활동
advocate 애드버킷 ; 대변자
aeration 에어레이션 ; 통기
affected part of the body 아픈 쪽 ; 환측
affective congruency 정서일치
affective disorders 정서장애
affiliation between outpatient clinics
의원간 진료연계
affiliation between outpatient clinics and
hospitals 병의원간 진료연계
affiliation of medical care and social
welfare 의료복지연계
affirmative action 차별수정계획
affluent society 풍요사회
after-care 사후보호
against medical advice : AMA
의학지시거부 ; 자주퇴원
age of maximum criminality
최고범죄연령

aged care home 고령자케어제공주택 ;
노인수발제공주택 ; 노인케어제공주택 ; 케어제공
고령자주택
aged care home 케어제공주택
aged deaf 농고령자 ; 농노인
aged retiree household 노인무직세대
aged society 고령사회
Aged Society Basic Act 고령사회대책기본법
Aged's Day 노인의 날
ageism 에이지즘 ; 연령차별
agency 사업소
agency delegated function 기관위임사무
Agency for International Development :
AID 국제개발기구
Agency of the Work of the Elderly
고령자취업알선센터
agency program of the work of the
elderly 고령자취업알선사업
agent 대행자
Agent Orange 고엽제
age-related disease 가령성 질환 ; 고령성 질환
age-related macular degeneration
가령황반변성
aggregate old age pension 통산노령연금
aggression 공격
aggressive behavior 공격적 행동
aggressive casework 어그레시브 케이스워크
aggressive child 공격적 아동
aggressive mechanism 공격기제
aging 가령 ; 노화
aging index 노년화지수
aging population 고령화
aging society 고령화사회
agnosia 실인
agonist 주동근
agoraphobia 광장공포증
agraphia 필기불능증 ; 실서증
agreement 동의서
aid for extended reach 원격조작용구
aid for grasping 파지용구
Aid to Families with Dependent Children :
AFDC 요보호아동가족부조
Aid to the Permanently and Totally

Disabled : APTD 완전·영속적 중증장애인부조
air bronchogram 공기기관지조영
air conditioning 공기조화
air curtain 에어커튼
air embolism 공기색전증
air filter 공기여과장치 ; 에어필터
air insufflation 환기
air leak 에어리크
air mattress 에어매트
air pollution 공기오염 ; 대기오염
air sampler 공기시료채집기
air sampling 공기시료채집
air shower 에어샤워
air sleeping pad 에어패드
air trapping 에어트래핑
airborne bacteria 공중부유균 ; 공중세균
airborne infection 공기감염
airborne infection isolation : AII
공기감염격리
airborne microbe sampler
공중세균측정기 ; 공중부유균 측정기
airborne particle 부유입자 ; 공중먼지
airborne precaution 공기예방책
airborne transmission 공기감염
airborne transmission 공기전파
airplane splint 어깨뼈 외전보조기
airway 기도 ; 에어웨이
airway burn 기도화상
airway cleaning 기도세정 ; 기도클리닝
airway closure 기도마개 ; 기도폐쇄
airway collapse 기도허탈
airway conductance 기도전도도
airway maintenance 기도확보
airway management 기도관리
airway obstruction 기도폐쇄
airway occlusion 기도폐쇄
airway pressure 기도내압
airway pressure-time curve
기도내압 시간곡선
airway resistance 기도저항
airway stenosis 기도협착
airway stent 기도스텐트
akathisia 정좌불능 ; 좌불안석증 ; 아카티시아

Al-Anon 알아논
alarm 경보 ; 알람
Alaska Natives 알래스카 원주민
albuminuria 단백뇨
alcohol 알코올
alcohol abuse 알코올남용
alcohol consumption 알코올소비
alcohol-based handrub 알코올 손세정제
alcohol-containing antiseptic handrub
알코올 손세정제
alcoholic encephalopathy 알코올성 뇌장애
alcoholic hallucinosis 알코올환각증
alcoholic hepatitis 알코올성 간염
alcoholic psychosis
알코올정신병 ; 알코올성 정신병
alcoholics 알코올중독
Alcoholics Anonymous : AA
알코올중독자갱생회
alcoholics patient 알코올중독환자
alcoholism 알코올의존증 ; 알코올중독
alcohol-related psychosis 알코올환각증
Aldactazide 알닥타자이드
Aldactone 알닥톤 ; 이뇨제
alendronate 알렌드로네이트
alert safety system 경보안전시스템 ; 알람
alexia 난독
Alfred C. Pigou 피구
algesia 통각 ; 통각과민증
alien 외국인
Alien Labor Certification Division
외국인노동관리소
alienation 인간소외 ; 소외
alignment 얼라이먼트
alimony 위자료
alkalemia 알칼리혈증
alkalosis 알칼로혈증
allergic bronchitis 알레르기성 기관지염
allergic pruritus 알레르기성 소양증
allergic reaction 알레르기 반응
allergic rhinitis 알레르기성 비염
allergy 알레르기
Alli 알리 ; 지방흡수억제제
allocated money 배분금

allocation 배분
allocation plan 배분계획 ; 할당계획
allograph 대필
allotted charge 분담금
allowance 수당
allowances for the aged 노령수당 ; 노인수당
all-you-can-eat buffet
뷔페식 ; 마음껏 먹기 뷔페 ; 바이킹식
Alma-Ata Declaration 알마아타선언
almoner 알모너
almshouse 구빈원 ; 양로원 ; 암스하우스
alpha-blocker α 차단제
alpha-glucosidase inhibitor α
글루코시다아제 억제제
alternate three-point gait 교차3점 보행
alternative medicine
대체요법 ; 올터너티브메디슨 ; 대체의학
alternative work schedule 교대제 근무
altruism 이타주의
alveolar 치조농루
alveolar air 폐포기
alveolar air equation 폐포기식
alveolar cell 폐포상피세포
alveolar collapse 폐포허탈
alveolar damage 폐포상해
alveolar dead space 폐포사강
alveolar edema 폐포수종 ; 폐포부종
alveolar epithelial cell 폐포상피세포
alveolar epithelium 폐포상피
alveolar gas exchange 폐포가스교환
alveolar hypoventilation 폐포저환기
alveolar hypoxia 폐포성 저산소
alveolar lavage 폐포세정
alveolar macrophage
폐포대식세포 ; 폐포매크로파지
alveolar membrane 폐포막
alveolar pressure 폐포내압
alveolar recruitment 폐포리크루트먼트
alveolar space 폐포강
alveolar structure 폐포구축
alveolar surface tension 폐포표면장력
alveolar surfactant
폐포표면활성물질 ; 폐포서팩턴트

alveolar ventilation 폐포환기
alveolar-arterial oxygen tension
difference 폐포기·동맥혈 산소분압교차
alveolar-capillary barrier
폐포·모세혈관관문 ; 폐포·모세혈관장벽
alveolus 폐포
Alzheimer's Association Japan
일본치매노인가족회
Alzheimer's Association Korea
한국치매가족협회
Alzheimer's disease 알츠하이머병
Ambien 수면제 ; 암비엔
ambivalence 앰비밸런스 ; 양가감정 ; 양면가치 ;
감정의 양면성
ambulance 구급차
ambulation 보행
ambulation activity 보행동작
ambulatory care 이동보호 ; 외래케어
ambulatory clinic 외래진료소
ambulatory community-based
rehabilitation 지역밀착형통소재활
ambulatory health care services 통원의료
ambulatory medicine 외래진료
ambulatory rehabilitation 외래재활 ; 주간재활 ;
통소재활
amenity 어메니티
American Indian 아메리칸 인디언
amino acid 아미노산
Amiodarone 아미오다론
Amitriptyline 아미트립틸린
Amlodipine 암로디핀
ammonia 암모니아
ammonia detoxification 암모니아 해독
amnesia 기억상실증 ; 건망증
amnesty 사면
amniocentesis 양수검사 ; 양수진단
amount of National Pension Insurance
benefit 국민연금피보험자의 수급금액
amphetamine 암페타민
ampholyte 양성전해질
amphoteric electrolyte 양성전해질
amphoteric surface active agent
양성계면활성제

amputation 절단
amputation for peripheral vascular
disease 혈관원성 절단
amputation stump 단단 ; 절단단
amylase 아밀라아제
amylum 전분
amyotrophic lateral sclerosis : ALS
근위축성측색경화증
An Independent NGO in the Public
Service 대한은퇴자협회
anabolism 동화작용
anaclitic 의존성
anaerobe 혐기성 균
anaerobic exercise 무산소훈련 ; 무산소성 훈련
anaerobic threshold : AT
무산소성 역치 ; 젖산역치
Anafranil 아나프라닐
anakinra 아나킨라
anal dilator 항문확장기
anal endosonography 항문관초음파검사
anal manometry 항문내압측정
anal mucosal electrosensitivity
항문점막전류감각역치
anal personality 항문기 성격
anal phase 항문기
anal speculum 항문경 ; 항문벌리개
anal sphincter muscle 항문괄약근
anal stimulator 항문자극장치
analgesic 진통제
analgesic drug 진통약
analysand 정신분석을 받는 환자
analysis 분석
analysis of defenses 방위의 분석
analysis of variance : ANOVA 분산분석
analytical psychology 분석심리학
anamnesis 기왕경험연수
anaphylactic shock
과민성 쇼크 ; 아나필라틱 쇼크
anaplastic thyroid cancer 갑상선미분화암
Anaprox 아나프록스
anarchism 무정부주의
anatomical position 해부학적 자세
androgen 안드로겐

androgen deprivation therapy : ADT
안드로겐 제거요법
androgyny 양성 소유
anemia 빈혈
anesthesia 무감각증 ; 촉각소실 ; 감각소실 ; 마취
anesthetic 마취제
anethole trithione 아네톨트리티온
aneurysm 동맥류
aneurysmectomy 동맥류 절제
aneurysmorrhaphy 동맥류 봉축술
Angel Plan 엔젤플랜
anger 분노
angina attack 협심증 발작
angina pectoris 협심증
angiogram 혈관조영
angioplasty 혈관형성술
angiotensin 앤지오텐신
angiotensin II receptor antagonist
엔지오텐신 II 수용체 길항제
angiotensin-converting-enzyme inhibitor :
ACE inhibitor 앤지오텐신 변환효소 억제제
animal assisted activity : AAA 동물개재활동
animal assisted therapy : AAT 동물개재요법
animal food product 동물성 식품
animal therapy 동물요법
anionic surface active agent
음이온 계면활성제
Aniridia cerebellar ataxia mental
deficiency 무홍채-소뇌성운동실조-정신박약증
anisakis 아니사키스
ankle joint 족관절
ankle-brachial index : ABI 발목상완지수
ankle-foot orthosis : AFO 단하지보조기
ankylosing 경직성
ankylosing spondylitis 경직성 척추염
ankylosis 경직
Annual Health 후생노동백서
annual survey 연차조사
annually managed expenditure : AME
매년관리지출액
anode 양극
anomie 사회적 무질서 ; 아노미 ; 무규범
anorectal prolapse 직장항문탈출

anorexia 거식증
anorexia nervosa 신경성 무식욕증
anorexia nervous 신경성 식욕부진증
anoscope 항문경
anoscopy 항문경검사
anosmia 후각소실증
anosognosia 질병인식불능증
anoxemia 무산소혈증 ; 저산소혈증
anoxia 산소결핍증 ; 저산소증 ; 무산소증
Antabuse 앤터뷰스
antacid 제산제
antagonism 길항작용
antagonist 길항근
antalgic gait
　동통회피성 보행 ; 절뚝걸음 ; 진통보행
antegrade colonic enema : ACE
　선행성 결장관장
anterior spinal artery syndrome
　전척수동맥증후군
anterograde amnesia 전향성 건망
anteroom 전실
anthelmintic 구충제
antianemia drug 빈혈치료제
antianxiety medication 항불안제
antibacterial agent 항균제 ; 항균물질
antibacterial and deodorization material
　항균·방취소재
antibacterial drug 항균제
antibacterial soap 항균제함유비누
antibacterial spectrum 항균스펙트럼
antibiotic 항생물질 ; 항생제
antibiotic resistant infection
　항생물질내성균감염
antibody 항체
antibody titer 항체가
antibody valence 항체결합가
anticancer drug 항암제
anticoagulant 항응고제
Anti-Defamation League of B'nai B'rith
　인신공격방지위원회
antidepressant medication 항우울제
antidiabetic 항당뇨병제
antidiscrimination education 동화교육

antidiuresis 항이뇨
antidote 해독제
antidromic conduction 역방향성 전도
antiedemic 항부종성 ; 항구토제
antiepileptic drug 항간질제
antifungal 항진균제
antifungal antibiotic 항진균성 항생물질
antigen 항원
antigenicity 항원성
antigravity muscle 항중력근
antihistamine 항히스타민제
antiinflammatory drug 항염증제
antiinflammatory medication 항염증제
antimicrobial 항균
antimicrobial agent 항균물질 ; 항균제
antimicrobial resistance 항균제저항성
antimicrobial soap
　항균성 비누 ; 항균제함유비누
antimicrobial spectrum 항균스펙트럼
antioxidant 항산화물
antioxidant agent 항산화제
antioxidant therapy 항산화요법
antioxidant vitamin 항산화비타민
anti-Parkinsonian drug 항파킨슨병제
anti-Parkinsonian medication 항파킨슨병약
antiplatelet agent 항혈소판제
antipodagric 항통풍제
antipoverty programs 빈곤퇴치 프로그램
antipruritic 진양제
antipruritic drug 진양제
antipruritic medication 진양제
antipsoriatic drug 항건선제
antipsychotic 항정신병약 ; 항정신병제
antipsychotic drug 항정신병제
antipsychotic medication 항정신병 치료제 ;
　항정신병약
antipyretic 해열제 ; 해열제
antipyretic drug 해열제 ; 해열제
antipyretic medication 해열제 ; 해열제
antisepsis 소독 ; 생체소독
antiseptic 방부제
antiseptic agent 생체소독제 ; 생체소독약
antiseptic handrub 손 소독마찰

antiseptic handwash 손씻기 소독
antiserum 항혈청
anti-social group 반사회성 ; 반사회적 집단
antisocial personality 반사회적 성격
antithrombotic drug 항혈전제
antithrombotic medication 항혈전제
antithyroid 항갑상선약 ; 항갑상선제
antithyroid drug 항갑상선제 ; 항갑상선약
antithyroid medication 항갑상선제
antitussive drug 진해제 ; 진해약
antitussive medication 항갑상선약
antiviral 항바이러스
antiviral drug 항바이러스제
anuria 무뇨증
anus 항문
anxiety 불안증 ; 불안
anxiety disorder 불안장애
anxiety for long-term caregivers
　개호자 불안
anxiety neurosis 불안신경증
anxiolytic 항불안제
anxiolytic medication 항불안제
aortic stenosis 대동맥변협착증
apartheid 아파르트헤이트
apartments for the aged 노인아파트
apathy 무관심
aperture color mode 개구색 모드
apex beat 심첨박동
aphasia 실어 ; 실어증
aphonia 무성증 ; 실성증
aplastic anemia 재생불량성 빈혈
apnea 무호흡 ; 호흡정지
apnea index 무호흡지수
apnea-hypopnea index : AHI
　무호흡저호흡지수
apneic spell 무호흡발작
apneic threshold 무호흡역치
apneusis 지속성 흡식
apolipoprotein 아폴리포 단백질
apoplexy 중풍 ; 뇌졸중
appeal 불복제기 ; 이의신청 ; 진정
appeal system 불복제기제도 ; 이의신청제도
appetite 식욕

appetite center 식욕중추
applicant 신청자
applicants on the waiting list 대기자
applied psychology 응용심리학
applied research 응용조사
applying pad 지지패드
appointment 예약 ; 약속
appointment of curator of minor
　미성년보좌인 선임
appointment of guardian 후견인선임
appointment of guardian of minor
　미성년후견인 선임
apprentice 견습생
apprentice system 도제제도
apprenticeship
　양성훈련제도 ; 직장실습형 훈련제도
apprenticeship period 견습기간
apprenticeship system 도제제도
apprenticing 도제
approach to the critically injured patient
　중증외상환자에 대한 접근법
appropriation 정부지출금
approval 인가
approved non-profit corporation 인정NPO
　법인
apraxia 실행증
apraxia of speech 말 실행증
apron 에이프런 ; 앞치마
aptitude test 적정검사
aquatic exercise 아쿠아운동
arch support 아치서포트 ; 오목발바닥 받침
area services 에어리어 서비스
Area wise Social Welfare Center
　지역사회복지관
Aricept 아리셉트
arm sling 암 슬링 ; 팔걸이
arm support 암 서포트
armrest 암 레스트 ; 팔걸이
Arnold Toynbee 토인비
Arnold's neuralgia 후두신경통
Arnold-Chiari malformation
　아놀드키아리증후군
aromatherapy 향기치료

arrhythmia 부정맥
arsenic poisoning 비소중독
art therapy 예술치료 ; 미술치료
arterial blood 동맥혈
arterial blood gas 동맥혈가스
arterial blood gas analysis 동맥혈가스분석
arterial blood pressure 동맥압
arterial blood sampling 동맥혈채취
arterial bruit 동맥잡음
arterial carbon dioxide tension
　동맥혈이산화탄소분압
arterial compliance 동맥경직도
arterial conduit 동맥도관
arterial continuous murmur 동맥연속잡음
arterial desaturation 동맥혈포화도저하
arterial disease 동맥질환
arterial distensibility 동맥신장성
arterial embolism 동맥색전
arterial occlusive disease : AOD 동맥폐쇄질
　환
arterial oxygen saturation 동맥혈산소포화도
arterial oxygen tension 동맥혈산소분압
arterial partial pressure of carbon
　dioxide : PaCO2 동맥혈탄산가스분압
arterial pulse 동맥박동
arterial puncture 동맥천자
arterial remodeling 동맥 재구축
arterial resistance 동맥저항
arterial systolic murmur 동맥수축기잡음
arterial to end-tidal carbon dioxide tension
　difference 동맥·호기종말 이산화탄소분압교차
arterial tonometry 동맥안압측정
arterial tree 동맥수
arterial valve 동맥변
arterial-mixed venous oxygen content
　difference 동맥·혼합정맥 산소교차
arteriogenesis 동맥신생
arteriography 동맥조영
arteriole 세동맥
arteriosclerosis 동맥경화
arteriosclerosis obliterans 폐쇄성 동맥경화증
arteriosclerotic heart disease : ASHD
　동맥경화성 심질환

arteriospasm 동맥경련 ; 동맥연축
artery 동맥
arthralgia 관절통
arthritis 관절염
arthrokinematic approach : AKA
　관절운동접근법
articles of incorporation 정관
articulation disorder 구음장애
articulation training 구음훈련
artificial anus 인공항문
artificial bladder 인공방광
artificial blood vessel 인공혈관
artificial cochlea 인공내이
artificial feeding 인공영양
artificial fiber 인조섬유
artificial heart 인공심장
artificial heart valve 인공심장변
artificial hybrid organ 하이브리드 인공장기
artificial insemination 인공수정
artificial lens 인공렌즈
artificial limb 의지(義肢)
artificial lung 인공폐
artificial organ 인공장기
artificial respiration 인공호흡
artificial respirator 인공호흡기
artificial teeth 의치
artificial ventilation 인공호흡 ; 인공환기
as needed : PRN 필요시
asepsis 무균
aseptic barrier 무균적 차폐 ; 무균적 피복
aseptic intermittent catheterization : AIC
　무균적 간헐도뇨법
aseptic procedure 무균조작
Ashworth Scale 애쉬워스척도
Asian American 아시아계 미국인
Asian American Social Workers : AASW
　아시아계미국인사회사업가협회
Asperger syndrome 아스퍼거증후군
aspergillosis 국균증 ; 아스페르질루스증
asphyxia 질식
aspiration 흡입
aspiration cytology 천자흡인세포진
aspiration pneumonia

오연성 폐렴 ; 연하성 폐렴

aspirin 아스피린

aspirin therapy 아스피린요법

Assembly of Health Gymnastics for the Aged 노인건강체조경연대회

assertive community treatment 포괄형지역생활지원

assertiveness 자기주장

assertiveness training 자기주장훈련

assessed value 평가액

assessment 평가 ; 사정 ; 어세스먼트 ; 감별

assessment item 평가항목

Assessment of Motor and Process Skills : AMPS 운동기능·프로세스기능평가

assessment of urinary incontinence 실금평가

assessment sheet 어세스먼트 시트

assessment tool 평가툴

assets 자산

assign 배치

assignment 과제 ; 임무

assignment program 위탁사업

assimilation 동화

assist and/or controlled mechanical ventilation 보조조절환기

assist mode 보조양식 ; 보조모드

assistance 돌봄 ; 수발 ; 원조 ; 보조 ; 부조 ; 구원

assistance dog 보조견

assistance for people with mental disabilities 정신장애인부조

assistance for people with mental retardation 지적장애인부조

assistance for the aged 노인부조

assistance for the disabled 장애인부조

assistance for the disabled children 장애아부조

assistance for the elderly 고령자부조

assistance for the physically disabled 신체장애인부조

assistance services agency for the elderly 고령자부조서비스기관

assistance services for the elderly

고령자부조서비스

assistance services office for the elderly 고령자부조서비스사업소

assistance services provider for the elderly 고령자부조서비스사업자

assistance with delivery 분만보조

assistance with eating 식사보조 ; 식사원조 ; 식사케어

assistance with the self-administration of medication 투약

assistant 돌봄 ; 수발 ; 원조

assistant administrator 부시설장

assistant director of nursing 부간호사장

assistant mover 보조동근

assistant service division of nursing 간호조무사

assisted coughing 기침보조

assisted suicide 자살방조

assistive device 지원기기

assistive exercise 보조훈련 ; 돌봄훈련

assistive listening and technology device 복지전화

assistive technology 보조기술

associated movement 연합운동

association 협회 ; 결사체

Association for Technical Aids 테크노에이드협회

Association of Area Welfare Institutes 지역복지협력사업

asthenopia 안정피로

asthma 천식

asthmatic attack 천식발작

astigmatism 난시

astringent 수렴제

asylum 수용시설

asylums 보호시설

asymmetry 비대칭

asymptomatic carrier 무증후성 보균자 ; 무증후성 캐리어

at bedtime 취침시

ataxia 운동실조

ataxic gait 실조성 파행 ; 실조보행

atheroma 아테롬 ; 분류 ; 죽종

athetosis 무정위운동증 ; 아테토시스 ; 아테토제

Ativan 아티반

atom 원자

atomic bomb 원자폭탄

atomic bomb survivor 피폭자

atopic cough 아토피기침

atopic dermatitis 아토피성 피부염

atopy 아토피

atrial fibrillation 심방세포

atrial septal defect 심방중격결손증

atrium 심방

atrophic gastritis 위축성 위염

atrophic vaginitis 위축성 질염

atrophy 위축 ; 퇴화

attachment 애착

attendance allowance 간병수당

attendant 간병인

attending doctor 주치의

attending system 개방병원

attention deficit disorder 주의력 결핍장애

attention deficit hyperactivity disorder :
ADHD 주의결함·다동성장애

attitudes toward care 장기요양자세

attorney-at-law 변호사

attorney-in-fact 대리인

attributable risk 기여위험

attributable risk percent : ARP 기여위험비율

attribution 귀속

atypical antipsychotic 비정형 항정신병약

atypical mycobacteria 비정형 항산균증

atypical psychosis 비정형 정신병

audible pedestrian traffic signal
시각장애인용 신호기

audio visual education 시청각교육

audio visual library 시청각라이브러리

audiogram 오디오그램 ; 청력도

audiologist 청능훈련사

audiology assessment 청각적 평가

audiometer 오디오미터

audiometry 청력검사

audit of financial accounts 회계감사

auditorially disabled 청각장애자

auditorially impaired 난청자

auditorially impaired child 난청아

auditorially impaired elderly 난청고령자

auditorially impaired infant 난청유아

auditory agnosia 청각실인

auditory deficit 청각장애

auditory disability 청각장애

auditory disorder 청각장애

auditory hallucination 환청

auditory impairment 청각장애

auditory sense 청각

auditory-verbal center 청각음성센터

auditory-verbal therapist 청각음성테라피스트

aural hematoma 이개혈종 ; 이혈종

authoritarian 권위적인

authoritarian management 권위적인 관리

authority 권력 ; 권위

autism 자폐증

autism spectrum disorder : ASD
자폐증 스펙트럼장애

autistic child 자폐아

autoclave 고압증기멸균기 ; 오토클레이브

autoclaving 고압증기멸균 ; 증기멸균

autogenic training 자율훈련법

autoimmune hepatitis 자기면역성 간염

autoimmunity 자기면역

autolysis 자가분해 ; 자기분해 ; 자기용균

automated auditory brainstem response
자동청성 뇌간반응

automated auditory brainstem response
evaluation 자동청성 뇌간반응평가

automated endoscope reprocessor : AER
자동내시경세정장치

automated external defibrillator 자동제세동기

automatic peritoneal dialysis 자동복막투석

automatism 자동기술법

automobile allowance 자동차수당

autonomic dysfunction 자율신경기능장애

autonomic dysreflexia 자율신경과반사

autonomic hyperreflexia 자율신경과반사

autonomic nerve 자율신경

autonomic nerve disorder 자율신경장애

autonomic nervous system 자율신경계

autonomic thought 자동사고

A

autonomous affairs 자치사무
autonomous choice 자주선택성
autonomous practice 자율사회사업
autonomy 자주성 ; 오토노미 ; 자율성
autonomy versus shame and doubt
자율성 대 수치심과 의심
autophobia 단독공포증
autopsy 검시 ; 부검 ; 사체해부
autoreceptor 자가수용기 ; 자기수용체
autoregulation 자동조절 ; 자기조절
autosomal dominant 상염색체 우성
autosomal dominant disorder
상염색체 우성유전병
autosomal dominant inheritance
상염색체 우성유전
autosomal recessive 상염색체 열성
autosomal recessive disorder
상염색체 열성유전병
autosomal recessive inheritance
상염색체 열성유전
autosome 상염색체
average cost of bringing up a child
평균양육비용
average household size 평균세대인원
average length of stay : ALOS 평균입원일수

average life span 평균수명
average price of drugs 평균약가
average size of households 평균세대인원
aversion therapy 혐오요법 ; 혐오치료제
aversive stimulus 혐오자극
Avodart 아보다트 ; 탈모치료제
avoidance 회피
avoidance conditioning 회피조건형성
avoidance learning 회피학습
avoidant personality disorder
회피성 성격장애
awake 각성
awakening drug 각성제
awakening recovery center 약물갱생시설
axilla 겨드랑이
axillary artery 겨드랑이동맥
axillary crutch 목발
axillary osmidrosis 암내 ; 액취
axillary temperature 액와체온
axis 축
Axis Ⅱ disorder 제2축 장애
axonal degeneration 축색변성
ayurvedic medicine 아유르베다 의학
Azathioprine 아자티오프린
azotemia 고질소혈증

B

baby boom generation
베이비붐 세대 ; 단카이세대

baby boomer 베이비부머 ; 단카이세대

baby with mental retardation 지적장애유아

babysitter 베이비시터 ; 보모

bachelor of social work : BSW
사회복지학사학위

bachelor's degree 학사호

back ground music : BGM 환경음악

back knee 반장슬

back support 백서포트

back to Richmond 리치먼드로 돌아가라

backrest 백레스트 ; 등받이

bacteremia 균혈증

bacteria 세균

bacterial pneumonia 세균성 폐렴

bactericidal action 살균작용

bacteriostatic action 정균작용

bacterium 세균 ; 감염균

bacteriuria 세균뇨

bag lady 유랑여성

bail 보석

balance 밸런스

balance billing 차액청구

balance in a sitting position 좌위유지

Baller-Gerold syndrome 밸라-제롤드 증후군

balloon catheter 벌룬도뇨카테터

balloon expulsion test 벌룬배출시험

balloon retaining test 벌룬보지시험

balneotherapy 온천요법

bandage 붕대

bar soap 고형비누

Baraclude 바라크루드

barbiturates 신경안정제

Barclay Report 바클레이 보고서

bargaining 교섭

barium contrast radiography 바륨조영

barium enema 바륨주장조영

barium meal 바륨죽

barium small bowel enema 역행성 바륨소
장조영

barrier 배리어

barrier equipment 배리어기재

barrier free 배리어프리

barrier free design 배리어프리 디자인

barrier free home 배리어프리 주택

barrier free map 배리어프리 지도

barrier nursing 배리어널싱

barrier precaution 배리어 예방책

barrier-free threshold 배리어프리 문지방

Barthel index 바델척도

basal body temperature 기초체온

basal metabolic rate : BMR
기초대사량 (기초대사율)

basal metabolism 기초대사

Basic Act for Persons with Disabilities
장애인기본법

Basic Act for the Elderly 고령사회기본법

Basic Act for the Low Birth Rate and
the Aging Society 저출산·고령사회기본법

basic activities of daily living : BADL
기본적 일상생활활동

basic allowance 기본수당

basic anxiety 기본적 불안

basic care fee 기본장기요양비

basic color term 기본색채어

B

basic daily fee 일일 이용료 ·
basic disability pension 기초장애연금
basic encounter group 엔카운터집단
basic food group 기초식품
basic human rights 기본적 인권
basic needs 기본적 욕구
basic nursing education 간호기초교육
basic old-age pension 노령기초연금
basic pension 기초연금
basic pension for persons with disabilities 장애인기본계획
basic pension number 기초연금번호
basic pension system 기초연금제도
basic reimbursement rate 기초상환점수
basic resident registration 주민기본대장
basic resident registration card 주민기본대장 카드
basic standard deduction 기초공제
Basic Structural Reform of Social Welfare 사회복지기초구조개혁
basic survey 기본조사
basic survivors pension 유족기초연금
basin method 수반법 ; 침투지법
basket forceps 바스켓 겸자
bath board 배쓰보드
bath ratio 욕비
bathing 목욕
bathing activity 목욕동작
bathing assistance 목욕보조
bathing equipment 목욕용구
bathing services 목욕서비스
bathrobe 목욕용 가운 ; 배스로브
bathroom 욕실
bathtub 욕조
battered child 매 맞는 아동
battered spouse 매 맞는 배우자
battery 구타
beadhouse 양로원
Beck Depression Inventory : BDI
    BECK 우울증 진단
Becker muscular dystrophy
    벡커형 근육퇴행위축
bed 침대 ; 베드

bed lift 침대 리프트
bed making 침구정리
bed mobility 침상동작
bed positioning 침상 상지위
bed rest 안정침상 ; 장기침상요양
bedclothes 침구
bedding 침상
bedpan 변기
bedpan washer 변기세정기
bedridden 와상
bedridden elderly 와상고령자 (와상노인)
bedridden eradication campaign
    와상노인제로작전
bedridden level 와상도
bedridden long-term care recipient
    요개호와상노인
bedridden period before death : BPbd
    최종장기침상요양기간
bedridden status 와상생활상태
beds with an extra charge 차액침상
bedside commode
    포터블화장실 ; 휴대용 화장실 ; 이동화장실
bedside rail 침대난간
bedside table 베드사이드 테이블 ; 침대 옆 탁자
bedsore 욕창
Beers criteria 고령자약제처방기준 ; 비어스 기준
Beers list 비어스 기준
behavior 행동
behavior assessment 행동평가
behavior modification 행동수정법 ; 행동수정
behavior modification approach
    행동수정접근법
behavior pattern 행동양식 ; 행동패턴
behavior rehearsal 행동리허설
behavior science 행동과학
behavior therapy 행동요법 ; 행동치료
behavioral and psychological symptoms of dementia : BPSD 치매의 행동정신증상
behavioral assessment 행동사정
behavioral language 행동언어
behavioral observation 행동관찰
behavioral rehearsal 예행
behavioral science 행동과학

B

behaviorism 행동주의
bell and pad 벨패드법
Bell's palsy 벨 마비 ; 안면신경마비
below-elbow amputation 전완절단
below-knee amputation 하퇴절단
beneficence 선행
beneficiary 수익자
beneficiary-to-pay principle 수익자부담의
  원칙
benefit for medical care expenses
  의료비급여
benefit in kind 현물급여
benefit level 급여수준
benefit management form 급여관리표
benefit management services 급여관리업무
benefit period 급여기간
benefit principle
  수익자부담 ; 응익원칙 ; 응익자부담
Benefit Review Committee 급여비심사위원회
benefit-received principle 응익부담
benefits 급여
benefits priority list 급여우선리스트
benefits standards 급여기준
Benicar 베니카
Benicar 항고혈압제
benign prostatic hyperplasia 전립선비대증
Benztropine 벤즈트로핀 ; 약물항콜린제
bereavement 사별 ; 애도증
Berg Balance Scale 버그균형척도
Bertolotti's syndrome 베르토로티 증후군
best practice 최선의 치료
beta receptor blockage β 수용체 차단제
beta-amyloid peptide β 아밀로이드 펩티드
beta-blocker β 차단제
beta-carotene β 카로틴
Beveridge Report 베버리지 보고서
bias 편견
bibliotherapy 독서치료
Biestek's 7 principles 비에스틱 7대 원칙
Biestek's principles 바이스테크의 7원칙
Big Brothers and Sisters Movement
  BBS운동
big government 큰 정부

bigamy 중혼
Biguanide 비구아니드
bilateral support 쌍무적 부양
Bill for Care Services Insurance for the
  Elderly 노인수발보험법안
Bill of Rights 권리장전
billing period 청구대상기간
billing statement 청구서
bimodal 양자발생
Binet Intelligence Test 비네 지능검사
Binet-Simon Test 비네시몬 지능검사법
binge drinking 폭음 ; 통음
Binswanger's disease 빈스완거병
Bioburden 바이오버든
bioclean system 바이오크린 시스템
bioelectromagnetic 생체전자기학
bioengineering 생체공학 ; 생명공학
bioethics 생명윤리 ; 유기체적 윤리
biofeedback 바이오피드백
biofeedback therapy 바이오피드백요법
biofilm 바이오필름
biohazard mark
  바이오해저드마크 ; 생물재해표시
biologic response modifier
  생물학적 응답조절물질
biological age 생물연령
biological clean room
  바이오클린병실 ; 생물학적 클린룸
biological indicator
  바이얼라지컬 인디케이터 ; 생물지표
biological paradigm 생물학 패러다임
biological rhythm 생체리듬
biological therapy 생물학적 지료빕
biomechanics 생체역학
biomedical ethics 생명·의료윤리
biopsy 생체검사 ; 생검
biopsy forceps 생검겸자
biotin 비오틴
bipolar disorder 쌍극성 장애 ; 양극장애 ;
  조우울증
bipolar I disorder 쌍극 I 형 장애
bipolar II disorder 쌍극 II 형 장애
birth certificate 출생증명서

B

birth control 산아제한
birth palsy 분만마비
birth-order theories 출생서열이론
birthrate 출산율
bisexuality 양성애
bisphosphonate drug 비스포스포네이트 제재
bitter 쓴 맛
bivariate analysis 변화분석
Bjornstad syndrome 비욘스타드 증후군
Black Lung program 진폐증 보상프로그램
black market adoption 불법입양
black power 흑인 민권운동
blacks 흑인 소수민족
bladder hypotonia
　긴장성 방광 ; 신경성 방광 ; 저긴장성 방광
bladder training 배뇨훈련
bleach solution 표백액
bleaching 표백
bleaching agent 표백제
bleeding 출혈
blended diet 믹서식
blended family 혼합가족
blennorrhoea alveolaris 치조농루
Blessed Orientation-Memory-Concentration
　Test 브레스트지남력 기억집중검사
blind child 농아아동
blind child institution 맹아시설
blind elderly 농아고령자 ; 농아노인
blind infant 농아유아
blind person 농아자 ; 맹인
blindness 맹 ; 맹증 ; 실명
blister 물집 ; 수포
block contract 블록계약
block grant 정액교부금
block organizations 가구주민협의회
block placement 지역실습배치
Blood and Blood Products Division
　혈액대책과
blood bank 혈액은행
blood donation 헌혈
blood plasma 혈장
blood poisoning 패혈증
blood pressure 혈압

blood pressure manometer 혈압계
blood seller 매혈자
blood serum 혈청
blood sugar 혈당
blood sugar level 혈당치
blood test 혈액검사
blood transfusion 수혈
blood urea nitrogen : BUN 혈액요소질소
bloodborne infection 혈액매개감염
bloodborne pathogen 혈액유래병원체
bloodborne virus infection 혈중바이러스
　감염증 ; 혈액매개바이러스감염증
bloodstream infection 혈류감염
blue collar 블루칼라
Blue Cross Association 청십자사
blue-collar worker 육체노동자
board and care home 보드 앤드 케어홈
board of directors 기관장위원회
body composition 신체조정
body fluid 체액
body image 신체상
body mass index : BMI 체질량지수
body mechanism 신체메커닉스
body reflection 신체반사
body substance isolation 생체물질격리
body surface isolation 생체표면격리
body temperature 체온
body-centered psychotherapy
　신체지향심리요법 ; 하코미테라피
boiling sterilization 자비소독
boiling water 끓는 물 ; 비등수
bonding 결속
bone atrophy 골위축증
bone density 골밀도
bone disease 골질환
bone mineral density 골밀도 ; 골염량
Boniva 보니바
borderless 보더리스
borderline 경계선
borderline class 경계선층
borderline family 저소득자세대
borderline personality disorder
　경계선 성격장애

Borstal system 영국청소년비행 프로그램
Boston Naming Test 보스톤 이름대기검사
Bouchard's node 부샤르결절
boundary 경계
boutonniere deformity 단추구멍변형
bovine spongiform encephalopathy : BSE
소해면상뇌증 ; 우해면양뇌증
bowel and bladder dysfunction 방광직장장애
bowel function 장기능
bowel incontinence 변실금
bowel irrigation 장세정
bowel management 배변관리
bowel movement 변통 ; 변의
bowel preparation 관장 ; 장 전처치
bowel training 배변훈련
Bowie-Dick Test 공기제거 및 증기침투시험 ;
보위딕 테스트
box joint 상자형 이음새
boxer's fracture 복서골절
boy's house 소년의 집
boycott 보이콧
brace 보조기 ; 장구 ; 보장구
brachial plexus palsy 상완신경총마비
Braden Scale for Predicting Pressure
Sore Risk 욕창발생예측척도
Braden Scale for Predicting Pressure
Ulcer Risk 욕창발생예측척도
bradycardia 느린맥 ; 서맥
bradypnea 느린호흡 ; 서호흡
Braille 브라이유식 점자 ; 시각장애인용 점자 ;
점자
Braille block 점자블록 ; 시각장애인용 점자블록 ;
브라이유식 점자블록
Braille library 점자도서관
Braille reading
시각장애인용 촉독 ; 촉독 ; 브라이유식 촉독
Braille typewriter 시각장애인용 점자타이프라
이터 ; 브라이유식 점자타이프라이터 ; 점자타이프
라이터
Braille writing equipment
시각장애인용 점자용구 ; 점자용구 ; 브라이유식 점
자용구
brain damage 뇌장애

brain death 뇌사
brain edema 뇌부종
brain stem 뇌간
brain tumor 뇌종양
brainstorming 브레인스토밍
brand name medication 선발약품
breast cancer 유방암
breast prosthesis 유방보철물
breast reconstruction 유방재건술
breast-sparing surgery 유방온존수술
breathing 호흡
breathing exercise 호흡훈련
bridge job 교량직업
Brief Fatigue Inventory : BFI 간이피로평가
Brief Oral Health Status Examination :
BOHSE 간이구강위생검사
Brief Pain Inventory : BPI 간이동통조사표
brief therapy 간단한 치료 ; 브리프테라피 ;
단기치료
brightness 밝기
bringing up 양육
Broca's aphasia 브로카실어증
Broca's area 브로카영역
broken home 결손가정
broker role 중개자 역할
bronchial asthma 기관지천식
bronchial drainage
배담 ; 기관지드레나지 ; 기관지배액
bronchitis 기관지염
bronchodilator 기관지확장제
bronchoscopy 기관지내시경
Brown-Sequard syndrome
브라운씨퀴드증후군
bruise 내출혈 ; 타박상
Brunnstrom stage 운동신경기능 회복단계 ;
브론스트롬 스테이지
brushing 브러싱
brushing cytology 찰과세포진
bubble bath 기포욕 ; 버블배스
Buddhist social work 불교사회사업
budget 예산
budget buster 재정파탄
budgeting 예산편성

B

B

budgeting loans 가계대출
building rapport 신뢰관계의 구축
bulbar palsy 구마비
bulimia 과식증
bulimia nervosa 신경성 대식증 ; 폭식증
bull's eye appearance 표적상 소견
bullying 괴롭힘 ; 왕따 ; 집단괴롭힘 ; 집단따돌림
bunion 건막류 ; 무지외반증 ; 버니언
burden 부담
burden interview 부담질문표
burden of care 장기요양부담 ; 개호부담
burden of health care 의료부담
burden rate 부담율
Bureau of Indian Affairs 인디언 업무국
bureaucracy 관료제 ; 관료정치

bureaucratization 관료화
burial 매장
burial and funeral assistance 상제부조
burial and funeral benefit 상제급여
burial and funeral costs 상제비용
burial and funeral expenses allowance
　상제수당
burn 화상 ; 열상
burnout 극도의 피로 ; 번아웃 ; 소진
burnout syndrome 탈진증후군 ; 번아웃신드롬
busing 강제 버스통학
button aid 버튼에이드
Buzz Session 버즈세션
by mouth : PO 경구
bypass surgery 바이패스수술 ; 혈관우회로술

C

C bar C바
C. W. Beers 비어스
C2 neuralgia 후두신경통
cabinet 내각
cable housing 케이블하우징 ; 케이블보관집
cadherin 유착물질 ; 케드헤린
caffeine 카페인
Calan 칼란
calcitonin 칼시토닌
calcium 칼슘
calcium channel blocker
  칼슘길항제 ; 칼슘통로차단제
calcium deficiency 칼슘결핍증
calcium pyrophosphate deposition
  disease 칼슘 파이로인산염 축적질환
calculating public-private competition
  costs 관민경쟁의 비용산정
caliper 캘리퍼
caloric intake 섭취열량
caloric restriction 칼로리 제한
Calvinism 칼비니즘
campaign 캠페인
Canadian-type hip disarticulation
  prosthesis 캐나다식 고의족
cancellation of certification 지정취소
cancellation of certification of long-term
  assistance-required 요지원인정의 취소
cancellation of certification of long-term
  care-required 요개호인정의 취소
cancellation of designation 지정취소
cancer 암
cancer patient 암환자
cancer treatment 암치료

cancerous growth 악성종양
candesartan 칸데사르탄 ; 항고혈압제
candida albicans 칸디다 알비칸스
cane 지팡이
cane-assisted gait 지팡이 보행
cannabis 칸나비스
cannula 캐뉼라
canteen for the senior citizen 경로식당
capital gains tax 양도소득과세
capital punishment 극형
capitalism 자본주의
capitated payment 인두지불제
capitated plan 인두제 선불정액제
capsaicin 캡사이신
carbamazepine 카르바마제핀 ; 항간질제
carbohydrate 탄수화물
carbon dioxide 이산화탄소
carbon monoxide 일산화탄소
carbon monoxide poisoning 일산화탄소 중독
carcinogenesis 발암
carcinomatous pain 암성동통
cardiac dysrhythmia 심장부정맥
cardiac ECHO 심에코
cardiac massage 심장마사지
cardiac nuclear medicine 심장핵의학
cardiac output 심박출량
cardiac rehabilitation 심장재활
cardiac shock 심원성 쇼크
cardiac shunt 심장분로
cardiac surgery-related infection
  심장외과관련감염
cardiac surgical intensive care unit
  순환기외과집중치료실

C

cardiogenic pulmonary edema 심원성
폐수종
cardiology 순환기 ; 심장병학
cardiometabolic risk 심혈관·대사질환리스크
cardiopulmonary cerebral resuscitation :
CPCR 심폐뇌소생법
cardiopulmonary resuscitation : CPR
심폐소생법
cardiothoracic ratio 심흉곽비 ; 심흉비
cardiovascular disease 심혈관질환
cardiovascular risk 심혈관리스크
Cardizem 칼디젬
care 장기요양 ; 개호 ; 케어
care advisor 개호상담원
care and education 양육
care and education for the disabled
children 양육지도
care and welfare 장기요양복지 ; 개호복지
care assistant 장기요양원조자 ; 개호원조자
care card 케어카드
care conference 케어컨퍼런스
care coordination 케어코디네이션
care device 장기용양기기 ; 개호용구 ; 개호기기
care equipment 복지용구 ; 복지용품 ; 장기요
양기기 ; 개호용구 ; 개호기기
care for people with mental retardation
지적장애인개호
care for the disabled 장애인개호
care for the disabled children disabled
children's care 장애아개호
care for the physically disabled
신체장애인개호
care goal 장기요양목표 ; 개호목표 ; 케어목표
care guidance 장기요양지도 ; 개호지도
care guideline 케어가이드라인
care home 케어주택 ; 케어하우스
care home for the aged 노인홈 ; 양로원
care management 케어매니지먼트
care management center for the aged
노인개호지원센터
care management for people with
mental disabilities 지적장애인개호지원
care management for the disabled

children 장애아개호지원
care management for the disabled
장애인케어매니지먼트
care management for the people with
mental disabilities 정신장애인개호지원
care management for the physically
disabled 신체장애인개호지원
care management for the physically
disabled children 신체장애아개호지원
care management model 케어매니지먼트모델
care management provider
케어매니지먼트기관
care management services 개호지원서비스
care management services plan
개호지원서비스계획
care manager
케어매니저 ; 개호지원전문원 ; 장기요양지원전문원
care mix 케어믹스
care pathway 케어패스
care plan 장기요양계획 ; 케어플랜 ; 개호계획
care plan for home care 재가케어플랜 ;
방문개호계획
care plan for institutional care 시설케어플랜
care practice 장기요양행위
care process 장기요양과정 ; 개호과정
care profession 개호전문
care professional 개호전문 개호전문직
care provider-recipient relationship
장기요양관계 ; 개호관계
care robot 장기요양로봇 ; 개호로봇
care service and health service facilities
for the aged 노인요양원
care service and welfare facilities for the
aged 노인요양복지시설
care service facilities for the aged
노인요양시설
care services 케어서비스
care services manager 개호서비스제공책임자
care services plan 장기요양서비스계획 ;
개호서비스계획
care skills 장기요양기술 ; 개호기술
care team 케어팀
care versus cure 치료 대 케어

C

care with education for the disabled children 장애아양육
care work 장기요양노동 ; 케어워크 ; 개호노동
Care Work Foundation : CWF 개호노동안정센터
care worker 요양보호사 ; 장기요양노동자 ; 케어복지사 ; 케어워커 ; 개호노동자
career counseling 직업상담
caregiver 장기요양자 ; 개호자 ; 케어기버
caregiver burden 장기요양자 부담
caregiver burden interview 장기요양자 부담질문표
Caregiver Burden Scale 장기요양자 부담척도
caregiver burnout 장기요양자의 감정적 탈진증후군
caregiver strain index : CSI 장기요양자 부담지표
caregiver stress 장기요양자 스트레스
care-preventive services 장기요양예방서비스 ; 개호예방서비스
carer's allowance 장기요양자 수당 ; 개호자 수당
caring for people with mental retardation 지적장애인개호
caring for people with mental disabilities 정신장애인개호
caring for the disabled 장애인개호
caring for the disabled children 장애아개호
caring for the dying 임종간호
caring for the elderly 고령자개호 ; 노인개호
caring for the physically disabled 신체장애인개호
caritas 카리타스
Caritas Internationals 국제카리타스
Carl Ransom Rogers 로저스
Caroli disease 카롤리병
carotid artery stenosis 경동맥협착
carrier 보균자
case 케이스
case aid 케이스에이드
case aid worker 케이스에이드워커
case conference 사례회의 ; 케이스컨퍼런스
case control study 대조군연구 ; 케이스컨트롤연구
case file 케이스파일
case finding 사례발견
case history 케이스히스토리 ; 사례사
case investigation 사례조사
case load 케이스담당량 ; 케이스로드
case management 케이스매니지먼트 ; 사례관리
case meeting 케이스회의
case mix 케이스믹스
case mix index : CMI 케이스믹스지수
case record 사례기록 ; 케이스기록 ; 처우기록
case research 사례연구
case study 사례검토 ; 케이스스터디
case supervision 케이스슈퍼비전
case supervisor 케이스슈퍼바이저
case work 케이스워크 ; 개별원조기술
case worker 케이스워커
case worker aide 보조사회사업가
case-fatality rate 치사율
case-mix reimbursement 혼합사례 상환
casework diagnosis 케이스워크 진단
casework process 케이스워크 과정
casework relationship 케이스워크 관계
cash benefit 현금급여 ; 금전급여
cash grant 현금급부
cast 기브스
caster 캐스터 ; 자재고리
castration 거세
castration anxiety 거세불안
catalyst role 촉매자 역할
cataplasm 습포
cataract 백내장
catastrophic health care expenses 고액요양비
catastrophic long-term care expenses 고액장기요양비용 ; 고액개호비용
catastrophic long-term care services expenses 고액장기요양서비스 ; 고액개호서비스
catastrophic medical expenses 고액의료비
catchment area 수혜지역
catechol-O-methyltransferase : COMT 카테콜-오-메틸트랜스라제

C

categorical assistance 절대부조
category of long-term care status
요개호상태구분
catharsis 정화
cathartic method 카타르시스법
catheter 카테터
catheter-associated bloodstream
infection : CABSI 카테터관련피유행성 감기염
catheter-associated infection 카테터관련감염
catheterization 카테터유치법
catheter-related bacteremia 카테터유래균혈증
catheter-related bloodstream infection :
CRBSI 카테터유래피유행성 감기염
catheter-related infection 카테터유래감염
cathexis 부착
Catholicism 카톨리시즘
Caucasians 백색인종
causalgia 작열통
cause-oriented organization 원인지향적 조직
cause-versus-function issue
원인 대 기능 논쟁
Celebrex 셀레브렉스
celecoxib 셀리콕시브
cellulitis 봉와직염
cemetery 묘지
centenarian 100대
Center for Disease Control and
Prevention : CDC 질병관리예방센터
Center for Epidemiological Studies
Depression Scale : CES-D 우울자기평가척도
Center for Independent Living : CIL
자립생활센터
Center for Intergenerational Learning of
Temple University 템플대학 세대간 학습센터
Center for Searching Runaway Aged
가출노인찾기종합센터
center of gravity : CG 중심
Center of Social Welfare Promotion and
National Examination 사회복지진흥 · 시험센터
Centers for Disease Control 질병통제센터
central auditory processing disorder
중추성 청각처리장애
central catheter 중심정맥카테터 ; 중심카테터

central cord syndrome : CCS 중심성 경골수
손상
Central Labour Relations Commission
중앙노동위원회
central nervous system 중추신경계
central parenteral nutrition 중심정맥영양법
central scotoma 중심암점
central sterile and supply department
중앙멸균공급부 ; 중앙멸균재료부
central supply 중앙공급
central venous pressure 중심정맥압
centralization 중앙집중화
centrifugal family structure 원심적 가족구조
centrifugal sampler 원심 공중부유물질채집기
centripetal family structure 구심적 가족구조
cerebellum 소뇌
cerebral anemia 뇌빈혈
cerebral angiography 뇌혈관조영
cerebral arteriosclerosis 뇌동맥경화증
cerebral contusion 뇌좌상
cerebral embolism 뇌색전
cerebral hemorrhage 뇌출혈
cerebral infarction 뇌경색
cerebral nerve 뇌신경
cerebral palsy : CP 뇌성마비
cerebral thrombosis 뇌혈전 ; 뇌혈전증
cerebral vascular accident 뇌혈관장애
cerebrovascular dementia 뇌혈관성 치매
cerebrovascular disorder : CVD 뇌혈관장애
certificate 증명서
certificate of health examination
건강진단증명서
certification 인정 ; 지정 ; 자격증
certification appeal 심사청구
certification of disability 장애인정
certification of disability level
장애정도구분의 인정
certification of incurable disease
난병인정 ; 불치병인정
certification of long-term care
assistance-required 요양등급지원인정 ;
요지원인정
certification of long-term care-required

요양등급인정 ; 요개호인정
certification standards 인증기준
certification standards for long-term
  care insurance benefits 요개호인정기준
certified care worker : CCW 개호복지사
Certified Care Worker Registry
  요양보호사 등록 ; 개호복지사 등록
certified child care worker 보육사 ; 보모
certified health education specialist
  인정건강교육사
certified home care worker 재가개호복지사
certified medical facility for health
  insurance 특정승인 보험의료기관
certified nurse : CN 인정간호사
certified nurse midwife 인정간호조산사
certified psychiatric social worker : CPSW
  정신보건복지사
Certified Psychiatric Social Workers Act
  정신보건복지사법
certified social insurance and labor
  consultant 사회보험노무사
certified social worker : CSW 사회복지사 ;
  공인사회사업가
Certified Social Worker and Care Worker
  Act 사회복지사 및 개호복지사법
certified welfare equipment trade
  특정복지용구판매
cervical cancer 자궁경암
cervical cord injury 경수손상
cervical dysplasia 자궁경부형성장애증
cervical orthosis 경추보조기
cervical radiculopathy 경부신경근증
cervical spinal cord injury 경수손상
cervical spine 경추
cervical spine collar 경추보호대
cervical spondylosis 변형성 경추증
cervical traction 경추견인
cervicogenic headache 경추성 두통
Chadwick Edwin 채드위크
chaining 연쇄
chamber pot 침실용변기
CHAMPUS 챔푸스
change agent 변화매개인

change agent system 변화매개체계
change of position 체위변환
change of residence 이사
changing bed sheets 시트교환
changing clothes
  갈아입기 ; 의복 갈아입기 ; 착탈의
character 캐릭터 ; 성격
character disorder 성격이상 ; 성격장애
Charcot joint 샤르코관절 ; 신경성 관절
charette 재해복구
charges for recipients 이용자부담금
charges to beneficiaries 수익자청구금
charitable trust 공익신탁
charity 자선
charity hospital 자선병원
Charity Organization Movement
  자선조직화운동
Charity Organization Societies : COS
  자선조직협회
charity pot 자선남비
charity work 자선사업
Charter for the Elderly 노인헌장
Chartist Movement 차티스트운동
cheap government 값싼정부
chemical fiber 화학섬유
Chemical Hazards Control Division
  화학물질대책과
chemical indicator 화학적 지시약
chemical restraint 약물구속
chemoembolization 화학색전
chemotherapy 화학요법 ; 화학치료
chest compression 흉부압박
chest pain 가슴통증 ; 흉통
chest physical therapy 흉곽물리요법
chest respiration 흉식호흡
chest strap 흉곽밴드
chest X-ray : CXR 흉부 X선
chewing problem 저작문제
Cheyne-stokes psychosis 체인스토크스
  정신병
Cheyne-stokes respiration 체인스토크스
  호흡
Chicano 치카노

chicken pox 수두
chief 주임 ; 치프
chief complaint 주소 ; 주요호소증상
chief home helper 주임 홈헬퍼
child 아이
child abuse 아동학대
Child Abuse Prevention Law 아동학대방지법
child advocacy 아동옹호
child allowance 아이수당
Child Allowance Law 아동수당법
child and family care leave benefit
육아 · 개호휴업급여
child and family care leave system
육아 · 개호휴업제도
child care 아동보호
child care allowance 육아수당
child care benefit 육아급여
child care leave 육아휴업
child care worker 아동보호 사회사업가
child centered education 아동중심적교육
child culture 아동문화
child custody
감독과 보호권 ; 아동후견 ; 자녀양육권
child day care center 보육소 ; 보육원
child disability allowance 장애아복지수당
child guidance center 아동상담소
child in need of protection 양호아동
child neglect
육아방기 ; 아동방임 ; 아동방치 ; 육아태만
child protective service 아동보호서비스
child protective services 아동학대보호서비스
child psychoanalysis 아동 정신분석
child psychology 아동심리학
child psychotherapy 아동 정신치료
child rearing in the family 기정양육
child sexual abuse 아동 성적학대
child snatching 아동유괴
child welfare 아동복지
child welfare agency 아동복지기관
child welfare facility 아동복지시설
Child Welfare Law 아동복지법
child welfare officer 아동복지사
child welfare plan 아동복지계획

child welfare residential facility 아동관
child welfare services 아동복지서비스
child with mental retardation 지적장애아
childbearing 출산
childbearing age 출산적령기
childbed fever 산욕감염증 ; 산욕열
childhood 아동기
childhood autism 소아자폐증
childhood disintegrative disorder
소아기 붕괴성 장애
childhood disorder 아동기 장애
Childhood schizophrenia 아동기 정신분열증
childless family 무자녀가족
Child-Rearing Promotion Division 육성환경과
children 아동 ; 아이
Children Welfare League 미국아동복지연맹
children with acquired severe disabilities
중도장애아
children with acquired severe mental
disabilities 중도정신장애아
children with acquired severe mental
retardation 중도지적장애아
children with acquired severe physical
disabilities 중도신체장애아
children with delayed mental
development 정신발달지체아
children with emotional disturbances
정서장애아
children with mental disabilities 정신장애아
children with severe physical and
mental disabilities 중증심신장애아
Children's Aid Society
아동구호협회 ; 아동원조협회
children's allowances 아동수당
Children's Bureau 아동과
Children's Charter 아동헌장
Children's Defense Fund 아동보호기금
children's hall 아동관 ; 아동원
children's home 양호시설
children's house 아동관
children's problems 아동문제
children's recreational facility 아동후생시설
children's shelter 아동긴급보호시설

chill 오한
chiropractic 척주지압요법 ; 카이로프랙틱
Chlordiazepoxide 클로르디아 제폭사이드
chlordiazepoxide-amitriptyline
클로르디아 제폭사이드 아미트리프틸린
chlorpromazine 클로르프로마진
chlorzoxazone 클로르족사존
cholesterol 콜레스테롤
cholinergic therapy 콜린성 요법
cholinesterase inhibitor 콜린에스터레이즈억제제
chondroitin sulfate 콘드로이친황산
chopped diet 페이스트식
Christian Lorenz Ernst Engel 엥겔
Christian social work 그리스트교 사회사업
chromaticity 색도
chromosomal abnormality 염색체이상
chromosome 염색체
chronic 만성
chronic arsenic poisoning 만성비소중독
chronic bronchitis 만성기관지염
chronic disease 만성질환
chronic fatigue syndrome 만성피로증후군
chronic illness 만성병
chronic inflammatory demyelinating
polyneuropathy 만성염증성 탈수초성 다발신경
병증 ; 만성염증성 탈수성 다발뉴로파치 ; 만성염증
성 탈수성 다발신경염
chronic kidney disease 만성신장병
chronic lymphoid leukemia : CLL
만성림프액성 백혈병
chronic myelocytic leukemia
만성골수성 백혈병
chronic obstructive airway disease
만성폐쇄성 기도질환
chronic obstructive pulmonary disease :
COPD 만성폐쇄성 폐질환
chronic pain 만성동통
chronic pyelonephritis 만성신우신염
chronic renal failure 만성신부전
chronic stage 만성기
chronic tension-type headache
만성긴장형 두통
chronic unemployment 만성적 실업

chronological age
달력나이 ; 실연령 ; 실역연령 ; 역연령
church for the senior citizen 경로당
Church World Service 기독교세계봉사회
cicatricial contracture 반흔구축
cimetidine 시메티딘
cinedefecography 배변영화촬영술
cineradiography 방사선동영상촬영
cineration and any other things
necessary for funerals 납골·기타 상제를
위해서 필요한 것
circadian rhythm 서커디안리듬 ; 활동일주기
circadian variation 일내변동
circle mat 원좌
circle of Willis 대뇌동맥륜 ; 윌리스 써클
circular causality 순환적 인과성
circumduction 순환운동 ; 원회전
circumduction gait 원회전 보행
cirrhosis 경화증
citizen 시민
citizen autonomy 주민자치
citizen leader 주민리더
citizen movement 시민운동
citizen participation 시민참가
citizen's advice bureau 시민생활상담소
citizenship 시민권
citizenship theory 시민권이론
city and wards 시군구
City Council of Social Welfare
시사회복지협의회
city designated by government ordinance
정령지정도시
city hospital 시립병원
Civic Code 민법전
civic consciousness 시민의식
Civil Law 민법 ; 시민법
civil liberties commission 인권옹호위원회
civil minimum 시빌미니멈
civil rights 공민권
civil rights movement 공민권운동
civil servants 공무원
civil society 시민사회
civilization 문명

claim form for the lump-sum withdrawal payments 탈퇴일시금재정청구서
claimant of medical benefits 의료급여수급자
claimant of national basic human needs benefits 국민기초생활수급자
claims for refund 반환청구
clarification 명확화
class 계급
class action suit 집단민원
classical conditioning 고전적 조건형성 ; 고전적 조건화
Classification Code of Technical Aids : CCTA 복지용구분류코드
classification of medical devices 의료기기분류
classified admission 분류수용
classless society 무계급사회
classroom for the aged 노인교실
claudication 파행
clay work 도예
clean area 청결구역
clean bench 크린벤치
clean intermittent catheterization : CIC 청결간헐도뇨법
clean room 클린룸 ; 청정실
clean surgery 청결수술
clean wound 청결창
clean zone 클린존
clean-contaminated operation 준청결수술
clean-contaminated wound 준청결창
cleaning 청소
cleaning equipment 청소용구
cleaning of the patient care unit 병동청소
cleanliness class 청정도 클래스
cleanness 청결
cleanup 청소
clearing technique 클리어링법
clerical personnel 사무직원
clidinium-chlordiazepoxide 클로디아 제폭시드 클리디늄
client 의뢰인 ; 클라이언트 ; 내담자 ; 이용자
client allocation cost 조치비용
client allocation system 조치제도

client evaluation 이용자평가
client participation 클라이언트 참가
client payment 이용자지불
client system 클라이언트 체계
client-centered therapy 의뢰인중심요법 ; 클라이언트 중심요법 ; 클라이언트 중심치료 ; 환자중심요법
client-oriented 클라이언트 본위
clinic 진료소
Clinical Dementia Rating Scale : CDR 임상적 치매평가척도
clinical diagnosis 임상적 진단
clinical engineering technologist 임상공학기사
clinical examination 임상검사
clinical intervention 임상적 개입
clinical interview 임상적 면접
clinical laboratory technologist and technician 임상검사기사
clinical microbiological technician 임상세균검사기사
clinical nutritional assessment 임상영양평가
clinical pathway 임상경로 ; 클리니컬 패스웨이
clinical pharmacist 임상약제사
clinical psychologist 임상심리사
clinical psychology 임상심리학
clinical radiologic technologist 진료방사선기사
clinical respiratory care and services 임상호흡치료서비스
clinical skill 클리니컬 스킬
clinical social work 임상사회사업
clinical trial 임상시험
clinical trial result 임상시험결과
clinician 임상의 ; 임상가
Clock Drawing Test : CDT 시계그리기 검사
clock position 클락포지션
clomipramine 클로미프라민
clonazepam 클로나제팜
clopidogrel 클로피도그렐
clorazepate 클로르제페이트 ; 클로르제프산
closed drainage 폐쇄식 드레이니지 ; 폐합유역
closed endotracheal suction tube

폐쇄식 기관내흡인튜브
closed family 폐쇄가족
closed kinetic chain 폐쇄운동사슬
closed panel 한정명부제
closed system 폐쇄 ; 폐쇄체계
closed system of urinary drainage
　system 폐쇄식 지속도뇨시스템
closed-ended questions 폐쇄형 질문
clostridium difficile 클로스트리듐 디피실리균
clothes 의복 ; 피복
clothing allowance 피복수당
clothing climate 의복기후
clothing irritation 의류장애
clothing life 의복생활
clothing pressure 의복압
clouding of consciousness 의식혼탁
clozapine 클로자핀
club activity 클럽활동
cluster headache 빈발두통 ; 군발두통
coalition 연합
coating drug 피복제
coating flux 피복재
cocaine 코카인
cochlear implant 인공내이
Cochrane review 코크런리뷰
cock-up wrist hand orthosis 수관절배굴장구
code of ethics 윤리강령
code of ethics for nurses 간호사의 윤리강령
codeine 코데인
co-dependency 공의존
coder 부호기
coding 부호화
coefficients for diagnosis procedure
　combination : DPC 진단군분류별 계수
coercion 강제
Cognex 코그넥스
cognition 인지
cognitive behavioral therapy 인지행동요법
cognitive development 인지발달
cognitive disorder 인지장애
cognitive dissonance 인지 불일치
cognitive experiential self theory
　인지적 · 경험적 자기이론

cognitive impairment 인식장애
cognitive map 인지도
cognitive models 인지모델
cognitive paradigm 인지패러다임
cognitive rehabilitation 인지재활
cognitive remediation 인지훈련 ; 인지요법
cognitive restructuring 인지적 재구성
cognitive status 인지상태
cognitive style 인지유형
cognitive theory 인지이론
cognitive therapy 인지요법 ; 인지치료
cohabitation 동거
cohabiting dyad 의제가정
cohort 코호트
cohort analysis 코호트분석
cohort isolation 집단격리
cohort sequential analysis 일군연계분석
cohort study 코호트연구
cohorting 코호팅
co-insurance 공동보험
cold compress 냉찜질
cold pack 냉습포
cold sterilant 냉각멸균제
cold sterilization 저온살균 ; 냉멸균
cold stress 한랭스트레스
cold therapy 한랭요법
cold zone 경계구역
collaboration 제휴 ; 합동
collaborative therapy 합동치료 ; 협동치료
collagen 콜라겐
collagen disease 교원병
collateral sources of data 방계적자료원
collection 징수
collection agency 채권회수회사
collection letter 독촉장
collection of costs 비용징수
collection of insurance premiums
　보험료징수
collection of wrongful gain 부정이득의 징수
collection to make up a difference 차액징수
collective bargaining 단체교섭 ; 단체협상
collective child care 집단보육
collective responsibility 집단책임

C

C

collective unconscious 집합적 무의식

colloquy 커러퀴

colon cancer 대장암

colon preparation 결장전처치

colonic lavage 결장세정

colonic mucosal biopsy 결장점막생검

colonic transit study 결장통과검사

colonization 군체형성 ; 칼러니제이션

colonization catheter 세균정착카테터

colonoscope 결장내시경

colonoscopy 결장내시경검사

colony 콜로니

colony forming unit : CFU 칼러니형성단위

color blindness 색맹

color constancy 색각항상

color matching function 등색함수

color opponent cell 반대색세포

color weakness 색약

colorectal cancer screening 대장암검진

colorectal polyps 대장폴립

colorimetry 측색

coma 혼수

comatose 혼수상태

comfort 안락

comfortable position 안락한 체위

comfortable urinary aid 안락뇨기

coming out 극복

commercial activity 상업적 활동

Commission for Promotion of Home Care 재가의료추진회의

commissioned child welfare volunteer 아동위원

commitment 위탁행위

Committee for the Advancement of Social Work with Group 집단사회사업발전위원회

Committee of Ways and Means 재무위원회

Committee on Dietary Allowances 영양소요량위원회

Committee on Mental Health 정신의료심사회

commode 포터블화장실

commode chair 이동의자

common stock price 일반주가지수

common work place for the aged 노인공동작업장

communicable disease 전염병

Communicable Diseases Prevention Law 전염병예방법

communication 의사소통 ; 커뮤니케이션

communication aid 의사전달장치 ; 커뮤니케이션 에이드

communication board 커뮤니케이션 보드

communication disorder 커뮤니케이션 장애

communication notes 커뮤니케이션 노트

communication theory 의사소통이론 ; 커뮤니케이션이론

communicative ability 커뮤니케이션 능력

communism 공산주의

community 공동사회 ; 커뮤니티 ; 지역사회 ; 지역

community action agency 커뮤니티활동기관

community advocacy services 지역복지권리옹호사업

community approach 지역사회접근방법

community bond 지연성

community care 지역보호 ; 지역사회보호 ; 지역케어 ; 커뮤니티케어

community care meeting 지역케어회의

community care network 지역케어네트워크 ; 커뮤니티케어네트워크

community care system 지역케어시스템 ; 커뮤니티케어시스템

community center 지역사회센터 ; 커뮤니티센타

community chest 공동모금 ; 커뮤니티체스트

Community Chest 공동모금회

community chest campaign 공동모금활동

community decision network 지역사회 의사결정 조직망

community development 지역개발 ; 지역사회개발

community diagnosis 지구진단 ; 지역사회진단

community difference 지역격차

community disorganization 지역사회해체

community forum 지역사회포럼

community general hospital 지역일반병원

community health 지역보건

Community Health Act 지역보건법

community health and medical care

지역보건의료
community health and medical care plan
지역보건의료계획
community hospital 지역병원 ; 커뮤니티병원
community living for the elderly
고령자거주공동체
community living support center for
people with mental disabilities 정신장애
인지역생활지원센터
community living support for people with
mental disabilities 정신장애인지역생활원호
community living support program for
people with mental disabilities
정신장애인지역생활지원사업
community medical care 지역의료
community medical care plan 지역의료계획
community mental health center
지역사회정신건강센터
community mental health service
지역정보보건활동
community nursing 지역간호
community organization : CO
지역활동조직 ; 커뮤니티조직 ; 지역사회조직 ;
지역사회조직 ; 커뮤니티오거니제이션
community organization activity 지역조직활동
community organization for welfare
복지커뮤니티
community organization model
지역사회조직의 실천모델
community organizer 지역사회조직가
community plan 지역계획
community planning 지역사회계획 ; 지역계획
Community Planning and Development
Office 지역사회조직 및 개발사무소
community psychiatry 지역사회정신의학
community rehabilitation 지역재활
community relations 지역사회관계
community residential care
지역거주시설서비스
community residential care services
지역거주시설케어서비스
community revitalization 커뮤니티재생
community self-help 지역사회자조

Community Service Block Gran program
지역사회서비스 정액교부금 프로그램
community social development
지역공동사회개발
community social work 커뮤니티소시얼워크
community study 지역조사
community support 지역지원
community support project 지역지원사업
community welfare 지역복지
community welfare activities for the
aged 지역노인복지활동
community welfare activities for the
disabled 지역장애인복지활동
community welfare activities for the
elderly 지역고령자복지활동
community welfare activity 지역복지활동
Community Welfare and Services
Division 지역복지과
community welfare center 지역복지센터
community welfare facility
지역복지시설 ; 지역복지기관
community welfare for the aged
지역노인복지
community welfare for the disabled
지역장애인복지
community welfare for the elderly
지역고령자복지
community welfare fund 지역복지기금
community welfare office 지역복지사업소
community welfare planning 지역복지계획
community welfare program 지역복지사업
community welfare provider 지역복지사업자
community welfare services 지역복지서비스
community welfare services coordinator
지역복지 코디네이터
community welfare work 지역복지원조기술
community work 지역사회사업 ; 커뮤니티워크
community worker
지역사회사업가 ; 커뮤니티워커
community-acquired infection 보조감염
community-based and outpatient
rehabilitation 지역밀착형통소재활
community-based care center

C

지역포괄지원센터
community-based day care services
지역밀착형통소개호
community-based rehabilitation
지역밀착형재활
community-based service 지역밀착서비스
commuting for care 당일치기 개호
commuting for rehabilitation 외래재활 ;
주간재활 ; 당일치기 재활
companion 동반자 ; 컴패니언
compartment syndrome
구획증후군 ; 컴파트먼트증후군
compassion fatigue 공감피로
compensation 보상 ; 대상
Compensation Division 보상과
compensation for leave 휴업보상
compensation for long-term health care
costs 요양비용보상
Compensation Operation Office
노재보험업무실
compensatory education 보상교육
compensatory movement 대상운동
competence 능력
competence 역량
competency-based practice 실무능력
competent evidence 적법 증거
competitive employment
경쟁적 고용 ; 일반고용
complaint 불평
complaints handling 불평처리
Complaints Resolution Committee
운영적정화위원회
complementarity 보충성
complementary and alternative medicine :
CAM 보완대체의료
complementary medicine 대체의학 ; 보완의료
complete blood count : CBC 총혈구수
complete survey 전수조사
complex 컴플렉스 ; 콤플렉스
compliance 법령준수 ; 컴플라이언스
Compliance and Narcotics Division
감시지도 · 마약대책과
compliance rate 준수율

complication 합병증
composite institute 복합시설
compound fracture 개방성 골절
comprehensive community care 지역포괄케어
comprehensive community care system
포괄적 지역케어시스템
comprehensive consultation 종합상담
comprehensive counseling center for the
aged 노인종합상담센터
Comprehensive Employment and Training
Act 종합고용 및 직업훈련법
Comprehensive Geriatric Assessment :
CGA 고령자종합평가
comprehensive health care 포괄적 의료
comprehensive hospital 종합병원
comprehensive medicine 포괄의료
comprehensive order 포괄적 지시
comprehensive planning 종합기획
comprehensive spending review
포괄적 지출리뷰
comprehensive surveillance 포괄적 감시
compressed recording 압축기록
compression fracture 압박골절
compression of morbidity 병적상태의 압축
compromise 타협
compromised host 약화된 숙주 ; 타협숙주 ;
역감염숙주
compromised patient
감염방어능저하환자 ; 면역부전환자 ; 역감염환자
compulsion 강박
compulsive manipulation of tools
도구의 강박적 사용
compulsive personality disorder
강박적 성격장애
compulsory admission 강제입소
compulsory collection 강제징수
compulsory education 의무교육
compulsory enrollment 강제가입
compulsory insurance 강제보험
compulsory measure 강제조치
computed tomography : CT
CT검사 ; 컴퓨터단층촬영
computerized axial tomography : CAT

컴퓨터체축단층촬영
conation 의욕
concentrations 전공학습
concentric contraction 구심성 수축
concentric contraction of the visual field
구심성 시야협착
concentric needle EMG 동심형 침전극
concept of disability 장애의 개념
concept of the disablement 장애의 개념
concepts of independence 자립의 개념
concern for the dying 죽음에 대한 관심
conciliation 화해
concrete operations stage 구체적조작기
concurrent review 동시성검토
concurrent treatment 병행치료
conditional release 가퇴원 ; 가출소
conditional voluntary admission 임의입원
conditioned inhibition 조건부 금지
conditioned reflex 조건반사
conditioned response 조건반응
conditioned stimulus 조건자극
conditioner 컨디셔너
conditioning 조건화
conduct disorder 행위장애 ; 행동장애
conduction aphasia 전도성 실어증
conductive deafness 전도성 ; 전도성 난청
cone 원추 ; 추체
confabulation 작화증 ; 지어낸 이야기
conference 컨퍼런스
Conference on Aging 고령화위원회
confidentiality 묵비 ; 비밀보지 ; 비밀보장
conflict 갈등
conflict between mothers-in-law and
  brides 고부갈등
conflict between mothers-in-law and
  daughters-in-law 고부갈등
conflict induction 갈등유발
conflict management 갈등관리
conflict resolution 갈등해결
conflict theories 갈등이론
conformity 동조
confrontation 대립
Confucianism 유교

congenital anomaly 선천이상
congenital hip dislocation 선천성 고관절탈구
congenital hypotonia 선천성 근긴장저하
congenital malformation 선천기형
congenital muscular dystrophy
  선천성 근이영양증
congenital nephrotic syndrome
  선천성 신증후군
congestion 울혈
congestive heart failure 울혈성 심부전
congregate home 집단주택
congregate housing center 집단주택센터
congregate housing for the aged 노인주택
congregate housing for the elderly
  노인집합주택
congregate meal program 집단급식서비스
Congressional Budget Office : CBO
  국회예산국
conjoint family therapy 합동가족치료
conjoint therapy 공동치료
conjugal family 부부가족
conjunctivitis 결막염
consanguinity family 혈연가족
conscience 양심
conscientization 의식화
conscious 의식의
conscious manipulation 의식적 조정
consciousness 의식
consciousness-raising 의식고양
consensual validation 합의적 입증
consensus 합의
consensus building 합의형성
consequence 결과
conservatism 보수주의
conservative and corporatist welfare
  state 보수주의적 · 조합주의적 복지국가
conservative treatment
  보존적 요법 ; 보존적 치료
consolidation of municipalities 시정촌 합병
conspiracy theory 음모이론
constant friction joint 정마찰 이음새
constipation 변비
constitution 헌법

Constitution of the World Health Organization 세계보건기구헌장
constraint 속박
construct validity 타당성 구축
constructional apraxia 구성실행 ; 구성실행증
constructive disability 구성장애
consultation 자문
consultation-liaison psychiatry 자문조정정신의학
Consultative Body Promoting Activation of Senior Citizen Churches 경로당활성화협의체
consumer 소비자
Consumer Affairs Agency 소비자청
consumer education 소비자교육
consumer price index : CPI 소비자물가지수
consumer protection 소비자보호
consumer protection office 소비자보호사무소
consumer rights group 소비자권리그룹
Consumer's League National 전국소비자연맹
consumer-directed care 소비자중시의 케어
consumerism 소비자주의 ; 소비자운동
consumers' cooperative association 소비생활협동조합
consumption tax 소비세
contact infection 접촉감염
contact method 접촉법
contact plate 접촉한천배지 ; 접촉배양지
contact precaution 접촉예방책
contact reflection 접촉반사
contact transmission 접촉전파
contaminated area 오염구역
contaminated operation 오염수술
contaminated wound 오염창 ; 오염상처
contamination 오염
contamination control 오염관리 ; 오염통제
contemporary capitalism 현대자본주의
contestable market 경쟁가능한 시장
contextual factor 배경인자
continence 자제
continence care product 배설관련용구
contingency 수반성 ; 우연성
contingency contracting 조건부 계약
contingent fee 성공보수

continuative passive motion : CPM 지속타동운동
continuing care 계속적 케어
continuing education 평생교육
continuity theory 계속이론
continuous ambulatory peritoneal dialysis : CAPD 연속적 휴대식복막투석
continuous cold therapy 계속적 냉각요법
continuous positive air pressure : CPAP 지속적 양압호흡
continuous quality improvement 계속적 개선활동
continuous reinforcement 지속적 강화
continuous traction 지속견인
continuum 연속체
contraception 피임법
contract 계약
contract document 계약서
contract system 계약제도
contracting 계약수립
contracture 구축
contracture prevention 구축예방
contrast bath 교대욕
contrast sensitivity 대비감도 ; 콘트라스트감도
contribution for basic pension 기초연금거출금
contribution in proportion to income 보수비례거출
contributory benefit 거출급여
contributory benefit system 거출급여제
contributory scheme 갹출제
control 통제
control and prevention 제어
control group 통제집단
control of hospital bed 병상규제
control variable 통제변수
controlled emotional involvement 통제된 정서적 관여
controlled substances 규제약물
convalescent carrier 회복기 보균자
convalescent home 회복기 시설
convalescent rehabilitation 회복기 재활
conventional 재래형
conventional care 인습적 장기요양

conventional medicine 인습적 의료
convergence theory 수렴이론
conversion 전환
conversion disorder 전환성 장애 ; 전환장애
conversion symptoms 전환증상
convulsion 경련
cooking 조리
cooking recipe 조리방법
cooking space 조리공간
cooking tool 조리기구
cooking utensil 요리도구
cooling off 쿨링오프
cooperation 연계
cooperation of commission volunteers
　민생위원의 협력
cooperation with physicians 의사와의 연계
cooperative association 협동조합
co-operative union : CO-OP 생활협동조합
cooptation 포섭
coordination 협조
coordination disorder 협조운동장애
coordinative function 조정적 기능
coordinator 조정자 ; 코디네이터
co-pay 공동부담
co-payment 면책정률부담 ; 일부부담금 ;
　자기부담금
coping 대처 ; 코핑
coping behavior 코핑행동 ; 대처행동
coping strategy 대처전략
copy of certificate 증명서의 사본
copy of proof 증명서의 사본
copycat medication 모방약품
copyright 저작권
core time 코어타임
corneal reflex 각막반사
Cornell medical index : CMI
　코넬건강지수 ; 코넬메디컬인덱스 ; 코넬의학조사표
Cornell Scale for Depression in
　Dementia : CSDD 코넬치매우울척도
coronary angiography 관상동맥조영
coronary angioplasty 동맥형성술
coronary artery 관상동맥
coronary artery bypass graft surgery :

CABG 관상동맥우회술
coronary artery disease : CAD
　관상동맥질환 ; 관동맥질환
coronary care unit : CCU
　관상동맥질환집중치료실
coronary heart disease : CHD
　관상동맥성 심질환
corporate pension 기업연금
Corporate Pension and National Pension
　Fund Division 기업연금국민연금기금과
corporate union 기업조합
corporate volunteer 기업자원봉사
corporate welfare 조합복지
corporation 법인
corporation tax 법인세
corporatism 조합주의
corporatist welfare state
　조합주의적 (보수주의적) 복지국가
corporatist welfare state
　코포라티스트 복지국가
corporatization 기업화
correctional education 감화교육
correctional facility 교정시설
correctional relief activities 감화사업
corrections 교정
corrective orthosis 교정용보조기
corrective shoes 교정화 ; 구두형 장구 ;
　정형구두
correlation 상관관계
correlation coefficient 상관계수
corset 코르셋
corticosteroids 코르티코스테로이드
cosmetic ← non-functional → upper limb
　prosthesis 장식용 의수
cosmetic hand 장식핸드
cost containment 비용억제
cost estimation 비용산정
cost of living 생활비용 ; 생계비
Cost of Living Adjustment : COLA
　생계비용조정
cost of social welfare 사회복지비용
cost of standard benefits 표준급여비용액
cost of standard payment 표준부담액

cost sharing 비용분담
cost-benefit 비용편익 ; 비용효익
cost-benefit analysis 비용편익분석
cost-effective 비용효율
costochondritis 골연골염 ; 늑연골염
cost-of-living adjustment : COLA 생활비용조정
cost-of-living index 생계비지수
costs for bringing up a child 양육비용
costs of Social Security benefit
　사회보장급여비
cost-sharing formula 비용부담방식
cost-volume contract 코스트계약
cottage system 소숙사제도
cotton 솜
cotton swab 면봉
cough 기침
cough variant asthma : CVA 기침형천식
coughing up of blood 각혈
Coumadin 쿠마딘
council 위원회 ; 협의회 ; 심의회
Council of Economic Advisers : CEA
　경제자문위원회
Council of Social Welfare 사회복지협의회
Council on Economic and Fiscal Policy
　경제재정자문회의
Council on International Programs : CIP
　국제사회사업가훈련프로그램협의회
counseling 카운셀링 ; 상담
counseling and support 상담원조
Counseling Center for Elderly Abuse
　노인학대상담센터
counseling center for women 부녀상담소
counselor 상담원 ; 카운셀러
counselor for people with mental
　retardation 지적장애인상담원
counselor for the aged 노인상담원
counselor for women 부녀복지상담원
countertransference 역전이
county hospital 군립병원
couple therapy 커플요법
course for development of care worker
　요양보호사양성강좌
court assistance 법정원조

court assistant 보좌인
court assistant for minors 미성년보좌인
coxarthrosis 변형성 고관절증
Cozaar 코자
crack 크랙
cradle 이피가 ; 크래들
crawling 네발 기어가기
C-reactive protein C반응성 단백
creaming 크리밍
cream-skimming 크림스키밍 ; 탈지행위 ;
　편의적 선취
creeping 네발 기어가기 이동 ; 팔꿈치 기어가기
cremation 매장 ; 화장
cretinism 크리티니즘
Creutzfeldt-Jakob disease : CJD 야콥병
crib death 영아사망
crime 범죄
crime by the elderly 노인범죄
crime prevention education 방범교육
crime prevention policy 방범대책
crime victimization 범죄피해
crimes against the elderly 노인에 대한 범죄
criminal code 형법전
criminal justice policy 형사 사법정책
criminal justice system 형사 사법제도
criminal law 형법
criminal psychology 범죄심리학
criminology 범죄회학
crippled 지체부자유
crippled child 지체부자유아
crippled people 지체장애인
crippled person 지체부자유자
crisis 공황 ; 위기
crisis bargaining 위기교섭
crisis care centers 위기보호센터
crisis hot line 위기긴급전화
crisis intervention 위기중재 ; 위기개입
crisis intervention approach 위기개입접근법
crisis management 위기관리
crisis sequence 연속위기
crisis theory 위기이론
criteria for bedridden 와병도 판정기준
critical 크리티컬 ; 결정적 ; 침습적

critical failure factor
주요실패요인 ; 중요실패요인 ; 핵심실패요인

critical pathway : CP 위기경로

critical success factor : CSF
중요성공요인 ; 주요성공요인 ; 핵심성공요소

Cronkhite-Canada syndrome : CCS
크론카이트-카나다 증후군

cross contamination 교차오염

cross infection 교차감염

cross tab 크로스집계

cross tabulation 크로스집계

crossed leg sitting 양반다리 앉기

cross-sectional area of muscle 근육단면적

cross-sectional research 횡단적 조사

cross-sectional survey 횡단면조사

cross-subsidization 내부상호보조

cross-tabulation 교차표

crouch posture 구부린 자세

crowding-out theory
구축현상 ; 크라우딩아웃이론

crude birth rate 조출생률 ; 보통출생율

crude mortality rate 조사망률

crutch 목발 ; 크러치

crutch gait 목발보행

cryotherapy 냉동요법

crypt hook 크리프트 후크

crystal arthropathy 결정관절증 ; 유사관절염

crystal induced arthritis 결정유발성 관절염

crystal lens 수정체

crystallized ability 결정성 능력

crystallized intelligence 결정성 지능

cuff 반월

culdocentesis 더글라스와천자 ; 천자술

cult 종파 (예식)

cultural anthropology 문화인류학

cultural assimilation 문화적 동화

cultural barrier 문화적 장벽

cultural deprivation 문화적 박탈

Cultural Festival for the Aged 노인문화제

cultural lag 문화지체

cultural pattern 문화양식

cultural relativism 문화적 상대주의

culture of poverty 빈곤문화

culture shock 문화충격

cumulative effect 축적효과

cumulative incidence rate 누적이환율

curandero 민간요법의사 ; 주술치료사

curator 보좌인

curator of minor 미성년보좌인

cure 치료 ; 큐어

curriculum hours 이수시간

curriculum policy statement
교과과정정책설명서

Cushing's syndrome 쿠싱증후군

cushion 쿠션

custodial care 보호형 케어 ; 보조적 케어 ; 요호

custodial care facility
개호형 양로원 ; 보호형 개호시설

custodial care facility for crippled
children 지체부자유아요호시설

custodial care facility for the people
with mental disabilities 정신장애인요호시설

custodial care facility for the physically
disabled 신체장애인요호시설

custody 감독과 보호 ; 보호권

custody of children 아동양육보호권

Customary, Prevailing and Reasonable :
CPR 상환액결정방식

customer 고객

customer satisfaction : CS 고객만족

Customer Service Promotion Division
서비스추진과

cutaneous pruritus 피부소양감

cyanamide 시안아미드

cyanosis 청색증 ; 치아노제

cyber government 전자정부

cybernetics 인공두뇌학

cyclical unemployment 주기적 실업

cyclobenzaprine 사이클로벤자프린

cyclosporine 사이클로스포린

cyclothymic disorder 기분순환성장애

Cymbalta 심발타

cystocele 방광류 ; 방광헤르니아

cystometrography 방광내압측정

cystometry 방광내압측정

cystoscopy 방광경검사

D

daily life guidance counselor 생활지도원

daily living training facility for people
with mental disabilities 정신장애인
생활훈련시설

daily money management : DMM
일상적 금전관리

daily program 일안

daily treatment 일상적 처우

daily-needs assistance 생활부조

damper 댐퍼

danger to others : DTO 타해행위

danger to self or others 자상타해

dark adaptation 암순응

dark/light adaptation 암명순응

Darvon 다르본

database 데이터베이스

date of birth 생년월일

David Ricardo 리카드

David Wechsler 웩슬러

day care 데이케어 ; 탁아보호 ; 주간보호(보육)

day care center 데이케어센터 ; 주간보호시설 ;
주간보호센터

Day Care Division 보육과

day care facilities for the aged 노인주간보
호시설

day care office 주간보호사업소

day care project 주간보호사업

day care services 통소개호

day care services center 통소개호시설

day care services facility for crippled
children 지체부자유아통원시설

day care services for people with
dementia 치매대응형주간보호 ; 인지증대응형통

소개호

day care services for people with
mental retardation 지적장애인주간보호서비스

day care services for the physically disabled 신체장애인주간보호서비스

day care services program for children
with severe physical and mental
disabilities 중증심신장애아통원사업

day care services program for people
with mental retardation 지적장애인주간보
호서비스사업

day care services program for people
with severe physical and mental
disabilities 중증심신장애인통원사업

day home 데이홈

day hospital 주간병동 ; 낮병원 ; 데이호스피탈

day labor 일고

day labor employee 날품팔이 노동자

day laborer 일용근로자 ; 날품팔이 노동자

Day Laborers Health Insurance
날품팔이 노동자건강보험

day nursery policy 보육정책

day nursery system 보육제도

day services 데이서비스

day services center 데이서비스센터

day services center for people with
mental retardation 지적장애인주간보호서비스
센터

day services center for the physically
disabled 신체장애인주간보호서비스센터

day services facility for the auditory loss
infants 난청유아통원시설

day/night care

데이 · 나이트서비스 ; 주 · 야간보호
daylighting 채광
de jure 합법성
dead on arrival : DOA
내원시 심장정지 ; 도착즉시사망 ; 도착직후사망
deaf 귀머거리 ; 농자
deaf elderly 농고령자 ; 농노인
deaf-blind and mute 맹농아인
deaf-blind and mute child 맹농아아
deaf-blind and mute infant 맹농아유아
deaf-blind child 맹농아
deaf-blind infant 맹농유아
deaf-blind person 맹농인
deaf-mute 농아자
deaf-mute child 농아아 ; 농아유아
deaf-mute elderly 농아고령자 ; 농아노인;
귀머거리 노인
deafness 난청 ; 농 ; 귀먹음 ; 귀머거리
death 사망 ; 죽음
death certificate 사망진단서
death rate 사망율
death tax 상속세
death with dignity 존엄사
Death with Dignity Act 존엄사법
debate 토론
debate forum 토론회
debt collector 채권회수회사 ; 회수대행업자
deceased 고인 ; 사망자 ; 사자
December divorce 황혼이혼
decentralization 분권화 ; 지방분권화 ; 지방분권
decertification 자격 제거
decibel : dB 데시벨
decimal distribution ratio 십분위분배율
decimal reduction time D치
decimal reduction value D치
decision for the placement 배치결정
decision theory 의사결정이론
decision-making 의사결정
decision-making meeting 판정회의
Declaration of Alma-Ata 알마아타선언
Declaration of Helsinki 헬싱키선언
Declaration of the Rights of the Child
아동권리선언

Declaration on the Rights of Disabled
Persons 장애인의 권리선언
Declaration on the Rights of People with
Mental Retardation 지적장애인의 권리선언
decompression 감압 ; 제압
deconditioning prevention 약화예방
decongestant 충혈제거제
decontaminate hands 손가락의 오염제거
decontamination procedure 오염제거처리
decriminalization 기소대상면제
decubitus 욕창
decubitus ulcer 욕창 ; 압박궤양
deductible 정액자기부담 ; 면책정액부담
deduction 공제
deduction for elderly dependents
노인부양공제
deduction for employment 근로공제
deduction for medical care 의료공제
deduction for medical expenses 의료비공제
deduction for National Health Insurance
premiums 국민건강보험료감면
deduction for National Pension
premiums 국민연금보험료감면
deduction for the aged 노년자공제
deduction of long-term care insurance
premiums 장기요양보험료감면제도 ;
개호보험료감면제도
deductive method 연역법
deductive reasoning 연역적 추론
deemed status 간주지정
deemed status accreditation 간주지정인정
deep brain stimulation 심부뇌자극술
deep sensation 심부감각
deep vein thrombosis 심부정맥혈전증
defamation 명예훼손
default judgment 궐석재판
defecation 배변
defecation disorder 배변장애
defecography 배변조영검사
defecometry 배변내압검사
defense 방어 ; 방위
defense mechanism 방어기제
defensiveness 방어행동

deficit 적자
defined contribution 확정거출연금
deflation 디플레이션(통화수축)
deformity 변형
degeneration 변성
degenerative disease 변성질환
deglutition pneumonia 연하성 폐렴
degree of disability 장애등급구분
degree of freedom of motion 동작의 자유도
degree requirements for social work
사회복지전공과목
dehydration 탈수증
dehydroepiandrosterone : DHEA 프라스테론
deinstitutionalization 탈시설화 ; 탈시설
deliberate self-harm
계획적 자상행위 ; 고의적 자상행위
delinquency 비행
delinquent gang 비행집단
delinquent subculture 비행하위문화
delinquent tax collection organization
세금체납정리기구
delirium 섬망
Delirium Rating Scale
섬망평가검사 ; 섬망평가척도
delirium tremens : DTS 섬망증 ; 진전섬망
deliver 배달
delivered meals 식사택배서비스
delivery program of domestic helpers
가정봉사원파견사업
delusion 망상
delusion of persecution 피해망상
delusional disorder 망상성 장애
Demand and Supply Adjustment Division
수급조정사업과
demands 수요 ; 요구 ; 디맨즈
dementia 치매 ; 인지증
Dementia Care Information Network
인지증개호정보네트워크
Dementia Care Research and Training
Center 인지증개호연구・연수센터
Dementia Rating Scale
치매평가검사 ; 치매평가척도
dementia special care unit

인지증케어전문병동
Demerol 데메롤
democracy 민주주의
democratic socialism 민주사회주의
democratic society 민주주의사회
democratization 민주화
demogrant 데모그란트
demogrants 일반급부
demographic dependency ratio
인구학문적 종속인구비율
demographic statistics 인구통계
demographic transition theory 인구전환론
demography 인구학 ; 인구통계학
demonology 악마연구 ; 악마학
demonstrative 과시행위
demyelinating disease 탈수초성 질환
demyelination 탈수 ; 탈수초
denarian 10대
denervation 신경제거 ; 탈신경
denial 거부 ; 부인
denial of illness 질병부인
dental disease 치과질환
dental floss 치실 ; 덴탈프로스
Dental Health Division 치과보건과
dental hygienist 치과위생사
Dental Hygienists Law 치과위생사법
Dental Practitioners Law 치과의사법
dentist 치과의사
dentistry 치과
denture 틀니 ; 의치
Denver Developmental Screening Test :
DDST 덴버발달선별검사
Department of Food Safety 식품안전부
Department of Health and Welfare for
Persons with Disabilities 장애보건복지부
department public services agreement
부처별 공공서비스협약
Departmental Expenditure Limit : DEL
부처별 세출한도액
dependency allowance 부양수당
Dependency and Indemnity
Compensation : DIC 유족보상금
dependency and indemnity compensation

군인유족수당
dependency ratio 종속인구지수
dependent 피부양자
Dependent Care Service Coverage
  Payment Application Form 가족요양비지급
  신청서
dependent health care coverage 가족요양비
dependent personality disorder
  의존성 성격장애
dependent population 종속인구
dependent service business
  가정봉사원파견사업
dependent variable 종속변수
depersonalization disorder 이인장애 ; 이인증
depopulation 과소 ; 소자녀화 ; 저출산화
depopulation and aging 저출산고령화
depreciation 감가상각
Deprenyl 데프레닐
depression 우울증 ; 억울
depression economic 경제불황
depression type 억울형
depressive neurosis 우울신경증
depressive reaction 우울한 반응
depressive state 우울상태
depressurized room 감압실
deprivation 박탈
deregulation 규제완화
dermatologist 피부과 전문의 ; 피부과의사
dermatology 피부과학
dermatomyositis 피부근육염증
dermatophyte 피부사상균 ; 피부진균
dermatophytosis 백선 ; 피부사상균증
desegregation 차별대우폐지
desensitization 탈감각화
desertion 유기
designated activity 특정활동
designated cancer hospital 암진료 연계거점병원
designated donation 지정기부금
designated emergency hospital 구급지정병원
designated employment 직종지정
designated home-based care
  management provider 지정주택개호지원사업자
designated home-based care services

지정주택서비스
designated hospital 지정병
designated medical care agency 지정의료기관
designated psychiatrist 정신보건지정의
designated public information center
  지정정보공표센터
designation 지정
designation of curator of minor
  미성년보좌인의 지정
designation of guardian 후견인의 지정
designation of guardian of minor
  미성년후견인의 지정
designation system for medical providers
  지정의제도
designation system for teeth and areas
  of the oral cavity 치아 및 구강부위 호흡시스템
desipramine 데시프라민
detention and classification 관호조치
detergent 세제
detergent allergy 세제알레르기
determinism 결정론
detoxification 해독
detrusor-sphincter dyssynergia : DSD
  배뇨근괄약협동부전 ; 실조
developed country 선진국
developing country 발전도상국 ; 개발도상국
development 발달
development of the aged 노년개발
development protection 발달보장
developmental age 발달연령
developmental delay 발달지연
Developmental Disabilities Assistance Act
  발달장애인지원법
developmental psychopathology
  발달정신병리학
developmental quotient : DQ 발달지수
developmental social welfare 개발적사회복지
developmental stages 발달단계
developmental tasks 발달과제
developmental test 발달검사
developmental theory 발달이론
deviance 일탈
deviant behavior 일탈행동

D

deviate sexual intercourse 비정상적 성관계
device-related infection 기구관련감염
dexterity 민첩 ; 손재주
dextromethorphan 덱스트로메토르판
diabetes food exchange list 당뇨병식품교환표
diabetes medication 당뇨병약
diabetes mellitus : DM 당뇨병
diabetic coma 당뇨병성 혼수
diabetic ketoacidosis : DKA 당뇨병성 케톤산증
diabetic nephropathy 당뇨병성 신부전
diabetic neuropathy 당뇨병성 신경증
diabetic retinopathy 당뇨병성 망막증
diagnosis 진단
diagnosis casework 진단주의 케이스워크
diagnosis of dementia 치매진단
diagnosis procedure combination : DPC
진단군분류
diagnosis-related groups prospective
payment system : DRG-PPS 진단군별정액
지불방식 ; 진단군별포괄지불제 ; 질병군별포괄수가제
Diagnostic and Statistical Manual of
Mental Disorders 정신장애 진단 통계편람
Diagnostic and Statistical Manual of
Mental Disorders : DSM 정신장애진단 및
통계편람
diagnostic category 진단범주
diagnostic criteria for clinical diagnosis
of brain death 뇌사판정기준
diagnostic imaging 화상진단
diagnostic related groups 진단관련집단
diagnostic school in social work
진단주의 사회사업학파
dialysis 투석
dialysis therapy 투석요법
diaper 기저귀
diaper change 기저귀 교환
diaper cover 기저귀 커버
diaper removal 기저귀 폐기 ; 기저귀 제거
diaphragm 횡격막
diarrhea 설사
diary 일지
diastolic pressure 확장기혈압
diathermy 고주파요법 ; 고주파투열요법 ;

디아테르미
diazepam 디아제팜
dichromatic reflection model 2색형 반사모델
didactic analysis 교육분석
dietary fiber 식물섬유
dietary habit 식습관
dietary life 식생활
dietary prescription 영양처방
dietary restriction 식사제한
dietary supplement 영양보조식품
diethylstilbestrol : DES 디에틸스틸베스트롤
dietitian 영양사
Dietitian Law 영양사법
differential culture 분리배양
differential response 차별적 반응
differentiated welfare state 분화복지국가
differentiation 분화
difficult delivery 이상출산
difficult urination 배뇨곤란
diffuse axonal injury : DAI 미만성 축색손상
diffusion theory 확산이론
digestion 소화
digestion and absorption 소화흡수
digestive disease 소화기질환
digital anorectal examination 항문직장수지검사
digital examination 수지검사
digital rectal examination 직장수지검사
digital subtraction angiography
디지털혈관조영
dignity 존엄
dignity of the disabled 장애인의 존엄
dignity of the elderly
고령자의 존엄 ; 노인의 존엄
digoxin 디곡신
dilemma 딜레마
diltiazem 딜티아젬
diminished capacity 심신모약
diminished responsibility 한정책임능력
diphtheria 디프테리아
diplegia 양측마비
direct care profession 개호전문
direct care professional 개호전문 개호전문직
direct care section 개호부문

direct care staff 장기요양담당자 ; 장기요양종
사자 ; 장기요양직원 ; 개호담당자 ; 개호종사자 ;
개호직원
direct contact infection 직접접촉감염
direct contact transmission 직접접촉감염
direct contract model 직접계약모델
direct cost 직접비용
direct influence 직접영향
direct language 직접언어
direct light reflex 직접대광반사 ; 직접빛반사
direct practice 직접실천
direct questions 직접질문
direct social work practice 직접원조기술
direct tax 직접세
direct treatment 직접처우 ; 직접치료
direct treatment staff 직접처우직원
directive therapy 지시적 치료
director 임원
director of nursing 간호사장
dirty area 불결구역
dirty behavior 불결행위
dirty utility room 오물처리실
dirty wound 더러운 상처 ; 불결창
dirty/infected operation 불결·감염수술
disability 능력저하 ; 무능력 ; 장애
disability allowance 장애인수당
disability benefit 장애급여
disability care management
신체장애인개호지원 ; 장애인케어매니지먼트
disability care management 장애인개호지원
disability certification 장애인정
disability compensation 장애보상급부
disability freeze 장애동결
disability insurance : DI 장애보험
disability levels 장애등급 ; 장애정도구분
disability living allowance
장애인생활수당 ; 장애인생활지원수당
disability movement 장애인운동
disability pension 장애연금
disability rights movement 장애인권리운동
disability standards for education
교육에 있어서의 장애기준
disability study 장애학

disability welfare allowance
장애복지수당 ; 장애인복지수당
disability welfare pension
장애복지연금 ; 장애인복지연금
disabled 장애인
disabled abuse 장애인학대
disabled child 장애아
disabled elderly 장애고령자 ; 장애노인
disabled infant 장애유아
disabled parking permit 장애인주차허가증
Disabled Peoples' International KOREA :
DPI 한국장애인연맹
disabled sports 장애인스포츠
disarmament 군비축소
disarticulation 탈구 ; 관절이단
disaster 재난
disaster benefit 재해급여
disaster prevention 방재 ; 재해예방
disaster science 재해과학
disaster syndrome 재해증후군
discharge 퇴원
discharge cleaning 퇴원시 청소
discharge from the facility 퇴소
discharge from the hospital 병원퇴원
discharge information 퇴소시 정보
discharge management 퇴원조정
discharge planning 퇴원계획
disciplinary punishment 징계
discoloration 변색
discomfort index 불쾌지수
Discomfort Scale for Dementia of the
Alzheimer's Type : DS-DAT 알츠하이머형치
매 불쾌평가척도 ; 알츠하이머형인지증 불쾌평가척도
discount price 할인요금
discretionary funds 임의성 자금
discrimination 차별
discriminative stimulus 변별자극
disease 병 ; 질환
disease management : DM
질병관리 ; 질환관리 ; 병관리
disease-modifying antirheumatic drug :
DMARD 질환수식성 항류마티스약제
diseases of adult people 성인병

D

diseases of the elderly 노인병
disengaged family 분리가족
disengagement 유리 ; 이탈
disengagement theory 이탈이론
disguised unemployment 위장실업
disinfectant 소독제
disinfection 소독
disinhibition 탈억제
disorder of environmental origin
환경유래질환
disorder of executive function 수행기능장애
disorders of the heart function 심장기능장애
disorders of the kidney function
신장기능장애
disorders of the small intestinal function
소장기능장애
disorientation
견당식장애 ; 방향감각상실 ; 지남력장애 ; 혼미
dispatch worker 파견노동자
dispensary 의무실
disperser 미생물 살포자 ; 미생물 비산자
displaced homemaker 기능상실주부
displacement 전치
disposable 디스포저블 ; 일회용
disposable income 가처분소득
disposal 처리 ; 폐기
disposal of garbage and swill
음식물쓰레기처리
disruptive tactics 전략적 파괴행동
disseminated intravascular coagulation
파종성 혈관내응고증
dissemination of information 정보제공
dissociated sensory disturbance
해리성 감각장애 ; 해리성 지각장애
dissociative disorder 해리성 장애 ; 분열장애
dissociative identity disorder 해리동일성 장애
distal 원위 ; 말초
distal end 원위단 ; 말단부
distal latency 원위잠복기
distal radius fracture 요골원위단 골절
distance education 원격교육
distance learning 원격학습
distracter role 전환자 역할

distractibility 전도성
distribution 분포
distribution quota 배급할당
district court 지방재판소
disturbance of balance 평형기능장애
disturbance of consciousness 의식장애
disturbance of thermoregulation
체온조절장애
disturbance of urinary storage 축뇨이상
disulfiram 디설피람
disuse 폐용
disuse atrophy 폐용위축
disuse bone atrophy 폐용성 골위축
disuse muscle atrophy 폐용성 근위축
disuse syndrome 폐용증후군
diuretic 이뇨제
diversional occupational therapy
심리재활을 위한 작업치료
diversity 다양성
diversity and inclusion 다양성과 포괄성
diverticular disease 게실질환
Division of the Heath for the Elderly
노인보건과
divisions of labor 분업
divorce 이혼
divorce certificate 이혼증명서
divorce mediation 이혼중재
divorce therapy 이혼치료
divorced person 이혼자
dizziness 현기증
DNR〈 Do Not Resuscitate 〉 심폐소생술거부
Do Not Resuscitate : DNR 소생조치거부
doctor 의사
doctor appointment 진료예약
Doctor of Philosophy (Ph.D.) in Social
Work 소시얼워크박사호
Doctor of Philosophy degree 박사호
doctor referral services 의사소개서비스
doctor's home visit 왕진
doctor's note 주치의 의견서
doctor's office visit 통원
doctoral programs 박사과정
doctorate degree 박사호

do-gooder 공상적 사회개량가
dole 실업수당
domestic help 가정봉사
domestic helper 가사도움
domestic labor 가사노동
domestic violence : DV
가정내폭력 ; 더메스틱 바이오런스
domiciliary care 재가복지
dominant inheritance 우성유전
donation 기부 ; 기부재산
donation practice 기부행위
donepezil 도네페질
donor 기증자 ; 도너
donor card 증명카드
door 도어
dopamine 도파민
dopamine receptor blockade
도파민 수용체 차단
dopamine receptor D2 blockade
D2 도파민수용체길항제
Doral 도랄
dormitory matron 요모
dormitory system 대사제
dorsiflexion 배굴
dosage modification 투약량 조정
double bag technique 더블백 손기술
double bind 이중구속 (이중맹검)
double bind theory 이중구속이론
double bucket system 이중양동이법
double contrast roentgenography
이중방사선조영법
double stance phase 동시입각기
double support 두발지지
double support period 두발지지기
doughnut phenomenon 도너츠현상
Down Syndrome 다운증후군
downers 진정제
downsize 경량화
drain 드레인 ; 배수관
draining board (sunoko) 목욕탕 발판 ; 스노코
drama therapy 드라마테라피
drape 복포 ; 드레이프
drastic medicine 극약

D

dream analysis 꿈 분석
dressing 옷갈아입기 ; 드레싱 ; 갱의
dressing activity 갱의동작
dressing change 붕대교환
dressing room 탈의실 ; 탈의장
dressing skill 드레싱스킬 ; 착의스킬
drinking giving-up organization 절주회
drip infusion cholecystography
점적주입담도조영술
drive 충동
drive-through delivery 드라이브스루 출산
drooling 유연
drooling 침흘리기
droplet infection 비말감염
droplet nuclei 비말핵
droplet precaution 비말예방책
droplet transmission 비말전파
dropout 낙오자 ; 드롭아웃
drowsiness 경면
drug 약
drug abuse 약물남용
drug abuse detection 약물남용 적발
drug addiction 약물중독
drug allergy 약물알레르기
drug dependence 약물의존
drug free 약물미사용
drug habituation 약물탐닉
drug price controls 약값규제
drug rash 약물발진 ; 약진
drug tariff standards 약가기준
drug tolerance 약물내성
drug-induced acute pancreatitis
약물유발성 급성췌장염
drug-induced chronic pancreatitis
약물유발성 만성췌장염
drug-induced hepatitis 약물유발성 간염
drug-induced liver disease 약물유발성 간질환
drug-induced lupus 약물유발성 루푸스
drug-induced lupus erythematosus
약물유발성 홍반성낭창
drug-induced osteoporosis
약물유발성 골다공증
drug-induced pancreatitis 약물유발성 췌장염

drug-induced Parkinsonism
약물유발성 파킨슨증
drug-induced psychosis
약제기인성 정신병 ; 약물유발성 정신병
drug-induced Schizophrenia
약물유발성 정신분열증 ; 약물유발성 통합실조증
drug-induced suffering 약해
drug-induced thrombocytopenia
약제기인성 혈소판감소증
drug-induced thrombocytopenic purpura
약물유발성 혈소판감소성 자반병
drunkenness 만취 ; 명정 ; 취한 상태
dry cleaning 드라이크리닝 ; 연식세탁 ;
건식세탁
dry heat 건열
dry heat sterilization 건열멸균
dry mouth 드라이마우스 ; 구갈 ; 구강건조증
dry shampoo 드라이샴푸
dry wiping 마른 걸레질
dual career family 맞벌이가족
dual economy 이중경제
dual-energy X-ray 이중에너지 방사선
dual-energy X-ray absorptiometry : DEXA
이중에너지 방사선흡수법
Duchenne muscular dystrophy
듀센느형 근이영양증
dull-normal 정상둔자
duloxetine 둘록세틴
dumbbell 덤벨 ; 아령
dumping syndrome 덤핑증후군
Dupuytren's contracture 듀피트렌구축
durable medical equipment : DME

내구의료기기
dutasteride 두타스테리드
duty of confidentiality 묵비의무
D-value D치
dwelling welfare facilities for the elderly
노인주거복지시설
dyad 한 쌍 (한 단위로서)
dying 임종
dynamic 역동성
dynamic computed tomography
동적 컴퓨터단층촬영
dynamic diagnosis 역동적 진단
dynamic stability 동적 안정성
dysarthria 구음장애
dysarthria training 구음훈련
dysautonomia 자율신경장애 ; 자율신경실조
dyschezia 배변장애
dysesthesia 이상지각
dysexecutive syndrome
수행기능장애증후군 ; 집행기능장애증후군
dysfunction 기능장애 ; 역기능
dysgraphia 실서증
dyskinesia 이상운동증 ; 운동장애
dyslipidemia 이상지질혈증 ; 지방질이상증
dyspareunia 성교동통 ; 성교동통증 ; 성교통
dysphagia 연하장애
dysphagia of swallowing function
연하기능장애
dysplasia 이형성증
dyspnea 호흡곤란
dysthymic disorder 비관우울증
dystonia 근육긴장이상 ; 디스토니아

D

E

E. O. Seguin 세간
ear, nose and throat evaluation
이비인후검사
ear, nose and throat specialist
이비인후전문의
early adolescence 소년전기
early ambulation 조기이상
early detection 조기발견
early intervention 조기개입
Early Speech Perception Test
초기 단음절 말지각검사
early-onset Alzheimer's disease
조기발생 알츠하이머병
earmarked revenue 특정재원
earmarked taxes 목적세
earned income tax credit : EITC
근로소득세액공제
earnings test 소득조사
Easter Seal Society 이스터 실 협회
eastern philosophies 동양철학
easy fatigability 역피로성
eating 식사동작
eating assistance 식사보조 ; 식사원조 ;
식사케어
eating disorder
섭식장애 ; 식이장애 ; 식행동 이상
eating habit 식습관
eating tool 식사용구
Eaton-Lambert syndrome 이튼람베르트 증후군
eccentric contraction 원심성 수축
eccrine gland 에크린샘 ; 외분비샘
echo boomer 에코부머
echo housing 에코주택

echocardiogram 심초음파도 ; 초음파심장진단도
echocardiography 심초음파 ; 초음파심장진단 ;
심에코
eclectic 절충적
eco map 에코맵 ; 이코맵
ecological approach 생태학적 접근법
ecological perspective 생태학적 관점
ecological psychology 생태학적 심리학
ecology 생태학
ecology movement 에콜로지운동 ; 환경운동
ecomap 생태도
econometrics 계량경제학
Economic & Social Council 경제사회이사회
Economic Affairs Division 경제과
economic development 경제발전
economic education 경제교육
economic growth 경제성장
economic growth rate 경제성장률
economic liberalism 경제적자유주의
economic of scale 규모의경제
Economic Opportunity Act 경제기회법
Economic Partnership Agreement : EPA
경제연계협정
economic planning 경제계획
economic policy 경제정책
economic predation 경제적 약탈
economic system 경제체제
ecosystem 생태계
ectopic kidney 이소신
ectopic pregnancy 자궁외임신
ectopic rhythm 이소성 리듬
ectopic sebaceous gland 이소성 피지선
ectopic ureter 이소성 요관

E

ectopic ureterocele 이소성 요관류
eczema 습진
edema 부종
Eden Alternative 에덴대안
edentulism 무치증
editing 편집
educable 교육 가능한
education 교육
Education for All Handicapped Children
　Act 장애아동교육법
education for the aged 노인교육
education for the blind 맹인교육
education for the disabled 장애인교육
education for the disabled children
　장애아교육
education of supporting nursing for the
　home visiting nurses 방문간호보조사교육
educational aid 교육부조
educational benefit 교육급여
educational class for the aged 노인학급
educational class for the elderly 고령자학급
educational expenses 교육비
educational home visit 방문지도
educational home visiting 방문교육
educational maintenance allowance
　교육보조수당
educational maintenance allowance
　교육유지수당
educational meeting 교육미팅
educational psychology 교육심리학
educational rehabilitation 교육적 재활
educator role 교육자역할
Edward Denison 데니슨
Edward T. Devine 디바인
effective demand 유효수요
effective width of doorway 출입구유효폭
Effexor 이펙사
efficacy 효과
effort angina 노력협심증
effort respiration 노력호흡
ego 자아 ; 에고
ego analysis 자아분석
ego defense 자기방어

ego functioning 자아기능
ego ideal 이상적 자아
ego identity 자아동일성
ego integration 자아통합
ego psychology 자아심리학
ego strengths 자아력
egocentrism 자기중심주의
ego-oriented social work 자아지향적 사회사업
EKG〈 electrocardiogram 〉 이케이지
elasticity 탄력성
Elberfeld System 엘버펠드제도
elbow bathing 주관절욕 ; 팔꿈치 욕
elbow disarticulation prosthesis 주관절의지
elbow fracture 주관절골절
Eldepryl 엘데프릴
elder abuse 노인학대
elder abuse and neglect 고령자학대·니글렉트
Elder Abuse Prevention Act 고령자학대방지법
elder abuse prevention activity
　고령자학대방지활동
elder care housing 고령자케어제공주택 ;
　노인수발제공주택 ; 노인케어제공주택 ; 케어제공
　고령자주택
elder neglect 고령자개호포기 ; 고령자무시
elder to elder care 노노개호
elderly 고령자
elderly abuse 노인학대 ; 고령자학대
elderly aged 75 and above 후기고령자
elderly aged between 65 and 74 전기고령자
elderly care 고령자개호 ; 노인개호
elderly care management
　고령자개호지원 ; 노인개호지원
elderly care management services
　고령자개호지원서비스
elderly care management services
　agency 고령자개호지원서비스기관
elderly care management services
　provider 고령자개호지원서비스사업자
elderly care management services office
　고령자개호지원서비스사업소
elderly care provided by elderly 노노개호
elderly health 노인보건
elderly health services 노인보건서비스

elderly home care management
고령자재가개호지원 ; 노인재가개호지원
elderly hospital 노인전문병원
elderly household 고령자세대
elderly housing 고령자주택
elderly idle work force 노인유휴노동력
elderly legal assistance program
고령자법률지원프로그램
elderly market 실버산업
Elderly Market Development & Promotion
Committee 실버산업육성추진위원회
elderly mistreatment 고령자학대
elderly person with mental retardation
지적장애고령자
elderly personnel utilization policy
노인인력활용대책
elderly population 고령자인구 ; 노년인구
elderly remarriage 노인재혼
elderly volunteers 노인자원봉사
elderly welfare system 노인복지제도
elderly with dementia 치매성 고령자 ;
치매성 노인 ; 인지증노인
elderly with mental disabilities
정신장애고령자 ; 정신장애노인
elderly with mental retardation
지적장애노인
elderly-onset rheumatoid arthritis : EORA
고령발생 류마티스관절염
elective abortion 인공임신중절
elective cardiac catheterization
대기적 심장카테터검사
Electra complex 엘렉트라 콤플렉스
electric aspirator 전동흡인기
electric bed 전동침대
electric Braille writer 전동점자타자기 ;
전동브라이유식 점자타이프라이터 ; 전동점자타이
프라이터
electric records 전자기록
electric toothbrush 전동칫솔
electric upper limb prosthesis 전동의수
electric wheelchair 전동휠체어
electrocardiogram : ECG 심전도
electroconvulsive therapy : ECT 전기경련요법

electrode 전극
electrodermal responding 피부전위반응
electrodiagnosis : EDX 전기진단법
electroencephalogram : EEG 뇌전도 ; 뇌파
electrogoniometer 전기관절각도계
electromyogram : EMG 근전도
electromyography : EMG 이엠지 ; 근전도검사
electromyography of anal sphincter
항문괄약근 근전도검사
electron beam computed tomography
컴퓨터단층촬영 ; 전자빔 전산화단층촬영 ;
전자빔CT
electron beam sterilization 전자선멸균
electronic endoscopy 전자내시경검사
electronic health records
전자건강기록 ; 전자진료기록카드
electrophysiology 전기생리학
electroshock therapy : EST
전기충격치료 ; 전기쇼크요법
electrostimulation 전기자극
electrostimulator 전기자극장치
electrotherapy 전기요법
elektrotherapie 전기치료
elementary school children 학동
eletriptan 일레트립탄
elevation 들어올리기
eligibility 앨리지빌리티 ; 적격성
eligibility of employee pension 연금수급자격
eligible population 노동가능인구
elimination of thresholds 단차해소
Elizabeth Fry 프라이
Elizabethan Poor Laws 엘리자베스 구빈법
emancipation 해방
embezzlement 횡령
embolism 색전
emergency alarm system 긴급통보장치
emergency assistance : EA 긴급부조
emergency call 긴급통보
emergency call services 긴급통보서비스
emergency call system 긴급통보시스템
emergency contact information 긴급연락처
emergency first aid 응급수단 ; 응급처치
emergency medical services 구급의료

emergency medical technician : EMT
구급구명사

emergency planning 방재대책

emergency room : ER 구급구명실 ; 구급외래

emerging infectious disease 신종감염질병

EMG biofeedback EMG 바이오피드백

emigrant 출이민

emollient 연화제

emotion 정동 ; 정서

emotional abuse 심리적 학대

emotional dependency 정신적 의존

emotional development 정서발달

emotional divorce 정서적 단절

emotional incontinence 감정실금증

emotional insecurity 정서불안정

emotional lability 정서적 불안정

emotional release 감정방산

emotional test 정서테스트

empathic understanding 공감적 이해

empathy 공감 ; 감정이입

emphysema 기종 ; 폐기종

emphysematous pyelonephritis
기종성 신우신염

empiric therapy 경험주의적 치료 ; 경험적 치료

empirical 경험의

empirically-based practice 관찰에 기초한 실천

employee 피고용자 ; 종업원 ; 피용자

employee assistance programs : EAPs
고용인원조계획

employee credit system 대부금제도

employee insurance 피고용자보험 ;
피용자보험 ; 후생보험

employee pension 피고용자연금 ; 피용자연금 ;
후생연금

employee pension for disability 장애후생연금

employee representation 종업원대표제도

employee rules and regulations 취업규칙

employee satisfaction : ES 종업원만족도

employees health insurance 피고용자건강보험

employees pension fund : EPF 후생연금기금

Employees' Health Insurance Division
보험과

employees' insurance 피용자보험 ; 후생보험

employees' pension 피용자연금

employees' pension insurance 후생연금보험

Employees' Pension Insurance Law
후생연금보험법

employment 고용

Employment Act 고용법

employment adjustment 고용조정

employment agreements and contracts
고용계약

Employment Antidiscrimination Law
고용차별금지법

employment assistance 취업지원

Employment Basic Law 고용정책기본법

employment contract 노동계약

Employment Development Division
고용개발과

employment insurance 고용보험

Employment Insurance Division 고용보험과

Employment Insurance Law 고용보험법

Employment Insurance System 고용보험제도

Employment Measures for Persons with
Disabilities Division 장애인고용대책과

Employment Measures for the Elderly
and Persons with Disabilities Department
고령·장애인고용대책부

Employment Measures for the Elderly
Division 고령자고용대책과

employment of older workers 고령자고용

employment of the aged 노인고용

employment of the disabled 장애인고용

employment of the elderly 고령자고용

employment of the people with mental
disabilities 정신장애인고용

employment of the physically disabled
신체장애인고용

employment period 고용기간

employment policy 고용정책

Employment Policy Division 고용정책과

employment programs 고용계획

employment promotion for people with
mental disabilities 정신장애인고용촉진

employment promotion for the aged
노인고용촉진

employment promotion for the disabled
장애인고용촉진
employment promotion for the elderly
고령자고용촉진
employment promotion for the physically
disabled 신체장애인고용촉진
employment promotion policy for people
with mental disabilities 정신장애인고용촉진
대책
employment promotion policy for the
aged 노인고용촉진대책
employment promotion policy for the
disabled 장애인고용촉진대책
employment promotion policy for the
elderly 고령자고용촉진대책
employment promotion policy for the
physically disabled 신체장애인고용촉진대책
employment quota 할당고용
employment rate 고용율
employment rates for older people
노인고용율
employment rates for persons with
mental disabilities 정신장애인고용율
employment rates for persons with
physically disabilities 신체장애인고용율
employment rates of the aged 노인고용율
employment rates of the disabled
장애인고용율
employment rates of the physically
disabled 신체장애인고용율
Employment Security Bureau 직업안정국
Employment Security Law 직업안정법
Employment Statistics Division 고용통계과
employment structure 취업구조
Employment training programs
고용훈련 프로그램(ET프로그램)
empowerment 권리부여 ; 임파워먼트 ; 권한부여
empowerment approach 임파워먼트 접근법
empowerment model 권한부여모델
empowerment plan for long-term care
개호력 강화계획
empty nest syndrome
공소증후군 ; 빈 둥지증후군

empty-chair technique 빈 의자기법
enable role 조장자 역할
enabler 인에이블러 ; 조장자
enalapril 에나라프릴
enamel 에나멜질
Enbrel 엔브렐
enclosure movement
둘러쌓기운동 ; 엔클로우저운동
encoding disturbance 기명력장애
encopresis 장기능장애
encounter group
대면집단 ; 인카운터그룹 ; 집단경험 ; 참만남 집단
encouragement 말걸기 ; 말붙이기
endarteritis 동맥내막염
end-bearing socket 단단부하소켓
endemic 풍토병
endocrine 내분비
endocrine disease 내분비질환
endocrinologist 내분비의사 ; 내분비학자
endocrinology 내분비학
end-of-life care 종말기케어 ; 엔드 오브 라이프
케어
endogenous 내인성
endogenous infection
내인성 감염증 ; 내인성 감염
endogenous psychosis 내인성 정신병
endorectal coil 직장내 코일
endorectal ultrasonography
경직장적 초음파검사법 ; 직장내 초음파검사법
endoscope 내시경
endoscopic 내시경수술
endoscopic retrograde cholangiopancreatography 내시경적 역행성 담관췌관조영
endoscopic ultrasonography 내시경적
초음파검사
endoscopy 내시경검사
endosonography 내시경초음파검사
endotoxin test 내독소시험 ; 엔도톡신검사
endotracheal anesthesia 기관내 마취
endowment 기금
endowment facilities at cost 실비양로시설
endowment facilities for the aged
노인양로시설

end-stage renal disease : ESRD 말기신부전
endurance 내구성 ; 지구성
endurance exercise 지구력운동
enema 관장
energy 에너지
energy expenditure 에너지소비
energy requirement 에너지필요량
energy storing prosthetic foot
고기능 인공발연구
enervation 무기력
enforcement notice 강제통고 ; 집행통고
Enforcement of Long-Term Care and
Insurance Act for the Aged
노인장기요양보험법시행규칙
Engel's coefficient 엥겔계수
Engel's Law 엥겔법칙
enlarging reading device 확대독서기
enmeshment 그물화 ; 병적인 얽힘
enrollee 등록자 ; 입회자 ; 가입자 ; 참가자
enrollment 등록 ; 입회 ; 가입 ; 참가
enrollment restriction 등록제약 ; 입회제약 ;
가입제약 ; 참가제약
entacapone 엔타카폰
entecavir 엔테카비어
enteral tube 외부튜브
enteric-coating 장용성 제피 ; 장용코팅 ; 장용피
Enterocele 장 탈장
enterovirus 엔테로바이러스 ; 장바이러스
entitlement 권리 (자격)
entrapment neuropathy 교액성 신경장애
entrepreneurial practice 유로복지사업
entropy 엔트로피
enuresis 야뇨증 ; 유뇨증
environment 환경
environment of care 케어환경
environmental assessment 환경평가
environmental control system : ECS
환경제어장치
environmental coordination 환경조정
environmental determinism 환경결정론
environmental factor 환경인자
environmental hazards 환경위험물질
Environmental Health Division 생활위생과

environmental maintenance 환경정비
environmental modification 환경수정
environmental pollution 환경오염
environmental problem 환경문제
environmental protection 환경보전
environmental protection agency
환경보호기관
environmental reform 환경개선
environmental rights 환경권
environmental sampling 환경조사
environmental surveillance 환경감시
environmental treatment 환경요법 ;
환경치료
epidemic 유행성
epidemic keratoconjunctivitis : EKC
유행성 각결막염
epidemiological study 역학조사
epidemiology 역학
epidural analgesia 경막외진통법
epidural hematoma 경막외혈종
epigenesis 후성설
epilepsy 간질
epileptic seizure 간질발작
episodic memory 에피소드기억 ; 일화기억
epistemology 인식론
e-prescription 전자처방
Equal Employment 고용균등 · 아동가정국
Equal Employment Opportunity Laws
남녀고용기회균등법
Equal Employment Policy Division
고용균등정책과
equal participation of women and men
남녀공동참가
equal rights 평등권
equality 평등
equality of opportunity 기회의 평등
equality of result 결과의 평등
equilibrium 평형 ; 평형상태
equinovarus foot 내반첨족
equipment 기기 ; 도구 ; 용구
equipment management services
기기관리서비스
equipments for daily living activities

일상생활용구
equity 공평 ; 형평
erectile dysfunction : ED 발기부전
erection 발기
erector spinae 척주기립근
ergometer 에르고미터
ergonomics 인체공학 ; 인간공학 ; 에르고노믹스
Erich Fromm 프롬
Eros 에로스
erosion 미란 ; 짓무름 ; 침식
errors in long-term care 개호사고
erythrocyte sedimentation rate : ESR
혈침치 ; 적혈구침강속도
erythropoietin 에리스로포리에틴
esophageal manometry 식도내압검사
esophageal motility disorder 식도운동장애
esophageal phase 식도단계
esophagus 식도
essential amino acid 필수아미노산
essential hypertension 본태성 고혈압
essential nutrition 필요영양량
establishment of the team care
팀케어의 확립
estate planning 상속재산설계 ; 에스테이트플래닝
estate tax 유산세
estazolam 에스타졸람
esteem needs 자아욕구
esterase 에스테라제
estimated daily intake 추정일일섭취량
estrangement 불화
estrogen 에스트로겐
estrogen replacement therapy : ERT
에스트로겐 보충요법
etanercept 에타너셉트
ethical code 윤리규정
ethics 윤리
ethics in research 연구윤리
ethics of long-term care 개호의 윤리
ethnic discrimination 민족차별
ethnic group 민족
ethnic minority 소수민족
ethnicity 에스니시티 ; 민족성
ethnocentrism 자기민족중심주의

Ethology 인성학
ethopropazine 에토프로파진
ethylene oxide gas sterilization
산화에틸렌 가스멸균 ; 에틸렌옥시드 가스멸균
Étienne Laspeyres 라스파이레스
유료노인홈
etiological diagnosis 원인적 진단
etiology of criminal behavior 비행원인론
etiquette 예의 ; 에티켓
Eugenic and Maternal Protection Law
우생보호법
eugenic operation 우성수술
eugenic protection 우성보호
eugenics 우성학 ; 우생학
eurage 경찰법 (輕擦法)
eurhythmia 정맥
euthanasia 안락사
evacuation site 피난장소
evaluation 평가
Evaluation and Licensing Division 심사관리과
evaluation criteria 평가항목
evaluation of services 서비스평가
evaluation research 평가조사
evening care 이브닝케어
event-related potential : ERP
사건관련전위 ; 사상관련전위
eversion 외반 ; 외전
every 2 hours : Q2H 2시간 마다
every 3 hours : Q3H 3시간 마다
every 4 hours : Q4H 4시간 마다
every 6 hours : Q6H 6시간 마다
every 8 hours : Q8H 8시간 마다
every day : QD 날마다 ; 매일
every hour : QH 1시간 마다
every morning : QAM 매일아침
every night : QHS 매일아침시간전
every other day : QOD 이틀에 한번 ; 하루 걸러
eviction 퇴거
evidence-based care : EBC
증거에 기초한 개호 ; 증거에 기초한 장기요양 ;
증거에 기초한 케어
evidence-based community planning
증거에 기초한 지역계획

E

E

evidence-based medicine : EBM
증거에 기초한 의료
evidence-based nursing 증거에 기초한 간호
Evista 에비스타
evoked electromyogram 유발근전도
evoked potential 유발전위
ex office member 직책에 의한 성원
Examination Committee of Social
Insurance 사회보험심사회
examination fee 수험수수료
exceptional children 특수아동
exceptional eligibility 특수자격
excessive daytime sleepiness 주간과다졸림증
excessive drooling 과도한 침흘림
excretion 배설
excretion care 배설장기요양 ; 배설개호 ;
배설케어
excretion disorder 배설장애
excretion exercise 배설훈련
excretion tool 배설용구
Exelon 엑셀론
exercise 운동 ; 체조
exercise capacity 운동내용능
exercise instructor 운동전문사
exercise load 운동부하
exercise physiology 운동생리
exercise prescription 운동처방
exercise strength 운동강도
exercise test 운동시험
exercise tolerance test : ETT 운동부하검사
exercises for maintaining muscle
근력유지훈련
exfoliative cytology
박리세포진 ; 탈락세포검사 ; 박리세포학검사
existential therapy 실존적 요법
existentialism 실존주의
exit-site infection 출구부감염

exogenous 외인성
exogenous hormone 외인성 홀몬
exogenous infection 외인성 감염
exorcism 악마추방 ; 엑소시즘
expenditure 지출
expenses for bringing up a child 양육비지출
experience rating 경험요율 ; 경험율
experienced illness 장애체험 ; 체험으로서의 장애
experiential self 경험자기
experiential therapy 경험치료
expert witness 전문가증언
experts designing post retirement life
노후생애설계전문가
exploring electrode 탐색전극
exposure 폭로
expressions of desires 의사전달
extended care 연장장기요양
extended care facilities : ECT 연장보호시설
extended childcare 연장보육
extended family 확대가족
extension 신장(伸長)
extension contracture 신장구축
extension ladder theory 사다리이론
extension of maximum life span 생명의 연장
extension shoe 굽높은 구두
external frame of reference 외적 조합범위
external rotation 외회전
externalization 외면화
extinction 멸종현상 ; 소거현상 ; 소멸현상
extinctive prescription 소멸시효
extrapolation 외삽법
extraversion 외향성
extrovert 외향성의 사람
eye bank 아이뱅크 ; 안구은행
eye disease 안질
eye drop 점안액
eye goggle 보호용 안경

F

F wave F파
Fabian socialism 페비안 사회주의
Fabianism 페이비안주의 (페이비어니즘)
face cleaning 세수 ; 세안
face mask 페이스마스크
face sheet 페이스시트 ; 표지
face shield mask 안면보호실드마스크
face validity 표면적 타당성
facial paralysis 안면신경마비 ; 안면마비
facial reflection 표정반사
facilitation 촉진
facilitation technique 촉진기법
facilitator role 촉진자 역할
facilities for development of care worker
요양보호사양성시설
facility 시설
facility administration 시설운영
facility for children with mental
retardation 지적장애아시설
facility for children with severe physical
and mental disabilities 중증심신장애아시설
facility for crippled children 지체부자유아시설
facility for deaf-blind children 맹농아아시설
facility for people with severe physical
and mental disabilities 중증심신장애인시설
facility for the blind 맹인시설
facility for the blind children 장님아시설
facility for the blind persons 맹자시설
facility for the deaf-mute children
농아아동시설
facility for the physically and mentally
disabled 심신장애인시설
facility for the physically and mentally

disabled children 심신장애아시설
facility management 시설관리
facility volunteer 시설자원봉사
facility-based services 시설기반형 서비스
facioscapulohumeral muscular dystrophy
안면견갑상완근이영양
factitious disorder 인위적인 장애
factor analysis 요인분석 ; 인자분석
Factory Act 공장법
failure to thrive : FTT 성장장애
fainting 실신
fair share plan 페어쉐어플랜
fall 낙상
fall incident 낙상사고
fall risk 낙상위험도
falling asleep 입면 ; 잠들기
falls prevention 낙상예방
false eye 의안
famciclovir 팜시클로버
familial adenomatous polyposis : FAP
가족성 대장포리포시스 ; 가족성 선종성용종증
familism 가족주의
family 가족
family adviser 가정상담원
family allowance 가족수당
family benefit 가족급여
family budget 가계
family care allowance 장기요양휴가수당금
family care leave 장기요양휴가 ; 개호휴가
family care leave system 개호휴가제도
family care work 가족케이스워크
family caregiver 가족개호자
Family Caregiver Burden Scale

가족부양부담감척도
family case work 패밀리케이스워크
family case worker 가족케이스워커
family centered casework 가족중심케이스워크
family child care 가정양호
Family Classroom for the Dementia/Cere-
brovascular Disease 치매·뇌졸증가족교실
family composition 가족구성
family conflict 가족갈등
family court 가정법원 ; 가정재판소
family diagnosis 가족진단
family disorganization 가족해체
family doctor 가정의 ; 단골의사
family doctor's function 가정의 기능
family down 가정붕괴
family dynamics 가족역동성
family education 가족지도
family environment 가정환경
family function 가족기능
family group home 패밀리 그룹홈
family history 가족력
family homeostasis 가족항상성
family in need of public assistance
요보호가족
family interview 가족면접
family issue 가족문제
family labor 가내노동
family law 가족법
family life cycle 가족생활주기 ; 가족주기
family map 가족도
family myths 가족신화
family of orientation 방위가족 ; 지향가족
family of origin 기원가족
family of procreation
생식가족 ; 창설가족 ; 출산가족
family pathology 가족병리
family planning 가족계획
family planning guidance 가족계획지도
family policy 가정정책 ; 가족정책
family projection process 가족투사 과정
family relationship 가족관계
family resistance 가족저항
family right 가족권

family role 가족역할
family rule 가족 룰
family rules 가족규칙
family sculpting 가족조각
family secrets 가족비밀
family service organizations 가족봉사기관
family social work 가족소시얼워크 ;
패밀리소시얼워크
family social worker 가족소시얼워커
family structure 가족구조 ; 세대구조
family support 패밀리서포트 ; 가족지원 ;
가족부양
family support center
가족지원센터 ; 패밀리서포트센터
family system 가족시스템
family system theory 가족시스템이론
family systems approach 가족시스템접근법
family tention 가족긴장
family therapy 가족요법 ; 가족치료
family trouble 가정불화
family violence 가족폭력 ; 가정폭력
family welfare 가족복지 ; 가정복지
Family Welfare Division 가정복지과
family welfare service center 가족복지기관
family-based care 가족중심케어
family-oriented care 가족지향케어
family-provided care 가족개호
Famvir 팜비어
fango therapy 팡니요법 ; 팡고테라피
fantasy wandering 판타지배회 ; 환상배회 ;
공상배회
fasciculation potential 섬유속전위 ;
섬유속자발수축
fasciitis 근막염
fasting blood sugar 공복시 혈당
fat 지방
fatal familial insomnia 치명적 가족성 불면증
fatherless families advisor 모자지도원
fatherless family 모자가정
fatherless household 모자세대
fatigue 피로
fatigue study 피로연구
fat-soluble vitamin 지용성 비타민

fatty acid 지방산

fault tree analysis 결함수분석

feasibility study 타당성 연구

feather allergy 깃털알레르기

fecal chymotrypsin test 분변키모트립신시험

fecal examination 대변검사 ; 분변검사

fecal impaction 숙변

fecal incontinence 변실금

fecal occult blood test : FOBT
대변잠혈검사 ; 변잠혈검사

fece 배설물

feces examination 대변검사

feces sampling 채변

Federal Crime Insurance Program
연방범죄보험 프로그램

federal government 연방정부

Federal Housing Administration : FHA
연방주택청

Federal Insurance Contributions Act :
FICA 연방보험기여법

federal plan for the disabled 장애인플랜

Federation of Inochi No Denwa Inc.
일본 생명의 전화연맹

fee 이용료

feedback 피이드백 ; 환류

feeding activity 식사동작

feeding restriction 섭식제한

fee-for-service : FFS 행위별수가제

Feeling Tone Questionnaire : FTQ
감정기분질문표

feet 피트

felonies 중죄

felt needs 감득욕구 ; 느낀 욕구

female elderly project 여성노인사업

feminism 페미니즘 ; 여권론

feminist social work 페미니스트소시얼워크

feminist theory 페미니즘이론

feminist therapy 여권주의 치료

feminization of poverty 빈곤의 여성화

femoral neck fracture 대퇴골 경부골절

fence 장물아비

Ferguson Report 퍼거슨리포트

fertility 출산력

fertility rate 출생율

fetal alcohol spectrum disorder
태아알코올스펙트럼장애

fetal alcohol syndrome
태아기 알코올증후군 ; 태아알코올증후군

fetal disorder 태아기 장애

fetology 태아학

fetus 태아

feudal society 봉건사회

feudalistic thought 봉건사상

fever 발열

fever of unknown origin 불명열

feverfew 피버퓨

fiber 섬유

fiber type grouping 섬유형 그룹화

fibrillation potential 섬유자발전위 ; 세동전위

fibrin 섬유소 ; 피브린

fiduciary abuse specialist team : FAST
경제적학대 전문가팀

field instruction 실무교육

field instructor 실습지도자

field of group work 그룹워크의 분야

field of microscope 현미경시야

field placement 현장실습

field research 현지조사

field study 현장연구

fields of practice 실무분야

filial duty 아동으로서의 의무

filial piety to parents 효도

filial responsibility 자식의 책임

filling-in 끼움 ; 메꿈 ; 필링인

film forum 필름 포럼

filtration sterilization 여과멸균

financial asset 금융자산

financial capability index 재정력지수

financial management 재무관리

financial stability fund 재정안정기금

financial statement 재무제표

financial welfare 재정복지

finasteride 피나스테라이드 (피네스테리드)

finding abnormality 이상발견

fines for default 과태금

finger agnosia

손가락실인증 ; 수지실인증 ; 지실인증
finger ladder 손가락사다리
finger print plate method 지문법
finger streak plate method
손가락도말평판법 ; 손가락평판도말배양법
fingernail 손톱
fingerspelling 손가락문자
Fire Department 소방서
fire prevention 방화대책
fire risk 화재위험도
Firefighter 소방대원
first aid 구급법
first insured 제1호 피보험자
first-order change 제1단계 변화
fiscal intermediaries 재정중재기구
fiscal year 회계년도
fitness 피트니스
fitting 적합
fitting evaluation 적합판정
Five Giants 대악 ; 5대 사회악
five major nutrients 5대 영양소
five stages of grief 퀴블러로스 사망단계
five times daily : 5D 하루 5회
five times weekly : 5W 주 5회
five-stage hierarchy of needs 욕구5단계설
fixation 고착
fixator 고정기
fixator muscle 고정관계
fixed amount system 정액제
fixed assets 고정자산
fixed charge 정액부담 ; 정액청부
fixed charge rate 정률부담
fixed dystonia 고정근육긴장이상 ; 고정디스토니아
fixed price 정액청부
fixed-interval schedule 조정간격 계획표
flaccid 이완
flaccid paralysis 이완성 마비
flame sterilization 화염멸균
flame-resistant material 방염소재
flash pulmonary edema 급성폐부종 ;
급성폐수종
flashback 플래시백현상
flat rate benefit 균일급여

flat rate contribution 균일거출
flat rate scheme 균일제
flat-rate fee 정액요금
flavor 풍미
Flexeril 플렉세릴
flexibility 유연성
flexibility exercise 유연체조
flexible working hours system 플렉스 타임제
flexion 굴곡
flexion contracture 굴곡구축
Flexner Report 플렉스너 보고서
flextime 플렉스타임
flight into illness 질병편력
floating particle 공중부유분진 ; 부유미립자 ;
공중먼지
Flomax 프로막스
flooding 홍수(법)
floor cleaning 바닥청소
floor level 바닥
flooring 플로어링
floppy infant 근육긴장저하아 ; 영아저긴장증후군
flora 식물군 ; 식물상
Florence Nightingale 나이팅게일
flossing teeth 치간치솔
fluid 수분
fluid ability 유동성 능력
fluid balance 수분밸런스
fluid intake 수분섭취
fluid intake and output 수분출납
fluid intelligence 유동성 지능
flu-like symptom 감기와 같은 증상
fluorescein endoscopy 형광내시경검사
fluoride 불소
fluoroscopy 방사선투시검사 ; X선투시검사
fluoxetine 플록세틴 ; 플로옥세틴
fluvoxamine 플루복사민
focal 병소 ; 국한성
focal infection 병소감염
focus 조준
focus of colonization 세균증식의 병소
focusing 초점맞추기 ; 초점조정 ; 포커싱
fogging 분무
Folie à Deux 이인정신병

folk medicine 민간요법
folktale 민화
folkways 원규
follicular thyroid cancer 갑상선여포암
follow-up 팔로우업 ; 추수지도 ; 폴로우업
follow-up process 추수과정
follow-up study 추적조사
follow-up visit after discharge 퇴소후
방문지도
foment 찜질
food 음식
Food Bank 푸드뱅크
food bank food items 푸드뱅크식품
food box 푸드박스
food contamination 식품오염
food exchange list for diabetes
당뇨병식품교환표
food inspector 식품위생감시원
food intake 섭식
food poisoning 식중독
food preparation 식품조리
food safety and sanitation supervisor
식품위생관리자
food sanitation 식품위생
Food Sanitation Law 식품위생법
food stamps 식품구입권
food-borne infection 음식매개감염
food-related disorder 음식관련장애
foot bath 족욕 ; 발목욕
foot board 발판
foot drop 첨족
foot flat 발바닥접지
foot orthosis with lateral corrective
wedge 외측쐐기첨부 발바닥보조기
foot plate 족판
foot problem 발의 문제
foot rest 발걸이 ; 풋레스트 ; 발판
foot slap 전족부 접촉 ; 발때림
foot support 발판 ; 발받침대
footboard 풋보드
footwear 신발
force plate 힘측정판
forced crying 강제울음

forced laughing 강제웃음
forceps 겸자
forceps biopsy 겸자생검
forcible collection 강제징수
fordism 포드주의
foreclosure 차압
foreign care worker 외국인장기요양노동자
Foreign Workers' Affairs Division
외국인고용대책과
foreign-born elderly 외국태생고령자
forensic anthropologist
법의학인류학자 ; 사법인류학자
forensic anthropology
법의학인류학 ; 사법인류학
forensic autopsy 사법해부
forensic nurse 법의사간호 ; 사법간호
forensic nursing 법의학간호학 ; 사법간호학
forensic pathologist
법의학병리학자 ; 사법병리학자
forensic pathology 법의학병리학 ; 사법병리
forensic psychiatric nursing
법의학정신간호 ; 사법정신간호
forensic psychologist
법의학심리학자 ; 사법심리학자
forensic psychology 법의학심리학 ; 사법심리학
forensic social work 법의학복지 ; 사법복지
forequarter amputation
전사반부절단 ; 견갑흉간절단술
forequarter amputation 포오쿼터절단
forequarter amputation prosthesis
견갑흉간절단용 의수
forgetfulness 건망증
formal care 포멀케어
formal network 포멀네트워크
formal operations stage 형식적 조작기
formal organization 공식적조직
formal sector 포멀섹터
formal service 포멀서비스
formed group 형성집단
formulary 처방집
for-profit organization 영리단체 ; 민간영리조직
forum 포럼
Fosamax 포사맥스

F

foster care 가정위탁 ; 양연보호 ; 수양부모
foster care system 수양부모제도
foster grandparent program
수양조부모 프로그램
foster grandparents 조부모 양연
foster parent 양친자관계
foster-child care 사회적 (아동) 보호
foundations 재단(기금)
foundling hospitals 기아보호소
four basic food groups 네개의 식품군
four food groups 네개의 식품군
four system 4체계 모델
four times daily : QID 하루 4회
four times weekly : 4W 주 4회
four types of pain in elderly 노인4고
four-legged cane 네발 지팡이
four-point gait 4점 보행
four-year nursing school 간호계 대학
Fowler's position 파울러씨 체위
fracture 골절
fracture management 골절관리
frail child 허약아
frail elderly 허약고령자 ; 허약노인
frail joint 동요관절
frailty 허약
frame 프레임
Francis Galton 갈톤
Frankel classification 프란켈분류
fraternity 우애
fraud 사기
Frederic Morton Eden 이든
Frederic Winslow Taylor 테일러
free access 무료접속 ; 프리엑세스 ; 무료진입
free association 자연연상 ; 자유연상
free endowment facilities 무료양로시설
free endowment facilities for the aged
무료노인양로시설
free enterprise system 자유기업제도
free health care 무상의료
free health care service facilities for the
aged 무료노인요양시설
free medical care 무상의료
free of charge 무료

free rationing to the aged 노인무료급식
free rider 프리라이더 ; 무임승차
free specialized health care service
facilities for the aged 무료노인전문요양시설
Free Trade Agreement : FTA 자유무역협정
Freedmen's Bureau 프리드먼 사무소
Freedom of Information Act 정보자유법
free-floating anxiety 막연한 불안
freeter 프리터
frequent bowel movements 빈변
Freudian slip 프로이트 과실
Freudian theory 프로이트이론
friction lock joint 마찰잠금 이음새
frictional unemployment 마찰실업
Friedrich Engels 엥겔스
friend 친구 ; 지인
friendly society 우애조합
friendly visit services 우호방문서비스
friendly visiting 우애방문
friendly visitor 우애방문원
frigidity 불감증
fringe benefits 부가급여 ; 부가급부
Frits Jules Roethlisberger 레스리스버가
front wheel folding walker 전륜절첩보행기
frontal lobe 전두엽
frontal lobe dysfunction 전두엽장애
frontal lobe syndrome 전두엽증상
front-temporal dementia 전두측두엽치매
front-wheel walker 전륜보행기
frovatriptan 프로바트립탄
frozen gait 움츠러진 걸음걸이
frozen shoulder 오십견 ; 동결어깨
frustration 욕구불만 ; 요구저지 ; 좌절 ; 좌절감
frustration tolerance
인내력 ; 욕구불만내성 ; 좌절감내성
Fukuyama type congenital muscular dystrophy 후쿠야마형 선천성 근이영양증
full denture 총의치
full employment 완전고용
full participation and equality 완전참가와 평등
full-body bath 전신욕 ; 전신목욕
full-body sponge bath 전신세정 ; 전신닦기
full-time employment 정규고용

full-time equivalent : FTE 상근환산

function 기능

function trainer 기능훈련사

Functional Activities Questionnaire : FAQ
기능적 활동질문표

functional age 기능연령

functional approach 기능적 접근법

functional assessment 기능평가 ; 기능사정

Functional Assessment Inventory : FAI
기능평가표

Functional Assessment of Cancer
Therapy : FACT 암치료기능평가

Functional Assessment of Chronic Illness
Therapy : FACIT 만성질환요법기능평가

functional brace 기능적 장비

functional casework 기능주의 개별사회사업

functional community 기능지역사회

functional differentiation 기능분화

functional electrical stimulation : FES
기능적 전기자극

functional exercise 기능훈련

functional group 기능집단

functional impairment 기능손상

functional independence 기능적 자립

Functional Independence Measure : FIM
기능적 자립도평가법

functional localization
기능국소화 ; 기능적 국재화

functional magnetic resonance imaging :
fMRI 기능적 MRI

functional maintenance 기능유지

functional mental illness 기능적정신병

functional occupational therapy
기능적 작업요법

functional position 기능성 체위 ; 기능적 지위

functional prognosis 기능적 예후

functional reconstruction 기능재건

functional recovery 기능회복

functional residual capacity 기능적 잔기량

Functional Status Questionnaire : FSQ
기능상태질문표

functional training 기능훈련

functionalism 기능주의 ; 기능심리학

fundamental habits 기본적 생활습관

fundamental human rights 기본적 인권

fundamental position 기본적 지위

fundamental rights at work 노동기본권

funding 기금조성

funding for employment of the elderly
고령자고용지원금

funding-holding 기금소지

funeral care 장제보호

funeral expenses 상제비지출

fungal endophthalmitis 진균성 안내염

fungal infection 세균감염 ; 진균감염

fungemia 진균혈증

furosemide 푸로세미드 ; 푸로세마이드

fusion 용해

futon mattress drying service 이불건조서비스

future of care 케어의 미래

G

gabapentin 가바펜틴

Gabitril 가비트릴

Gabriel needle 가브리엘바늘

Gaffky table 가프키도표

gait 보행

gait ability 보행능력

gait analysis 보행분석

gait apraxia 보행실행

gait assessment 보행기능평가

gait cycle 보행주기

gait difficulty 보행곤란

gait disability 보행장애

gait disorder 보행장애

gait disturbance 보행장애

gait pattern 보행패턴

gait training 보행훈련 ; 보행연습

gait velocity 보행속도

galantamine 갈란타민

gallstone 담석

Gallup Korea 한국갤럽

gambling 도박 ; 갬블

gamma sterilization 감마선멸균

gang 깽 ; 패거리

gang age 갱에이지

gangrene 괴저 ; 회저

garbage 음식물쓰레기

Garden classification system of fracture 가든골절분류

gargling 양치질

garnishment 채권압류 통고

gas sterilization 가스멸균

gastrectomy 위절제술

gastric cancer 위암

gastric lavage 위세정

gastric ulcer 위궤양

gastritis 위염

gastroenterologist 소화기내과의

gastroenterology 소화기병학

gastroesophageal reflex disease : GERD 위식도역류증

gastrografin enema 가스트로그라핀관장

gastrointestinal physiology 소화관생리학

gastrostomy 위루형성술 ; 위루

gastrostomy tube 위루튜브

gatch bed 개치베드

gauze 가제

gay elder 노년기 동성애자

gender 젠더 ; 성 ; 성별

gender difference 성차

gender identity disorder : GID 성동일성장애

gender role 성역할

gender track 젠더트랙

gender-equal society 남녀공동참가사회

gender-related development index : GDI 성개발지수

gene 유전자

general account 일반회계

general administrative field 일반행정부문

General Affairs Division 총무과

general assistance 일반부조

general bathtub 일반욕조

general bed 일반병상

general condition survey 개황조사

general health education 일반건강교육

general hospital 일반병원

general household survey : GHS 일반세대

조사 ; 종합세대조사
general medical clinic 일반진료소
general practitioner : GP 일반의
general practitioner fundholder
예산직접관리일반개업의
general system theory
일반시스템이론 ; 일반체계이론
general welfare center of elderly
노인종합복지관
generalist 일반개업자
generalization 일반화
generalization behavioral 행동의 일반화
generalized anxiety disorder 범불안장애
generation boundary 세대간 경계
generatively 차세대육성능력 ; 생식성
generic drug 후발의약품
generic social work 일반사회사업 ;
일반소시얼워크
generic social worker 일반사회사업가
generic-specific controversy
일반적-특수적 논쟁
genetic counseling 유전상담 ; 유죄답변 거래
genetic diagnosis 유전자진단
genetic diseases 유전병
genetic testing 유전자검사
genetics 유전학
genital hygiene 음부세정 ; 음부닦기
genital stage 생식기 ; 성기기 ; 성기단계
genocide 집단학살
genogram 가계도
genomic imprinting
유전체각인 ; 제노믹각인 ; 제노믹임프린팅
gentrification 주택지구 상류화
genuineness 진실성 ; 진지
geographic adjustment factor : GAF
지역차조정계수
geriatric care 고령자개호 ; 고령자케어 ;
노인개호
geriatric care expenditures 요양비지출
geriatric care management
고령자 케어매니지먼트
geriatric case management
고령자 케이스매니지먼트

geriatric case manager 고령자 케이스매니저
geriatric dentistry 고령자 치과학분야
Geriatric Depression Scale : GDS
노인우울증척도 ; 노년우울증스케일
geriatric disease 노년병
geriatric evaluation and management
program 고령자평가 매니지먼트프로그램
geriatric health and welfare 고령자보건복지
geriatric health and welfare facility
노인보건복지시설
geriatric health care facilities
개호노인보건시설
geriatric health care facilities 노인보건시설 ;
장기요양노인보건시설
geriatric hospital 노인병원
geriatric hospital 노인전문병원
geriatric intensive care unit 노인집중치료실
geriatric interdisciplinary health care
team 연계·협동고령자헬스케어
geriatric medical care 노인의료
geriatric medical fee system 노인진료보수
제도
geriatric medicine 노인의료
Geriatric Medicine Fellowship Program
고령자의료 펠로우십프로그램
geriatric mental health care 노인정신보건
geriatric mental health care system
노인정신보건제도
geriatric nursing 고령자간호 ; 노인간호
geriatric syndrome 노년증후군
geriatric welfare facilities 노인복지시설 ;
장기요양노인복지시설 ; 개호노인복지시설
geriatric welfare home 특별양호노인홈
geriatrician 고령자전문의
geriatrics 노년의학
germicide 살균제
gerontological social work 노년사회복지학
gerontology 노년학 ; 노인학
gerontophobia 노인공포증
Gerstmann syndrome
거스트만 증후군 ; 게르스트만 증후군
gestalt psychology 게스탈트 심리학
gestalt therapy 게슈탈트요법 ; 게스탈트 치료

G

gestation 임신
gestational diabetes 임신당뇨병
getting in and out of the car 차 승강
getting up 일어나기
Get-up and Go Test 기립보행검사
giant cell arteritis : GCA 거대세포동맥염
Gilbert Act 길버트 법
gingival 잇몸
Gini coefficient 지니계수
ginkgo biloba 은행
Ginnie Mae 지니 매
glare 눈부심 ; 눈부신 빛
glasses 안경
glaucoma 녹내장
global aging 세계적 노화
Global Assessment of Functioning : GAF
  전반적 기능평가 ; 총괄기능평가
Global Assessment Scale : GAS
  전반적 평가척도
global standards 글로벌스탠다드
globalization 글로벌리제이션
glossopharyngeal breathing 설인호흡
glossopharyngeal neuralgia 설인신경통
glove juice method 글로브쥬스법
glucocorticoid
  글루코코르티코이드 ; 당질코르티코이드
Glucophage 글루코파지
glucosamine 글루코사민
glucose 포도당 ; 글루코스
glucose anhydride 글루코스무수물
glucose level 혈당치 ; 혈당량
glucose tolerance test 포도당 부하시험
glucose-non-fermentative bacteria
  포도당 비발효균
glutaraldehyde 글루타르알데히드
gluteus maximus muscle 대둔근
goal 목표
goal of care 케어목표
goal of services 서비스목표
goal-setting 목표설정
go-between role 중재역할
goiter 갑상선종
Gold Plan 골드플랜 ; 고령자보건복지추진 10개년

전략
Gold Plan 21 골드플랜21
Gold Plan for 21st century 골드플랜21
gold sodium thiomalate 금티오말산나트륨
gonarthrosis 변형성 슬관절증
goniometer 관절각도계
gonorrhea 임질
good cholesterol HDL 콜레스테롤
Good Finders 좋은 이웃들
goodness of fit 호적상태
gout 통풍
gouty arthritis 통풍성 관절염
government administered 정부관장
government administered health
  insurance 정부관장건강보험
government ordinance city 정령지정도시
government sponsored health insurance
  정부관장건강보험
government subsidy to care providers
  개호급여비납부금
gown technique 가운착용법 ; 가운테크닉
grab bar 이동대 ; 이동바
grace period 유예기간
graft 횡령
grandfather clause 조부 조항
grandiosity 허세
grandparenting 손자손녀양육 ; 손자손녀키우기
grant for basic pension 기초연금교부금
grant-in-aid 교부금 ; 조성금
grant-in-aid for scientific research
  과학연구비보조금
grants-in-aid 보조금
grantsmanship 연구보조금 획득수완
grass roots democracy 풀뿌리민주주의
grating 그레이팅 ; 회절격자
Graves' disease 그레이브스병
gray market adoption 그레이마켓 입양
Gray Panthers 그레이팬서
Great Depression 세계대공황
Great Society 위대한 사회
greater trochanter 대전자
greater trochanter fracture 대전자부 골절
greater trochanteric pain syndrome

대전자동통증후군
greatest happiness for the greatest
  number 최대다수의 최대행복
green card 외국인입국허가증
green medical care card 녹색의료보호수첩
greenhouse effect 온실효과
greenlining 그린라이닝
Gresham's Law 그레셤의 법칙
grief work 고난
Grievance Committee of the National
  Health Insurance 국민건강보험단체연합회불평
  처리위원회
grievances and complaints resolution
  불평해결
grip strength 악력
gross domestic product : GDP 국내총생산
gross motor function 대동작기능
gross national product : GNP 국민총생산
gross national welfare : GNW 국민총복지
ground reaction force 지면반력
group 집단
group cohesiveness 집단응집성
group counseling 그룹카운셀링 ; 집단상담
group delinquency 집단비행
group development 집단발달
group dynamics 집단역학 ; 그룹다이내믹스
group eligibility 집단적격성
group examination for the large bowel
  cancer 대장암집단검진
group exercise 그룹운동
group experiences 집단경험
group function 집단기능
group home 그룹홈 ; 공동생활가정
group home for people with dementia
  치매대응형공동생활장기요양 ; 치매대응공동생활개
  호 ; 인지증대응형공동생활개호
group home for people with mental
  retardation 지적장애인그룹홈
group home for the aged 노인요양공동생활가정
group home for the elderly with
  dementia 치매성 노인그룹홈 ; 인지증그룹홈
group identity 집단정체성
group institutional care 집단시설보호

group interaction 집단상호작용
group leader 집단지도자
group life insurance 단체보험
group living 그룹리빙
group living assistance for the elderly
  고령자공동생활부조
group living for the aged 노인공동생활
group living for the elderly 고령자공동생활
group living management for the elderly
  고령자공동생활지원
group living support for the aged
  노인공동생활지원
group living support for the elderly
  고령자공동생활원조
group medical examination 집단검진
group model 그룹모델
group of beds for long-term health
  care 요양형병상군
group of elderly volunteer services
  노인자원봉사단
Group of Elderly Volunteers 장년봉사단
group physical examination 집단검진
group practice 그룹진료
group pressure 집단압력
group process 집단과정
group psychotherapy
  집단심리치료 ; 집단정신치료법
group recreation 그룹레크리에이션
group structure 집단구조
group supervision 그룹슈퍼비전
group therapy 집단요법 ; 집단치료
group treatment 집단처우
group work 그룹워크 ; 집단사회사업 ;
  집단지도 ; 집단원조기술
group work recording 그룹워크기록
group worker 그룹워커 ; 집단사회사업가
growth hormone 성장호르몬
GS civil service ranks 일반공무원제도 서열화
guaiac test 잠혈검사 ; 구아이악검사
guarantee 보증
guaranteed annual income 연간보증소득
guaranteed minimum standard of living
  최저생활보장

guarantor 보증인
guardian 후견인 ; 보호자
guardian of minor 미성년후견인
guardianship 감호
guess-who test 게스 후 테스트
guidance 생활지도 ; 보도 ; 가이던스
guidance counselor 안내상담역 ; 진로지도교관
guidance for career direction 진로지도
guidance for the blind 맹인 가이드헬프
Guidance of Medical Service Division
　지도과
guide dog 맹도견
guide helper 가이드헬퍼

guide helper for the blind 맹인 가이드헬퍼
Guide to Physical Therapist Practice
　물리치료료사 실습가이드 ; 이학요법사 실습가이드
guidelines 가이드라인
Guillain-Barre syndrome : GBS 길랑바레증후군
guilt 죄의식
gum disease 치주병
guns or butter 대포냐 버터냐
gustation 미각
gymnastics 체육
gynecologist 산부인과의사 ; 부인과의사
gynecology 산부인과 ; 부인과 ; 산부인과의학 ;
　부인과의학

G

H

H reflex H반사
H wave H파
habeas corpus 인신보호영장
habilitation 훈련
habituation 순응 ; 해빌리테이션
haemoptysis 각혈
Haglund's deformity 헤이글런드 기형
Haim G. Ginott 지노트
hair 머리카락
hair removal 제모 ; 털 제거
haircut 이발
halazepam 하라제팜
half lotus sitting position 반가부좌
half-body bath 반신욕
half-life 반감기
half-sitting position 반좌위
halfway house 하프웨이하우스
halfway houses 중간시설
hallucination 환각
hallucinogen 환각제
hallux valgus 외반모지
halo effect 후광효과
halo orthosis 할로보조기
haloperidol decanoate 할로페리돌데카노에이트
halo-vest orthosis 할로베스트 ; 경추보조기
Hamburg System 함부루크제도
Hamilton Gordon 해밀턴
Hamilton Rating Scale for Depression :
 HamD 해밀턴우울평가척도
hand 손 ; 핸드
hand antisepsis 손가락소독
hand bath 수욕
hand hygiene 손가락소독 ; 손가락위생

hand wash 손씻기 ; 핸드워시
hand-assisted escort 안내서
handedness 잘 쓰는 손
handicap 핸디캡 ; 사회적 불리
Handicapped Children Act 장애아동법
handrail 손잡이 ; 핸드레일
handrail installation 손잡이 설치
handrim 핸드림
Hansen's disease 한센병
Hansen's disease 한센씨병
Hansen's disease control policy 한센병대책
hard-to-reach clients 접근하기 어려운
 클라이언트
hardware 하드웨어
harness 안전벨트 ; 하니스
Harold Maslow Abraham 아브라함
Harriet M. Bartlett 바트레트
Harris R. Perlman 펄만
Harris-Benedict caloric intake equation
 하리스베네딕트 기초에너지방정식 ; 하리스베네딕
 트 열량섭취 방정식
Harris-Benedict equation 하리스베네딕트 방정식
Harry Hopkins 홉킨즈
Hartnup disease 하트넙병 ; 하아트누프병
Hartnup disorder 하트넙증 ; 하아트누프증
Harvard Medical Malpractice Study
 하버드 의료과오연구
Hasegawa Dementia Scale : HDS
 하세가와 치매척도
Hasegawa Dementia Scale-Revised
 HDS-R 하세가와 치매척도개정판 ; 하세가와식
 간이지능평가스케일 개정판
Hashimoto disease 하시모토병

Hashimoto's thyroiditis 하시모토병 ; 하시모토 갑상선염

hashish 해시시

Hawthorne effect 호손효과

Hawthorne experiment 호손 실험

hay fever 꽃가루 알레르기

Hazard Analysis Critical Control Point system : HACCP 위기분석중점관리제도 ; 해썹

hazardous material 위험물 ; 위험유해물질

HDL〈 high-density Lipoprotein 〉고밀도지단백

HDL cholesterol HDL 콜레스테롤

Head Start 조기교육

head trauma 두부외상

headache 두통

Headache Classification Committee of the International Headache Society 국제두통학회 두통분류위원회

health 건강 ; 보건

Health and Medical Services Law for the Elderly 노인보건법

health and welfare 보건복지

health and welfare agency 보건복지기관

health and welfare agency for the aged 노인보건복지기관

Health and Welfare Bureau for the Elderly 노건국 ; 노인보건복지국

Health and Welfare Committee for the Aged 노인보건복지대책위원회

health and welfare education 보건복지교육

health and welfare facility 보건복지시설

health and welfare for the aged 노인보건복지

Health and Welfare Law for People with Mental Disabilities 정신보건 및 정신장애인복지에 관한 법률

Health and Welfare Law for People with Mental Disabilities 정신보건복지법

health and welfare office 보건복지사무소 ; 보건복지사업소

health and welfare office for the aged 노인보건복지사업소

Health and Welfare Plan for the Aged 노인보건복지계획 ; 노인보건복지서비스계획

health and welfare program for the aged 노인보건복지사업

health and welfare provider for the aged 노인보건복지사업자

health and welfare services 보건복지서비스

health and welfare services plan for the aged 노인보건복지서비스계획

health and welfare standards 보건복지기준

health and welfare system for the aged 노인보건복지제도

health assessment 건강사정

health behavior 건강행동 ; 보건행동

health behavior theory 건강행동이론

health belief model 건강신념모델

health care 건강보호 ; 헬스케어

health care and welfare services organization for the aged 노인보건복지종합대책

health care cost containment 의료비억제책

health care expenditures for the elderly 고령자의료비

health care expenditures for the elderly 고령자보건의료비

Health Care Financing Administration 건강보호재정국

health care for the elderly 고령자보건의료

health care proxy 의료위임장

health care reform 의료제도개혁

health care services facilities for the aged 노인보건의료시설

health care services for the elderly 고령자보건의료서비스

health care system for the elderly 고령자보건의료제도

health care systems for the aged 노인보건제도

health center 보건센터

health check-ups for the aged 노인건강진단

health condition 건강상태

health counseling 건강상담

health culture 건강문화

health education 건강교육

health education guidelines

건강교육 가이드라인
health examination 건강진단
health expenditure rationalization plan
의료비적정화계획
health food 건강식품
Health Frontier Strategic Plan
건강프론티어전략
health guidance 보건지도
health handbook 건강수첩
health hygiene 보건위생
health indicator 건강지표
health industry 건강산업
health insurance 건강보험
health insurance benefit 건강보험급여
Health Insurance Bureau 보험국
health insurance card 건강보험증
Health Insurance Division 의료보험과
Health Insurance Finance Operations Agency 건강보건재정운영국
Health Insurance Fiscal Stability Policy
건강보험재정안정종합대책
Health Insurance Review Agency 건강보험
심사평가원
health insurance society 건강보험조합
health insurance system 의료보험제도
Health Insurance System for Elderly Aged 75 and Above 장수의료제도
Health Insurance System for the Elderly Aged 75 and Above 후기고령자의료제도
Health Japan 21 건강일본21
health maintenance 건강유지
health management 건강관리
health observation 건강관찰
health plan for the aged 노인보건계획
health planning 보건계획 ; 의료계획
health policy 의료정책
Health Policy Bureau 의정국
health profession 의료전문
health professional 의료전문직
health professional shortage area
의료전문직 부족지역
health programs for the aged 노인보건사업
health promotion 헬스프로모션 ; 건강증진

Health Promotion Act 건강증진법
health risk management 건강위기관리
Health Science Division 후생과학과
Health Service Bureau 건강국
health services 보건시설
Health Services Commission 의료서비스위원회
health services for the aged 노인보건서비스
health services package 의료서비스패키지
health services plan for the aged
노인보건서비스계획
health-related quality of life 건강관련 QOL
health-related services 의료관련서비스
healthy carrier 건강보균자
healthy control 건강대조자
Healthy Japan 21 21세기에 있어서의 국민건강
만들기 운동
healthy person 정상인
healthy volunteer 건강자원봉사 ; 정상인
healthy volunteer healthy subject
건강한 사람
hearing 청력
hearing ability 청력
hearing aid 보청기
hearing aid used in connection with implant 인공내이
hearing level 청력레벨
hearing loss : HL 난청
hearing test 청력검사
heart 심장
Heart Building Law 허트빌딩법
heart catheterization 심장카테터법
heart disease 심질환
heart failure 심부전
heart rate 심박수
heartburn 속쓰림
heat exhaustion 열피로 ; 열피페
heat rash 땀띠
heat retention 울열
heat stroke 열사병 ; 열중증
heat therapy 온열요법
heating ventilation and air-conditioning : HVAC 공기조화기
hebephrenic schizophrenia 파괴성 정신분열증

Heberden's nodes 헤버덴결절 ; 헤베르덴결절
heel bumper 발뒤꿈치 범퍼
heel contact 발뒤꿈치 접지
heel off 발뒤꿈치 들림
hegemony 헤게모니
Heimlich Maneuver 하임리히법
Heinrich's law 하인리히 법칙
Helicobacter pylori 헬리코박터 파일로리
Hellen, Bosanquet 보산케트
Heller's syndrome 헬러 증후군
help 구원
Help Age International
　한국노인복지회 ; 한국헬프에이지
help the clients help themselves 자립조장
hematemesis 토혈
hematochezia 혈변
hematocrit 적혈구용적률 ; 헤마토크릿
hematology 혈액학
hematoma 혈종
hematuria 혈뇨
hemianopia 반맹
hemiarthroplasty 인공골두치환술
hemipelvectomy 골반반절제술 ; 편측골반절단
hemipelvectomy prosthesis
　천장골하지절단의지 ; 편측골반용의족
hemiplegia 반신불수 ; 편마비
hemodialysis 인공투석 ; 혈액투석
hemoglobin : Hb 헤모글로빈
hemolytic anemia 용혈성 빈혈
hemophilia 혈우병
hemophilic arthropathy 혈우병성 관절증
hemoptysis 각혈 ; 객혈
hemorrhagic bullae 출혈성 수포
hemorrhagic stroke 출혈성 뇌졸중
hemorrhaging 대출혈
hemostasis 지혈
Hendrich's Fall Risk Assessment Tool
　헨드릭 낙상위험사정도구
Henri Wallon 와롱
Henrician Poor Law 헨리 구빈법
heparin 헤파린
hepatic arterial infusion 간동맥동주요법
hepatitis 간염

hepatitis A A형 간염
hepatitis A virus A형 간염바이러스
hepatitis B : HBV B형 간염
hepatitis B virus B형 간염바이러스
hepatitis C C형 간염
hepatitis C virus C형 간염바이러스
hepatitis D D형 간염
hepatitis D virus D형 간염바이러스
hepatitis E E형 간염
hepatitis E virus E형 간염바이러스
hepatologist 간 전문의
hepatology 간장학 ; 간장병학
Hepsera 헵세라
herb doctor 한방의
herbal medicine 한방약
Herceptin 허셉틴 ; 헤르셉틴
hereditary nonpolyposis colorectal
　cancer : HNCC 유전성 비용종성 대장암
heredity 유전
hernia of the intervertebral disc
　척추간반헤르니아
heroin 헤로인
heroin dependence 헤로인 의존
herpes 포진
herpes zoster 대상포진
hertz 헤르쯔
heterogeneous 이질의
heterosexuality 이성애
heterostasis 정체이형
heterotopic bone formation 이소성 골화
hiatus hernias 열공헤르니아
hibernating myocardium 동면심근
hibernation 동면
hiccups 딸꾹질
hidden cultural barrier 숨은 문화적 장벽
hierarchical society 계급사회
hierarchy of needs 욕구서열 ; 욕구계층
high altitude cerebral edema 고소뇌부종
high altitude pulmonary edema 고소폐수종
high deductible health insurance plan
　고면책액의료보험
high dependency unit 고도치료실
high economic growth 고도경제성장

high efficiency particulate air filter
초고성능여과공기기 ; 초고성능필터

high industrialized society 고도산업사회

high level disinfection 고수준소독

high level of welfare 고복지 · 고부담

high risk 하이리스크

high touch surface 고빈도접촉면

high-density lipoprotein : HDL
고비중리포단백질

high-density lipoprotein cholesterol
HDL 콜레스테롤

higher apprenticeships 고등양성훈련제도

higher brain dysfunction 고차뇌기능장애

higher brain function 고차뇌기능

highly advanced medical technology :
HAMT 고도선진의료

high-quality rental housing for the
elderly 고령자대상 우량임대주택

hindquarter amputation 후사반부절단

hip disarticulation prosthesis 고관절의족

hip fracture 고관절골절

hip-knee-ankle-foot orthosis : HKAFO
골반대부 하지보조기

Hippocratic Oath 히포크라테스의 맹세

hiring older workers 고령자고용

Hispanics 라틴아메리카계인

histamine H1 receptor blocker
히스타민 H1 수용체차단제

histamine H2 receptor blocker
히스타민 H2 수용체차단제

histamine receptor blocker
히스타민 수용체차단제

histrionic personality disorder
연기성 성격장애

Hoehn-Yahr stage
혼-야 단계 ; 혼과 야의 스케일

holiday 축일

holiday sharing 축일보조

holism 전체론

holistic 전체론적 연구

holistic medicine 홀리스틱의학 ; 전인적의료

holistic rehabilitative intervention
포괄적 재활접근법

holistic-faceted development 전면발달

Hollis-Taylor Report 홀리스-테일러 보고서

holon 홀론

holter electrocardiogram 홀터심전도

home 가정

home and community-based care
지역밀착형방문개호

home and community-based health care
지역밀착형방문간호케어

home assistance 재가부조

home assistance for the elderly
고령자재가부조

home bathing 방문입욕

home bathing care 방문입욕

home bathing services 방문입욕서비스

home bathtub 가정욕조

home beauty services 방문이미용서비스

home care 방문요양 ; 방문개호 ; 재가개호 ;
재가케어 ; 가정보호

home care advisor 재가개호상담원

home care aide 재가개호사

home care assessment
재가케어평가 ; 오아시스

home care management 재가개호지원

home care management center
재가개호지원센터

home care management center for the
aged 노인재가개호지원센터

home care management for people with
mental disabilities 정신장애인재가개호지원

home care management for people with
mental retardation 지적장애인재가개호지원

home care management for the disabled
신체장애인재가개호지원

home care medicine 재가의학

home care nurses station 방문간호스테이션

home care office 방문개호사업소

home care physician 재가의사

home care project 방문개호사업

home care promotion plan 홈케어촉진사업

home care provider 방문개호사업자

home care rehabilitation 방문재활

home care service

재가보호서비스 ; 홈케어서비스 ; 재가케어서비스 ;
재가서비스
home care services agency 재가서비스기관 ;
재가케어서비스기관 ; 재가개호서비스기관
home care services for the aged
재가노인개호서비스
home care services for the disabled
재가장애인개호서비스
home care services for the elderly
재가고령자개호서비스
home care services office 재가서비스사업소 ;
재가케어서비스사업소 ; 재가개호서비스사업소
home care services provider 재가서비스사
업자 ; 재가서비스제공자 ; 재가케어서비스사업자 ;
재가개호서비스사업자
home care worker 방문개호원
home care worker development
curriculum 요양보호사양성커리큘럼
home care worker training program
방문개호원양성연수
home dialysis therapy 재가투석요법
home elevator 홈 엘리베이터
home fire 자택화재
home for the aged 양로시설
home for the blind 맹인홈
home for training and education of
juvenile delinquent 교호원
home health 방문간호 ; 재가간호
home health aide 방문요양보호사 ; 재가간호사
home health care
방문간호케어 ; 재가간호케어 ; 재가요양
home health care agency
방문간호케어기관 ; 재가간호케어기관
home health care for the aged
노인방문개호케어
home health care support clinic
재가요양지원진료소
home health medication management
방문약제관리지도
home health nurse 방문간호사
Home Health Nurses Association
방문간호협회
home health nurses station 방문간호스테이션

home health plan of care 방문간호계획
home health services
홈헬스서비스 ; 가정건강서비스
home help 홈헬프
home help coordinator 홈헬프 코디네이터
home help for the aged 노인홈헬프
home help services 홈헬프서비스
home help services for the aged
노인홈헬프서비스
home help services for the physically
and mentally disabled
심신장애인홈헬프서비스
home help services for the physically
disabled 신체장애인홈헬프서비스
home help services for the physically
and mentally disabled children
심신장애아홈헬프서비스
home help services people with mental
retardation 지적장애인홈헬프서비스
home helper 홈헬퍼
home helpers 가정도우미
home helpers for household activities
가사활동도우미
home helpers of elderly program
노인가정도우미사업
home helping 생활원조
home improvement 주택개량 ; 주택개선 ;
주택개조
home laundry services 방문세탁서비스
home living assistance for the elderly
고령자재가생활부조
home living support for the elderly
고령자재가생활원조
home modification 주택개량 ; 주택개선 ;
주택개조
home modification allowance 주택개량수당
home modification benefit 주택개량급여
home nutrition education services
방문영양식사지도
home oxygen therapy : HOT 재가산소요법
home parenteral nutrition : HPN
재가중심정맥영양
home program 홈프로그램

home rehabilitation 재가재활
home repair scam 가옥수리사기
home safety 주택안전
home support 재가원조
home support for the elderly 고령자재가원조
home treatment 재가치료
home visits 가정방문
home-based assistance 거택부조
home-based assistance for the elderly
고령자거택부조
home-based assistance services
거택부조서비스
home-based assistance services plan
거택부조서비스계획 ; 거택부조계획
home-based care 거택개호
home-based care for people with mental
disabilities 정신장애인거택간호
home-based care for people with mental
retardation 지적장애인거택간호
home-based care for the aged 노인거택개호
home-based care for the elderly
고령자거택개호
home-based care for the physically disabled 신체장애인거택간호
home-based care management 거택개호지원
home-based care management center
for the aged 노인거택개호지원센터
home-based care management for
people with mental disabilities 정신장애
인거택개호지원
home-based care management for
people with mental retardation 지적장애
인거택개호지원
home-based care management for the
disabled 신체장애인거택개호지원
home-based care management for the
elderly 고령자거택개호지원
home-based care management office
거택개호지원사업소
home-based care management program
거택개호지원사업
home-based care management program
for people with mental retardation

지적장애인거택개호지원사업
home-based care management provider
거택개호지원사업자
home-based care management the aged
노인거택개호지원
home-based care services 거택개호서비스
home-based care services office
거택개호서비스사업소
home-based care services plan
거택개호서비스계획
home-based care services plan 거택서비스
계획
home-based care services provider
거택개호서비스사업자
home-based living assistance 거택생활부조
home-based living assistance for the
aged 노인거택생활부조
home-based living assistance for the elderly 고령자거택생활부조
home-based living assistance program
거택생활부조사업
home-based living assistance services
거택생활부조서비스
home-based living assistance services
office 거택생활부조서비스사업소
home-based living assistance services
provider 거택생활부조서비스사업자
home-based living support 거택생활원조
home-based living support for the
elderly 고령자거택생활원조
home-based living support program
거택생활원조사업
home-based living support services
거택생활원조서비스
home-based living support services
office 거택생활원조서비스사업소
home-based living support services
provider 거택생활원조서비스사업자
home-based living supportive program
거택생활원조사업
home-based living supportive services
거택생활원조서비스
home-based living supportive services

office 거택생활원조서비스사업소
home-based living supportive services
 provider 거택생활원조서비스사업자
home-based nutrition education
 방문영양식사지도
home-based services 거택서비스
home-based services office 거택서비스사업소
home-based services program
 거택서비스사업
home-based services provider
 거택서비스사업자
home-based support 거택원조
home-based support for the elderly
 고령자거택원조
home-based support services
 거택원조서비스
home-based supportive services
 거택원조서비스
homebound 귀가조치
homeless 노숙자 ; 노상생활자 ; 홈리스
homeless child 부랑아
homelessness 집 없음
homemaker 가사원조자 ; 가정조성자
homemaker service 가정봉사원서비스
homemaker services 가사원조 ; 가정조성서비스
homemaker services provider
 가사서비스제공자
homeopathic remedies 동종요법
homeostasis 항상성 ; 항상성유지기능
Homestead Act 홈스테드 법
homosexuality 동성애
homosexuality latent 잠재적 동성애
honorary position 명예직
hooked probe 갈고리 소식자 ; 갈고리 존데
hope 희망
Horatio Alger story 출세이야기
hormone 호르몬
hormone receptor test 호르몬수용체검사
hormone replacement therapy
 호르몬보충요법
Horner syndrome 호너증후군
horticultural therapy 원예요법
hospice 호스피스

hospice care 말기환자보호치료 ; 호스피스 보호
hospital 병원
hospital accreditation 병원기능평가
hospital bed-control 병상규제
hospital environment 병원환경
hospital infection 병원감염
Hospital Infection Control Practices
 Advisory Committee : HICPAC
 병원감염관리실천자문위원회
hospital information system 병원정보시스템
hospital insurance : HI 입원보험
hospital level of care 입원치료단계
hospital social work 병원사회사업
hospital stay 재원
hospital transfer 전원
hospital volunteer 병원자원봉사
hospital-acquired infection 원내감염 ;
 병원감염
hospital-acquired pneumonia
 원내폐렴 ; 병원감염폐렴
hospital-based services 병원기반형 서비스
hospitalism 호스피털리즘 ; 시설병
hospitalization 입원 ; 병원입원
hospitalization with consent 동의입원
hostile work environment 열악적 직장환경
hostile work environment harassment
 직장환경 악화형 성희롱
host-parasite relationship 숙주기생체관계
hot air sterilizer 건열멸균기
hot biopsy 고온생검
hot compress 온찜질
hot foment 온엄법
hot line 핫라인
hot pack 핫팩 ; 온습포
hot water disinfection 열수소독
hot zone 오염구역 ; 위험구역
hotel costs 호텔비용
house evaluation 가옥평가
house fire 가옥화재
house repair allowance 주택보수자금
housebound 두문불출
housebound elderly
 두문불출고령자 ; 두문불출노인

housebound syndrome 두문불출병후군
household 가구 ; 세대 (世帶)
household budget 가계
household duties adjustment 가사심판
household in need of public assistance
요보호세대
household work 가사 ; 가정일
households on public assistance
피보호자세대
housekeeper 가정부
housekeeping 가사 ; 가정일 ; 가사노동
housekeeping assignment 가사분담
housekeeping service providers 가정봉사원
housekeeping service providers
dispatching 가정봉사원파견사업
housekeeping service providers
dispatching facilities 가정봉사원파견시설
housekeeping service providers
dispatching office 가정봉사원파견사업소
housing allowance 주택자금
housing and environment coordinator
복지주거환경 코디네이터
housing assistance 주택부조
housing for mothers and children 모자주택
housing for the aged 노인전용주택
housing for the elderly 고령자용주택
housing loan 주택융자
housing management 주택관리
housing policy 주택정책
housing policy for the elderly 고령자주택정책
housing programs 주택프로그램
hub 허브
hubbard tank 허바드탱크
hue 색상
hue cancellation 색상해제
Hull House 헐 하우스
human behavioral science 인간행동과학
human capital 인적 자본
human development 인간개발
human dignity 인간의 존엄
human engineering 인간공학
human epidermal growth factor
receptor-2 : HER2 사람표피증식인자수용체 2형

Human Genome Project 인간게놈프로젝트
human immunodeficiency virus : HIV
사람면역결핍바이러스
human lymphocyte antigen 사람백혈구항원
human poverty index 인간빈곤지수
human relation management 인간관계관리
human relations 인간관계
Human Resource Agency of the Elderly
고령자인재은행
Human Resource Development Bureau
직업능력개발국
human resources 인적자원
Human Resources Development Division
능력개발과
human rights 인권
human rights advocacy 권리옹호
Human Rights Watch : HRW
국제인권단체 ; 휴먼라이츠워치
human science 인간과학
human services 휴먼서비스
humanism 휴머니즘 ; 인도주의
humanistic and existential therapy
인간적 실존치료
humanistic orientation 인본주의적 지향
Humira 휴미라
humoral regulation 체액조절 ; 액성조절
Huntington's chorea 헌팅턴무도병
Huntington's disease 헌팅턴병
hydralazine 하이드랄라진
hydrocodone 하이드로코돈
hydrocollator 하이드로컬레이터
hydrogen peroxide gas plasma
sterilization 과산화수소가스 플라스마멸균
hydrotherapy 수치료 ; 하이드로테라피 ; 물요법
hydroxychloroquine 하이드록시클로로퀸
hygiene 위생
hygiene laboratory technician 위생검사기사
hygienic hand washing 위생적 손씻기
hygienics 위생학
hygroscopic fiber 흡습성 섬유
hyperactive child syndrome
아동행동과다증후군
hyperactivity 행동과다증

hyperacusis 청각과민
hyper-aged and depopulating society
초저출산고령사회
hyperalgesia 통각과민
hyperalimentation 고칼로리수액
hypercapnia 고탄산가스혈증
hypercholesterolemia 고콜레스테롤혈증
hyperemia 충혈
hyperesthesia 촉각과민 ; 감각과민
hyperextension 과신장
hyperglycemia 고혈당증
hyperglycemic hyperosmolar nonketotic
  coma : HHNKC 당뇨병성 고혈당성 고삼투압성
  혼수
hyperkeratosis 과각화증
hyperkinesia 다동 ; 운동항진 ; 운동과다증
hyperlipidemia 고지혈증
hyperosmolar hyperglycemic syndrome :
  HHS 고혈당성 고삼투압증후군
hypersalivation 타액과다분비
hypertension 고혈압
hyperthermia 고체온
hyperthyroidism 갑상선기능항진증
hypertonia 근긴장항진 ; 긴장항진
hypertrophic cardiomyopathy 비대형 심근증

hypertrophy 비대
hyperuricemia 고요산혈증
hyperventilation 과호흡증
hypesthesia 감각감퇴 ; 감각둔마 ; 촉각둔마
hypnosis 최면 ; 최면상태
hypnotherapy 최면치료 ; 히프노테라피 ; 최면요법
hypnotic drug 수면제
hypochondria 심기증 ; 건강염려증
hypoglycemia 저혈당 ; 저혈당증
hypokinesia 운동저하
hypomania 경조병
hyponatremia 저나트륨혈증
hypotension 저혈압
hypothermia 저체온
hypothesis 가설
hypothyroidism 갑상선기능저하증
hypotonia 근긴장저하 ; 긴장저하
hypotonic dehydration 저장성 탈수
hypovolemic shock 순환혈액량감소성쇼크
hypoxemia 저산소혈증
hysteria 히스테리
hysteric 히스테리적인
hysterical neurosis, conversion type
  전환성 히스테리 신경증
hysterosalpingography 자궁난관조영

I

iatrogenesis 의원병
iatrogenic 의원성
ibandronate 이반드로네이트
ibuprofen 이부프로펜
ice bag 빙낭 ; 얼음주머니
ice pack 아이스팩
ice pillow 빙침 ; 얼음베개
Icelandic roll on silicone socket :
  ICEROSS 실리콘제내 소켓
icing 아이싱
ICU-acquired infection 집중치료실감염 ;
  ICU감염
Ida M. Cannon 캐넌
ideal body weight : IBW 기준체중비
idealization 이상화
ideas of Confucianism 유교사상
ideas of reference 관계사고
ideation 관념화
ideational apraxia 관념실행
identification 동일화 ; 신분증명서 ; 동일시
identified patient (or client)
  확인된 환자 (또는 클라이언트)
identity 아이덴티티 ; 정체성
identity crisis 동일성 위기 ; 정체성 위기
identity theft 개인정보절도
identity versus role confusion
  정체성 대 역할 혼란
ideology 이데올로기
ideomotor apraxia 관념운동실행
idiopathic thrombocytopenic purpura : ITP
  특발성 혈소판감소성 자반병
idiosyncratic 특이한
ignorance 무지

ileus 장폐쇄 ; 이레우스
illegal employment 불법취업
illegal residence 불법체류
illegitimate 사생아
illiteracy 문맹
illiterate functional 기능적문맹
illness behavior 병행동
illness experience 병경험 ; 병체험
illusion 착각
image 심상
imbalance 불균형
imbecile 저능
I-message 나-전달법
imipramine 이미프라민
imitation 모방
Imitrex 이미트렉스
immigrant 이민자
immigrant elder 고령이민
immigration 이민
immobility 부동성
immobilization 부동
immoral family 부도덕가정
immune system 면역시스템
immunity 면역
immunity from premium contributions
  보험료면제
immunization 예방접종
immunoassay fecal occult blood test
  면역화학적 변잠혈검사
immunocompromised host
  면역저하숙주 ; 면역저항성 감약숙주 ; 면역결핍자
immunocompromised patient
  면역저하환자 ; 면역저항성 감약환자 ; 면역결핍환자

immunodeficiency 면역결핍증 ; 면역부전증
immunoglobulin : Ig 면역글로블린
immunoglobulin A : IgA 면역글로블린 A
immunoglobulin E : IgE 면역글로블린 E
immunoglobulin G : IgG 면역글로블린 G
immunoglobulin M : IgM 면역글로블린 M
immunologic fecal occult blood test
면역학적 변잠혈검사
immunoscintigraphy 면역신티그라피
immunosuppressed
면역결핍 ; 면역부전 ; 면역억제
immunotherapy 면역요법
impact analysis 영향분석
impaired fasting glucose : IFG 공복시 고혈당
impaired glucose tolerance : IGT 내당능이상
impairment 손상 ; 임페어먼트 ; 기능장애
impairment of balance function 평형장애
impingement 음위 ; 인핀지먼트
implantable defibrillator 이식형 제세동기
implied consent 암시된 동의
imposition system 부과방식
impotence 임포텐츠
impounding 가압류
imprinting 각인
improvement 향상
improvement of body functions
운동기 기능향상
improvement of oral functions 구강기능향상
impulse 임펄스 ; 자극
impulsiveness 충동성
in vitro diagnostic reagent 체외진단제
in vitro diagnostic test 체외진단검사
inactivation factor 불활성화계수
inadequacy 부적격
inanimate surface 무생물 표면
inapparent infection 불현성 감염
inappropriate prescription for elderly
고령자에 대한 약제부적절투여
inattention 주의장애
incarceration 투옥
incentive 유인
incentive contracting 유인적 계약
incentives for employment of the elderly

고령자고용장려금
incentives for promoting employment of
the elderly 고령자고용촉진장려금
incentives for the continued employment of
the retired people 정년퇴직자계속고용장려금
incest 근친상간
incestuous desire 근친상간욕망
inching technique 인칭술
incidence 감염 ; 이환 ; 발생
incidence rate 이환율 ; 발생률 ; 감염율
incidence survey 감염율조사
incinerator 소각로
inclusion 인클루전 ; 포함
inclusive evaluation 포괄평가
income distribution 소득분배
income limit 소득제한
income maintenance 소득유지
income other than actual income
실수입 이외의 수입
income policy 소득정책
income redistribution 소득재분배
income security 소득보장
income tax 소득세
income test 소득검사 ; 소득조사
incomplete cervical cord injury 부전경수손상
incomplete quadriplegia 부전사지마비
incongruence 불일치
incontinence 실금
incontinence care 실금케어
incorporated association 사단법인
incorporated foundation 재단법인
incremental social change 점진적 사회변화
incremental threshold 증분역
incrementalism 점진주의
incubation carrier 잠복기 보균자
incurable disease 난치병
incurable disease certification
난병인정 ; 불치병인정
indemnity 배상
indenture 고용계약서
independence 자립
independence center 자립센터
independence center for the disabled

장애인자립센터
independence level of elderly with dementia 치매성 고령자의 일상생활자립도 ; 치매노인일상생활자립도 ; 인지증고령자의 일상생활자립도 ; 장애고령자의 일상생활자립도
independence support 자립지원
independence support for children 아동자립지원
independent administrative institution 독립행정법인
independent living : IL 자립생활
independent living aid 자립생활기구
independent living center for the disabled 장애인자립생활센터
independent living for the disabled 장애인자립생활
independent living movement IL운동 ; 자립생활운동
independent living movement of the disabled 장애인자립생활운동
independent living skill 자립생활스킬
independent source of revenue 자주재원
independent variable 독립변수
Inderal 인데랄
indeterminate sentence 부정기형
index of independence in activities of daily living 일상생활자립도 판정기준
India ink method 먹물법
indicator 인디케이터 ; 지표
indigenous bacterial flora 상주세균총
indigenous social worker 토착인 사회복지사 ; 토착인 사회사업가
indirect contact infection 간접접촉감염
indirect contact spread 간접접촉전파
indirect cost 간접비
indirect language 간접언어
indirect practice 간접활동
indirect questions 간접질문
indirect social work 간접원조기술
indirect tax 간접세
indirect treatment 간접처우 ; 간접치료
indirect treatment staff 간접처우직원
indiscrimination 무차별

individual family session 개별가족세션
individual guidance 개별지도
individual management 개별관리
individual manipulation 개별적조정
individual psychology 개인심리학
individual quota 개인할당
individual retirement account : IRA 개인퇴직연금계산
individual treatment 개별처우
individual understanding 개별이해
individualism 개인주의
individualization 개별화
individualization service 개별사회사업
individualized care 개별케어 ; 개인케어 ; 개별개호
individualized education program 개별교육프로그램
individualized educational plan 개별교육계획
Indocin 인도신
indomethacin 인드메타신
indoor climate 실내기후
indoor relief 수용보호 ; 원내구조
inductive logic programming 귀납논리프로그래밍
inductive method 귀납법
inductive reasoning 귀납적 추론 ; 귀납추리
industrial accident compensation 노동자피해보상보험보상
industrial accident compensation insurance 산업재해보상보험
industrial casework 산업케이스워크
industrial counseling 산업카운셀링
industrial democracy 산업민주주의
Industrial Health Division 노동위생과
industrial psychology 산업심리학
industrial revolution 산업혁명
Industrial Safety and Health Act 노동안전위생법
Industrial Safety and Health Department 안전위생부
industrial social work 산업사회사업
industrial sociology 산업사회학
industrialism 산업주의

industrialization 공업화 ; 산업화
industry versus inferiority 근면성대열등감
indwelling catheter 유치카테터 ; 유치도뇨관
indwelling catheter infection 유치도뇨관 감염
inequality 불평등
inequity 불공평
infant 유아
infant institute 영아시설
infant mortality rate 유아사망률
infant with mental retardation 지적장애유아
infanticide 유아살해
infantile autism 유아자폐증
infantilization 유치함
infants with mental disabilities 정신장애유아
infection 감염
infection clinical nurse specialist
감염전문간호사
infection control 감염관리 ; 감염대책 ; 감염제어
infection control and prevention
감염관리예방 ; 감염대책예방 ; 감염제어예방
infection control committee
감염관리위원회 ; 감염대책위원회 ; 감염제어위원회
infection control doctor
감염관리의사 ; 감염대책의사 ; 감염제어의사
infection control nurse
감염관리간호사 ; 감염대책간호사 ; 감염제어간호사
infection control practitioner
감염관리전문가 ; 감염대책전문가 ; 감염제어전문가
infection control program 감염관리프로그램;
감염대책프로그램 ; 감염제어프로그램
infection control team
감염관리팀 ; 감염대책팀 ; 감염제어팀
infection prevention 감염예방
infection surveillance 감염증감시
infectious disease 감염증
infectious medical waste 감염성 의료폐기물
infectious waste 감염성 폐기물
infective endocarditis 감염성 심내막염
inferiority complex 열등감
inflamed gum 치은염
inflation 인플레이션
infliximab 인플릭시맙
influence tactics 영향력 전술

influenza 인플루엔자
Influenza vaccine 인플루엔자 백신
influenza virus 인플루엔자 바이러스
informal 인포멀
informal care 인포멀케어 ; 사적개호 ;
사적장기요양
informal group 비공식적 그룹 ; 자연집단
informal network 인포멀네트워크
informal organization 비공식조직
informal resources 인포멀자원
informal sector 비공식부문
informal services 인포멀서비스
informal system 인포멀시스템
information and referral service
정보 및 의뢰서비스
Information and Referral Service for the
Aged 노인의 전화
Information Center for Employment of
the Elderly 고령자고용정보센터
information disclosure 정보공개 ; 정보개시
information network 정보네트워크
information network for the disabled
장애인 정보네트워크
information of the work for the elderly
고령자취업정보
information services facility for the
people with auditory impairments
청각장애인 정보제공시설
information services facility for the
visually and auditorially impaired
시청각장애인 정보제공시설
information services facility for the
visually impaired 시각장애인 정보제공시설
information system 정보시스템
information technology : IT 정보기술
information theory 정보이론
informationalized society 정보화 사회
informed choice 인폼드초이스
informed consent : IC
인폼드콘센트 ; 사전동의 ; 동의
infrared therapy 적외선요법
infrastructure 하부구조
infusate-related bloodstream infection

주입제관련 혈류감염 ; 주입기재관련 혈류감염
ingrown toenail 함입조
inhalation 흡식
inhalation 흡입
inherently governmental activity
정부고유활동
inheritance 상속
inhibitor 저해인자
inhibitor for rehabilitation 재활중지기준
in-home welfare facilities for the aged
노인재가복지시설
in-home welfare office for the aged
노인재가복지사업소
in-home welfare policy 재가복지대책
in-home welfare program for the aged
재가노인복지사업
in-home welfare service center
재가복지봉사센터
in-home welfare service project
재가복지사업
in-home welfare services 재가복지서비스
in-home welfare services agency
재가복지서비스기관
in-home welfare services agency for the
disabled 재가장애인복지서비스기관
in-home welfare services agency for the
disabled 재가장애인복지서비스사업소
in-home welfare services for the
disabled 재가장애인복지서비스
in-home welfare services for the aged
재가노인복지서비스
in-home welfare services for the elderly
재가고령자복지서비스
in-home welfare services office
재가복지서비스사업소
in-home welfare services provider
재가복지서비스사업자
in-home welfare services provider for
the disabled 재가장애인복지서비스사업자
initial assessment 일차판정
initial cost 초기비용
initial intake 초기면접
initiative versus guilt 자발성 대 죄악감

injection 주사
injection plug 인젝션 플러그
injunction 금지명령
injury 상해
inkblot test 잉크블롯 테스트
inmate 수용자
inner-city phenomenon 이너시티현상
innocuous drug 무해한 약제
innovation 기술혁신
inpatient 입원환자
inpatient hospice 입원형 완화케어
input-output analysis 투입-산출분석
insanity 심신상실
insecurity 불안정성
in-service training 현직훈련 ; 현임훈련
insight 통찰
insight into disease 병식
insight therapy 통찰요법
insole 깔창 ; 안창 ; 인솔 ; 중창
insolvency 지급불능
insomnia 불면증
inspection 사찰
Inspection and Safety Division 감시안전과
Inspection Division 감독과
inspector 사찰지도원
institution 제도
institution of family welfare 가족복지시설
institutional care 시설케어 ; 시설보호 ;
시설개호
institutional care provider 개호시설사업자
institutional care services 시설케어서비스 ;
시설장기요양서비스 ; 시설개호서비스
institutional concept 제도적 개념
institutional environment 시설환경
institutional network 제도망
institutional services 시설서비스
institutional services plan 시설서비스계획
institutional training 시설실습
institutional welfare 시설복지
institutional welfare provision
제도적 복지급여
institutional welfare services 시설복지서비스
institutionalism 시설주의 ; 인스티튜셔널리즘

instrumental activities of daily living :
IADL 수단적 ADL ; 수단적 일상생활활동 ;
수단적 일상생활동작능력
insulin 인슐린
insulin self-injection 인슐린자기주사
insulin-dependent diabetes mellitus :
IDDM 인슐린의존성 당뇨병
insurance 보험
insurance agency 보험기관
insurance benefit 보험급여
insurance card 보험증
insurance company 보험회사
insurance doctor 보험의
insurance period 보험기간
insurance premium 보험료
insurance premium level 보험료수준
insurance premium rate 보험료율
insurance premium rate calculator
standard 보험료산정기준
insured 피보험자
insured event 보험사고
insured of long-term care insurance
개호보험피보험자
insured period 피보험자기간
insurer 보험자
intake 인테이크 ; 접수단계
intake conference 인테이크 컨퍼런스
intake interview
인테이크면접 ; 접수면접 ; 수리면접
intake worker 접수면접원
integrated delivery system : IDS
통합공급시스템
integrated education 통합교육
integrated health care delivery system
통합의료공급시스템 ; 의료복합체
integrated method 통합방법론 ; 통합적 방법
integrated setting 통합된 환경
integrated welfare state 통합된 복지국가
integrating method 방법론통합화
integration 인테그레이션 ; 통합 ; 통정
integration of the public pension
schemes 공적연금일원화
integumentary 외피

integumentary system 외피계
intellectual age 지능연령
intellectual disorder 발달지체
intellectual level 지적수준
intellectual property 지적재산
intellectual property right 지적소유권
Intellectualization 지성화
intelligence 지능
intelligence diagnosis 지능진단
intelligence disorder 지능장애
intelligence quotient : IQ 지능지수 ; 아이큐
intelligence standard score 지능편차치
intelligence test 지능검사
intelligent prosthesis 인텔리전트 의족
intensity-duration curve : I-D curve
강도기간곡선
intensive care management
집중적 케어매니지먼트
intensive care unit : ICU 집중치료실
intensive casework 심층케이스워크
intensive caseworker 인텐시브 케이스워커
intensive reform plan 집중개혁플랜
intercostal neuralgia 늑간신경통
interdisciplinary 학제적
interdisciplinary activity 학제간 활동
interdisciplinary approach 학제적 연구
interdisciplinary team : IDT 다직종팀
interest group 이익집단 ; 이익단체
interest group theory 이익집단이론
interface 인터페이스
interface reflection 계면반사
interferon 인터페론
interferon alfa 인터페론α
interferon beta 인터페론β
interferon gamma 인터페론γ
intergenerational care 세대간 케어
intergenerational conflict 세대간 분쟁
intergenerational redistribution
세대간 재분배
intergenerational relations 세대간 관계
intergenerational support 세대간 부양
intergroup relations 집단관계
intergroup work

인터그룹워크 ; 집단간의 집단지도
interim order 가명령
intermediary 중간지불기관
intermediate disinfection 중수준소독제
intermediate facility 중간시설
intermittent claudication 간헐성 파행
intermittent leave 단속적 휴가
intermittent pneumatic compression
간헐적 공기압박치료
intermittent positive-pressure breathing
therapy IPPB요법 ; 간헐적 양압호흡법
intermittent reinforcement 간헐적 강화
intermittent traction 간헐견인
intermittent urethral catheterization
간헐도뇨
internal disorder 내부장애
internal environment 내부환경
internal frame of reference 내적 조합범위
internal medicine 내과
internal rotation 내회전
internalization 내면화
International Affairs Division 국제과
International Association of Schools of
Social Work : IASSW 국제사회사업대학협의회
International Bill of Human Rights
국제인권헌장
International Classification of Disease
10th revision : ICD-10 국제질병분류 제10판
International Classification of Diseases :
ICD 국제질병분류 ; 국제질병분류법
International Classification of Functioning,
Disability and Health : ICF
국제생활기능분류
International Classification of Impairments
Disabilities and Handicaps : ICIDH
국제장애분류
International Council on Social Welfare :
ICSW 국제사회복지협의회 ; 국제사회복지협회
International Covenant on Civil and
Political Rights 시민적 및 정치적 권리에
관한 국제규약
International Covenant on Economic,
Social and Cultural Rights 사회적 및

문화적 권리에 관한 국제규약
International Covenant on Human Rights
국제인권규약
International Cultural and Art Festival
for the Elderly 국제노인문화예술제
international health 국제보건
international health and welfare
국제보건복지
International Labour Organization : ILO
국제노동기구
International Longevity Center 국제장수센터
international medicine 국제의료
International Organization for
Standardization : ISO 국제표준화기구
International Pension Division 국제연금과
International Psychogeriatric Association
국제노년정신학회
international social welfare 국제사회복지
international social work 국제사회사업
International Standard : IS 국제규격
International Union for Child Welfare
국제아동복지연합
International Union for Child Welfare :
IUCW 국제아동복지연맹
international welfare 국제복지
International Women's Day 국제여성의 날
International Women's Year : IWY
국제부인의 해 ; 국제여성의 해
international year 국제년
International Year of Biodiversity : IYB
국제생물다양성의 해
International Year of Chemistry : IYC
국제화학의 해
International Year of Disabled Persons :
IYDP 국제장애인의 해
International Year of Older Persons :
IYOP 국제고령자의 해
International Year of Peace 국제평화의 해
International Year of Sanitation : IYS
국제위생의 해
International Year of the Child
국제아동의 해
International Year of the Family

국제가족의 해
International Year of Youth 국제청년의 해
interpersonal helping skill 대인원조기술
interpersonal relationship 대인관계
interpersonal relationship skill
대인관계스킬
interpretation 해석
interprofessional education 다직종연계교육
interprofessional team 관련전문가 팀
interprofessional work 다직종연계
inter-rater reliability 평가자 간의 신뢰도
intersectoral planning 교차계획
intersex 인터섹스 ; 간성
intertrochanteric fracture 대퇴전자간골절
interval measurement 등간측정
intervention 개입 ; 인터벤션
intervention study 개입연구
interventional angiography 개입적 혈관조영
interventional radiology : IVR
화상진단적 개입치료 ; 개입적 화상진단
interview 인터뷰 ; 면접
interview survey 면접조사
intestinal string 장끈 ; 장줄
intimacy versus isolation 친밀감 대 고립감
intoxication 중독
intraarterial 동맥내
intraarterial digital subtraction
angiography 동맥내 디지털감산혈관조영술
intractable disease 특정질환 ; 특정질병
intramuscular 근육내
intraocular lens : IOL 안내렌즈
intraocular pressure 안내압 ; 눈내압
intraoperative endoscopy 수술중 내시경검사
intraoperative ultrasonography
수술중 초음파검사
intrapsychic 정신 내면의
intratracheal foreign body 기관내 이물
intratracheal injection 기관내 주입
intravascular catheter 혈관내 유치카테터
intravascular catheter-related infection
혈관내 유치카테터관련감염증
intravascular ultrasound 혈관내 초음파법
Intravenous 링겔

intravenous hyperalimentation : IVH
중심정맥고칼로리수액법 ; 중심정맥영양법
intravenous pyelogram : IVP 경정맥신우조영
intravenous therapy 링겔치료
intrinsic motivation 자연발생적 동기부여
intrinsic sphincter deficiency : SD
내인성 괄약근부전
introjection 투입
Intron A 인트론 A
introversion 내향성
introversion extroversion test
향성검사 ; 성반응검사
inverse relationship 역전관계
inversion 도치 ; 반전 ; 전화
investigation questionnaire 질문지조사
investment-versus-consumption concept
투자 대 소비 개념
invisible hand 보이지 않는 손 ; 인비져블 핸드
invisible loyalties 잠재적 충성
involuntary admission 강제입소
involuntary client 비자발적인 클라이언트
involuntary hospital admission 입원조치
involuntary hospitalization 강제입원
involuntary movement 불수의운동
involuntary unemployment 비자발적실업
iodine 옥소
iontophoresis 이온도입법
IQ test 아이큐 테스트 ; IQ검사
iron 철분
iron deficiency 철분결핍증
iron deficiency anemia 철분결핍빈혈증
irrational belief 비합리적 신념
irritability 과민성 ; 자극감수성 ; 화를 잘 냄
irritation response theory 자극반응이론
ischemic colitis 허혈성 장염
ischemic heart disease : IHD 허혈성 심질환
ischemic stroke 허혈성 발작
ischial weight-bearing 좌골지지
ISO International Classification for
Standards : ICS ISO국제규격분류
isoarea map 분포도 ; 등면적도
Isocarboxazid 이소카복사지드
isokinetic contraction 등속성 수축

isokinetic exercise 등속성 운동
isolation 격리 ; 고립
isolation precaution 격리예방책
isolation room 격리실
isolation unit 격리병동
isolator 격리장치 ; 아이솔레이터
isometric contraction 등척성 수축
isometric exercise 등척성 운동
Isoptin 이솝틴
isotonic contraction 등장성 수축
isotonic exercise 등장성 운동
isovolumetric 등용
isovolumetric contraction 등용수축 ;
　등용성 수축
isovolumetric contraction time : ICT
　등용성 수축시간 ; 등용수축시간
isovolumetric relaxation 등용이완

isovolumetric relaxation time : IRT
　등용이완시간
isovolumic 등용
isovolumic contraction 등용수축 ;
　등용성 수축
isovolumic contraction time
　등용성 수축시간 ; 등용수축시간
isovolumic relaxation 등용이완
isovolumic relaxation time : IRT
　등용이완시간
Itai-itai disease 이타이이타이병
itching 소양감
item record 항목기록
items of intermediate assessment
　중간평가항목
Ivan Petrovich Pavlov 파블로프

J

jacuzzi 거품목욕 ; 기포목욕

Janz syndrome 청소년근육간대경련간질

Japan Association for Clinical Engineering Technologists 일본임상공학기사회

Japan Association of Certified Care Workers 일본개호복지사회

Japan Association of Certified Social Workers 일본사회복지사회

Japan Association of Radiological Technologists : JART 일본방사선기사회

Japan Coma Scale : JCS 일본식 혼수척도

Japan Dental Association 일본치과의사회

Japan Eye Bank Association 일본아이뱅크협회

Japan Federation of Senior Citizens' Club 전국노인클럽연합회

Japan International Corporation of Welfare Services : JICWELS 국제후생사업단

Japan Medical Association 일본의사회

Japan National Council of Social Welfare 전국사회복지협의회

Japan Pharmaceutical Association 일본약제사회

Japan Society for Dying with Dignity 일본존엄사협회

Japan Trace Nutrients Research Society 일본미량영양소학회

Japanese Association of Medical Technologists : JAMT 일본임상위생검사기사회

Japanese Association of Retirement Housing 전국유료양로원협회

Japanese Association of Social Workers 일본소시얼워크협회

Japanese Center for the Prevention of Elder Abuse 일본고령자학대방지센터

Japanese Industrial Standards : JIS 일본공업규격

Japanese orphans in China 중국잔류고아

Japanese Paramedics Association 일본구급구명사협회

Japanese Society of Intensive Care Medicine 일본집중치료의학회

Japanese Society of Oral and Maxillofacial Surgeons 일본구강외과학회

Japanese Version of Denver Developmental Screening Test : JDDST-R 일본판 덴버식 발달스크리닝검사

jaundice 황달

Jean Henri Dunant 듀낭

Jean Marc Gaspard Itard 이타드

Jean Piaget 피아제

Jean-Jaques Rousseau 루소

Jewish social agency 유대인 사회기관

job analysis 직무분석

Job Corps 직업단

job description 직업설명 (회)

job placement guidance 취업지도

job placement program 직업안정프로그램

job seeker 구직자

job seeker's benefit 구직자급여

job training 직업훈련

Job Training Partnership Act 직업훈련협력법

jobless 무직

jobs program 직업 프로그램

Johann Heinrich Pestalozzi 페스탈로찌

John Dewey 듀이

John Howard 하워드

John Locke 로크
John M. Bowlby 볼비
John Maynard Keynes 케인즈
John Stuart Mill 밀
joining 합류
joint 관절 ; 이음새
joint and several liability 연대책임
joint and several obligation 연대채무
joint and several obligation for payments
연대납부의무
Joint Association of Elderly Welfare
Facilities for the Aged 노인복지시설연합회
joint budgeting 공동예산책정
Joint Commission on Mental Illness and
Health 정신병 및 건강공동위원회
joint contracture 관절구축
joint custody 공동보호양육원
Joint Economic Committee 공동경제협력위원회
joint family 복합가족
joint funding 공동기금
joint interview 공동면접
joint moment 관절모멘트
joint prosthesis 관절보철
joint replacement 관절치환술
joint stiffness 관절구축
Joseph Chamberlain 챔버린
judgment 판정
judicial review 사법심사
judo orthopedist 유도접골사
Jungian psychology 융 심리학
juridical person 법인

juvenile 청소년 ; 소년 ; 청년성
juvenile classification office 소년감별소
juvenile court system 소년법원제도
juvenile crime offence 청소년범죄
juvenile delinquency 청소년비행 ; 소년범죄 ;
소년비행
juvenile delinquent 비행소년
juvenile diabetes 청소년당뇨병
juvenile idiopathic arthritis
청소년특발성 류머티즘
juvenile justice 소년심판
juvenile Justice and Delinquency Prevention Act 청소년사법과 비행방지법
juvenile justice policy 청소년사법정책
juvenile justice system 청소년사법제도
juvenile labor 연소근로자
Juvenile Law 소년법
juvenile myoclonic epilepsy
청소년근육간대경련간질
juvenile offender 범죄소년
juvenile offenders 청소년범죄자
juvenile Parkinsonism 청소년파킨슨병
juvenile police 소년경찰
juvenile polyps 청소년폴립
juvenile prison 소년교도소
juvenile probation 소년보호
juvenile probation officer 소년보호사
juvenile prosecution 소년검찰
juvenile protection 청소년보호
juvenile rheumatoid arthritis
청소년관절류머티즘

J

K

Karl Marx 마르크스
katharsis 카타르시스
Katz ADL index 카츠 ALD 도구
KBS 한국방송공사
Kegel exercise 케겔운동
Kelly pad 켈리패드
Kenny Self-Care Evaluation
　케니식 자기건강관리평가
keratosis 각화증
keratotic lesions 각화성 병변
Kerner Commission 커너 위원회
kernicterus 핵황달
key child 열쇠아이
key person 중요인물
keyhole surgery 열쇠구멍수술 ; 키홀수술
Keynesian economics 케인즈경제학
Keynesian Welfare State 케인즈주의적 복지국가
Keynesianism 케인즈주의
Kibbutz 키브츠
kidney 신장(腎臟)
kidney cancer 신암
kidney disease 신장질환
kidney failure 신부전
kidney stone 신결석
kindergarten 유치원
kinematic analysis 운동학문적 분석
Kineret 키너렛
kinesiology 운동학
kinesthesia 운동감각
kinesthetic sense 운동각
kinetics 운동역학
Kingsley Hall 킹슬리 홀
kinship 친족

kinship care 친족케어
Klebsiella pneumonia 클렙시엘라폐렴
Klenzak ankle joint 클렌자크식 발목관절 이음새
Klonopin 클로노핀
Kluver-Bucy syndrome 클뤼버부시증후군
knee disarticulation prosthesis 슬관절의족
knee extension assist 슬관절 신장보조장치
knee giving way 무릎굽힘 ; 무릎불안정
knee joint 무릎이음새
knee orthosis : KO 무릎보조기
knee pad 무릎보호대 ; 니패드
knee replacement 슬관절치환술
knee-ankle-foot orthosis : KAFO 하지보조기
kneel sitting 슬좌위 ; 정좌위
knowledge base 지식기초
knuckle bender
　MP굴곡보조기 ; 너클벤더 ; 손등관절보조기
Kohlberg moral development theory
　콜버그의 도덕발달 이론
Kohs Block Design Test 코스정신발달검사
Kondylen Bettung Munster transtibial
　KBM식 하퇴의족
Korea Academy of Mental Health Social
　Work 한국정신보건사회복지학회
Korea Association in Community Care
　for the Elderly 한국재가노인복지협회
Korea Association of Community Senior
　Club 한국시니어클럽협회
Korea Association of Family Relations
　한국가족관계학회
Korea Association of Senior Welfare
　Centers 한국노인종합복지관협회
Korea Association of social workers

한국사회복지사협회
Korea Care Association 한국요양보호협회
Korea Catholic Old People's Welfare Organization 한국가톨릭노인복지협의회
Korea Consumer Agency 한국소비자보호원 ; 한국소비자원
Korea Counseling Development Institute 한국상담개발원
Korea day care center 한국노인복지센터
Korea Deposit Insurance Corporation 예금보험공사
Korea Elderly Healthcare Association 한국노인치매건강협회
Korea Federation of Senior Welfare 한국노인복지중앙회
Korea Geriatrics Society of Volunteer Service 한국노년자원봉사회
Korea Health Industry Development Institute 한국보건산업진흥원
Korea Housing Association 한국주택협회
Korea Industrial Relations Association 한국노사관계학회
Korea Institute for Health and Social Affairs 한국보건사회연구원
Korea Insurance Research Institute 보험연구원
Korea Labor Force Development Institute for the aged 한국노인인력개발원
Korea Labor Institute 한국노동연구원
Korea Long-Term Care Worker Association 한국요양보호사협회
Korea National Council on Social Welfare 한국사회복지협의회
Korea noin Broadcast 한국노인방송
Korea Qualification Association 한국민간자격협회
Korea Research Institute of Gerontology 한국노년학연구회
Korea Senior Citizens Association 대한노인회
Korea Teachers' Pension 사립학교교직원연금
Korea World Vision 한국선명회
Korean Academy of Clinical

Geriatrics 대한임상노인의학회
Korean Academy of Geriatric Rehabilitation Medicine 대한노인재활의학회
Korean Academy of Oral Health 대한구강보건학회
Korean Academy of Psychiatric and Mental Health Nursing 정신간호학회
Korean Academy of Rehabilitation Medicine 대한재활의학회
Korean Academy of Social Welfare 한국사회복지학회
Korean Aging Society Academy 한국노화학회
Korean Anti-Aging Medical Society 대한노화방지의학회
Korean Association for Dementia 한국치매협회
Korean Association for Geriatric Psychiatry 대한노인정신의학회
Korean Association for Local Government studies 한국지방자치학회
Korean Association for the Study of the Liver 대한간학회
Korean Association of Care Work 한국케어사회복지대학협의회
Korean Association of Family Therapy 한국가족치료학회
Korean Association of Geriatric Hospitals 대한노인요양병원협회
Korean Association of Health Economics and Policy 한국보건경제정책학회
Korean Association of Leisure Time Specialized Coach for the Aged 한국노인여가전문지도자협회
Korean Association of Personal Welfare Facilities for the Aged 한국노인복지개인시설협회
Korean Association of Schools of Social Work 한국사회사업 (복지) 대학협의회
Korean Association of Senior Industry 대한실버산업협회
Korean Athletic Association for the Aged 한국노인체육협회
Korean Bar Association 대한변호사협회

K

Korean Care and Welfare Association
대한전인케어복지협회

Korean Care Serves Center for the Aged
한국노인요양센터

Korean Care Welfare Academy
대한케어복지학회

Korean Care Workers' Association
전국요양보호사협회

Korean Center for Human Rights for the
Aged 한국노인인권센터

Korean church aged school 한국교회노인학
교연합회

Korean College of Neuropsychopharmacology 대한정신약물학회

Korean Council of Geriatric Physical
Therapy 한국노인시설물리치료사협의회

Korean Council of Hospitals for the
Elderly 대한노인병원협의회

Korean Counseling Association
한국상담학회

Korean Counseling Center for the
Suffered Mistreated Aged 한국노인학대피
해상담센터

Korean Cultural Center for the Aged
한국노인문화센터

Korean Dementia Art Therapy
Association 한국치매미술치료협회

Korean Dementia Association 대한치매학회

Korean Dementia Family Information
Network 한국치매가족정보망

Korean Diabetes Association 대한당뇨병학회

Korean Elderly Welfare Newspaper
대한노인복지신문

Korean Family Studies Association
한국가족학회

Korean Federation of Elderly Voters
한국노년유권자연맹

Korean Foundation for Supporting Life
of the Aged 한국노인생활지원재단

Korean Geriatric Medical Association
대한노인의학회

Korean Geriatrics Society
대한노인병학회

Korean Gerontological Society
한국노년학회

Korean Hip Society 대한고관절학회

Korean Information Network for
Preventing Mistreatment to the Aged
한국노인학대방지정보망

Korean Institute for Medical Cares
대한요양보호사협회

Korean Institute of Geriatrics
한국노인병연구소

Korean Institute of Science and
Inventions for the Elderly
대한노인과학발명협회

Korean Insurance Academic Society
한국보험학회

Korean Joint Association of Scientific
Institutions for the Aged
한국노인과학학술단체엽합회

Korean Joint Association of the Aged
한국노인연합회

Korean Leisure Recreation Association
한국여가레크리에이션협회

Korean Lifetime Education University
Council for the Aged 한국평생교육노인대학
협의회

Korean Long-Term Care Institutes
Association for the Aged 한국노인복지장기
요양기관협회

Korean Management Institute of Care
Serves Facilities for the Aged 한국노인요
양시설경영연구회

Korean medicine 한방의학

Korean Mutual Aid Society for the
Elderly 한국노인상조회

Korean Nurses Association 대한간호협회

Korean Nurses Welfare Foundation
대한간호복지재단

Korean Physical Therapy Academy for
the Elderly 대한노인물리치료학회

Korean Research Center for the
Mistreated Aged 한국노인학대연구소

Korean Research Institute for the
Problems of the Aged 한국노인문제연구소

Korean Research Institute of Sexual
 Education for the Aged 한국노인성교육연구소
Korean Research Institute of the Univer-
 sities for the Aged 한국노인대학연구회
Korean Retired Worker's Association
 한국정년퇴직인협회
Korean Social of Welfare for the Aged
 한국노인복지학회
Korean Society for Correction Service
 한국교정학회
Korean Society for the Prevention of
 Lost Dementia Patients 한국치매미아방지협회
Korean Society of Family Law
 한국가족법학회
Korean Society of Internal Medicines for
 the Elderly 대한노인내과학회
Korean Society of Physical Therapy
 대한물리치료학회
Korean Specialized Agencies for
 Protection of the Aged 한국노인보호전문기관
Korean Standard Classification of
 Disease-Cause of Death 한국표준질병·사

인분류
Korean Stroke Society 대한뇌졸중학회
Korean Universities and Welfare Council
 for the Aged 한국노인대학복지협의회
Korean War veteran 한국전쟁퇴역군인
Korean Welfare Counseling Association
 for the Aged 한국노인복지상담협회
Korean Welfare Facilities Association for
 the Aged 한국노인복지시설협회
Korean Welfare Missionary Council for
 the Aged 한국노인복지선교협의회
Korean Welfare Movement for the Aged
 한국노인복지운동
Korsakoff's psychosis 코르사코프 정신병
Koryeo Funeral (leaving one's parents
 when they get older) 고려장
Kubler-Ross model 퀴블러로스 사망단계
Kubler-Ross's five stage of grief
 퀴블러로스 사망단계
kurtosis 첨도
kyphosis 척추후만증 ; 후만

K

L

label 라벨
labeling 낙인 ; 라벨링
labetalol 라베타롤
labile hypertension 동요성 고혈압증
labor collective agreement 단체협약
labor economics 노동경제학
Labor Federation of Government
 Related Organizations 정부관계법인노동조합
 연합
labor force 노동력
labor force population 노동력인구
labor management 노무관리
labor management committee 노사협의회
labor market 노동시장
labor policy 노동정책
labor problem 노동문제
labor productivity 노동생산성
labor relation 노사관계
labor relation commission 노동위원회
labor relations board 노동조정위원회
labor standards inspector 노동기준감독관
labor union 노동조합
labor welfare 노동복지
Labour Insurance Contribution Levy
 Division 노동보험징수과
Labour Market Center Operations Office
 노동시장센터업무실
Labour Standards Bureau 노동기준국
labour welfare 노동복지 ; 복지노동
labyrinthitis 내이염
lacunar dementia 일부치매
lacunar stroke 라크나경색
lady bountiful 여성자원봉사자

laissez-faire 자유방임 ; 자유방임주의
laissez-faire type leadership 방임형 지도
Lamictal 라믹탈
laminar air flow : LAF 충류
lamivudine 라미부딘
lamotrigine 라모트리진
language 언어
laparoscopic surgery 복강경수술 ; 복강경하수술
larceny 절도죄
large intestine polyps 대장폴립
laser doppler flowmetry
 레이저도플러혈류측정기
laser surgery 레이저수술
laser therapy 레이저치료
Lasix 라식스
last hired-first fired 후임자 우선해고원칙
last will 유언장
latchkey child 맞벌이부부 아동
late adolescence 소년후기
late marriage 만혼화
late phase rehabilitation 유지기 재활
latency 잠시
latency period 잠복기
latency stage 잠재기
latency-age child 잠재연령기
latent autoimmune diabetes in adults :
 LADA 성인잠재성 자기면역성 당뇨병
latent content 잠재내용
latent homosexual 잠재적 동성애자
latent infection 잠복감염
latent needs 잠재적 욕구
latent overpopulation 잠재적 과잉인구
latent schizophrenic 잠재적 정신분열증 환자

latent unemployment 잠재실업
late-onset Alzheimer's disease
지발성 알츠하이머병
lateral pinch 측면잡기 ; 파악
lateral whip 외측휘프
later-life activity 고령기 활동
Latino elder 라틴아메리카계고령자
laundry 세탁
laundry room 세탁실
laundry soap 세탁용 비누
laundry synthetic detergent 세탁용 합성세제
lavage cytology 세정세포진
Law 법 ; 법률
Law for Employment Promotion of
Persons with Disabilities 장애인고용촉진법
Law for Medical Benefits/Care 의료급여법
Law for Medical Surgeons 의료기사등에 관
한 법률
Law for Promotion of Nursing Care
Industry 고령친화산업진흥법
law of codetermination 공동결정법
law of domestic relations 친족법
law of effect 효과의 법칙
Law of Settlement and Removal
정주법 및 이주법
law of value 가치법칙
Law to Promote Specified Non-Profit
Activities : NPO Law 특정비영리활동촉진법
law violation 법령위반
lawmaker 입법자
laxative 완하제
layered clothing 겹쳐입음
lay-off 레이오프 ; 임시휴직
LDS Social Services 엘디에스 사회서비스
lead poisoning 납중독
leadership 리더쉽
League of Nations : LON 국제연맹
League of Woman Voters 여성유권자연맹
lean body mass : LBM 제지방체중
learned helplessness
학습성 무력감 ; 학습된 무기력
learned helplessness theory 학습성 무력감
이론

learning ability 학습능력
learning disability : LD 학습장애
learning disability screening LD 스크리닝검사
learning disabled 학습불능자
learning experience 학습경험
learning paradigm 학습패러다임
learning society 학습사회
learning theory 학습이론
least developed country : LDC 최빈국
leather work 가죽세공
leave 휴직
leave benefit 휴직급여
leave of absence : LOA 휴가
leave of absence by menstruation 생리휴가
leaving care 리빙케어
lecture forum 렉추어포룸
leflunomide 레플루노마이드
left lateral recumbent 좌측와위
left ventricular hypertrophy 좌심실비대
leftist 좌파
left-right disorientation 좌우실인
leg length 다리길이 ; 각장 ; 하지장
leg length inequality 각장부동
leg rest 레그레스트 ; 발받침대
legal aid 법률부조
legal aid service 법률부조사업
legal assistance 법률지원
legal capacity 권리능력
legal consultation 법률상담
legal employment 합법취업
legal guardian 법정대리인
legal issue 법적 문제
legal obligation 법적 의무
legal reception services 법정대리수령서비스 ;
대리수령
legal regulation 법적 규제
legal separation 법적 별거
legally designated communicable disease
법정전염병
legitimation 정당화
leg-support 레그서포트
leisure 여가
leisure guidance 여가지도

leisure program 여가프로그램 ; 레저프로그램
leisure time management
여가관리 ; 여권주위 사회사업
leisure time of the aged 노인여가
leisure time welfare facilities for the
aged 노인여가복지시설
lending of welfare equipments 복지용구대여
length of stay : LOS 입소기간 ; 입원기간
leprosy 한센병 ; 나병
leprosy control policy 한센병대책
lesbian 레즈비언
lesbian elder 고령동성애자 ; 레즈비언고령자
less-eligibility principle 열등처우의 원칙
leukemia 백혈병
level of consciousness 의식수준
level of dementia 치매도 ; 인지증도
level of health and welfare 보건복지수준
level of independent 자립도
level of pension benefits 연금급여수준
level of social welfare 사회복지수준
level of welfare 복지수준
levodopa 레보도파
levy 강제할당
Lewy body dementia 루이소체치매
liaison critical pathway 지역연계패스
liberal 자유주의자
liberal welfare state 자유주의적 복지국가
libido 성욕 ; 리비도 ; 성적충동
Librax 리브락스
Librium 라이브리엄 ; 리브리엄
licensed clinical social worker : LCSW
유자격 임상소시얼워커 ; 임상사회복지사
licensed heath care practitioner : LHCP
유자격 의료복지직
licensed nurse 유자격 간호사
licensed social worker 유자격 소시얼워커
lidocaine 리도카인
life course 라이프코스
life cycle 라이프사이클 ; 생활주기
life design 생활설계
life event 라이프이벤트
life expectancy 평균여명
life extension 수명연장

life functioning 생활기능
life history 생활력
life insurance 생명보험
life insurance premium 생명보험료
life line 생명의 전화
life management advisor 생활상담원
life model 생활모델 ; 생활모형
life needs 생활욕구
life review 라이프리뷰 ; 회상
life satisfaction 생활만족도
life skills training 생활기능훈련
life space 생활공간
life space crisis intervention
생활공간위기개입
life stage 라이프스테이지 ; 생활단계 ;
인간발달단계
life structure 생활구조
life table 생명표
life with dignity 존엄있는 생활
life worth living 사는보람이 있는 생활
lifelong education 생애교육 ; 평생교육
lifelong employment 종신고용
lifelong employment system 종신고용제도
lifelong housing 생애주택
lifelong learning 평생학습
lifelong pension 종신연금
lifelong sports 생애스포츠
lifelong wages 생애임금
life-prolonging treatment 연명치료
lifespan 수명
lifespan development 생애발달
lifestyle 생활습관 ; 라이프스타일
lifestyle-related disease 생활습관병
life-sustaining treatment 연명치료
lift 리프트
lift bus 리프트버스
lifter 들어올리기
lifting platform 단차해소기
light adaptation 명순응 ; 광순응
light house 라이트하우스
light reflex 대광반사
light/dark adaptation 명암순응
lighting 조명

lightness 밝기 ; 명도

lightness constancy 밝기 항등성 ; 흑백도항등성

limb kinetic apraxia 지절운동실행

limb-girdle muscular dystrophy
지대형 근이영양증

Limbitrol 린비트롤

limbs 사지

limited assistance 부분원조 ; 부분보조 ;
일부보조

limited liability non-profit mutual benefit
corporation 유한책임중간법인

limited medical care 제한진료

line of old age (age when a person is
treated as old) 노령선

line sepsis 유치카테터감염 (유치카테터패혈증)

linear causality 직선적 인과율

link nurse 제휴간호사 ; 링크널스

lipid 지방질

lipid storage disease 지방질축적증

lipoprotein 리포단백질

lipoprotein receptor-related protein : LRP
리포단백질수용체관련단백

lip-reading 독순술 ; 독화

liquid diet 유동식

liquid soap 액체비누

list of disability grading
신체장애인장애정도등급표

literacy 해독력

literacy program 리터러시 프로그램

literature review 문헌소개 ; 문헌리뷰

lithium 리튬

livelihood aid 생계보호

livelihood problem 생활문제

liver 간장

liver cancer 간암

liver cirrhosis 간경변

liver function test : LFT 간기능검사

liver spots 간반 ; 기미

living assistance for the elderly
고령자생활부조

living assistance services 생활원조

living donor liver transplantation 생체간이식

living environment 생활환경 ; 주거환경

living expense 생활자금

living institution 생활시설

living management center for the aged
노인재가생활지원센터

living support services 생활지원서비스

living trust 생전신탁

living will 리빙윌 ; 자신의 사망처리에 관한 유서 ;
정리의향서 ; 존엄사선언서

loan shark 고리대금업자

loaned executive 론드 이그재큐티브

local administration 지방행정

local allocation tax 지방교부세

local authority association 지방자치체연합

local autonomy 지방자치

Local Autonomy Law 지방자치법

local governing authority 지방행정부

local government 지방자치체

local public enterprise personnel
공영기업직원

local public entity 지방공공단체

locked facility 폐쇄시설

locked unit 폐쇄병동

locked-in syndrome 감금증후군

locomotion 이동

locomotion activity 이동동작

locomotive syndrome
로커모티브신드롬 ; 운동기증후군

locus of center of gravity 중심도

Lofstrand crutch 로프스트랜드 목발

logic of pie 파이의 논리

logotherapy 로고테라피 ; 의미치료

loneliness 고독

lonely people 환과고독

long opponens wrist hand orthosis
장대립보조기

long-distance care 원거리장기요양

long-distance medicine 원거리의료

longevity 장수

longevity science 장수과학

longevity society 장수사회

longitudinal arch 종족궁 ; 세로발활

longitudinal study 종단적 연구 ; 종단적 조사

long-range planning 장기기획

long-sitting position 장좌위
long-term assistance-recipient 요지원자
long-term assistance-required 요지원
long-term care 장기요양보호 ; 장기요양 ;
요양보호 ; 장기치료 ; 장기케어 ; 장기개호 ; 개호
long-term care advisor 개호상담원
long-term care agency for the aged
노인개호기관
long-term care agency for the elderly
고령자개호기관
long-term care allowance 개호수당
long-term care approval score
장기요양인정점수
long-term care approval survey
장기요양인정조사표
long-term care assistance 개호부조
long-term care assistance recipient
지원대상자
long-term care assistance-required
지원대상
long-term care assistant
장기요양원조자 ; 개호원조자
long-term care business 개호비즈니스
long-term care certification 장기요양인정서
Long-Term Care Certification Committee
장기요양인정심사회 ; 개호인정심사회
Long-Term Care Classification Committee
장기요양등급판정위원회
Long-Term Care Classification Committee
장기요양판정위원회
long-term care classification levels
장기요양등급 ; 요개호도
long-term care classification levels
authorization 장기요양등급인정
long-term care costs 장기요양비용
long-term care facilities 장기보호시설
long-term care facility 장기요양시설 ;
개호시설
long-term care facility for the aged
노인개호시설
long-term care facility for the elderly
고령자개호시설
long-term care for the aged

노인장기요양 ; 노인장기요양보장
long-term care home for the elderly
blind 맹인양로원
long-term care industry 장기케어시장
long-term care institute 장기요양기관
long-term care insurance 개호보험
long-term care insurance benefit
장기요양급여 ; 개호급여
long-term care insurance certified
provider 개호보험지정사업자
Long-Term Care Insurance Division
개호보험과
long-term care insurance eligibility
assessment 장기요양인정조사 ;
개호보험인정조사
long-term care insurance for the aged
노인장기요양보험
long-term care insurance for the elderly
고령자개호보험
Long-Term Care Insurance Law
장기요양보험법 ; 개호보험법
Long-Term Care Insurance Law for the
Aged 노인장기요양보험법
long-term care insurance payment
장기요양급여비용 ; 개호보수
long-term care insurance plan
장기요양보험사업계획 ; 개호보험사업계획
long-term care insurance premium
장기요양보험료 ; 개호보험료
long-term care insurance premium rate
장기요양보험료율 ; 개호보험료율
long-term care insurance system
장기요양보험제도 ; 개호보험제도
Long-Term Care Insurance System for
the Aged 노인장기요양보험제도
Long-Term Care Insurance System for
the Disabled People 장애인장기요양보험제도
long-term care model 장기요양모델 ;
개호모델
long-term care needs 장기요양욕구 ;
개호욕구
long-term care office for the aged
노인개호사업소

long-term care ombudsman
장기요양옴부즈맨

long-term care premium 장기요양보험료 ;
개호보험료

long-term care pricing 장기요양수가

long-term care provider for the elderly
고령자개호사업자

long-term care recipient
장기요양등급자 ; 요개호자

Long-Term Care Referee's Committee
장기요양심판위원회

Long-Term Care Review Committee
장기요양심사위원회

long-term care services 장기요양서비스

long-term care services agency for the
aged 노인개호서비스기관

long-term care services agency for the
elderly 고령자개호서비스기관

long-term care services for the aged
노인개호서비스

long-term care services for the elderly
고령자개호서비스

long-term care services office for the
aged 노인개호서비스사업소

long-term care services office for the
elderly 고령자개호서비스사업소

long-term care services package
개호서비스패키지

long-term care services provider for the
aged 노인개호서비스사업자

long-term care services provider for the
elderly 고령자개호서비스사업자

long-term care status 요개호상태

long-term care system 공적노인요양제도

long-term care-required
장기요양대상 ; 요개호

long-term goal 장기목표

long-term health care 요양

long-term health care bed 요양병상

long-term health care beds 요양형병상군

long-term health care benefit expenses
요양급여비용

long-term health care benefits 요양급여

long-term health care expenses
요양병원요양비

long-term health care expenses 요양비

long-term health care facilities 요양형의료
시설

long-term health care facility
개호요양형의료시설

long-term institutional care 장기시설케어

long-term memory 장기기억

long-term stay 장기입소

long-term volunteer 장기자원봉사

loperamide 로페라미드

Lopressor 로프레소

lorazepam 로라제팜

lordosis 전만 ; 척추전만증

Lorenz Curve 로렌쯔곡선

losartan 로살탄

loss 상실

loss of appetite 식욕부진 ; 식욕저하

loss of smell 후각저하

loss of taste 미각저하

loss of touch sensation 촉지각저하 ;
접촉감저하

lost experience 상실체험

lotus position 연화좌

Lou Gehrig's disease 루게릭병

love belonging needs 사회적 욕구

low back pain 요통

Low Birth Rate and Aging Society
Commission 저출산·고령사회위원회

low birth weight infant 저출생체중아

low cost care service facilities for the
aged 경비노인양로시설

low cost health care service facilities
for the aged 경비노인요양시설

low cost pension for the elderly
감액노령연금

low cost specialized health care service
facilities for the aged 경비노인전문요양시설

low floor bus 저상버스

low frequency current therapy 저주파요법

low income 저소득

low income class 저소득층

low income country 저소득국
low income family 저소득가정
Low Income Home Energy Assistance
  program 저소득가정 에너지원조 프로그램
low income household 저소득세대
low level disinfection 저수준소독
low salt diet 감염식
low sodium diet 감염식
low temperature burn 저온화상
low vision 저시력
low-density lipoprotein : LDL
  LDL 콜레스테롤 ; 저밀도콜레스테롤 ; 저밀도지단백
lower class 하류계층
lower esophageal sphincter : LES
  하부식도괄약근
lower esophageal sphincter dysfunction
  하부식도괄약근 기능장애
lower extremity 하지
lower extremity orthosis 하지보조기
lower gastrointestinal 하부소화관
lower limb amputation 하지절단
lower limb prosthesis 의족
lower motor neuron
  하위운동뉴런 ; 하위운동신경원
lower social stratum 하층사회
low-fat diet 저지방식
low-income rental housing for the
  elderly 저소득고령자대상 임대주택
low-wage labor 저임금노동
low-wage labor market 저임금노동시장
lumbago 요통

lumbago exercise 요통체조
lumbago prevention 요통예방
lumbar puncture 요추천자
lumbar radiculopathy 요골신경근증
lumbar spinal cord injury 요골손상
lumbar traction 요추견인
lumbar vertebrae 요추
lumbosacral orthosis 요선추보조기
lumbrical bar 충양근대
luminance 밝기 ; 휘도
lump sum payment for outpatient
  외래시 일부부담금
lumpectomy 유선종양적출방법
lump-sum withdrawal payments 탈퇴일시금
lung cancer 폐암
lung capacity 폐활량
lung transplant 폐이식
lung volume reduction surgery 폐용량감소술
lupus 낭창 ; 루프스
lutein 루테인
Luvox 루복스
luxatio coxae congenita 선천성 고관절탈구
luxation 탈구
lycopene 리코펜
lying position 와위
lying position for rest 안정침상
Lyrica 리리카
Lysosomal diseases 리소솜병
Lysosomal storage disease 리소좀 ; 리소좀병
Lysosomal storage diseases 리소좀축적병

M

M wave M파
M. William Beveridge 베버리지
MacArthur Competence Assessment Tool
for Treatment : MacCAT-T 동의능력평가도
구 ; 맥아더치료 동의능력평가도구
macro level 마크로레벨
macro orientation 거시적 지향
macro practice 거시적 실천
macrocytic anemia 대적혈구성 빈혈증
macular degeneration 황반변성
mad-cow disease 광우병
Madelung deformity 마데룽변형
magic hand 마법의 손 ; 매직핸드
magnesium 마그네슘
magnetic resonance angiography : MRA
자기공명혈관촬영
magnetic resonance imaging : MRI
자기공명장치
magnetic stimulation 자기자극
magnifying endoscopy 확대내시경검사
mail survey 우송조사법
mainstreaming 주류화 ; 메인스트리밍
maintain a sitting position 좌위보지
maintenance 메인트넌스
maintenance of the dignity 존엄의 보지
major affective disorder 주요정서장애
major depression 대우울증 ; 주우울증
malacia 이식증 ; 연화증
maladjusted behavior 부적응행동
maladjustment 부적응
maladjustment disorder 적응장애
male nursery teacher 보부
malignant rheumatoid arthritis

악성관절류머티즘
malignant tumor 악성종양
mallet finger 망치수지 ; 추상지 ; 해머지 ; 추지
malnutrition 영양실조 ; 영양불량
malposture 불량자세 ; 불량지위
malpractice 부정행위
malpractice insurance 의료과오보험
Malthusianism 맬더스주의
maltreatment 학대
mammogram 유방촬영술
mammography 만모그라피
managed care 매니지드케어
managed care plan 매니지드케어프랜
managed competition
관리경쟁 ; 매니지드콘페티션
managed cost
비용관리 ; 관리가능고정비 ; 자유재량고정원가
managed health care 매니지드헬스케어
managed long-term care 개호판 매니지드케어
management information systems : MISs
관리정보체계
management participation 경영참가
management system 매니지먼트시스템
management system of growth rate
성장율관리제도
management tasks 관리과업
Management Training Program : MTP
관리자훈련계획
mandatory retirement 정년퇴직
mandatory retirement system 정년제
mania 매니아 ; 조증 ; 광기
manic depressive psychosis 조울증 ; 조우울증
manic depressive psychosis in the

elderly 노년기 조우울증
manic episode 조증 에피소드
manic-depressive illness 조울병
Manifest Anxiety Scale 현재성 불안척도
manifest content 현재내용
manifested needs 현재적욕구
manometry 검압법
Manpower Development and Training Act 인력개발 및 훈련법
manpower planning 인력기획
manslaughter 고살죄
manual attendant controlled wheelchair 탑승자제어 휠체어
manual Braille writer 수동점자타이프라이터 ; 수동점자타자기 ; 수동브라이유식 점자타이프라이터
manual cleaning 수작업 세정 ; 용수세정
manual muscle testing : MMT 도수근력검사
manual therapy 도수요법 ; 맨손요법
manual-type Braille writer 수동브라이유식 점자타이프라이터
mapping technique 매핑기법
marasmus 노쇠 ; 마라스무스 ; 쇠약
marginal village 한계취락
Maria Montessory 몬테소리
marijuana 대마
marital contracts 결혼계약
marital deduction 배우자공제 ; 부부간 공제
marital property agreement 부부재산계약
marital relationship 부부관계
marital role 부부역할
marital skew 결혼왜곡
marital therapy 부부요법 ; 부부치료
market basket method 마켓바스켓방식 ; 시장바구니방식 ; 이론생계비방식
market economy 시장경제
market failure 시장의 실패
market mechanism 시장원리
market success 시장의 성공
market testing 시장성 테스트 ; 마켓테스팅
Marplan 마플란
marriage 결혼 ; 혼인
marriage certificate 혼인증명서

marriage counseling 결혼상담 ; 부부상담
marriage counseling center 결혼상담소
Marriott Seniors Volunteerism Study 매리어트 노인자원봉사조사
Martin-Gruber anastomosis 마틴그류버접합
Marxism 마르크스주의
Maslow's hierarchy of needs 매슬로의 욕구5단계설 ; 매슬로의 욕구단계
masochism 피학성
mass communication 매스커뮤니케이션 ; 매스컴
mass leisure 대중여가
mass media 대중매체 ; 매스미디어
mass society 대중사회
massage 맛사지
massage therapy 맛사지요법
masseur 안마사(남성)
masseuse 안마사(여성)
mastectomy 유방절단술
master of social work : MSW 사회복지학석사
master's degree 석사호
mastication 저작
masticatory disorder 저작기능장애 ; 저작장애
masticatory disturbance 저작장애
masticatory myositis 저작근염
masturbation 마스타베이션
mat 매트
mat activity 매트동작
mat exercise 매트운동
matching gift 매칭기프트제도
material abuse 물질적 학대
material culture 물질문화
maternal 임산부
maternal and child health care 모자보건
Maternal and Child Health Division 모자보건과
maternal and child health handbook 모자수첩 ; 모자건강수첩
maternal and child pension 모자복지연금 ; 모자연금
maternal and child problem 모자문제
Maternal death rate 임산부사망율
maternity 모성
maternity allowance 출산수당 ; 출산수당금

maternity assistance 출산부조
maternity home 조산시설
maternity homes 모자원
maternity leave 출산휴가
maternity neurosis 육아노이로제
maternity protection 모성보호
matrix metalloprotease enzyme
기질금속단백질분해효소
mattress 매트리스
mattress pad 매트리스패드
mature 원숙
Maxalt 맥살트
maximal gait velocity 최대보행속도
maximum conduction velocity : MCV
최대전도속도
maximum muscle strength 최대근력
maximum oxygen consumption
최대산소소비량
maximum resting pressure : MRP
최대정지압
maximum squeeze pressure : MSP
최대수의수축압
maximum tolerable volume 최대내용량
McGill Pain Questionnaire : MPQ
맥길 통증질문지
meal 식사
meal delivery service 밑반찬배달서비스
meal delivery services 배식서비스
meal management 식사관리
meal preparation 식사준비
meal services 식사서비스
meal services for the elderly 고령자급식
meal tray services 상차리기
mean 평균
means test 재산조사 ; 자산조사 ; 민즈테스트 ;
수입조사 ; 자본조사
measles 홍역
measure of central tendency 중심경향측정
measurement 측정
measurement of body temperature
체온측정
mechanical cleaning 기계세정
mechanical diet 연식

mechanical soft diet 연식
mechanism 기제
Medecins Sans Frontieres : MSF
국경없는 의사회
media 매체
medial single hip joint system
내측단고이음새 시스템
medial whip 내측휘프
median 중간값
mediation 조정 ; 절충 ; 중재
mediation divorce 중재 이혼
mediator role 중재자 역할
Medic Alert 의료경보
Medicaid 메디케이드
medical aid 의료보호
medical aid for children with potential
disability 육성의료
medical aid for premature infants 양육의료
medical aid for specific chronic diseases
of children 소아만성특정질환치료연구사업
medical and health care for the aged
노인보건의료
medical and health care plan for the
aged 노인보건의료계획
medical and health care services for the
aged 노인보건의료서비스
medical and health care system for the
aged 노인보건의료제도
medical and welfare facilities for the
aged 노인의료복지시설
medical anthropologist 의료인류학자
medical anthropology 의료인류학
medical assistance 의료부조
medical benefit 의료급부
Medical Benefits Law 의료보호법
medical care and education for the
disabled children 요육의료
medical care benefit 요양급여 ; 의료급여
medical care expenditures for the aged
노인의료비
medical care expenses 요양비 ; 의료비
medical care for people with mental
disabilities 정신장애인의료

M

medical care for people with mental
retardation 지적장애인의료
medical care for the disabled 장애인의료
medical care for the disabled children
장애아의료
medical care for the elderly 고령자의료
medical care for the physically disabled
신체장애인의료
medical care service 의료보호사업
medical care services agency for the
elderly 고령자의료서비스기관
medical care services for the aged
노인의료서비스
medical care services for the elderly
고령자의료서비스
medical care services office for the
elderly 고령자의료서비스사업소
medical care services provider for the
elderly 고령자의료서비스사업자
medical care system for remote areas
벽지의료체제
medical care system for the aged
노인의료제도
medical care system for the elderly
고령자의료제도
medical casework 의료개별사회사업
medical caseworker 의료케이스워커
medical certificate of the cause of death
시체검안서
medical check-up 건강체크
medical coder 진료정보관리사계
medical corporation 의료법인
medical delivery system 의료전달체계
medical device 의료기기 ; 의료기재 ; 의료도구 ;
의료용구
medical director 의사장
medical economic 의료경제
medical economic index 의료경제지수
Medical Economics Division 의료과
medical education system
의사양성제도 ; 의료교육제도
medical equipment 의료기기 ; 의료기재 ;
의료도구 ; 의료용구

medical error 의료미스 ; 의료사고
medical ethics 의료윤리
medical expenses 의료비 ; 요양비
medical expenses for the aged
고령자보건의료비 ; 노인의료비
medical expenses for the elderly
고령자의료비
medical facility for public assistance
recipients 의료보호시설
medical fee 진료보수
medical history 기왕력 ; 치료력 ; 치료경험연수 ;
기왕경험연수
medical home care 재가의료
medical home care plan 재가의료대책
medical home care services 재가의료서비스
medical home-based care 거택의료
medical home-based care services
거택의료서비스
medical home-based care services
agency 거택의료서비스기관
medical home-based care services
provider 거택의료서비스사업자
medical home-based care services office
거택의료서비스사업소
medical home-based care services plan
거택의료서비스계획
medical industrial complex 의료산업복합체
medical inspector 의료감시원
medical insurance 의료보험
medical insurance card recipient
의료수급자증
medical insurance system 의료보험제도
medical interview 의료면접
medical issue 의학분야문제
medical leave 병휴가
medical letter 메디컬레터
medical malpractice 의료과오 ; 의료과실
medical malpractice liability insurance
의료과오보상보험
medical malpractice suit 의료과오소송
medical marijuana 의료대마
medical model 의학모델 ; 의료모델

medical model of disability 장애의 의학모델
Medical Outcomes Study 36-Item Short-Form Health Survey : MOS SF-36 36항목 건강설문지
medical personnel 의료관계자
medical practice 의료행위 ; 의술업 ; 의업 ; 의행위
Medical Practitioners Law 의사법
Medical Practitioners' Registration Act 의사등록법
medical problem 의료문제
medical profession 의료전문
medical professional 의료전문직
Medical Professions Division 의사과
medical records 의료기록
medical rehabilitation 의료적 재활 ; 의학적 재활
medical rehabilitation services 갱생의료
medical resources 의료자원
medical security 의료보장
medical security program 의료보장프로그램
medical service plan 의료서비스계획
Medical Services Law 의료법
medical social security 의료보장제도
medical social services 의료사회복지사업
medical social work : MSW 메디컬소시얼워크 ; 의료사회사업 ; 의료사회복지
medical social worker 의료사회복지사 ; 의료사회사업가
medical specialist 전문의
medical staff 의료종사자
medical supply 의료품
medical support assistant 의료원조자
medical team 의료팀
medical thermometer 체온측정계
medical treatment fee system 진료보수제도
medical waste 의료폐기물
medically needy 의료보호대상자 ; 의료곤궁대상자
medically underserved area 무의촌 ; 무의지구 ; 의료서비스부족지역 ; 의료과소지역
Medicare 메디케어
Medicare system 건강보험제도

medication 약제
medication adherence 복약치료지속성
medication compliance 복약준수
medication error 투약과오 ; 오약
medication interaction 약물상호작용
medication management 약제관리 ; 복약관리
medication restriction 투약제한
medicine 의료
medicine and welfare 의료복지
medicine ball 메디신볼
Medicredit 의료신용제
medulla oblongata 연수
medullary thyroid cancer 갑상선수양암
megaloblastic anemia 거적아구성 빈혈
megatrend 메가트렌드
meiosis 감수분열
melanocyte 멜라닌세포
melatonin 멜라토닌
melena 하혈 ; 흑색변 ; 멜레나
memantine 메만틴
membrane filter 막여과기 ; 멤브레인 필터
memorial hospital 기념병원
memory 기억
memory disorder 기억장애
memory disturbance 기명장애
Memory Impairment Screen : MIS 기억장애검사
memory retention 기명력
menarche 초경
Meniere's disease 메니에르병 ; 메니에르신드롬
meningeal leukemia 수막백혈병
meningitis 수막염
menopausal disorder 갱년기장애
menopause 폐경 ; 갱년기 ; 메노포즈
mental age : MA 정신연령
mental and behavioral disorder 정신 및 행동장애
mental and physical disability 심신장애
mental capacity assessment 의사능력평가
mental competency 정신적 적응력
mental cruelty 정신적 학대
mental disability 정신장애
mental health 정신보건 ; 정신건강 ; 정신위생

M

M

mental health administration 정신보건행정
Mental Health and Disability Health
  Division 정신·장애보건과
mental health and welfare 정신보건복지
mental health and welfare center
  정신보건복지센터
mental health and welfare counselor
  정신보건복지상담원
mental Health Association 정신건강협회
mental health care 정신위생케어 ; 마음의 케어
mental health center 정신보건센터
mental health clinic 정신위생클리닉
Mental Health Committees 정신의료심사회
mental health counselor 정신보건카운셀러
mental health professional 정신건강 전문가
mental health services 정신보건서비스
mental health team 정신건강 팀
mental health workers 정신건강 사회사업가
mental hospitals 정신병원
mental hygiene movement 정신위생운동
mental illness 정신질환
mental retardation : MR
  지적장애 ; 정신박약 ; 정신지체 ; 발달지체
mental status exam 정신상태검사
mentally retarded infant 지적장애유아
menu 메뉴 ; 식단
meralgia paresthetica 대퇴통 지각이상
mercantilism 중상주의
mercury poisoning 수은중독
Meridia 메리디아
merit goods 메리트재
merosin-deficient congenital muscular
  dystrophy 메로신결핍 선천성 근이영양증
mesmerize 최면술 ; 심령치료 ; 메스메리즘
metabolic disease 대사성 질환
metabolic disorder 대사이상
metabolic equivalent of task : MET
  대사당량 ; 메츠
metabolic inhibitor 대사저해제
metabolic syndrome 메타보릭크증후군
metabolism 대사
metacognition 상위인지 ; 초인지 ; 메타인지
metal craft 금공세공

metamer 동위색 ; 조건등색지수
metamerism 조건등색
metamessage 메타메시지
metamorphosis of capital 자본의 전형운동
metaphor 은유 ; 메타포
metatarsal bar 중족골지지대
metaxalone 메탁살론
metered-dose inhaler 정량분무식 흡입기
metformin 메트포민 ; 메트포르민
methicillin-resistant staphylococcus
  aureus : MRSA 메티실린 내성 황색포도구균
methocarbamol 메토카르바몰
methods in social work 사회사업방법론
methotrexate 메토트렉세이트
methylprednisolone 메틸프레드니솔론
metolazone 메톨라존
metoprolol 메토프롤롤
metropolitan area 대도시권
Mettray 메트레이
mezzo level 메조레벨
mezzo practice 중도실천
micro balloon 마이크로벌룬
micro level 미크로레벨
microangiography 미소혈관조영
microbial sampling 환경미생물조사
microbial substitute 균교대현상
microclimate of sleeping floor 침상기후
micro-expressions 미표정
microorganism contamination 미생물오염
microwave therapy 극초단파요법
micturition center 배뇨중추
micturition disorder 배뇨장애
mid swing 유각중기
middle adolescence 소년중기
middle age 중년
middle range theory 중범위이론
middle-class consciousness 중류의식
midlife crisis 중년위기
mid-stance phase 입각중기
Midtown Manhattan Study
  미드타운 맨하턴 연구조사
midwife 조산사 ; 조산원
migraine headache 편두통

migrant care worker 외국인장기요양노동자
migrant laborer 이민노동자
migrant work 객지벌이
mild cognitive impairment : MCI 경도인지장애
miliary tuberculosis 속립결핵증
milieu therapy 환경치료
military social work 군대사회사업
Milwaukee brace 척추측만증보조기
minced meal 다진고기식
mind-body medicine 심신의학
mineral 미네랄 ; 무기질
mineral deficiency 미네랄결핍증
mineral excess 과잉미네랄
mineral supplementation 미네랄보급
Mini Mental State Examination : MMSE
　간이정신상태검사
Mini Nutritional Assessment : MNA
　간이영양상태평가
mini stroke 미니뇌졸중
minimal brain damage : MBD 미세뇌기능장애
minimal brain dysfunction 최소두뇌장애
minimal erythema dose : MED 최소홍반량
minimally invasive surgery 최소침습수술
minimum cost of living 최저생계비 ; 최저생
　활비
Minimum Data Set : MDS 미니멈 데이터세트
minimum market basket 최저생활가계부
minimum needs estimation 최저요구 측정
minimum standard 최저수준
minimum standard of living 최저생활
minimum subsistence level 최저생존수준
minimum wage 최저임금
minimum wage system 최저임금제도
Minipress 미니프레스
Ministry of Health 후생노동부
Ministry of Health and Welfare 보건복지부
Minnesota Multiphasic Personality
　Inventory : MMPI 미네소타 다면인격목록
minor 미성년 ; 미성년자
minor brain damage : MBD 미세뇌손상
minor child 미성년아이
minor offence 경범죄
minor registry 미성년자 등기부

minorities of color 유색소수인종
minority 마이너리티 ; 수수파
minority group
　마이너리티그룹 ; 소수집단 ; 소수파그룹
minutes 회의록
miosis 축동
Mirapex 미라펙스
mirror writing 거울문자 ; 경영문자
misdiagnosis 오진
missing child 미아
missing person 행불자
misuse 오용
misuse syndrome 오용증후군
mitochondrial disease 미토콘드리아병
mitral regurgitation 승모판폐쇄부전
mitral stenosis 승모판협착증
mixed dementia 혼합형 치매
mixed economy 혼합경제
mixed hearing loss 혼합성 난청
Miyake Paired Verbal Association
　Learning Test 미야케식 기명력검사
mob psychology 군중심리
mobile arm support
　만능팔 지지기 ; 거상 팔 지지대
mobile beauty services 방문이미용서비스
mobile dental hygiene and educational
　services 방문치과위생지도
mobile dental hygiene services 방문치과위생
mobile nursery service 순회보육
mobile oral health services 방문구강위생
mobile room air cleaner
　가동성 실내공기청정기
mobility 가동성 ; 이동성
mobility aid
　이동보조도구 ; 보행보조기기 ; 이동관련복지용구
mobility skill 이동기능
mobilization 모바라이제이션 ; 수동술
Mobilization for Youth 청소년을 위한 이동사업
MODAPTS 모답츠법
mode 중위수
model of disability 장애모델
modeling 모델링
moderation in medical care costs

M

의료비적정화
modernization 근대화 ; 현대화
modernization theory 근대화론
Modified Ashworth Scale 수정 애쉬워스척도
modified Barthel index 수정 바셸지수
Modified Water Swallow Test
수정 물마시기검사
modular prosthesis 모듈러 의지
modular seating system 모듈러식 좌위보지장치
modular wheelchair system 모듈러 휠체어
module 모듈
Mohs surgery 모스수술
moist heat sterilization 습열멸균
moist heating 습성온열
molded seating system 몰드형 좌위보지장치
monetary needs 화폐적 욕구
money management 금전관리
mongolism 몽고리즘
monitor 모니터
monitoring 모니터링
monitoring measurement 모니터측정
monoamine oxidase inhibitor
모노아민 산화효소저해약
monochromatic light 단색광
monogamy 일부일처제 ; 일처일부체
monoplegia 단마비
monopolization 업무독점
monosaccharide 단당류
monosaccharide anhydride 단당무수물
monosynaptic reflex 단시냅스반사
monthly : 1M 매월
monthly charge 월부과 ; 당월부과
monthly premium 월보험료 ; 소득월액보험료
mood 기분
mood disorder 기분장애
moral hazard 모럴헤저드 ; 도덕적 해이
morale 모럴
morality of long-term care 개호이념
moratorium 지불유예
morbid 질병
morbidity compression 질병의 압축 ;
병적상태의 압축
morbidity rate 질병률

morbilli 홍역
morgue 사체안치소
Morita therapy 모리타요법
moron 저능자
morpheme 형태소
morphine 모르피네
morphine dependence 모르피네 의존
morphogenesis 형태발생
morphostasis 형태안정
mortality rate 사망률
mothball 방충제
Mother without Custody
저녀보호권이 박탈된 어머니회
mother-headed family 모자가족
motherhood 모성
mothering 모성적 양육 ; 머더링
motherless family 부자가정
motherless household 부자세대
mother-to-child transmission 모자간염
motion analysis 동작분석
motion control 운동제어
motivated needs 동기부여된 욕구
motivation 동기 ; 동기부여 ; 동기화
motor age 운동연령
motor age test 운동연령검사
motor aphasia 운동실어 ; 운동성 실어
motor apraxia 운동실행
motor assessment 운동평가
motor ataxia 운동실조
motor development 운동발달
motor developmental evaluation
운동발달평가
motor evoked potential 운동유발전위
motor function 운동기능
motor impairment 운동장애
motor impersistence 운동유지곤란
motor learning 운동학습
motor nerve 운동신경
motor nerve conduction velocity
운동신경전도속도
motor neuron 운동뉴런
motor neuron disease 운동뉴런질환
motor paralysis 운동마비

motor point 운동점
motor point block 운동점블록 ; 모터포인트블록
motor skill 운동기능
motor unit 운동단위
motor unit action potential : MUAP
운동단위활동전위
motor vehicle accident 자동차사고
mourning 초상 ; 상복 ; 애도
mouth-to-mouth breathing
구강대 구강 인공호흡
mouth-to-nose breathing 구강대 비강 인공호흡
mouton 무톤
movement 운동 ; 동작
movement analysis 운동분석
movement disorder 운동장애
movement during swallowing 연하운동
movement dysfunction 운동장애
movement for people with mental
disabilities 정신장애인운동
movement for people with mental
retardation 지적장애인운동
movement for the physically disabled
신체장애인운동
movement scale 이동척도법
movement-related functional limitation
운동제한
moving around by wheelchair 휠체어이동
moving expenses 전근비용
moxibustion 뜸요법
moxibustion therapist 구사 ; 뜸사
muckrakers 폭로자
mucocutaneous lymph node syndrome
가와사키병
mucopolysaccharidosis 무코다당증
multidimensional functional assessment
다차원적 기능평가
multidimensional poverty index : MPI
다차원빈곤지수
multi-drug resistance : MDR 다제내성
multi-drug resistant tuberculosis :
MDR-TB 다제내성 결핵
multi-infarct dementia : MID 다발경색성 치매
Multilevel Assessment Instrument : MAI

다단계평가
multimodal therapy 다면적 요법
Multiphasic Environmental Assessment
Procedure : MEAP 포괄적 환경요인조사표
multiple cerebral infarction 다발성 뇌경색
multiple debtor 다중채무
multiple disabilities 중복장애
multiple handicapped 중복장애인
multiple handicapped child 중복장애아
multiple handicaps 중복장애
multiple interviews 중복면접
multiple organ dysfunction syndrome :
MODS 다장기기능부전증후군
multiple organ failure 다장기기능부전
multiple personality 다중성격
multiple personality disorder 다중인격성 장애
multiple sclerosis : MS 다발성 경화증
multiple system atrophy : MSA 다계통위축증
multipotent 다분화능 ; 다능
multipotent adult progenitor cell
성인형 다능성 간세포
multipotent drug 강력한 약
multiproblem family 복합문제 가족
multipurpose senior center
고령자다목적복지센터
multivariate analysis 다변량해석
mumps 유행성 이하선염
mumps 이하선염
municipal consolidation 시정촌 합병
municipal council of social welfare
시정촌 사회복지협의회
municipal court 자치체 재판소
municipal health center 시정촌 보건센터
municipality 시정촌
municipality's general account
시정촌 일반회계
municipality's long-term care insurance
program plan 시정촌 개호보험사업계획
Munsell color system 먼셀표색계
murder 살인
muscle 근육 ; 근
muscle biopsy 근생검
muscle contracture 근구축 ; 근구축증

muscle cramp 근 클램프 ; 근경련 ; 근경축 ; 열경련

muscle endurance 근지구력

muscle fatigue 근피로

muscle fiber conduction velocity 근섬유전도속도

muscle fiber type 근섬유형

muscle hypertonia 근긴장항진

muscle hypertrophy 근비대

muscle hypotonia 근긴장저하

muscle maintenance 근력유지

muscle reeducation 근재교육

muscle relaxant 근이완제

muscle relaxation technique 근육이완법

muscle strength 근력

muscle strength measurement 근력측정

muscle strengthening exercise 근력강화훈련

muscle tonus 근긴장

muscular atrophy 근위축

muscular dystrophy 근육위축증 ; 근이영양증

muscular strengthening 근력강화

muscular weakness 근력저하

musculoskeletal disease 근골격질환

musculoskeletal system 근골격계

music therapy 음악요법

mutations of genes 유전자의 돌연변이

muted voice 함축소리

mutism 함구증

mutual aid 상호부조

mutual aid association 공제조합

mutual aid groups 상호원조집단

mutual aid pension 공제연금

mutual aid system 공제제도

mutual assistance 상호부조

mutual help 상호협력

myalgic encephalomyelitis 근통성 뇌척수염

myasthenia gravis : MG 중증근무력증

mycosis 진균증

myelodysplastic syndrome 골수이형성증후군

myelopathy 척수증

myocardial infarction 심근경색

myocardial ischemia 심근허혈

myoclonic seizure 근경련발작 ; 근간대성 발작 ; 근육간대경련발작

myoclonus 근육간대경련 ; 간대성 근경련 ; 미오크로누스

myoclonus epilepsy 간대성 근경련간질 ; 마이오클로누스간질

myodesopsia 비문증

myoelectric upper limb prosthesis 근전의수

myofascial pain syndrome : MPS 근근막성 동통증후군

myofascial release 근막이완요법 ; 근막릴리스

myoglobin 미오글로빈

myopathy 근질환 ; 근육병 ; 미오파치

myositis 근염

myositis ossificans 골화성 근염

myotonia 근긴장증

myotonic dystrophy 근긴장성 이영양증

M

N

nail 손톱
naltrexone 날트렉손
Namenda 나멘다
nanny 베이비시터
Naprosyn 나프로신
naproxen 나프록센
narcissism 나르시시즘 ; 자아도취
narcissistic caregiver 자기애성 장기요양자
narcissistic personality disorder
　자기애성 인격장애
narcotic 마약
narcotic addicted 마약중독자
narcotic addicted infant 마약중독유아
narcotic addiction 마약중독
narcotics 마취제 ; 마약
Nardil 나딜 ; 나르딜
narrative approach
　내러티브적 접근 ; 이야기접근법
narrative therapy
　담화치료 ; 이야기치료 ; 내러티브테라피
nasal 경비
nasal tube feeding 경비경관영양
NASW Code of Ethics
　전국사회사업가협회 윤리강령
National Academy of Practice : NAP
　국립사회복지연수원
National Advisory Council on the Social
　Security System 사회보장제도심의회
national allocation plan 나라별할당계획
National Association of Social Workers
　Code of Ethics 미국소시얼워커윤리강령
National Basic Human Needs Security
　Law 국민생활기초생활보장법

National Basic Livelihood Security Act
　국민기초생활보장제도
national burden rate 국민부담율
National Cancer Institute 국립암연구센터
national census 국세조사
National Center for Child Health and
　Development 국립생육의료연구센터
National Center for Geriatrics and
　Gerontology 국립장수의료연구센터
National Center for Global Health and
　Medicine 국립국제의료연구센터
National Center for Health Statistics
　Research : NCHSR 국립보건통계조사사청
National Center of Neurology and
　Psychiatry 국립정신·신경의료연구센터
National Center on Child Abuse and
　Neglect 국립아동학대및방임예방센터
National Center on Social Work Policy
　and Practice 한국사회사업정책 및 실무센터
National Cerebral and Cardiovascular
　Center 국립순환기병연구센터
National Certification Examination and
　Practice Examination 국가시험·실기시험
National Certification Examination and
　Practice Examination for Care Workers
　개호복지사 국가시험·실기시험
National Certification Examination for
　Care Worker 개호복지사 국가시험
National Conference on Catholic
　Charities 전국카톨릭자선단체대회
National Consumer Affairs Center of
　Japan 국민생활센터
National Council of Hospitals for Elderly

전국노인병원협의회

national expenditures on long-term care services 국민개호비용

National Food Bank 전국푸드뱅크

National Health and Welfare Festival 전국건강복지축제

national health expenditures 국민의료비

National Health Festival for the Elderly 전국노인건강축제

National health Insurance 국민건강보험 ; 국민보건보험

National Health Insurance Act 국민건강보험법

National Health Insurance card 국민건강보험증

National Health Insurance Corporation 국민건강보험공단

National Health Insurance Division 국민건강보험과

National Health Insurance premiums 국민건강보험료

National Health Insurance society 국민건강보험조합

National Health Insurance System 국민건강보험제도

National Health Personnel Licensing Examination Board 한국보건의료인국가시험원

national health promotion movement 국민건강만들기 운동

National Health Promotion Movement in the21st Century 21세기에 있어서의 국민건강 만들기 운동

national health promotion policy 국민건강만들기 대책

national health service 국민보건서비스

national hospital 국립병원

National Hospitals Division 국립병원과

national income : NI 국민소득

National Information Society Agency 한국정보화진흥원

National Institute of Child Health and Human Development 국립아동건강 및 인간 발달연구원

National Institute of Health 국립보건원

National Institute of Health Sciences 국립의약품식품위생연구소

National Institute of Infectious Diseases 국립감염증연구소

National Institute of Mental Health : NIMH 국립정신보건연구원

National Institute of Population and Social Security Research 국립사회보장·인구문제연구소

National Institute of Public Health 국립보건의료과학원

National Institute of Welfare Association for the Elderly 전국노인복지단체협의회

national long-term care expenditures 국민개호비용

national medical expenditures 국민의료비

national minimum 내셔널미니멈 ; 최저국민수준

national minimum standards 국가최저기준

national minimum wage 국가최저임금

national minimum wage compliance officer 국가최저임금감독관

National Pension 국민연금

National Pension Corporation 국민연금공단

National Pension Council 연금심의회

National Pension Fund 국민연금기금

National Pension Insurance 국민연금보험

National Pension Law 국민연금법

National Pension premiums 국민연금보험료

National Pension registration number 국민연금의 기호번호

National Recovery Administration : NRA 국립부흥청

national responsibility 국가책임

national service framework : NSF 서비스체제 ; 서비스프레임워크

National Specialized Agency for Protection of Elderly 전국노인보호전문기관

National Union of Welfare Association for the Elderly 전국노인복지단체연합회

national universal medical insurance 전국민의료보험

National Urban League 전국도시연맹

National Welfare Center for the Elderly
전국노인복지관대회
nationalism 내셔널리즘 ; 국가주의
nationality 국적
Native American 네이티브아메리칸 ; 미국선주민
natural disaster 천재지변 ; 자연재해
natural fiber 천연섬유
natural group 자연집단
natural helping network 자연원조망
naturalization 귀화
naturally occurring retirement
community 자연발생적 퇴직자커뮤니티
nausea 구토 ; 구역질
near poor population 유사빈곤층
near-infrared 근적외선
nebulizer 의료용 분무기 ; 네블라이저
neck distortion 경추염좌
necrosis 괴사
nectar liquid diet 과즙액체식
need 니드
need for public assistance 요보호성
need group 욕구집단
needle biopsy 천자생검 ; 침생검
needle cytology 천자세포진
needle electromyogram 침근전도
needle puncture 침천자
needlestick 니들스틱
needlestick injury 니들스틱상처 ; 니들스틱사고
needs 니즈 ; 욕구
needs assessments 욕구사정 ; 욕구평가
needs survey 욕구조사
needs survey method 욕구측정법
needs-response principle 필요즉응의 원칙
needy person 곤궁자
negative income tax 부의 소득세
negative income tax : NIT 부의 소득세 ;
역소득세
negative mold 음성모델
negative pressure pulmonary edema
음압성 폐수종
negative punishment 부의 벌
negative reinforcement 부정적 강화 ;
부의 강화

negative transference 부정적 전이
neglect 방임 ; 무시 ; 니글렉트 ; 양육방치
neglected child 유기아
negligence 태만
negotiation 협상
neighborhood 근린
neighborhood association 반상회
neighborhood guild 네이버후드 길드
neighborhood information 근린정보센터
neighborhood movement 인보운동
Neighborhood Youth Corps 지역청소년단
neoconservatism 신보수주의
neo-Freudian 신프로이트학파
neoliberal 신자유주의
Neonatal Behavior Assessment Scale
신생아행동평가
neonatal deaths rate 신생아사망율
neonatal intensive care unit : NICU
신생아집중치료실
neonate 신생아
nephrectomy 신적제
nephritic syndrome 네프로제증후군
nephrologist 신장내과의 ; 신장전문의
nephrology 신장학
nerve block 신경블록
nerve conduction velocity : NCV 신경전도속도
nerve entrapment 신경교액
nervous tissue 신경조직
net balance of the settled account 실질수지
net national welfare 국민복지지표
net profit and loss 순손익
network 네트워크 ; 관계망
network model 네트워크모델
network therapy 관계망 치료
networking 네트워킹 ; 관계망 형성
neuralgia 신경통
neurocirculatory asthenia 신경순환무력증
neurodegenerative disease 신경변성 질환
neurodevelopmental approach
신경발달적 접근법
neurofeedback 뉴로피드백
neurogenic bladder 신경인성 방광
neurogenic muscle atrophy 신경원성 근위축

neurogenic pulmonary edema
신경원성 폐수종

neurogenic shock 신경원성 쇼크

neurological condition 신경학문적 상태

neurological examination 신경학문적 검사

neurologist 신경학자

neurology 신경학

neuromuscular disease 신경관계질환

neuromuscular facilitation technique
신경근촉통법

Neurontin 뉴론틴

neuro-oncologist 신경종양의

neuro-oncology 신경종양학

neuropathic pain 신경원성 동통

neuropathy 뉴로파치 ; 신경장애

neurophysiological approach 신경생리학적
접근법

neurophysiologist 신경생리학자

neurophysiology 신경생리학

neuropsychological evaluation 신경심리학적
평가

neuropsychological test 신경심리학적 검사

neuropsychologist 신경심리학자

neuropsychology 신경심리학

neurosis 노이로제 ; 신경증

neurosurgical care unit 뇌신경외과집중치료실

neurotic disorder 신경증성 장애

neutral detergent 중성세제

neutral position 중간위 ; 중립위

New Angel Plan for Children 신엔젤플랜

New Barrier Free Law 배리어프리 신법

new clinical training system of primary
care 신의료임상연수제도

new daily persistent headache : NDPH
일상지속적 두통

New Deal 뉴딜

New Deal Policy 뉴딜정책

new federalism 신연방주의

New Gold Plan for the Elderly 신골드플랜

new middle classes 신중간층

New Poor Law 신구빈법

New York Heart Association functional
Classification 뉴욕심장학회 분류

newborn infant period 유아기

newly blind 중도시각장애자

newly developed industrial city 신산업도시

Newly Introduced Plan 2015 (fundamental
plan for low birth rate and aging society)
새로마지플랜 2015 (저출산·고령사회 기본계획)

Niacin 나이아신

niche 니치

nidus 병소

night blindness 야맹

night care 나이트케어 ; 야간보호

night care for children 야간보육

night care project 나이트케어사업

night home care 야간대응형 방문개호

night hospital 야간병원 ; 나이트호스피털 ; 밤병원

night orthosis 야간보조기

night school 야간학교

night services 나이트서비스

night shift 야근

night sitter 나이트시터

night watchman state 야경국가

nightmare 악몽

night-time delirium 야간섬망

Nishimura Dementia Scale : NMS
N식 정신기능검사 ; NM스케일

nitrate 질산염

nitrogen dioxide 이산화질소

nitroglycerin : NG 니트로글리세린

no added salt : NAS 무염

no added salt diet 무염식

nocturia 야뇨증

noise 소음

nomadism 유랑생활

nominal wage 명목임금

nonagenarian 90대

non-atherosclerotic coronary artery
disease 비어테로머성 관상동맥질환 ; 비죽상동
맥경화증

non-cancer patient 비암질환환자

non-contributory benefit 무거출급여

non-contributory benefit system
무거출급여제

non-contributory pension 무거출연금

non-contributory retirement pension
무거출퇴직연금

noncontributory scheme 무갹출제

non-countable asset 산입불가능자산

non-critical 논크리티칼 ; 비침습적

non-discrimination and equality 무차별평등

non-distribution constraint 비배분의 원칙

non-esterified fatty acid 유리지방산

non-governmental organization : NGO
비정부조직

non-insulin-dependent diabetes mellitus :
NIDDM 인슐린비의존성 당뇨병

non-invasive diagnostic test 비침습성 검사

non-judgmental attitude 비심판적 태도

nonmaleficence principle 무해성 원리

non-monetary needs 비화폐적 욕구

non-partisan voter 무당파층

non-payment 체납

non-payment of premium 보험료체납

non-penal fine 과태료

non-prescription drug 비처방전약

non-pressure bedding 무압이불

nonprofit 비영리

non-profit advocacy 비영리 어드버커시

Non-Profit Mutual Benefit Corporation
Law 중간법인법

non-profit organization : NPO 비영리조직

non-rapid eye movement 〈 NREM 〉 sleep
논렘수면

non-slip 미끄럼방지 ; 논슬립

non-slip mat 미끄럼방지매트 ; 논슬립매트

non-slip tape 미끄럼방지테이프 ; 논슬립테이프

non-small cell lung cancer : NSCLC
비소세포폐암

non-steroidal antiinflammatory drug :
NSAID 비스테로이드계 항염증약

non-tuberculous mycobacterial infection
비결핵성 항산균증

nonverbal communication 비언어적 의사소통

non-verbal communication 비언어적 커뮤니
케이션

non-weight bearing brace 비체중부하보조기

non-weight bearing orthosis 비체중부하보조기

nonwhite 유색인

normal 정상

normal adjustment mechanism 정상적응기제

normal blood pressure 정상혈압

normal curve 정규곡선

normal distribution 정상분포

normal flora 정상세균총

normal pressure hydrocephalus
정상압수두증

normal temperature 정상온도 ; 표준온도

normal value 정상치

normalization 노멀라이제이션 ; 정상화

normative 규범적

normocytic anemia 정구성 빈혈

norms 규범

norovirus 노로바이러스

Norpramin 노르프라민

nortriptyline 노르트립틸린

Norvasc 노르바스크

nosocomial infection 원내감염 ; 병원감염

nosology 질병분류학

nostalgia 노스탤지어

not applicable : N/A 비해당

Not in Education, Employment or
Training : NEET 니트족

notarial deed 공정증서

notary public 공증인

nothing by mouth 〈 nulla per os 〉: NPO
절식

Notice of Determination of Long-Term
Care Benefit Cost Calculation 노인장기요
양급여비용정산심사결정통지서

noxious environment 유해환경

NPO tax support system NPO지원세제

NPV analysis 엔피브이분석

nuclear cardiology 핵심장학

nuclear family 핵가족

nuclear heart scan 핵심장스캔

nuclear scanning 핵스캔

null hypothesis 영 가설

number of patients receiving medical
care 진료환자수

Numeric Rating Scale : NRS

숫자등급척도 ; 숫자통증등급

nurse 간호사

nurse aide 간호조무사 ; 간호조수

nurse assistant 간호보조원

nurse practitioner 전문간호사

nursery care programming 보육계획

nursery child care 보육

nursery for the disabled children
장애아보육

nursery needs 보육니즈

nursery rhymes 동요

nursery school 보육원

nursery unit cost 보육단가

nursing 간호

Nursing Academy for the Aged 노인간호학회

**nursing care for people with mental
disabilities** 정신장애인간호

nursing care for the disabled 장애인간호

nursing care for the disabled children
장애아간호

nursing care for the physically disabled
신체장애인간호

nursing care industry 고령친화산업

nursing center for the aged 노인간호센터

Nursing Division 간호과

nursing home 널싱홈 ; 요양원

nursing notes 간호일지 ; 장기요양일지

nursing personnel 간호관계자

nursing profession 간호전문

nursing professional 간호전문직

nursing records 장기요양기록

nursing shortage 간호사부족

nursing staff 간호직원 ; 간호종사자

nurturance 육성

nutrient 영양소

nutrient intake 영양섭취량

nutrition 영양

nutrition care management
영양케어매니지먼트

nutrition care plan 영양케어계획

nutrition consultant 영양지도원

nutrition improvement 영양개선

nutrition screening initiative : NSI
영양스크리닝추진재단

nutrition services 영양서비스

nutrition therapy 식사요법

nutritional assessment 영양평가

nutritional disturbance 영양장애

nutritional education 영양지도

nutritional intake 영양섭취

nutritional management 영양관리

nutritional problem 영양문제

nutritional requirement 영양필요량

nutritional screening 영양스크리닝

nutritional status 영양상태

nutritional support 영양보급

nutritive value of foods 영양가

N

O

obesity 비만
obesity hypoventilation syndrome
비만저환기증후군
obesity index 비만지수
object relations theory 대상관계이론
objective needs 객관적욕구
objectivity 객관성
oblate 오브라이트
observation 관찰
observation unit 경과관찰병동
obsession 강박증
obsessive compulsive disorder : OCD
강박성 장애
obsessive compulsive disorder medication
강박성 장애제
obstructive sleep apnea 폐쇄형 수면무호흡
obstructive sleep apnea syndrome : OSAS
폐쇄형 수면무호흡증후군
occipital neuralgia 후두신경통
occult blood test 잠혈시험
occupancy rate 병실점유율
occupational aid 생업부조 ; 자활보호
occupational assistance 생업부조
occupational change 전직
occupational disease 직업병
occupational exposure
업무상 폭로 ; 직업성 폭로
occupational group insurance 직역보험
occupational health 직장보건
occupational identity 직업적 아이덴티티
occupational infection 직업감염
occupational injury 노동재해
Occupational Safety and Health

Administration : OSHA 노동안전위생청
occupational social work 직장사회사업
occupational therapist : OT
작업치료사 ; 작업요법사 ; 오큐페이셔널테라피
occupational therapy 작업요법 ; 작업치료
octogenarian 80대
odynophagia 연하통
Oedipus complex 오이디푸스 콤플렉스
Oedipus phase 오이디푸스기
offenders rehabilitation 갱생보호
office 사업소
office automation 사무자동화 ; OA화
Office of Child Support Enforcement
아동지원국
Office of Economic Development : OED
경제개발국
Office of Economic Opportunity : OEO
경제기회국
Office of Management and Budget : OMB
예산관리국
Office of Voluntary Action : VAC
자원봉사활동국
official development assistance : ODA
정부개발원조
off-the-job-training : OFF-JT 직장외 훈련
ointment 연고
olanzapine 오란자핀
old aged 노인
old people's club 고령자클럽
old placement system 구조치입소
old-age 노년기
old-age assistance : OAA 노령부조
old-age dependency ratio 노년인구지수 ;

노인부양비
old-age disorder 고령기 장애
old-age employees' pension 노령후생연금
old-age insurance 노령보험
old-age pension 노령연금
old-age reserve account 노령적립구좌
old-age welfare pension 노령복지연금
older worker 고연령노동자
oldness 늙음
oliguria 핍뇨
olmesartan 오르메사르탄
Olympic for the disabled 장애인 올림픽
ombudsman 옴부즈맨
ombudsperson 옴부즈퍼슨
oncologist 종양의
oncology 종양학
one-child policy 한 아이정책 ; 외동이정책
one-handed activity 한손동작
one-minute time study 1분간 타임스터디
online education 통신교육
on-site assessment 방문조사
on-site evaluation 방문조사
on-site interview 방문면접
on-site survey 방문조사
on-the-job-training : OJT 직장훈련 ; 직업교육
onychia 손발톱염 ; 조염
onychodystrophy
　손톱이영양증 ; 발톱이영양 ; 조이영양증
onychogryphosis 손발톱굽음증 ; 조갑구만증
onychomycosis 조백선 ; 조진균증
open adoption 개방입양
open biopsy 직시하 생검
open drainage system 개방식 드레나쥐법
open enrollment period 개방등록기간
open facility 개방시설
open fracture 개방성 골절
open kinetic chain 개운동연쇄
open system 개방체계
open-ended group 개방집단
open-ended questions 개방형 질문
open-panel 개방명부제
operant conditioning
　자발적 반응조건부여 ; 조작적 조건화

operant technique 자발적 반응기법
operant therapy 조작적 치료
operating room : OR 수술실
operating suite 수술옷
operating theater 수술실
operation gown 수술용 가운
Operation PUSH 푸시
operation room registered nurse : ORRN
　수술실 간호사
operational definition 조작적 개념
ophthalmologist 안과의
ophthalmology 안과학
opiate addiction 아편중독
opiate dependence 아편의존
opinion leader 오피니언리더 ; 여론지도자
opinion survey 여론조사 ; 의식조사
opioid medication 오피오이드제
opioid-related disorder 아편류 관련장애
opponens bar 대립바
opponens splint 대립보조기
opponent color 반대색
opportunistic infection 기회감염
opportunity costs 기회비용
opportunity programs 기획프로그램
opportunity theory 기회이론
Optacon 옵타콘
optional categorically needy
　선택적 제도곤궁대상자
optional enrollment 임의가입
optometrist 검안의 ; 검안사 ; 안경사
optometry 검안
oral and maxillofacial surgeon
　구강악안면외과의
oral and maxillofacial surgery
　구강악안면외과
oral appliance 구강내장치
oral apraxia 구강실행증 ; 구두실행증
oral cancer 구강암
oral cavity 구강
oral character 구순성격
oral disease 구강질환
oral health 구강위생
oral health assessment 구강보건평가

oral health care 구강케어
oral hygiene 구강청소행동
oral intake 경구섭취
oral medication 내복약
oral method 구화법
oral phase 구순기
oral propulsive phase 구강단계
oral rehydration therapy 경구보액요법
oral stage 구강기
oral status 구강상태
oral temperature 구강온
oral thermometry 구강체온
oral transmission 경구감염
order for improvement of services
  처우개선명령
Order of Enforcement of Long-Term
  Care and Insurance Act for the Aged
  노인장기요양보험법시행령
ordinal measurement 서열측정
ordinance 조례
ordinary collection 보통징수
ordinary premium collection 보통보험료징수
ordinary tax collection 보통세징수
organ donation 장기제공
organ transplantation 장기이식
organic disturbance 기질적 장애
organic mental disorders
  기질성 정신장애 ; 기질성 정신질환
organization 조직
Organization for Economic Co-operation
  and Development : OECD 경제협력개발기구
organization for long-term cares for the
  aged 노인장기요양보호종합대책
organization for the disabled 장애인단체
organization man 조직인
organizational socialization 조직사회화
orgasmic impairment 오르가슴 장애
orientation 견당식 ; 방향정위 ; 지남력 ;
  오리엔테이션
orlistat 오르리스타트
orphanage 고아원
orphans 고아
orthodontic appliance 교정장치

orthopedic appliance 장구 ; 보장구
orthopedic shoes 정형구두
orthopedics 정형외과
orthopnea 기좌호흡
orthopsychiatry 교정정신의학
orthoptist : ORT 시능훈련사
orthosis 보조기 ; 장구 ; 보장구
orthosis and prosthesis 의지보조기
orthostatic hypotension 기립성 저혈압
orthotic treatment 보조기요법
orthotics 보조기학
osmidrosis axillae 액취
ossification of the posterior longitudinal
  ligament : OPLL 후종인대골화증
osteoarthritis : OA 변형성 관절증
osteomalacia 골연화증
osteopenia 골감소성 ; 골결핍증
osteoporosis 골다공증
ostomate 장루설치환자 ; 오스트메이트
ostomy aid 스토마 용품
other sanitary supplies 그 밖의 위생재료
otitis media 중이염
otolaryngologist 이비인후과의
otolaryngology 이비인후학
ototoxic substance 청각기독성물질
Ottawa Charter for Health Promotion
  오타와 헌장
Otto Eduard Leopold Bismarck 비스마르크
out of bed 이상
outbreak 집단발생 ; 대발생 ; 아웃브레이크
Outcome and Assessment Information
  Set : OASIS 재가케어평가 ; 오아시스
outdoor relief 원외구조
out-of-pocket 자기지불
outpatient 외래환자 ; 통원환자
outpatient care 외래케어
outpatient clinic 외래진료소
outpatient medicine 외래진료
outpatient rate 통원자율
outpatient rehabilitation 당일치기 재활
outpatient rehabilitation 외래재활 ; 주간재활
outreach 아웃리치
ovarian cancer 난소암

O

over behaviors 현성행동
over work weakness 과용성 근력저하
overbed table 오버베드테이블 ;
　침대용 접이식 탁자
overbedding 과잉병상
overcompensation 과잉보상 ; 과보상
overeating 과식
overflow incontinence 일류성 요실금
overgrowth 과중성장
overkill 오버킬
overloving 과잉애
overpayment of premium 과오납액
overpopulation 과잉인구 ; 과밀인구
overprotectiveness 과잉보호
overprotectiveness of children 과보호
Overseas Cooperation Division 해외협력과

overseers of the poor
　빈민감독관 ; 빈민감독원
over-the-counter medication 시판약
overuse 과용
overuse syndrome 과용증후군
own house 자기집
owner's payment 사업주부담금
oxycodone 옥시코돈
OxyContin 옥시콘틴
oxygen 산소
oxygen concentrator 산소농축기
oxygen consumption 산소소비
oxygen intake 산소섭취
oxygen therapy 산소요법
ozone 오존

O

P

P. M. Symonds 사이몬드
pacemaker 페이스메이커
Pacific Islander 태평양제도(諸島) 출신자
Pacific Islanders 태평양 섬주민
pad 패드
paid endowment facilities 유료양로시설
paid endowment facilities for the aged
유료노인양로시설
paid health care facilities for the aged
유료노인요양시설
paid specialized health care facilities for
the aged 유료노인전문요양시설
paid time off : PTO 유급휴가
paid voluntary 유상볼룬터리
paid volunteer 유상자원봉사
paid welfare houses for the aged
유료노인복지주택
pain 동통
pain clinic 페인클리닉 ; 통증클리닉
pain control 동통관리
Pain Disability Assessment Scale : PDAS
통증생활장애평가척도
pain disorder 동통성 장애
pain management 동통관리 ; 동통 매니지먼트
pain medication 동통제
pajamas 파자마
palliative 완화
palliative care 완화케어
palliative care bed 완화케어병상
palliative care unit 완화케어병동
palmar flexion 장굴
palpitation 동계 ; 심계항진 ; 심장고동
palsy 마비

Pamelor 파메라
pancreas 췌장
pancreatic cancer 췌장암
pancreatitis 췌장염
pandemic 유행병
panel discussion 패널토의
panel heater 패널히터
panic disorder 패닉장애
pantothenic acid 판토텐산
paper diaper 종이기저귀
Papez circuit 파페츠회로
papillary thyroid cancer 갑상선유두암
paradigm 패러다임
paradoxical directive 역설적 지시
paradoxical incontinence
역설적 실금 ; 기이성 요실금
paradoxical intention 역설적 지향
paraffin bath 파라핀욕
paralinguistics 주변언어학
parallel bar 평행봉
parallel bars theory 평행봉이론
Paralympics 패럴림픽
paralysis 마비
paralytic side 마비측
paramedical staff 준의료직원 ;
파라메디컬 스태프
paranoia 피해망상증
paranoid 편집증
paranoid disorders 편집장애
paranoid ideation 편집형 사고
paranoid personality disorder
편집형 성격장애
paranoid schizophrenia 편집형 정신분열증

paraparesis 대부전마비 ; 불완전대마비 ;
부전대마비
paraphasia 착어
paraphilic coercive disorder
강제적 성도착장애
paraphrasing 의역
paraphrenia 편집성 치매 ; 파라프레니아
paraplegia 대마비
paraplegic 하반신마비
parapraxis 착행증
paraprofessional 준전문가
parasite single 패러사이트싱글
parasympathetic nerve 부교감신경
Parent Effectiveness Training : PET
부모교육훈련
parent group 부모모임
parent patriot 국친사상
parental authority 친권
parental leave 육아휴업
parental leave allowance 육아휴업수당금
parent-centered 보호자중심
parent-child relationship 친자관계
parenteral feeding 비경구영양
parenteral nutrition 정맥영양법
parenthood tax rebate 부양자세액공제
parenting 육아
parenting support 육아지원
Parents Anonymous : PA 이동학대부모모임
parents patriae 국가보호
paresis 마비 ; 부전마비
Pareto optimum 파레토 최적
Parish Poor Rate 교구빈민구제
Parkinson's disease 파킨슨병
Parkinson's syndrome 파킨슨증후군
Parkinsonism 파킨소니즘
Parnate 파네이트
parole 가석방 ; 보호관찰부가석방
parole board 가석방심의위원회
parole officer 보호사
paroxysmal supraventricular tachycardia
발작성 상실성 빈맥
part time 파트타임
partial affairs association 일부사무조합

partial bath 부분욕 ; 부분목욕
partial enumeration 부분조사
partial hepatectomy 부분간절제
partial hospital 부분입원
partial pension 부분연금
partial sponge bath 부분세정
partialization 부분화
participant 참가자 ; 가입자
participant modeling 참여모델
participant observation 참여관찰
participation 참가 ; 가입
participation restriction 참가제약 ; 가입제약
participative management 참여관리
particle counter 공중부유미립자측정기 ; 미세먼
지측정기 ; 파티클 카운터
partner dog 보조견
part-time staff 비상근직원
part-time work 파트타임노동
Part-Time Work and Home Work
Division 단시간・재가노동과
part-time worker 파트타임노동자
Party Protecting Interests of the Aged
노인권익보호당
passive exercise 타동운동 ; 타의적 운동
passive range of motion 타동가동역
paste meal 페이스트식
pasteurization 저온살균 ; 파스퇴르제이션
pasteurizer 저온살균기
patellar tendon bearing ankle-foot
orthosis PTB식 체중부하식 하지보조기 ; PTB식
단하지보조기 ; PTB식 하퇴의족
paternalism
패터널리즘 ; 온정주의 ; 부성적 온정주의
path analysis 경로분석
pathogenic organism 병원체
pathological bone fracture 병적 골절
pathology test 병리검사
patient advocacy 환자옹호
patient records 진료기록카드 ; 환자기록
patient safety 환자의 안전
patient satisfaction survey 환자만족도조사
patient survey 환자조사
patient's instructions for use 사용상 주의

patient-centered medicine 환자중심의료
patient-centered therapy 환자중심요법
patient-controlled analgesia : PCA
자기조절진통법
patient-provider relationship
환자 제공자간 관계
patients 환자
patients' rights 환자의 권리
patriarchalism 가부장제
pauper 빈민
Paxil 팍실
Paxipam 팍시팜
payment fund 지불기금
payment of pension premiums
연금보험료납부
payments to care providers 개호비용지불
payroll deduction 급여공제
payroll tax 인두세
peace 평화
Peace Corps 평화봉사단
peace movement 평화운동
peace study 평화학
Pearson's r correlation 피어슨의 알 상관
pectus excavatum
새가슴 ; 오목가슴 ; 누두흉 ; 깔때기가슴
pediatric 소아과
pediatric advanced life support
소아에 대한 2차 구명심폐소생법 및 처치
pediatric advanced life support
소아전문소생술
pediatric endoscopy 소아내시경검사
pediatric home care 소아재가케어
pediatric home health 소아재가의료
pediatrician 소아과의사
peer counseling 피어카운셀링
peer group 피어그룹 ; 동료집단 ; 또래집단
peer group supervision 피어그룹 슈퍼비전
peer relationship 동료관계
peer supervision 피어슈퍼비전
peer support 피어서포트
Pegasys 페가시스
pegboard 페그보드
pegylated interferon 페그인터페론

pellagra 펠라그라
pelvic band 골반대
pelvic floor relaxation 골반저이완
pelvic fracture 골반골절
penal code 형법전
penal regulation 벌칙
penalty 벌금
pendulum test 진자시험 ; 펜듈럼테스트
penicillin 페니실린
penology 형벌학
pension 연금
pension benefit 연금급여
pension benefits standards 연금급여기준
Pension Benefits Standards Act
연금급여기준법
Pension Bureau 연금국
Pension Division 연금과
pension for the senior citizen 경로연금
pension fund 연금기금
pension handbook 연금수첩
pension insurance 연금보험
Pension Insurance Division 연금보험과
pension insurance premiums 연금보험료
pension insurance system 연금보험제도
pension mathematics 연금수리
pension of government servants
공무원연금
pension reserve fund 연금적립기금
pension system 연금제도
pensionable age 연금지급개시연령 ;
연금수급자격연령
pensionable right 연금수급권
pensioner 연금수급자
people with acquired severe disabilities
중도장애인
people with acquired severe mental
disabilities 중도정신장애인
people with acquired severe mental
retardation 중도지적장애인
people with acquired severe physical
disabilities 중도신체장애인
people with auditory impairments
청각장애자

P

people with dementia 치매노인 ; 인지증고령자

people with mental disorders 정신장애인

people with mental retardation 지적장애인

people with severe physical and mental disabilities 중증심신장애인

people's capitalism 인민자본주의

People's Life Indicators 신국민생활지표

People-to-People Committee for the Handicapped 장애인의 참이웃 모임

peptic ulcer 소화성 궤양

peracetic acid 과초산

percentage of patients receiving annual dental exams 치과검진수료율

percentage of patients receiving medical care 수료율

perception 지각

perceptual distortion 지각왜곡

percussion 타진

percutaneous endoscopic gastrostomy : PEG 경피내시경적 위루조설술

percutaneous ethanol injection 경피적 에탄올주입요법

percutaneous implantable electrode 경피적 매입전극

percutaneous infection 경피감염

percutaneous transhepatic cholangiodrainage 경피경간적 담관드레나지

percutaneous transluminal coronary angioplasty 경피경관적 관상동맥형성술

percutaneous transluminal coronary recanalization 경피경관적 관상동맥재개통술

perfect society 완전사회

performance principle 실적주의

peri ⟨ perineal ⟩ care 음부세정

periarteritis nodosa 결절성 동맥주위염

perinatal mortality rate 주산기 사망율

perindopril 페린도프릴

perineal ⟨ peri ⟩ care 음부세정

perineum 회음

period for the premium payment 보험료납부필기간

period of apprenticeship 견습기간

period of employment 고용기간

period of insurance 보험기간

periodic health evaluation : PHE 정기적 건강진단

periodic leg movement 주기성 사지운동

periodic leg movement disorder : PLMD 주기성 사지운동이상증

periodic limb movement disorder 주기성 사지운동장애

periodontal disease 치주병

periodontitis 치주병

periodontium 치주조직

peripheral arterial disease : PAD 말초동맥질환

peripheral edema 말초부종

peripheral facial nerve palsy 말초성 안면신경마비

peripheral nerve 말초신경

peripheral nerve palsy 말초신경마비

peripheral neuropathy 말초신경장애

peripheral parenteral nutrition : PPN 말초정맥영양법

peripheral vascular disease 말초순환장애

peripheral vestibular dysfunction 말초전정기능부전

peripheral vision 주변시야

peristalsis 연동운동

peritoneal dialysis : PD 복막투석

peritoneal lavage 복강세정

peritoneography 복막조영

permanency planning 영속적 기획

permanent domicile 본적

permanent tooth 영구치

permissible exposure limit : PEL 폭로허용농도

permissiveness 개방성

pernicious anemia 악성빈혈

perseveration 보속증

persistent activity 활성지속

persistent disturbance of consciousness 지체성 의식장애

person authorized to submit applications on behalf of the applicant 제출대행자

person bringing up 양육자

person in need of public assistance
요보호자

person responsible for dependent family
부양의무자

person responsible for dependent family
members 부양의무자

person responsible for protection
보호의무자

person submitting application on behalf
of the applicant 제출대행자

person with acquired hearing impairment
중도청각장애자

person with acquired visual impairment
중도시각장애자

Person, Problem, Place, Process 4P

personal assistance services 개인지원서비스

personal care 신체장기요양 ; 신체개호 ; 신체보조

personal care services 대인케어서비스

personal change 개인내 변동

personal communication 개인적 커뮤니케이션

personal emergency device 개인적 구조기구

personal guardianship
신상감독과 보호 ; 신상감호

personal hygiene 정용 ; 개인위생

personal hygiene activity 정용동작

personal hygiene assistance
신체활동지원 ; 정용보조

personal hygiene care 정용개호

personal income distribution 소득분포

personal information 개인정보

Personal Information Protection Act
개인정보보호법

personal insurance 사적보험

personal pension 개인연금

personal pension premium 개인연금보험료

personal pension scheme 개인연금플랜

personal protective equipment : PPE
개인보호물품

personal social services
대인사회서비스 ; 인적서비스 ; 대인적 사회서비스

personal-controlled analgesia : PCA
환자조절진통법

personality 성격 ; 인격 ; 퍼스낼리티

personality diagnosis methods 성격진단법

personality disorder 인격장애

personality inventory
인격검사질문지 ; 성격특성항목표

personality structure 성격구조

personality test 성격검사 ; 인성검사 ; 인격검사

person-in-environment perspective
환경 속의 인간관점

personnel costs 인건비용

personnel expenditures 인건비지출

person-oriented 이용자본위

person-oriented record 클라이언트 중심기록
방법

pervasive developmental disorder : PDD
광범성 발달장애

pes planus 편평족

pessary 페서리

pest house 격리병원

PET〈positron emission tomography〉펫

petition 탄원 ; 청원 ; 진정

phacoemulsification 수정체유화흡인술

phallic stage 남근기

phantom limb pain 환지통

phantom limb sensation 환상사지감각 ; 환지

Pharmaceutical Affairs Law 약사법

Pharmaceutical and Food Safety Bureau
의약식품국

pharmaceutical costs 약제비

pharmaceutical inspection 약사감시

pharmaceutical inspector 약사감시원

pharmaceutical services 조제서비스

pharmacist 약제사

pharmacodynamic change 약리학적 변화

pharmacokinetic change 약물동태적 변화

pharmacotherapy 약물요법 ; 약품요법

pharmacy 약국

pharyngeal passage time 인두통과시간

pharyngeal phase 인두단계

pharynx 인두

phenelzine 페넬진

phenol block 페놀블록

phenomenology 현상학

philanthropy 자선활동 ; 박애 ; 박애사업

philological research 문헌연구
philological study 문헌검토
philosophy of technology 기술철학
phobia 공포증
phobic disorder 공포장애
Phones for the Aged, Korea 한국노인의 전화
photoaging 광노화
photodynamic therapy 광선역학요법
photophobia 광선혐기증
photopigment 감광색소
photoreceptor 시세포
physiatrist 재활의
physical abuse 신체적 학대
physical activities of daily living : PADL
신체적 일상생활동작능력
physical activity 신체활동량
physical aggression 신체적 공격
physical assistance 신체원조
physical barrier 물리적 장벽
physical conditioning 신체조정
physical contact 스킨십
physical deconditioning 신체둔감
physical dependence 신체의존
physical disability 신체장애
physical disability certificate handbook
신체장애인수첩
physical exercise for Parkinson's disease
파킨슨병 체조 ; 파킨슨체조
physical fitness 체력
physical function 신체기능
physical handicapped person
신체장애인 (아)
physical independence 신변자립
physical medicine 물리의학
physical performance test : PPT
신체기능검사
physical restraint 신체구속
physical therapist : PT
물리치료사 ; 이학요법사
physical therapy 물리치료 ; 이학요법
physically and mentally disabled
심신장애인
physically and mentally disabled

child 심신장애아
physically disabled aged person
신체장애노인
physically disabled child 신체장애아
physically disabled elderly
신체장애고령자
physically disabled infant 신체장애유아
physically frail elderly
허약고령자 ; 허약노인
physically weak 허약
physician 의사
physician fee 치료보수
physician referral services 의사소개서비스
physician rounds 회진
physician-assisted suicide 의사조력자살
physiological needs 생리적 욕구
Piaget's theory 피아제이론
Pick's disease 픽병
Picture Speech Intelligibility Evaluation :
PSINE 회화음성양해도검사
Pierre Guillaume Frédéric Le Play
르프레이
piety 효행
pillow 베개
pilocarpine hydrochloride
염산필로칼핀 ; 축동제
pilot campaign 파이로트 캠페인
pilot study 파일로트 스터디
pinch 집기
pink noise protocol 핑크노이즈 프로토콜
placater role 화해자 역할
placebo 위약
placebo effect 플라시보효과
placement 배치
placement period 조치기간
placement questionnaire 유치조사
plain soap 보통비누
planning 플래닝 ; 기획
Planning Division of War Victims' Relief
원호기획과
plantar flexion 발바닥굽힘 ; 족저굴곡
plasma glucose 혈장글루코스
plastic orthosis 경직성 보조기 ; 플라스틱보조기

P

plasticity 가역성
plateau 플래토
platform crutch 플랫폼크러치 ; 플랫폼형 지팡이
Plavix 플라빅스
play therapy 놀이치료 ; 유희요법
pleasure principle 쾌락원칙
plug-fit socket 플러그피트소켓
pluralistic society 다원화된 사회
pneumococcal meningitis 폐렴구균성 수막염
pneumococcal pneumonia 폐렴구균성 폐렴
pneumococcal vaccination 폐렴구균예방접종
pneumonia 폐렴
pneumonia in the elderly 노인성 폐렴
pocket infection 포켓감염 ; 포켓러스감염
podiatric medicine 족병
podiatrist 족병의
podiatry 발병치료 ; 발병학
point gait 동작보행
point of maximum intensity 최강점
point prevalence 유행점
point-of-service 자유진료 ; 진찰선택
polarization 양극화
police social work 경찰사회사업
police work with juveniles 소년경찰제도
policy 정책
policy analysis 정책분석
policy community 정책커뮤니티
policy decision-making theories 정책결정론
policy for dementia
　치매고령자대책 ; 인지증고령자대책
policy for elderly with dementia
　치매노인대책 ; 인지증노인대책
policy for incurable diseases
　난병대책 ; 불치병대책
policy for the bedridden elderly
　와상고령자대책
policy for the elderly with dementia
　치매고령자대책 ; 인지증고령자대책
policy implementation 정책실시
policy of geriatric mental health care
　노인정신보건대책
policy of health and medical care of the
　elderly 노인보건의료대책

policy of health and welfare 보건복지시책
policy statement 정책성명서
policymaker 정책입안자
poliomyelitis 폴리오 ; 회백수염
political action 정치적 행위
political activism 정치적 활동
pollakiuria 빈뇨
pollution 공해
polyarticular gout 다관절성 통풍
polyester allergy 폴리에스테르 알레르기
polygamy 일부다처제 (일처다부제)
polymyalgia rheumatica 류마티스성 다발근통증
polyneuropathy 말초신경병증 ; 다발뉴로파치
polypharmacy 다제처방 ; 다제병용
polyps 폴립
polysynaptic reflex 다시냅스반사
polyunsaturated fatty acid : PUFA
　다가불포화지방산
polyuria 다뇨
Pompe van Meerdervoort 폼베
poor 빈곤자
poor family 빈곤가정
poor law 구빈법
poor law guardians 빈민구제위원 ;
　빈민보호위원
poor relief 구빈사업
poor relief system 구빈제도
poor strata 빈곤층
poorhouse 구빈원
popular sovereignty 국민주권
population aging 고령화
Population Association of Korea
　한국인구학회
population census 인구조사
population dynamics 인구동태
population explosion 인구폭발
population movement 인구이동
population policy 인구정책
population problem 인구문제
population projection 장래추계인구
population structure 인구구조
portable bathtub 이동욕조 ; 포터블욕조
position 체위

positioning 체위설정 ; 포지셔닝
positive connotation 긍정적내포
positive discrimination 긍정적 차별
positive finding 양성소견
positive mold 양성모델
positive punishment 정적 처벌
positive reinforcement 긍정적 강화 ; 정적 강화
positive sharp wave 양성예파
positive symptom 양성증상
positive transference 긍정적 전이
positivism 실증주의
positron emission tomography : PET
　양전자방출 단층촬영술 ; PET법 ; 포지트론단층법 ;
　포지트론CT ; 포지트론에미션 토모그래피
post retirement farming 은퇴농장
post-assessment 사후평가
post-evaluation 사후평가
post-fall syndrome 전도후 증후군
post-herpetic neuralgia : PHN
　대상포진후 신경통
post-infection cough 감염후 기침
post-modern 포스트모던
postmortem care 사후처치
post-nasal drip syndrome : PNDS
　후비루증후군
postoperative infection 수술후 감염
postpartum depression 산후우울증
post-polio syndrome : PPS 폴리오후증후군
posttraumatic stress disorder
　정신후유증(외상후유증)
post-traumatic stress disorder : PTSD
　외상후 스트레스장애
postural drainage 체위배액 ; 체위드레나지
postural exercise 자세훈련
postural reaction 자세반응
postural reflex 자세반사
posture 자세
post-viral fatigue syndrome
　바이러스감염후 피로증후군
potable water 음료수
potential need 잠재욕구
potential needs 잠재니즈
pouch 파우치

poverty 빈곤
poverty among the elderly 노인빈곤
poverty index 빈곤지수
poverty level 빈곤수준
poverty line 빈곤선
powdered drug 가루약 ; 분말약품
power 능력 ; 힘 ; 권력
power group 권력집단
power of attorney 위임권
power rehabilitation 파워재활
practical skills training for long-term care
　개호기술강습회
practical training for long-term care
　개호강습
practice 행위
practice and promotion center for
　long-term care 개호실습·보급센터
practice manual 업무메뉴얼
practice theory 실무이론
practice wisdom 실무지식
pragmatism 실용주의 ; 프래그머티즘
pramipexole 프라미펙솔
prazosin 프라조신
pre-assessment 사전평가
precipitating cause 촉진원인
preconscious 전의식
predation 약탈
predictor variable 예측변수
prednisone 프레드니손
pre-evaluation 사전평가
prefabricated home 조립주택
preferential 우선적
preferential certificate for the senior
　citizens 경로우대증
preferential placement 우대조치
preferential rights 우선적 권리 ; 선취특권
pregabalin 프리가발린
pregenital 전성기기
prehension 파지
prehension orthosis 파지보조기
preimplantation genetic diagnosis
　착상전진단
prejudice 편견

prejudice against the elderly
고령자에 대한 편견
preliminary assessment 1일차판정
preliminary survey 예비조사
premature atrial contraction : PAC
심방기외 수축
premature birth 조산
premature infant 미숙아
premature ventricular contraction : PVC
심실기외 수축
premium collection 보통보험료징수
premium rate of long-term care
insurance 장기요양보험료율 ; 개호보험료율
premium reduction 보험료감면
premiums on a per capita basis
피보험자균등할
prenatal 태아기
prenatal diagnosis 출생전진단
prenuptial agreement 혼전합의
preoperational stage 전조작기
preoperative anxiety 수술전불안
preoperative bowel cleaning 수술전장관처치
preoperative bowel preparation
수술전장관세정 ; 수술전장관준비 ; 수술전장관처리
prepaid group practice : PGP
선불제 집단개원
prepaid medical practice 선불제 진료
preparatory education for the elderly
노인준비교육
prerequisite criteria 필요전제기준
presbycusis 노년성 난청
presbyopia 노안
preschool education 취학전교육 ; 유아교육
prescribing the symptom 증상설명
prescription 처방전
prescription medical 처방
prescription medication program
처방약제프로그램
presenile dementia 초로기 치매
presenile depression 초로기 우울증
presenting problem 표출된 문제
press campaign 캠페인
pressure 압박

pressure group 압력단체
pressure sore 욕창 ; 압박궤양
pressure ulcer 욕창 ; 압박궤양
pressure ulcer prevention 욕창예방
pressure ulcer prevention and treatment
욕창예방 및 치료
Pressure Ulcer Scale for Healing : PUSH
욕창치유과정스케일
pressure ulcer treatment 욕창치료
pressure wave 압력파
pressure zone 내압대
pressurized room 양압실
presyncope 의식소실발작
pre-test 프리테스트 ; 사전조사
prevalence 유병
prevalence rate 유병율
prevalence survey 유행조사
prevention 예방
prevention of becoming bedridden
와상예방
prevention of becoming bedridden
elderly 와상고령자예방
prevention of contracture 구축예방
prevention of dementia 치매예방
prevention of elder abuse 고령자학대방지
prevention of infection 감염예방
prevention of long-term care
장기요양예방 ; 개호예방
prevention of lumbago 요통예방
prevention of poverty 빈곤예방
prevention of pressure ulcer 욕창예방
preventive aged-care approach for the
independent 개호예방일반고령자시책
preventive aged-care approach for the frail
개호예방특정고령자시책
preventive benefit 예방급여
preventive care 예방케어
preventive care management
개호예방케어매니지먼트
preventive gerontology 예방노년학
preventive health programs
예방건강 프로그램
preventive home bathing care

preventive long-term care plan
장기요양예방사업 ; 개호예방사업
preventive medicine 예방의학
preventive psychiatry 예방정신의학
preventive rental services of welfare
equipments 개호예방복지용구대여
preventive services 예방서비스
preventive short-term care
accommodation 개호예방단기입소생활개호
preventive treatment 예방처치
preventive vaccination 예방접종
prevocational 직업전
price controls 가격통제
price discrimination 가격차별
price grant 현물급부
price indexation 물가슬라이드제 ; 물가연동제
price of common stock 일반주가지수
price supports 가격유지
primal therapy 일차적 치료
primary afferent fiber 일차구심성 섬유
primary bacteremia 원발성 균혈증
primary biliary cirrhosis 원발성 담즙성 간경변
primary blood stream infection
원발성 혈류감염
primary care 프라이머리케어 ; 예방진료
primary care physician : PCP
단골의 ; 단골담당의사 ; 예방진료의
primary care physician : PCP 단골의사
primary caregiver 주장기요양자 ; 주개호자
primary doctor 주치의 ; 단골의사
primary gain 일차이득
primary group 일차집단 ; 원초적집단
primary health care : PHC 프라이머리헬스케어
primary medical care 일차 진료
primary needs 일차적 욕구
primary open angle glaucoma : POAG
원발개방우각녹내장
primary poverty 일차 빈곤
primary prevention 일차예방
primary process 일차과정
primary process thinking 일차적 사고과정
primary progressive aphasia

원발성 진행성 실어
primary progressive nonfluent aphasia
원발성 진행성 비유창성 실어
primary stimulus 원자극
prime mover 주동근
primitive reflex 원시반사
principle of acceptance 수용의 원칙
principle of beneficence 선행원리
principle of client self-determination
자기결정의 원칙
principle of competition 경쟁원리
principle of confidentiality 비밀보장의 원칙
principle of controlled emotional
involvement 통제된 정서적 관여의 원칙
principle of equalization of income and
expenditure 수지상등의 원칙
principle of equivalence 수지균등의 원칙
principle of individualization 개별화의 원칙
principle of justice 공정원리
principle of less eligibility 처우제한의 원칙
principle of natural law 자연법사상
principle of non-judgmental attitude
비심판적 태도의 원칙
principle of nonmaleficence 무해성 원리
principle of private/public dichotomy
공사분리의 원칙
principle of public assistance based on
application 신청보호의 원칙
principle of public assistance on a
household basis 세대단위의 원칙
principle of purposeful expression of
feelings 의도적인 감정표현의 원칙
principle of respect for autonomy
자립성 존중원리
principle of self-help 자조원칙
principle of standards and extent
기준 및 정도의 원칙
principle of supplementary nature of
public assistance 보충성의 원리
print disabled 독서장애
priority seat 우선석 ; 우선좌석
prison 형무소 ; 교도소
prisoner 복역수

privacy 프라이버시 ; 사생활
privacy protection 프라이버시보호
private activity 민간활동 ; 사적활동
private activity bond 사적사업채권
private assistance 사적부조
private association 민간단체
private care home 실비요양시설
private enterprise 민간기업
private facility 민간시설
private foundation 민간조성단체
private home 민간홈
private hospital 민간병원 ; 사립병원
private industrial welfare 민간산업복지
private insurance 민간보험
private investment 민간투자
private long-term care insurance
　민간장기요양보험 ; 민간개호보험
private medical insurance 민간의료보험
private non-profit organization
　민간비영리조직
private organization 민간기관
private pension 민간연금
private practice 개업사회사업
private program 민간사업
private program provider 민간사업자
private residential home for the elderly
private room 개인실
private school corporation 학교법인
private sector 민간섹터
private services 민간서비스
private services for people with mental
　retardation 지적장애인대상 민간서비스
private services for the aged
　노인대상 민간서비스
private services for the disabled
　장애인대상 민간서비스
private services for the elderly
　고령자대상 민간서비스
private services for the physically
　disabled 신체장애인대상 민간서비스
private services for the psychiatric
　patient 정신장애인대상 민간서비스
private social agencies 자영 사회복지기관

private social welfare 민간사회복지
private social welfare organization
　민간사회복지단체
private social welfare program
　민간사회복지사업
private support 사적부양
private welfare 민간복지
private welfare activity 민간복지활동
privatization 민영화 ; 사영화 ; 민간화 ;
　사유화 ; 프라이버타이제이션
privatization of public enterprise 공설민영
privatization of Social Security
　사회보장의 민영화
probability sampling 확률표본 추출
probation 보호관찰 ; 보호관찰부선고
probation and parole officer 보호감찰관
probation and parole system 보호감찰제도
probation officer 보호사
probationary employment period 시용기간
probationer system 집행유예자 보호관찰
probe 프로브
probing 추가질문
problem behavior 문제행동
problem child 문제아
problem of the aged 노인문제
problem solving 문제해결
problem solving approach 문제해결접근법
problem solving model 문제해결모형
problem solving process 문제해결과정
problematic family 문제가족
problem-oriented system : POS
　문제지향형 시스템
procedures of long-term care 개호순서
process model 과정모형
process recording 과정기록
process-centered social work 과정중심주의
process-goal 프로세스 골
proctography 직장조영
proctoscope 직장경
proctoscopy 직장경검사
proctosigmoidoscope 직장S장결장경
proctosigmoidoscopy 직장S장결장경검사
prodromal phase 프로드로말 현상

production fatigue 생산피로설
productive aging 프로덕티브에이징
productive welfare 생산적 복지
productivity 생산력
profession 전문직 ; 전문
professional association 전문직단체
professional association of social
 workers 사회복지전문직단체
professional attitude 전문적 태도
professional practice examination 실기시험
professional social work
 사회복지전문직 ; 복지전문직
Professional Standards Review
 Organizations 전문기준심의기구
professionalism 전문성 ; 직업의식
professionalization 전문화
profile 프로필
profit-making business 수익사업
progeria 조로증
progesterone therapy 프로게스테론요법
prognosis 예후
prognosis prediction 예후예측
Program Evaluation and Review Technique
 프로그램 평가 및 검토기법
Program Planning and Budgeting system
 프로그램 기획 및 예산제도
progress note of the home visiting nurses
 방문간호경과기록부
progress record 경과기록
progressive bulbar palsy 진행성 구마비
Progressive Era 진보주의적 시대
progressive muscular dystrophy : PMD
 진행성 근이영양증
progressive myoclonus epilepsy
 진행성 마이오클로누스간질
progressive resistance exercise
 점증저항훈련
progressive systemic sclerosis
 전신성 진행성 경화증
progressive tax 누진세
prohibition of acts causing discredit
 신용실추행위의 금지
Prohibition of Acts to Damage

Impartiality 신용실추행위의 금지
project 프로젝트
project for activation of senior citizen
 churches 경로당활성화사업
projection 투영 ; 투사
projective identification 투사 동일시
projective method 투영법
projective test 투영검사 ; 투시검사법
prokinetic medication 위운동촉진제
prolonged stretching 신장지속
promotion center of social participation
 for the physically disabled 신체장애인사회
 참가촉진센터
Promotion Division 진흥과
promotion of social participation
 사회참가촉진
pronation 회내
prone position 복와위
proof of employment letter 재직증명서
proof of immunization 예방접종증명서
proof of work experience 실무경험증명서
proper functional position 양지위
property division 재산분여
property tax 자산세
prophylactic medication 예방투여 ; 예방내복
proportional mortality indicator : PMI
 사망비율
proportional mortality rate 사인별사망비율
propoxyphene 프로폭시펜
propranolol 프로프라놀롤
proprietary 유료사회단체
proprietary medicine 특허매약
proprietary practice 유료행위
proprietary social services 유로사회봉사
proprioception 고유감각
proprioception deficit 고유수용성 결함
proprioceptive neuromuscular facilitation :
 PNF 고유수용성 신경근촉통법
Proscar 프로스카
prosocial behavior 친사회행동
ProSom 프로섬
prosopagnosia 안면실인증
prospective payment system 포괄지불제도

P

prospective review 예견적 감사 ; 전망적 리뷰
prospective study 전망적 연구 ; 예견적 연구
prostate cancer 전립선암
prostate disease 전립선질환
prostate specific antigen 전립선특이항원
prostatitis 전립선염
prosthesis 장구 ; 보장구 ; 의지 (義肢)
prosthesis fitting 의지장착
prosthetic 보철 ; 의지학
prosthetic equipment 보조기구
prosthetic training 의지훈련
prosthetist and orthotist : PO 의지장비사
prostitution 윤락행위 ; 매춘 ; 매음
Prostitution Prevention Law 매춘방지법
protection 원호
protection care 보호
protection of human rights 인권존중
protection/social security of the elderly
  first by the family, then by the society
  선가정보호 · 후사회보장
protective care for women 부녀보호
protective clothing 감염방어복 ; 방호의복
protective custody 보호감호 ; 보호구치
protective environment : PE 방호환경
protective isolation 예방격리
protective measure 보호처분
protective service 보호서비스 ;
  프로텍티브 서비스
protective services 보호국
protein 단백질
protein energy 단백질에너지
protein-energy malnutrition : PEM
  단백질에너지결핍증
Protestant ethic 청교도 윤리
Protestantism 프로테스탄티즘
proton pump inhibitor 플로톤펌프 저해약
provider 공급자 ; 공급주체 ; 제공자 ; 판매자 ;
  사업자
provision systems 공급체계
provisional collection 가징수
provisional release 가출옥
proximal 근위
proximal end 근위단

proximal tibia fracture 경골근위부골절
proxy decision maker 의사결정대리자
Prozac 프로작
prudent lay person 상식적 아마추어
pruritus 가려움증 ; 소양증
pseudo delinquent 가성불량소년
pseudobulbar paralysis 가성구마비
pseudodementia 가성치매
pseudomonas pneumonia 녹농균성 폐렴
pseudomutuality 의사성숙
psychiatric day care 정신과데이케어
psychiatric day care center
  정신과데이케어센터
psychiatric disorder 정신장애
psychiatric drug 정신제
psychiatric emergency 응급정신질활
psychiatric home health care
  정신과방문간호케어
psychiatric medication 정신약
psychiatric patient 정신병환자
psychiatric rehabilitation 정신과재활
psychiatric social work 장신의료사회사업
psychiatric social worker : PSW 정신보건사
  회복지사 ; 정신보건복지사 ; 정신과소시얼워커 ;
  정신의료사회사업가
psychiatrist 정신과의사 ; 정신의학자
psychiatry 정신의학
psychic trauma 심리적 외상
psycho drama 사이코드라마
psycho therapy 사이코세라피
psychoactive drug 정신작용제
psychoactive drugs 정신병약
psychoanalysis 정신분석 ; 정신분석학
psychoanalyst 정신분석가
psychoanalytic paradigm 정신분석의 패러다임
psychoanalytic theory 정신분석이론
psychoanalytic therapy 정신분석요법
psychoanalytical psychotherapy
  정신분석적 심리요법
psychodrama 심리극
psychodrama therapy 심리극요법
psychodynamics 정신역학 ; 정신역동론
psychogenesis 심인

P

psychogenic 정신병학적
psychogenic reaction 심인반응
psycholinguistics 언어심리학
psychological abuse 심리적 학대
psychological assessment 심리평가
psychological dependence 정신의존
psychological development theory
심리사회발달이론
psychological evaluator 심리판정원
psychological rehabilitation 심리적 재활
psychological support 심리적 지지
psychological test 심리테스트 ; 심리검사
psychological therapy 정신요법
psychologist 심리학자
psychology 심리학
psychopath 정신병질적
psychopathic personality 정신병질적 인격
psychopathologist 정신병리학자
psychopathology 정신병리학
psychopharmacology 정신약리학
psychosexual development
심리 · 성적 발달이론
psychosexual development theory
정신성적 발달이론
psychosexual disorder 정신성적 장애
psychosexual dysfunction 정신성적 역기능
psychosexual stages 심리 · 성적 단계
psychosis 정신병
psychosocial assessment 심리사회평가
psychosocial therapy 심리사회치료
psychosomatic 정신신체증
psychosomatic disease : PSD 심신증
psychosomatic medicine 정신신체의학
psychotherapist 심리치료자
psychotherapy
심리치료 ; 정신치료 ; 심리요법 ; 정신요법
psychotic 정신병적
psychotic behavior 정신병적 행동
psychotropic 향정신제
psychotropic drug 향정신약
PTSD 〈 post-traumatic stress disorder 〉
피티에스디
ptyalism 유연증 ; 유수증 ; 타액분비과다

puberty 사춘기
public assistance 생활보호 ; 공적부조
public assistance committee 생활보호위원회
public assistance costs
생활보호비용 ; 공적부조비용
Public Assistance Division 보호과
public assistance fraud 부정수급
Public Assistance Law 생활보호법 ; 부조법
public assistance ratio 보호율
public assistance recipient
생활보호수급자 ; 공적부조수급자 ; 피보호자
public assistance standards
생활보호기준 ; 공적부조기준
public assistance system 생활보호제도
public bath house 대중목욕탕 ; 대중탕
public benefit corporation 공익법인
public businesses account
공영기업등 회계부문
public choice theory 공공선택이론
public defender 관선변호인
public economics 공공경제학
public employment security office : PESO
공공직업안정소
public enterprise 공적기업
public guardian 공적후견인
public health 공중보건 ; 공중위생
public health care insurance 공적의료보험
public health care insurance system
공적의료보험제도
public health center 보건소
public health doctor 공중보건의
public health nurse : PHN 보건사
Public Health Service 공중보건서비스청
Public Health Service Act 공중위생법
public hearing 공청회
public hospital 공립병원
public hospital reform 공립병원개혁
public housing 공공주택 ; 공영주택
public housing for the aged
노인대상 공영주택
public housing for the elderly
고령자대상 공영주택
public institution 공립시설

public intervention 공적개입
public long-term care insurance
공적개호보험
public long-term care insurance
공적장기요양보험
public long-term care insurance system
공적장기요양보험제도 ; 공적개호보험제도
public opinion 여론
public pawnshop 공익전당포
public pension 공적연금
public pension plan subscription process
공적연금제도가입경과
public pension system 공적연금제도
Public Planning Committee for Protection
and Promotion of Care Services for the
Elderly 공적노인요양보장추진기획단
public policy 공공정책
public prosecutor 검찰관
public relations : PR 피알 ; 홍보
public relations education 홍보교육
public relief 공적구제
public reporting of long-term care services
개호서비스정보공개
public responsibility 공적책임
public services 공적서비스
public support 공조
public transportation 공공교통기관
public utility 공익사업
public vocational training 공공직업훈련
public welfare 공공복지
public welfare administration 민생행정
public work 공공사업
Public Works Administration : PWA
공공사업청
public/private dichotomy 공사분리
publicity 퍼블리시티
public-private competition 관민경쟁
puerperal fever 산욕감염증 ; 산욕열
puerperal sepsis 산욕열
pulley 활차
pulmonary aspiration 오연
pulmonary atelectasis 무기폐
pulmonary atresia 폐동맥폐쇄증

pulmonary disease 폐질환
pulmonary disorders 폐기관장애
pulmonary edema 폐수종
pulmonary embolus 폐쇄전
pulmonary emphysema 폐기종
pulmonary function test 폐기능검사
pulmonary nocardiosis 폐노카르디아증
pulmonary rehabilitation 호흡재활
pulmonary tuberculosis 폐결핵
pulp pinch 가볍게집기
pulse 맥박
pulse oximeter 펄스옥시미터
punch biopsy 펀치생검법 ; 세절채취법 ;
찍어냄생검
punishment 처벌
pupil rejecting school attendance
등교거부아
pupillary light reflex 동공대광반사
purchase of welfare aids 복지용구구입
purchase of welfare equipments
복지용구구입
pureed diet 반유동식 ; 퓌레식
pureed solids 퓌레상태
purine metabolism inhibitor 푸딩대사저해제
Puritanism 퓨리터니즘 (청교도주의)
purposeful expression of feelings
의도적인 감정표현
purposeful wandering 의도적 배회
pursed lip breathing 오므린 입술 호흡법 ;
입술 오므리고 숨쉬기
push off 푸시오프 ; 오르기
push up 푸시업
push up workout 팔굽혀펴기운동
put clothing on the affected side and
take the clothing off the unaffected
side 탈건착환
pyelography 신우조영
pyelonephritis 신우신염
pyorrhea 치조농루
pyramidal tract 추체로
pyrazinamide 피라지나마이드
pyrogen 발열물질 ; 파이로젠
pyrogen test 발열물질검사 ; 파이로젠검사

P

pyrophosphate deposition disease
파이로인산염침착증

pyuria 농뇨

q-sort technique 큐분류법
quad cane 네발 지팡이
quadragenarian 40대
quadriceps femoris 대퇴사두근
quadrilateral socket 사변형 소켓
quadriplegia 사지마비
qualitative investigation 질적조사
qualitative research 질적연구
quality affordable health care
적당하고 질 좋은 케어
quality assurance 품질보증
quality control : QC 품질관리활동 ; 품질관리
quality home care 질 좋은 재가장기요양
quality home health care
질 좋은 재가간호케어
quality improvement : QI 개선활동
quality nursing home care 질 좋은 널싱케어
quality of care
장기요양의 질 ; 케어의 질 ; 개호의 질
quality of life : QOL 생활의 질
quality of life assessment 생활의 질 평가

quality of medical care 의료의 질
quality of service : QOS 서비스의 질
quality of well-being : QWB 건강복지의 질
quantitative investigation 양적조사
quantitative research 양적연구
quasi-market 준시장 ; 의사시장
quasi-medical practice 의업유사행위
quazepam 쿠아제팜
Queen Elizabeth Ⅰ 엘리자베스 1세
questioning 질문
questionnaire 조사표 ; 설문지 ; 질문지
questionnaire method 질문지법
quiet sleep 안면
quinapril 퀴나프릴
quinine sulfate 황산염 ; 황산 키니네
quinquagenarian 50대
quorum 정족수
quota employment system 할당고용제도
quota restriction 할당제한
quota share 비례분배
quota system 할당 (고용) 제도 ; 할당제

R

R. C. Cabot 캐보트
racial and ethnic difference
인종적 민족적 차이
racial quotas 인종할당
racism 인종차별주의
radial artery 요골동맥
radial artery aneurysm 요골동맥류
radial artery cannulation 요골동맥카뉴레삽입법
radial artery catheter 요골동맥카테터
radial deviation 요굴 ; 요측편위
radiation emergency medical management
긴급피폭의료관리
radiation therapy 방사선치료
radical social work
급진적사회사업 ; 래디컬소시오워크
radiculopathy 신경근증
radioactive iodine 방사성옥소
radioallergosorbent test
방사성알레르겐흡착시험
radiography 방사선촬영 ; X선촬영
radioisotope 방사성동위체
radionuclide angiography 방사성핵종혈관조영
rage 광기
raloxifene 랄록시펜
ramelteon 라멜테온
ramp 경사로
random assignment 무작위할당
random sampling 무작위추출
range of motion : ROM 관절가동역
range of motion exercise 관절가동역운동
range of motion testing : ROM-T
관절가동역검사
rape 강간

rapid eye movement〈REM〉sleep 렘수면
rapport 라포르 ; 라포 ; 신뢰관계
rate of population aging 고령화율
ratio 비율
ratio of the elderly population 노년인구비율
rational casework 합리적 개별사회사업
rational-emotive therapy 합리적・정서적 치료 ;
논리정동요법
rationalization 합리화
rauhaus 라우에 하우스
Raven's colored progressive matrices
레이븐의 색채매트릭스검사
Razadyne 라자다인
reach out 리치아웃
reacher 리처
reaching out 출향(적극적) 원조
reaching out casework 적극적개별사회사업
reaction formation 반동형성
reaction time 반응시간
reactive psychosis 반응성 정신병
readiness 준비성 ; 래디니스
reading assistance 대독
reading glasses 독서안경
reading volunteer 낭독봉사원
reading volunteer services 낭독봉사
ready-to-serve dish 조리필
real expenditure 실지출
real income 실수입
reality orientation
현실견당식 ; 현실지남력 ; 리얼리티오리엔테이션
reality orientation training : ROT
현실견당식훈련 ; 현실지남력훈련
reality principle 현실원칙

reality testing 현실검증
reality therapy 현실치료
reanalysis of problems 재과제분석
reapportionment 의원 재할당
rearfoot varus deformity 후족부 내반변형
reassessment 재평가
reassurance 재보증
rebellious stage 반항기
recap 리캡
Receipt of Written Statement of Claim
  for Long-Term Care Benefit Cost
  노인장기요양급여비용청구명세서접수증
receptive attitude 수용적 태도
re-certification 재지정 ; 재인정 ; 재교육증명
recession 일시적 경기침체
recessive inheritance 열성유전
recidivism rate 재범(재발)률(상습적 범행률)
recidivist 재범자(상습자)
recipient 수급자 ; 이용자
recipient evaluation 이용자평가
reciprocal Ia inhibition Ia 상호억제
reciprocal interactions 상호작용
reciprocal walking frame 교호식 보행기
reciprocating gait orthosis 교호보행보조기
reclassification 재분류
reclining wheelchair 리클라이닝형 휠체어
recognition 재허가 ; 인식
recommendation 권고
recommended dietary allowance : RDA
  영양권장량 ; 영양소요량 ; 추장량
reconstituted family 재결합가정
recording 기록
recording style 기록양식
records 기록
recovery phase rehabilitation 회복기 재활
Recovery, Inc. 갱생협회
recreation 레크리에이션
recreation program 레크리에이션 프로그램
recreational activity 레크리에이션활동
recreational home for the aged 노인휴양홈
rectal 직장내
rectal biopsy 직장생검
rectal examination 직장진찰

rectal irrigation 직장세정
rectal prolapse 직장탈
rectocele 직장혹
recurrent expenditures 경상비
red blood cell : RBC 적혈구
Red Cross 적십자 ; 적십자사
red feather community chest movement
  빨간깃털모금 ; 무브먼트
rediscovery of poverty 빈곤의 재발견
redistribution 재분배
redistributive effect 재분배효과
red-light district 홍등가
redlining 적색지대
redneck 촌놈
redness 발적
reduction of taxes for widow 과부공제
reductionism 축소주의
re-education of sensation 지각재교육
re-emerging infectious diseases 재흥감염증
reemployment arrangements 재고용
reevaluation 재평가
reference daily intake : RDI 하루섭취권장량
reference electrode 기준전극
reference group 준거집단
reference group theory 준거집단론
referendum 국민투표
referral 위탁
referral fee 소개료
referral services 소개서비스
referred pain 관련통
reflection benefit 반사적 이익
reflection of feeling 감정반사
reflex 반사작용 ; 반사
reflex movement 반사운동
reflex sympathetic dystrophy : RSD
  반사성 교감신경성 이영양증
reformatory 소년원 ; 감화원
Reformed Poor Law 개정구빈법
reformer 개혁자
reformism 개량주의
reframing 재구성 ; 리프레이밍
refugee 난민 ; 피난민(망명자, 도피자)
refugee relief program 난민구제

R

refugee services 난민서비스
refuse disposal 폐기물처리
regeneration 갱생
regeneration medicine 재생의료
regional gap 지역격차
regional planning 지역계획
registered dietitian 관리영양사
registered nurse : RN 등록간호사 ; 정규간호사
registration 등록
registration number 등록번호
regression 퇴행
regression analysis 회귀분석
regression behavior 퇴행행동
regressive tax 역진세
regular diet 보통식 ; 주식
regular employee 상용노동자
rehabilitation 재활 ; 리허빌리테이션 ; 재활서비스
rehabilitation and assistance center for people with acquired severe physical disabilities 중도신체장애인갱생원호시설
rehabilitation and assistance center for the physically disabled 신체장애인갱생원호시설
rehabilitation approach 재활접근법
rehabilitation center 주간재활센터
rehabilitation center for people with mental disabilities 정신장애인사회복귀시설
rehabilitation center for the disabled 장애인갱생센터
rehabilitation counseling center for people with mental disabilities 정신장애인갱생상담소
rehabilitation counseling center for people with mental retardation 지적장애인갱생상담소
rehabilitation counseling center for physically disabled 신체장애인갱생상담소
rehabilitation counseling center for the disabled 장애인갱생상담소
rehabilitation engineering 재활공학
rehabilitation equipment 재활기기
rehabilitation facility for crippled children 지체부자유아갱생시설

rehabilitation facility for people with acquired severe physical disabilities 중도신체장애인갱생시설
rehabilitation facility for people with mental retardation 지적장애인갱생시설
rehabilitation facility for persons with disabilities 신체장애인갱생시설
rehabilitation facility for persons with disabilities 신체장애인갱생원호시설
rehabilitation facility for the auditorially impaired 청각장애자갱생시설
rehabilitation facility for the physically disabled 신체장애인갱생시설
rehabilitation facility for the visually impaired 시각장애인갱생시설
rehabilitation fund for the physically disabled 신체장애인갱생기금
rehabilitation institute 재활시설
Rehabilitation International : RI 세계재활협회
rehabilitation medicine 재활의학
rehabilitation nurse 재활간호사
rehabilitation nursing 재활간호
rehabilitation prescription 재활처방
rehabilitation program 재활프로그램
Rehabilitation Specialty's Handbook 재활전문 안내서
rehabilitation worker 재활사회사업가
rehabilitative care 재활개호
rehabilitative facility for people with internal disorders 내부장애인갱생시설
rehydration 수분보급
reimbursement 상환지불
reinforcement 강화
reinforcer 강화물 ; 강화인자
Reiter's syndrome 라이터증후군
reiterative reflection 반복반사
rejection 거부
relabeling 재명명
relation over population 상대적 과잉인구
relationship 관계
relationship therapy 관계요법
relative metabolic rate : RMR 에너지대사율
relative risk 상대적인 위험 ; 상대위험

R

relative's responsibility 친족의무
relaxation 릴랙세이션 ; 이완
release on parole 가출소
reliability 신뢰도
Relief Division 원호과
relief institution 구호시설
relief work 구제사업
religion 종교
religious corporation 종교법인
religious social work 종교사회사업
relive 구조
relocation stress 이사스트레스
Relpax 렐팍스
remaining function 잔존능력 (잔존기능)
remaining sense 잔존감각
remaining sense of pain 통각잔류
remarriage 재혼
remarriage in matured age 황혼재혼
remarried family 재혼가정
remedial model 치료모델
remedial order 개선명령
Remicade 레미케이드
reminiscence 라이프리뷰 ; 회상
reminiscence therapy 회상법 ; 회상치료
Reminyl 레미닐
remission 회복 ; 관해
remote area medicine 원격지의료
remote care 원격케어
remote medical system 원격의료시스템
remote medicine 원격의료
renal failure 신부전
renal function 신장기능
Rene Sand 상드
renewal 갱신
renewal application 갱신신청
rent control 임대료통제
rent strike 임대료쟁의
rental housing 임대주택
rental housing for low-income elderly
　저소득고령자대상 임대주택
reorganization 재조직화 ; 리오가나이제이션
repetitive saliva swallowing test : RSST
　반복 타액연하검사 ; 반복 침삼키기검사

report 보고
report from the primary doctor
　주치의 의견서
repression 억압
reputation 명예 ; 평판
Requip 리큅
requirements for benefits 지급요건
requirements for establishment 설치기준
requirements to receive benefits 수급요건
rescue 구조
rescue breathing 인공호흡
research 조사
Research and Development Division
　연구개발진흥과
Research Center for Health Check-ups &
　Welfare of the Aged 노인건강&복지연구소
Research Institute of Dwelling of the
　Elderly 노인주거연구소
Research Institute of Life Science of
　Elderly 노인생활과학연구소
research institution 연구소
research subjects 조사대상
resettlement 재정착
residency laws 주거제한법
resident 입소자 ; 널싱홈 이용자 ; 주민 ; 이용자
resident bacteria 상재균
resident flora 상재세균총
resident movement 주민운동
resident participation 주민참가
resident tax 주민세
residential care 거주케어
residential care home for children
　양호시설
residential care work 레지덴셜케어워크
residential environment 거주환경
residential facility 입소시설
residential home for the elderly
　양호노인홈
residential social work 레지덴셜소시얼워크
residential treatment 수용치료
residential welfare facilities for the aged
　노인거주복지시설
residual conception 보충적개념

R

residual functional capacity
잔존능력 (잔존기능)
residual functional capacity assessment|
잔존능력평가
residual sensation 잔뇨감
residual urine 잔뇨
residual versus institutional model
잔여적 모델 대 제도적 모델
residual welfare provision 잔여적 복지시책
resistance 저항
resistance exercise 저항운동
resistance training 저항훈련
resocialization group 재사회화 집단
resource allocation 자원할당
resource systems 자원체계
Resource-Based Relative Value Scale :
RBRVS 자원기준 상대가치측정법
resources 자원
respect for the aged 경로사상
Respect for the Aged Day 경로의 날
respect for the elderly 경로
Respect for the Elderly Day 경로의 날
respecting filial obligation 경로효친사상
respiration 호흡
respirator 인공호흡기
respirator dependent quadriplegia
인공호흡기의존 사지마비
respiratory disease 호흡기질환
respiratory disorder 호흡장애
respiratory exercise 호흡연습
respiratory failure 호흡부전
respiratory functional disorder
호흡기능장애
respiratory infection 호흡기감염
respiratory isolation 기도감염격리
respiratory organ 호흡기
respiratory paralysis 호흡마비
respiratory therapy 호흡요법
respiratory training 호흡훈련
respite care 레스파이트케어
respite care services 레스파이트케어서비스
respite service 휴식서비스
respondent behavior 반사행동 ; 반응행동

response cost
반응비용 ; 리스폰스코스트 ; 반응대가 ; 행동대가
response hierarchy 반응계층
responsibility 책임
responsibility to support dependents
부양의무
responsible for aging parents 노친부양
responsible for an aging parent 노친부양
responsible for family 가족부양
responsible for the age 노인부양
rest areas for the aged 노인휴양소
rest equipment 휴양설비
rest facilities for the aged 노인휴양시설
rest home 레스트홈
rest home for the aged 노인휴양홈
resting energy expenditure : REE
안정시 에너지소비량
restitution 원상복구
restless legs syndrome : RLS 하지불안증후
군 ; 근질근질 다리증후군
restorative training 기능회복훈련
restraining tie 억제대
restraint 억제 ; 구속
restricted mobility 운동제한
restrictive services 제한적 서비스
restroom 화장실
restructuring 구조조정
retardation 지체
retina 망막
retinal sensitivity 망막감도
retired immigrants 은퇴이민
retiree health care insurance system
퇴직자 의료보험제도
retiree health care system 퇴직자 의료제도
retirement 퇴직 ; 은퇴 ; 정년
retirement allowance 퇴직수당
retirement community 은퇴촌 ; 노인촌락
retirement earnings test 퇴직소득조사
retirement lump sum grant 퇴직일시금
retirement pension 퇴직연금
retirement process 과정으로서의 퇴직
retirement test 퇴직조사 ; 퇴직검사
retribution 응보

retroactive indication 소급적용
retroactive premium payment
보험료소급부과
retrograde amnesia
역행성 건망 ; 퇴화성 기억상실증
retrograde pyelography 역행성 신우조영
retroperitoneal hematoma 후복막혈종
retrospective charge 소급부과
retrospective review 회고적 감사
retrospective study
기왕조사 ; 뒷방향연구 ; 회고적 연구법 ;
후향성 연구
return to work 직업복귀
reuse 재사용
Reuter centrifugal sampler
RCS 공중부유물질채집기
revascularization 혈행재건술
reverse discrimination 역차별
reverse mortgage 리버스모기지
reverse mortgage program
리버스모기지 프로그램
reversed isolation 보호격리 ; 역격리
Revia 레비아
Review Committee on Long-Term Care
Insurance 개호보험심사회
Revised Children's Manifest Anxiety
Scale : RCMAS 개정판 아동발현불안척도
Revised Hasegawa's Dementia Scale :
HDS-R 하세가와식 간이지능평가스케일 개정판
Revised Wechsler Adult Intelligence
Scale : WAIS-R 개정판 웩슬러 성인지능척도
Revised Wechsler Memory Scale :
WMS-R 개정판 웩슬러 기억검사
Revision of the Eight Acts related to
Social Welfare 사회복지관계 8법의 개정
revocation 취소
Rey figure copy 레이 복합도형검사
rheumatic disorder 류머티즘
rheumatoid arthritis : RA
관절류머티즘 ; 만성관절류머티즘
rheumatologist 류머티즘전문의
rheumatology 류머티즘학
rhinitis 비염

Richard Morris Titmuss 티트머스
rickets 구루병
Riemenbugel method 리멘뷰겔법
rifampin 리팜핀
right lateral recumbent 우측와위
right of freedom 자유권
right of labor 노동권
right to a decent standard of living
생존권
right to demand the compensation
for damage 손해배상청구권
right to live 생활권
right to receive benefits 수급권 ;
수익권
right to refuse treatment 치료거부권
right to strike 쟁의권
right to the pursuit of happiness
행복추구권
right to treatment 치료권
righting reaction 회복반응 ; 정위반응
rights 권리
rights of caregivers 돌보는 사람의 권리
rights of caregivers 장기요양자의 권리
rights of patients 환자의 권리
rights of residents 입소형 시설이용자의 권리 ;
널싱홈 이용자의 권리
rigid scope 경성경
rigid sigmoidoscopy 경성S상 결장경검사
rigidity 오그라듦 ; 강직
rigor mortis 사후경직
Rilutek 리루텍
riluzole 릴루졸
ring lock 고리 자물쇠
rinse 린스
risedronate 리세드로네이트
risk 리스크
risk assessment 위험율평가
risk control 리스크관리
risk factor 위험인자
risk management 리스크매니지먼트 ; 위기관리
risk prevention 위험방지
risk-sharing plan
위험분담의 원칙 ; 리스크 공유플랜

R

risky shift 모험이행 ; 리스키시프트
Risperdal 리스페달
risperidone 리스페리돈
rite of passage 통과의식
ritual 의례
rivastigmine 리바스티그민
Rivermead Behavioural Memory Test :
 RBMT 리바미드 행동기억검사
rizatriptan 리자트립탄
Robaxin 로박신
Robert D. Vinter 빈터
Robert Owen 오웬
rocking chair 안락의자 ; 흔들의자
rocking chair-type 안락의자형
rod 간상 ; 간체
roentgen X레이 ; 뢴트겐
Roger Barker 바카
role 역할
role ambiguity 역할모호성
role behavior 역할행동
role complementary 역할보충성
role conflict 역할갈등
role distance 역할거리
role expectation 역할기대
role perception 역할인지
role performance 역할수행
role play 롤플레이 ; 역할연기
role playing 롤플레잉 ; 역할연기
role re-equilibration 역할재평형
role reversal 역할전환
role strain 역할긴장
role theory 역할이론
role vigor 역할강도
roll over 돌아눕기
room climate 실내기후

Roosevelt F. D. 루즈벨트
root avulsion injury 신경근결출손상
ropinirole 로피니롤
Rorschach Inkblot Test
 로르샤흐잉크반점검사 ; 로샤검사잉크반점검사
Rorschach test 로오샤크테스트 ; 로르샤흐검사 ;
 로샤검사
rotational vestibulo-ocular reflex
 회전전정동안반사
rotator cuff injury 건판손상 ; 견견판손상
rotator strap 선회대
roundback 척추후만증 ; 후만
routes of infection 감염경로
routine daily-life guidance 일상생활지도
routine health examination 정기건강진단
royal commission 왕립위원회
Rozerem 로제렘
rubbing board 빨래판
rubbing method 마찰접종법 ; 러빙법
rubella 풍진
rubeola 홍역
rugged individualism 극렬개인주의
rumination disorder of infancy
 유아기 반추장애
run away from home 가출
runaway 가출자
runaway aged 가출노인
running cost 런닝코스트
rural elder 농촌부의 고령자
rural over population 농촌과잉인구
rural problem 농촌문제
rural society 농촌사회
rural village 농촌
Russell Sage Foundation 러셀세이지재단

R

S

saccharide 당질
sacral region 선골부
sadist 새디스트
sadistic 가학성애
sadistic personality disorder 가학성 성격장애
sadomasochism 가학피학성애
safeguard for human rights 인권보장
safekeeping 보관
safety and health control 안전보건관리
safety confirmation 안부확인
safety confirmation system 안부확인시스템
safety control 안전관리
safety control system 안전관리체제
Safety Division 안전대책과 ; 안전과
safety education 안전지도
safety issue 안전문제
safety needs 안전욕구
safety net 세프티네트 ; 안전망
salary calculator 급여계산
salary peak 임금피크제
saliva 타액
saliva functioning 타액기능
salmonella 살모넬라균
salmonella food poisoning 살모네라균식중독
salt 식염
salty 짠맛
salvation army 구세군
sample 표본
sample survey 표본조사 ; 추출조사
sampling 표본추출
sampling design 표본추출법
sampling error 표본오차 ; 추출오차
sampling method 추출법

sanctuary 피난처
sand bag 모래주머니
sand play technique 상정요법 ; 모래놀이치료
sanding 샌딩
sanitarium 결핵요양소 ; 새니토리움
sanitization 소독위생처리
santeria 산테리아
saponated cresol solution 크레졸비누액
sarcopenia 사르코페니아
satellite system 새틀라이트 방식
satisfaction 만족
satisfaction in caregiving 장기요양만족감
satisfaction measurement 만족도측정
satisfying 만족도
saturated vapor 포화증기
saturation 채도
save 구조
Save the Children Federation 아동구호연
scabies 옴 ; 개선
scaling stairs 계단승강
scam 사기
scapegoat 희생양
scapulohumeral rhythm 견갑상완리듬
schedule of reinforcement 강화계획
schema 스키마
schizoaffective disorder
　분열감정장애 ; 분열정서장애
schizoid 정신분열성
schizoid personality disorders
　정신분열성 성격장애
schizophrenia 통합실조증 ; 정신분열증
schizophreniform disorder 정신분열증 장애
schizophrenogenic parent

S

정신분열증 유발형 부모

scholarship program 육영사업

school absenteeism 등교거부 ; 불등교

school counseling 학교상담

school counselor 스쿨카운슬러 ; 진로지도교관

school for the aged 노인학교

school for the blind 맹학교 ; 맹인학교

school for the deaf 농학교

school for the deaf mute 농아학교

school for the disabled children 양호학교

school for the elderly 고령자학교

school for the physically and mentally disabled children 양호학교

school infirmary 양호실 ; 보건실

school instructor for the aged 노인학교지도사

School Lunch program 학교급식 프로그램

school nurse 양호교사

school of social work 사회복지사양성시설

school phobia 학교공포증

school social work 학교사회사업

school social worker 스쿨소시얼워커

science 과학

scientific method 과학적 방법

scintigraphy 섬광조영술 ; 신티그래피

scoliosis 측만

scotopic luminance 암소시휘도

scratching 스크래칭 ; 긁금

screening 스크리닝 ; 검진

scripts 각본

scrub method 스크러브법

sculpting 조각기법

Seamen's Insurance 선원보험

Seamen's Insurance Law 선원보험법

seasonal affective disorder : SAD 계절성 정서장애

seasonal day nursery 계절보육소

seasonal unemployment 계절적 실업

seasonal work 계절노동

seating aid 좌위보조구

seating system 좌위보지장치

Sebivo 세비보

second opinion

세컨드오피니언 ; 다른 의사의 의견

secondary assessment 2차 판정

secondary disorder 2차 장애

secondary gain 2차적 이득

secondary group 2차 집단

secondary infection 2차 감염

secondary insured 제2호 피보험자

secondary medical care 2차 진료

secondary medical service area 2차 의료권

secondary physician 부주치의

secondary poverty 제2차 빈곤

secondary prevention 2차 예방

secondary process 2차 과정

secondary stress on caregivers 장기요양자의 2차적 스트레스

secondhand smoke 수동흡연

second-order change 제2단계 변화

secrecy obligation 비밀보지의무

sectarian services 종교적 사회복지

sectoral planning 구획계획

security 보장

sedative-hypnotic drug 진정최면제

sedatives 진정제

Seddon's classification 세돈분류

Seebohm Report 시봄보고서

seeing eye dog 맹도견

seizure disorder 발작이상

seizure disorders 발작성 장애

seizure medication 발작제

selective abstraction 선택적 추출

selective dissemination of information : SDI 선택적 정보배포

selective optimization with compensation 선택적 최적화론

selective placement 선택고용

selective programs 선별적 프로그램

selective serotonin reuptake inhibitor : SSRI 선택적 세로토닌재흡수저해제

selective services 선별적 서비스

selectivism 선별주의 ; 선택주의

selegiline 셀레길린

selenium 셀레늄

self-actualization 자아실현 ; 자기실현

self-advocacy movement
셀프어드보카시 무브먼트

self-advocacy movement
자기옹호운동 ; 자기권리주장운동

self-assisted exercise 자기타동운동

self-awareness 자기인식 ; 자기각지

self-care 셀프케어 ; 자기건강관리

self-care management
자기건강관리 매니지먼트

self-care plan 자기건강관리 플랜

self-catheterization 자기도뇨

self-concept 자기개념

self-control 셀프콘트롤 ; 자기통제

self-control theory 자기컨트롤이론

self-defeating personality disorder
자기파괴적 성격장애

self-determination 자기결정

self-disclosure 자기폭로

self-efficacy 자기효력감

self-employed 자영업자

self-employed health insurance deduction
자영업자 건강보험공제

self-employment 자영업

self-esteem 자존심

self-evaluation 자기평가

self-expression 자기표현

self-fulfilling prophecy 자아성취 기대

self-government association 자치회

self-harm : SH 자상행위

self-hate 자동안전장치

self-hatred 자기혐오

self-help 자조

self-help activity 당사자활동

self-help device 자조도구

self-help group : SHG 셀프헬프그룹

self-help group for families 가족회

self-help groups 자조집단

self-help organization 자조조직

self-identity 자기동일성

self-improvement 자기개선

self-infection 자기감염

self-injury 자상행위

self-instructional training 자기교시훈련

self-invested personal pension
자기투자형 개인연금

self-maintenance 자기조정

self-medication 자기치료

self-neglect 자기방임

self-poisoning 자가중독

self-protection type 자기방위형

self-realization 자기실현

self-reliant living assistance services
자립생활원조

self-responsibility 자기책임

self-restraint 자제

self-understanding 자기이해

semantic dementia : SD 의미성 치매

semantic memory 의미기억

semicritical 세미크리티컬 ; 반침습적

semi-Fowler's position 반좌위

semiotics 증후학

semi-prepared dish 반조리

semi-private room 2인실 ; 준개인실

semi-unemployment 준실업

senile deafness 노인성 난청

senile dementia 노인성 치매 ; 노년치매 ;
노년인지증 ; 노인성 인지증

Senile Dementia Center 노인성 인지증질환센터

senile dementia of the Alzheimer's type :
SDAT 알츠하이머형 치매

senile depression 노인성 우울증

senile plaque 노인성 반점 ; 노인반점

senility 노쇠

senior care advisor 고령자케어 어드바이저

senior center 시니어센터 ; 고령자복지센터 ;
노인복지센터

Senior Citizen Charter 미국노인헌장 ;
경로헌장

senior citizens club 노인클럽 ; 고령자클럽 ;
경로회

Senior Companion Program
시니어컴퍼니언 프로그램 ; 노인동료프로그램

senior home 실버홈

senior housing 시니어주택

senior lifestyle 실버라이프스타일

senior living community 고령자거주공동체

S

senior rental housing 고령자전용임대주택
senior volunteer 시니어자원봉사
senium 노년기
sense 감각
sense of hearing 청각
sense of shame 수치심
sense of sight 시각
sense of smell 후각
sense of taste 미각
sense of touch 촉각
sense of value 가치관
sensitivity group 감수성 훈련집단
sensitivity test 감수성 시험
sensorimotor stage 감각운동기
sensorineural deafness 감음난청
sensorium 지각중추(감각)
sensory aphasia 감각성 실어
sensory change 지각능력변이
sensory disorder 감각장애
sensory disturbance 감각장애
sensory enhancement 감각강화법
sensory function 감각기능
sensory impairment 지각장애
sensory integration 감각통합
sensory nerve 감각신경
sensory nerve conduction velocity
  감각신경전도속도
sensory paralysis 감각마비 ; 지각마비
sensory substitution 감각대행
Sentencing Project
  형선고문제연구 ; 판결감시프로젝트
separation 분리
separation anxiety 분리불안
separation anxiety disorder 분리불안장애
separation of dispensary from medical
  practice 의약분업
sepsis 패혈
septic shock 패혈증성 쇼크
septicemia 패혈증
septuagenarian 70대
sequela 후유증
serial section 연속절편
serologic test for syphilis 혈청학적 매독검사

serotonin 세로토닌
serotonin norepinephrine reuptake
  inhibitor : SNRI 세로토닌 노르에피네프린
  재흡수억제제
sertraline 설트랄린
service area 서비스제공권
service code 서비스코드
service contract 서비스계약
service coordination 서비스조정
service dog 보조견 ; 보호견
service level 서비스수준
service management team for the
  elderly 고령자서비스조정팀
service manager 서비스제공책임자
service menu 서비스메뉴
service provider report 개호서비스제공표
service recipient 서비스이용자
service skill 서비스기술
service staff meeting 서비스담당자회의
services package 서비스패키지
setting plate sampling 낙하균측정법
settlement 세틀먼트
Settlement Act 정주법
settlement house 세틀먼트하우스 ; 인보관
settlement house work 인보사업
severance package 퇴직수당
severe acute respiratory syndrome :
  SARS 중증급성 호흡증후군 ; 사스
severe physical and mental disabilities
  중증심신장애
sex chromosome 성염색체
sex crime 성범죄
sex discrimination 성차별
sex education 성교육
sexagenarian 60대
sexism 성차별주의
sexual abuse 성적학대 ; 성학대
sexual activity 성행위
sexual assault nurse examiner
  성폭력피해자지원 간호직
sexual division of labor 성별역할분업
sexual dysfunction 성기능장애
sexual equality 성평등

sexual harassment
성희롱 ; 성적희롱 ; 섹슈얼 해러스먼트
sexual health 성건강
sexual minority 성적 소수자
sexual orientation disturbance 성지향장애
Sexual violence 성폭력 ; 성적폭력
sexuality 섹슈얼리티
sexually transmitted disease : STD
성행위감염증 ; 성감염증
shadow work 쉐도우워크
shadowing 쉐도윙
shampoo 샴푸
shampooing 머리감기
shank 섕크
shantytowns 빈민굴
shaping 쉐이핑 ; 조형
share of cost 부담금분담
share of cost of medical care
의료비부담금분담
shared housing 공유주택
shared paranoid disorder 공유성 편집장애
sharps injury 주사침 등의 손상 ; 예리물질손상
shave biopsy 면도생검
shaving 제모 ; 수염깍기
sheltered employment 보호고용
sheltered housing 보호주택
sheltered workshop facility 수산시설
sheltered workshop for people with
acquired severe physical disabilities
중도신체장애인수산시설
sheltered workshop for people with
mental disabilities 정신장애인수산시설 ;
정신장애인통소수산시설
sheltered workshop for people with
mental disorders 정신장애인수산시설
sheltered workshop for people with
mental retardation 지적장애인수산시설
sheltered workshop for the physically
disabled 신체장애인수산시설 ;
신체장애인통소수산시설
sheltered workshop services 수산사업
shelters 쉼터
shingles 대상포진

shock 쇼크 ; 충격
shock therapy 충격치료
shoe horn 구두주걱
shoe horn brace : SHB 구두주걱보조기
short leg brace : SLB 단하지보조기
short opponens hand orthosis 단대립보조기
short stump 단단단
short wave diathermy 초단파요법
shortness of breath 숨가쁨
short-stay 단기보호
short-stay care 단기입소케어
short-stay care facilities 단기보호시설
short-stay facility for the aged
노인단기입소시설
short-stay for people with mental
retardation 지적장애인단기입소
short-stay for the aged 노인단기입소
short-stay for the physically disabled
신체장애인단기입소
short-stay health care 단기입소요양개호
short-stay office 단기보호사업소
short-stay program for people with
mental retardation 지적장애인단기입소사업
short-stay project 단기보호사업
short-stay services 단기보호서비스
short-term care facility 단기케어시설
short-term goal 단기목표
short-term memory 단기기억
short-term treatment facility for children
with disabilities and emotional
disturbances 정서장애아단기치료시설
short-term volunteer 단기자원봉사
shoulder disarticulation prosthesis 견의수
shoulder dislocation 견관절탈구
shoulder impingement syndrome
어깨 인핀지먼트 증후군
shoulder subluxation 견관절아탈구
shoulder suspension system
숄더서스펜션 ; 어깨걸이띠
shoulder wheel 어깨회전운동기
shoulder-hand syndrome 견수증후군
shower bath 샤워욕
shower chair 샤워의자 ; 샤워체어

S

shower wheelchair 샤워용 휠체어

Shy-Drager syndrome : SDS
샤이드래거 증후군

sialorrhea 침과다증 ; 과유연 ; 유연증 ;
타액분비과다

sibling conflict 형제 < 자매 > 간 갈등

sibling rivalry 형제 < 자매 > 간 경쟁

Sibutramine 시부트라민

sick leave 병휴가 ; 질병휴가

sickle-cell anemia 겸상 적혈구성 빈혈

sickness and injury allowance 병수당 ;
상병수당금

sickness benefit 질병급여 ; 상병급여금

sickness impact profile : SIP
질병영향 프로파일

sickness insurance 질병보험

sickness pension 질병연금

side effect 부작용

side job 부업

side pinch 옆으로 집기

side-lying position 측와위

siderail 사이드레일

side-taking 편파적 중재

sigmoid colon S장결장

sigmoidoscopy S장결장경검사

Sigmund Freud 프로이드

sign language 수화 ; 수화법

sign language interpreter : SLI 수화통역사

sign language support 수화원조

sign language supporter 수화원조자

sign language volunteer 수화봉사원

sign language volunteer work 수화봉사

signage 기호

significance level 유의도

significant change 현저한 변화

significant difference 유의차

significant others 중요한 타자

signs of disease 병의 징조

silent aspiration 불현성 오연

silent infection 불현성 감염

silent killer 사일런트 킬러

silent myocardial ischemia 무증후성 심근허혈

Silesian bandage 실레지아 밴드

silicone soft liner 실리콘제 소프트라이너

silver city 노인촌

silver service 실버서비스

silver town 실버타운

simple bathtub 간이욕조

Sims' position 심스위

simultaneous contrast effect 동시대비효과

single axis joint 단축이음새

single parent home 모자가정 ; 부자가정

single photon emission computed
tomography : SPECT 단일포톤방출단층촬영

single-father household 부자세대

single-mother household 모자세대

single-parent family 편부모가정

single-payer 통합지불

single-session group 일회성 집단

single-use device 1회사용기재

sink 싱크대 ; 개수대

sinobronchial syndrome 부비강기관지증후군

sinopulmonary infection 기도감염

sinus headache 부비동성 두통

sit to stand 일어서기

site investigation 방문조사

site investigator 방문조사원

sitting exercise 좌위훈련

sitting position 좌위 ; 단좌위 ; 기좌위

sitting posture 좌위자세

sit-to-stand exercise 기립운동 ; 일어서기운동

situational reflection 상황반사

six basic food groups 여섯가지 기초식품군

six times weekly : 6W 주 6회

Sjogren's syndrome 쇼그렌 증후군

Skelaxin 스케락신

skeletal muscle 골격근

skeleton 골격

skill of group work 그룹워크의 기술

skilled nursing facility 전문요양시설

skilled nursing home
고도간호시설 ; 스킬드 널싱홈

skin 피부

skin antiseptic 피부소독

skin barrier 피부보호제

skin cancer 피부암

skin disease 피부질환
skin disorder 피부장애
skin pruritus 피부소양증
skin rash 발진
skin surface culture method
  피부표면세균배양법
skin tear 피부손상
Skinner box 스키너상자
Skinnerian theory 스키너이론
sleep 수면
sleep apnea 수면시 무호흡
sleep apnea syndrome : SAS
  수면시 무호흡증후군
sleep disorder 수면장애
sleep disturbance 수면장애
sleep medicine 수면제
sleep-driving 졸음운전
sleeping pill 수면제
sleeplessness 불면
sleep-related breathing disorder
  수면관련호흡장애
slide-on-ceiling type of lift 천장주행형 리프트
sliding scale 슬라이딩 스케일 ; 신축법 ;
  슬라이드제
sliding scheme of pension 연금슬라이드제
sliding tube 슬라이딩 튜브
slight fever 미열
sling 삼각건 ; 슬링
slope 슬로프
slowly progressive insulin dependent
  diabetes 저속진행성 인슐린의존 당뇨병
slum 빈민가 ; 슬럼
slum area 불량주택지역
small cell lung cancer : SCLC 소세포폐암
small government 작은 정부
small group discussion 소집단토의
small intestinal polyps 소장폴립
small intestine 소장
small-scale custodial facility for the
  physically disabled 소규모신체장애인요호시설
small-scale geriatric welfare home for
  the aged 소규모특별양호양로원
small-scale multi-functional home-based

care service 소규모다기능형거택장기요양 ; 소
  규모다기능형거택개호
small-scale multi-functional services
  소규모다기능서비스 ; 소규모다기능형서비스
small-scale workshop 소규모작업소
small-scale workshop for people with
  metal disabilities 정신장애인소규모작업소
smoke alarm 연기감지기
smoking 흡연
snare 스네어
snare electrocoagulation 스네어 전기응고
snoring 코골이
social action 사회적 행위 ; 사회적 행동 ;
  사회행동
social activist 사회행동가
social activity 사회활동
social adequacy 사회적 적용
social adjustment 사회적 적응
social administration
  사회복지관리 ; 사회행정 ; 사회복지경영
Social Administration Office 사회복지관리사
  무소
social agency 사회기관
social allowance 사회수당
social assistance 사회부조 ; 사회적 부양
social barrier 사회적 장벽
social bond 사회유대
social capital 사회자본
social care 사회적 양호
social case work 소시얼케이스워크
social change 사회변동 ; 사회적 부담비
social class 사회계급
social cognitive theory 사회인지이론
social consciousness 사회의식
social control 사회통제
social cost 사회비용
social democracy 사회민주주의
social democratic welfare state
  사회민주주의적 복지국가
social development 사회개발
social diagnosis 사회진단
social disorganization 사회해체
social distance 사회적 거리

S

social ecology 사회생태학
social education 사회교육
social employment 사회고용
social engineering 사회공학
social environment 사회환경
social evil 사회악
social evolutionism 사회진화론
social functioning ability : SFA 사회생활력
social geography 사회지리학
social gerontology 사회노년학
social group 사회집단
social group work 소시얼그룹워크 ; 집단사회사업
social hand washing
사회적 손씻기 ; 일상적 손씻기
social handicapped 사회적 장애
social hospitalization 사회적 입원
social inclusion 사회적 통합 ; 사회적 수용 ;
소시얼인클루전 ; 사회적 포섭
social indicators 사회지표
social institution 사회제도
social insurance 사회보험
Social Insurance Agency 사회보험청
social insurance costs 사회보험비용
social insurance examiner 사회보험심사원
social insurance expenses 사회보험비
Social Insurance Medical Fee Payments
Fund 사회보험진료보수지불기금
social insurance office 사회보험사무소
social insurance operation center
사회보험업무센터
social insurance premium 사회보험료
social insurance system 사회보험방식
social integration 사회통합 ; 사회적 상호작용
social intergroup work 소시얼인터그룹워크
social isolation 사회적 격리
Social Law 사회법
social learning theory 사회학습 이론
social maturity scale 사회성숙도척도
social medicine 사회의학
social mobility 사회이동
social model 사회모델
social model of disability 장애의 사회모델
social movement 사회운동

social movement theory 사회운동론
social needs 소시얼니드 ; 사회적 요구 ; 사회욕구
social network 사회적 네트워크
social norm 사회규범
social order 사회질서
social organization 사회조직
social participation 사회참가
social participation of women 여성의 사회참가
social pathology 사회병리 ; 사회병리학
social phobia 사회공포증
social planning 사회계획
social policy 사회정책
social policy analysis 사회복지정책분석
social problems 사회문제
social problem-solving 사회적 문제해결법
social program 사회사업
social psychology 사회심리학
social reform 사회개혁 ; 사회개량
social rehabilitation 사회적 재활
social rehabilitation and training facility for
people with mental disabilities
정신장애인사회복귀시설
social rehabilitation and training for
people with mental disorders 정신장애인
사회적응훈련
social relation 사회관계
social research 사회조사
social resource 사회자원
social rights 사회권 ; 사회적 기본권
social risk 사회적 위험
social risk management
사회적 위기관리 ; 소시얼위기관리
social role 사회적 역할
social role theory 사회적 역할론
social safety net 사회안전망
social science 사회과학
Social Security 사회보장
Social Security Act 사회보장법
Social Security benefit 사회보장급여
Social Security burden 사회보장부담
Social Security Charter 사회보장헌장
Social Security costs 사회보장비용
Social Security system 사회보장제도

S

Social Security tax 사회보장세
social service 소시얼서비스
social service exchange 사회봉사교환소
social services 소시얼서비스 ; 사회서비스
social services for fatherless families
모자복지
social settlement 정착
social skill 소시얼스킬
social skills training : SST 소시얼트레이닝 ;
사회기능훈련 ; 사회생활기능훈련 ; 소시얼스킬훈련
social skills training for people with
mental disabilities 정신장애인사회적응훈련
social solidarity 사회연대
social statistics 사회통계
Social Statistics Division 사회통계과
social status 사회적 지위
social stratification 사회계층
social stratum 계층
social structure 사회구조
social study 소시얼스터디
social support 소시얼서포트 ; 사회적지지 ;
사회적 지원 ; 소시얼지원
social support network
소시얼서포트네트워크 ; 사회적 지원네트워크
social support services 사회지원서비스
social system 사회체제
social tension 사회적 긴장
social theory 사회이론
social treatment 사회치료
social unrest 사회불안
social value 사회적 가치
social welfare 사회복지
Social Welfare Administration
사회복지운영관리 ; 사회복지행정
social welfare agency 사회복지기관
Social Welfare and War Victims' Relief
Bureau 사회·원호국
social welfare center 사회복지관
social welfare corporation 사회복지법인
social welfare day 사회복지의 날
social welfare facility 사회복지시설
Social Welfare Funds for Longevity
Society 장수사회복지기금

social welfare information 사회복지정보
social welfare legislation 사회복지의 법제
Social Welfare National Center for Social
Service Human Resources 복지인재정보센터
social welfare office 사회복지사무소
social welfare office staff 사회복지사무소직원
social welfare officer 사회복지주사
social welfare organization 사회복지단체
social welfare planning 사회복지계획
social welfare planning method
사회복지계획법
social welfare policy 사회복지정책
social welfare registration 사회복지법제
social welfare research 사회복지조사
Social Welfare Service Law
사회복지법 ; 사회복지사업법
social welfare services
사회복지서비스 ; 사회복지사업
social welfare services agency
사회복지사업단
social welfare standards 사회복지기준
social welfare system 사회복지제도
social withdrawal 두문불출
social work 소시얼워크
social work and welfare activity
사회복지원조활동
social work and welfare education
사회복지교육
social work and welfare practice
사회복지원조기술
social work education 사회사업교육
social work in rehabilitation 재활소시얼워크
social work practice 사회사업실천
social work practicum 사회복지현장실습
social work profession 사회복지전문
social work research
소시얼워크연구 ; 사회사업조사
social work skills 사회사업기술
social worker : SW 소시얼워커 ; 사회사업가
social worker for rehabilitation
재활소시얼워커
social worker for the elderly
노인복지지도주사

S

socialism 사회주의
socialization 사회화
socialization of care 요양의 사회화
socialization of medical care 의료의 사회화
socialization of medicine 의료의 사회화
socialized long-term care 사회적 개호
socially advantaged person 사회적 강자
socially disadvantaged person 사회적 약자
society with the declined birth rate
소자사회 ; 출생률 감소사회
society-managed health insurance
조합관장건강보험
sociofugal arrangements 역효과 치료환경
sociogram 소시오그램 ; 교우도식
sociology 사회학
sociology of the family 가족사회학
sociology of welfare 복지사회학
sociometry 소시오메트리 ; 사회측정
sociopetal arrangements 효과적 치료환경
socket 소켓
sodium 나트륨
sodium hypochlorite 차아염소산나트륨
sodium intake 염분섭취
softener agent 유연처리제
soil-borne infection 토양감염
soil-resistant material 오염방지소재 ; 방오소재
solar disinfection 일광소독
solar water disinfection : SODIS
태양광 식수살균법
soldiers' pension 군인연금 ; 보훈연금 ; 은급
solid ankle cushion heel foot : SACH 의족
solitary death 고독사
solitary-living 독거
solitary-living disabled person 독거장애인
solitary-living elderly 독거노인 ; 독거고령자 ;
독신생활고령자 ; 독신생활노인
solo practice 단독개업
solo practitioner 단독개업의사
solution-focused approach 해결지향적 접근법
solvency 지불능력
somatic sensation 체질감각
somatoform disorders 신체형장애
somatogenesis 신체적 원인론

somatosensory evoked potential : SEP
체성감각유발전위
somnipathy 수면장애
somnolence 졸림 ; 경면
Sonata 소나타
sound amplifier 음성증폭기
soup kitchen 무료급식소
sour 산미
source isolation 감염원격리
source of infection 감염원
span of control 통제범위
spasm 경련 ; 연축 ; 쥐
spastic 경성
spastic diplegia 경직형 양마비
spastic paralysis 경성마비
spastic paraparesis 경성대마비
spastic quadriplegia 경직형 사지마비
spastic torticollis 경성사경
spastic type 경직형
spasticity 경성 ; 경축
special account 특별회계
special benefit allowance 특별수당
special benefit and discounts programs
for the senior citizens 경로우대할인제도
special benefit programs for the senior
citizens 경로우대제도
special benefits for the senior citizens
경로우대
special benefits service 경로우대서비스
special care unit 치매전문병동 ;
치매케어전문병동 ; 인지증전문병동
special cash benefits 특별현금급여
special class for children with
disabilities 특별지원학급
special collection 특별징수
special deduction for people with
disabilities 특별장애인공제
special disability allowance 특별장애인수당
special education 특수교육
special education school 특수교육제학교
special exemption 특별공제
special home care benefits 특례요양비
special interest group 특수이익집단

special juridical person 특수법인
special meal 특별식
special municipal benefit 시정촌 특별급부
special needs education 특별지원교육
special needs plan 특별니즈플랜
special notes 특기사항
special occupation retirement pension
특수직역연금
special premium collection 특별보험료징수
special school 특별지원학교
special school for crippled children
지체부자유아양호학교
special standard 특별기준
special tax deduction for people with
disabilities 특별장애인세공제
special tax rebate 특별세액공제
special therapeutic diet 특별치료식
special volunteer fund 특별자원봉사기금
special ward 특별구
special welfare equipment 특정복지용구
specialist 전문가
specialized bathtub 특수욕조
specialized bed 특수침대
Specialized Central Organization for Care
of Elderly 중앙노인보호전문기관
specialized health care service facilities
for the aged 노인전문요양시설
specialized hospital for people with
dementia 치매전문병원
specialized institute for the protection of
the aged 노인보호전문기관
specific care home for the preventive
long-term care 개호예방특정시설입소자생활개호
specific casework 전문개별사회사업
specific developmental disorder : SDD
특정발달장애
Specific Diseases Control Division
질병대책과
specific disorder of arithmetical skills
특정산수능력장애
specific geriatric care costs 특정요양비
specific reading disorder
특정독서장애 ; 특이적 독서장애

specific social work 전문사회사업
specific spelling disorder 특정철자장애
specimen collection 검체수집
spectral luminous efficiency 분광시감효율
speech 언어능력
speech and language training 언어훈련
speech clarity 언어의 명료성
speech disorders 언어장애인 ; 언어기능장애 ;
음성기능장애
speech perception instructional curriculum
and evaluation 발화지각지도 커리큘럼과 평가
speech reception threshold : SRT
어음청취역치
speech reception threshold test
어음청취역치검사
speech therapist : ST 언어치료사 ; 언어요법사
speech therapy 언어치료 ; 언어요법 ; 어치료
speech-language impediment 언어장애
speech-language rehabilitation 언어청각재활
speech-language training
언어청각훈련 ; 언어청각요법
speech-language-hearing therapist : ST
언어청각사
speech-reading 독순술 ; 독화
speed 각성제
Speenhamland 스핀햄랜드
Speenhamland system 스핀햄랜드제도
spending down 고의적 자산축소
sphincter disturbance 활약근장애
sphincteroplasty 활약근형성술
spina bifida 이분척추 ; 척추뼈 갈림증 ; 척추파열
spinal canal stenosis 척주관협착증
spinal cord injury : SCI 척수손상
spinal orthosis 체간보조기
spinal reflex 척수반사
spinal tap 척추천자
spinal X-ray 척추방사선 ; 척추 X선
spinocerebellar degeneration 척수소뇌변성증
spiral ankle-foot orthosis
나선상 지주단하지보조기
spiritual care 스피리츄얼 케어
spiritual pain 스피리츄얼 페인
Spiritual Well-Being Scale

S

영적만족감측정기구 (영적안녕척도)
spirituality 정신성 ; 영성
spirometry 폐기량측정법
spironolactone 스피로놀락톤
splint 스프린트 ; 부목 ; 접골치료용 부목
split hook and specialized tool
능동훅 작업용 수선구
split-half reliability 이분할 신뢰도검사
splitting 분열
sponge bath 스폰지목욕 ; 깨끗이 닦기
sponsorship service program 결연사업
spontaneous activity 자발활동
spontaneous group 자연발생적집단
spore 홀씨 ; 포자 ; 아포
sports facility 스포츠시설
sports for the elderly 고령자스포츠
spouse 배우자
spouse abuse 배우자학대
sprain 염좌
spray 살포
sprinkler 스프링클러
squamous cell carcinoma 편평표피암
square corner 사각코너
squat toilet 일본식 변기
squeezing pain 쥐어짜는 듯한 아픔
stability 안정성
stabilizer 스테빌라이저 ; 입위보지장치
staff conference 직원회의
staff development 직원연수 ; 직원개발
staff model 스탭모델
staffing 인사관리 ; 직원배치
stage of dementia 인지증도
stage theories 단계이론
stagflation 스태그플레이션 (불황)
stain removal 얼룩빼기
stair lift 계단승강기
stairs 계단
stall bar 늑목
stammer 말더듬이
stamp agar method 접촉배양지법 ;
스탬프한천법
stance phase 입각기
standard benefits package 표준급여패키지

standard cost of living 표준생계비
standard deduction 표준공제
standard deviation 표준편차
standard for remuneration 표준보수
standard household 표준가구
standard labor agreement 표준근로계약서
standard language test of aphasia : SLTA
표준실어증검사
standard long-term care usability document
표준장기요양이용계획서
standard of living 생활수준
standard pay system 표준보수제
standard pension 표준연금
standard precaution 표준예방책
standard rate of insurance premium
보험료기준액
standard text book for development of
care worker 요양보호사양성표준교과서
standard wheelchair 보통형 휠체어
standardization 표준화
standardization of services 서비스의 표준화
standardized care 기준개호
standardized long-term care 기준개호
standardized mortality ratio : SMR
표준화 사망비
standardized nursing 기준간호
standardized tests 표준검사
Standards and Evaluation Division
기준심사과
standards of care 장기요양의 기준
standards of medical practice
의료의 기준 ; 진료의 기준
standards of nursing 간호의 기준
standards of nursing practice 간호의 기준
standards of public assistance
생활보호기준 ; 공적부조기준
standing exercise 기립훈련 ; 입위운동 ;
기립운동
standing position 입위
standing table 기립대
Stanford Binet test 스텐포드비네법
staphylococcal pneumonia
황색포도상구균성 폐렴

S

staphylococcus aureus 황색포도상구균
starch 전분
stasis dermatitis 울체성 피부염
state monopolistic capitalism
국가독점자본주의
state of depressed mood 우울상태
state subsidy 국고보조금
State Supplemental Program 주보충프로그램
state-centered theory 국가중심이론
static stability 정적 안정성
stationary bicycle 고정자전거 ;
훈련용 고정자전거
statistical hypothesis test 통계적 가설검정
statistical research 통계조사
statistical significance 통계적 유의도
statistical test 통계적 검정
statistics 통계
Statistics and Information Department
통계정보부
Statistics Korea 통계청
status 지위
status offender 지위위반자
statutory functions entrusted 법정수탁사업
statutory instrument 행정입법
statutory rates of employment 법정고용율
steam sterilization 고압증기멸균 ; 증기멸균
stem cell 줄기세포
stem family 직계가족
step length 보폭
stepfamily 의붓가정
step-up contribution 단계적 보험료
step-up elbow hinge 배동주경첩 이음새
stereotype 스테레오타이프 ; 상동증
stereotyped behavior 상동행동 ; 상동행위
sterilant 멸균제
sterility assurance 멸균보증 ; 무균보증
sterility assurance level : SAL
무균성 보증레벨 ; 멸균보증수준
sterility test 무균시험
sterilization 멸균
sterilization process 멸균공정
sterilization validation 멸균바리데이션
sterilized water 멸균수

sterilizer 멸균기
sterno-occipital-mandibular- immobilizer
brace 소미브레이스
steroid 스테로이드
stigma 스티그마
stigmatization 스티그마티제이션 ; 낙인화
stimulant abuse 물질남용
stimulation method 자극법
stimulus generalization 자극일반화
stirrup 늑근 ; 등자
stoma 스토마
stoma care 스토마케어
stomach cancer 위암
stool 변
stool extraction 적변
stool microbiology 분변세균검사
stool production 변생성
stool specimen 대변검사
Stop Drinking Alcohol Support Group
절주회
strained back 급성요통증
straining 거르기
stranger anxiety 이방인 불안 (낯가림)
strangling pain 질식할 것 같은 아픔
Strassburger System 슈트라스부르그시스템
strategic family therapy 전략적 가족치료
strategic marketing 전략적 마케팅 ;
전략적 계획
stratified sampling 층화추출법
street guidance 가두보도활동
street value 소비자가격
strength 강점
strength exercise 강화운동
strength model 강점모델
strength-based model 강점모델
strengths perspective 강점관점 ; 스트렝스 시점
streptococcus pneumoniae
폐렴연쇄구균 ; 폐렴연쇄상구균
stress 스트레스
stress electrocardiogram 부하심전도
stress incontinence 복압성 요실금
stress inoculation training 스트레스 면역훈련
stressor 스트레서

S

stretcher 스트레처
stretching 스트레칭
stretching exercise 신장운동
strict isolation 엄중격리
stride 스트라이드
stride length 보폭 ; 스트라이드
stride width 보폭너비
strike 노동쟁의
stroke 뇌졸중
stroke care unit 뇌졸중 집중치료실
Stroke Impairment Assessment Set : SIAS
뇌졸중 기능장애평가법
stroking 강찰법
structural family therapy 구조적 가족치료
structural incrementalism 구조적 증분주의
structural reform of Social Security
사회보장구조개혁
structural social change 구조적 사회변동
structural social work 구조적 사회사업
stubby 스터비
student aid programs 학생보조 프로그램
student nurse 견습간호사
study 조사
stump care 단단관리
stump pain 단단신경통 ; 단단통
stump sock 단단대
styling and setting hair 머리정돈
subacute care facility 아급성 케어시설
subacute myeloopticoneuropathy : SMON
스몬병
subarachnoid hemorrhage : SAH
지주막하출혈
subchorionic hematoma 융모막하혈종
subclavian vein catheterization
쇄골하정맥도관삽입술 ; 쇄골하정맥직접천자법
subconscious 하의식
subconscious mind 잠재의식
subcortical arteriosclerotic encephalopathy
동맥경화성 피질하백질뇌증
subcortical vascular dementia
피질하 혈관성 치매
subcutaneous : Sub-Q 피하
subcutaneous bleeding 피하출혈

subdural hematoma 경막하혈종
subemployment 불완전고용
sub-group 하위집단
subject 대상자
subjective happiness 주관적 행복감
Subjective Happiness Scale
주관적 행복감척도
subjective needs 주관적 욕구
subjective well-being 주관적 행복도
sublimation 승화
sublingual gland 설하선
sublingual tablet 설하정
subluxation 아탈구
subsidized adoption 입양보조금
subsidy adjustment 조정교부금
subsistence level 생계수준
substance-induced psychosis 물질유발정신병
substance-related disorder 화학물질관련장애
substantivity 지속성
substitute 대용 ; 대역
substitute care 대리보호
substitute function 대체기능
substitute medication 대체조제
substituted judgment 대리판단
substitution 치환 ; 대리
subsystem 하부체계
subtrochanteric fracture 대퇴골 전자부골절
subungual hematoma 조하혈종
successful aging 석세스풀 에이징 ;
성공적인 노화 ; 행복한 늙음
suction 흡인 ; 석션
suction biopsy 흡인생검
suction socket 흡착식 소켓
suctioning 흡인
sudden death 돌연사
sudden infant death syndrome : SIDS
유아급사증후군 ; 유아돌연사증후군
Sudeck atrophy 수덱위축
sugar 당분
suicidal ideation 자살성 사고
suicide 자살
suicide by the aged 노인자살
suicide prevention 자살예방

sulfasalazine 설파살라진
sulfonylurea 설폰요소제
sumatriptan 수마트립탄
summary records 요약기록
sunbathing 일광욕
sundown syndrome 일몰증후군
sundowning 일몰행동
sunk costs 기관개발기금
sunlight disinfection 일광소독
sunshine laws 의사공개법
super-aged society 초고령사회
supercentenarian 110세 이상
superego 초자아
superficial sensation 피부감각 ; 표재감각
superinfection 균교대증
superintendent of public welfare office
  복지사무소소장
superstition 미신
supervisee 슈퍼바이지
supervision 슈퍼비전 ; 수퍼비전 ; 지도감독
supervisor 슈퍼바이저 ; 수퍼바이저
supervisor of adult guardian 성년후견감독인
supervisor of guardian of minor
  미성년후견감독인
supervisor of the curator 보좌감독인
supination 외전
supine position 앙와위
supplemental coverage 보충적용
supplemental payment to the aged 노령가산
Supplemental Social Security Insurance :
  SMI 보완적 의료보험
supplementary benefit 보충급여
Supplementary Benefit Scheme 보충급부제도
supplementary nature of public
  assistance 보호의 보충성
supply subsidy 공급보조금
support 돌봄 ; 수발 ; 원조 ; 부양 ; 구원 ;
  서포트 ; 지지
support bar 지지봉
Support Center for the Nursing Care
  Industry 고령친화산업지원센터
Support Center for the Work of the
  Elderly 고령자취업지원센터

support for business of the elderly
  고령자창업지원
support for people with mental
  disabilities 정신장애인원조
support for people with mental
  retardation 지적장애인원조
support for the aged 노인원조
support for the disabled 장애인원조
support for the elderly 고령자원조
support for the physically disabled
  신체장애인원조
support group 서포트그룹 ; 지원집단 ; 지원그룹
Support of Employment 사회취로센터
support of quiet sleep 안면원조
support payment system 지원비제도
support repellent phenomenon observed
  in elderly 노인부양기피현상
support services agency for the elderly
  고령자원조서비스기관
support services for the elderly
  고령자원조서비스
support services office for the elderly
  고령자원조서비스사업소
support services provider for the elderly
  고령자원조서비스사업자
support system 서포트시스템 ; 지원체계
supported employment 원조첨부고용
supporter 보조원 ; 원조자 ; 조수 ; 수발자
supporter of sign language 수화원조자
supporting nurse 간호보조사
supportive casework 지지적 케이스워크
supportive occupational therapy
  지지적 작업요법
supportive services agency for the
  elderly 고령자원조서비스기관
supportive services for the elderly
  고령자원조서비스
supportive services office for the elderly
  고령자원조서비스사업소
supportive services provider for the
  elderly 고령자원조서비스사업자
supportive treatment 지지적 치료
support-required elderly 요원호노인

S

suppository 좌약
supraglottic swallow 기도폐쇄법 ; 성문위삼킴
surface color mode 표면색모드
surface electrode 표면전극
surface electromyogram 표면근전도
surgery 수술
surgical hand antisepsis 수술시 손가락소독
surgical hand washing 수술시 손씻기
surgical intensive care unit
　외과계 집중치료실
surgical mask 외과용 마스크 ; 서지컬마스크
surgical scrub 수술시 손씻기
surgical site infection 수술부위감염 ; 술야감염
surgical wound 수술창
surgical wound classification 수술창분류
surgical wound infection 수술창감염
surrogacy 대리출산
surrogate decision 대리결정
surrogate delivery 대리출산
surveillance 감시 ; 서베일런스 ; 감리
survey 조사 ; 감사
surveyor 감사관
survival of the fittest 적자생존
survivors allowance 유족급여
survivors pension 유족연금
suspension frame 서스펜션프레임 ; 현수프레임
suspension system 현수장치
sustaining procedures
　지지적 과정 ; 지속적 지지수속
sustenance 부양
sustenance food 기탁식품
swab collection 면봉채취 ; 스와브 채취
swab method 면봉법 ; 스와브법
swallowing 연하
swallowing difficulty 연하곤란
swallowing function 연하기능
swallowing problem 연하문제
swallowing reflex 연하반사
swallowing training 연하훈련
Swan neck deformity 스완네크변형 ;
　백조목변형
Swan-Ganz catheter 스완간즈 카테터
sweating industry 고한산업

Swedish knee cage 스웨덴식 무릎장구
sweet 감미
swelling 종창
swing phase 유각단계
swing-through gait 스윙드루보행 ; 진요통과보행
swing-to gait 뛰기보행 ; 지유각보행
Swiss lock 스위스형 무릎고정대
Sydney Webb and Beatrice Potter Webb
　웹부처
symbiosis 공생
symbiosis society 공생사회
symbolic barrier 물리적 장벽 ; 상징적 장벽
Syme's amputation 사임절단
Syme's prosthesis 사임의족
sympathetic muscle nerve activity
　근교감신경활동
sympathetic nerve 교감신경
sympathetic skin response 교감신경피부반응
sympathy 동정
symposium 심포지움
symptom 증상
symptomatic anemia 증후성 빈혈
symptomatic therapy 대증요법
synchronicity 신크로니시티 ; 동시발생
syncope 의식상실
syndrome 증후군
synergist 공동근
synergy 공동운동
synovectomy 활막절제술
synthetic detergent 합성세제
synthetic fiber 합성섬유
syphilis 매독
system 체계
system for appointing a qualified person
　자격임용제도
system for appointing qualified persons
　자격임용제도
system theory 체계이론
systematic and rational reconstruction
　계통적 논리재구성법
systematic desensitization 체계적 탈감각화
systematic sampling 체계적 추출법 ;
　계통추출법

S

systemic failure 조직적 실패
systemic lupus erythematosus : SLE
　전신성 홍반성 낭창 ; 전신성 홍반성 루프스
systemic requisites 체계적 필수조건

systemic success 조직적 성공
systems perspective 시스템적 시점
systolic pressure 수축기압

S

T

table of random numbers 난수표

tablet 정제

tabulation 집계분석

tachycardia 빈맥

tachypnea 빈호흡

tacrine 타크린

tactics of influence 영향력 전술

tactile floor tile 점자블록

tai chi 태극권

tailor sitting 양반다리 앉기

Talcott Parsons 파슨즈

Talent Bank of the Aged 노인능력은행

talipes calcaneus 종족변형

talipes valgus 외반족

tamsulosin 탐스로신

Tanaka-Binet Intelligence Test
다나카 비네식 지능검사

Tanaka-Binet Scale of Intelligence
다나카 비네식 지능검사

tannin 탄닌

tap water 수도물

Tarasoff 타라소프

tardive dyskinesia 지발성 디스키네지아

target behavior 표적행동

target population of geriatric medicine
노인의료수급대상자

target system 표적체계

targeted surveillance 대상한정감시

task analysis 과제분석

task performance ability 과제수행능력

task-centered approach
과제중심접근법 ; 과제중심접근방법

task-centered model 과제중심모델

task-centered treatment 과업중심치료

tattooing 점묵법

tax 세금 ; 조세

tax burden 조세부담

tax burden ratio 조세부담률

tax code 택스코드

tax collection 조세징수

tax cost 조세비용

tax deduction 세금공제

tax deduction at source 원천징수

tax deduction for a spouse 배우자세공제

tax deduction for charity donations
기부금세공제

tax deduction for dependents 부양세공제

tax deduction for elderly dependents
노인부양세공제

tax deduction for employment 근로세공제

tax deduction for medical care 의료세공제

tax deduction for medical care expenses
의료비세공제

tax deduction for National Pension
premiums 국민연금보험료감면

tax deduction for social insurance
premiums 사회보험료료공제

tax deduction for the disabled 장애인세공제

tax deduction for the seniors 노년자세공제

tax deduction for widows 과부세공제

tax delinquency 세금체납

tax exemption 면세조치

tax expenditure 조세지출

tax quake 감세지진

tax rebate 세액공제 ; 세금환부

tax revolt 납세자의 반란

tax-exempt allowance 비과세수당
tax-exempt household 비과세세대
tax-exempt organization 비과세단체
taxpayer's revolt 납세자의 반란
tax-privileged 조세우대
Taylor's Manifest Anxiety Scale : TMAS
테일러의 표출불안척도
Tay-Sachs disease 테이색스병
T-cane T자 지팡이
team approach 팀접근법
team care 팀케어
team medicine 팀의료
teamwork 팀워크
technical aid 보조도구
technical aid for the disabled 복지용구 ;
복지기기
teeth 이 ; 이빨 ; 치아
Tegretol 테그레톨
telbivudine 텔비부딘
telephone assistance 대리전화
telephone assistive device 복지전화
telethon 텔레톤
temporary 일시적
temporary aid 일시부조
temporary allowance 일시급여금
temporary allowance for the disabled
장애일시급여금
temporary appointment 임시적 임용
temporary assistance 일시부조
temporary disability allowance
장애인 일시급여금 ; 장애일시급여금
temporary disability child allowance
장애아일시급여금
temporary disability leave
일시적 신체장애휴업제도
temporary employment 일시고용
temporary lower limb prosthesis
훈련용 가의족
temporary prosthesis 훈련용 가의지
temporary prosthesis of upper limb
amputee 가의수
temporary protection 일시보호
temporary services 일시적 서비스

temporary worker 템퍼러리 워커
tendency to escape from reality
현실도피경향
tendency to fall 역전도성
tennis elbow 테니스엘보 ; 동통성 주관절증후군
tenodesis 건고정
tenodesis effect 건고정 효과 ; 힘줄고정작용
tenodesis splint 파지부목
tension 긴장
tension-type headache 긴장형 두통
tentative plan for home-based care
services 잠정거택서비스계획
Ten-Year Strategy to Promote Health
and Welfare for the Aged 고령자보건복지
추진 10개년전략
teratoma 테라토마
terminal care 터미널케어 ; 종말기케어 ;
말기치료 ; 노인의 종말간호 ; 종말기장기요양
terminal impact 무릎충격
terminal medical care 종말기의료 ; 종말기간호
terminal stage 종말기
terminal sterilization 최종멸균
terminal treatment 종말기치료
termination of employment 해고 ; 고용종료
termination phase 종결단계
tertiary education 제3차 교육
tertiary health care 3차 진료
tertiary processed food 인스턴트식품
test bias 검사 편견
testament 유언서
testator 유언자
testosterone 테스토스테론
test-retest reliability 조사-재조사 신뢰도
tetanus 파상풍
tetany 테타니
T-group 집단생활지도집단
thalassemia 사라세미아
thalidomide 탈리도마이드
thallium scanning 탈륨스캔검사
thanatology 생사학
the ideas of Confucianism 유교사상
The Workhouse Act 작업장법
thematic apperception test : TAT

T

주제통각검사
theme group 주제집단
theophylline 테오피린
theoretical maximum daily intake
이론적 최대일일섭취량
theories of social development 사회발전론
theory 이론
theory of deterioration 궁핍화이론
theory of multiplier 승수이론
theory of planned behavior 계획적 행동이론
theory of social action 사회적 행위이론
theory of social contract 사회계약설
therapeutic community
치료공동체 ; 치료적 지역사회
therapeutic diet 치료식
therapeutic education 치료교육
therapeutic electrical stimulation : TES
치료적 전기자극
therapeutic endoscopy 치료적 내시경검사
therapeutic exercise 운동요법
therapeutic relationship 원조관계 ; 구원관계
therapeutic technique 치료기법
therapist 세라피스트 ; 치료자
therapy 세라피 ; 치료
thermometer 체온계
thermoregulation 체온조절
thermotherapy 온열요법
thiamine deficiency 티아민결핍증
thiazide diuretic 타이아자이드계 이뇨제
thiazolidinedione 치아졸리딘다이온계 약제
thickened 걸쭉함
thickened diet 걸쭉한 음식
thickened liquid 농축음료 ; 농후음료
thickening agent 연하보조제
Thioredoxin 티오레독신
third age 제3의 인생
third sector 제3섹터 ; 제3부문
Third Way 제삼의 길
Third World 제삼세계
third-party panel 제삼자위원
third-party payment 제3부문 지불
third-party quality certification system
for welfare services 복지서비스 제삼자평가제도

third-party quality endorsement 제삼자평가
third-party quality endorsement system
제삼자평가제도
Thomas Chalmers 찰머즈
Thomas Robert Malthus 맬더스
thoracic spinal cord injury 흉수손상
thoracocentesis 흉강천자
thought disorder 사고장애
three act concerning with labor 노동3법
three biggest causes of death 3대사인
three major nutrients 삼대 영양소
three times daily : TID 하루 3회
three times weekly : 3W 주 3회
three-dimension CT 삼차원 CT
three-dimensional gait analysis
삼차원 보행분석
three-dimensional motion analysis
삼차원 동작해석
three-generation family 3세대가족
three-jaw chuck pinch 세손가락 집기
three-person transfer 3인 이승법
three-point gait 3점 보행 ; 3동작 보행
threshold 단차 ; 역치
throat swab culture 인두배양
thrombolytic 혈전용해제
thrombolytic therapy 혈전용해요법
thrombosis 혈전 ; 혈전증
thumb post 엄지손가락 버팀목
thumbprint 엄지손가락 지문
thyroid cancer 갑상선암
thyroid disease 갑상선질환
thyroid-stimulating hormone : TSH
갑상선자극호르몬
tiagabine 티아가빈
tibial plateau 경골고원
ticket system 티켓제도
Ticket System for the Elderly
노인승차권제도
Tietze's syndrome 티에체 증후군
tile mosaic 타일모자이크
tilting table 기립침대 ; 틸팅테이블
Timed Get-Up and Go Test
기립 보행동작측정법

time-out 타임아웃
tinea 백선
tinea pedis 무좀 ; 족백선
Tinel sign 티넬징후
tinnitus 귀 울림 ; 이명
tip pinch 손가락 끝으로 집기
tipping lever 템핑레버 ; 티핑레버 ; 지지대
tissue perfusion 조직관류
Title XX 타이틀 20
toddler class 유아반
toe contact 발끝접지
toe in 내향발굽 ; 토우 인
toe off 발끝떼기 ; 이지
toe out 외향발굽
toe-break 토우 브레이크
toenail 발톱
Tofranil 토프라닐
toggle brake 토글 브레이크
toilet 변기
toilet screen 화장실 스크린
toileting assistance 배설보조
toileting schedule 배설스케줄
token economy 금전보상기법
Tokyo Metropolitan Institute of
  Gerontology index of competence :
  TMIG-IC 동경노인종합연구소 활동능력지표
tolcapone 톨카폰
tolerable daily intake 내용일일섭취량
tolerance 내성 ; 내용성
tomography 단층촬영
tongue swallowing 설근침하
tonic neck reflex 긴장성 경반사
tonometry 안압계
tonsil 편도선
tools for eating 식사용구
tooth brushing 이닦기
tooth loss 치아상실
topical : TOP 경피 ; 국소
topiramate 토피라메이트
topographical agnosia 지적 실인
torsional phacoemulsification
  회선 수정체유화흡인방법
total aphasia 전실어

total artificial heart 완전인공심장
total assistance 전면원조 ; 전면보조
total blindness 전맹
total care 전면장기요양 ; 전면개호
total cholesterol 총콜레스테롤
total color blindness 전색맹
total contact socket 전면접촉 소켓
total dependence 전면의존
total disability 폐질
total fertility rate : TFR
  총출산율 ; 합계출산율 ; 합계특수출생률
total health promotion : THP
  종합건강증진운동 ; 토털헬스프로모션
total hip arthroplasty 인공고관절형성술
total hip replacement : THR
  고관절인공관절 전치환술
total incontinence 완전성 요실금
total medical costs 총의료비용
total medical expenditures 총의료비지출
total parenteral nutrition : TPN 완전정맥영양
total period fertility rate : TPFR
  총출산율 ; 합계출산율 ; 합계특수출생률
total personal care 전인격적 케어
total purchasing 종합구입
total quality management : TQM
  종합적 품질관리활동 ; 종합적 품질경영활동
total surface bearing below-knee prosthesis
  TSB 하퇴의족 ; TSB 소켓
Tourette's disorder 토레트병
TOWER system 타워법
Townsend Plan 타운센드 계획
toxic psychosis 중독정신병
toxoids 유독소
Toynbee Hall 토인비 홀
trace nutrient 미량영양소
trachea 기관
tracheostomy 기관절개
traction 견인
traction treatment 견인요법
trade school 직업학교
Trade Union Law 노동조합법
trade unionism 노동조합주의
traffic drug 부정약품

T

Trail-Making Test 선추적검사
trainer 트래이너
training 훈련
training benefit 훈련급여
Trandate 트란데이트
tranquilizer abuse 신경안정제 남용
transactional analysis 교류분석
transactions 교류
transanal ultrasonography 경항문적 초음파검사
transcranial magnetic stimulation : TMS
경두개자기자극
transcutaneous electrical nerve
stimulation : TENS 경피적 전기신경자극
transdermal 경피 ; 국소
transfemoral prosthesis 대퇴의족
transfemoral socket 대퇴소켓
transfer 이승 ; 트랜스퍼
transfer aid 이승보조도구 ; 이승관련용구
transfer and locomotion 이동 ; 이승
transfer assistance 이동개호
transfer bar 이동대 ; 이동바
transfer board 트랜스퍼보드
transfer exercise 이승훈련
transfer from bed to wheelchair
침대에서 휠체어로
transfer from wheelchair to bed
휠체어에서 침대로
transfer from wheelchair to parallel bar
휠체어에서 평행봉
transfer income 이전소득
transfer motion 이승동작
transfer motion training 이승동작훈련
transfer payments 이전지급
transference 감정전이 ; 전이
transference focused psychotherapy
전이초점화 정신요법
transference neurosis 전이신경증
transhumeral prosthesis 상완의수
transient bacteria 통과균
transient flora
일과성 세균총 ; 일과성 균총 ; 통과세균
transient ischemic attack : TIA
일과성 뇌허혈발작

transintestine nutrition method 경장영양법
transit study 장관 이송능검사
transition zone 이행역
transitional care 이행기 케어
transitional syndrome 통과증후군
translation into Braille 점역
translational vestibulo-ocular reflex
병진전정동안반사
transmissible disease 전염성 질환
transmission-based precaution
감염경로별 예방책
transportation 송영 ; 수송
Transportation Accessibility Improvement
Law 교통장애물제거법
transportation allowance 교통수당
transportation and escort services
외출지원
transportation fee 이송비
transportation services 이송서비스 ;
송영서비스
transportation vehicle 송영차
transracial adoption 타인종 입양
transradial prosthesis 전완의수
transrectal ultrasonography
경직장적 초음파검사
transtheoretical model 범이론적 모델
transtibial prosthesis 하퇴의족
transtibial socket 하퇴소켓
transurethral incision of prostate
경요도적 전립선절제술
transurethral microwave therapy : TUMT
경요도적 마이크로파 온열요법
transurethral resection : TURP 경요도적 절제
transverse arch 횡족궁 ; 횡단아치 ; 횡축족궁
Tranxene 트랑센
tranylcypromine 트라닐시프로민
trastuzumab 트라스투주맙
trauma 트라우마 ; 마음의 상처 ; 외상
traumatic brain injury : TBI
뇌외상 ; 외상성 뇌손상 ; 두부외상
traumatic injury 외상성 손상
travel-associated legionellosis
여행감염 레지오넬라증

T

traveling clinic 순회진료
treadmill 트레드밀
treadmill testing 트레드밀 부하시험
treasury investment and loan 재정투융자
treatment 치료 ; 트리트먼트
treatment based classification 분류처우
treatment plan 처우계획
treatment policy 처우방침
treatment prior to and after delivery
분변전 및 분변후 처치
tree analysis 나무기법 ; 나무분석 ; 트리법
tree diagram 수형도
tremor 진전
Trendelenburg position 트랜델렌버그 체위
Trendelenburg sign 트랜델렌버그 징후
triangle corner 삼각코너
tricenarian 30대
trick motion 속임동작 ; 트릭모션
trickle-down theory 통화침투이론
tricyclic antidepressant : TCA 삼환계 항우울제
trigeminal neuralgia : TN 삼차신경통
trigger 트리거
trigger point 트리거 포인트
triglyceride 중성지방
triplegia 삼지마비
tripod cane 삼각지팡이
triptan drug 트리프탄 제재
trisomy 21 21트리소미
tristimulus value 삼자극치
trochanteric bursitis 전자활액포염
trochanteric fracture 전자부 골절
truancy 무단결석
true emergency 진성구급
true incontinence 진성요실금
truncus 체간
trust versus mistrust 신뢰 대 불신
truth telling 암선고 ; 선고
T-strap T스트랩

t-test t검정
tube feeding 경관영양 ; 튜브영양
tuberculoma 결핵종
tuberculosis 결핵
Tuberculosis and Infectious Diseases
Control Division 결핵감염증과
tuberculosis patient 결핵환자
tumor necrosis factor : TNF 종양괴사인자
tumor necrosis factor-alpha inhibitor
종양괴사인자α 저해제
tunnel infection 피하터널감염
turf issues 케이스할당문제
turnover rate 이직율
twenty-four-hour care 24시간 케어
twenty-four-hour on call 24시간 연락체제
twenty-four-hour protective oversight
24시간 주시
twice every month : 2M 월 2회
two times daily : BID 하루 2회
two times weekly : 2W 주 2회
two-days off a week system 주휴 2일제
two-point gait 2족 보행
Tylenol 타이레놀
tympanic membrane 고막
tympanoplasty 고실형성술
type 1 diabetes 제1형 당뇨병
type 1 diabetes mellitus 제1형 당뇨병
type 2 diabetes 제2형 당뇨병
type 2 diabetes mellitus 제2형 당뇨병
Type A personality 에이형 성격
type of poverty 빈곤의 유형
types and scope of public assistance
보호의 종류 및 범위
typhoid fever 장티푸스
typologies 유형학
typology of casework treatment
개별사회사업 치료의 유형학
Tyzeka 타이제카

T

U

ulcer 궤양
ulceration 궤양형성
ulnar deviation 척굴 ; 척측편위
ulnar flexion 척굴 ; 척측편위
ultimate gift 마지막 기부
ultra low penetration air filter ULPA 필터
ultra violet radiation 자외선조사
ultraclean air 초청정공기
ultra-honey-thick diet 농후 벌꿀상 액체식
ultrasonically activated device : USAD
초음파응고절개장치
ultrasonically guided puncture
초음파유도천자
ultrasonography : US 초음파검사
ultrasound 초음파
ultrasound cardiography 심장초음파검사
ultrasound therapy 초음파요법
ultraviolet 자외선
ultraviolet disinfection 자외선살균
ultraviolet rays protection material
자외선차폐소재
ultraviolet therapy 자외선요법
umami 우마미
unaffected side of the body 건측
unauthorized 무인가
unconditional positive regard
무조건의 긍정적 배려
unconditioned response 무조건반응
unconditioned stimulus 무조건자극
unconscious 무의식
under age 미성년 ; 미성년자
under arm hair 겨드랑이털 ; 액모
underarm brace

겨드랑이보조기 ; 언더암 브레이스
underclass 하층계급
underemployment 불안전고용
undernutrition 저영양상태
underutilization 활용부족
underwater exercise 수중운동
underwear 내의
undifferentiated 미분화
undifferentiated status 미분화상태
undocumented alien 밀입국자
unemployment 실업 ; 완전실업 ; 무직
unemployment benefit 실업급여
unemployment compensation 실업보상
Unemployment Insurance 실업보험
unemployment problem 실업문제
unemployment rate 실업률
unfair charge 부정청구
unfair labor practice 부당노동행위
unification of health care insurance
programs 의료보험제도의 일원화
uniform chromaticity scale diagram
균등색도도
uniform color space 균등색공간
unilateral neglect 편측무시
unilateral spatial agnosia 편측공간실인
unilateral spatial neglect : USN 편측공간무시
unilateral support 편무적 부양
unincorporated association 임의단체
uninhibited bladder 무억제방광
uninsured 무보험자
union 조합
unique hue 유니크 색상
unit 병동

unit of attention 개입초점
unit price contract 단가계약
unit-based care 유니트케어 ; 신형특별양호케어
United Fund 합동모금 ; 연합모금
United Nations : UN 국제연합
United Nations Children's Fund : UNICEF
유니세프
United Nations Decade of Disabled
Persons 국제장애인 10년
United Nations Declaration of Human
Rights 유엔인권선언
United Nations Educational, Scientific
and Cultural Organization : UNESCO
유네스코
United Nations High Commissioner for
Refugees : UNHCR 유엔난민고등판무관사무소
united way 유나이티드웨이
universal access 보편적 편리성
Universal Declaration of Human Rights :
UDHR 세계인권선언
universal design 유니버설디자인
universal fashion 유니버설패션
universal health insurance system
전보험제도
universal insurance 전보험
universal long-term care insurance
전개호보험
universal long-term care insurance
system 전개호보험제도
universal medical care insurance
전의료보험
universal medical care insurance system
전의료보험제도
universal needs 보편적 욕구
universal pension 전국민연금 ; 전연금
universal pension insurance 전연금보험
universal pension insurance system
전연금보험제도
universal precautions 보편적 예방책
universalism 보편주의
university for the elderly 고령자대학
university for the senior citizens for
lifetime learning 경로대학

University of Lifelong Learning for the
Aged 노인대학
unlimited liability non-profit mutual
benefit corporation 무한책임중간법인
unmarried mother 미혼모
unpaid labor 무상노동
unpaid work 무상노동
unqualified person for public pension
무연금자
unsaturated fatty acid 불포화지방산
unskilled long-term care worker
미숙련장기요양노동자
unskilled worker 미숙련노동자
unsocial behavior 비사회성
upper airway cough syndrome
상기도기침증후군
upper esophageal sphincter : UES
상부식도괄약근
upper esophageal sphincter dysfunction
상부식도괄약근장애
upper extremity 상지
upper extremity amputation 상지절단
upper extremity orthosis 상지보조기
upper gastrointestinal 상부소화관
upper income class 고소득층
upper limb prosthesis 의수
uppers 각성제
urban planning 도시계획
urban problem 도시문제
urbanism 도시생활
urbanization 도시화
urbanizing society 도시화 사회
uremia 요독증
uresiesthesia 요의
urethra 요도
urethral catheter 요도카테터
urethral catheterization 요도카테터법
urethrocele 요도류
urge incontinence 절박성 요실금
urgent involuntary hospitalization
긴급조치입원
uric acid 요산
urinal 소변기 ; 요강

U

urinalysis 요검사
urinary bottle holder 소변기 ; 요강
urinary disorder 배뇨장애
urinary incontinence 요실금
urinary management 배뇨관리 ; 요로관리
urinary retention 요폐
urinary storage disorder 축뇨장애
urinary tract 요로
urinary tract infection : UTI 요로감염
urination 배뇨
urine 소변 ; 오줌
urine collector 수뇨기
urine sampling 채뇨
urocystitis 방광염
urodynamic test 요역동학검사
urologist 비뇨기과의
urology 비뇨기과
urosepsis 요로감염패혈증

urostomy 요로스토미
usage cost 이용료
use of leisure time 여가이용
use rate 사용율
useful field of view 유효시야
user fee 이용자부담
usual cleaning 일상청소
usury 고리대금
utensil 부엌도구 ; 가정도구
uterine prolapse 자궁탈
utilitarianism 공리주의
utility hand 능동핸드
utility theory 효용이론
utilization management : UN 이용관리
utilization population 가동인구
utilization rate 가동률
utilization review : UR 이용감사 ; 효용재고
Utopia 유토피아

U

V

vaccination 백신주사 ; 예방접종
vacuum cleaner 청소기
vaginal care 질케어
vaginitis 질염
vagrancy 방랑
valacyclovir 발라시클로버
valgus 외반
validation 밸리데이션
validation therapy 밸리데이션요법
validity 타당성
Valium 바륨
valproic acid 밸프로산 ; 밸프로인산
Valtrex 발트렉스
value 가치
value added tax : VAT 부가가치세
value judgment 가치판단
value orientation 가치지향
value-for-money : VFM 금전가치
values clarification 가치 명료화
valvular disease 판막증
valvular heart disease 심장판막증
vancomycin resistant enterococci : VRE
　반코마이신 내성 장구균
vancomycin-resistant enterococcus : VRE
　반코마이신 내성 장구균
vandalism 파괴행위
variable 변수
variable friction joint 가변마찰 이음새
variance 변량
varicella infection 수두감염
varicella zoster 수두대상포진
varicella zoster virus 수두대상포진 바이러스
varix 정맥류

varus 내반
vascular dementia 혈관성 치매
vascular imaging 혈관조영
vasodilator 혈관확장제
vasogenic shock 혈관원성 쇼크
vasospastic angina pectoris
　관상동맥 연축성 협심증
Vasotec 바소텍
vaulting 발돋움 보행 ; 뒷꿈치돋움 보행
vegetable food 식물성 식품
vegetative state 식물상태
vein 정맥
venlafaxine 벤라팍신
venous blood 정맥혈
ventilation 환기법 ; 환기
ventricular fibrillation 심실세동
ventricular septal defect : VSD
　심실중격결손
ventriculoperitoneal shunting : VP
　뇌실복강단락술 ; VP션트
verapamil 베라파밀
verbal aggression 언어적 공격
verbal apraxia 발어실행
verbal communication
　구화 ; 언어적 커뮤니케이션
verbal disorder 언어장애
verbal encouragement 말걸기 ; 말붙이기
verbal memory 언어성 기억
Verelan 베렐란
vertebral angiography 추골뇌저동맥조영
vertebral artery 추골동맥
vertebral compression fracture
　척추압박골절

V

verteporfin 베르테포르핀
vertical disease transmission 수직감염
vertical relationship 상하관계
vertigo 현기증
very premature infant 극저출생체중아
vestibular dysfunction 전정장애
vestibulo-ocular reflex 전정동안반사 ;
전정안반사
vesting 수급권 부여
veteran 퇴역군인
Veterans Disability Pension Program
장애군인연금 프로그램
Veterans Disability Program
장애군인 프로그램
vibration 바이브레이션 ; 진동법
vibrio parahaemolyticus 장염 비비리오
vice 비행행위
vicenarian 20대
vicious circle of poverty 빈곤의 악순환설
victim blaming 피해자 책임전가
victim care 범죄피해자 구제
victim compensation 피해자 보상
victimology 피해자 연구(학)
video endoscopy 비디오 내시경검사
videofluorography : VF 연하조영검사
view of life and death 사생관
violence 폭력
viral hepatitis 바이러스성 간염
viral infection 바이러스감염증
virus 바이러스
visibly soiled hands 육안적으로 오염된 손가락
vision 시력
Vision 2030 비전2030
vision loss 시력저하
vision substitution 시각대행
visitation rights 면접교섭권
visiting teacher service 방문교사 서비스
visual acuity 시력
visual agnosia 시각실인
Visual Analog Scale : VAS
시각통증척도 ; 시각상사척도
visual deficit 시각장애 ; 시력장애 ; 시야장애
visual disability 시각장애 ; 시력장애 ; 시야장애

visual disorder 시각장애 ; 시력장애 ; 시야장애
visual disturbance 시각장애 ; 시력장애 ; 시야장애
visual field restriction 시야협착
visual hallucination 환시
visual impairment 시각장애 ; 시력장애 ;
시야장애
visual limitation 시각제한
visual perception 시지각
visual spatial agnosia 시공간실인
visually impaired 시각장애인
visually impaired; visually disabled
시각장애인
Vital and Health Statistics Division
인구동태·보건통계과
vital signs 바이탈사인
vital statistics 인구동태통계
vitamin 비타민
vitamin A deficiency 비타민 A 결핍증
vitamin B1 deficiency 비타민 B1 결핍증
vitamin B12 deficiency 비타민 B12 결핍증
vitamin B2 deficiency 비타민 B2 결핍증
vitamin B6 deficiency 비타민 B6 결핍증
vitamin C deficiency 비타민 C 결핍증
vitamin D deficiency 비타민 D 결핍증
vitamin E deficiency 비타민 E 결핍증
vitamin K deficiency 비타민 K 결핍증
vocational 직업적
Vocational Ability Evaluation Division
능력평가과
vocational aptitude assessor 직능판정원
vocational counseling 직업카운셀링
vocational counselor 직업지도원
vocational evaluation 직업평가
vocational guidance 직업지도(직업안내)
vocational guidance parent 보호수탁자
vocational rehabilitation 직업적 재활 ;
직업재활
vocational training 직업훈련
vocational training allowance 직업훈련수당
vocational training facility 직업훈련시설
vocational training facility for the
disabled 장애인직업훈련시설
vocational training for the disabled

V

장애인직업훈련
Vocational Training Promotion Division
육성지원과
voice generator 인공후두
voice guidance 음성안내
voice-speech disorder 음성언어기능장애
volitional disorder 의욕장애
Volkmann's contracture 폴크만연축
voluntarism 볼런터리즘 ; 자원정신 ; 자원주의
voluntary 볼런터리 ; 자발적
voluntary bankruptcy 자기파산
voluntary closing hook 자동잠김식 훅
voluntary contraction 수의수축 ; 자동수축
voluntary guardianship system 임의후견제도
voluntary insurance 임의보험
voluntary movement 수의운동
voluntary opening hook 자동열림식 훅
voluntary unemployment 자발적 실업
voluntary work 봉사
volunteer 볼런티어 ; 자원봉사 ; 자원봉사자 ;

봉사원
volunteer activity 볼런티어활동 ; 자원봉사활동
volunteer adviser 자원봉사 어드바이저
volunteer Braille services 점역봉사자
volunteer bureau 볼런티어뷰로 ; 자원봉사국
volunteer card 자원봉사자카드
volunteer center 볼런티어센터 ; 자원봉사센터
volunteer coordinator 자원봉사 코디네이터
volunteer fund 자원봉사기금
volunteer group 자원봉사그룹
volunteer plan 볼런티어계획 ; 자원봉사계획
Volunteer Probation Officers Act 보호사법
volunteer school 볼런티어스쿨
volunteer service providers development
  association 자원봉사자육성사업
volunteering 사회봉사
volunteerism 자원봉사주의
vomiting 구토
voucher system 바우처방식 ; 증서제도
voyeurism 관음증

V

W

wage 임금
wage controls 임금통제
wage disparity 임금격차
wage indexation 임금슬라이드
wage system 임금체계
Wages and Labour Welfare Statistics Division 임금복지통계과
waist circumference 허리둘레
waiting list 대기자 리스트
waiting period 대기기간
waiver 면제
walk in room 실내보행
walker 보행기
walking ability 보행능력
walking aid 보행보조도구
walking cane 보행용 지팡이
walking rate 보효율
wandering 배회
War on Poverty 빈곤과의 전쟁
warfarin 와파린
wash method 세정법
washbowl 세면기
washer disinfector 세정소독기
washer sterilizer 세정멸균기
washing 세정
washing machine 세탁기
Wassermann reaction 바세르만반응
Waste Disposal and Public Cleaning Law 폐기물처리법
water cooler 냉수공급장치
water leakage test 누수시험
water pill 워터필 ; 이뇨제
water pollution 수질오염

Water Supply Division 수도과
water-absorbing fiber 흡수성 섬유
waterborne infection 수계감염
waterless antiseptic agent 속건성 찰식소독약
waterless handwashing product 속건성 손씻기용 제재
waterproof sheet 방수시트
water-soluble bag 수용성 가방
water-soluble vitamin 수용성 비타민
way of life style 생활양식
weak eye sight 약시
weakness 허약
wearable identification 착용신분증명서
wearing-off phenomenon 약효과 소실현상
weather 날씨
Wechsler Adult Intelligence Scale : WAIS 웩슬러 성인용 지능검사
Wechsler Intelligence Scale 웩슬러 지능검사
Wechsler Intelligence Scale for Children : WISC 웩슬러 아동용 지능검사
Wechsler Intelligence Scale for Children-Revised : WISC-R 웩슬러 아동용 개정판
wedge 쐐기
wedged insole 쐐기상 족저판
WeeFIM 소아용 기능독립성평가
weekly care plan 주간케어계획
weekly schedule 주안
weekly service plan 주간케어계획
weight-bearing 체중부하
Weimarer Verfassung 바이마르헌법
welfare 복지
welfare activity 복지활동
welfare administration 복지행정

welfare administration district and
health-welfare of the aged
노인보건복지권영역
welfare adviser for the aged 노인복지상담원
welfare adviser for the disabled
장애인복지상담원
welfare agency for people with mental
retardation 지적장애인복지기관
welfare agency for the aged 노인복지기관
welfare allowance 복지수당
welfare and medical service network
system : WAM NET 왐네트 (의료복지기구)
welfare and recreation 복지레크리에이션
welfare assistance 복지원조
welfare assistant 복지원조자
welfare backlash 복지반동
welfare benefit 복지급여
welfare capitalism 복지자본주의
welfare card 복지카드
welfare center for fatherless families
and widows 모자과부복지센터
welfare center for the aged 노인복지센터
welfare center for the elderly
고령자생활복지센터
welfare center for the physically disabled
신체장애인복지센터
welfare commission volunteer 민생위원
Welfare Commission Volunteers Act
민생위원법
welfare counseling for the aged
노인복지상담
welfare culture 복지문화
Welfare Division for Persons with
Disabilities 장애복지과
welfare economics 복지경제학 ; 후생경제학
welfare education 복지교육
welfare equipment 복지용구 ; 복지기기
welfare equipment industry 복지용구산업
Welfare Equipment Law 복지용구법
welfare equipment rental services
복지용구대여서비스
welfare equipment rentals 복지용구대여
welfare equipments advisor

복지용구전문상담원
welfare equipments planner 복지용구플래너
welfare equipments trade 복지용구판매
welfare ethics 복지윤리
welfare expenditure 복지비
welfare facilities for fatherless families
모자과부복지시설
welfare facility 복지시설
welfare facility for fatherless families
and widows 모자과부복지시설
welfare facility for people with mental
retardation 지적장애인복지시설
welfare facility for the elderly 노인복지시설
welfare for fatherless families and
widows 모자과부복지
welfare for people with mental
retardation 지적장애인복지
welfare for the aged 노인복지
welfare for the disabled 장애인복지
welfare for the elderly 고령자복지
welfare for the physically disabled
신체장애인복지
welfare fund 복지기금 ; 생활복지자금
welfare fund loan for widows
과부복지자금대여
welfare fund loan system
생활복지자금대출제도
welfare funds 복지재원
welfare halls for the aged 노인복지회관
welfare home 복지홈
welfare home for people with mental
disabilities 정신장애인복지홈
welfare home for people with mental
disorders 정신장애인복지홈
welfare home for people with mental
retardation 지적장애인복지홈
welfare home for the physically disabled
신체장애인복지홈
welfare houses for the aged 노인복지주택
welfare housing at cost for the aged
실비노인복지주택
welfare indicator 복지지표
welfare information 복지정보

Welfare Law for the Elderly 노인복지법
welfare loan for fatherless families and widows 모자과부복지대부금
welfare manpower 복지인재
welfare needs 복지욕구
welfare office 복지사무소
welfare office for people with mental retardation 지적장애인복지사업소
welfare office for the aged 노인복지사업소
welfare officer for people with mental retardation 지적장애인복지사
welfare officer for the physically disabled 신체장애인복지사
welfare pension 복지연금
welfare personnel 복지관계자
welfare policy 복지정책
welfare policy for the aged 노인복지시책
welfare profession 복지전문
welfare program 복리후생
welfare program for the aged 노인복지사업
Welfare Promotion Division 복지기반과
welfare provider for the aged 노인복지사업자
welfare public corporation 복지공사
welfare regime 복지제도
welfare rights 복지권
welfare services 복지서비스
welfare services for the aged 노인복지서비스
welfare services for the elderly 고령자복지서비스
welfare society 복지사회
welfare staff 복지직원
welfare standards 복지기준
welfare state 복지국가
welfare state in crisis 복지국가의 위기
welfare supervisor for the elderly 노인복지지도주사
welfare system 복지제도 ; 복지시스템
welfare system for the aged 노인복지제도
welfare system for the elderly 노인복지제도
welfare taxi 복지택시
welfare taxi services 복지택시
welfare vehicle 복지차량
Welfare Vision for the 21st Century 21세기 복지비전

welfare worker for the aged 노인복지사
welfare workshop for people with mental disabilities 정신장애인복지작업소
welfare workshop for people with mental retardation 지적장애인복지작업소
welfare workshop for the disabled 복지공장
welfare workshop for the physically disabled 신체장애인복지작업소
Well Aging Community Law : WAC Law WAC법
well-being 웰빙
Wellbutrin 웰부트린
Werner Syndrome : WS 베르너 증후군 ; 워너 증후군
Wernicke's aphasia 베르니케실어
Wernicke's area 베르니케영역
Wernicke's encephalopathy 베르니케뇌증
Wernicke-Korsakoff syndrome 베르니케 코르사코프 증후군
western aphasia battery : WAB WAB 실어증검사
western medicine 서양의학
wet cleaning 습식세탁
wheel 구동륜
wheelchair 휠체어
wheelchair activity 휠체어동작
wheelchair assistance 휠체어보조
wheelchair sports 휠체어스포츠
wheelchair to parallel bar 휠체어에서 평행봉
wheelchair transfer 휠체어이승
wheelchair transfer assistance 휠체어이승원조
wheeze 숨을 헐떡임 ; 쌕쌕거림 ; 천명
whiplash 교통사고 목손상 ; 편타손 손상
whiplash injury 교통사고 목손상 ; 편타손 손상
whirlpool bath 와류욕
whirlpool spa 거품목욕탕 ; 기포목욕탕 ; 기포목욕
whistle-blowing 고발
white blood cell : WBC 백혈구
white cane 흰 지팡이
white collar 화이트칼라
white-collar crime 화이트칼라 범죄

W

white-collar worker 사무직노동자
WHO Association of Japan 일본WHO협회
WHO's three-step pain ladder
  WHO 3단계 진통제사다리
whole-body bathing 전신샤워욕
WIC program 윅 프로그램
widow 미망인 ; 과부 |여성|
widow benefit 과부급여
widow's pension 과부연금
widower 과부 |남성|
width 폭
wild analysis 잠정적 분석
Wild Boy of Aveyron 아베이론의 야생아
will 유언서 ; 의지 (意志)
Wilson's disease 윌슨병
withdrawal 금단
withdrawal symptoms 금단증상
withdrawal syndrome 두문불출병후군
withdrawn child 퇴보형 아동
withhold 지불보류
withholding tax 원천과세
Women for sobriety 여성금주조직
Women's economic activity 여성경제활동
women's franchise 여성참정권
women's labor 여성노동
women's liberation movement 여성해방운동
women's movement 여성운동
women's problems 여성문제
women's welfare 부녀복지
woodworking 목공
word finding difficulty 단어찾기의 어려움 ;
  단어찾기장애 ; 환어곤란 ; 환어장애
word finding disorder 단어찾기의 어려움 ;
  단어찾기장애 ; 환어곤란 ; 환어장애
word-for-word reflection 순어반사 ; 축어적 반사
work 일
work ability index 노동적응능력지표
work absence 결근
work adjustment 작업조정
Work and Family Harmonization Division
  직업가정양립과
work arm 작업용 의수
work capacity 작업능력

work environment 노동환경
work for the elderly 고령자취업
work force 노동인구
work hours 노동시간
work house 워크하우스
work incentive program : WIN 노동장려계획
work incentives 작업동기
work sample method 워크샘플방법
work sharing 워크쉐어링
work tolerance 작업내성
workability 문제해결능력 ; 워커빌리티 ; 가동성
workaholic 일중독자 ; 워커홀릭
worker's collective
  워커즈콜렉티브 ; 노동자생산협동조합
Worker's Compensation Department
  노동자재해보험보상부
worker-client relationship 워커-내담자관계
workers accident 산업재해
workers' compensation 산업재해보상
Workers' Compensation Administration
  Division 노동자재해보험관리과
workers' compensation insurance
  노동재해보험
Workers' Life Department 근로자생활부
Workers' Life Division 근로자생활과
workfare 노동유인정책
workhouse 작업장
Workhouse Test Act 작업장테스트법
working conditions 노동조건
working memory 작업기억
working poor 노동빈곤자
working population 취업인구
working rule 취업규칙
working through 탐색과정
working women's welfare 근로여성복지
working youth welfare 근로청소년복지
working-age population 생산연령인구
workshop 워크숍
workshop for people with mental
  disabilities 정신장애인작업소
workshop for people with mental
  retardation 지적장애인작업소
workshop for the disabled 장애인작업소

W

workshop for the physically disabled
신체장애인작업소
work-table 작업테이블
World Health Organization : WHO
세계보건기구
World Human Rights Day 세계인권의 날
worthy poor 가치 있는 빈민
wound care 창상케어 ; 운드케어
wound classification 상처의 분류
wound dressing 상처도포제 ; 창상피복제

wound infection 상처감염 ; 창감염
wrist joint 손이음새
writ 영장
writing exercise 글씨쓰기훈련
Written Claim for Long-Term Care Benefit Cost 노인장기요양급여비용심사청구서
written communication 필담
written examination 필기시험
Written Statement for Long-Term Care Benefit Cost 노인장기요양급여비용심사명세서

W

X chromosome 엑스 염색체
xanthines 크산틴
Xanthogranulomatous pyelonephritis
　황색육아종성 신우신염
Xenical 제니칼
xenophobia 외국인혐오증

xerosis 건조증
xerostomia 구강건조증
X-linked dominant inheritance
　X연쇄우성유전 ; X염색체 연관우성유전
X-ray 방사선 ; X선
xy chromaticity diagram xy색도도

Y

Y chromosome 와이 염색체
Yankee City Study 양키시티조사
Yatabe-Guilford Personality Test
  야타베 기르포드 성격검사
Yates Report 예이츠보고서
yearly paid-holiday 연차유급휴가
yellow medical care card 황색의료보호수첩
yoga 요가
Young Men's Christian Association :
  YMCA 기독교청년회 ; 그리스도교 청년회
young population 연소인구

Young Women's Christian Association :
  YWCA 그리스도교 여자청년회 ; 기독교여성청년회
young-old 전기고령자
youth adolescent 청년기
youth counselor 청소년상담사
youth culture 청년문화
youth hostel : YH 유스호스텔
youth organization 청소년단체
youth programs 청소년대책사업
youth service organization 청소년봉사기구

Z

z value Z치
zaleplon 잘레플론
Zancolli classification 수절지배분류
Zaroxolyn 자록솔린
zero population growth 인구의 제로성장
zero position 제로자세 ; 제로지위
zero sum orientation 영합지향
zero-base budgeting 영점기준예산제
zero-based budgeting 제로베이스 예산편성
Zestril 제스트릴
zinc 아연
zolmitriptan 졸미트립탄

Zoloft 졸로프트
zolpidem 졸피뎀
Zomig 조믹
zoning 지대설정 ; 지역설정계획 ; 조닝 ; 지역제
zoonose 동물원성 감염증
zoonosis 인수공통전염병
Zostavax 조스타박스
Zovirax 조비락스
Zung Self-Rating Depression Scale : SDS
　Zung 자가평가우울척도
Zutphen Elderly Study 주프텐 고령자연구
Zyprexa 자이프렉사

PART 3

GLOSSARY OF
KOREAN TERMS

한어
용어
해설

ㄱ

가계 가정생활의 경제적 운영.

가령 일반적으로 나이를 먹는 것.

가사 건강하고 안전하고 쾌적하게 가정생활을 영위하기 위한 일련의 노동.

가정 생활의 변화에 대응하면서 가정경영, 식생활, 의생활, 주생활 등을 운영해, 한 가정의 생활을 잘 꾸려가는 것.

가정부 주로 가정관리 이외의 생활수단(물건)을 정돈하거나 가족성원과 관련되는 일을 그 집 가족(주로 주부)을 대신해서 하는 것을 직업으로 하는 여성.

가족 부부관계나 부모와 자식·형제 등의 혈연관계에 의해서 연결되어 있는 친족관계로부터 구성되어 있는 소집단.

가족개호 장기요양을 필요로 하는 고령자나 장애인 등에 대해서 그 가족이 장기요양을 하는 것.

가족개호자 장기요양을 하고 있는 가족.

가족관계 부부관계, 부자관계, 형제관계, 시어머니와 며느리관계 등 가족집단내의 구성원 상호간의 인간관계의 총칭.

가족회 가족 중에 장애인·장기요양대상자, 난치병 환자 등이 있어 공통된 문제를 안고 있는 가족들이 모여서 만든 단체.

간경변 간에 염증이 반복해서 일어나 간이 딱딱해져 제대로 기능하지 않게 되어 버리는 병.

간호 대한간호협회의 정의에 의하면, 「간호란 모든 개인, 가정, 지역사회를 대상으로 하여 건강의 회복, 질병예방, 건강유지와 증진에 필요한 지식, 기력, 의지와 자원을 갖추도록 직접 도와주는 활동」임.

간호 일본개호협회(1973년)의 정의에 의하면, 간호란 건강의 모든 면에 있어서 개인이 건강하게 정상적인 일상생활을 할 수 있도록 원조하는 것.

간호사 의료법(제2장 제1절)에서 정하는 전문교육을 받고 국가시험에 합격한 후 보건복지부 장관의 면허를 받은 자로서 의사의 진료를 돕고 상병자나 해산부를 돌보는 업무를 수행하는 자.

간호사 일본의 보건사조산사간호사법(제5조)에 의하면, 「후생노동대신의 면허를 받고, 상병자 또는 해산부에 대한 요양상의 도움 또는 진료를 보조하는 것을 업무로 하는 것이다」라고 정의되어 있는 자.

갈아입기 입고 있던 의복을 벗고 다른 의복을 입는 것.

감각기능 인간의 외부환경 및 내부환경에 관한 정보를 수용기로 받아서 중추신경계에 전달하는 기능.

감염 어떤 병원미생물이 인체의 조직이나 장기 속에 비집고 들어가서 거기서 증식을 계속하는 상태.

감염균 감염에 의해 병을 일으키는 병원균.

감염예방 병원체가 체내에 침입·정착·증식하는 것을 예방하는 것.

감염증 생체에 감염을 일으키는 병원균이 조직에 침입·정착하여 그 염증에 의해 세포장애나 기능장애를 일으킨 상태.

감음난청 내이로부터 청신경을 통해 대뇌의 청각중추까지의 경로 상에서 일어난 난청.

개별개호 개인을 존중하고 존엄을 중시해서 서비스 이용자의 개성에 맞추어 장기요양을 실시하는 것.

개선 개선충이라고 하는 매우 미세한 진드기가 피부에 기생함으로써 일어나는 피부병.

개치베드 등이나 무릎을 들어 올리는 기능이 있는 침대로서 특수침대라 불림.

개호 심신이 부자유해 자기 스스로 신변 처리를 할 수 없게 되었을 때에 그 사람을 돌보는 것.

개호계획 장기요양대상자에게 장기요양급여를 적절하게 제공하기 위해서 작성한 구체적인 계획서.

개호과정 이용자의 욕구를 중심으로 한 장기요양을 실시하기 위해서 필요한 일련의 과제달성 프로세스

개호급여 일본의 개호보험제도에 있어서 요개호인정 결과, 피보험자가 요개호(1~5)로 인정된 요개호자에 대한 급여.

개호기술 장기요양에 관한 전문적 지식을 기본으로 해서 실천하는 행위.

개호노동자 장기요양서비스 제공에 종사하는 노동자.

개호노인보건시설 일본의 개호보험법에 근거한 시설서비스의 하나.

개호노인복지시설 일본의 특별양호노인홈이 개호보험제도하의 개호보험시설로서 역할을 할 경우의 명칭.

개호목표 장기요양계획을 방향 짓는 목표.

개호보수 일본의 개호서비스 사업자가 일본국내에서 개호서비스를 제공했을 경우, 그 대가로서 개호보험으로부터 9할, 이용자의 자부담 1할이 사업자에게 지불되는 보수.

개호보험 치매나 와병생활 때문에 요지원 또는 요개호 상태가 되었을 때에 필요한 개호서비스를 제공하고 그 비용을 보장하기 위한 일본의 사회보험.

개호보험법 일본의 개호보험제도에 있어서 요지원 또는 요개호 상태가 된 고령자 등에게 필요한 개호서비스를 제공하는 것 등을 정한 법률.

개호보험사업계획 일본의 개호보험법에 의해 시정촌과 도도부현(都道府縣)이 5년간을 한주기로해서 3년마다 책정하는 사업계획.

개호보험심사회 보험자의 보험급여에 관한 결정 또는 보험료 등의 징수 결정에 관한 불복에 대한 심사청구를 심리·재결하기 위해 일본의 각 도도부현에 설치되는 기관.

개호보험인정조사 일본의 개호보험제도에 있어서 요지원 또는 요개호인정의 신청 또는 갱신을 위해서 30일 이내에 실시하는 조사.

개호보험제도 일본의 지방자치체가 개호를 필요로 하는 40세 이상의 중고령자 등에게 개호서비스를 제공하는 사회보험제도.

개호복지 사회복지분야의 전문적인 교육을 받은 사람이 고령이나 심신장애 등에 의해 사회 생활상에 곤란을 가지는 사람 또는 원조를 필요로 하는 사람에 대해서 직접적인 원조나 생활원조를 중심으로 신체적 측면·정신심리적 측면·사회적 측면에서 원조하는 것.

개호복지사 신체나 정신에 장애가 있는 사람들에게 개호급여를 제공하는 일본의 전문 국가자격을 가진 자.

개호복지사 국가시험 개호복지사로서 필요한 지식 및 기능에 관한 일본의 국가시험.

개호복지사 등록 일본의 개호복지사가 되기 위해서 국가시험에 합격한 후에 등록하는 것.

개호부담 와병생활 또는 치매 등의 장기요양대상자 등을 돌보고 있는 장기요양자나 그 가족의 신체적, 정신적, 경제적인 부담.

개호서비스계획 장기요양계획, 케어플랜.

개호예방 일본의 개호보험제도에 있어서 요지원 상태가 될 가능성이 있는 사람, 또는 요지원 상태에 있는 사람이 요개호 상태가 되지 않도록 실시하는 개호서비스

개호예방사업 개호예방을 위해서 일본의 시정촌(市町村)이 실시하는 개호보험제도에 의한 지역지

원사업 중의 한 사업.

개호요양형의료시설 일본의 개호보험제도에 있어서 의료와 개호의 필요성이 높은 요개호자 전용의 의료형 개호보험시설.

개호욕구 신체상 또는 정신상의 장애에 의해 일상생활을 영위할 수 없는 경우, 그것을 충족시키기 위한 신체적·정신적·사회적 요구, 욕구, 필요.

개호용구 장기요양에 관련된 복지용구.

개호인정심사회 일본의 개호보험제도에 있어서 피보험자가 개호보험의 급여를 받기 위해서 개호서 비스가 필요한가 필요하지 않는가, 필요하다면 어느 정도 필요한가, 요지원 또는 요개호 상태의 심사판정업무를 실시하는 시정촌에 설치된 기관.

개호자 신체상 또는 정신상의 질환이나 장애가 있는 사람에게 장기요양을 실시하는 간호사나 요양 보호사 등.

개호지도 고령자나 장애인을 돌보고 있는 가족 등에게 장기요양에 관한 지식이나 기술을 직접 지 도하거나 조언하는 것.

개호지원전문원 일본의 개호보험제도에 있어서 요개호자 등의 개호욕구를 만족시켜 개호급여를 제 공하고 연락·조정하는 전문직(케어매니저).

개호직원 장기요양을 일로 하고 있는 자.

개호휴가 장기요양이 필요한 가족이 있는 노동자가 그 장기요양을 하기 위해서 휴가를 얻을 수 있 는 제도.

건강 WHO에 의하면, 「신체적, 정신적 및 사회적으로 완전하게 양호한 상태이며, 단지 병이 없거나 허약한 상태가 아닌 것만은 아닌 상태」.

건강관찰 건강상태를 평가해 파악하는 것.

건강보험 사업소에 고용되는 사람을 피보험자로 하는 강제 의료보험.

견당식장애 자신이 있는 장소나 현재의 시간 등을 모르는 상태.

경관영양 입을 통해서 소화관에 카테터를 삽입하여 유동식을 주입하는 영양보급법.

경수손상 경수가 손상되어 완전 또는 부전마비를 일으키는 장애.

경청 이야기 내용과 거기에 따른 정서적 측면을 수용적으로 듣는 것.

계단 높이가 다른 곳에 있는 단차가 있는 승강로.

계단승강 계단을 오르거나 내리거나 하는 것.

계약 서로 의사표시하고 약속한 것을 합의하는 것.

고령기 장애 가령 및 노화에 의해 고령기에 일어나는 장애.

고령사회 노년인구비율(총인구 중에서 65세 이상의 노인이 차지하는 비율)이 14%를 넘은 사회.

고령자 일반적으로는 65세 이상인 자.

고령자세대 65세 이상의 사람만으로 구성된 세대.

고령자학대방지법 고령자의 학대가 심각한 경우에 고령자를 보호조치하고 양호자의 부담을 경감시 키기 위해서 제정한 법률(2005년 성립).

고령화 총인구에 차지하는 노인비율이 높아지는 것.

고혈압 동맥혈압이 정상보다 높은 상태에 있는 것.

골다공증 뼈의 양이 감소하고 석회성분이 줄어들어 뼈의 강도가 약해져서 골절이 일어날 가능성이 높은 상태.

골절 뼈가 외부압력에 의해서 변형되거나 파괴되는 것.

공감 일반적으로 타인의 감정 등을 자신도 똑같이 느끼거나 이해하거나 하는 것.

공익법인 공익사업을 하는 사람의 모임이나 재산을 중심으로 한 모임에 부여하는 법적인 인격.

공익사업 공익을 목적으로 실시하는 사업.

공정증서 공정인이 작성한 유언이나 금전대차에 관한 증서.

공증인 민사에 관한 공정증서를 작성하는 자.

과부 일반적으로 남편이 먼저 사망한 여성.

과용증후군 과도의 운동이나 훈련에 의해 생기는 운동기능의 저하 또는 장애.

관념실행 인지기능은 충분히 유지되고 있어 운동을 하는 기능에도 아무 이상이 없는데 물건을 올바르게 움직이지 못하는 것.

관리영양사 영양사가 행하는 업무가운데 복잡 또는 곤란한 것을 행하는 적격성을 지닌 자로서 등록된 영양사.

관리영양사 일본의 영양사법(제1조2)에 규정된 전문직으로서 후생노동대신으로부터 면허를 받아 건강을 유지관리하기 위한 영양지도를 하거나 시설에서 급식관리를 하는 자.

관장 직장이나 결장에 액체를 넣어 대장내의 대변이나 가스를 제거하는 것.

관절 골격을 형성하고 있는 두 개 또는 그 이상의 뼈마디에 일정한 간격이 존재함으로써 그 뼈마디가 완전히 분리되어 가동적으로 결합된 조직.

관절가동역 관절을 타동적 또는 자동적으로 운동시켰을 경우의 가동범위.

관절류머티즘 다발성의 관절염을 주된 증상으로 하는 원인불명의 만성 전신성 질환.

괴사 신체의 세포나 조직의 죽음.

구강기능향상 일본의 개호보험제도에 있어서의 예방급여에 의한 선택 서비스의 하나로서 구강기능을 향상시키는 훈련.

구강케어 구강내를 청결하게 함으로써 구강 내 상태를 개선하는 것.

구급구명사 중증 의식상태에 있는 환자를 병원으로 반송할 시에 의사의 지시 하에 응급처치를 할 수 있는 전문직.

구속 억제하는 것.

구역질 인두에서 위부에 걸쳐서 구토의 전단계에서 일어나는 막연한 불쾌감(구토).

구음장애 발음기관의 장애에 의해 확실하게 소리를 내서 발음할 수 없는 상태.

구축 관절을 움직이지 않아서 관절 자체가 단단해져 움직임이 나빠진 상태.

구축예방 관절가동역이 저하되지 않도록 예방하는 것.

구토 위의 내용물이 역류되어 식도, 구강을 거쳐 밖으로 배출되는 현상.

국제생활기능분류 세계보건기구(WHO)가 2001년에 제창한 개정판의 국제장애분류.

국제장애분류 1980년에 세계보건기구(WHO)로부터 제시된 장애의 개념 및 거기에 기초를 두는 분류.

국제질병분류 세계보건기구(WHO)가 정한 질병이나 사인에 관한 국제적 통계의 분류기준.

국제표준화기구 1947년에 성립된 각국의 표준화 기관으로서 160개국 이상이 참가하고 있으며 전기분야 이외의 공업분야의 국제표준규격을 책정하는 연합체.

권리옹호 이용자의 권리침해에 대한 보호·구제.

궤양 피부나 점막의 일부분이 짓물러 문드러진 상태.

그룹레크리에이션 많은 장기요양대상자 등과 함께 레크리에이션을 그룹으로 실시하는 것.

그룹리빙 보통 60세 이상의 비교적 건강한 노인이 친족 이외의 사람과 함께 공동생활을 하는 거주형태.

그룹워크 의도적인 그룹 경험을 통해서 원조하는 소시얼워크 원조기술의 하나.

그룹홈 소규모의 가족적인 집단생활을 통해 일상생활에 장애를 가지고 있는 사람의 자립을 지원하는 서비스

극약 사람 또는 동물의 체내에 이것이 흡수되었을 경우, 비록 미량이라도 해를 끼치거나 해를 끼칠 우려가 있는 약.

근위축 질환이나 부동화 등에 의해 골격근이 양적으로 감소하는 것.

금전관리 실제로 금전을 보관하거나 적절하게 금전을 관리하는 것.

기관 호흡운동에 의해 들어온 공기를 폐를 통해 넣었다 내보냈다 하는 도관의 일부.

기능유지 신체운동을 하기 위한 여러 가지 기능을 현재 수준으로 유지시키는 것.

기능장애 세계보건기구(WHO)의 국제장애분류(1980년)에 의하면, 심리적, 생리적, 해부적인 구조 또는 기능에 어떤 상실이나 이상이 일어난 상태.

기능훈련 병이나 가령 등에 인해서 심신기능이 저하된 사람의 건강유지와 증진을 도모하고 일상생활의 자립을 도와 장기요양예방 등을 목적으로 실시하는 훈련.

기록 서비스 등에 관한 실천과정·결과·평가 등의 사실을 적는 것.

기립성 저혈압 와위에서 좌위 또는 입위로 갑작스럽게 체위를 바꿀 때 발생하는 혈압저하.

기명력 새롭게 지각하고 체험한 것 등을 기억 속에 포함시켜 지속시키는 능력.

기억장애 기억의 일련의 과정의 어디엔가 장애가 일어난 상태.

기저귀 배설물을 흡수해서 음부의 오염을 막아 청결하게 유지하기 위한 것.

기저귀 교환 배설물을 흡수해서 음부의 오염을 막아 청결하게 유지하기 위해서 기저귀를 바꾸는 것.

기저귀 떼기 기저귀를 대고 있는 상태에서 기저귀를 사용하지 않고 배설할 수 있는 상태로 이행하는 것 또는 그것을 위한 원조

기저귀 커버 기저귀로부터 배설물이 새어나와 오염되는 것을 막는 것.

기좌위 침대를 위로 일으켜서 상반신을 일으킨 자세.

기초대사 신체적, 정신적으로 안정된 상태로 살아가기 위해서 필요한 최소 에너지 소비량.

기초장애연금 생활이 어려운 중증장애인의 소득을 보장하기 위해 마련된 연금제도

기회감염 생체에 상주하여 병원성을 나타내지 않았던 미생물이 생체에 감염증을 발생시키는 것.

긴급연락처 응급상황이나 재해발생 등의 긴급 시에 연락하는 상대편.

깨끗이 닦기 혼자서 목욕을 할 수 없는 장기요양대상자 등의 신체를 온탕이나 비누를 이용하여 때수건 등으로 닦아서 청결하게 하는 것.

ㄴ

난청 회화나 소리 등 신변의 소리가 구별하기 어려워지게 되는 것.

난치병 「불치병」 등의 난치성 질환에 대해 일반적으로 사용되어 온 말.

내부장애 내장 기능에 장애가 있는 상태.

네발지팡이 지팡이 끝이 네 개로 나누어져 있는 지팡이.

노령기초연금 노령을 이유로 지급되는 국민연금.

노령복지연금 일본에서 국민연금보험이 시작된 1961년에는 이미 보험료를 납부할 수 없는 연령에 이르고 있던 사람에게 지급되는 연금.

노령연금 노령기초연금 참조.

노멀라이제이션 모든 아동, 장애인, 고령자 등이 한사람의 인간으로서 인격이 존중되어 한사람의 시민으로서의 권리가 보장되고, 지역사회에서 자기 스스로 생활할 수 있는 사회를 목표로 하는 것.

노안 가까이의 것이 보기 어려워지는 중년기 이후에 일어나는 원시.

노인보건시설 일본의 개호보험제도에 있어서 병상이 거의 안정되어 입원치료보다 간호·개호·재활이 필요한 고령자를 대상으로 하는 입소시설.

노인성 난청 가령에 수반해서 서서히 고음부의 소리가 듣기 어려워져 점차 중음부와 저음부가 듣기 힘들어지는 난청.

노인성 우울증 노년기에 발병하는 우울증.

노인성 치매 노년기에 많이 발생하는 진행성 치매를 주증상으로 하는 뇌의 변성질환.

노인장기요양보험법 고령이나 노인성 질병으로 독립적인 일상생활의 영위가 불가능한 노인 등에게 신체활동과 가사지원 서비스를 제공하여 가족의 부담을 완화하고 노인의 삶의 질을 향상시키려는 목적으로 제정된 법률.

노인장기요양보험제도 고령이나 노인성 질병 등의 사유로 다른 사람의 도움을 받지 않고서는 생활하기 어려운 노인들에게 신체활동 또는 가사지원 등의 장기요양급여를 제공하는 사회보험제도.

노인학대 노인에 대한 신체적, 심리적, 경제적, 성적, 방임에 의한 학대.

노화 시간의 경과와 함께 일어나는 생물의 변화 가운데 성숙기 이후에 일어나는 현상.

논렘수면 급속안구운동(REM)을 수반하지 않는 수면.

농 양쪽 귀의 청력레벨이 약 100dB (데시벨) 이상의 청각장애.

뇌경색 뇌의 혈관이 막혀 뇌에 혈액이 흐르지 않게 되어 그 부근의 뇌세포가 죽어 버리는 병의 용태.

뇌사 뇌간을 포함한 뇌기능이 완전히 없어진 상태.

뇌색전 심장이나 경동맥 등에 형성된 혈전 등이 혈류에 의해서 뇌내에 옮겨져 뇌의 동맥을 막아버리는 병의 용태.

뇌성마비 발달도상의 뇌에 여러 가지의 원인이 더해져서 비진행성의 병변을 일으킨 결과, 주로 영속적인 중추 운동장애를 불러일으킨 상태의 총칭.

뇌출혈 뇌의 혈관이 손상됨으로써 출혈한 병의 용태.

뇌혈관성 치매 뇌혈관의 장애에 기인한 치매의 총칭.

뇌혈관장애 뇌의 혈관이 막히거나 찢어져서 뇌가 기질적으로 손상되어 손상된 곳에 의해서 반신마비, 의식장애, 언어장애 등이 나타나는 질환군의 총칭.

뇌혈전 뇌의 혈관 내벽에 이물질이 조금씩 부착(죽장경화) 함으로써 혈관이 점점 좁아져서 결국에는 꽉 막혀버리는 병의 용태.

능력저하 어떤 일을 할 수 있는 능력이 저하되는 것.

ㄷ

다운증후군 돌연변이 염색체 질환으로서 21번 염색체가 정상인보다 한 개 많은 세 개가 존재하는 선천성 유전질환.

단골의사 자기 가까이에서 건강상담을 해주거나 치료를 해주는 의사.

단기보호 수급자를 보건복지가족부령으로 정하는 범위 안에서 일정 기간 동안 장기요양기관에 보호하여 신체활동 지원 및 심신기능의 유지·향상을 위한 교육·훈련 등을 제공하는 장기요양급여.

단기보호 재가의 요개호자 등이 일시적으로 시설에 입소하여 받는 일본의 개호보험서비스.

단좌위 침대 또는 시트 끝에서 양종아리를 늘어뜨리고 앉은 자세.

단하지보조기 무릎 이하에 사용하는 보조기.

당뇨병 혈중 포도당 농도가 높아져 소변에 포도당을 배출하는 대사이상의 질환.

대독 이용자가 글을 읽을 수 없게 되었을 시에 대신 읽어주는 원조.

대리전화 전화통화가 곤란한 사람을 대신해서 전화를 하는 것.

대마비 양측 하지가 마비되어 있는 상태.

대상포진 수두 바이러스가 재발해서 띠 모양의 발진이 나타나는 증상.

대장암 대장에 생긴 암.

대퇴사두근 슬관절에서 신전을 만들어내는 대퇴전면에 위치하는 근육.

대필 이용자를 대신해서 편지·서류 등을 써 주는 것.

도수근력검사 로버트 러벳≪Lovett, R.≫이 개발한 항중력 근력검사법.

독거 가족이나 친족 등과 함께 살지 않고 혼자서 살고 있는 것.

독화 청각장애인의 커뮤니케이션 수단의 하나로서 상대의 표정이나 입의 움직임으로부터 음성언어를 읽어내는 것.

돌아눕기 위를 보고 누워있던 상태에서 우측 또는 좌측으로 눕는 것.

동맥경화 동맥의 퇴행성 병변에 의해서 동맥의 벽이 두꺼워지고 딱딱해진 상태.

동통 신체적인 아픔.

두통 머리 부분의 아픔.

라이프리뷰 자신의 인생을 되돌아보며 말하는 것으로서 자신이 걸어 온 인생의 의미를 찾아내서 자기를 긍정할 수 있게 되는 것.

라이프사이클 사람의 출생에서 사망까지를 한 주기로 한 인생의 과정.

라이프스타일 의, 식, 주, 교류, 여가활동 등을 포함한 생활의 방법.

라포르 원조하는 측과 원조 받는 측의 사이에 친근감이나 신뢰감이 흘러넘치는 관계.

레크리에이션 생활 속의 여유와 안락함, 즐거움을 창조해 나가는 다양한 활동의 총칭.

렘수면 급속안구운동으로서 자고 있는데 안구가 격렬하게 움직이고 있는 수면상태.

롤플레이 시나리오를 만들어 이야기하는 사람, 듣는 사람, 관찰하는 사람을 결정해서 연기하는 수법.

ㅁ

마비 신경계의 비정상에 의해서 일어나는 근력저하나 지각소실 또는 운동장애.

말걸기 신뢰관계를 형성하기 위한 중요한 커뮤니케이션의 하나.

말기치료 그 이상 연명치료가 곤란하게 된 종말기에 제공되는 케어.

말붙이기 말걸기 참조.

망상 실제로 있을 수 없는 사고내용이나 관념.

매트 크기나 형태가 다양한 사이즈의 깔개.

맥박 심장의 박동을 나타내는 동맥의 압력변동.

머리감기 두발을 청결하게 유지하기 위해서 실시하는 신체의 청결 원조법의 하나.

머리정돈 빗이나 브러쉬를 사용하여 머리카락을 빗어 손질하는 것.

메뉴 식품의 올바른 선택이나 조리법, 요리의 종류 등을 결정하는 식사계획.

메타보릭크증후군 내장지방형 비만만이 아니라 고혈당, 고혈압, 지방질 이상증 중에 두 개 이상이 있
는 경우에 진단되는 증후군.

멸균 어느 장소(기재, 신체, 식품재료 등)로부터 모든 미생물을 배제해서 무균, 즉 세균이 없는 상태로 하는 것.

모니터링 클라이언트의 문제가 해결되고 있는지를 판별하는 것.

목발 상처 등에 의해 하지가 부자유스러운 사람의 보행을 보조하기 위한 목제 또는 알루미늄제의
보조도구.

목욕 일상적인 생활행위의 하나로서 욕조에 몸의 일부 또는 전신을 담그는 것.

묵비 복지전문직, 의사, 변호사 등이 그 직무를 통해서 알게 된 개인정보를 외부에 누설해서는 안
되는 것.

문제행동 문제로 여겨지는 행위.

미네랄 생체에 필요한 무기성분의 하나.

믹서식 죽을 믹서로 간 것으로서 브랜드식이라고도 하는 유동식.

바이탈사인 생명유지를 나타내는 활력징후.

반신욕 욕조내의 수위를 가슴아래에서 배꼽 위 사이로 조절하여 목욕하는 것.

반조리 자르기, 익히기 등 음식을 조리하는 과정 중 일부를 어느 정도 미리 손질하여 조리 과정을 단축시키는 조리법.

반좌위 배위로부터 상반신을 약 20에서 30도 정도 일으켜서 고관절과 슬관절을 가볍게 굽힌 자세.

발달장애 일반적으로 발달기에 일어나는 지적장애, 자폐증, 학습장애, 뇌성마비, 간질 등의 장애.

발열 근수축이나 질환 등에 의해 열이 많이 발생함으로서 말초혈관이 수축되어 열방사가 억제된 상태.

발적 선홍색을 띠며 압박되면 퇴색하고 압박을 하지 않으면 다시 원래의 색으로 돌아오는 붉은 반점이 피부에 생기는 것.

발진 혈류량의 감소, 색소침착이나 감소 또는 결핍, 염증, 종양의 진피내로의 침윤, 표피의 비후 등이 생기는 상태.

발판 휠체어를 구성하는 일부로서 족부를 지탱하는 것.

방문간호 장기요양요원인 간호사 등이 의사, 한의사 또는 치과의사의 방문간호지시서에 따라 수급자의 가정 등을 방문하여 간호, 진료의 보조, 요양에 관한 상담 또는 구강위생 등을 제공하는 장기요양급여.

방문간호* 방문간호가 필요하다고 주치의가 인정했을 경우에 방문간호스테이션의 간호사 등이 요개호자 등의 자택을 방문해서 요양상의 도움 또는 필요한 진료를 보조하는 일본의 개호보험서비스

방문간호스테이션* 간호사, 준간호사, 보건사 등이 배치되어 있는 일본의 방문사업소.

방문개호* 방문개호원(홈헬퍼)이나 개호복지사가 요개호자 등의 자택을 방문해서 배설·목욕·식사 등에 관한 신체 개호나 쇼핑·요리·세탁·청소 등의 생활원조, 일상생활 전반에 걸친 상담 조언 등의 서비스를 제공하는 일본의 개호보험서비스.

방문목욕 장기요양요원이 목욕설비를 갖춘 장비를 이용하여 수급자의 가정 등을 방문하여 목욕을 제공하는 장기요양급여.

방문요양 장기요양요원이 수급자의 가정 등을 방문하여 신체활동 및 가사활동 등을 지원하는 장기요양급여.

방문입욕개호* 요개호자 등의 자택을 방문해서 욕조를 제공해 입욕을 실시해서 신체의 청결을 유지하거나 심신기능을 유지하고 향상시키는 일본의 개호보험서비스

방문재활* 요개호자 등에 대해서 이학요법사·작업요법사·언어청각사 등이 주치의의 지시 하에 각 가정에 가서 재활이나 지도 등을 하는 일본의 개호보험서비스

방염소재 불에 접근시켰을 경우에도 타지 않고 불에 타도 확산되지 않는 소재.

방오소재 음식의 얼룩이나 때가 잘 안 타는 소재 또는 더러워져도 세탁을 하면 때가 잘 빠지는 소재.

배뇨 노폐물을 포함한 혈액이 신장에서 여과되어 노폐물이 소변이 되어 요관을 통해 방광으로 옮겨져서 요도로부터 체외로 배출되는 것.

배뇨곤란 방광에 저장된 소변이 나오기 어려워지는 것 또는 잔뇨가 있는 상태.

배뇨장애 빈뇨, 배뇨곤란, 요실금 등 배뇨기능에 장애가 생긴 상태.

배리어프리 공공 건축물이나 교통기관 등의 물리적인 장벽뿐만 아니라 제도적 장벽, 문화·정보적 장벽, 정신적 장벽 등의 모든 장벽을 제거하는 의미의 용어.

배변 대변을 체외로 배출하는 것.

배변장애 변비, 설사 등, 대변을 배설하는 기능에 장애가 생긴 상태.

배설 체내의 불필요한 것을 체외로 배출하는 것.

배설보조 신체적·정신적·사회적인 장애에 의해 배설 행위를 스스로 할 수 없게 된 사람을 지원하는 것.

배회 목적도 없이 무작정 걸어 다니는 상태.

백내장 안구의 수정체가 탁해지는 것.

백서포트 휠체어 사용자가 등을 의지하는 부위로서 이른바 등받이 부분.

벌룬도뇨카테터 소변이 자동적으로 체외의 주머니에 저장 되도록 방광에 삽입하는 관.

변기 배설한 소변이나 대변을 위생적으로 수집하는 용구.

변비 대장의 기능적, 기질적 비정상으로 인해 발생해, 비정상적으로 길게 장내에 분변이 저장되거나 대변을 자주 못 보아서 불쾌감과 고통을 수반하는 상태.

변실금 자신의 의지대로 조절할 수 없어 무의식적으로 대변이 새어나옴.

보건사 보건소, 보건센터, 병원, 일반기업 등에서 주민이나 사원에 대해 보건지도업무 등을 실시하는 국가자격의 전문직.

보건소 지역에 있어서의 주민의 질병예방, 공중위생의 향상과 증진을 도모하는 것을 목적으로 하고 있는 기관.

보육사 전문적 지식 및 기술을 가지고 아동의 보육 및 아동의 보호자에 대한 보육에 관한 지도를 실시하는 것을 일로 하는 자.

보조 고령자나 장애인이 생활하는데 있어서 실제로 어떤 행위를 할 때에 당사자의 필요에 따라서 다른 사람(장기요양자나 가족 등)에 의해 행해지는 보완적인 행위.

보청기 소리를 크게 하는 기능을 가진 난청자의 보장구.

보충급여 소득에 따라 부담한도액을 설정해서 저소득자의 부담이 무겁지 않도록 기준비용액과 부담한도액과의 차액을 급여하는 것.

보행 양쪽 하지를 교대로 딛으면서 이동하는 것.

보행기 좌우의 프레임과 이것을 연결하는 중앙부의 파이프로 구성되어 있는 것으로서 이용자는 그 사이에 서서 보행을 실시하는 용구.

보행연습 어떤 원인으로 보행에 장애가 발생했을 경우에 평행봉·목발·지팡이를 사용하거나 이학요법사·작업요법사 등에 의한 보조 또는 지도 하에 재활훈련실이나 실외에서 걷는 기본적 동작의 연습.

보험료 보험사업에 필요로 하는 비용을 충당하기 위해서 피보험자가 거출하는 비용.

보험자 보험료를 징수해서 보험제도를 운영하며, 사고 등이 발생하면 피보험자에게 보험급여(서비스 제공)를 하는 자.

복식호흡 횡격막을 상하시키는 것으로서 복부의 운동에 의한 호흡.

복와위 엎드려서 상지를 몸측에 붙이고 하지를 뻗은 자세.

복지 쾌적한 생활이나 보다 나은 생활의 행복을 위한 본연의 모습.

복지기기 장기요양대상자 등의 생활을 지원하기 위해서 만들어진 기구 전반.

복지사무소 사회복지행정의 중심적인 기관.

복지용구 심신의 기능이 저하되어 일상생활을 하는데 있어서 지장이 있는 사람의 일상생활을 보다 편리하게 보조하는 도구.

복지용구대여 복지용구 중에 일상생활용구를 공비로 급여 또는 대여하는 것.

부분세정 병이나 부상, 체력의 저하가 현저해서 목욕할 수 없을 때, 50~55℃의 더운 물을 준비해서 때수건 또는 워쉬크로스로 신체의 일부분을 닦는 것.

부분욕 병이나 부상, 체력의 저하가 현저해서 목욕할 수 없을 때, 신체의 일부만을 뜨거운 물에 담 그어 씻는 것.

부분원조 이용자의 행동을 부분적으로 원조하는 것.

부작용 치료효과를 기대하는 작용(주작용) 이외에 나타나는 작용.

부종 임상적으로는 이른바 「부어오름」으로서 세포간격에 체액이 과잉하게 저장되는 상태.

불평해결 서비스 이용자 등이 신청한 불평이나 불만을 처리해서 해결하는 것.

뷔페식 다양한 요리를 테이블에 늘어놓고 셀프서비스로 좋아하는 음식만 먹는 식사스타일.

비만 지방조직이 과잉하게 축적되어 체중이 표준을 초과한 상태.

비밀보지 클라이언트가 원조과정 중에 털어놓은 비밀정보를 지키는 것.

비언어적 커뮤니케이션 시선, 표정, 태도, 몸짓 등의 비언어적 수단에 의해 서로가 자신의 주장이나 생각, 감정 등을 교환하는 것.

비에스틱 7대 원칙 미국의 비에스틱≪Biestek, F. P.≫이 원조자와 클라이언트의 기본적인 관계로서 명시한 일곱 개의 원칙.

비타민 인체의 생명유지, 성장, 생식을 위한 적은 양의 필수 영양소.

빈변 대변을 여러 차례에 걸쳐서 배설하는 상태.

빈혈 어떤 원인으로 인해 혈액의 단위 용적 중의 적혈구 또는 혈색소량이 감소한 상태.

빙낭 고무 자루에 얼음과 물을 넣은 것.

빙침 얼음과 물을 넣은 고무제의 베개.

사고장애 정신질환에 의해서 발생하는 장애.

사례검토 문제가 있는 어떤 일에 대해 그 상황을 분명히 해서 원인을 찾아 그 해결방법 등을 검토하는 것.

사생관 생과 사에 대한 생각.

사회보장 국민의 인간다운 생활을 보장하기 위해 국가책임 하에 국민생활의 안정과 건강을 보장하는 제도.

사회보장심의회° 일본의 후생노동성의 부속기관으로서 사회보장에 관한 후생노동대신의 자문기관.

사회보험 강제적 보험기술을 이용하여 사회정책을 실현하려고 하는 경제보장정책.

사회복지 사회관계의 곤란을 생활면으로부터 파악해서 개인의 최저생활을 원조하는 것.

사회복지사 사회복지에 관한 전문지식과 기술을 가진 자로서 보건복지부 장관으로부터 자격증을 교부받아 사회복지사업에 종사하는 자.

사회복지사° 일본의 사회복지사법 및 개호복지사법 제2조에 의하면, 전문적 지식·기술을 가지고 복지에 관한 상담을 하고, 조언, 지도, 복지서비스를 제공하는 사람 또는 의사 그 외의 보건의료 서비스를 제공하는 사람 그 외의 관계자와의 연락 및 조정 그 외의 원조를 실시하는 것(「상담원조」)을 직업으로 하는 자.

사회복지사업 사회복지를 목적으로 계획해서 활동하는 사업.

사회자원 개인이나 집단이 사회생활상의 욕구를 충족시키기 위한 시설, 설비, 자금, 물자, 인재, 기능 등의 총칭.

사회적 불리 기능장애 또는 능력저하의 결과로서 사회로부터 받는 불이익.

상실체험 중요한 것을 잃는 경험을 하는 것.

생명윤리 생명에 관련되는 윤리.

생명의 연장 생명의 유지기간을 최대한으로 지연시키는 것.

생활력 현재에 영향을 미치는 과거의 생활기록.

생활부조 생활이 궁핍해서 최저한도의 생활을 영위하는 것이 어려운 사람에 대해서 식비, 피복비, 교통비, 광열비, 가구비 등, 일상생활의 수요를 지원하기 위해서 설정되어 있는 부조.

생활습관병 생활습관과 깊이 관련되어 가령과 함께 증가하는 병.

생활원조 정든 곳에서 심신의 건강을 유지하면서 보낼 수 있는 가정생활을 할 수 있도록 의·식·주·그 외의 측면에서 지원하는 것.

생활의 질 개인에게 있어서 생활의 질적 측면을 묻는 장면에 사용되는 개념.

생활환경 생활에 있어서 인간과 관련되는 주위의 사상이나 상태.

샤워욕 샤워로 실시하는 목욕.

서비스담당자회의 케어플랜 작성이나 변경 시에 개최하는 회의.

서포트시스템 병이나 장애, 노령으로 생활이 어려워졌을 시의 지원구조.

설사 대변의 수분량이 증가해서 액체상 또는 거기에 가까운 대변을 하루 몇 차례에서 수차례 배설하는 증상.

섬망 환각이나 망상 등을 동반하는 의식혼탁에 의해 혼란해진 상태.

섬유 가늘고 긴 실 소재.

섭식 입으로부터 음식을 받아들이는 것.

섭식장애 입으로부터 음식을 받아들이는 것에 지장이 생긴 상태.

성년후견제도 정신적 제약으로 인해 재산이나 신상에 관한 일처리가 어려운 사람의 의사결정과 일처리를 지원함으로서 당사자의 권리를 보호하는 제도(2013년 7월 시행).

성년후견제도 판단능력이 불충분한 성년자가 손해를 받지 않게 여러 가지 권리를 지킴과 동시에 사회적으로 지원하는 일본의 제도.

세계보건기구 유엔의 전문기관의 하나로서 보건분야에 관한 국제기관.

세대(世帶) 동일한 주거로 거주하면서 생계를 같이 하는 사람의 집단.

세안 피부의 때를 없애 청결을 유지하기 위해서 얼굴을 씻는 것.

세정 씻어 내림으로서 오염물질을 깨끗이 제거해서 청결하게 하는 것.

세제 개체의 표면에 부착한 오염물질을 제거해서 청결하게 하는 것을 목적으로 이용되는 물질의 총칭.

세탁 착용 시에 부착한 의류의 때를 씻어 제거해서 의류를 다시 청결·쾌적하게 하는 것.

셀프헬프그룹 공통의 문제를 안고 있는 사람이나 그 가족에 의해 자발적으로 결성된 당사자 그룹으로서 멤버끼리 서로 도우면서 문제의 해결을 위해서 활동하는 그룹.

소규모다기능형거택개호 일본의 개호보험서비스의 하나로서 25명 이하가 이용하는 소규모 사업소가 자택에 거주하는 요개호 고령자 등에게 통소, 방문, 숙박 서비스를 제공하는 지역밀착형 서비스.

소변 혈액중의 노폐물 등이 신장에서 여과되어 추출된 수분.

소시얼워커 사회복지전문직로서의 일정한 교육·훈련을 받아 전문적 가치나 이론 및 기술을 습득하여 사회복지를 실천(소시얼워크)하는 자의 총칭.

손씻기 손가락을 비비면서 흐르는 물로 씻는 것.

손잡이 넘어지는 것을 방지하거나 이동하기 쉽고 휠체어에 타는 것을 돕기 위해서 벽 등에 붙이는 봉.

수단적 일상생활활동 자립된 사회생활을 보내기 위해 필요한 가사나 약 관리, 쇼핑, 전화사용법, 금전 관리 등의 응용적인 활동.

수면 자는 것.

수분밸런스 신체에 대한 수분공급과 손실의 대사.

수분보급 신체에서 손실된 수분을 보충하는 것.

수욕 손을 더운 물에 담그어 씻는 것.

수익사업 수익을 얻을 목적으로 실시하는 사업.

수포 표피 밑에 세포액이 고여서 생긴 물집.

수화 주로 손동작에 의해서 의사를 전하는 언어로서 청각장애인의 자립생활을 위한 중요한 커뮤니케이션 수단.

슈퍼바이저 스퍼바이지에 대해서 슈퍼비전을 실시하는 지도자.

슈퍼바이지 슈퍼바이저로부터 지도를 받는 자.

슈퍼비전 지도자의 피지도자에 대한 지도·감독에 의한 대인원조법.

스트레스 심신의 부담이 되는 자극에 의해서 생체 내부에 생기는 긴장상태.

스트레처 이동이 곤란한 사람을 눕힌 채로 이송하는 들것.

스트렝스 시점 클라이언트가 가지고 있는 힘에 초점을 맞추어 그것을 강화하고 최대한으로 발휘할 수 있도록 지원하는 것.

스피리츄얼 케어 육체적인 것만이 아니라 자기존재나 가치관을 바탕으로 한 내면으로부터 영혼의 절 규에 관련된 케어.

시각장애 장기적 또는 영속적으로 시각기능이 저하된 상태.

시각장애인 시각기능이 선천적 또는 후천적인 원인에 의해 영속적으로 기능이 저하되어 있는 자.

시력저하 시력이 저하된 상태.

시설개호 장기요양대상자 등을 대상으로 실시하는 시설서비스

시야장애 눈에 보이는 범위에 장애가 있는 상태.

시야협착 눈에 보이는 범위가 좁아지는 것.

시트교환 이용자가 쾌적하고 기분 좋게 잘 수 있은 침상이 되도록 시트를 정돈하는 기술.

식물상태 대뇌의 기능이 정지되어 일어나는 의식장애를 수반한 중증 와병생활이지만 뇌간기능이 유 지된 상태.

식물성 식품 곡류, 감자류, 야채류, 해조류, 버섯류, 열매류 등의 식물만으로 완성되는 식품.

식사 살기 위해 필요한 영양소를 섭취하기 위해서 음식을 먹는 것.

식사동작 식사와 관련된 일련의 동작.

식사보조 식사원조 참조.

식사요법 어떤 종류의 영양장애나 생리적 또는 병적상태를 시정하기 위해서 실시하는 영양치료법.

식사원조 심신의 다양한 장애에 의해서 자력으로 식사할 수 없는 사람에게 필요한 원조를 실시하는 것.

식욕 음식이나 음료를 먹고 마시고 싶다는 욕구.

식욕부진 식사시간이 되어도 식욕이 솟지 않는 것.

식중독 음식중에 포함된 세균이나 화학물질을 입을 통해 섭취함으로서 일어나는 급성 위장염 등의 총칭.

식품위생 음식물이 원인인 건강장애를 막고 건강을 유지하도록 하기 위한 대처.

신뢰관계 라포르 참조.

신상감호 판단능력이 불충분한 성년자의 일상생활을 돕는 지원.

신체기능 신체동작 등의 활동을 하기 위한 능력.

신체메커닉스 골격이나 근육, 내장을 포함한 자세나 동작 등의 역학적 상호관계를 과학적으로 생각 한 생체역학.

신체보조 자립생활이 곤란한 고령자나 장애인에게 도움을 주는 사람이 직접 신체에 접촉해서 보조 하는 것.

실금 배설기능을 조절하지 못하여 자신의 의사와는 관계없이 소변 또는 대변을 배설하는 것.

실기시험 필기시험에 합격한 사람만이 치를 수 있는 개호기술 등에 관한 전문적 기능을 시험하는 일본의 개호복지사 국가시험의 2차 시험.

실무경험증명서 실무경험을 증명하는 서류.

실수입 실질적으로 가정의 둔재산고(자산−부채)를 증가시키는 수입.

실어 뇌혈관장애나 두부외상 등에 의해 대뇌의 언어에 관련되는 부분이 손상되어 일어나는 언어장애.

실인 시각 · 청각 · 촉각 등의 기능은 유지되고 있지만 그것을 올바르게 인식할 수 없는 상태.

실지출 소비지출과 비소비지출을 합계한 지출로서 생활을 하기 위해서 지출되는 비용.

심계항진 평상시에는 의식하지 않는 심장의 맥박을 불쾌하게 느끼는 자각증상.

심기증 심신의 사소한 증상에 얽매어 의학적인 검사로는 아무 문제가 없음에도 불구하고 그것에 구 애되어 중대한 병의 징조가 아닌가하고 그것을 타인에게 집요하고 계속적으로 호소하는 상태.

심신증 그 진단이나 치료에 있어서 심리적 인자에 대한 배려가 특히 중요한 의미를 가지는 병의 용태.

심장판막증 심장의 네 개의 변 중에서 어느 하나에 장애가 일어나는 심장병.

아동기 장애 6세에서 12세까지의 아동기에 일상생활에 적응 못하는 상태.

아테토시스 완만하게 구부러지는 것 같은 불수의운동의 하나로서 규칙성이 없는 움직임이 연속해서 일어나고 있는 상태.

아테토제 아테토시스 참조.

안내서 장애인 또는 시각장애인을 유도할 경우에 이용하는 보조법의 하나.

안락 신체적, 정신적, 사회적으로 불쾌감 없이 만족하고 편한 상태.

안락한 체위 신체적으로도 정신적으로도 고통이 없는 편한 자세.

안면 기분 좋은 편안한 잠.

안면원조 기분 좋게 안면할 수 있도록 원조하는 것.

안전관리 장기요양을 하는데 있어서 장기요양대상자 등에게 피해가 없도록 안전하게 관리하는 것.

알츠하이머병 치매를 일으키는 퇴행성 뇌질환으로서 1907년에 알로이스 알츠하이머 ≪Alzheimer, A.≫ 박사에 의해 보고된 뇌내의 특유한 신경원섬유의 변화와 노인반점이 나타나는 치매.

알츠하이머형 치매 노년기의 알츠하이머병에 기인한 뇌의 변성에 의해서 발병하는 치매의 일종.

암 악성종양.

앙와위 팔을 몸에 붙이고 발을 뻗고 배와 가슴을 위로 하고 반듯이 누운 자세.

애드보커시 대변기능이나 권리옹호에 의해 이용자가 필요로 하는 사회적 자원에 대해 유연하게 대응하고 개선을 요구해 가는 것.

액와체온 겨드랑이 밑의 체온.

액티버티 「활동」이라는 의미.

야간섬망 환각이나 망상 등을 동반하는 의식혼탁에 의한 혼란상태.

약물요법 약제를 이용해서 병의 증상 등을 억제하는 것.

약제 생물학적 작용을 필요로 하는 약을 조제하는 것.

약제관리 약을 적절히 복용을 할 수 있도록 약을 보관하고 복약을 지도하는 것.

약제사 조제, 의약품의 공급, 그 외 약사위생을 주관하는 국가자격을 지닌 전문직.

양호노인홈 일본의 노인복지에 있어서 환경상의 이유 및 경제적 이유에 의해 자택에서 양호를 받는 것이 곤란한 65세 이상의 노인을 입소시켜서 양호함과 동시에 그 외의 원조를 실시하는 것을 목적으로 하는 시설 (노인복지법 제11조).

어세스먼트 관찰이나 정보 수집을 통해서 입수한 이용자의 상황을 분석해, 이용자의 욕구와 그것을 저해하는 요인을 명확히 해서 평가하는 것.

억제 신체구속이라고도 하는데 추락하거나 넘어지는 것을 방지하고 링겔이나 경관영양의 관을 뽑는 것을 막기 위해서 강제적으로 행동을 제한하는 행위.

언어장애 이야기하고 듣고 이해하고 쓰고 읽는 언어능력에 장애가 생긴 상태.

언어청각사 언어장애나 청각장애 때문에 커뮤니케이션이 어려워진 사람에 대해 재활을 실시하는 전문직.

에어매트 욕창이 발생되기 쉬운 압박부위의 압력을 덜어주기 위해서 사용되는 공기매트.

에어패드 체위변환 등에 사용하는 것으로서 펌프로 공기를 보냄으로써 돌려 눕힐 수 있는 것.

에이즈 후천성면역부전증후군 참조.

에이지즘 의식 속에 잠재하는 노인에 대한 차별의식.

엥겔계수 가계의 총소비지출액에서 식료품비가 차지하는 비율.

연금 본인이나 유족에게 지급함으로서 소득을 보장하고 생애에 걸쳐서 지급되는 생활지원 보험금.

연하 음식물을 구강에서 음식덩어리로 만들어서 그 음식덩어리 및 구인강의 분비물을 인두와 식도를 통해서 위까지 보내는 과정.

연하곤란 연하장애 때문에 구강중의 음식물을 삼킬 수 없는 상태.

연하보조제 오연방지를 위해서 음식물이 목구멍에 잘 넘어가도록 하거나 음식물이 덩어리로 잘 만들어지게 하기 위해서 더하는 보조제.

연하성 폐렴 음식조각, 위내용물 또는 토한 것이 기관지에 들어감으로서 일어나는 기관지폐렴.

염색체이상 염색체의 수와 구조에 이상이 일어나는 것.

영양 생물의 생명활동 중에서 체외로부터 섭취하는 단백질이나 지방질, 탄수화물, 미네랄, 비타민 등.

영양개선[*] 일본의 개호보험제도에 있어서의 장기요양 예방급여에 의한 선택적 서비스의 하나로서 저영양상태를 예방・개선하기 위한 영양교육.

영양관리 식생활과 관련된 개인 또는 집단의 영양상태관리의 총칭.

영양권장량 대부분(약 98%)의 집단에 있어서 충분한 영양소량.

영양사 식품위생법 제30조에 규정된 전문직으로서 보건복지부 장관으로부터 면허를 받아 국민의 질병예방과 건강증진을 위해 급식관리 및 영양서비스를 수행하는 자.

영양사[*] 일본의 영양사법 제1조에 규정된 전문직으로서「도도부현 지사로부터 면허를 받아 영양사의 명칭을 사용하여 영양지도에 종사하는 것을 직업으로 하는 자.

영양소 음식물로부터 섭취되어 생체가 생명을 유지하고 성장 및 발육하기 위해서 필요한 물질.

예방급여[*] 일본의 개호보험제도에 있어서 요개호인정의 결과, 피보험자가 요지원 1 또는 2로 인정된 요지원자에 대한 급여.

오연 물이나 음식물 등이 잘못해서 식도가 아니라 기도에 들어가 버리는 것.

오연성 폐렴 연하성 폐렴 참조.

와상 일상생활에 있어 어떠한 도움을 필요로 하는 장기요양 상태.

와상도 장애노인의 일상생활자립도 판정기준의 약칭.

와위 옆으로 누운 자세.

완화케어 종말기를 맞이한 환자에 대해서 치료 중심의 의학적인 대응만이 아니라 정신적인 원조를 중심으로 하는 방법을 도입한 케어.

요강 화장실에 이동이 곤란한 경우에 소변을 담기 위한 용기.

요개호[*] 일본의 개호보험제도에 있어서 피보험자가 시정촌의 개호인정심사회에서 요개호 상태로 인정되는 것.

요개호도[*] 일본의 개호보험제도에 있어서의 요지원 상태와 요개호 상태의 구분.

요개호인정[*] 일본의 개호보험제도에 있어서 요개호 상태에 있는지 아닌지를 전국일률의 기준에 의거해 공평하고 객관적으로 인정하는 것.

요개호자[*] 일본의 개호보험법에 의하면 요개호 상태에 해당하는 자.

요로감염 소변이 신장에서 만들어져서 요관을 지나 방광에 머물러 있다가 요도로부터 배출될 때까지의 요로에서 발생하는 감염병.

요실금 본인의 의사와 관계없이 소변이 나와 버리는 것.

요양보호사 치매·중풍 등 노인성 질환으로 독립적인 일상생활을 수행하기 어려운 노인들을 위해 노인요양 및 재가시설에서 신체 및 가사 지원 서비스를 제공하는 자.

요원호노인 일상생활을 영위하는데 지장이 있어 원조, 보호, 장기요양 등이 필요한 노인.

요의 방광 내에 소변이 꽉 차 있을 때에 대뇌에 일어나는 감각.

요지원＊ 일본의 개호보험제도에 있어서 피보험자가 시정촌의 개호인정심사회에서 요지원 상태로 인정되는 것.

요지원인정＊ 일본의 개호보험제도에 있어서 요지원 상태에 있는지 아닌지를 전국일률의 기준에 의거해 공평하고 객관적으로 인정하는 것.

요지원자＊ 일본의 개호보험법에 의하면 요지원 상태에 해당하는 자.

요통 허리부분과 그 주변에 다양한 동통을 수반하는 통증.

요통예방 요통을 일으키지 않게 예방하는 것.

요통체조 요통에 대한 치료 또는 요통을 예방하기 위한 체조.

욕구 필요, 니즈, 요구 등.

욕조 목욕할 때 사용하는 목욕통.

욕창 신체의 일부분에 장시간 압력이 가해져서 혈액이 차단되어 피부에 발적이나 궤양, 괴사 등이 생긴 상태.

욕창예방 욕창이 생기는 원인을 줄이고 발생이나 진행을 예방하는 것.

우울증 주로 기분장애를 수반하는 정신병으로서 기분이 침체하는 억울 상태가 장기간 계속 되어 다양한 심신증상이 나타나는 정신장애.

운동기 기능향상＊ 일본의 개호보험제도에 있어서의 장기요양 예방급여에 의한 선택적 서비스의 하나로서 개호예방을 위해서 실시하는 운동훈련.

운동실조 근육의 상호협조가 유지되지 않아 운동에 장애를 받고 있는 상태.

운동요법 운동장애나 운동부족 등을 완화하기 위해서 체조·운동을 실시하는 치료법.

운동장애 운동기에 관련된 신체기능의 장애에 의해 발생하는 장애로서 자기가 맘먹은 대로 신체를 움직일 수 없는 상태.

운영적정화위원회＊ 일본의 개호보험제도에 있어서 복지서비스 이용에 따른 불평이 발생했을 경우에 그것을 해결하는 기관.

원좌 도너츠형의 둥근 깔개.

위기경로 필요한 치료나 검사, 간호 등의 내용을 입원 후의 시간경과와 더불어 제시하는 치료 예정표.

위축 정상적인 크기로 발육한 기관이나 조직이 부상이나 병 등에 의해서 축소되는 것.

위험방지 장기요양대상자 등을 원조할 시에 위험이 발생하거나 사고가 안 나도록 궁리하는 것.

유니버설패션 연령, 체형, 사이즈, 장애에 구애되지 않고 모든 생활자에게 기능적이고 멋있는 패션상품을 추천하고 제공하려고 하는 것.

유니트케어＊ 일본의 노인복지실천에 있어서 장기케어시설 등에 입소해 있는 요개호자 등을 케어 할 때에 적은 인원을 그룹으로 나누어 케어 하는 것.

유동성 지능 새로운 것을 학습하거나 기억하거나 하는 경험의 영향을 거의 안 받는 지능.

유동식 구강 내에서 빨리 유동체가 되어 소화되기 쉽고 찌꺼기가 없고 자극이 적은 음식.

유료양로원 식사 등의 제공 그 외 일상생활상 필요한 편의를 제공하는 것을 목적으로 하는 시설이며 노인복지시설이 아닌 것.

유족기초연금 국민연금보험 또는 노령기초연금의 가입자가 사망했을 시에 그 사망자의 유족에게 지급되는 기초적인 연금.

유지기 재활 급성기에서 회복기를 경과한 후에 기능이나 능력을 유지하기 위해서 계속적으로 실시하는 재활.

유치카테터 소변을 배설시키는 것을 목적으로 요도로부터 방광 내에 설치하는 카테터.

음부닦기 음부를 닦아서 청결하게 하는 것.

음부세정 음부를 씻어서 청결하게 하는 것.

응급수단 응급처치를 하기까지 해 두는 수단.

응능부담 서비스 이용자의 소득 상황을 파악해서 그 소득 상황에 따라 지불 상황을 판단해 필요한 부담액을 결정하는 방식.

응익부담 서비스 이용자의 소득 상황을 고려하지 않고 일률적으로 서비스 이용 상황에 따라 비용부담을 결정하는 방식.

의료보험제도 질병, 부상, 사망 또는 분만 등의 의료행위에 대해서 보험자가 보험급여를 실시하는 제도.

의료소시얼워커 병원이나 진료소 등에서 환자나 가족이 안고 있는 생활상의 문제 등에 대해서 상담원조를 하는 보건의료분야의 소시얼워커.

의류장애 의복에 의해서 신체에 장애를 일으킨 상태.

의복 몸 전체를 감싸는 것.

의복 갈아입기 의복을 입거나 벗거나 하는 것.

의사소견서 장기요양보험제도에 있어서 요양등급판정에 이용되는 의사의 소견서.

의식장애 정신활동이 저해되고 그 기능저하가 인정되는 상태로서 사물을 올바르게 이해할 수 없는 상태.

의지장비사 일본의 의지장비사법(1987년)에 의해 국가자격화 된 전문직.

의치 부러지거나 빠진 이를 대신하는 인공적인 의치.

이뇨제 신장의 기능 단위인 네프론의 세뇨관이나 집합관에 작용해서 체내의 나트륨 수분의 배설인 이뇨를 촉진시키는 약.

이동 신체의 중심을 옮김으로서 그 위치가 변화하는 것.

이동개호 장기요양대상자 등이 혼자서 이동이 곤란한 경우에 요양보호사가 도움을 주거나 복지용구 등을 이용해 이동시키는 것.

이동관련복지용구 고령자나 장애인 등이 이동이 곤란한 경우에 그 능력저하를 경감시키기 위해서 이용하는 복지용구.

이동변기 이동 가능한 휴대용 변기.

이동욕조 체력저하나 와병생활 등에 의해서 욕조까지 이동이 곤란한 장기요양대상자 등을 목욕시키기 위해 이동시킬 수 있는 욕조.

이발 성장한 머리카락을 자르고 손질하는 것.

이송비 의사의 지시에 의해서 긴급입원 등이 필요한 환자를 이송했을 시에 그 교통비가 나중에 의료보험으로부터 지급되는 비용.

이승동작 이용자가 대상물에서 다른 대상물로 갈아타는 동작.

이완 근긴장이 저하된 상태로서 근육에 발생하는 장력이 느슨해지는 상태.

이용료 장기요양서비스의 이용자가 부담하는 비용.

이학요법사 의사의 지시 하에 이학요법을 실시하는 일본의 전문직.

인공호흡 스스로 호흡할 수 없는 사람에 대해, 긴급적으로 대상자의 기도를 확보해서 인공적으로 호흡을 보조하는 것.

인슐린 랑겔한스섬 β 세포로부터 분비되는 혈당을 저하시키는 호르몬.

인지증 뇌의 다양한 기질적 질환 때문에 생긴 후천성의 회복 불가능한 지능의 결손상태.

인지증고령자 인지증을 발병한 고령자.

인지증고령자의 일상생활자립도 일본의 후생성이 1993년에 정한 인지증고령자의 일상생활자립도를 결정할 때의 판정 기준.

인지증대응형공동생활개호° 일본의 개호보험제도에 있어서 인지증이 있는 요개호자에게 개호서비스를 제공하는 지역밀착형 서비스.

인지증대응형통소개호° 일본의 개호보험제도에 있어서 인지증이 있는 요개호자에게 통소개호로 개호서비스를 제공하는 지역밀착형 서비스.

인테이크 케이스워크 과정에 있어서 최초의 면접 단계.

인포멀 「비공식」형태에 사로잡히지 않음.「평상복차림」 등의 의미.

일내변동 생체내의 기능이 주기적으로 변동하는 생체리듬에 있어서의 24시간의 주기.

일상생활활동 한 인간이 살기 위해서 행하는 기본적이고 공통적인 매일 반복되는 신체활동.

일어나기 자고 있는 상태(와위)에서 앉은 상태(좌위)가 될 때까지의 동작.

일어서기 앉은 자세에서 선 자세를 취할 때까지의 자세전환동작.

임파워먼트 본래 가지고 있는 능력을 충분히 발휘할 수 없는 상태에 있는 개인이나 그룹에 대해, 자신의 힘을 자각하고 자기결정능력을 높일 수 있도록 지원해서 자기가 안고 있는 문제를 스스로 해결하려고 하는 힘을 가질 수 있도록 원조하는 과정.

임페어먼트 기능장애 참조.

입면 피로를 풀고 에너지를 축적하기 위해서 잠에 들어가는 것.

입위 서있는 자세.

자기각지 원조자가 자신의 가치관이나 판단기준, 감정, 행동경향 등에 대해서 자기이해하는 것.

자기건강관리 기본적으로는 자기스스로 자신의 건강상태의 유지, 생명의 안전, 자립을 위해 대처하는 것.

자기결정 개인이 생활해 가는데 있어서 자기책임 하에 자기가 선택해서 결정하는 것.

자기실현 개인이 자신의 생활이나 인생에 대하여 스스로가 목표로 하는 삶의 방법을 실현하는 것.

자동운동 자신의 의지와 힘으로 움직이고 싶은 신체부위를 움직이는 것.

자립 스스로 다른 사람에게 의존하지 않는 것.

자립도 일상생활에 있어서 어느 정도 자립해 있는지를 판정하는 척도

자립지원 자립과정에 있어서 그 권리를 충분히 발휘할 수 없는 개인에 대해서 실시하는 원조자의 지원.

자상행위 자기의 육체의 일부를 손상하는 행위.

자외선차폐소재 자외선을 흡수 또는 확산하는 물질을 첨가해 차폐율을 향상시킨 소재

자원봉사 현대사회의 다양한 문제를 해결·예방하기 위해서 자유의지에 의해서 타인을 돕거나 금품을 제공하는 것.

자조도구 어떠한 신체장애 등을 가지고 있는 사람이 일상생활을 할 수 있도록 궁리해서 이용하는 도구의 총칭.

자존심 자기 자신에 대한 자부심 또는 자신의 존엄을 의식하는 것에 의해서 자신의 품위를 유지하려고 하는 심리 또는 태도

자폐증 뇌기능의 발달지연 등에 의한 장애로서 범용성 발달장애로부터 정의된 증후군.

작업요법 신체 또는 정신에 장애가 있는 사람이 자발적으로 생활할 수 있도록 하기 위해서 실시하는 재활의 일종.

작업요법사 일본의 이학요법사 및 작업요법사법(1965년)에 의하면,「신체 또는 정신에 장애가 있는 사람에 대해서 주로 그 응용적 동작 능력 또는 사회적응능력의 회복을 도모하기 위해, 수예, 공작, 그 외의 작업을 실시하게 하는 것」을 의사의 지시에 따라 실시하는 전문직.

잔존능력(잔존기능) 심신에 있는 전 기능 중에 장애를 받은 기능 이외에 남겨진 기능.

장구 체간의 기능장애의 경감 등을 목적으로 사용하는 보조도구.

장기요양급여 노인장기요양보험제도에 있어서 장기요양등급판정 결과, 요양등급(1~3) 자로 인정된 장기요양대상자에 대한 급여.

장기요양급여비용 장기요양기관이 장기요양급여를 제공했을 경우, 그 대가로서 노인장기요양보험으로부터 사업자에게 지불되는 비용.

장기요양보험 치매나 와병생활 등에 의해서 장기요양대상자가 되었을 때에 필요한 장기요양급여를 제공하고 그 비용을 보장하기 위한 사회보험.

장수사회 건강을 유지하면서 즐기면서 적극적으로 사는 긍정적인 고령자상을 희구하려는 것을 배경으로 한 사회.

장애 질병이나 사고 등에 의해 지적, 정신적, 청각, 시각 등에 결함이 생겨서 정상적인 생활이 곤란하거나 불가능한 상태.

장애* 일본의 장애자기본법의 정의에 의하면, 「계속적으로 일상생활 또는 사회생활에 상당한 제한을 받는다」는 것.

장애기초연금* 일본의 국민연금보험(기초연금)에 가입중인 사람 또는 국민연금보험에 가입하고 있던 60세 이상 65세 미만인 사람이 병이나 사고로 일정한 장애를 입었을 경우에 지급되는 연금.

장애의 수용 자기의 신체장애를 객관적이고 현실적으로 인정해서 받아들이는 것.

장폐쇄 장이 막혀서 내용물이 통과할 수 없게 되는 상태.

재가간호 간호사 등이 집에서 요양하는 환자에게 제공하는 서비스.

재가개호* 가정이나 그 사람이 정든 곳에서 생활의 질을 유지하면서 생활을 계속할 수 있도록 보건·의료·복지 분야로부터 지원하는 서비스.

재가케어 재가장기요양 참조.

재평가 서비스가 계획대로 제공되고 있는지를 확인하고 새로운 과제에 대해서 계획을 세우기 위한 평가.

재활 어떠한 장애에 의해서 한 번 없어진 기능을 회복시키는 것.

재활개호* 장기요양을 필요로 하는 사람들에 대한 재활이념에 근거한 장기요양의 실천.

재활의학 질환에 수반되는 장애에 대해서 심신의 기능유지나 향상을 목표로 하는 의료분야의 재활.

저작 소화의 제1단계로서 구강에 들어온 음식물을 치아로 씹어서 잘게 잘라서 침과 혼합하여 인두에 보내기 쉽게 하는 것.

저출산고령화 출생률이 낮아서 해마다 아동이 감소하는 한편 고령자는 해마다 증가하는 상태.

저출산화 한 사회에 있어서 자녀수의 비율이 지속적으로 저하되는 것.

저혈당 혈액중의 포도당량이 정상보다 저하된 상태.

저혈압 혈압이 정상보다 저하하여 박출량이 저하된 상태.

적변 대변이 딱딱해서 직장 하부에 차 있을 때에 손가락 끝으로 대변을 긁어내는 것.

전도성 난청 고막에서 중이까지의 사이에서 소리가 진동해서 전해지는 부분에 장애가 발생해서 일어나는 난청.

전동침대 리모트 콘트롤(리모콘)에 의해 전기로 높이를 조절하거나 체위를 변환시키는 조절 기능이 달린 침대.

전동휠체어 전동모터로 구동하는 휠체어.

전면원조 중증 심신장애 때문에 전면적인 보조를 필요로 하는 상태.

전신세정 전신을 닦아서 깨끗이 함.

전신욕 목에서부터 아래의 전신을 욕조에 담그는 목욕 방법.

전인격적 케어 모든 욕구를 파악해서 종합적으로 케어를 제공하는 것.

점자 손가락 끝의 촉각만으로 읽을 수 있는 특수한 촉독문자.

정맥영양법 정맥혈관내에 영양소를 직접 투여하는 방법.

정신과소시얼워커 정신장애인과 그 가족이 갖고 있는 문제에 대한 상담 원조자.

정신보건복지사* 1997년에 제정된 정신보건복지 영역의 소시얼워커의 일본의 국가자격.

정신보건사회복지사 의료기관, 사회복지시설, 정신보건센터 등에서 환자의 치료, 재활과 사회복귀를 돕기 위해 사정, 진단, 상담, 프로그램 개발, 기획, 실시, 평가, 지원, 교육 등의 업무를 수행하는 자.

정신장애 정신질환의 총체로서 정신상태의 편향이나 이상을 총칭한 것.

정신장애자 정신의 장애로 사물을 변별할 능력이나 의사를 결정할 능력이 없는 자 또는 그 능력이

미약한 자.

정신장애자 일본의 정신보건 및 정신장애자복지에 관한 법률(제5조)에 의하면, 통합실조증, 정신 작용 물질에 의한 급성중독 또는 그 의존증, 지적장애, 정신질환을 가진 자.

정용 얼굴을 씻거나 이를 닦거나 머리카락을 솔질하거나 수염을 깎는 등의 몸가짐.

제압 신체의 일부를 극단적으로 압박하는 것을 경감하는 것.

조기발견 자각증상이 없을 때에 병이나 장애를 발견하는 것.

조리 생야채나 날고기 등의 식품 소재를 가열하거나 가열하지 않고 음식으로 만드는 것.

조리방법 영양이 있도록 식품 재료를 요리하는 방법.

조울증 기분이 들뜨는 조증과 기분이 가라앉는 우울증이 반복되어 나타나는 정신병.

조정교부금 일본의 모든 시정촌이 개호서비스를 원활히 안정적으로 제공할 수 있도록 정부로부터 교부되는 재원.

조치비용 조치제도에 근거한 복지서비스 제공에 드는 비용.

조치제도 법률 등에 의거해서 판단을 내려 처분하는 제도.

족욕 발의 일부를 더운 물에 담그어 씻는 것.

종말기 사람의 생애에 있어서의 임종이 확실히 가까워진 시기.

종말기케어 인생의 종말기를 맞이한 사람에 대한 케어.

종속인구 부양자인 생산연령인구에 의해서 부양되는 사람들.

종이기저귀 흡수성이 높은 종이를 층층이 겹친 기저귀.

좌위 상반신을 90도 또는 그에 가까운 상태로 일으킨 자세로서 팔을 몸에 붙이고 늘어뜨려 둔부와 대퇴후면을 지지면으로 해서 체중을 지탱하는 자세.

주·야간보호 수급자를 하루 중 일정한 시간 동안 장기요양기관에 보호하여 신체활동 지원 및 심신 기능의 유지·향상을 위한 교육·훈련 등을 제공하는 장기요양급여.

주치의 자기가 담당하는 환자를 책임지고 의료를 실시하는 의사.

주치의 의견서 개호보험제도를 이용하기 위한 요지원 또는 요개호 인정의 판정에 이용되는 주치의 의 의견서.

주택개량 일상생활의 자립과 사고방지, 장기요양의 부담을 경감하기 위해 장애나 가령에 맞추어서 주택을 개량하는 것.

중복장애 장애가 중복되어 있는 상태, 즉 하나의 장애는 아니라 두 종류 이상의 장애를 갖고 있는 상태.

지능 지능의 정의는 다양한데, 단지 기억 또는 학습한 지식과 경험을 응용하는 것이 아니라 자신에 게 있어서의 새로운 과제나 사태를 해결하는 능력.

지능지수 지능의 정도를 정신연령과 생활연령 비율의 지수로 나타낸 지능검사결과에 근거하는 지표.

지방질이상증 혈액중의 콜레스테롤이나 중성지방이 이상치를 나타내는 것.

지역밀착서비스 요개호 상태가 되어도 정든 곳에서 생활을 계속할 수 있도록 하기위해 2005년의 개 호보험법개정에 의해서 창설된 일본의 개호보험서비스.

지역포괄지원센터 일본의 개호보험제도에 있어서의 지역지원사업 중의 하나로서 포괄적 지원사업을 실시하는 기관.

지적장애 지적기능의 장애가 발달기에 나타나 일상생활에 지장이 생겨 어떠한 특별한 원조를 필요 로 하는 상태.

지적장애인 지적장애가 있는 자.

지주막하출혈 뇌에서 출혈한 혈액이 뇌의 지주막 아래 공간에 혼입되는 것.

지체부자유 뼈·관절계·신경계·근계, 혈관계, 운동제어에 관련된 중추신경계 등의 운동기의 기능 장애에 의해서 생기는 신체운동능력의 저하에 의한 장애.

지팡이 막대에 잡는 부분을 단 보행을 보조하는 복지용구.

지팡이 T자 보행을 보조하는 지팡이의 하나로서 손잡이가 T자형인 지팡이.

지팡이 보행 지팡이를 짚고 걷는 것.

지혈 출혈을 멈추게 하는 것.

직업적 재활 정신·신체장애인이 가지고 있는 능력을 발휘할 수 있는 직업을 가질 수 있도록 원조하고 그것을 계속할 수 있도록 직업훈련이나 직업지도 등을 실시하는 재활.

직접원조기술 사람과 사람의 관계에 의한 직접적인 대인관계를 기반으로 한 원조의 방법.

진전 신체의 일부 또는 전신의 규칙적인 불수의운동.

찜질 냉수·온수, 약제 등을 신체의 일부분에 대어서 염증이나 통증을 완화하는 것.

ㅈ

착탈의 의복을 입거나 벗거나 하는 행위.

척수손상 척수가 손상을 받은 상태.

척추압박골절 척추가 압력을 받아서 부러지는 골절.

첨족 족관절이 저측굴곡위에 구축되어 발꿈치가 땅에 닿지 않는 발.

청각장애 듣는데 지장이 있는 장애.

청결 위생적으로 깨끗하게 유지하는 것.

청력레벨 들을 수 있는 능력인 청력의 정도를 나타내는 척도

청소 쓸고 닦아서 먼지나 쓰레기를 없애는 것.

체온 신체의 각 부위에 있어서 보지되는 온도.

체온측정 신체의 생리적 변화를 관찰하는 방법의 하나로서 체온을 측정하는 것.

체위변환 신체자세의 방향을 바꾸는 것.

체인스토크스 호흡 호흡의 변화가 주기적으로 일어나는 생명의 위기를 초래하는 이상 호흡.

초로기 치매 40세 이상 64세 이하의 연령대에 발병하는 뇌의 변성에 의해서 생기는 치매.

총의치 이가 빠지거나 부러져서 하나도 없는 경우에 이 대신에 넣는 인공적 치아.

추천량 집단의 대부분(약 98%)에 있어서 충분한 영양소량.

축뇨장애 소변을 저장해두는 기능에 장애가 생긴 상태.

출혈 혈관이 손상되어 혈액이 혈관 밖으로 유출되는 것.

측와위 옆으로 누워 다리를 뻗은 자세.

치과위생사 치과의사의 지도 하에 치석제거, 충치예방을 위한 약물도포, 치약지도 등을 실시해, 치과 진료 보조를 하는 국가자격의 전문직.

치매 뇌의 다양한 기질적 질환 때문에 생긴 후천성의 회복 불가능한 지능의 결손상태.

치매노인 치매를 발병한 노인.

치매노인 일상생활자립도 인지증고령자 일상생활자립도 참조

치아노제 저산소혈증에 의해 피부 및 점막이 파랗게 된 상태.

침구정리 이용자가 쾌적하고 기분 좋게 잘 수 있는 침대를 만들기 위한 침대상의 정리.

침대 자거나 눕기 위한 침대.

침대에서 휠체어로 장기요양대상자등이 침대에서 휠체어로 이동할 때의 동작.

침상 자기 위해서 이용하는 이불이나 베개, 잠옷 등.

커뮤니케이션 지각, 감정, 사고 등을 표출해, 몸짓, 기호, 언어 등을 구사해서 그 내용을 전달하는 행위.

커뮤니케이션 에이드 발성·발어가 곤란한 경우에 의사전달의 보조·대체수단으로서 이용하는 기기나 용구.

케어 일반적으로 마음 써 주는 것, 그 사람이 바라도록 돕는 것.

케어매니지먼트 이용자가 갖고 있는 사회생활상의 여러 가지 욕구의 해결이나 충족을 위해서 적절한 사회자원을 연락·조정하는 방법.

케어매니저 개호지원전문원 참조

케어워크 케어에 근거한 대인원조서비스이며 그 기술을 의미함.

케어컨퍼런스 이용자에 대한 원조과정에서 적절한 케어를 실시하기 위해서 케어업무에 종사하는 사람이 모여서 토론하는 회의.

케어팀 이용자의 자립지원을 위해서 다양한 멤버로 구성하는 팀.

케어플랜 지원을 필요로 하는 사람에 대한 서비스 공급시스템 계획.

케어하우스 노인시설의 일종으로 자유로운 환경에서의 자립생활을 지원하는 공동주택.

케이스워크 이용자와 원조자와의 직접적 또는 개별적인 대인간 관계를 통한 원조기술.

케이스컨퍼런스 사례를 검토하기 위한 회의나 검토회의.

콜레스테롤 세포막, 담즙산, 각종 호르몬 등의 원재료가 되는 지방질의 일종.

클락포지션 물건의 배치 등을 시계의 문자판에 가정한 위치.

ㅋ

ㅌ

타동운동 타인의 힘이나 기구의 힘을 빌려서 몸을 움직이는 운동.

탈구 어떠한 외적 인자 등에 의해 관절면 상호의 위치관계가 없어져 있는 상태.

탈수증 신체의 체액, 특히 세포외액이 없어진 상태.

탈진증후군 극도의 심신피로와 감정의 고갈이 나타나는 증후군.

토혈 소화관계, 특히 식도나 위로부터 출혈한 혈액을 토출하거나 토출된 것이 혈액에 혼입되는 상태.

통소개호 송영을 하는 주간개호로서 데이서비스라 불리는 일본의 개호보험제도에 있어서의 거택개호서비스의 하나.

통소재활 주간재활개호로서 데이케어라 불리는 일본의 개호보험제도에 있어서의 거택개호서비스의 하나.

통합실조증 생활환경으로부터 들어오는 정보를 잘 종합할 수 없는 인지장애, 환각이나 망상 등이 나타나 대인접촉 장애를 초래하는 정신병.

퇴행 정신·생리적 기능 또는 상태가 미발달·미분화된 시점까지 퇴보해 버리는 것.

투석 의료행위의 하나로서 신부전 환자의 혈액중의 노폐물이나 불필요한 수분을 인공적으로 여과해서 혈액을 깨끗하게 하는 것.

특별양호노인홈 신체상 또는 정신상에 현저한 장애가 있어 상시 개호를 필요로 하는 65세 이상의 고령자가 집에서 개호서비스를 받기 어려워졌을 때에 입소하는 일본의 개호보험시설.

특별치료식 병 치료를 목적으로 특정의 병에 대해 환자 개개인의 상황에 따라 영양소를 제한한 식사.

특수욕조 일반적인 욕조에서는 목욕이 곤란한 이용자가 목욕할 수 있도록 개발된 특수한 욕조.

특수침대 특수한 기능을 갖춘 침대.

팀어프로치 다양한 직종이 팀을 편성해서 이용자에게 접근하는 것.

팀케어 보건·의료·복지 등의 전문직이 제휴·협동하여 이용자의 케어를 하는 것.

파울러씨 체위 침대에서 상반신을 약 45도 일으킨 체위.

파킨슨병 떨림, 경직, 운동완만의 3대 징후가 나타나는 불수의운동을 수반하는 중추신경질환.

팔로우업 일본의 개호보험제도에 있어서 입안한 개호서비스계획(케어플랜)에 근거한 개호서비스가 이용자 및 그 가족과 함께 설정한 목표를 향해 적절히 제공되고 있는가를 평가하고 확인하는 것.

페이스시트 이용자의 이름, 성별, 연령, 직업, 학력 등의 속성에 관한 정보가 기재되어 있는 용지.

편마비 장애를 입은 대뇌반구쪽과는 반대쪽의 상하지에 운동마비가 생기는 상태.

평균수명 사망하는 정도가 장래에도 변하지 않는다고 가정했을 경우에 총계적으로 계산되는 영세아의 평균여명.

평균여명 각 연령의 개인이 평균적으로 앞으로 몇 년 살 수 있을지를 나타낸 지표의 하나.

폐기종 폐가 과다하게 팽창해서 호흡을 충분히 하지 못해 폐에 공기가 쌓여버리는 만성질환.

폐렴 병원균 등 다양한 원인에 의해서 일어나는 폐의 염증의 총칭.

폐암 폐에 생긴 표피성의 악성종양.

폐용위축 폐용증후군의 한 증상으로서 신체의 저활동에 의해서 생기는 뼈와 근육의 위축.

폐용증후군 신체의 비활동에 의해서 발생하는 신체기능의 저하.

포지셔닝 안정되고 편안함을 얻을 수 있는 자세 또는 위치설정.

포터블욕조 거실 등에서 목욕을 쉽게 실시할 수 있는 휴대용 간이욕조.

포터블화장실 운반을 할 수 있는 실내용 의자변기.

프라이머리케어 한 개인이나 가족을 최초로 진료하는 초기진료 또는 기초진료라는 의미인데, 의사가 초진환자의 질병을 정확하게 파악하여 적절한 지시를 내리고 긴급처방을 실시한 다음 다른 전문의에게 환자의 진료를 위탁하거나 혹은 환자의 지속적인 건강진단과 만성질환의 계속적인 치료를 담당하는 주치의로서의 역할을 수행하는 것.

프라이머리케어 일본의 후생노동성에 의하면, 「개인이나 가정이 최초로 접하는 보건의료시스템이며, 의사는 초기 환자의 문제를 정확하게 파악해서 적절하게 지시하고 긴급히 필요한 처치를 하거나 다른 의사를 소개해서 개인이나 가정의 계속적인 건강유지, 만성 질환의 계속적인 치료나 재활에 대해서 이른바 주치의로서의 역할을 완수하는 것」이라고 정의되고 있음.

프라이버시 다른 사람과 구별된 자신만의 영역이며 사적인 일 또는 사적비밀이라는 의미.

프로필 간단한 인물소개.

피보험자 보험제도에 있어서 보험금을 지불하여 급여를 받을 권리를 가지고 있는 자.

피해망상 자신이 다른 사람으로부터 피해를 받고 있다는 근거 없는 생각.

필기시험 필기로 행해지는 일본의 개호복지사 국가시험.

ㅍ

하세가와 치매척도개정판 치매의 스크리닝용으로서 1974년에 하세가와 가즈오 등에 의해서 개발된 대표적인 노인용 지능평가척도.
하혈 항문에서 배출되는 혈액.
학대 부당하고 부적절하게 대응하는 행위로서 비참한 대우를 하거나 잔혹한 행위를 하는 것.
합계특수출생률 여성 한명이 평생 동안 낳을 수 있는 평균 자녀수.
합병증 하나의 병이 일어남으로서 다른 병도 동시에 발생하는 것.
항균·방취소재 섬유제품에 항균제를 첨가해 세균의 증가를 억제하고 악취 발생을 막는 항균 방취 가공된 소재.
항생물질 미생물에 의해서 만들어져 미생물이나 그 외의 생활세포의 발육 등을 저해하는 물질.
핵가족 부부와 그 미혼의 자녀로 구성되는 가족의 기초단위.
허약 체력이 없고 심신이 쇠약한 것.
혈압 혈류에 의해서 혈관 벽에 미치는 내압.
호르몬 내분비선에서 혈액이나 림프액 중에 직접 분비되는 미량물질.
호흡 밖으로부터 산소를 도입해 체내에서 배출된 이산화탄소를 배설하는 기능.
호흡기능장애 호흡기의 병에 의해서 발생하는 장애로서 산소와 이산화탄소를 교환하는 기능에 일어나는 장애.
홈헬퍼 일본의 개호보험제도에 있어서 요지원 또는 요개호 고령자, 장애인, 난치병 환자 등의 자택에 방문해 배설·입욕·식사 등에 관한 신체개호나 쇼핑·조리·세탁·청소 등의 생활원조, 일상생활 전반에 걸친 상담 조언 등의 서비스를 제공하는 자.
화상 고열의 액체, 기체, 고체 등에 의해서 일어나는 피부 및 점막의 화상.
환각 현실에는 존재하지 않는 것이 마치 존재하는 것 같이 지각되는 것.
환경정비 안전하고 쾌적한 생활공간을 만드는 것.
환기 생활공간에 있어서의 공기교체.
회복기 재활 발병 직후인 급성기 이후의 약 반년 정도의 재활.
회상법 과거의 경험에 대해서 되돌아보며 그것을 다른 사람에게 말하거나 평가하거나 하는 심리적 원조의 한 방법.
후기고령자 일본의 노년인구 구분 시의 75세 이상의 노인.
후천성면역부전증후군 자기조직 이외를 배제하는 면역기능이 부전증상을 일으키는 바이러스에 감염되어 일어나는 증후군의 약칭.
휠체어 이동에 이용되는 바퀴가 달린 의자.
휠체어보조 이용자가 휠체어로 이동하거나 이승할 때에 도움을 주는 것.
휠체어에서 침대로 이용자가 휠체어에서 침대로 이승하는 것.
휠체어이동 휠체어를 이용해서 목적지에 가는 것.
흰 지팡이 시각장애인 등이 장애물 등을 탐색하기 위해 또는 장애인인 것을 다른 사람에게 알려 안전하게 보행하기 위해서 사용하는 지팡이.

PART 4

GLOSSARY OF
ENGLISH
TERMS

영어
용어
해설

A

abdominal respiration Breathing that occurs primarily by moving the diaphragm up or down.

ability-to-pay principle A method to decide the necessary amount of money that should be paid according to an individual's level of income or wealth.

abuse A term used to describe improper or inappropriate acts/treatment toward a person.

acceptance of disability Realizing and accepting one's own physical disorder objectively and realistically.

acquired immune deficiency syndrome : AIDS A term used for an infectious disease caused by the human immunodeficiency virus (HIV) that progressively reduces the effectiveness of the immune system.

active listening A communication skill that requires the listener to listen to the emotional undertone of what a person is saying and comprehend, interpret and evaluate what the listener hears.

active movement The movements of intended parts of the body with one's own will and strength.

activities of daily living : ADL The basic activities of everyday life that individuals perform such as eating, toileting, bathing, dressing and transferring.

activity A term that refers to recreation, action or movement.

actual expenditure The sum of expenditures of individuals or nations on consumption and non-consumption expenses for daily life.

actual income The income of individuals or nations after paying income taxes and adjusting for inflation.

adjustment subsidy A federal governmental subsidy paid to municipal governments to support the provision and delivery of a steady long-term care service.

adult guardianship system A legal assistance program that was implemented in 2013 to protect and support judgment-impaired adults and/or minor children who have some difficulty in protecting their rights.

adult guardianship system The system that protects and supports judgment-impaired adults who have some difficulty in protecting their rights.

Advisory Council on Social Security The affiliated organization of Japan's Ministry of Health, Labour and Welfare that has the power or duty to advise on the Social Security system.

advocacy An individual or organization that advocates on behalf of others to influence organizations, governments or societies to improve social resources.

aged society A society with more than 14% of the population aged 65 and above.

ageism Stereotyping and discrimination on the basis of age, especially prejudice against the elderly.

A

aging In general, the process of getting older.

agnosia The inability to recognize common objects persons, sounds, shapes or odor while the major senses of sight, hearing, smell, touch and taste are not defective nor is there any significant memory loss.

air mattress An inflatable mattress that is used to reduce and relieve pressure on tissues to prevent ulcers from forming.

air sleeping pad An inflatable pad that is used for changing position by inflating air with a pump.

allograph Writing letters/other documents on behalf of individuals who cannot write.

all-you-can-eat buffet A meal where a variety of dishes are set out on the table or sideboard for self-service.

Alzheimer's disease A progressive and degenerative disease of the brain which causes the irreversible loss of neurons ; reported by Alois Alzheimer in 1907.

ambulatory rehabilitation A type of home-based care service in which individuals travel to a so-called "day care center" to have rehabilitation therapy.

anemia A state where a number of red blood cells or quantity of hemoglobin measured in unit volume is reduced below normal levels.

ankle-foot orthosis : AFO An appliance used for the lower leg and foot to support the ankle.

antibacterial and deodorization material A fabric or material that contains antibacterial and anti-odor chemicals that kill and/or slow down the growth of bacteria and decreases odor production.

antibiotic A compound or substance derived from special microorganisms that fight bacterial infections by killing or slowing down their growth, for example, penicillin or streptomycin.

aphasia A partial or total loss of the ability to produce and comprehend language caused by an illness or injury to the related part of the brain.

appetite A physical desire to eat or drink.

arteriosclerosis A chronic disease in which thickening, hardening or changing in the shape of the artery walls result in impaired blood circulation.

articulation disorder An inability to pronounce particular sounds correctly due to speech impairments.

artificial respiration An act of supporting respiration in emergency cases to individuals who cannot breath on their own.

aspiration pneumonia Bronchopneumonia caused by inhaling a foreign substance into the bronchial tree such as vomit or a piece of food.

assessment The act of evaluating the status of an individual, clarifying his or her needs, and identifying the underlying causes of each need based on observations and information obtained.

assistance The supplemental or alternative help supplied by people such as care workers and family members to people such as the elderly and disabled, based on their daily needs.

assistance with eating An act of providing necessary assistance to individuals who cannot eat on their own due to various types of physical and mental disabilities.

assistance-required A person who is classified into "assistance-required (level 1 and 2)" based on the results of an on-site assessment of each individual's physical and mental status under the long-term care insurance system : in need of long-term assistance.

ataxia A neurological sign or symptom that results in loss of coordination of the muscle movements.

athetosis A symptom that is characterized by involuntary convoluted writhing and continuous movements of the hands and feet typically caused by lesions in the corpus striatum of the brain.

atrophy   A reduction in the size of an organ or body part due to injury or disease.

auditory impairment   A disability or impairment of hearing.

autism   A disorder in the neural development that can lead to impaired social interaction and communication and is a term used to describe a diagnostic category called pervasive developmental disorders (PDD).

average life span   The length of time a new born is expected to live between birth and death assuming mortality trends stay constant.

axillary temperature   A method of measuring body temperature by holding the thermometer under the armpit.

B

back support A backrest on the wheelchair which provides support and positioning.

bacterium A single celled organism/pathogen that can cause sickness upon infection.

balloon catheter A tube inserted in the urinary bladder in order to withdraw or introduce fluid.

barrier free A term that refers to the elimination of not only the structural and architectural boundaries found in public and transportation facilities, but also the political, cultural, informational and emotional biases found in various situations.

basal metabolism The minimum amount of energy consumption required by a person in a physically and mentally resting state.

basic disability pension A program that provides support for people with physical disabilities and/or impairments.

basic disability pension° A form of pension provided when people who are enrollees of the Basic Pension program or enrollees of the National Pension Insurance program aged between 60 and 64 become disabled and are unable to work due to an illness or disability.

basic old-age pension The national pension available to the elderly.

basic survivors'pension° Japan's pension benefit that is paid to eligible dependents upon the death of a person who had enrolled in the National Pension Insurance or Basic Old-Age Pension.

bathing One of the activities of daily living in which one's body is wholly or partially washed.

bathtub A bathtub used for taking a bath.

bed A piece of furniture used for sleeping and reclining.

bed making Restoring a bed to an unslept-in condition so that individuals can feel comfortable.

bedding Materials used for sleeping such as a futon, mattress, pillow and pajamas.

bedpan A bowl shaped like a toilet seat that collects excreted urine and stool in a sanitary manner.

bedridden An individual who cannot leave the bed due to severe impairment or illness.

bedridden level The abbreviation for criteria for determining the independent level of daily living of elderly people suffering from disabilities.

bedside commode A chair-like movable and portable toilet with a container below the toilet.

benefit-received principle The idea that the cost burden should be proportional to the amount of benefit or number of services that the individual receives, irrespective of income or wealth level.

Biestek's 7 principles Seven principles of the casework relationship between workers and clients identified by Biestek, F. P. from the United States of America.

bioethics Ethical issues related to life.

bleeding Occurs when a blood vessel is damaged and blood flows outside of the vessel.

blended diet A type of diet in which foods have been blended into a smooth consistency.

blister A fluid filled pocket in the upper layers of the skin called the epidermis.

blood pressure The pressure exerted by the flow of blood on the walls of the arteries.

BMI : body mass index An indicator for determining obesity status calculated from an individual's height and weight.

body mechanics The study of posture and movement of bones muscle and internal organs and the relationship between them also known as biomechanics.

body temperature The temperature of the body.

Braille Special reading and writing tool for the blind that is made up of tactile dots and can be read only with the sense of touch.

brain death A state where all functions of the brain including the brainstem lose their functionality.

burden of care The physical mental and financial burden on the caregivers providing care for the bedridden and/or demented person.

burn Injuries to skin due to liquids, gases or solids that come into contact with the skin and or mucosa.

burnout syndrome A syndrome principally involving extreme physical and mental fatigue and depletion of emotions.

B

C

cancer Group of diseases characterized by uncontrolled cell growth.

cane A slender walking aid which has a hand grip on the support bar.

cane-assisted gait Ambulation with a stick or cane.

care A variety of services provided to aid people when they are unable to care for themselves due to physical and/or mental impairments.

care In general, the term refers to helping individuals based on their wishes and needs.

care and welfare An act of providing direct care and assistance by a person with knowledge and skills in providing care to people who have difficulties in their social life or require care, by looking into their physical, mental, psychological and social aspects of their needs.

care conference A meeting of health care professionals who are involved in the care of patients to discuss appropriate care for the patients.

care goal A goal that will give direction for the care plan.

care guidance An act of providing direct guidance and suggestions about long-term care to families who take care of the elderly and disabled.

care home One type of residential care setting where a number of elderly people live and have access to various services for independent living.

care management A multi-step process which coordinates necessary social services with resource providers on behalf of an individual to resolve and fulfill his or her multiple social needs.

care manager* A professional who is responsible for the assessment, development, coordination and implementation of care plans for elderly and disabled persons.

care plan A plan or sequence of actions undertaken by the caregivers to aid an individual to meet his or her medical and non-medical needs.

care process A process of accomplishing a suit of assignments which are necessary to provide nursing care with a focus on an individual's needs.

care services plan A term that refers to care plans.

care skills The special techniques related to nursing care, especially for long-term care patients.

care team A team formed by a variety of health care professionals to provide care to maximize and maintain the highest level of independence.

care work A term that refers to the techniques of providing personal support based on a sense of responsibility to provide care for other people.

care worker A worker who is licensed by the government to provide a variety of care services to the elderly people or people with disabilities, such as help with activities of daily living.

caregiver A person such as a nurse or care worker responsible for the supervision, prevention and treatment of physical or psychological illness and disability.

case conference A meeting or investigation performed to analyze a case.

case study An investigation of an individual or an event to determine causes and solutions for a positive outcome.

case work The social work that involves directly and interpersonally working with individuals who need support.

cataract Clouding or loss in the transparency of the lens in the eye.

cerebral embolism An obstruction of the cerebral artery by an embolus such as a blood clot formed inside a blood vessel, that is carried by the bloodstream to the brain where it blocks the artery.

cerebral hemorrhage A medical condition in which blood vessels in the brain are ruptured and cause bleeding.

cerebral infarction A medical condition in which the blood vessel in the brain is blocked, causing a disturbance in blood supply to the brain.

cerebral palsy : CP An inclusive term for a group of conditions that can cause the development of an immature brain and produce non-progressive lesions, which can result in a permanent central impairment of motions.

cerebral thrombosis A medical condition in which a foreign body slowly adheres to the inner wall of a blood vessel in the brain and eventually blocks the vessel.

cerebrovascular dementia A type of dementia caused by cerebrovascular disease.

cerebrovascular disorder : CVD An inclusive term for a group of brain dysfunctions caused by blockage or the bursting of blood vessels in the brain, which may cause paralysis, impaired consciousness, speech impairment and so forth depending on the parts of the brain damaged.

certification of assistance-required An act of equally and objectively assessing and classifying an applicant into either "assistance-required" level 1 or 2 for preventive care benefits under long-term care insurance based on the classification standards.

certification of care-required An act of equally and objectively assessing and classifying an applicant into one of five levels (care-required level 1 to 5 for long-term care benefits under long-term care insurance) based the classification standards.

certified care worker : CCW An individual who has acquired a national qualification for caring and assisting persons with a physical and/or mental disability.

Certified Care Worker Registry Japan's registration program that requires all certified care workers to be registered after passing the National Certification Examination for Care Workers, to perform care worker tasks. It ensures that they meet the qualifications for a certified care worker.

certified child care worker A person who has specialized knowledge and techniques to provide care to children and instructions regarding childcare to their parents.

certified psychiatric social worker : CPSW A person who has a national license to help people with mental disorders and their family.

certified social worker : CSW A specialized social worker who obtained a special license from the Ministry of Health and Welfare to support low-income earners.

certified social worker : CSW A person with the expertise and techniques to provide advice, education, referrals to other professionals who provide health and welfare services such as

C

physicians and health care personnel, and coordinate those services.

cervical spinal cord injury An injury to the cervical spinal cord that may result in partial or total paralysis.

change of position To change the orientation of one's physical posture.

changing bed sheets A technique of making an occupied bed to make an individual feel comfortable to sleep.

changing clothes An act of removing clothes one is wearing and putting on other clothes.

Cheyne-stokes respiration An abnormal breathing pattern marked by alternating periods of decreased and increased breathing.

childhood disorder A disorder which commonly occurs in children between the ages of 6 to 12 and causes difficulty in daily life.

cholesterol A lipid that is used to produce essential substances such as cell membrane bile acids and hormones.

chromosomal abnormality Abnormality in the number of chromosomes and/or its structure.

circadian variation The biochemical and physiological or behavioral processes that occur during a 24-hour cycle.

circle mat A round donut-shaped mat.

cleaning An act of removing dirt, dust, stains or impurities by sweeping or wiping.

cleanness Keeping oneself or surroundings clean and sanitized.

client allocation cost All costs that are paid for allocating an individual to a particular facility/ service, including the cost of labor, operations, maintenance, in-service education and so forth.

client allocation system A system of assigning each individual to a particular facility/service for all their needs according to the regulations.

clock position Noting the position of an object or item using the positions shown on the clock face.

clothes Mainly, materials used to cover the body.

clothing irritation Physical imperfections caused by clothing.

colon cancer Large intestine (colorectal) cancer.

comfort A peaceful state having no physical, mental or social discomfort.

comfortable position A relaxed position having no physical discomfort or mental pain.

commode A portable toilet chair used inside the room.

communication An act of transmitting information such as thoughts, messages and feelings as by gestures, signals and language.

communication aid An instrument or tool used as an aid or alternative medium for communication when verbalization is difficult.

community-based care center A community-based organization implementing comprehensive support operations.

community-based service A type of service established by Japan's Long-Term Care Insurance Law in 2005 that aims to promote independent living for people in need of long-term care in the community.

Complaints Resolution Committee An organization that resolves any reported complaints regarding welfare services.

complication A medical condition in which one disease occurs with another at the same time.

conductive deafness A hearing impairment caused by a defect in the part of the ear that conducts sound, specifically the area between the eardrum and middle ear.

confidentiality The duty that requires all health care professionals such as doctors and attorneys to respect the confidentiality of their patients/clients and not to divulge any information obtained during the course of consultation/treatment.

constipation A state of discomfort or pain occurring due to feces accumulating inside the intestine and difficulties occurring with defecation.

contract A written or verbal agreement made by one party to another.

contracture Stiffness of the joints as a result of lack of joint movements that limits full extension.

contracture prevention Preventing the deterioration of joint mobility.

cooking The act of converting commodities such as raw plant or animal materials into edible foods using heating or non-heating processes.

cooking recipe A set of instructions for cooking food.

crippled A functional damage to the bone joint nerve muscle blood vessel and/or central nerve system that regulates motor function caused by injury or illness

critical pathway : CP An algorithm that documents the medical and nursing procedures including treatments and diagnostic tests during a patient's hospitalization.

crutch A support tool, either wooden or aluminum, used by people with a leg injury as an aid in ambulation.

cyanosis The appearance of a blue coloration of the skin due to hypoxemia.

D

daily living aid for people with disabilities A device which assists and makes daily life activities convenient for those whose physical and mental functions are reduced and face difficulties in performing daily life activities.

daily-needs assistance A type of assistance provided to low income people who have difficulty maintaining the minimum standard of living of paying for their daily expenses such as food/drink, transportation, utility bills, clothes and household appliances.

day care services A community-based center that provides care supervision and transportation to persons who require assistance with daily living activities.

day care services for people with dementia A community-based care service for people with dementia who are in need of care.

day/night care A variety of services provided to low-income earners during the day and at night, such as home help services, visitation services, and accommodation in nursing care centers.

deafness A loss of ability to hear sounds greater than 100 dB (decibels) in both ears.

decompression An act of reducing extreme compression occurring in any part of the body.

defecation An act of eliminating feces from the digestive tract via the anus.

dehydration An excessive loss of body fluids, especially extracellular fluids.

delirium A confused state where the individual can suffer from drowsiness disorientation and hallucination.

delusion A false or deceptive belief and thought.

delusion of persecution A false belief and thought of being hurt by others that is maintained in spite of evidence against it.

dementia A defect of one's acquired intellectual ability which cannot be recovered due to various diseases or injuries of the brain.

dental hygienist A specialist in oral hygiene with a national qualification to provide dental services such as teeth cleaning applying medication and educating patients on oral hygiene under the supervision of a dentist.

denture A partial or complete set of artificial teeth used for one or more missing teeth.

dependent population A group of people who do not work and rely on others.

depopulation A reduction in the number and percentage of children in society.

depopulation and aging A condition where the number of children decreases and the number of elderly increases every year.

depression A psychosomatic symptom, mainly a mood disorder resulting in prolonged extreme sadness despair and anxiousness, which also causes some physical symptoms.

detergent A substance used to remove the dirt and stains in the laundry.

developmental disorder A group of disorders that usually occur during childhood, including intellectual disability, autism, learning disability, cerebral palsy and epilepsy.

diabetes mellitus : DM A disease of metabolic abnormality where glucose in the blood increases chronically and gets discharged in the urine.

dialysis One of the medical practices that removes the waste and excess water from the blood of a patient suffering from renal failure.

diaper An absorbent garment used to absorb bodily waste, avoiding infection of the genitals and maintaining cleanliness.

diaper change An act of changing diapers in order to remove the absorbed bodily waste avoiding infection of the genitals and maintaining cleanliness.

diaper cover A cloth cover used to prevent leaks of bodily waste from a diaper.

diaper removal A term used for providing assistance with toileting or implementing a scheduled toileting program to help incontinent people become continent so they no longer need to wear diapers.

diarrhea A condition in which an individual has frequent and liquid bowel movements.

dietitian A specialized person qualified by Chapter 32 of Food Sanitation Law. Dietitians have a national qualification to provide nutritional guidance to all citizens. They are usually employees of public health centers, hospitals, and private or public sector organizations.

dietitian According to Japan's Dietitian Law (Article 1) a dietitian is "a person designated by the prefecture governor who engages in nutritional guidance using the name of dietitian."

difficult urination A condition in which a person has difficulties ejecting urine from the bladder or is unable to empty the bladder completely.

direct care staff Nursing staff responsible for providing direct care for the sick and disabled.

direct social work practice A method of delivering direct support/therapy though a worker-client relationship based on bonding.

disability A team that refers to any people who suffer from a substantial limitation in daily or social life.

disability According to the Basic Act for Persons with Disabilities, it refers to any people who suffer from a substantial limitation in daily or social life.

disorientation A state where orientation is damaged and the person does not recognize time, location and persons.

disturbance of consciousness A change in cognition or a perceptual disturbance that causes a lack of awareness about the environment.

disuse atrophy A wasting or diminution in the size of bones or muscles occurring as a result of low activity.

disuse syndrome Various symptoms of decline in the body's functions as a result of immobilization of the affected body parts.

diuretic A medication used to increase the excretion of sodium moisture from the body by using the convoluted tubules of the nephron.

doctor's note A descriptive written report created by the applicant's doctor used to determine the eligibility for long-term care insurance benefits.

Down Syndrome A congenital disorder caused by the inheritance of three #21 chromosomes.

drastic medicine A drug that is specified as harmful or can cause harm to humans or animals if administered.

dyschezia A disorder in defecation such as constipation or diarrhea.

dyslipidemia An abnormal quantity of lipids within the blood.

early detection An act of finding a disease before it is fully developed.

eating An action related to consuming food.

eating disorder A disorder of taking in food.

edema An abnormal and excessive accumulation of liquid in the cellular intervals as a result of clinical swellings.

elder abuse The physical, emotional, financial or sexual mistreatment or neglect of older people.

Elder Abuse Prevention Act A law established in Japan in 2005 calling for increased national responsibility in protecting the elderly from abuse and neglect, and also relieving caregiver stress.

elderly In general, it refers to persons aged 65 and above.

elderly aged 75 and above Persons aged 75 and above.

elderly household A household consisting entirely of persons above the age of 65.

electric bed Bed with electric height, head and foot adjustment features that can be controlled by a remote control.

electric wheelchair A wheelchair operated by an electric motor.

emergency contact information List of emergency phone numbers and other information of people who can be contacted in case of any emergency like sudden illness or accidents.

emergency first aid The initial care or treatment provided to a sick or injured person until definitive medical treatment can be applied.

emergency medical technician : EMT A professional who is trained to provide emergency medical services in conjunction with a doctor while transporting a critically ill patient to a hospital.

empathy In general understanding of and sympathizing with others emotions similarly.

empowerment A process or set of processes that help to increase the political social economic and/or spiritual strength of people who don't have confidence in their own abilities, so they can increase their capability to make decisions to solve their own problems.

encouragement One of the important types of communication required to build rapport.

end-of-life care The supportive nursing care of people who are terminally ill.

enema A method of eliminating stool and gas inside the colon by inserting liquids into the rectum and colon.

Engel's coefficient The proportion of income spent on food in family expenditure.

environmental maintenance The arrangement of a safe and pleasant living space.

excretion An act of excreting bodily waste.

extension of maximum life span Reversing the process or reducing the rate of aging to extend the maximum amount of time a person or a group of people can survive between birth and death.

F

face cleaning Washing an individual's face to keep skin clean.

face sheet A document that contains information about the client such as name, gender, age, occupation and highest education level.

falling asleep Being in a state of sleep to relieve fatigue and gain energy.

family A small group of individuals of common ancestry ; composed of relatives who are related by marriage or blood, such as a husband and wife, siblings, parents and their children.

family care leave A system that permits an employee to be absent from his or her job to take care of a family member who requires care.

family caregiver A family member who provides care for his or her family.

family relationship An inclusive term for mutual relationships of individuals in one family group, such as the relationship between a husband and wife, parents and their children, siblings, mother-in-laws and daughter-in-laws and so forth.

family-provided care A family caring for the elderly or handicapped relative who is in need of care.

fecal incontinence Unconscious leakage of feces.

fee The quantity of payment given by a recipient for long-term care services.

fever A state characterized by an elevation of body temperature above normal due to muscle contradiction or disease, and where heat dissipation is reduced due to the contraction of surrounding blood vessels.

fiber An elongated filament ; threadlike structure.

flaccid A state where muscle tone is diminished and tension on muscle is loosened.

flame-resistant material A material which does not burn even when in close contact with a fire source or if it burned does not spread the fire.

fluid balance The balance between the amount of water taken into the body and the amount lost from the body.

fluid intelligence The ability to learn and recognize new things and is independent of acquired knowledge and experience.

follow-up An act of confirming and evaluating whether health care services provided based on the care goals and plan created by health care professionals along with clients and their family are appropriate.

foment The application of warm or cold liquids, or medications to the body to relieve inflammation and pain.

food intake Oral intake of food.

food poisoning A generic term for health problems caused by eating improperly stored, prepared or managed food that may be contaminated by a harmful pathogen.

food sanitation A set of protocols that should be used in the production and preparation of food products to remove the risk of introducing contaminating pathogens.

foot bath Washing one's feet by putting them in hot water.

foot drop A condition where a person has difficulty pointing their toes upward.

Fowler's position A body posture in which the upper half of the body is elevated approximately 45 degrees on the bed.

fracture A complete or incomplete break in a bone due to an excessive external force.

frailty Weakening of the mind and body due to the loss of physical strength.

frequent bowel movements A state where stool is excreted frequently.

full denture A complete set of artificial teeth used when there are no teeth left.

full-body bath A type of bathing where the whole body below the neck is dipped in the bathtub.

full-body sponge bath A type of bathing including wiping the whole body with a wet cloth or sponge.

functional maintenance An act of attaining or maintaining the highest level of physical function.

functional training A type of exercise provided to individuals with decreased physical ability due to illness or aging, and which involves maintaining and improving health and physical function to independently carry out activities performed in daily life and preventing them from requiring long-term care.

F

G

gait A movement of walking by alternately moving both of the lower extremities.

gait training An act of practicing the basic movements for walking inside or outside of a rehabilitation room with the support of physical/occupational therapists, parallel bars, crutches or a cane.

gatch bed A bed that has features such as lifting an individual's back and knees.

genital hygiene The washing practices involved in maintaining a healthy environment in the genital region.

getting up A movement that occurs when one arises from a sleeping position (supine position) to a sitting position.

grievances and complaints resolution A process or set of processes to solve complaints and dissatisfaction reported by an individual.

group home A small community-based facility or supervised home-like residence for impaired people with similar needs who cannot live alone without proper supervision.

group home for people with dementia A community-based home which provides supervision and care for people who suffer from dementia.

group living A type of residential facility for relatively healthy people aged 60 and above in which residents live with people other than family members.

group recreation An act of performing some type of recreation in a group with multiple members.

group work One of the techniques in social work through which individuals work in groups assisted by a staff member who guides their interaction in the program.

H

haircut An act of cutting and setting the extended hair.

half-body bath Taking a bath by maintaining the water level in the bathtub at below one's chest.

hallucination Perceiving something that does not exist.

hand bath Washing one's hands by putting them in hot water.

hand wash An act of washing hands using soap and running water.

hand-assisted escort One of the methods used for guiding impaired people by using a hand.

handicap Social disadvantages as a result of functional disabilities or impairments of one's ability.

handrail A narrow rail attached to the wall side of a stairway and so forth used to avoid fall incidents while providing stability and support when moving around or transferring to a wheelchair.

Hasegawa Dementia Scale-Revised : HDS-R A rating scale for dementia : a set of items developed by Kazuo Hasegawa in 1974 for assessing the cognitive status of the elderly.

headache A pain in the head area.

health According to World Health Organization (WHO), it refers to a state of complete physical, psychological and social well-being and not merely the absence of disease or infirmity.

health care equipment A general device made for supporting the life of a person in need of nursing care.

health care facility for the elderly A facility targeting elderly people whose health condition is in a stable stage and who require nursing care or rehabilitation rather than acute hospital treatment.

health insurance A mandatory insurance that provides health insurance coverage to almost all workers.

health observation Monitoring and evaluating the health status.

hearing aid A hearing-impaired person's equipment which has the function of increasing the volume of the sound.

hearing level A scale showing the level of hearing ability.

hearing loss : HL A wide range of hearing difficulties in determining the sounds and conversations in one's surroundings.

hematemesis The vomiting of blood or coffee-ground material due to hemorrhage in the gastrointestinal system.

hemiplegia Paralysis affecting only one side of the body opposite to the affected cerebral hemisphere.

hemostasis The biological processes involved in forming a blood clot to stop bleeding.

herpes zoster A viral disease characterized by a blistering skin rash caused by the varicella-zoster virus.

home bathing care A variety of actties providing bathing services to elderly people and people with physical disabilities in their own home.

home bathing care˚ A service whereby a nurse will visit the home of clients with a bathtub and provide bathing assistance to maintain the cleanliness of the body.

home care A series of activities for washing, meal help, daily activities, emotional care, and cleaning aged or handicapped people at home. These activities are covered by long-term care insurances.

home care˚ A type of care service provided in the individual's home. It can be provided by home helpers or certified care workers who provide assistance with to activities of daily living such as toileting, bathing and eating, and instrumental activities of daily living such as shopping, cooking, washing and cleaning.

home care rehabilitation A service whereby physical occupational and speech therapists will go to an individual's home and provide rehabilitation and education.

home health A form of health care services provided by health care professionals such as nurses in the patient's home that aims to improve the health of individuals with illness.

home helper A care professional who visits the home of elderly and disabled people in need of care ; offers support for patients with incurable or difficult-to-treat diseases provides assistance with activities of daily living such as toileting, bathing, eating and with instrumental activities of daily living such as shopping, cooking, washing, cleaning and so forth, and also provides consultation related to their overall daily lifestyle.

home modification An act of reforming one's house in response to disorders impairments or increasing age, with the aim of improving independent living, preventing accidents and reducing the burden of care.

hormone A trace substance secreted directly into the blood and lymph nodes from the endocrine glands.

household A basic residential unit consisting of the members of a family who live together and share the same living accommodation.

household budget A term that refers to household economy.

housekeeper A woman who is employed to perform the domestic work and is responsible for the maintenance and cleaning of the household on behalf of her employers, mainly housewives.

housekeeping A series of acts such as vacuuming rooms and disposing of rubbish to maintain a healthy, safe and comfortable environment for living.

human rights advocacy The protection and advocacy of the rights of persons.

hypertension High blood pressure ; a condition in which the arterial blood pressure is higher than normal.

hypochondria A disorder characterized by excessive preoccupation or repetitive complaints about having a serious illness, even when there is not any medical evidence to prove the presence of an illness.

hypoglycemia A state where the blood sugar levels drop below normal.

hypotension Blood pressure below normal, causing decreased cardiac output.

I

ICD A term that refers to the "International Classification of Diseases."

ice bag A thin waterproof rubber bag to hold ice and water.

ice pillow A rubber pillow which holds ice and water.

ICF A term that refers to the "International Classification of Functioning, Disability and Health."

ICIDH A term that refers to the "International Classification of Impairments, Disabilities and Handicaps."

ideational apraxia A neurological disorder characterized by the inability to plan for a specific movement and perform learned complex tasks involving the use of objects in the proper order in the absence of motor and sensory impairment.

ileus Being unable to eliminate feces or pass gas because of a partial or complete blockage of the intestine.

impairment According to International Classification of Impairments Disabilities and Handicaps (ICIDH) created by World Health Organization (WHO) in 1980, it refers to "any reduction or abnormality of psychological, physiological, or anatomical structure or function."

improvement of body functions One of the selective services provided by the long-term care insurance system whereby a beneficiary conducts motion exercise for care prevention.

improvement of oral functions One of the selective services provided by the long-term care insurance system that offers an exercise program for improving the function of the mouth.

incontinence An involuntary excretion of urine or passage of stool as a result of the inability to control bladder or bowel movements.

incurable disease A term commonly used in Japan for a disease that is difficult to cure.

independence Being independent, mainly not depending on others.

independence level of people with dementia A criteria for determining the independent level of daily living of elderly people suffering from dementia, established by Japan's Ministry of Welfare (currently known as the Ministry of Health, Labour and welfare) in 1993.

independence support Support given by health care professionals to individuals who cannot live independently.

individualized care Care which is planned to meet the needs of a patient with respect and dignity.

indwelling catheter A flexible plastic tube inserted from the urethra into the bladder to withdraw urine.

infection A state whereby a host organism is infected by a pathogenic organism often resulting in a diseased state.

infection prevention An act of preventing infectious agents from entering, settling, and growing in the body.

infectious disease A disease caused by infectious agents such as bacteria, viruses and so forth, causing tissue damage and impairing host function.

informal A term that refers to something not officially recognized ; not formal and/or casual.

institutional care A facility-based service geared towards the elderly who are in need of continuous care under long-term care insurance.

instrumental activities of daily living : IADL A term that refers to a series of life functions necessary for independent living in a community setting such as preparing meals, taking medications, shopping for groceries, using the telephone and managing money.

insulin A natural hormone secreted by the islets of Langerhans in the pancreas that reduces the levels of blood sugar.

insurance premium A periodic payment made by the insured to the company in order to cover the expenses required for carrying insurance business.

intake An initial casework screening interview that helps to gather basic information and evaluate the needs of the interviewee.

intelligence Although it has been defined in different ways, it is not only the ability to apply learned knowledge and experience, but also the capacity to solve new problems.

intelligence quotient : IQ An index derived from the results of an intelligence test, expressed as the ratio of the mental age in months to chronological age, multiplied by 100.

internal disorder The improper functions of the internal organs.

International Classification of Diseases : ICD The international classification codes concerning disease or cause of death issued by the World Health Organization (WHO).

International Classification of Functioning, Disability and Health : ICF The revised version of International Classification of Impairments, Disabilities and Handicaps (ICIDH) approved by World Health Organization (WHO) in 2001.

International Classification of Impairments Disabilities and Handicaps : ICIDH A common framework for classifying the consequences of disease issued by World Health Organization (WHO) in 1980.

International Organization for Standardization : ISO An international organization funded in 1947 and made up of approximately 160 countries, that determines the standards that should be applied for both technical and non-technical fields, except electric/electronic engineering.

IQ A term that refers to the "intelligence quotient."

J

joint An area that connects two or more bones, which is separated by short and tough fibers of cartilage for the purpose of body part motion.

L

late phase rehabilitation A rehabilitation program designed to assist patients to attain and maintain their highest level of functioning during the late stage.

laundry An act of washing soiled clothing, towels and bed linen.

level of independent Criteria for determining the independent level of daily living.

life cycle The cycle of life ; the period from birth to death.

life expectancy One indicator which shows how long an individual in each age group will live on average.

life history Records of the series of events that have happened in the past and still affect a person's life.

life review Looking back at one's life and reviewing the meaning of how one has lived his or her life.

life style A method of living including clothing, food, housing, entertainment and leisure activities.

lifestyle-related disease A disease deeply related to one's lifestyle and which worsens with age.

limited assistance An act of partially assisting the individual's actions.

lip-reading A method of understanding the speech of others by visually interpreting the facial expression and movements of the lips and mouth.

liquid diet Mild food in liquid or strained form that has no residue and is easy to swallow and digest.

liver cirrhosis A liver disease caused by repeated episodes of inflammation or hardening of the liver preventing proper function.

living assistance services An act of assisting people living in the community to maintain their physical, mental and emotional health by helping with their clothing, nutritional and housing issues.

living environment A wide range of circumstances, objects or conditions by which one is surrounded.

locomotion A change in position due to movement of the body.

longevity society A society who has the intention of maintaining the health of elderly people while they live happily actively and positively.

long-term assistance-recipient According to Japan's Long-Term Care Insurance Law (Article 7), it refers to a person who qualifies and receives preventive care services from long-term care insurance.

Long-Term Care Certification Committee A group of health care experts officially delegated to review the applications to determine whether or not the applicant qualifies for long-term care insurance benefits and if so how much and what kind of benefits are to be provided. They take into account the result of physical psychological and social assessments and a report from the applicant's doctor.

long-term care classification levels The classification levels of benefits under long-term care insurance.

long-term care insurance An insurance that covers certain health care costs and expenses, and provides services for those individuals who may require long-term care due to dementia or being bedridden.

long-term care insurance benefit Payments and services by long-term care insurance plan to elderly people with age-related illness such as dementia and stroke. This plan is for reducing family care costs.

long-term care insurance benefit The benefits provided to individuals who are classified into "care-required (level 1 to 5)" based on the results of an on-site assessment of each individual's physical and mental status under the long- term care insurance system.

long-term care insurance eligibility assessment An assessment of the functional and cognitive status of an applicant performed within 30 days of applying for long-term care insurance benefits.

Long-Term Care Insurance Law A law that established the provision of long-term care services for the elderly who are in need of assistance or care in Japan.

Long-Term Care Insurance Law for the Aged A long-term care insurance plan for elderly people with age-related illness such as dementia and stroke. This plan is for reducing family care costs.

long-term care insurance payment The costs that cover payments and services provided by long-term care insurance plan to elderly people with age-related illness such as dementia and stroke. This plan is for reducing family care costs.

long-term care insurance payment The long-term care insurance system in Japan pays the service providers 90% of the charges and the individual pays the remaining 10% co-insurance.

long-term care insurance plan As per Japan's Long-Term Care Insurance Law, it is the 5-year action plan for long-term care insurance that must be reviewed every three years by both municipal and prefectural governments in Japan.

long-term care insurance system A long-term care insurance plan for elderly people with age-related illness such as dementia and stroke. This plan is for reducing family care costs.

long-term care insurance system A social insurance program in Japan that provides health care services to persons aged 40 years and above if they qualify for the benefits.

Long-Term Care Insurance System for the Aged A policy or institution for long-term care insurance plan for elderly people with age-related illness such as dementia and stroke. This plan is for reducing family care costs.

long-term care needs The physical mental and social needs, wants and demands of people with difficulties in their daily life due to physical and psychological disorders.

long-term care recipient According to Japan's Long-Term Care Insurance Law (Article 7), it refers to a person who qualifies and receives the long-term care benefits from long-term care insurance.

long-term care-required According to Japan's Long-Term Care Insurance Law, it refers to a person who is classified into the "care-required (level 1 to 5)" based on the results of an on-site assessment of each individual's physical and mental status under the long-term care insurance system.

long-term health care facility A type of long-term care insurance-covered health care facility designed for people who require regular medical attention and nursing supervision/care.

loss of appetite A feeling of no desire to eat even at mealtime.

lost experience The experience of losing important things.

lumbago A condition where pain is experienced in the lower back and surrounding parts of the body.

lumbago exercise A type of nonsurgical treatment or exercise to prevent lower back pain.

lumbago prevention An act of reducing the risk of developing lower back pain.

lung cancer An epithelial malignant tumor that forms in the lungs.

luxation A displacement or misalignment of a joint due to some external cause.

lying position A body position in which the body is in a flat or horizontal position.

L

M

management of household affairs The maintenance and management of household affairs such as dealing with financial, nutritional and clothing matters, in response to changes in the environment.

manic depressive psychosis A mental disorder characterized by repeated episodes of mania and depression.

manual muscle testing : MMT A method of examining muscle power by using an electronic device developed by Robert Lovett.

mastication The first step of digestion in which food is crushed and ground by teeth, mixed with digestive enzymes and then sent down the throat.

mat A flat piece of fabric or carpet of various sizes, designs and colors.

meal Eating food items that provide nutrients necessary for survival.

measurement of body temperature An act of measuring body temperature as one of the methods for observing physiological changes.

medical insurance system A system in which the insurer provides insurance benefits to beneficiaries for medical treatment of diseases injuries death or childbirth and so forth.

medication A medicine or compound which exerts a biological effect.

medication management The monitoring of medications an individual takes to confirm that the individual is complying with the medication regimen.

melena The discharge of black tarry bloody stools containing decomposed blood.

memory disorder Disturbances that appear somewhere in encoding information and in the retention of acquired information or in the recall of information.

memory retention The ability to memorize and recall new information and experiences.

mental disorder A generic term for any pattern of psychological symptoms that causes a disruption and abnormality in an individual's thinking, feeling, moods and so forth.

mental retardation : MR A mental impairment that has occurred during the development stage and requires some kind of assistance in daily living activities.

mentally retarded person A person with intellectual difficulties.

menu The process of menu planning that includes applying the knowledge of food, nutrients, cooking methods and recipes.

metabolic syndrome A set of any two or more of the following signs in the same person meet the criteria for the metabolic syndrome : abdominal obesity, high blood sugar, high blood pressure and dyslipidemia.

mineral One of naturally occurring compounds that is required by the body for healthy functioning.

MMSE : Mini Metal State Examination A brief test created by Folstein S. E. et al. in 1975, widely used to screen for dementia and to assess cognitive/mental status including memory and orientation.

MMT : Manual Muscle Testing A method of examining muscle power by using an electronic device developed by Robert Lovett.

mobility aid A device specifically designed to aid in the movement of elderly or impaired people.

money management Managing and budgeting a money source appropriately.

monitoring A stage of carefully observing whether a client's difficulties are being resolved.

motor impairment A loss or limitation of function in voluntary movement or mobility resulting from dysfunction within the motor system.

moving around by wheelchair Traveling to a destination with a person using a wheelchair.

MRSA : methicillin-resistant staphylococcus aureus A type of staph bacteria called staphylococcus aureus that is resistant to the antibiotic methicillin and causes several infections that are difficult to treat.

MSW : Medical Social Worker A person from the health care field who usually works in a hospital or clinic and delivers psychosocial, emotional and counseling support to individuals and/or their families with multiple problems in their daily life.

multiple disabilities Having not only one impairment but a combination of two or more impairments at the same time.

muscular atrophy The loss of skeletal muscle mass in a quantitative manner due to disease or limb immobilization.

M

N

National Certification Examination for Care Workers[*] A national objective test provided to assess and evaluate the knowledge and skills of the applicant as a certified care worker.

nausea A vague feeling of uneasiness or discomfort of the throat or upper stomach with an involuntary urge to vomit.

necrosis The death of body cells and tissues.

needs A term that refers to necessity requirement and demand.

night-time delirium A confused state due to clouded consciousness accompanied by hallucination and delusion.

non-rapid eye movement〈 NREM 〉sleep The phase of sleep without rapid eye movement (REM).

non-verbal communication The process of exchanging information such as opinions thoughts and emotions with others through eye contact, facial expressions, attitudes and gestures.

normalization Aiming to build a society where all children, disabled and elderly people will be respected as individual human beings, their rights as citizens will be safeguarded and they would be able to lead independent lives in society.

notarial deed A legal document such as a living will or promissory notes created by the notary public.

notary public A public officer who creates notarized civil affairs related documents.

NPO : non-profit organization An organization which uses surplus revenues for self-preservation rather than distributing them as profit.

nuclear family A basic unit of family that consists of two married parents and their unmarried children.

nurse A person who has obtained a special nursing license from the central government or local government to provide comprehensive care services to people with illness.

nurse[*] According to Japan's Public Health Nurse Midwife and Nurse Law (Article 5) a nurse is "a person who has obtained a formal permission from the Minister of Health, Labour and Welfare in Japan being a professional in providing nursing care and support for medical treatments."

nurses station An area or station where nursing staff congregate and carry out their administrative duties.

nursing A profession that aims to improve the health of individuals with illness.

nursing[*] A profession that aims to provide assistance with all aspects of health to help a person be able to lead a healthy and normal daily life.

nutrient An essential substance taken in from foods to help the body grow, repair and sustain itself.

nutrition Intake of materials by an organism required for survival such as proteins, fats, carbohydrates, vitamins and minerals.

nutrition therapy An intervention that aims to treat certain kinds of malnutrition or illness.

nutritional counseling One of the selective services provided by Japan's long-term care insurance that helps educate and improve the nutritional uptake of the beneficiaries.

nutritional management A generic term for assisting an individual or a group of individuals with a balanced dietary intake.

N

O

obesity A medical condition caused by excessive accumulation of body fat causing one's weight to exceed his or her ideal body weight.

occupational therapist : OT* A health professional who provides therapy, primarily handcraft, under the direction of the doctor for individuals with physical and mental disabilities to promote the recovery of social skills and adaptive behavior skills.

occupational therapy A type of rehabilitation therapy that improves health and independence by enabling individuals with physical and mental disability to perform purposeful activities.

old-age disorder A health complication that occurs in older people due to aging-related changes in their functioning.

old-age pension The national pension available to the elderly.

old-age welfare pension* The pension that is paid to a person who had reached a certain age and retired where the premiums cannot be paid when National Pension Insurance was implemented in Japan in 1961.

opportunistic infection An infection caused by pathogens that do not normally infect a healthy host.

oral health care Any measures taken to improve or maintain one's oral cavity by brushing, flossing and cleaning.

orthosis An orthopedic device designed to support and improve movement of an injured or weak part of the body.

orthostatic hypotension A form of decreased blood pressure due to sudden changes in body positions such as the supine to the standing position.

osteoporosis A condition of reduced bone mass in which bones become prone to fracture due to a reduction in bone density.

overuse syndrome A group of body impairments that occur due to excessive exercise or training.

P

pain An unpleasant sensation occurring in the body.

palliative care The specialized care for individuals that have a terminal illness ; mainly provides mental and emotional support in addition to some medical treatments.

palpitation Abnormal pulsation of the heart which is usually not noticeable to the individual.

paper diaper A diaper layered with high absorbent paper.

paralysis Weakening of muscular strength, loss of sensory perception or damage in movements and so forth, usually caused by abnormalities in one's nervous system.

paraplegia Paralysis of the lower part of the body.

parenteral nutrition A method of providing the essential nutrients and fluids directly inside the venous vessels.

Parkinson's disease A degenerative disease that affects the central nervous system impairing motor skills and is characterized by the three cardinal motor symptoms of tremors, rigidity and akinesia.

partial bath An act of washing only some part of the body when bathing is not possible due to illness or injury or when body strength is remarkably low.

partial sponge bath An act of wiping a part of the body by soaking a towel or wash cloth in water that is 50~55°C (122-131°F) when bathing is not possible due to illness or injury or when body strength is remarkably low.

passive exercise Fitness performed with the assistance of a person or equipment which moves a part of the body.

pension An insurance benefit paid to people or their family members, which is paid throughout their lives to safeguard their income.

people with mental disabilities A person with mental disorders, such as schizophrenia, or a person who suffers from acute poisoning by psychotropic agents or addiction, mental retardation, intellectual disabilities and/or other related conditions.

perineal 〈 peri 〉 care Washing and cleaning of the genital and rectal areas.

personal care An act of providing direct care and assistance to aged or impaired people who have difficulties with activities of daily living.

personal guardianship A legal support service for those who lack the mental capacity to make decisions to carry out the activities of daily living.

personal hygiene A set of practices such as washing face and hair, brushing teeth or shaving, associated with ensuring good health and cleanliness.

pharmacist A health care professional in medicine with a national qualification to assist people with understanding what and how the medications they are taking will work.

pharmacotherapy The treatment of a disease or disorder by administering medications.

physical function The ability of the body to perform mobility tasks.

physical therapist : PT A health care professional who provides physical therapy under the supervision of a medical doctor.

pneumonia An inclusive term for an inflammatory condition of the lung caused by organisms such as viruses and bacteria and can result in the alveolar filling with fluid.

population aging The increase in the proportion of elderly people in the total population.

portable bathtub A bathtub that can be easily transported and carried for bathing services for immobile or bedridden individuals requiring care.

portable bathtub A simple portable bathtub through which bathing can be done easily in the room.

positioning An act of placing or arranging the body into a position in which a person feels comfortable and relaxed.

presbyopia An aging medical condition where the eye shows decreased ability to focus on close objects.

presenile dementia Dementia caused by organic deterioration in the brain occurring between the ages of 40 to 64.

pressure ulcer A wound or skin breakdown due to prolonged pressure applied to the skin.

pressure ulcer prevention An act of reducing the risk of developing and progressing pressure ulcers.

prevention of long-term care A system of health care which provides services designed to prevent individuals from being "care-" or "assistance-" required under long-term care insurance.

preventive benefit The benefits provided to individuals who are classified into the "assistance-required (level 1 and 2)" based on the results of an on-site assessment of each individual's physical and mental status under Japan's long-term care insurance.

preventive long-term care plan One of the community support plans developed and implemented by municipal governments that is involved in setting up preventative measures to ensure that their residents do not become weak and frail.

primary care A health care system by medical doctors/physicians who help maintain good health and provide the first consultation for a person or a group of people with a health concern as well as diagnosing providing appropriate orders and emergency medical treatments, referring to specialists or providing continuous treatments and rehabilitation.

primary doctor A medical doctor who offers health consultation to a person with an undiagnosed health concern and orders medical care/treatments as necessary.

privacy An area or condition which is separated or secured from the presence or view of other people; personal things; personal secrets.

private residential home for the elderly A facility aiming at providing some help with activities of daily living such as bathing as well as instrumental activities of daily living such as preparing meals. It is different from a welfare facility for the elderly that provides continuous nursing care.

problem behavior An action or reaction of a person that is troublesome or disruptive.

professional practice examination A hands-on practical exam that can be taken after a written test and is designed to evaluate the knowledge, skills and abilities required to become a certified care worker.

profile   A simple biography.

profit-making business   The business that aims to make a profit.

prone position   A body posture where one lies on the stomach, puts the upper extremities on the trunk and extends the lower extremities.

proof of work experience   A document that proves his or her professional work experience or qualification.

prosthetist and orthotist : PO   A health care professional who has skills and knowledge in making and fitting artificial parts of the human body.

psychiatric social worker : PSW   A social worker who obtained a special license from the Ministry of Health and Welfare to work with elderly people and people with mental disorders, physical disabilities and/or low income.

psychiatric social worker : PSW*   A person who helps people with mental disorders and their family deal with their problems.

psychosomatic disease : PSD   A disease in which physiological changes are facilitated by psychological stressors and may require to take into account those stressors for diagnosis and treatment.

public benefit corporation   A corporation involved in providing services to benefit the public.

public health center   A public agency aimed to prevent disease and promote and improve public health in the community.

public health nurse : PHN   A specialized professional who has a special national qualification to provide health guidance to all citizens. They are usually employees of public health centers, hospitals, private or public sector organizations.

public utility   An organization that supplies necessities to the public.

pulmonary aspiration   An act in which food, liquid or saliva accidentally enters into the airways instead of the esophagus.

pulmonary emphysema   A chronic lung condition in which the alveoli in the lung may be over-inflated and stretched and making it difficult to exhale air.

pulse   It represents the tactile arterial palpation of the heartbeat.

P

Q

quad cane A cane that has a four-legged rectangular base of support for providing extra stability.

quadriceps femoris A muscle group located on the front part of the thigh and is an extensor muscle of the knee.

quality of life : QOL A concept used to measure the general well-being of individuals.

quiet sleep A term that refers to blissful and peaceful sleep.

Q

R

range of motion : ROM The degree of movement that a joint can move voluntarily or involuntarily.

rapid eye movement〈 REM 〉sleep A sleeping condition where the eyes move quickly during sleep.

rapport A trusting and intimate relationship between the care provider and the care recipient.

reading assistance Reading on behalf of individuals who have difficulty with reading.

reassessment Re-evaluation for confirming whether the services are provided as previously planned and creating a care plan for new issues.

recommended dietary allowance : RDA The daily dietary intake levels of essential nutrients considered necessary to meet the requirements of most healthy people (98%) .

records Writing down the facts about the client such as his or her previous history, assessment results and other health care related information.

recovery-phase rehabilitation Rehabilitation provided approximately six months following the time of the onset of problems and acute phase of rehabilitation.

recreation An inclusive term for various activities for getting comfort, peace and enjoyment in one's life.

redness Red spots on the skin that disappear when pressure is applied and reappear when pressure is relieved.

registered dietitian A nutritionist who has a special national qualification to provide nutritional guidance to all citizens. Registered dietitians are usually employees of public health centers, hospitals, and private or public sector organizations.

registered dietitian° According to Japan's Dietitian Law (Article 1) a registered dietitian is a person designated by the Minister of Health, Labour and Welfare, who designs meal plans, engages in nutrition guidance and supervises food preparation for individuals at a facility for promoting health.

regression Reversion to earlier patterns of feeling or behavior, or stages of mental and physiological functioning.

rehabilitation The action of restoring the skills and abilities of an individual who has had an illness or injury so they can attain maximum self-sufficiency and function as normal as possible.

rehabilitation medicine Rehabilitation in the medical field that aims to maintain or restore the body function that was lost through injury or illness.

rehabilitative care Care provided to people in need based on the principle of rehabilitative care.

rehydration Restoring lost water to the body.

reminiscence therapy One of the psychotherapeutic techniques which reviews, discusses and assesses the experience or events of the individual's life.

residential home for the elderly˙ A facility which provides supportive care to people aged 65 and above and require continuous care, but can't be cared for at home or in the community due to some environmental and financial issues (Article 11 of the Welfare Law for the Elderly).

residual functional capacity The remaining capacity to function after a disease or illness has affected the individual.

respiration A natural act of inhaling and exhaling that exchanges oxygen and carbon dioxide.

respiratory functional disorder A disability of function in exchanging oxygen and carbon dioxide caused by a respiratory disease.

restraint Also called a physical restraint an act of limiting the movements of an individual forcefully in order to avoid fall incidents, rollover or to avoid removal of tubes used for intravenous drips or feeding.

restraint The act of restraining constricted or controlled.

Review Committee on Long-Term Care Insurance˙ A committee formed in each prefecture whose purpose is to monitor the use, delivery and cost-effectiveness of long-term care services provided to long-term care insurance beneficiaries and to review the appeal of the decision of the committee.

rheumatoid arthritis : RA A chronic, autoimmune and systemic inflammatory disorder that principally attacks synovial joints that can also affect other internal organs.

risk prevention The ideas or methods to avoid and decrease the chance of an unfavorable injury or event occurring in nursing practices.

role play A technique that uses scenarios to explore the different genres of practice such as writer, speaker, listener or observer.

roll over Rolling over on one's left or right side while sleeping.

R

S

safety control The management of safety in order to reduce the risk of harm to patients while providing care.

scabies A skin disease caused by tiny invisible parasites that burrow under the host's skin causing severe itching.

scaling stairs Climbing up and down stairs.

schizophrenia A psychological disorder including cognitive impairment where information obtained from one's surroundings cannot be synthesized properly, occurring as fantasies and delusions, and can affect interpersonal contacts.

self-actualization The act of developing or achieving one's full potential and life goals.

self-awareness An awareness of oneself including one's value, judgment standard, feelings and behaviors.

self-care It basically refers to any personal health maintenance activities performed by a person with the intention of maintaining health, protecting life and becoming independent.

self-determination The act of deciding what to do or think without external compulsion and to be responsible for that decision.

self-esteem Philosophy or attitude of retaining one's dignity and self awareness.

self-harm : SH An act of injuring one's own body.

self-help device A collective term for the tools used by people with physical or mental disorders to conduct daily life activities.

self-help group : SHG A group or organization formed by people or families having a common problem or situation and where activities are conducted to overcome and resolve problems by helping each other.

self-help group for families A group or organization formed by family memberswho have a common problem such as having a family member with a disability, the need for long-term care or an incurable and difficult-to-treat disease.

semi-Fowler's position A body posture when lying in a supine position with both legs either bent or straight and the head at approximately 20 to 30 degrees.

semi-prepared dish A technique of cooking by performing only the pre-process like cutting, crushing, mixing and heating, and not doing the cooking completely.

senile deafness A loss of the ability to hear high frequencies, followed by a loss in ability to hear mid and low frequencies due to aging.

senile dementia A disease caused by the degeneration of brain cells, often associated with old age and is the predominant symptom of progressive dementia.

senile dementia of the Alzheimer's type : SDAT One type of dementia that occurs in old age, resulting from the formation of plaques or nerve tangles in the brain of Alzheimer's patients.

senile depression Depression that occurs in elderly people.

sensorineural deafness A type of hearing loss caused by lesions somewhere in the inner ear, central auditory nerve that runs from the ear to the brain, or the brain itself.

sensory function An ability to sense stimuli in both the internal and external environment and send the stimuli to the central nervous system.

service staff meeting A meeting of health care professionals held at the time of creating or changing care plans.

shampooing An act of washing the hair and scalp with various liquid or cream preparations of soap.

short-stay The provision of short-term or temporary care provided at a nursing facility for those who are sick or disabled and live at home.

shower bath A way of bathing through a shower.

side effect A secondary effect of a drug or treatment in addition to the intended effects.

side-lying position A posture in which a person lies on one side with both legs straight.

sign language The important means of communication employing signs made mainly with hands, used usually by individuals with hearing impairments.

sit to stand The movement of changing position from a sitting to a standing position.

sitting position A position where the upper half of the body is in the standing position with the upper limbs hanging parallel and the body weight is put on the rear of the hips and thighs, which are used as a supporting surface.

sitting position The posture of a person whose upper body is lifted off the bed.

skin rash An eruption of the skin causing symptoms such as decreased blood flow, loss of or decreased pigment deposition, skin cancer, inflammation and hyperplasia of the epidermis.

sleep A state characterized by reduced or absent consciousness whereby the mind and body are resting.

small-scale multi-functional home-based care service A type of community-based day care facility that is small but provides a wide range of services such as day care, home care and institutional care for people who live at home.

social insurance A mandatory insurance program that aims to materialize social policies.

social resource A generic term for the facilities, equipment, capital, products or skills used to fulfill the needs of the social life of an individual or group.

Social Security A system that aims to provide social protection based on the state's responsibility so that all citizens can enjoy the decent minimum standard of living.

social welfare The various social services and assistance provided to people with social difficulties after determining and confirming the needs for every aspect of daily life.

social welfare services A field which includes the planning and implementation of activities aimed at improving the quality of life for individuals, groups and communities.

social worker : SW A generic term for a person with education, training, values, knowledge, theory and skills in social work involved in social welfare services.

soil-resistant material A material which is difficult to stain and can be washed easily.

solitary-living Leading life independently without any family or relatives.

special therapeutic diet A special diet designed to optimize the nutritional needs of the individual by taking into account the pre-existing medical condition and nutritional needs in order to treat a variety of diseases and disorders.

specialized bathtub A special bathtub for a person who has difficulties bathing in a general bathtub.

specialized bed A bed equipped with special features.

speech-language impediment A communication disorder that affects the ability to talk understand, write and read.

speech-language-hearing therapist : ST A professional who provides speech therapy to people who have difficulties with communication caused by speech and hearing impairments.

spinal cord injury : SCI Damage or trauma to the spinal cord.

spiritual care Care that focuses not only the physical aspects, but also on the mind and spirit of the individual.

sponge bath An act of washing the body with a wet cloth or sponge using warm water and soap to maintain the cleanliness of the body for those who cannot take a bath.

stairs A series of steps leading from one level to another.

standing position A body position in which the body is raised upright on the feet.

sterilization An act of removing or killing all living pathogenic organisms from the surface of instruments, body and food.

stool extraction Extraction of impacted stool in the lower rectum using a finger.

strengths perspective A method which helps individuals recognize their strengths and abilities to cope or overcome their personal issues and challenges.

stress An intense physical and/or psychological type of tension caused by strong external stimuli, both physiological and psychological.

stretcher A medical cart used for moving injured or immobile people from one place to another.

styling and setting hair Arranging and designing the hair by using a comb and brush.

subarachnoid hemorrhage : SAH Bleeding into the subarachnoid space.

supervisee An individual who is directed by a supervisor.

supervision A process of directing and overseeing the performance and activity of an individual or a group of individuals.

supervisor An individual who supervises, oversees, directs and evaluates the performance and activities of a supervisee.

supine position A lying down position with the face up, upper limbs near the body and lower limbs folded.

supplementary benefit An income-tested benefit provided to low income people for determining the difference between what they can afford and how much the service actually costs, to minimize their financial burden.

support of quiet sleep Support for blissful and peaceful sleep.

support system A network of persons that provides individuals with practical or emotional support after becoming sick, disabled or aged.

support-required elderly An elderly person who has difficulties in carrying out his or her daily living activities and is in need of support, protection and care.

swallowing   A process of sending alimentary bolus and oropharyngeal cavity juice through the pharynges/throat.

swallowing difficulty   A state where an individual is unable to swallow food and drink due to a disorder.

S

T

T-cane One type of walking stick which has a T-shaped grip.

team approach An approach made by a team composed of members with varied qualifications, skills and experiences that contribute to the improvement of a patient's care.

team care The act of taking care of the clients by an association or cooperation of health/medical care and long-term care professionals.

telephone assistance Making a call on behalf of individuals who have difficulty communicating by phone.

terminal care Supportive care provided to individuals with a terminal illness during the terminal phase.

terminal stage A period in one's life when the end of life is close.

the demented elderly An elderly person suffering from dementia.

the insured A person having rights to receive benefits from the insurance provider due to paying insurance premiums.

the insurer A person running an insurance system collecting insurance premiums and providing the insurance benefits to the insured in case of an accident.

therapeutic exercise A method of performing therapeutic exercise for motility disorders and lack of exercise.

thickening agent A substance that is added to liquid and food to increase the viscosity and improve the bolus formation during the digestive process.

thought disorder A pattern of disabled language or thought processing that can occur due to psychotic mental illness.

toileting assistance Providing support to a person who cannot egest independently due to a physical/mental/social disability.

total assistance A state where an individual is totally dependent due to physical and mental disabilities.

total fertility rate : TFR The average number of children born to one woman in her lifetime.

total personal care An act of providing necessary care for meeting all aspects of the needs of the person.

trachea The windpipe that connects the pharynx to the lungs.

transfer assistance A movement undertaken by an immobile or partially immobile individual, with the help of care workers or welfare aids.

transfer from bed to wheelchair The action when a person moves to a wheelchair from the bed.

transfer from wheelchair to bed An individual moving from wheelchair to bed.

transfer motion An individual moving from one object (e.g., chair/wheelchair) to another.

transportation fee When a patient is transferred to a hospital for emergency hospitalization as per doctor's order, the travelling and life support costs are paid by the health insurance.

tremor A repetitive and involuntary movement of one or more parts of the body.

tube feeding A nutrient supply method that gives liquid nutrition to a person who cannot take food or drink through swallowing by inserting a catheter in the opening of the digestive tract.

U

ulcer A partial break in the skin accompanied by the disintegration of tissues.

ultraviolet rays protection material A material that contains ultraviolet blockers or absorbers to block or absorb ultraviolet rays.

unit-based care An act of providing care in small groups for people in need of care in long-term care facilities.

universal fashion An idea that means to provide functional and fashionable items such as clothing and foot wear to as many individuals as possible regardless of age, body shape, size and ability.

uresiesthesia A sensation produced in one's brain at the time when urine is stored in the bladder.

urinal A urine collection container that is used when a patient has difficulty in moving to the rest room.

urinary disorder A disorder characterized by frequent urination, difficult urination or incontinence.

urinary incontinence Involuntary urination from one's body due to the loss of bladder control.

urinary storage disorder A disorder that causes an inability to store urine.

urinary tract infection : UTI An infection that occurs in the urinary tract, commonly associated with bacterial and yeast infections.

urination An act of eliminating urine from the urinary bladder after removing waste from the blood by the kidneys and passing it down to the ureters, bladder and urethra.

urine A liquid byproduct of the body after the body fluids have been filtered through the kidneys.

U

V

valvular heart disease A heart disease that involves one or more of the four valves of the heart.

vegetable food Any kind of plants such as cereals, potatoes, vegetables, seaweed, mushrooms, nuts and seeds.

vegetative state A state where the brainstem function is maintained but the larger brain functions have stopped so that the person's consciousness is damaged and they become bedridden.

ventilation The exchange of air or gasses in a room to provide high air quality.

verbal encouragement An act of providing verbal encouragement or cueing.

vertebral compression fracture A situation where the bones in the spine called vertebrae are broken or compressed due to trauma.

view of life and death An approach toward life and death.

vision loss A decrease in one's vision.

visual field restriction A medical condition where one's sight in scope becomes narrow.

visual impairment A medical condition where one or more blind spots exist in the normal field of vision.

visually impaired person A person whose visual functioning is permanently deteriorating because of a hereditary disease or due to some acquired disease or injury.

vital signs Signs that include the heart beat, blood pressure, temperature and breathing rate that show sustainment of life.

vitamin Any of various organic components required in minute amounts for maintaining good health, growth and reproduction of the human body.

vocational rehabilitation The teaching of life and work skills that will be needed to get and/or keep a job for individuals who suffer from mental or physical disorders, but who still have the ability to function.

volunteer Any type of practice on behalf of others such as providing assistance, money or goods without wanting to receive anything in return.

vomiting The expulsion of the contents of one's stomach through the throat and mouth.

walker A three-sided walking tool configured of left and right frames joined by a middle pipe that allows the user to stand and walk in the center of the frame.

wandering A state of walking around without any purpose.

washing Removing and cleaning the dirt by flushing it with water and detergent.

welfare A living blessed with a pleasurable lifestyle and better livelihood.

welfare equipment rentals Renting and leasing devices for daily life activities at the government's expense.

welfare facility for the elderly An inclusive term for a certified long-term care insurance facility that provides nursing and welfare services for the elderly.

welfare home for the elderly A facility which provides a wide range of care to people aged 65 and above, who have physical and psychological disorders and require continuous care but can't be cared for at home or in the community.

welfare office A central organization of social welfare policies.

wheelchair A chair having wheels used for the movement of an impaired individual.

wheelchair assistance Assistance provided to the individual while moving around by wheelchair or moving to the wheelchair.

wheelchair foot rest A constituting part of the wheelchair which supports the leg.

white cane A special cane for individuals who are blind or have low vision that makes it easier for those people to feel obstacles and alerts others that this person is visually impaired.

widow In general, it refers to a bereaved woman.

World Health Organization : WHO One of the specialized organizations of the United Nations acting as an authority on public health.

written examination for certification A national written examination of certified workers.

W

참고문헌

김득린(2013) 편. 『사회복지 종합 가이드북』. 한국사회복지협의회.

김미혜(2006). 『노인복지 간호론』. 동인.

김영경 외(2007). 『노인병 생리학』. 현문사.

김주희 외(2005). 『장기요양 노인 간호』. 군자출판사.

나눔의 집 편(1999). 『사회복지 대백과사전』. 나눔의 집.

노동순보사 사전간행위원회 편(1989). 『사회보장 사회복지 사전』. 노동순보사.

대한노인병학회 편(2005). 『노인병학』. 군자출판사.

류종훈(2008), 『노인건강생활과 호스피스 케어』. 학문사.

보건복지부(2008). 『요양보호사 표준교재』.

보건복지부(2013). 『보건복지백서』.

보건복지부(2014). 『노인보건복지 사업안내』.

서강훈(2013). 『사회복지용어사전』. 이담북스.

서울복지재단 편(2006). 『노인요양시설 서비스 매뉴얼』. 서울복지재단.

신섭중 · 임춘식 외(2001). 『세계의 사회보장』. 유풍출판사.

양정남 · 최선경(2009). 『사회복지 실천론』. 양서원.

오정수(2008). 『중국의 사회보장』. 집문당.

이영호(2008). 『정신건강론』. 공동체.

이우수 · 이용부(2013). 『사회복지 용어사전』. 문화문고.

이윤로(2005). 『정신보건과 사회복지』. 창지사.

임춘식 외(2005). 『세계의 노인복지정책』. 학현사.

임춘식 외(2008). 『노인복지학 개론』. 현학사.

임춘식 외(2009). 『사회복지학 개론』. 공동체.

임춘식(1999). 『사회문제와 사회복지』. 유풍출판사.

임춘식(2004). 『고령화 사회의 도전』. 나남

임춘식(2008). 『현대사회와 노인복지』. 유풍출판사.

임춘식 외(2009). 『노인장기 요양산업의 이해』. 공동체.

임춘식 · 선현규 역(2008). 『일본의 개호보험제도』. 학현사

장인협(1999). 『사회복지실천론』. 서울대학교 출판부.

전광석(2008). 『독일 사회보장과 사회정책』. 박영사.

정순둘(2006). 『사례관리 실천의 이해』. 학지사.

최영희 외(2006). 『노인과 건강』. 현문사.

한국노인복지학회 편(2004). 『한국노인복지의 새로운 도전』. 학현사.

한국노인복지학회 편(2005). 『노인복지학 사전』. 현학사.

한국사회복지사협회 편(2004). 『사회복지사 표준 매뉴얼』. 한국사회복지사협회.

현외성 외(2005). 『한국노인복지강론』. 유풍출판사.

홍봉선(2004). 『교정 복지론』. 현학사.

青木務 編(2003). 『福祉・住環境用語辞典 ハンドブック』. 保育社.

秋元美世・芝野松次郎・森本佳樹・ほか 編著(2003). 『現代社会福祉辞典』. 有斐閣.

秋山美栄子 編著(2006). 『介護の用語と英語』. NOVA.

足立正樹 編著(2003). 『各国の社会保障』. 法律文化.

米国ナースの労働環境と患者 編(2006). 『患者の安全を守る―医療・看護の労働環境の変革』. 日本評論社.

飯島渉・澤田ゆかり(2010). 『高まる生活リスク 社会保障と医療』. 岩波書店.

池上直己 訳(2005). 『MDS2.1―施設ケアアセスメントマニュアル改訂版』, 医学書院.

一番ケ瀬康子・井上千津子・中島紀恵子・ほか 編著(1991). 『介護ハンドブック』. 光生館.

伊藤善典(2006). 『ブレア政権の医療福祉改革―市場機能の活用と社会的排除への取組み.』. ミネルヴァ書房.

井部俊子・開原成允・京極高宣・前沢政次 編(2009). 『在宅医療辞典』. 中央法規出版.

林春植・宣賢奎・住居広士(2010). 『韓国介護保険制度の創設と展開―介護保障の国際的視点』. ミネルヴァ書房.

上田敏・大川弥生 編著(1996). 『リハビリテーション医学大辞典』. 医歯薬出版.

内薗耕二・小坂樹徳 監修(2002). 『看護学大辞典(第5版)』. メデカルフレンド社.

大田仁史・三好春樹 監修(2005). 『実用介護事典』. 講談社

大森正集 編著(2006). 『介護職・福祉職のための医学用語辞典』. 中央法規出版.

小田兼三(2002). 『コミュニティケアの社会福祉学―イギリスと日本の地域福祉』. 勁草書房.

小田兼三(1993). 『現代イギリス社会福祉研究―日本からみた理論・政策・実践と課題』. 川島書店.

小田兼三・桑原洋子・谷勝英・ほか 編著(1998). 『現代福祉学レキション(第2版)』. 雄山閣.

介護福祉用語研究会 編(2001). 『必携介護福祉用語の解説』. 建吊社

金沢美智 監修(2007). 『福祉住環境コーディネーター基本用語辞典』. エクスナレッジ.

川上正夫・辻和男 編著(2006). 『実用介護・福祉・ケア用語辞典(2006年版)』. 土屋書店.

木下康仁(2007). 『改革進むオーストラリアの高齢者ケア』. 東信堂.

京極高宣(2004). 『社会福祉学小辞典(第2版)』. ミネルヴァ書房.

郡司篤晃 編著(2004). 『医療と福祉における市場の役割と限界―イギリスの経験と日本の課題』. 聖学院大学出版会.

小池五郎・福場博保 編著(1992). 『栄養学事典』. 朝倉書店.

小山剛 監修(2008). 『介護支援専門員基本用語辞典(第2版)』. エクスナレッジ.

近藤克則(2004). 『医療費抑制の時代: を超えて―イギリスの医療・福祉改革』. 医学書院.

最新医学大辞典編集委員会 編(2005). 『最新医学大辞典(第3版)』. 医歯薬出版.

坂本忠次・住居広士 編著(2006). 『介護保険の経済と財政―新時代の介護保険のあり方』. 勁草書房.

島津淳・高橋信幸・内藤佳津雄・ほか 編著(2002). 『介護保険辞典(新版)』. 中央法規出版.

社会福祉辞典編集委員会 編(2002). 『社会福祉辞典』. 大月書店.

庄司洋子・武川正吾・木下康仁・ほか 編著(1999). 『福祉社会事典』. 弘文社.

シリーズ 21世紀の社会福祉編集委員会 編(2009). 『社会福祉基本用語集(七訂版)』. ミネルヴァ書房.

新村出 編著(2008). 『広辞苑(第六版)』. 岩波書店.

杉本敏夫・南武志・和田謙一郎・ほか 編著(2007). 『ケアマネジメント用語辞典(改訂版)』. ミネルヴァ書房.

鈴木幸雄 編著(2003). 『介護福祉用語辞典ハンドブック.\』. 保育社.

硯川真旬 編著(2006). 『国民福祉辞典』. 金芳堂.

住居広士 編(2004). 『医療介護とは何か―医療と介護の共同保険時代』. 金原出版.

生活福祉研究機構 編(1998). 『イギリスの実践にみるコミュニティ・ケアとケアマネジメント』. 中央法規出版.

袖井孝子・陳立行 編著(2008). 『転換期中国における社会保障と社会福祉』. 明石書店

染谷俶子(1999). 『オーストラリアの高齢者福祉―豊かな国の豊かな老後』. 中央法規出版.

竹内孝仁 編著(1987). 『図解リハビリテーション事典』. 廣川書店.

武久洋三 監修・山口典考(2011). 『早わかりリハビリテーション用語・略語・英和辞典』. ナツメ社

田中雅子 監修(2007). 『介護福祉士基本用語辞典』. エクスナレッジ.

田端光美(2003). 『イギリス地域福祉の形成と展開』. 有斐閣.

中央法規出版編集部 編(2007). 『介護福祉用語辞典(四訂版)』. 中央法規出版.

寺出浩司 監修(2005). 『介護・社会福祉用語辞典』. 新星出版社

中村磐男・池弘子・牛津信忠・ほか 監修(2006). 『標準社会福祉用語辞典』. 秀和システム..

中村永司(2006). 『英国と日本における医療福祉とソーシャルワーク』. ミネルヴァ書房.

仲村優一・小島蓉子・トムソン, LH 編著(1981). 『社会福祉英和・和英用語辞典』. 誠信書房.

那須宗一 監修(1989). 『老年学事典』. ミネルヴァ書房.

南山堂 編(2006). 『南山堂医学大辞典(第19版)』. 南山堂.

二木立(2001). 『21世紀初頭の医療と介護―幻想の「抜本改革」を超えて』. 勁草書房.

二木立(1994). 『世界一: の医療費抑制政策を見直す時期』. 勁草書房.

日本介護福祉士会 監修(2003). 『介護職のための実務用語集(改訂版)』. エルゼビア・ジャパン.

日本看護協会(1996). 『高齢者への質の高いケアをめざして』. 日本看護協会.

日本在宅ケア学会 監修(2007). 『在宅ケア事典』. 中央法規出版.

日本社会福祉実践理論学会 編(2004). 『社会福祉実践基本用語辞典』. 川島書店.

日本地域福祉学会 編(2006). 『地域福祉事典(新版)』. 中央法規出版.

橋本篤孝 編著(2004). 『介護・医療・福祉小辞典』. 法律文化社.

平岡公一(2003). 『イギリスの社会福祉と政策研究―イギリスモデルの持続と変化』. ミネルヴァ書房.

福地義之助(1993). 『長寿社会総合講座＜10＞高齢化対策の国際比較』. 第一法規出版.

舟場正富・斎藤香里(2003). 『介護財政の国際的展開―イギリス・ドイツ・日本の現状と課題』. ミネルヴァ書房.

見藤隆子・小玉香津子・菱沼典子 編著(2003). 『看護学事典』. 日本看護協会出版会.

宮原伸二 編(2006). 『福祉医療用語辞典』. 創元社.

村川浩一 編著(2003). 『介護保険・保健福祉辞典(新版)』. ジヤパンインターナショナル総合研究所.

森岡清美・塩原勉・本間康平 編著(1993). 『新社会学辞典』. 有斐閣.

山縣文治・柏女霊峰(2009). 編著「社会福祉用語辞典(第7版)』ミネルヴァ書房, 2009.

用語事典編集委員会 編(2006). 『イラストでみる介護福祉用語事典(第3版)』. 福祉教育カレッジ.

古川孝順・川村佐和子・白澤政和 編著(2006). 『社会福祉士・介護福祉士のための用語辞典(第2版)』. 誠信書房.

吉川春寿・芦田淳 編著(2004). 『総合栄養学事典(第4版新装版)』. 同文書院.

吉田聡編(2008). 『福祉・介護・リハビリ英語小事典』. 英文社.

吉田宏岳 監修(2001). 『介護福祉学習辞典(第2版)』. 医歯薬出版.

吉本光一・小松真 編著(2008). 『介護・福祉・医療用語集(改訂版)』. エルゼビア・ジャパン.

和田攻・南裕子・小峰光博 編著(2002). 『看護大事典』. 医学書院.

Barker RL(2003). *The Social Work Dictionary: 5th Edition*. NASW Press.Birren JE and Schaie KW(1996). *Handbook of the Psychology of Aging*. Academic Press Limited, 1996.

Collnan AM(2009). *Dictionary of Psychology*. Oxford University Press.

Davies M(2000). *The Blackwell Encyclopedia of Social Work*. Blackwell Publishing Ltd..

DiGiovanna AG(1994). *Human Aging: Biological Perspectives*. McGraw-Hill, Inc..

Editors of the American Heritage Dictionaries(2000). *The American Heritage Dictionary of the English Language*. Houghton Mifflin Company.

Evashwick C(1996). *The Continuum of Long-Term Care*. Delmar Publishers.

Ferrini AF and Ferrini RL(1992). *Health in the Later Years*. Brown Benchmark.

Gelfand DE (1993). *The Aging Network-Programs and Services*. Springer Publishing Company.

Hafen B, Karren KJ, Frandsen KJ, et al(1996). *Mind/Body Health: The Effects of Attitude, Emotions, and Relationships*. Allyn & Bacon.

Kandel J(2009). *The Encyclopedia of Elder care*. Facts on File.

Koff TH and Park RW(1993). *Aging Public Policy-Bounding the Generations*. Baywood Publishing Company, Inc..

Matcha DA(1997). *The Sociology of Aging-A Social Problems Perspective*. Allyn & Bacon.

Merriam-Webster(2009). *Merriam-Webster's Collegiate Dictionary*. Merriam-Webster Inc..

Mezey MD(2004). *The Encyclopedia of Elder Care: The Comprehensive Resource on Geriatric and Social Care.* Prometheus.

Moody HR(1994). *Aging: Concepts and Controversies.* Pine Forge Press.

Morris JN, Murphy K and Nonemaker S(1995). *Minimum Data Set 2.0.* Health Care Financing Administration.

Romaine-Davis A, Boondas J and Lenihan A(1995). *Encyclopedia of Home Care for the Elderly.* Greenwood Press.

World Health Organization(1990). *International Classification of Impairments, Disabilities and Handicaps.* World Health Organization.

저자 약력

스미이 히로시住居 廣士

일본 岡山大 대학원 의학박사
일본 県立広島大 대학원 보건복지학 전공 교수
介護モデルの理論と実践(1998)
介護福祉用語辞典(2009) 외 다수

사와다 유키澤田 如

일본 福祉大 대학원 사회복지학 박사
일본 福祉大 보건사회연구센터 객원연구원
福祉社会開発学-理論・政策・実際(2008)
アメリカ高齢者ケアの光と陰(2012) 외 다수

임춘식林春植

대만 中國文化大 대학원 사회학 박사
한남대 사회복지학과 교수
노인장기 요양산업의 이해(2009)
韓国介護保険制度の創設と展開(2010) 외 다수

선현규宣賢奎

일본 東北大 대학원 경영학 박사
일본 共栄大 경영학부 교수
介護ビジネス経営戦略(2009)
노인장기 요양산업의 이해(2009) 외 다수

한영 · 영한

장기요양보험
용어사전

초판인쇄   2014년 9월 15일
초판발행   2014년 9월 15일

공편저   스미이 히로시 · 사와다 유키 · 임춘식 · 선현규
펴낸이   채종준
펴낸곳   한국학술정보(주)
주소   경기도 파주시 회동길 230(문발동)
전화   031) 908-3181(대표)
팩스   031) 908-3189
홈페이지   http://ebook.kstudy.com
전자우편   출판사업부 publish@kstudy.com
등록   제일산-115호(2000. 6. 19)

ISBN   978-89-268-6453-1 93330